I0815011

レンタカー
ニコニコレンタカー
2,525円~
ENEOS
IN

Ulysses Voelker | Michael Schmitz
Principles, Inspirations, Challenges

niggli

how communication design works

A – D

E, F

Introduction

On the concept and style of this book

Welcome to this book. It deals with visual communication that influences our lives in varied ways. Your own behavior at this exact moment provides a good example: The title, the topic, the design – all of this visual information caught your interest, and now you are reading these lines. The way this book has reached you represents a classic case of visual communication. The book explains this process in detail and offers an introduction to the associated field of work – what we call communication design.

When we started working on this book, we asked ourselves to what extent it was necessary, what conceptual direction we would take, and what the process would look like. We noted down the results of our little quiz – and found that this method actually helped us determine the book's character:

For whom is this book?
The book is primarily geared towards students majoring in the field of communication design. It will also refresh the knowledge of those who have already been working in design for a while. Those who are new to the subject will learn how to decipher the visual communication they encounter in everyday life.

What does the book say?
It covers the subject area's basic competences and discusses current and future challenges. In addition, the book serves as a compendium of facts and sources that extend to the fringes of communication design.

Why is this book relevant?
Reflecting on the requirements of and environment in which design takes place is incredibly important because designers are currently facing a multitude of challenges. An overwhelming flood of information, fake news, bots, artificial intelligence, social media, amateurish design created with easily accessible design tools, rapid process speeds, efficiency pressure, as well as competition in the field of design and occasionally precarious

working conditions – all of this is putting pressure on communication designers, leaving them with little time to think about the way they work. But more so than ever before, the circumstances demand reflection, diversified education, and a perspective that extends beyond the confines of one's own profession.

What goals does the book pursue?

It aims to remedy deficits. It contains a wealth of knowledge and suggestions. It describes the intertwining of design and social issues, both current and future, which has far-reaching consequences. But the book features an overarching leitmotiv which states that communication design is always the result of its creators' *mindset*. They are the ones who determine the way their work influences communication, the values it conveys, and what our visual everyday life looks like. To reconcile the social relevance of communication design and the daily life of a designer – that's why we wrote this book.

Theory or practice?

Either or. Visual communication encompasses both – you will find this combination in the book.

Complicated or simple?

When you take your time, something complicated often becomes simple. This book serves as a companion – the more you peruse it, the more familiar you will become with the topics.

Linear or intuitive?

The first part of the book (chapters A – D) is intended to be read linearly. The second part (the E and F chapters) contain sources, references, and "finds" that arise from the text. The numbers on the edge of the text will guide you there. We encourage you to "jump" around between the beginning and the end, to browse through the information.

Expertise or opinion?

Every ambitious specialist book strives for correctness, clarity, and truthfulness. So does this one. That said, an individual's perspective on an occurrence is always subjective. That's why we would rather say: expertise and opinion.

The approach

Of course, the scope of a project like this cannot cover or fully consider every facet of the subject matter. As a result, we were unable to provide in-depth accounts of many subject details that make up the curricula of

communication design courses at the university level. But that's what other specialist books and the respective seminars are for.
Our approach lay in examining and describing theoretical and practical aspects on an interdisciplinary scale, as well as delineating their relationships. In this way, the book deviates from the traditional format, which generally looks as follows: Theoreticians discuss design even though they lack practical design skills; designers, on the other hand, rarely think beyond practical applications, as they prefer to talk about the visual results of their work (or the work of others).

Our approach was aided by our experiences – for one, as a designer who has spent decades working as a professor, both in a research and teaching capacity (Ulysses Voelker); complemented by a designer currently working in the profession (Michael Schmitz). Teamwork is important – but in the end, only one person can write. That's why you will come across the occasional sentence written in the first person (by Ulysses Voelker).

Topics of social discourse

While creating this book, we dealt with the following recurring topics: questions of gender, a perspective that revolves around a western view, and the risk of cultural appropriation.
How would we be able to set examples in this book and where would we reach our limits? We had some interesting discussions on this topic with each other and with quite a few colleagues.
In terms of *gender issues*, the people we quote in the texts and refer to in the sources are mostly male. This is because women struggled to make their voices heard in the male-dominated field of design for many years. Only in the past few years has this started to change.

The western perspective depicted in this book stems from our background and our audience (students at universities located in this region). We can merely advocate for a rise in sensitivity concerning the perspectives of other cultures and the curiosity to explore these. In particular, we discussed the question of how to deal with *cultural appropriation*. After all, picking up on existing approaches and combining these in new ways constitutes an essential feature of design (similarly to music and the visual arts) – everything is connected to everything and builds on one another. Undoubtedly, not a single designer exists who has not turned to previously published work at some point – including from other cultures – to find inspiration. Here too, we would like to call for increased sensitivity in the way we handle the cultural assets of other countries – despite all the participative tendencies that most designers have adopted over the last years. Global interconnection requires particularly respectful treatment of others' copyrighted work. Furthermore, "sharing" means just that – sharing, not stealing. And when it comes to the topic of "cultural appropriation," the same rules apply as for all social topics: You cannot replace independent thinking; in fact, it is our duty.

This book's special features

When citing sources, we used the *orthotypography* of the originals – aside from the spelling, this particularly applies to the preference for lower-case letters that some protagonists prefer.

Another special feature can and should form a basis for discussion, namely the use of information provided by the platform Wikipedia. By including various references to Wikipedia pages, we are reflecting a type of behavior demonstrated by many people – both in everyday life and for specialist research:
These sources prove useful to gain a brief initial overview. However, when delving further into the subject, the researcher needs primary sources. Many studies have shown that the quality of some information published in books appeared more questionable than the platform's community efforts, always subject to public corrections and consistently up to date. We therefore want the Wikipedia links to serve as an incentive and a call to conduct further research.

On knowledge

Initially, we had planned to include a few words of wisdom at the end of this introduction – on how it takes time to acquire knowledge, that there are no shortcuts, and to emphasize what lies in store for you the more you know (that you will keep wanting to learn more in the future). Instead, we will simply conclude with a warning that the following quote summarizes well and that condenses the book's aspirations in a wonderful way:

"Knowledge makes us accountable." (Che Guevara)

That is why we are convinced that, after finishing this book, you will see communication design, and the role that you want to play within this professional field, from a different perspective.

Visual communication follows a simple structure:
It always starts with a sender who wants to transmit a message to a recipient. In contrast to ordinary communication between people – which is characterized by action and reaction and therefore features a great deal of spontaneity – visual communication constitutes a one-sided conversation. As a rule, an action does not elicit an immediate reaction. This lack of interaction creates the opportunity for a methodical approach. For this purpose, we rely on proven basic principles.

Section A of this book delves into this topic. I will start by describing what happens on the part of the recipient.
Then I will describe what the typical visual communication process looks like and the role designers play in it.

Receiving Visual Communication

"All Around Us" – that was the title of an American schoolbook from the 1950s that my uncle from the USA brought my family as a gift many years 001 ago. As a pre-school child, I leafed through the pages again and again. It was one of the first books I ever encountered. The pictures and illustrated stories as well as the sparse English words had the goal of explaining the world.[B1] But as often as I scanned and examined the book, I failed to notice that, aside from the visible information, "All Around Us" also contained some "invisible" information. Some of it was trivial: I was supposed to read the book from front to back. That was the only direction that made sense, and I had learned the same pattern from other picture books. Furthermore, I could jump from one illustrated story to the next, as each was self-contained. The illustrated stories themselves were structured in such a way that they made sense when viewed from left to right. I couldn't understand the text in the first part of the book, so it was irrelevant to me – after all, I could barely read, let alone in English. But I "knew" that my parents and my older siblings could make sense of such texts. This left me with a subtle sense of envy and seemed to indicate the following:

Visual information does not always target everyone equally. This American 002 schoolbook communicated on multiple levels and impacted me in various ways. It demonstrates several facets of visual communication that play an important role in the average intake of information, even though we often remain unaware of this.

Sensory perception

Sight makes up by far the greatest proportion of all the senses involved in the intake of information. On a percentage basis, sensory perception is distributed as follows: taste: 1.0%, haptic: 1.5%, olfactory: 3.5%, acoustic: 11.0%, visual: 83%.* Correspondingly, visual media considerably influence the opinions we form.

The unknown sparks curiosity

Our eyes respond to the unknown first. Eye-tracking tests show that our focus gives lesser priority to the aspects we consider familiar or unimportant. 003 For one, this archaic reflex is designed to warn us of threats or give the all-clear. However, the unknown also piques our curiosity.

From the big picture down to the details

Our visual perception starts with the big picture and then whittles it on to the details. This is because of our desire to quickly categorize and evaluate

* **»Sensory Branding«, Paul Steiner, SpringerGabler Verlag, 2020, p. 84**

001 ------ All Around Us, Teachers Edition, Foresman et al.
002 ------ Voyager freight to unknown recipients in outer space
003 ------ The Economy of the Eye, Aicher

001.1 -------- Definition of the term "illustration"
001.2 -------- For Your Own Good, Miller
002.1 -------- The Politics of Design, Pater
002.2 -------- Long-term nuclear waste warning
003.1 -------- Eye tracking
003.2 -------- Die Entschlüsselung der Bilder, Petersen, Schwender

B 1
The American children's schoolbook conveys a specific adult perspective: that of a white population in the 1940s and 1950s.

what we see. Based on our experience, a first glance allows us to roughly assess what we are dealing with before we focus on the details. Our practiced 004 brain connects what we see with the information we've stored. "All Around Us" demonstrates this effect in three ways:

– Our first glance reveals, completely trivially, that the object lying on the table before us is a book. This is evident based on its shape, size, thickness, and the spot on which it lies.[B 2]

– The selected illustrated story shows a car stuck in the mud. The arrangement of the images and the repetition of image details signalize a sequence. Due to our cultural socialization, we assume that this sequence runs from top left to bottom right. We see all of this with a cursory first glance at the spread, which we initially perceive as a whole.[B 3]

– Writing also constitutes a type of picture. To begin with, we observe the layout shapes and their context. And we predict the medium we might be dealing with. At this point, however, we haven't read a single word through which we could draw any conclusions.
The style of the text's typography at the start of the book, which is geared towards adults, requires us to read in a linear way (we need to read the entire text from the top left to the bottom right to understand the content) and promises a longer contextual presentation based on the font size, format, and choice of font. The double page reveals all of this before we have even started reading.[B 4]

Neuronal and evaluative perceptions

Visual perception takes place on two levels: neuronal and evaluative. To answer the question of whether an ultimate reality exists, psychologist Paul 005 Watzlawick speaks of "reality of the first order" and its "ascriptions". He describes what he means using the example of the red light at a set of traffic lights: "Reality of the first order" refers to the effect that the light signal unfolds on the retina. However, he claims that the message of "stop" is just as arbitrary as the neologism "red."
According to Watzlawick, both should be considered ascriptions that are based on cultural agreements and differ by society. Any reader who travels will be able to share experiences that differ from everyday life in their home country (in terms of the behavior, public structure, cultural traditions, 006 and similar aspects). Sometimes, these are entirely mundane: Consider the significance of the color white, which represents a color of mourning in traditional Japanese culture but is connected to weddings in Europe. Or keep in mind that in the Orient, shaking hands with a person of the

004 ------ The MAYA principle
005 ------ Wie wirklich ist die Wirklichkeit? Watzlawick
006 ------ The world from different perspectives

004.1 -------- The KISS principle
005.1 -------- Visual Perception, Nänni
005.2 -------- The Four Sides of a Message, Voelker
006.1 -------- Shifts in Mapping, Schranz et al.
006.2 -------- Alles so schön bunt hier – Ein Zeitalter der Vielfalt? Bauer

B 2
We always perceive a book as an object to begin with.

B 3
Illustrated stories are presented in a linear way.

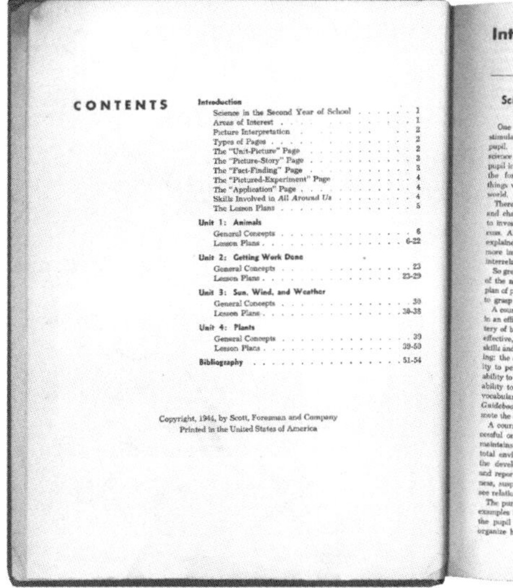

CONTENTS

Copyright, 1944, by Scott, Foresman and Company
Printed in the United States of America

Introduction

Science in the Second Year of School

One of the chief duties of the school is to stimulate and guide the all-round growth of the pupil. A fundamental aim of an adequate science program is to stimulate and guide the pupil in a constantly growing understanding of the forces, elements, materials, and living things which, together, make up his everyday world.

There is an abundance of things to interest and challenge pupils—things to watch, things to investigate, things to do, and things to discuss. All the world lies before the child, to be explained and understood in its parts and, more important still, to be understood in the interrelationships of these parts.

So great is the diversity, as well as the extent, of the natural environment that an organized plan of presentation is essential if the pupils are to grasp not only facts but also relationships.

A course in science must present information in an efficient manner. It must insure the mastery of basic understandings. But, to be really effective, it must also foster the intellectual skills and abilities necessary for scientific thinking: the ability to observe accurately, the ability to perceive likenesses and differences, the ability to infer, the ability to generalize, and the ability to understand and use an oral science vocabulary. *All Around Us* and the *Teacher's Guidebook* have been carefully planned to promote the development of these skills.

A course in science may be considered successful only if it so affects the pupil that he maintains a true scientific attitude toward his total environment. Such an attitude leads to the development of accuracy in observation and report, intellectual honesty, open-mindedness, suspended judgment, and the ability to see relationships.

The purpose of *All Around Us* is to present examples from the environment that will lead the pupil to see relationships and help him organize his thinking. *All Around Us* is the second step in a program that helps the pupil to an understanding of the principles and laws of science.

Areas of Interest

In *All Around Us* four centers, or areas, of pupil interest—animals, getting work done, weather, and plants—provide a framework upon which the pupil organizes his knowledge. They also form a basis for further exploration. This broad plan of organization leads to systematic understandings rather than to massed, unrelated factual information. (For a detailed list of concepts presented in *All Around Us*, see the Index to Concepts, pages 78-80.)

The scientific content of these broad centers of interest in *All Around Us* has been determined by four types of analysis:

1. An analysis of environment to determine the problems of living that are dependent upon science for intelligent solution
2. An analysis of these problems to determine the principles and concepts of science that provide solutions
3. An analysis of the age and grade level of the child at which these principles and concepts may be developed experientially and scientifically
4. An analysis of these principles and concepts to provide the basic experiences upon which learning must be based

Little of the actual content of *All Around Us* is new or strange to the pupils, and gaps in the pupils' background can usually be filled in quickly and efficiently. For example, few of the animals discussed in the first unit are animals that the pupils have not seen, talked about, or heard about in stories. Consequently, the basic subject matter is usually familiar; and the manner of viewing the subject matter, making inferences, and generalizing from it, provides the new element. The pupil is guided in the organization of his information through comparing

INTRODUCTION 1

B 4
Page layouts have their own informative value, even before you have read the page.

opposite gender is taboo, whereas we consider it a sign of politeness. Visual communication not only transports and manifests these ascriptions with what it shows and how, but also with what it doesn't show. In the case of the book "All Around Us," reality appears as follows: By depicting only white people, the 1950s book omits the multicultural composition (Native Americans, Afro-Americans, Asians, etc.) of US society; the genders are portrayed in a stereotypical manner – men have muscles and work, women look pretty and do housework; the book makes no mention of urban life, but instead shows an idyllic world of suburbs and small towns. [B 5 – 10]

Summary: visual communication can be misleading

This little excursion into the past aims to illustrate how visual communication relies on and caters to a wide range of cultural conventions. We consider the visuality that surrounds us in everyday life – whether in the form of a book, newspaper, sign, package insert, or website – to be a given. We fail to notice that it consists of visual "constructions" – as long as the relationship between the contextual message and creative form appears congruent, no foreign aspects interfere with the design, and it meets our expectations. I consciously chose the schoolbook "All Around Us" as an example because one thing is noticeable straight away: The content and design are products of their time, and the book would not exist today – neither in its graphical form, which seems antiquated now but was considered state-of-the-art back then, nor in its content, which reflects an outdated canon of values. The emancipatory movements of the last decades have led to the reduction of discriminatory depictions, omissions, and stereotypes in today's schoolbooks. I still loved the book as a child. The fragmented nature of the images, the stories they told, the illustration style, and the color climate: All of this strongly appealed to me. The multidimensional nature that characterizes visual communication bears a certain danger. Because even for adults, it remains nearly impossible to break down the content analytically and search for motives while at the same time absorbing the presented content. At any rate, this isn't feasible if visual communication makes use of its manipulative capacities. After all, we just need to ask ourselves what values we have internalized as truthful today and which ascriptions we accept without challenging them. Questioning something requires time and energy. And that's why we, the recipients of visual communication, are less robust and critical than we might think. That brings us to those responsible for visual communication – the senders.

007

007 ------ Addressing target groups, using the example of "All Around Us"

B 5

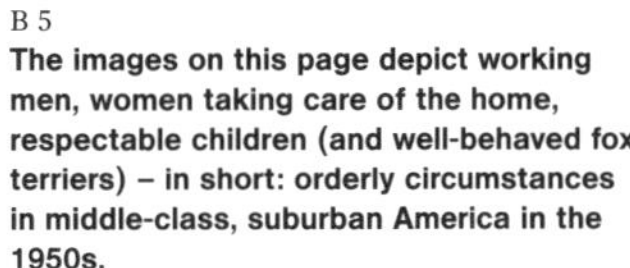

The images on this page depict working men, women taking care of the home, respectable children (and well-behaved fox terriers) – in short: orderly circumstances in middle-class, suburban America in the 1950s.

B 6

B 7

B 8

B 9

B 10

Sending Visual Communication

All humans communicate visually. They make use of various options and media, from their first self-drawn picture, early writing exercises, shopping lists, homework, postcards, photos, letters through to social media. This individual communication is targeted at a wide range of recipients, its design generally takes shape intuitively and/or is determined by the respective medial circumstances. For other types of visual communication, the sender aims to trigger a calculated effect on their target group using designed content. These processes require the input of designers. Their work is based on their knowledge of the three basic principles of visual communication. 008

First principle: the process

If we wanted to present a form of visual communication in a schematic way, as in diagram[B 11], the basic pattern would appear as follows: We have a communication situation in which a sender wants to transmit information to recipients (generally, we are dealing with target groups, not individuals) and wants to do so in a visual manner. In a similar vein to verbal communication – where the style, tone, gestures, and facial expressions are responsible for the way the spoken content comes across to the recipient – visual communication relies on tools that influence the effect of the transmitted content. As a rule, lay designers lack the respective knowledge and require professional help for the visual communication process. They need a designer. To begin with, the designer needs to understand what the sender is trying to say and how the sender wants to influence their recipients. Next, the designer takes a closer look at the recipients:
What is their taste like, what values are important to them, what is their educational level, what patterns of reception are discernible? Based on this background, the designer and sender develop a briefing together: Here, they define the impact they want to achieve, select suitable media, determine the budget, and define timeframes. Only once these factors have been settled does the design process begin.

Second principle: visual rhetoric

The design process is based on the effect mechanisms of visual rhetoric. Before I describe this term in more detail, I would like to address its origins, with which you will already be familiar from the area of verbal communication: Here, the goal frequently lies in triggering previously calculated and therefore desired reactions in the recipients. The method for achieving this goal stems from the high art of (ancient) oratory – or as we would call it, rhetoric (defined as "the art of speech"). As we know from the linguistics of 009

008 ------ Definition of the term "Design", Erlhoff, Marshall
009 ------ Definition of the term "Rhetoric"
009.1 -------- Declaration by Design: Rhetorik, Argument und Darstellung in der Designpraxis, Buchanan

everyday life, the use of rhetorical devices increases a person's persuasiveness. You will all remember lectures you found particularly persuasive. This appraisal is usually influenced by a compelling arc of tension, vivid examples, varied language, supporting gestures and facial expressions, moments that liven up the atmosphere, and credible argumentation. In short: The lecturer used rhetorical techniques. But you will also remember lectures that lacked all of this and left you longing for the end of a seemingly endless monolog.

Rhetorical aspects also play a crucial role in the design process. Here, the aim lies in using relevant visual devices to persuade others. This is referred to as visual rhetoric. It simplifies design work tremendously because all considerations revolve around the previously defined parameters. As a result, the design process becomes more predictable and loses the ambivalence that arises when you proceed purely based on instinct. In the following, I will clarify why this is the case.
Dialectic thought processes underpin both verbal and visual rhetoric. These, in turn, influence the quality of a (linguistic or graphical) piece. In other words: If you don't think rhetorically, you cannot create compelling designs (except perhaps accidentally). Only those who communicate rhetorical thoughts through adequate means can develop convincing designs. The internal logic of this relationship becomes clear when you "zoom into" a visual communication process:
Before your rhetorical thoughts can take shape, you need to gain an understanding of the imagination of those you are trying to reach with your visual message. This "anticipation" of a target audience's needs gives you an idea of the visual aspects you will have to incorporate into your argumentation. For this purpose, you can take advantage of a range of visual/verbal rhetorical devices. 010

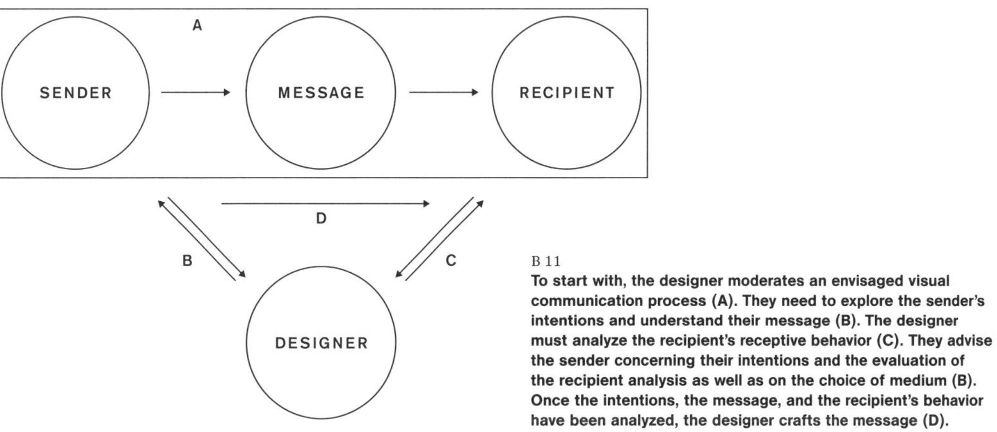

B 11
To start with, the designer moderates an envisaged visual communication process (A). They need to explore the sender's intentions and understand their message (B). The designer must analyze the recipient's receptive behavior (C). They advise the sender concerning their intentions and the evaluation of the recipient analysis as well as on the choice of medium (B). Once the intentions, the message, and the recipient's behavior have been analyzed, the designer crafts the message (D).

010 ------ Visuell-verbale Rhetorik, Bonsiepe

Analogies are some of the best-known rhetorical devices. Anyone interested in design will be familiar with these: You create an analogy by visualizing a verbal statement in a semantically equivalent way for illustrative purposes. Sounds complicated, but if we use our imagination, we can come up with a few examples – for example, how could attributes such as loud, quiet, exciting, calm, rebellious, or compliant find their visual equivalent in typography and in the layout? If we want to design a loud and exciting layout, we can resort to certain tools – such as bold and large fonts, significant differences in the font sizes and image formats, an asymmetrical grid, narrow edges, signal colors, and so on. Here, in the layout, it actually starts to take shape: rhetorical communication through design. Because even if we omitted all the listed preliminary considerations and simply started designing "unthinkingly," we could not prevent the design from sending signals – solely by means of its presence, entirely in the spirit of Watzlawick's axiom: "You cannot not communicate." * 011

Third principle: the medial laws

The selected medium makes up another important component of the design process. Without it, design wouldn't be conceivable. We find ourselves confronted with all kinds of media in everyday life. They have their own typical visual characteristics with which they signal from afar how we are meant to observe them. We categorize them accordingly – this is a newspaper, this is more of a magazine, these signs guide us as part of an orientation system, while this package insert provides us with information, this is a form, this will open a website, and so on. Every type of medium specifies a certain way in which it should be read and at the same time is confronted with the recipient's reading expectations: Sometimes reading serves an informative purpose (newspaper, magazine), sometimes an advisory purpose (package insert, guidance system), sometimes linear reading (novel), sometimes activating reading (advertising posters). This list shows that the various media have their own laws that govern how they work. 012

All in all, we can conclude that visual communication requires a structured approach. We need to take three basic principles into account:
The process starts with the analysis, which leads to a concept. Visual rhetoric helps translate this concept into design measures. Medial laws create the respective settings for this.

*
You can find the passage (p. 19, line 19 – p. 20, line 16) in the book "Read + Play" (p. 121). **See 068.1 for details on the book.**

011 ------ Die fünf metakommunikativen Axiome
012 ------ Different ways of reading

012.1 -------- Lesen – Ein interdisziplinäres Handbuch, Rautenberg, Schneider

NTT
西日本

注意

重要電話線あり

この付近を掘る
ときは必ず
事前にご連絡ください

サンキュウ サーイクヨ

連絡先 0120-39-3194

NTT西日本

（立会等無料）

To start with, section B of this book covers the basics of sign theory in relation to visual communication. On this basis, we can derive components and factors for design practice.

The components relate to both the general conventions that prevail within a society and the tastes that are prevalent within target groups. On the one hand, these factors constitute a time-related influence on design in line with the relevant dominant technique. On the other hand, we will present factors that arise from social circumstances and cultural trends and are discernible under the label of "zeitgeist" in the visual communication of different eras.

The aspects of "subjectivity" and "speculation" highlight the roles that designers play within this field of tension.

Sign Theory and Visual Communication

The principles introduced in Chapter A are based on general findings on the essence and use of signs. The academic field that revolves around signs is called semiotics. To introduce readers to its concepts, philosopher and sociologist Umberto Eco addressed the significance of signs in human communication in his book “Signs – Introduction to a Term and its History.” To start with, the book introduces Signor Sigma, who suffers from a stomachache during a stay in Paris. Signor Sigma then attempts to interpret this pain and takes the necessary steps to consult a doctor. He picks up a Parisian phone book, in which characters indicate who is a doctor and what number he can dial to reach them. Since Signor Sigma does not have a phone, he walks into a Parisian bar. He knows that he will find a pay phone here (Eco wrote the story in 1977). In Italy, his home country, he would know exactly where to find such a phone in a bar – right next to the cash register. But in Paris, he needs to look around first because he is not familiar with these bars. Here, pay phones are always located on the way to the restroom. He finds the phone and now needs to start the calling process. To do so successfully, he must understand what coins he has to insert into which slots. He also needs to know how to operate a rotary dial in order to enter the number consisting of letters and digits (the number is DAN 0019). The doctor gives him an address and schedules an appointment. Signor Sigma takes a taxi to get there. In the car, he needs to communicate with the taxi driver. Once he has arrived at his destination, the doorbell panel and door sign guide him to the practice. The doctor examines him and starts to interpret the signs he perceives by feeling the patient’s stomach and listening to Signor Sigma’s account of his ailment... Over the course of this story that spans just a few pages, Signor Sigma is confronted with all kinds of communication processes. This little story is teeming with signs that transmit impulses, signals, and messages to ALL human senses. Eco refers to a “network of sign systems” that (provided we are dealing with interpretive common knowledge based on cultural conventions) makes it possible for Signor Sigma to engage in this social interaction.

Umberto Eco describes the academic field he is introducing as follows: “The field of semiotics examines all cultural processes as communication processes. It aims to show how systems underpin cultural processes. The dialectic of system and process leads to the assembly of the dialectic of code and message.”* This means that semiotics targets all forms of communication; it represents a component of various academic disciplines, including epistemology and linguistics. Umberto Eco dedicated a whole chapter of his book “A Theory of Semiotics” to visual communication, titled “Semiotics of

013

*
“Einführung in die Semiotik,”
Umberto Eco,
Wilhelm Fink Verlag 1972, p. 38

013 ------ Zeichen – Einführung in einen Begriff und seine Geschichte, Eco

013.1 -------- Scents of the City, Baur, Naegele

Visual Codes." Here, he discusses signs' general modes of action; how they relate to what they depict and intend to depict; why they look the way they look, and how we perceive them. The explanations of sign and perception theory describe the structures and levels of meaning based on which all humans communicate visually.*

Relevance for communication design

You, the reader of this text, surely understand that we cannot offer an in-depth discussion of semiotics here. After all, this field constitutes an academic discipline that must be studied independently and is highly complex. For designers, whose task not only lies in creating concepts of visual communication, but also in designing such visual communication, semiotics offers few connecting points that are directly applicable to design practice – but there are some. In our view, it is helpful to confer such sign-theory fragments to the field of communication design. A model was developed for this purpose that addresses theoretical reflections from the perspective of design practice.** If we apply this model to the story of Signor Sigma, we can divide the different forms of communication into three categories:

1) *Cultural conventions* – examples: phone calls as a form of communication, the nature of the phone, coding of participants by means of phone numbers, taxis as a mode of transport, doorbell panels and door signs, physical symptoms, and diagnostic methods.
2) *Subjective sensations* – examples: Signor Sigma's feeling of pain, his decision to consult a doctor, the challenges presented by a foreign language, the doctor's range of interpretations while making a diagnosis.
3) *Time-specific influences* – examples: the phone book; the circumstances of not having your own telephone line; the pay phone's location and properties; the rotary dial. All of this describes the reality of 1977.

The three listed categories refer to components and factors that play a crucial role in creating visual communication and that make up the model:

Constant components: These refer to the codes that are determined by general cultural conventions.

Modifying components: These refer to the codes that are based on subjective feelings, habits (and standards of taste), and perceptions (influenced by socialization).

Time-related factors: These refer to visual codes' reliance on society's currently prevailing conditions as well as the patterns of value and meaning

*
You can find the passage (lines 10 – 45) in the book "Read + Play" (p. 119). See 068.1 for details on the book.

**
The terms used in the model may overlap with those common in semiotics. Here, their meaning is related to the presented model and refers to design practice.

typical of the respective time period. The following chapters are dedicated to these components and factors.

Constant Components

In visual communication, constant components all represent codes that are embedded in a culture as conventions and do not change, or change very slowly. Constant components allow for quick orientations and assessments. Even if its inhabitants remain unaware of this, all kinds of regulative systems are interwoven into the society in which they live. These span an infinitely vast spectrum and range from value standards, laws, constructions, and procedures through to behavioral conventions and visual communication.

015

Conventions condition people

There are countless examples of ways to assess whether something corresponds to what we think belongs to a classification system or convention. Simply imagine what something would need to look like if it were considered outside the norm. You would just need to picture an upside-down world in which stop signs are suddenly round and passports come in an A1 format, in which the color green tells you to stop and the color red tells you to go – a world in which everything is turned around. But we don't even need to resort to such drastic examples. Even minor deviations can lead to a sense of irritation. Font designer Adrian Frutiger came up with an example for this. Imagine a game die with its dot values from one to six. When you picture a die like this, you will most likely be able to draw the arrangements of the dots on the respective die sides from memory. Then Frutiger changed the arrangement – but the values remained the same. [B 13] As a result, the die looks wrong. Playing with it would prove difficult, even though it would theoretically be possible without causing any issues. This shows that we are conditioned in many different ways and are reluctant to accept something new if there seems to be no reason for it. This has obvious consequences for design practice – designers need to know the prevailing conventions, how to detect deviations, and how to evaluate these.

Examples from the "morphological table," also devised by Frutiger, demonstrate the extent to which humans have been conditioned in an unconscious way. *(see p. 29)*.

016

Take a look at the square, which consists of lines. Viewed from the top, it appears like a closed room. When you open the bottom side of the square, this clearly depicts the symbol for a dwelling from the side view. If you turn the square around, with the open side facing upwards, the figure

015 ------ Otto Neurath – The Language of the Global Polis, Vossoughian
016 ------ Signs and Symbols, Frutiger

015.1 -------- Die Transformierer – Entstehung und Prinzipien von Isotype, Kinross et al.
015.2 -------- Design von Frauen, Fiell, Fiell
015.3 -------- HerStories in Graphic Design, Breuer
016.1 -------- Proust and the Squid, Wolf

B 13
Irritation breaks trust: Imagine someone challenged you to gamble using these dice.

resembles a vessel. Both assessments are based on the human experience of gravity: Something can fall from above (such as rain); however, anything that gathers the bottom (such as liquids or objects) remains in place. If you turn the square to have the open side facing left, this could signify a symbol for “entrance;” if the open side faces the right, it could represent a symbol for “exit.”[B 14-18] Why do we Central Europeans share this perception? Because we learned that, in our culture, dynamic movement runs from left to right. This is what we learned when we started to read and write.
Written languages in general serve as the ultimate examples of constant components. They demonstrate reading processes that people in their respective cultures have learned and internalized. Fonts are based on unchangeable alphabets, and these, in turn, determine our reading behavior. The Latin letters with which we are familiar not only set the reading direction (from left to right), but also impact the way we read: Our eye jumps from one fixation point to the next. We refer to this process as reading in saccades.[B 19]

017

During this process, our gaze scans the top part of the words. The ascents and the upper edges of the x-height give us sufficient information about a word (unlike the descents and the bottom edge of the x-heights). This means that the reading process consists more of guessing and affirming rather than moving from letter to letter. This finding has a few simple implications: We can easily read writing that uses mixed cases (i.e., a mixture of lower-case and upper-case letters, as is common in our part of the world), whereas we struggle to read texts using only upper-case letters due to their lack of differentiated upper edges.

We consider these and many other practiced habits natural parts of a cultural reality. These self-evident factors contain further findings. To continue with our examples from the area of reading: We can easily read the lines of a longer text if they consist of no fewer than 45 and no more than 70 characters. Lines that contain more characters become more difficult to read because it takes longer to find the start of the next line. A left-justified layout is easier to read than a right-justified or centered layout. This is because we read from left to right, so a unified layout edge on the left helps us find the next line. The list of (typo)graphical stipulations that support access to textual information in a specific way is long, but it also varies depending on the medium and should therefore be explored further by consulting relevant specialist publications.

018

Fonts draw their aesthetic finesse from the conditions specified by the language’s country of origin, as demonstrated by examples from the past in which you would expect significant differences, as all three are based on the Latin alphabet – the fonts “Bodoni” from Italy, “Times” from Great Britain, and “Garamond” from France.[B 20] The crucial factors that determine the

017 ------ Decodeunicode, Bergerhausen, Poarangan

018 ------ Detailtypografie, de Jong, Forssman

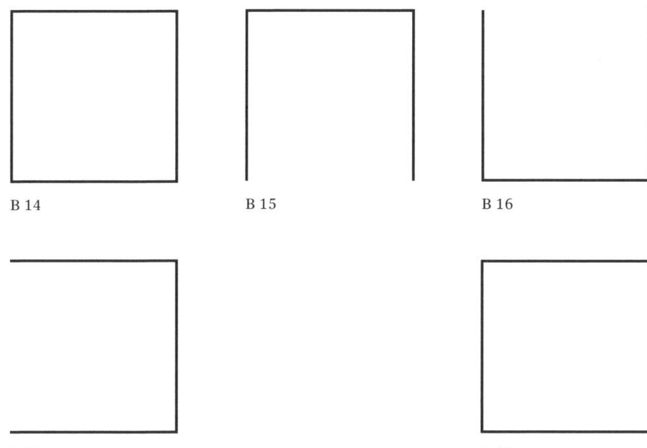

B 14 B 15 B 16

B 17 B 18

Ich komme aus einem fernen Lande. Einst
lebte dort ein friedliches und gottesfürchtiges
Volk, das ein gütiger König regierte.

B 19
We read in saccades:
Our eyes flit from one fixation point to the next.

aesthetic effect of a font when written in its language of origin are orthographic features – for example, how it uses uppercase letters or accents, or the frequency of certain letters in the respective language.

As the small number of examples – from dice to fonts – have already shown, culture-specific conventions have permeated our everyday lives and thus also visual communication. The fact that these have developed differently in various regions and cultures of the world comes as no surprise, since they stem from specific traditions (in terms of alphabets and reading direction, for example). Other experiences (such the effect of gravity and other irrefutable scientific conditions) shape all of humanity.

Conditioning creates expectations

Visual communication serves internalized conventions and at the same time sends signals that tell us how to classify graphic products. The creators select formats and typographical standards that cater to this interplay of acquired expectations and satisfying these in relation to the different media. That is why novels are published in the form of a book that you can easily hold in your hands, and its typography is designed in such a way that it enables "linear reading." We refer to the reading process as "linear" because we need to the many lines and pages of the full text of the novel if we want to understand its content.

However, we read newspapers for an "informative" purpose: They offer plenty of information pieces placed next to or below one another. Each of these is self-contained. The reader can jump from one "information island" to the next. Accordingly, this type of publication requires a larger format (bigger than a book, for example). We do not perceive the clutter created by multiple differing and competing pieces of information as a flaw, but essentially expect this as a typical characteristic of a newspaper. However, if we saw large, homogenous masses of unstructured text, this would lead to considerable irritation. At first glance, we would not refer to such a publication as a newspaper. The medium of a magazine also presents a form of clutter, though on a different level. But again, we expect this of magazines, as we also read them for "informative" purposes. Perhaps we should replace the term "clutter" with "liveliness." This applies to various content-based formats. For example, magazines will have sections such as "Title story," "Report," "Documentary," which include infographics, a lot of large and small images with captions, pages for brief reports on many different events (these may fall under a heading such as "Panorama"), categories such as "Business," "Sports," "Politics," or "Culture." All of these different editorial formats may vary in terms of font and layout within one theoretical design

Times (8 pt, Line spacing 9,5 pt)

English

I come from a distant land. Once upon a time, a peaceful and God-fearing people lived there, ruled by a benevolent queen. She was advised by great scholars and bold scientists. One day, however, a noble man rode up on a magnificent horse, whom no one had ever seen before, who wanted to see the queen. The queen was without guile, for her advisors saw no reason for suspicion. And so they held a royal feast, during which the wine flowed in torrents and as much boiled and roasted food as they wanted was served. At an advanced hour, the stranger paid the queen great compliments.

German

Ich komme aus einem fernen Lande. Einst lebte dort ein friedliches und gottesfürchtiges Volk, das eine gütige Königin regierte. Beraten wurde sie von großen Gelehrten und kühnen Wissenschaftlerinnen. Doch eines Tages kam ein edler Mann auf einem prächtigen Pferd daher geritten, den keiner je zuvor gesehen hatte, der begehrte die Königin zu sehen. Die Königin war ohne Arglist, denn ihre Berater sahen keinen Grund für Misstrauen. Und so hielten sie ein königliches Gelage, während dessen der Wein in Strömen floss und Gesottenes wie Gebratenes gereicht wurde, soviel man wollte. Zu vorgerückter Stunde machte der Fremde der Königin große Komplimente.

Garamond (8 pt, Line spacing 9,5 pt)

French

Je viens d'un pays lointain. Il y vivait autrefois un peuple paisible et pieux, gouverné par une reine bienveillante. Elle était conseillée par de grands savants et des scientifiques audacieux. Mais un jour, un homme noble, que personne n'avait jamais vu auparavant, arriva sur un cheval magnifique et demanda à voir la reine. La reine était sans malice, car ses conseillers ne voyaient aucune raison de se méfier. Ils organisèrent donc un festin royal au cours duquel le vin coula à flots et où l'on servit des viandes bouillies et rôties à volonté. À une heure avancée de la nuit, l'étranger fit de grands compliments à la reine.

German

Ich komme aus einem fernen Lande. Einst lebte dort ein friedliches und gottesfürchtiges Volk, das eine gütige Königin regierte. Beraten wurde sie von großen Gelehrten und kühnen Wissenschaftlerinnen. Doch eines Tages kam ein edler Mann auf einem prächtigen Pferd daher geritten, den keiner je zuvor gesehen hatte, der begehrte die Königin zu sehen. Die Königin war ohne Arglist, denn ihre Berater sahen keinen Grund für Misstrauen. Und so hielten sie ein königliches Gelage, während dessen der Wein in Strömen floss und Gesottenes wie Gebratenes gereicht wurde, soviel man wollte. Zu vorgerückter Stunde machte der Fremde der Königin große Komplimente.

Bodoni (8 pt, Line spacing 9,5 pt)

Italian

Vengo da una terra lontana. C'era una volta un popolo pacifico e timorato di Dio, governato da una regina benevola. La consigliavano grandi studiosi e audaci scienziati. Un giorno, però, arrivò un uomo nobile su un magnifico cavallo, che nessuno aveva mai visto prima, che voleva vedere la regina. La regina non aveva alcuna intenzione di fare il furbo, perché i suoi consiglieri non vedevano alcun motivo di sospetto. Così si tenne un banchetto regale, durante il quale il vino scorreva a fiumi e venivano serviti tutti i cibi bolliti e arrostiti che si volevano. A un'ora avanzata, lo straniero fece alla regina grandi complimenti.

German

Ich komme aus einem fernen Lande. Einst lebte dort ein friedliches und gottesfürchtiges Volk, das eine gütige Königin regierte. Beraten wurde sie von großen Gelehrten und kühnen Wissenschaftlerinnen. Doch eines Tages kam ein edler Mann auf einem prächtigen Pferd daher geritten, den keiner je zuvor gesehen hatte, der begehrte die Königin zu sehen. Die Königin war ohne Arglist, denn ihre Berater sahen keinen Grund für Misstrauen. Und so hielten sie ein königliches Gelage, während dessen der Wein in Strömen floss und Gesottenes wie Gebratenes gereicht wurde, soviel man wollte. Zu vorgerückter Stunde machte der Fremde der Königin große Komplimente.

B 20
The three examples show how fonts appear in their native languages – and how different their impact is in German.

climate. The impression the reader wants to gain is triggered in this way – in this case, the dominant features are a wealth of information and entertainment. If we look back at the magazines of a certain genre over a period from the more distant past, we can see that the structure has not changed much over the years – even if the design is subject to era-appropriate transformations now and again.

Constant components also appear in guidance systems, although in this case, technological developments are still most likely to bring about progressive [020] structural changes – consider navigation systems, for example, which are making many sign systems obsolete. Still, little has changed in terms of the distance from which fonts on (analog and digital) signs are easy to read and the clearest way to arrange information.

Whether we are dealing with old technologies or new ones, as in the example of navigation systems, or the many network-based apps or websites: They all attempt to cater to reading conventions (regarding expectations). A smartphone, for one, requires a "responsive" design: A website appears different (than on a computer) and reacts to the smaller size of display by enlarging the font. The goal lies in enabling comfortable reading that aligns with traditional standards (proportionately large font depending on the [021] reading distance). In this case, a new medium is providing the traditional form of "informative reading." The reader is no longer turning the pages, but instead scrolling. In addition, new media open up the option to include links, videos, and more. But the structure of an article (with the hierarchy of headline, sub-headline, running text, images plus captions) has not changed at all.

Perceptive processes start with the big picture before they move on to the details. Based on the format, layout arrangement, and use of font, we likely already "know" what kind of medium we are dealing with before we have read a single line. And even if readers are close enough to a medium to read the text, they trust in their experience and first observe the arrangement of texts, images, and other graphic information to make an initial judgment: Large text consisting of few words is most likely a headline, while small text beneath an image is a caption, body text divided into several columns provides detailed information.

Constant components form the foundation

The way humans perceive their visual environment affects the way we design visual communication. This represents a reciprocal reinforcement: If readers have very specific expectations of a medium, designers will do their

020 ------ Orientierungssysteme und Signaletik, Uebele
021 ------ The Grid in Web Design, Voelker
020.1 -------- Visual Coexistence. Informationdesign and Typography in the Intercultural Field, Baur, Felsing

best to meet these expectations. This not only applies to media, but also to different genres and assumed preferences. One downside of this reciprocal reinforcement: It confirms ingrained expectations. Visual communication occurs within this field of tension. It relies on viewing habits – and at the same time continuously tries to expand them with new approaches. After all, we also have this expectation when it comes to visual communication – we want to see something new, something unusual, something surprising. This means that, on the one hand, the basis for everything new as well as for tried-and-tested practices comprises universally applicable conventions that I refer to as the components of design. On the other hand, we need scope for differentiation that allows us to develop new facets within visual communication. These expanding margins are defined by another component and a factor, which I will discuss in the next two chapters.

Modifying Components

Modifying components are visual codes that are based on subjective feelings (such as taste standards) and perceptions (influenced by socialization).

We are familiar with comparable modifications from everyday communication between people: We have an individual sense of the kind of tone appropriate for a certain situation and types of gestures and facial expressions that best support our verbal communication. The type of communication not only depends on what we want to say, but above all, who we are speaking to. Whether communicating with authorities, trusted individuals, or in different professional roles: In every situation, we adapt our communication to the individuals we are communicating with. The content and tone result from the intentions and goals we are pursuing during a conversation. Over the course of this conversation, we readjust our communicative behavior again and again, tailoring it to the reactions of the person we are talking to and their conversational behavior.

Target groups and their expectations

This aspect differs somewhat in visual communication because we are "sending" messages in a one-sided manner and do not receive immediate feedback. We have the time to prepare our communication, so it takes place under different conditions. 022 But aside from interpreting the content correctly, it is essential to take the recipients into account. And this is where we inevitably encounter individual or group-specific trends that fall under the term "taste." Design must respond to taste in order to communicate successfully. Accordingly, the means to make this happen vary by target group.

022 ------ Stimulus and Response, Voelker

023

As the saying goes, there is no accounting for taste. This is due to its subjective character. Taste is derived from diverse sociocultural components. As a designer, when addressing your visual message, you are dealing with countless different tastes and thus with diverse educational levels, varying social groupings, individual tendencies, wide-ranging morals, and diverging cultural backgrounds. All readers will understand that this also leads to significant differences in terms of clarity, differentiation, humor, intellectual levels, design finesse, and value standards – depending on with whom you are communicating visually. In a society like ours, in which individuality ranks as one of the highest assets, we can – despite this sense of individuality – assign every person to a group that has its own specific taste standards. We only need to look at one example to illustrate this: We can say with near certainty that single and childless communication design students between the ages of 20 and 25 who live in shared accommodation have more in common on a national scale than, for example, business students who live alone. In addition to the identical goal of completing the same degree program and their corresponding professional interests, these individuals' similarities extend to their preferred clothing style, a certain range of music, the importance of specific social values, or their general lifestyle. The lack of similarities with other groups – such as non-academic professionals under 40 or 18-year-old construction apprentices or retired professors – is even more obvious.

With this in mind, we can conclude that as long as the sender designs a message that convinces the recipient, their visual communication can be considered successful – no matter how others perceive it. This verdict does not apply to general graphical or typographical standards that the designer did or did not follow. While this might sound irritating, it ultimately makes sense: A punk flyer [B 21], for example, composed of copied pictures, typewriter typography, and glued-on or handwritten letters, will fail to win over a mainstream audience.

In line with the expectations within the subculture, it is teeming with "incorrect" typography: Letters do not stay within the type line and feature irregular spacing, lines are crooked, texts have been damaged by the copy technology and are therefore hard to read, images are full of flaws – also due to the copy technology –, not to mention the lack of a grid-based structure that would allow for a good reading orientation. Even though the poster is filled with "mistakes" (if you apply the standards of traditional graphics rules), the design is appropriate. It consists of modifying components that are employed only for this purpose and this target group but would be out of place in other contexts. When we speak of successful communication, this means that it fulfilled the specific expectations of a target group. It does not

023 ------ Definitions of the term "Taste"

B 21

Some consider it a well-designed collection of taboo breaches, others consider it bad taste through and through. Who is right?

try to cater to the average understanding of what "proper" design should look like. The extent to which the design process was intuitive and the extent to which it was planned are also related to the designer's proximity to the recipient group. But whatever the weighting that gave rise to the design: If the flyer reaches the recipients, the designer has managed to empathize with them in some way that gives the design an authentic appearance and suits their taste.

You will encounter this approach for all target group-oriented designs. Whether an investment brochure from a financial institution, a service provider's website, or a customer magazine: The presumed expectations of previously determined target groups as well as patterns of taste and value always have a considerable impact on the design process. In all cases, conventions (that are reflected in the constant components) form the foundation. But these conventions are then differentiated through the modifying components in line with the occasion and recipient.

Required knowledge of target groups

We mentioned the example of "single and childless 20- to 25-year-old communication designers who live in shared accommodation." The description sounds oddly specific, but for good reason: The more we know about a target group, the more focused the visual/rhetorical conclusions we can draw and the more accurate the design will be as a result. If we expanded our list to include that the students have nearly completed their studies and have chosen to focus on typography, you can already guess – regardless of the content – what kinds of considerations would need to precede their design work. The fact that descriptions of target groups are often vague constitutes a discipline-specific dilemma (take the prime example of descriptions such as "individuals between the ages of 19 and 49"). As an initial priority, we should make sure we do not simply accept imprecise descriptions, but instead insist on learning more details. Admittedly, this is not always easy. Frequently, we receive tasks with target groups that are simply heterogeneous. However, getting to know them to the greatest extent possible makes up part of the work process for communication designers. Only after conducting a differentiated analysis of the situation can we determine the design scope within which we can design in a targeted way. For large projects (such as advertising campaigns, product launches, or developing new magazines), precise target-group observations already form part of the agenda, but they come at a high cost. These involve market-research experts who compile, review, and evaluate all necessary data on a target group using complex processes. Market research is a component of marketing.

024

024 ------ On marketing. On market research

Taste and quality

The taste, receptive behavior, and the expectations of a target group therefore contribute to the design to a considerable extent. However, understanding target groups is only the first step on the journey to good design. Because the "success" of visual communication alone does not serve as evidence of the quality of the work. It merely confirms that the designer has fulfilled a basic requirement: In principle, they have understood their recipients. The visual/rhetorical considerations and the resulting consequences then reveal the ramifications of this circumstance. This tension field of understanding and consequence is of crucial importance during the design process. After all, the resulting quality is often measured based on the way the interplay is interpreted: Are you catering to tastes in a clichéd manner or emphasizing new, additional features? Are you overestimating or underestimating the intelligence and tolerance of the target group? Are you surprising them or confirming routines? Of course, these are all questions that you will need to address and answer on a case-by-case basis.

If we apply this to the example of the punk flyer, we need to ask the following questions: What generation of punks are we addressing? Is the interplay between content and form coherent? Does the graphic implementation appear unauthentic in the subculture's current environment? How do we deal with clichés? Does the design emphasize new features? Do the modifying components sufficiently support the communication goal or is something missing?

These questions show that design processes come with a range of conceptual challenges linked to aspects of quality. Every form of visual communication presents a different relationship within the triad of sender – message – recipient. If conception and design can achieve more for the specific constellations than just being understood by the target group, then a "successful" visual message most likely turns into a "good" visual message.

In chapters C and D, we will address the ways to gauge what "good" design might mean beyond the aspects discussed here.

Time-Related Factors – Technology

Time-related factors include events and developments that can shape society, and therefore also visual communication, from the time of their initial appearance – before new events and developments supersede them. We have picked out two factors that we will examine in detail. To start with, we will take a look at the influence of technology. In the following chapter, we will discuss the influence of social developments.

Hot metal typesetting

The invention of hot metal typesetting is considered to be the beginning of typography. The term refers to typeface design under the auspices of mechanical reproducibility. In this way, hot metal typesetting also heralded the democratization of knowledge, since the ability to duplicate writing expanded access to texts to the wider population. The procedure, invented by Johannes Gutenberg around 1450, entailed filling letters to create printable alphabets (including all punctuation). To start with, the printer would produce a back-to-front hard-metal mold, which was then hammered into copper. Next, they would fill the resulting negative molds with a liquid lead alloy. After cooling, the molds were reworked and then sorted into a typecase as cast lead letters.[B 22]

Now the printer arranged the ready-to-use characters into words. To add spaces between words, spacing material was used, also known as slugs or leading. To create the justified layout that was common at the time, the spaces needed to be filled to ensure that all lines had the same length. This meant minimally stretching or shortening the spaces using the spacing material without creating visible "holes" between the words. After completing the printing process through manual typesetting, the printing plate would be dismantled into its individual components and arranged back into typesetting cases. The described technique shows that the design focused on aspects of craftsmanship, particularly to ensure good readability and harmonious proportions.[B 23]

Accordingly, craftsmen such as typesetters and printers were responsible for the entire process. Over the course of industrialization in the 19th century, mechanical typesetting became prevalent alongside manual typesetting for reasons of speed and streamlining (for example, for printing newspapers). The typesetting machines cast entire lines at once, which were melted down after use and then recast for the next application. The lead type had a significant impact on visual communication. While during Gutenberg's era, the works that were set and printed included almost exclusively religious works (in book form) and letters of indulgence, the types of printed

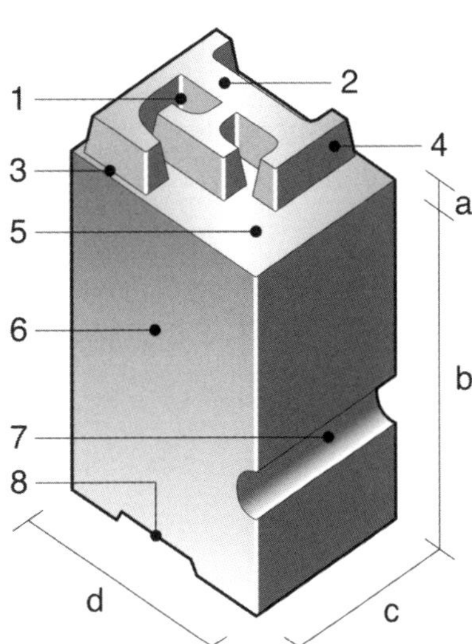

B 22

The example of a moveable lead letter.
Here is the hot metal type body of the uppercase "F":

1. Counter
2. Typeface
3. Non-printing part
4. Taper
5. Axle surface
6. Body
7. Signature
8. Pouring groove

Dimensions:
a Head
b Shoulder height
a+b Character height

Details:
c Width
d Body height

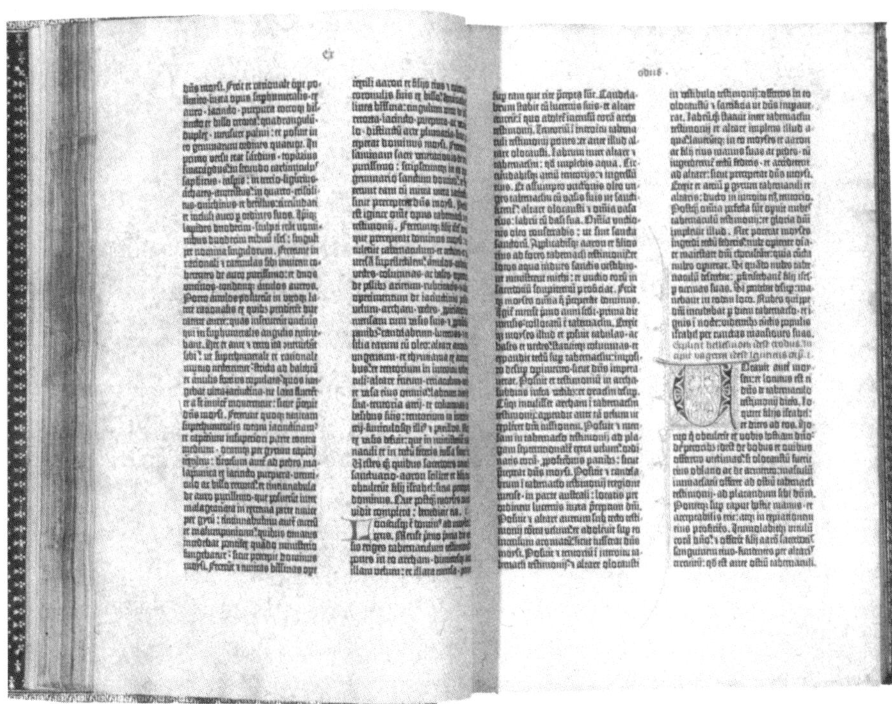

B 23

42-line bible, also known as the *Gutenberg Bible*, 1452 – 1454, Gutenberg-Museum, Mainz

media steadily increased as the technique grew more and more widespread over the course of the century. Soon the printed products included pamphlets, newspapers, scientific reference material, and many more. But while the design varied throughout the different cultural epochs, the technique remained largely unchanged.
As illustrated by the description of the procedure, the typesetting process was laborious and inflexible compared to later techniques. Due to its style and restrictions, lead type created a very special aesthetic characterized by the strict rules of the craft and limited variability (compared to today) of the layout structures.[B 24]

Phototypesetting

In the 1960s, phototypesetting began to replace lead type – and ushered in many new possibilities. Now designers were able to carry out creative work that had not been possible for centuries due to the tapers of the letters used in the era of lead type: for example, moving letters and lines closer together or varying font sizes as needed in a simple way, without having them on hand as physical objects. From a technical perspective, phototypesetting represented a real advancement and simplification, since it did not rely on physical letters. Films served in their stead. To turn the designer's draft into a finished product, they commissioned filming of the final type and any photographs. Then the designer would assemble the films into a print template. In a photographic procedure, the template would be exposed on a printing plate. This was required for the offset print. It is not hard to imagine that working with film material offered considerably more flexibility and could be completed much more quickly than lead typesetting. Phototypesetting inspired designers to experiment with the new possibilities it offered.[B 25] The designs of Wolfgang Weingart, for one, demonstrate the scope provided by the new technique.[B 26]

026

Computer typesetting

Computer typesetting, also called desktop publishing, started to supersede phototypesetting in the mid-1980s. Ever since, print templates have been produced digitally and sent to printing companies. The printing plates for offset printing are exposed digitally or even printed digitally. Since the inception of this technique, computer typesetting has significantly expanded the boundaries of what design can do. Technical limitations due to physical procedures (lead letters, films) are a thing of the past. The fact that designers can create a draft without the assistance of typesetters or lithographers has led to the possibility of interpreting typographic rules without critical feedback on the manual process. While this liberates designers, it also comes with an increased necessity for designers to acquire an even

026 ------ Phototypesetting

026.1 -------- Weingart: My Way to Typography

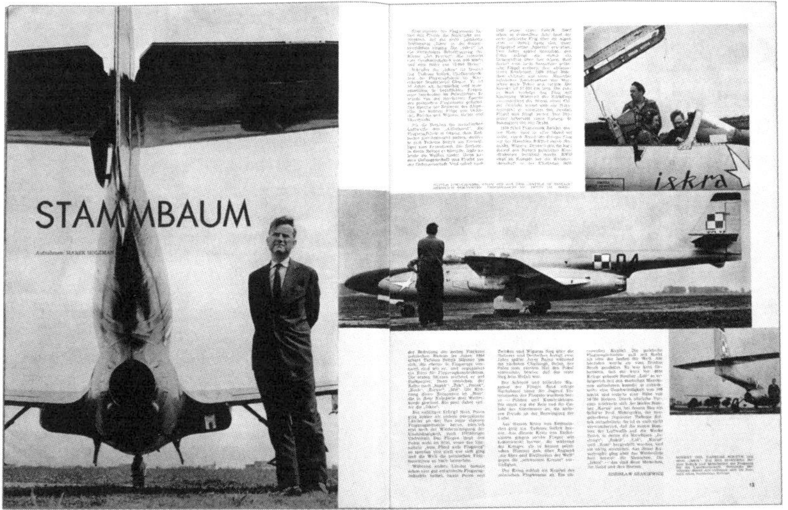

STAMMBAUM

B 24
***Polen* magazine, no. 8, 1963**

twen

scene

Axel Eggebrecht

Düstere Dramen – in Deutschland und anderswo

Drei linke Schriftsteller unter sich: Axel Eggebrecht zu zwei neuen Büchern von Gert von Paczensky und Sebastian Haffner

Lernen wir aus der Geschichte? Eine alte Frage. In unserem Jahrhundert fällt es schwer, sie zu bejahen. Allzu oft wiederholten sich die gleichen Torheiten und Katastrophen, jedesmal wurden sie gründlich dokumentiert und analysiert. Geholfen hat das kaum. Freilich verhalten die Historiker sich nicht selten so, als wollten sie eine bissige Bemerkung des alten Goethe bestätigen: „Geschichte schreiben ist eine Art, sich das Vergangene vom Halse zu schaffen." Sie finden es unwissenschaftlich, aus ihren Forschungen aktuelle Erkenntnisse zu gewinnen.

Gerade das aber möchten manche engagierten Publizisten, denen die Fachgelehrten dann flugs jegliche Kompetenz absprechen. Ich meine, daß wir solche Amateur-Historiker ermutigen sollten, auch wenn ihre Arbeiten Kritik herausfordern; etwa durch methodische Mängel oder allzu unverhohlene Parteinahme. Dergleichen Fehler entspringen meist der lebendigen Anteilnahme am jeweiligen Gegenstand. Ein aufmerksamer Leser wird eben dadurch angeregt, selber mitzudenken, weiterzudenken. Also aus der Historie zu lernen.

Zwei solche Fälle haben mich jüngst lebhaft beschäftigt. Sebastian Haffner beschreibt auf 240 Seiten „Die verratene Revolution"; die Ereignisse in Deutschland während des Winters 1918—19, in dem so viele Hoffnungen aufflammten und enttäuscht wurden, bis dann die schwache Republik von Weimar übrigblieb, deren Schicksal heute gern als warnendes Beispiel beschworen wird. Es ist der Bericht über eine bezeichnend deutsche Tragödie.

Gert v. Paczensky

Um eine Tragödie im Weltmaßstab geht es in dem umfangreichen Bande „Die Weißen kommen" von Gert von Paczensky. Er will, so der Untertitel, „Die wahre Geschichte des Kolonialismus" vorführen; die Ursachen des Problems aufdecken, von dessen Lösung die Zukunft der Menschheit ohne Zweifel abhängt: Der Aufstand der erwachenden Völker Asiens, Afrikas und Lateinamerikas.

Zwei wichtige Bücher. Als ich sie las, geriet ich in ein sonderbares Dilemma. Einer wesentlichen These Haffners muß ich nämlich, aus eigener Erfahrung, rundweg widersprechen — dennoch verliert seine kluge, klare Darstellung dadurch nichts von ihrem Wert. Bei Paczensky ist es umgekehrt: Mit seiner Haltung, seiner Tendenz, seiner humanen Absicht stimme ich völlig überein — und kann doch nicht verschweigen, daß mich die Ausführung bedenklich stimmt. Um es gleich zu sagen: Er steht sich selber im Wege.

Da ist auf 560 Seiten ein schier erdrückendes Material zusammengetragen. Eine grauenhafte Chronik von der Schande Europas. Kaum eine Nation ist davon ausgenommen. Auch wir Deutschen sind mitbetroffen, obwohl wir uns heute auf unsere kolonialpolitische Unschuld berufen, seit wir 1919 alle überseeischen Besitzungen verloren haben. Doch was vorher in Ostafrika und Kamerun, in Deutsch-Südwest und Togo geschah, belastet uns schwer. Wir haben das nur verdrängt. Ähnlich verhalten sich die anderen Kolonialmächte. Mit Recht kann Paczensky im Vorwort sagen, sein Buch solle „im Bewußtsein der weißen Welt eine Lücke schließen, die ebenso groß wie verhängnisvoll ist".

Sebastian Haffner

Wer heute die Rückständigkeit der Dritten Welt beklagt, macht sich nicht immer wie Paczensky klar, es könnten „an dieser Armut die reichen Weißen schuld sein — nicht etwa Gottes Gebot, die Rasse oder das Klima". Solchen Scheinargumenten wird allzugern geglaubt.

Die Wahrheit sieht anders aus. Zum Beispiel: Belgien. Bis in unser Jahrhundert errichtete König Leopold II. die Prachtbauten Brüssels von den üppigen Einkünften aus dem Kongostaat, der sein Privateigentum war. Er vergab Konzessionen an Firmen, die durch unsägliche Foltermethoden ihre Gewinne erpreßten. 1903 berichtete der Anglo-Ire Sir Roger Casement über die Greuel. In diesem einen Fall wurde das Weltgewissen alarmiert, doch nach ein paar Jahren beruhigte es sich wieder: Da verkaufte der tüchtige Monarch den suspekt gewordenen Besitz an sein Land.

Doch in der nunmehrigen Kolonie ging die Auspowerung weiter. Der Lebensstandard blieb erbärmlich, fast nichts geschah für die Bildung.

Kein Wunder, daß eine Handvoll Intellektueller fasziniert wurde durch Lenins Parole von der Befreiung der farbigen Völker, stärker noch durch das Vorbild Chinas. Es kam zu Unruhen. Abrupt entließen die erschrockenen Belgier den Kongo in die Unabhängigkeit, für die jede Voraussetzung fehlte. In jahrelangen blutigen Stammesfehden spielten fremde Interessen an Katangas Bodenschätze eine böse Rolle. Mühsam versucht der junge Staat sich zu festigen. Die Schuldigen aber höhnen: Da sieht man es, die Schwarzen sind eben unfähig, sich selbst zu regieren.

124

B 25
from: *Twen* no. 9, September 1970, detail

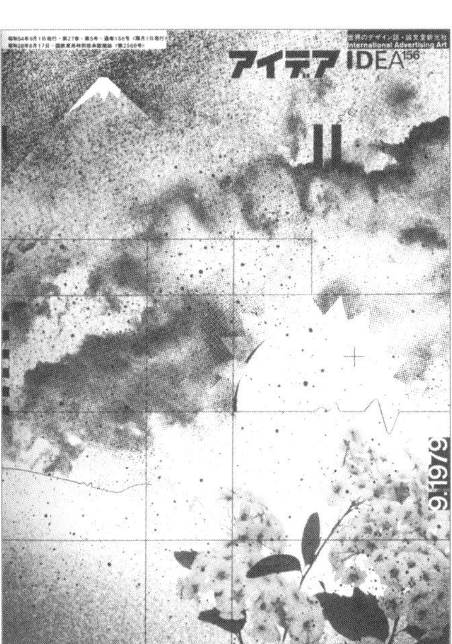

B 26
Wolfgang Weingart, cover of *Idea* no. 156, 9/1979, Experiments with screentone

higher level of expertise than they used to, specifically in the laws of reading, creation of printing templates, and other manual/technical aspects. In addition, the rise of digital media has led to a multiplication of communication methods. However, it would be a misconception to claim that design has fully freed itself from technical influences: The framework conditions offered by the layout programs result in a typical computer aesthetic. If we look at visual communication over the last forty years, we can see which programs designers preferred to use and which new features successively expanded the design options over time.[B 27, 28]
To find a current example, we can turn to rendered 3D graphics, which are now popular in communication design, often for illustrative purposes. Increasingly powerful computers have made this possible.

027

Developments in web design

The medium of "websites" has also developed over time and influenced the field of design in various ways.
Initially (in the late 1990s), websites were inflexible: If the visible section grew smaller, you would need to scroll horizontally to see any content on the edges. This inconvenience required a solution. To enable a grid-based adjustment to various sizes, layouts became "liquid," meaning that if the screen width became narrower, the layout columns would also grow narrower (as far as tolerable). However, in the meantime, the number of devices on which users could access websites had risen thanks to integrated browsers. Now websites needed to be displayed on all of these without sacrificing information and convenience – on smartphones (portrait and landscape format), on tablets (portrait and landscape format), on laptops, on stand displays, etc. Because of this, layouts needed to be more than just "liquid." They also became "adaptive": When the width of the layout changes, there are so-called "breakpoints" (display widths embedded into the source code). If these breakpoints are exceeded or not reached, either due to the respective device itself or the narrowing window, this triggers a modification of the display as defined in the source code. This ensures that the layout rapidly changes after a phase of "liquid" narrowing – for example, by turning a three-column layout into two columns from a certain width, and then into a single column. We refer to this structural flexibility, consisting of liquid and adaptive control mechanisms, as responsive web design. As of 2024, this is the gold standard, as it allows for an optimal depiction of content on the respective device. In terms of the design, this is something new: The layout becomes less important, and along with it the singular grid as the sole principle of order – because design now relies on multiple grids. To meet the needs of all the different formats, content must be split up into many little "information figures." These modular

027 ------ Technology's influence on typography, updated 2024

B 27
Kulturkampf, a publication from the University of the Arts, Bremen, 1990. In the early 1990s, rendered image sections like those on the double page from _032c_ (image 28) were still a long way off.

B 28
Double page from _032c_, no. 34, 2018

figures can be arranged flexibly around one another. Depending on the reading device, the designer can place them side by side, in a row, on top of or below one another, in line with the requirements and as defined by the programmer.

Technology impacts visual communication, as illustrated by these examples. It expands the range of options because the different printing processes, the selection of paper, binding techniques, the various reading devices, the diverse programs, the growing programming options, the costs, and the distribution options for the various media help define the scope within which designers make decisions during the design process. All of these factors form an invisible backdrop for the things that develop in society at a steady pace and then disappear again: They are passing fads that reveal themselves in visual communication. B 29 – 34

Time-Related Factors – Society

Time-related factors always also reflect the state of a society. They manifest themselves in various forms, for example in opinions, fashions, certain styles, or trends. They succeed each other, whether in art, music, clothing, language, behavior, or design. Every reader has been able to gain experiences in this regard. They just need to remember. And some might blush when they think back on the musicians they once idolized, the item of clothing that served as an essential staple, and the expressions they found especially cool. Looking back, we can get a pretty good idea of how values have changed. Their transformation is a reliable indication of the fact that society is movable – which also comes with implications for visual communication. Five examples from different decades demonstrate this.

The "Swiss style" of the 1950s and 1960s

"Typography is a tool of communication. It must be communication in its most intense form." This quote from László Moholy-Nagy from 1923 revealed the desire for an incorruptible form to aid a "pure" transmission of information. Since every designer might interpret this urgent dictate differently, typographers such as Jan Tschichold tried to define corresponding rules in the 1920s. This led to an aesthetic that resulted from a harmony of content, function, and form and ushered in the style of Modernism. During the Nazi era, this elementary or functional typography "hibernated" in neutral Switzerland. After World War II, a specific economic circumstance helped further functional typography – the concentration of chemical and pharmaceutical companies (Ciba, Geigy, Hoffman-La Roche,

B 29
***Bravo* cover, no. 1, Germany, 1962**

B 30
***Bravo* cover, no. 1, Germany, 2002**

B 31
***Easyriders tattoo*, USA, 1990**

B 32
***Tätowier-Magazin*, Mannheim, 2017**

Nr. 9. Deutsche 9. Jahrg.

Metall-Arbeiter-Zeitung.

Organ für die Interessen der Metallarbeiter.

Nürnberg, 28. Februar 1891.

Aus England.

B 33
***Deutsche Metall-Arbeiter-Zeitung*, no. 9, Nuremberg, 1891**

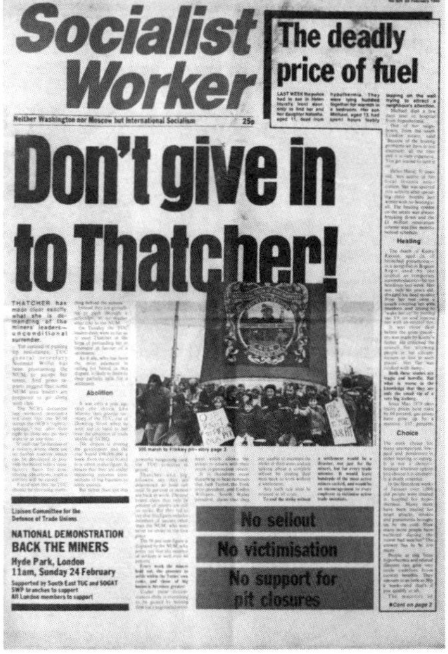
Socialist Worker

The deadly price of fuel

Neither Washington nor Moscow but International Socialism 25p

Don't give in to Thatcher!

Abolition

Healing

Choice

Liaison Committee for the Defence of Trade Unions

NATIONAL DEMONSTRATION
BACK THE MINERS
Hyde Park, London
11am, Sunday 24 February

No sellout
No victimisation
No support for pit closures

B 34
***Socialist Worker*, no. 924, UK, 1985**

Sandoz) and their visual communication requirements. In particular, the company Geigy adopted the functional style for its own purposes. It seemed to be made for this type of company: "objectivity" in advertising (thanks to matter-of-fact typography and the use of photography instead of illustrations), clear structures in the diverse product information. 029 Like its competitors, Geigy operated on a global scale. As a result, many of the designers – educated at the Allgemeine Gewerbeschule Basel (General Trade School Basel) – who were responsible for Geigy's visual communication relocated to offices abroad and thereby exported their design understanding to many parts of the world, but especially to the USA. That said, limiting the emergence of the Swiss style to the phenomenon just described would fall short of the mark. 030 As in the 1920s, the relationship between art, architecture, and visual communication was also tangible in the post-war years. The abstract painting of concrete art particularly influenced typography. Max Bill and Richard Paul Lohse helped drive forward the political/aesthetic aspirations of design. Lohse: "The essential task of art and architecture is to develop flexible modular systems (...) Serial and modular structures will serve as the design law of our time, and our task will lie in mastering these systems. The familiar realms (...) of simple relationships and proportions lie behind us. Ahead of us lies the field of the infinite law and infinite flexibility."*
The term "modular structures" refers to another characteristic of the Swiss style: the typographic grid. 031 The relationship between architecture and typography has been described multiple times, but it has never been as striking as in the construction of page layouts, the schematic structure of which resembles facade designs for functional buildings. There were also entirely pragmatic reasons for the efforts to establish a way of sensibly organizing a lot of information within a limited space: the fact that Switzerland is trilingual. The protagonists who developed this "constructive graphic" in the 1950s understood it to be a logical evolution of modernism. In the following years, the Swiss style increasingly established itself[B 35], and took a global 032 victory lap, accompanied by the Helvetica font, which would become one of the most widely used fonts. It competed with Akzidenz-Grotesk, the dominating font up until that point, and quickly grew more successful than its competitor. The Swiss style stood out thanks to its clarity and formal beauty.

Against this background, designer Karl Gerstner coined the term "integral typography" in the late 1950s. 033 His definition presents a summary of visual communication in the first half of the 20th century: "The designer's freedom doesn't hover on the margins of their task but forms a central aspect of it. As a typographer, they are only free to create something artistic if they understand and consider their task in all its parts. Any solution developed on this foundation will be an integral one, will form a unity of language and

*
"Elementarism. Series. Modulus", in: Anthony Hill "Data: Directions in Art", 1968, p. 63

029 ------ Typography, Ruder
030 ------ Die Schweizer Grafik, Hollis
031 ------ Grid Systems in Graphic Design, Müller-Brockmann
032 ------ Helvetica – Homage to a Typeface, Müller
033 ------ Programme entwerfen, Gerstner

032.1 -------- Die Univers von Adrian Frutiger, Friedl
032.2 -------- Imitat und Original, Voelker
032.3 -------- Neue Schriften. New Typefaces, Naegele et al.

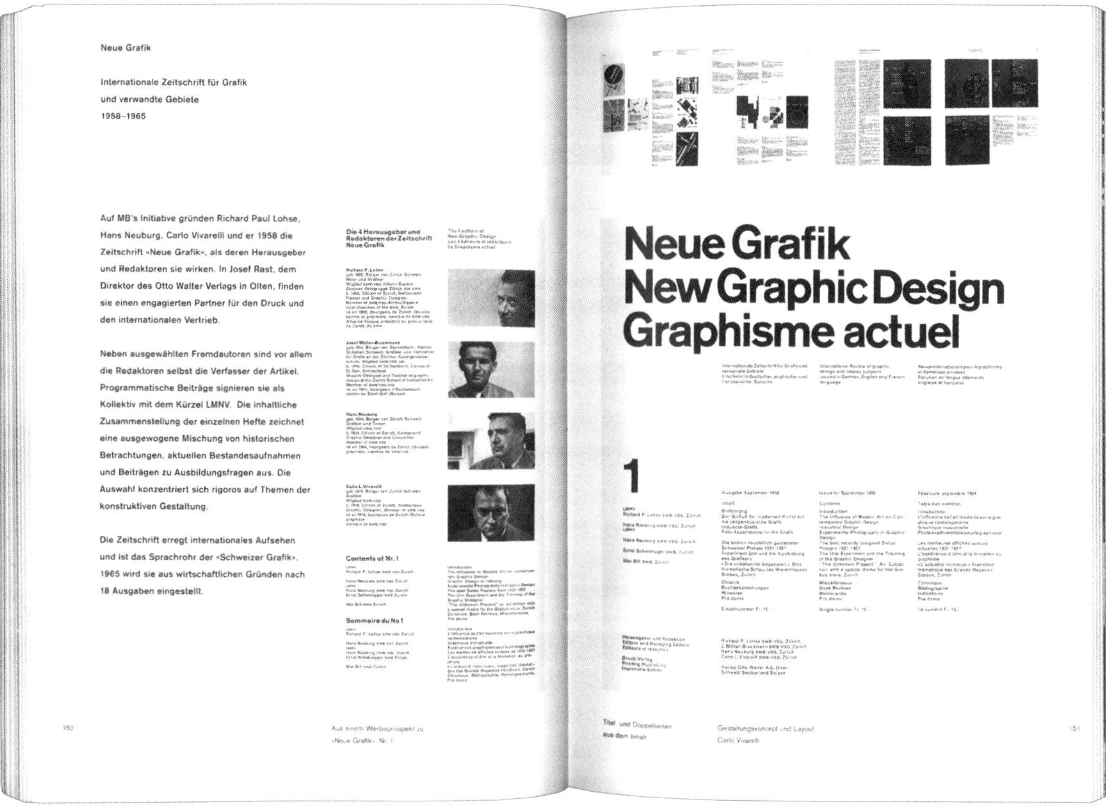

Neue Grafik

Internationale Zeitschrift für Grafik
und verwandte Gebiete
1958–1965

Auf MB's Initiative gründen Richard Paul Lohse, Hans Neuburg, Carlo Vivarelli und er 1958 die Zeitschrift «Neue Grafik», als deren Herausgeber und Redaktoren sie wirken. In Josef Rast, dem Direktor des Otto Walter Verlags in Olten, finden sie einen engagierten Partner für den Druck und den internationalen Vertrieb.

Neben ausgewählten Fremdautoren sind vor allem die Redaktoren selbst die Verfasser der Artikel. Programmatische Beiträge signieren sie als Kollektiv mit dem Kürzel LMNV. Die inhaltliche Zusammenstellung der einzelnen Hefte zeichnet eine ausgewogene Mischung von historischen Betrachtungen, aktuellen Bestandesaufnahmen und Beiträgen zu Ausbildungsfragen aus. Die Auswahl konzentriert sich rigoros auf Themen der konstruktiven Gestaltung.

Die Zeitschrift erregt internationales Aufsehen und ist das Sprachrohr der «Schweizer Grafik». 1965 wird sie aus wirtschaftlichen Gründen nach 18 Ausgaben eingestellt.

150

Aus einem Werbeprospekt zu «Neue Grafik» Nr. 1

Titel und Doppelseiten aus dem Inhalt

Gestaltungskonzept und Layout
Carlo Vivarelli

151

B 35
Double page from the book
Josef Müller-Brockmann – Pionier der Schweizer Grafik

font, of content and form."* The Swiss style and its underlying approach shaped the design field into the 1970s.

The "hippie movement" of the 1960s and early 1970s

In the 1960s, a graphic style emerged that can be described as the defining visual feature of the hippie movement. 034 This counter-culture youth movement started in the USA, but quickly spread to the rest of the western world. Its protagonists dabbled with things they discovered outside of societal norms: drugs, living in communes, free love, new music, dreams of equality and fraternity, an end to all wars (specifically the Vietnam War, which directly affected all Americans fit for military service).
In the media, the new style made its way into "free press" publications, album covers, posters, and underground comics. A graphic language emerged that was reminiscent of art nouveau due to its adaptation of organic shapes and became known as psychedelic art in its artistic expression. In particular, underground and alternative publications conveyed the radical political 035 conceptions and demands of this subculture. The hippie movement viewed itself as the antipole to the societies of the western hemisphere that they deemed to be bourgeois, dishonest, pro-discrimination, warring, and devoutly capitalist. The content of their publications included appeals, campaigns, essays, event calendars – and teemed with anarchistic humor. 036 They targeted a local audience and did not have the goal of turning a profit. These publications were cheaply produced, and their look gave this away. They resorted to affordable production means, such as Letraset letters (dry rub-down letters that were transferred to the layout), copied photos, typewriters, 037 hand lettering, stamps, and sketches, but also small offset presses made by the company Rotaprint, for their publications.
The designers were not tied to any requirements, especially not when it came to "proper" layouts or the "right" way to use typography. This resulted in an unmistakable graphic style that could be described as follows: raw, sensual, authentic, communicative, activating, also (frequently) "psychedelic."[B 36, 37]
The fact that the design worked within the target group – but was viewed with skepticism by large parts of society – comes down to the conventions and tastes of the time, those that formed the framework for evaluating visual communication. Back then, established design primarily relied on recognition and reproduction of "order." Generally speaking, "order" served as a keyword that was prevalent in the 1950s and 1960s and held positive connotations in the "Swiss style." It represented the graphical image of modernism, the essential cores of which included de-emotionalization,

*
Karl Gerstner in: »Typographische Monatsblätter (TM)«, Special edition: "Integrale Typographie," 1959, p. 340

034 –––––– Psychedelische Kunst und Gestaltung der 60er Jahre. Die Hippie-Bewegung, Grunenberg
035 –––––– Oz, East Village Other, Hotcha! Rogger et al.
036 –––––– Free Press – Underground & Alternative Publications 1965 – 1975, Bizot
037 –––––– Letraset letters
036.1 –––––––– Under the Radar: Underground Zines and Self-Publications 1965 – 1975, Bandel et al.
037.1 –––––––– Rotaprint, Kleinoffset

PARAPLUIE

PARAPLUIE
n° 4
105 BD MALESHERBES
PARIS 8
3 francs
IMPRIMERIE LE SOUTERRAIN
Depot legal 2ème TRIMESTRE
DIRECTEUR DE PUBLICATION HENRI-JEAN ENU
COLLABORATION JONATHAN FARREN
AVEC L'AIDE DE MARC
DOMINIQUE PATRICK BERNARD
ELISABETH CLAUDE
BARBARA LOWENGREEN

3 FRANCS

B 36
***Parapluie*, France, 1970**

MAY DAY celebration liberates Telegraph Ave. 7

LITTLE-REMIRO trial sparks new NWLF actions 8

JURY CONVICTS White Panthers in S.F. 8

TOM HAYDEN heralds new era of humanism 9

PINE RIDGE Goons indicted -- politely 11

THAILAND is a domino that won't fall 11

SLINKY SARAH Kernochan will fill up the holes in your soul 14

DAVE ALEXANDER and his jangling piano 18

LOUISIANA'S CLIFTON CHENIER and his Red Hot Band at the Boarding House . . . 19

Jill Johnston On Amazons As Warriors

Folsom Art Show: Creation In A Cage

Berkeley Barb

Tantric Runners

Issue 508, May 9 - 15, 1975

25¢ BAY AREA, 50¢ ELSEWHERE

WILL WE EVER SMOKE LEGAL DOPE?

B 37
***Berkeley Barb*, USA, 1975**

objectification, scientification, the aesthetic of reduction, and economic efficiency. Given the societal background and idealization of the principles of order, it seemed logical that the hippie movement would start to postulate opposing values: subjective, emotional, organic, anti-authoritarian, emancipated, subversive, and anti-capitalist.

Punk art of the 1970s

A subculture called "punk" emerged in the 1970s. It expressed itself through music, fashion, and design, always in ways that reflected their 038 shared values of nonconformism and rebelliousness. In contrast to the hippie movement, punks lacked a decisive political agenda, even though they shared the same enemies: bourgeois life, the establishment, capitalism, consumption. Punk placed greater value on public perception, on provocation.

"Pretty Vacant," "Kingdom Come," and "Touch and Go"[B 38 - 40] are a few typical examples of the graphic style. The design was shaped by a common theme that appeared in all punk genres and had also characterized the hippie style: a kind of self-empowerment, emancipation from everything so- 039 ciety considered professional, good, and proper. Punk was more radical, but at the same time less political and more focused on their external impact. On top of the design tools and materials already used in the hippie era, they turned to a new technique that was starting to become available to the wider public at the time – copy machines, which served as a cheap copying and layout tool.

Here, it is also interesting to observe how the state of society and the visual codes typical of the era shaped the design of this subculture.

Without its predecessors from the hippie period, punk's graphic style may not have evolved in the same way. Perhaps that is why punks were so noticeably focused on drawing a clear line between themselves and hippies ("Kill the Hippies" was a dictum). In any case, the emphatic distance could serve as an indication of the conceptual similarities between the two subcultures regarding shared enemies and anarchistic design. However, in the 1970s – in contrast to the still prospering 1960s – many indications pointed to economic transitions (the oil crisis, the incipient downfall of old industries) that impacted the era's youth on an existential and atmospheric level. The insignia of institutional power held by the state were questioned more and more (this was taking place in most western democracies). Various factors had contributed to this: social liberalization following the political disputes between the post-war generation and state institutions in the 1960s; infiltration by pop-cultural influences, particularly new subcultures, new music, new fashion, and pop art; and finally, the emancipatory movements of the time, including the US civil rights movement, the women's movement,

038 ------ Verschwende deine Jugend, Teipel
039 ------ Fucked up and Photocopied, Turcotte et al.

B 38
***Pretty Vacant*, UK, 1978**

B 39
***Kingdom Come*, UK, 1977**

B 40
***Touch and Go*, USA, 1982**

student revolts, and individual refusals, such as conscientious objection to military service.

"Postmodern" design of the 1980s and 1990s

In 1984, Apple launched its first MacIntosh – with low computing capac- 040
ities, but with a graphic interface. In the years that followed, the Apple computer evolved at rapid speed and not only offered increasingly powerful graphics programs, but also many design options. Now communication designers were able to visualize their design ideas instantly and in a realistic manner (not only as a sketch). It was comparatively cheap to use a computer for design work, as the process did not rely on external services (typesetting, films) and the designer merely needed a printer. In addition, they could save as many different versions of a draft as required. For designers, the autonomy and variability they gained was liberating.

Another development was making headway in the 1980s, one that affected
all cultural sectors: postmodernism. At its core, the term encompasses 041
the rejection of the certainties and mindsets of modernism. According to French philosopher Jean-Francois Lyotard, modernism's school of thought encompasses "narratives" that share a common factor: They rely on a "central principle" in order to make universally valid statements. Lyotard claims that this universal applicability excludes differences and diversity. Examples of modernist "narratives" include rationality, belief in progress, innovation, and industrialization. They are authoritative and, as maxims, leave no room for negotiation – just like the humanism and utopias of the best-possible life, which boil down to equality and general prosperity and therefore also have a political dimension. For individuals, this means being subordinate to these central "narratives." Postmodernism rejects such centralistic principles. However, other maxims apply: tolerance, diversity, freedom. It also opposes innovation (with the goal of constant societal progress) as the central motif behind all actions for reasons of one-dimensionality. It strives for the heterogeneity of a society to unfold itself, with its many different cultural and social influences. By negating modernism's value standards, postmodernism aims for different viewpoints and forms of expression to coexist on equal footing, without having to subject themselves to criticism.
The new computer technology was a perfect fit for postmodernism. All of its maxims now combined with the acquired design freedom and infiltrated visual communication on a design and mental level.
One of the first designers to make full use of these freedoms and achieve
worldwide fame was Neville Brody. Starting in the early 1980s, he turned 042
previously valid rules upside down, both regarding layouts and through his

040 –––––– Macintosh computer
041 –––––– Postmoderne, Heartney
042 –––––– The Graphic Language of Neville Brody

040.1 ––––––– 5. Bundestreffen Forum Typografie 1988, Thema: Desktop Publishing (DTP)
042.1 ––––––– Erik Spiekermann, Eckhard Jung, designer, teacher

numerous font designs. He is probably best known for designing the British magazine "Face" (GB 1980 – present) and for providing the Labour Party's corporate design. His most famous fonts include Industria and FF Blur. In 1990, he co-founded the font retailer Fontshop. Brody represents the many designers whose creations negated the rationality of modernism and gave visual communication a new spark. B 41

043

Another protagonist rang in the 1990s: David Carson. Between 1992 and 1995, the American designer worked on the music magazine "Ray Gun," through which he gained worldwide recognition.

Insiders were already familiar with Carson's work through his pioneering layouts for the surfer magazine "Beach Culture" (1989 – 1991). His layouts surpassed even the radical character of 1980s design – supported by the growing possibilities offered by layout programs and the resulting range of design options. Carson's work stands for a style that shaped the 1990s. B 42

B 41
Double page from *The Face* with typeface 3, 1984,
Layout and font design: Neville Brody

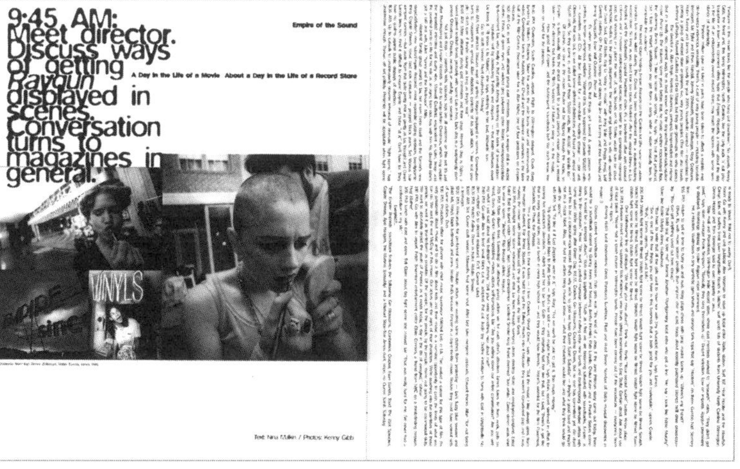

B 42
Double page from *Raygun*, no. 28, USA, 1995

Even more so than in the 1980s, typefaces were used for formal experiments; the focus was placed on the aesthetic, not the readability of texts; many new fonts were developed. The most innovative font designers included Rudy VanderLans and Suzanna Licko, who founded the font label 044 "Emigre" (San Francisco, 1984)[B 43] and published a magazine of the same name. They prioritized form over function, a development that designers around the world celebrated and that bore clearly postmodern traits. By neglecting design rules and customs in favor of a new and liberated form of design, they drew plenty of criticism claiming that they were undermining the purpose of visual communication – to ensure an appropriate relationship between content and form. This was partially the case, but overall, these instances were outweighed by successful solutions. They were successful because they catered to altered viewing habits and emerged in a social climate in which the sensual radiance of visual surfaces was given preference over the functionality of design.

"New Ugly Design" and "Authenticity" since approx. 2006

In 2007, designer and design critic Michael Bierut wrote an article for "The Design Observer" titled "How to be Ugly." 045 It was inspired by a new design trend derived from the typography of the magazine 032c [B 44] for one, for which art director Mike Meiré was responsible. In this article, Bierut writes that he thought nothing new could surprise him anymore after the design provocations and experiments of the 1990s – until he held a copy of the magazine in his hands and saw that, apparently, there was one last taboo left to break: that of twisting and distorting letters. This idea pervaded the entire magazine. Designers based in the USA – and now Meiré – first used the concept to draw attention to themselves and their work and present themselves as pioneering and bold. The trend of conscious flaws was visible in various publications in the late 2000s and did not only relate to distorted fonts. Frequently, it simulated the limitations of mere text programs such as Word, with its few means for distinction – for example, color gradients in fonts, strict layouts with disproportionately large font sizes compared to the width of the columns, holey typesetting, and more. All of this resulted in layouts that appeared extremely unprofessional. As summed up by Bierut and other critics: "The ugly is back."

This statement referenced an article by Steven Heller with the title "Cult of the Ugly" from 1993. 046 Heller was responding to the abandonment of the modernist principles that had established themselves in the work of young students and designers at the time – and served as inspiration around the world. This abandonment took place by redefining the relationship between form and content: Design no longer felt obligated to bow to content and celebrated itself in an experimental way *(see "postmodern" design).*

044 ------ Emigre. Zuzana Licko, Rudy VanderLans
045 ------ How to be Ugly, Bierut
046 ------ Cult of the Ugly, Heller

or some of the Variex characters. I am always very intrigued by experimental alphabets that either have no capitals or mix upper and lower characteristics, like Bradbury Thompson's Alphabet 26, or his typeface that has only lower case and uses boldface characters for caps. This is actually what Matthew Carter at Bitstream suggested I do with Variex, since there is no upper or lower case in Variex. I like that, although it is not always applicable. *Emigre: How did the computer give you creative inspiration specifically for typefaces, as opposed to graphic design?* Zuzana: I enjoy things that are like puzzles; anything that is tremendously restrictive, where there are very few choices but you have to make it work. If I get too many choices I become overwhelmed. I just don't have the time and patience to look at every possible scenario. This is the problem I have with graphic design. I never got the feeling that I found the final solution to a problem. Although today I can more easily design a typeface like Triplex, which is a bit more traditional and less modular, than I could have five years ago, I still get most of my creative energy out of solving these puzzles. When nobody is able to make something work, I get inspired to find out what I might do with it. Ever since I was first introduced to graphic design, I heard everybody say how bad digital type looked and how it was impossible to make it look any better. This really intrigued me. Whenever anybody makes a statement like that, I have difficulty agreeing. I was reading books on the history of graphic design and in the final chapter they would always mention something about digital type and show the same typefaces like OCR A or B. Some of them were actually interesting but never really good, especially for setting text. Then I read Chuck Bigelow's writings on the subject of digital type. I was fascinated and agreed with a lot of the things he was saying, but when I looked at the visual results I was a bit disappointed with how traditional his type still looked. So I saw that there was something unexplored and interesting there and I wanted to try my own hand at it. That's when I got involved with designing my first low resolution type in a computer class that I took. But every time I asked for advice, people kept telling me it was really a lost cause, that it couldn't be done. So I thought that anything I would do would be better than what was out there. *Emigre: When you look back at your early low resolution type, do you feel you succeeded?* Zuzana: For myself, yes. But then later I discovered quite a bit of material that I should have seen before I started. Issue number 6 of *Baseline* magazine, which was edited by Erik Spiekermann, was very good and informative. But then again, if I had read it beforehand, I might never have tried to explore the really basic ideas that I had. *Emigre: You mentioned that after five years of working on simple bitmap type designs you have acquired some confidence doing more humanist designs such as Triplex. Have you ever considered designing type entirely by hand, more calligraphic type?* Zuzana: I've never been very attracted to calligraphy. With calligraphy there was such a set way of doing things that unless you could technically outdo the next guy it became just a matter of production. How many hours could you spend doing this? That to me was more therapeutic than creative. I'm very concerned with maximizing our resources and not fighting with the medium. We do it in our design work as well. For example, we like to overprint offset colors, instead of knocking them out, in order not to kill ourselves in the stripping process. And that's not just a matter of money, it's also that things look better that way and are easier to produce. Why do it the difficult way, or why do it backwards? Simply because that's the way you happen to think and you haven't taught yourself to see things in a more direct way? When designers do things that don't come out of the medium, such as reproducing Goudy Old Style or Optima

CITIZEN

ggg

Ay

Citizen

bold or..

AaBbCcDdEeFfGgHhIiJjKkLlMmNnOoPpQqRrSsTtUuVvWwXxYyZz

1234567890

.Light

B 43

Double page from *Emigre*, no. 15, USA, 1990

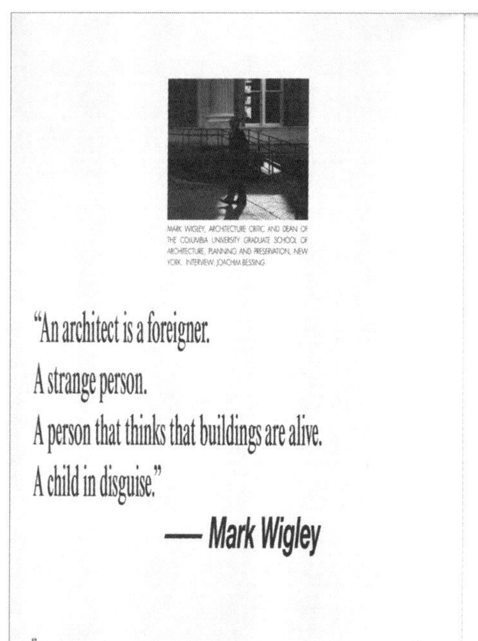

Did you ever experience a provocation from architecture, and of which kind was that?

More or less everyday. I think to be interested in architecture is to love buildings. And like any other form of love it means that you don't really know this thing that you love. So it's always a provocation. In other words: what I love is that buildings are a provocation. Always.

Could you remember the first time you were attracted to a piece of architecture, like when you were very young – please don't worry though, I'm not trying to talk you into being an objectophile ...

No, I had no idea! Since I was nine years old I wanted to become an architect. But I had no idea what that meant.

Were your parents involved in architecture?

No.

So you just felt you wanted to create spaces?

Yes. There were zero ingredients for incubating an architect in my history. I grew up in a more or less small city with a hundred thousand people in the middle of an island.

Can you imagine why works of architects like Rem Koolhaas, Zaha Hadid or Frank Gehry receive that much attention over here in Europe? Whenever they build something the public response is massive, like to a provocation. They do not stop wondering about the shapes, the surfaces, the materials used – all in all about these so-called new forms.

These people that you are describing are very intelligent. The architect is more than anybody else a public intellectual. It's not that the best architects are the ones that make the best buildings. The best architect is the one that makes us think again about buildings. You are describing a set of architects who don't just make good buildings – they do that, sure, but they do something else which is more important: they make us re-conceive of what a building is. The real purpose of the architect in my opinion is to make you hesitate, so that for a moment or a minute or a weekend or your lifetime you see things differently. And this ability of a good architect to see the world differently can become an invitation to maybe live your life differently. Most of these invitations are turned down. But every now and then an architect can trigger a hesitation that does change many other things. The great gift of the architect is just this very delicate thing. A jab in the normal rhythm.

Over here, the arguments against the works of these architects are that their buildings do not fit into the traditional structures of our cities, that they are destructive. These opponents vote for a rather mildly reconstructive or at least conservative style – to regain the structure, look and feel of cities as they were before World War II. In a way they argue that any other style is unnatural. Would you say that there is any one natural architecture?

No no. Architecture is interesting because it's unnatural! But you know nature is very strange. You know that. If architecture was natural, then it would be very strange – think about a cat! Surely a cat is natural. But a cat is a very crazy animal. If you really like nature a lot you should go to the African forests. Spend an evening. None of these people would say that they would like architecture to be natural. They don't want to be naked. They don't want to eat other people. They all have sets of rules for not being natural. In fact it is a political statement. You said it right: conservative. You mean exactly that moment where conservative means conservation. But there are many paradoxes here. Firstly, anybody who argues that we should always take the city back to its original older condition – this is a very stupid position. But anybody who says we should always change and make something new is also stupid. We are talking about a much more complicated relationship between what to change and what to keep. If you keep a building the same, paradoxically you have changed it. In the normal course of events, in changes in the environment, in the political, in the client, in the technologies of communication – everything changes and will change the building, too. So when you say, "Please, let's not change the building," you're actually asking for a real major change. In fact you are asking to stop the building from living. Because you say, "It will not breathe, it will not evolve." So when an architect says, "Please let's take everything back fifty years," what they are saying is, "I hate evolution. I hate change." But if you do for example take a piece of the city back it's a very strange thing to do. It can be very very beautiful. To walk

53

B 44

Double page from *032c*, no. 13, 2007, design: Mike Meiré

Heller wrote that, while others have turned away from such rules before – he gave the example of punk design of the 1970s –, this time, the "ugliness" had started to infect the institutions of established design (agencies, academies). He claimed that experiments are, in principle, the motor of progress and that their essence consists of instinct, intelligence, and discipline. But now the motor would start to stutter if instinct started to take over in place of intelligence and discipline. This, he said, was the case for many experiments at American and European universities. The style was one that claimed "more" was trendier than "less," cluttered better than simple, fragmented better than consistent, and that "ugliness" holds its own value. Heller opposed these views. He quoted American philosopher and writer Ralph Waldo Emerson, who wrote the following in his book "The Conduct of Life" (1860): "The secret of ugliness consists not of irregularity, but in being uninteresting." Heller recognized postmodern traits in the design style of the early 1990s that designer Paul Rand had already established in the 1980s. His verdict (Paul Rand: "A Designer's Art," 1985): "The separation of form and function, of concept and execution, is not likely to produce objects of aesthetic value" *(see chapter C).*

12 years after Heller's article, Michael Bierut was lamenting a return, a "new ugliness." The legitimation for consciously flawed design apparently lay in deviating from the mainstream and emphasizing originality in one's own designs. "Ugly design" and the revenant "New ugly design" point to three phenomena. First of all, they represent typical features of a postmodern spirit. Secondly, there are cycles in which design seems to repeat itself. Here, a remake encompasses style elements from past decades, enriched by era-typical features. Most of you will be familiar with such cycles in fashion. More experienced designers might remember the times when Swiss style made a comeback, when punk fragments of art nouveau elements left their traces in contemporary designs, when the 1970s, 1980s, or other decades were cited in design. In 2007, the mentioned case of "new ugly design"[B 45] recycled a design concept from the 1990s. The reasoning behind the imbalance of content and design in favor of form also struck a familiar tone. In 1995, Carson justified his style by saying, "My style has a very human side, because it requires interaction. It takes time to decipher the objects, the message. I hate the grid of American magazines, which engulf everything and ultimately embody only convenience."*
Mike Meiré, on the other hand, commented the following on his design of the 032c magazine and its warped typography: "I got a little tired of all these look-alike magazines. They are all very professionally designed, but I was looking for something more charismatic. I wanted to find an interesting look outside of the mainstream."**

*
"Typoundso," Hans Rudolf Lutz, see 143.1

**
"The ugly is back," Michael Bierut, see 045

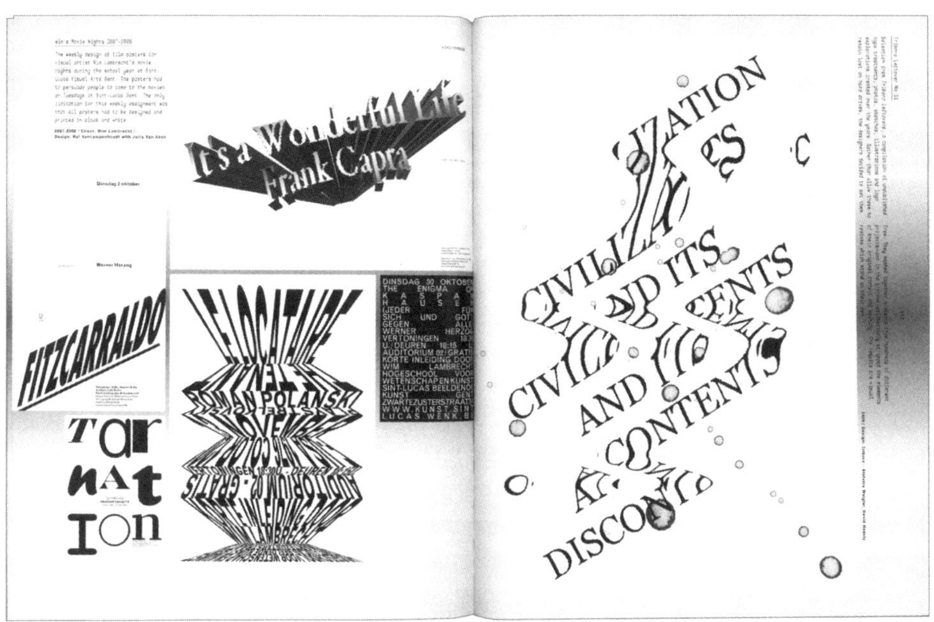

B 45
Double page from *Pretty Ugly*, Berlin, 2012

The third phenomenon arises through the innovation pressure placed upon visual communication. After all, audiences expect new design solutions expected over and over again. These should either serve to transport new content/products/ideas or transmit impulses to attract attention to something familiar. The innovation pressure stems from competition among similar content/products/ideas for which design is supposed to communicate their respective special features – and that as succinctly as possible in an increasingly overstimulated environment *(see chapter D)*. This competitive situation lends visual communication its typical dynamism. Of course, when vying for attention and acceptance, design also needs to take era-specific norms, values, and tastes into account. In this context, the difference between "ugly design" and "new ugly design" comes to light: In 1993, design shows the possibilities offered by computers. Nobody denounces this. On the contrary – anyone who has mastered this tool particularly well is considered a design virtuoso. By 2006, computers serve as an everyday tool for design, and there is ample proof of their range of possibilities. Now designers are flirting with technical limitations and amateurism. Both exude an aura of parochialism, but it comes across as genuine – the term used is "authentic." It is not just a topic of discussion in visual communication, but also in social discourse. Here, it dominates discussions on the environment, equality, cohesion, and political goals with related terms such as "credibility" and "sustainability." While the values of society are readjusting within social discourse, the protagonists in the field of visual communication respond in a similar way. This schema can be derived from activities in the design scene in the late 2000s and during the 2010s:

Countless workshops within and outside of universities explored chance and analog design methods. Many publications were self-published and printed in small numbers. These often used the risograph *(see 156)*, a duplication machine that enables color printing by using respective cartridges in a staggered manner. Due to the lesser printing quality on uncoated paper, it served as the ideal tool to create the rough, "authentic" look the designers aspired to (even in 2024, risographs are still very popular). During this time, a large number of self-organized book and art book fairs graced the publishing industry; sharing platforms were established; design collectives emerged. The fluctuation between actual authenticity, as was inherent in most of these activities, and pseudo-authenticity, which manifested itself in coquetry with design flaws, is a feature of the 2010s zeitgeist. Design became the calling card for individual creativity, which had to fight for its place in the narrow work and job market. This development – which saw its beginnings as postmodern design emerged in the 1990s – continued to pick up speed because "new ugly design" quickly lost its initial radicalness

and mutated into a more compliant and marketable design style. The audience's uncertainty on how to evaluate this design ("intentionally ugly or lack of skill?") soon gave way to the realization that designers are at work here. "New ugly design" turned into "pretty ugly design" B 46. In 2007, the 047
"design flaw" of Mike Meiré's typography in the 032c magazine came as a surprise that caused uncertainty and, at least temporarily, led to doubts about the professionality of its art direction. When "pretty ugly design" emerged in the early 2010s, the cult of flaws had long grown into a style 048
that defined the design tools and the scope of what is permitted – this is the only way to explain the worldwide similarity of design results.
An established style requires a definition. And so the book "Pretty Ugly" starts with the following self-description:
"Deviant – against established criteria of what good design is, embracing what is disliked und considered incorrect, mistakes become virtues, create authenticity and humanity."

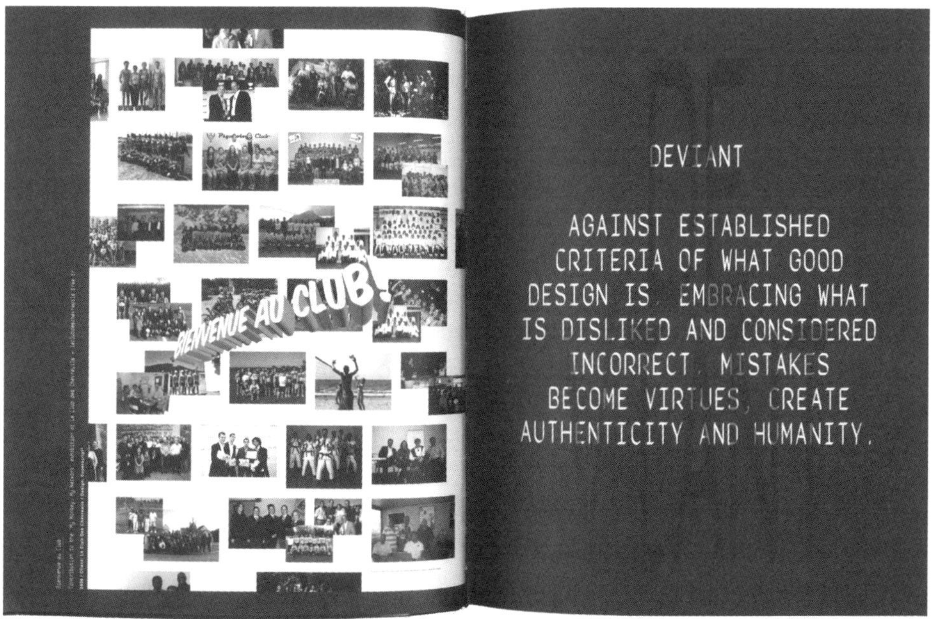

B 46
Double page from *Pretty Ugly*, Berlin, 2012

047 ------ Pretty Ugly Design, Twopoints.net et al.
048 ------ The Global Style – Modernist Typography after Postmodernism, Keedy

047.1 -------- Hipster – eine transatlantische Diskussion, Greif et al.

All versions of "ugliness" shared a commonality – despite attempts to root themselves in terms such as "authenticity," "honesty," and "credibility," – in that they granted their form an individual, content-independent aesthetic value. This approach corresponded with the altered viewing habits that preferred fast and attractive stimuli in a visually overstimulating world. Essentially, this description also applies to the early 2020s, but with different consequences. The section "Uniformity Versus Diversity" in chapter D describes the backgrounds that influence design in the year 2024.
There are many different social, technological, and cultural factors that influence design, and we were only able to address five examples. But two things become clear: Design does not emerge in a vacuum. It always builds on what already exists, it recomposes, rebuilds, reinterprets. And design is always infected by the topics of its time.

Subjectivity and Speculation

The illustrated differentiations provide for a certain unpredictability when it comes to the choice of design tools for creating visual communication. After all, the constantly changing fashions, trends, and tastes force designers to make adjustments again and again. There are specialist fields and disciplines with the expertise necessary to make temporary modifications of visual communication, ranging from trend research and media theory through to sociology. However, given the way our profession works on an everyday basis – demanding suitable solutions within a reasonable timeframe – designers rarely have the time to search for and study these sources. This reveals a discipline-specific dilemma: the fact that many design decisions are both subjective and speculative. In most cases that arise in day-to-day work, designers do not fall back on empirical surveys and statistical securities regarding the tastes of target groups and the impact of design methods, the latest fashions and the expected or current trends – with the exception of major campaigns and media developments, for which those responsible invest heavily in market research to learn about these aspects. Normally, this means that it is possible to find out whether audiences will accept or reject content/products/designs, but usually only through their usage at a later time. Even then, it remains difficult to ascertain the exact factors that led to success or failure and what proportion can be attributed to visual communication. 049

049 ------ Definition of the term "Advertising"

049.1 -------- Texte zur Theorie der Werbung, Baumgärtel et al.

Attempts to "objectify" visual communication

In the past, there have been a few attempts to minimize unpredictable factors in the design process, such as the speculative and subjective aspects. The founders of the Ulm School of Design, established in 1953, tried their hand at this. They viewed the institution as a Bauhaus successor, while the humanistic aspect emphasized during its founding was also a reaction to Nazi dictatorship. 050 In 1958, Otl Aicher, a member of the rectorate, wrote the following: "we are developing the ulm model: a design model based on technique and science, with designers no longer taking on the role of superordinate artist, but of an equal partner within the decision-making process of industrial production" (the quote uses lower-case letters because this was the trademark of the Ulm School of Design). And the "Stiftung HfG Ulm" writes:
"(...) However, the focus lies less on working on individual designs, but on complex solutions, for example for the phenomenon of traffic. This is analyzed in depth in interdisciplinary studies, a specific focal point of the HfG: from railcars to timetables, from stations to ticket machines (...)."*
Systems design shaped the curriculum. The Ulm School of Design described and taught a role of design that revolved around the principles of modernism: This centered around societal benefit, progress, and scientific principles. The choice of design style for this approach was obvious – the rational aesthetic and objective coolness resembled that of the Swiss style. Since the Ulm School of Design considered itself avantgarde, its protagonists not only set new standards in terms of holistic design work, but also awarded their touted design style the distinction of good design and emphasized its exemplary nature.

The "Conference on Design Methods" followed a similar approach. 051 It took place in the USA in 1962 and established the "Design Methods Movement." The movement's goal lay in driving the systematization of design processes. It aimed to reduce subjective – and therefore uncontrollable – influences to a minimum. A more recent example is the "Design Thinking" method, 052 which has grown in popularity over the last years. This method is founded on the assumption that it becomes easier to complete tasks and solve problems when people from different disciplines work together in a certain methodical way. Several quality assurance process steps aim to combine efficiency and creativity. In addition to the team-based approach, the central aspects of "Design Thinking" include the feasibility and profitability of a solution to be developed. The quality is measured by evaluating the degree of acceptance by the user, operator, or client.

*
https://www.hfg-ulm.de/de/hfg-ulm/geschichte/

050 ------ Die Hochschule für Gestaltung, neun Stufen ihrer Entwicklung, Aicher
051 ------ Design Methods Movement
052 ------ Design Thinking

051.1 -------- Das Design Methods Movement in den 1960er Jahren, Mareis

Subjectivity and its innovative potential

It certainly makes sense to follow such systematized design processes. However, they risk spreading the idea that thoroughly planned processes and feedback constitute the ultimate benchmark. But in actuality, subjective factors always influence a design process too: These include individual stances and evaluations, all kinds of irrationalities, and mere chance. This can certainly be viewed as a flaw. After all, it means that the quality of design clearly depends on the individual horizon of the designer and the environment in which they operate. On the other hand, the subjective perspective of the designer, their originality, and sometimes their (alleged) inefficiency give the design greater room to unfold. This scope is needed to create something new and expand the imagination of the users, operators, and clients, which does not stray far from familiar features.
You could say that without subjective perspectives and commitment, progress would stall. From the past to the present, every era has demonstrated a multitude of such perspectives that formed outside of an established understanding of visual communication, and which pushed efficiency and evaluations based on the status quo into the background, in favor of individual procedures and views. By incorporating their ideas, designers make significant contributions to design innovation, to the professional self-image – and not least to societal discourse.

Speculative Design

The research-conducting design duo of Anthony Dunne and Fiona Raby – who coined the term *speculative design* – have demonstrated the potential results of cultivating subjective perspectives. In their book "Speculative Everything – Design, Fiction, and Social Dreaming" (2013), they remove themselves from the traditional self-image of many designers who primarily view their work as a service in communication processes. They try to imagine what problems of the future could look like in order to draw conclusions about present-day design. For this purpose, they designed a table [B 47] that they described as follows: "Speculative Everything began as a list we created a few years ago called A/B, a sort of manifesto. In it, we juxtaposed design as it is usually understood with the kind of design we found ourselves doing. B was not intended to replace A but to simply add another dimension, something to compare it to and facilitate discussion."* The list appears remarkably obvious, and it becomes clear: With their help and by using the speculative design approach, the field of design can step out of its often reactive role and help develop solutions for the future early on.

053

*
"Speculative everything," Anthony Dunne & Fiona Raby, The MIT Press, 2013, p. VI

053 ------ Speculative Everything, Dunne, Raby

Critical Design

The design duo Dunne/Raby also belonged to the protagonists of *critical design*. This approach entails questioning the commercial purposes and usability of objects and falls under the umbrella of design research due to its design-theory approach. Changes of perspective play their part in raising awareness of cultural, ethical, and social matters among the public. The tools of *critical design* include creative analysis of existing concepts and ideologies and conscious caricaturing of the original goals and functions of an object. When broken down in this way, thought patterns create opportunities to combine tried-and-tested procedures with new perspectives. Questions – concerning social relevance or barrier-free usability, for example – as well as differentiated criticism of consumerism aid the development of products and designs. They are used to start a dialog between experts and the audience that ultimately increases the design quality thanks to the feedback received.

[a]	[b]
affirmative	critical
problem solving	problem finding
provides answers	asks questions
design for production	design for debate
design as solution	design as medium
in the service of industry	in the service of society
fictional functions	functional fictions
for how the world is	for how the world could be
change the world to suit us	change us to suit the world
science fiction	social fiction
futures	parallel worlds
the "real" real	the "unreal" real
narratives of production	narratives of consumption
applications	implications
fun	humor
innovation	provocation
concept design	conceptual design
consumer	citizen
makes us buy	makes us think
ergonomics	rhetoric
user-friendliness	ethics
process	authorship

B 47
A / B, London, 2013, Dunne & Raby

Anthony Dunnes' book "Hertzian Tales" (1999) first articulated the term *critical design* and its underlying ideas. FABRICA also became well-known – the center for communication research founded by the Italian fashion company Benetton joined the discourse with provocative visual projects and critical questioning. *Critical design* is based on the individual stances of designers. It is less of a style and more of a politicization of the occupational profile. The concept is mapped out in commentary on a wide range of topics ranging from consumer culture through to the MeToo movement. The socio-critical potential of *critical design* ties in with movements of the 1960s and 1970s, such as *social design* and *radical design* – and which *speculative design* draws on conceptually.

Social Design

The terms *speculative design* and *critical design*, introduced by Dunne/Raby, as well as their underlying ideas that extend beyond design practice, pick up on an emancipatory thread that began in the 1960s and 1970s. One of 054 the most famous protagonists of this critical wave was Viktor Papanek. He and many others laid the foundation for a school of design thought in which sustainability, criticism of growth, and ethics played an important role. The atmosphere of upheaval that pervaded the USA and Europe during those years, which became evident through the economy, technology, art, and politics, brought about many movements with one common factor: the rejection of a world view shaped by hierarchies and capitalism, the rejection of old role patterns and ideals, and the willingness assume responsibility. The movements started to critically question the focus on industry and rationality 055 – hallmarks of modernism – on different levels and to refine these ideas. In an interview from 1990, Viktor Papanek said: "Design is never silent. Design always impacts society, the environment, and ecology." * Today, his book "Design for the Real World" (1971) is considered a wake-up call to accept social responsibility. According to his idea of design work, critical ideas are linked with practical procedures in which users play a crucial role. The term *social design*, which is frequently used in this context, originated in the field of architecture and touts a comparable belief: that the people who eventually use the buildings should be included in their creation process. In Scandinavia, this idea was called *cooperative design*. It outlines the collaboration between designers and users with the goal of illuminating the problem presented by a design in the best possible way. In the 1970s, the term *participatory design* replaced *cooperative design* in the USA because the original term suggested too much of an egalitarian interaction between the developer and the user. Initially, this form of participation aimed to produce more clarity on the framework conditions of a design by conducting surveys. The present misconception that *participative design* turns anyone into a designer

*
"The Politics of Design," Victor Papanek, from the chapter "Nochmal scheitern, besser scheitern," Amelie Klein, Vitra Design Museum (ed.), 2018, p. 15

054 ------ The Politics of Design, Papanek
055 ------ First Things First Manifesto, 1964

054.1 -------- Design for the Real World, Papanek
055.1 -------- First Things First Manifesto, 2000
055.2 -------- First Things First Manifesto, 2020

has persisted. In fact, participation means that feedback from people's life experiences is viewed as an important contribution to the success of design processes. Over time, user participation in design development has steadily increased and now falls under areas such as *user experience design* (UXD, UED, or XD). A quote from the book "Design for the Real World" summarizes the idea of social design and other participatory approaches by placing the focus on the responsibility of the designer:
"We must stop filling the world with poorly designed objects," writes Viktor Papanek. "To be ecologically and socially responsible, design must be revolutionary and radical." This statement not only applies to products, but also to communication design.

Radical Design

Radical design represents a design trend that had its heyday in the late 1960s and early 1970s. It turned away from functionalism in design and architecture. Its protagonists were primarily based in Italy. *Radical design* saw itself as an avantgarde movement and produced correspondingly unconventional designs and manifestos, particularly when it came to product design and architecture. Interdisciplinary work structures characterized the movement, as did the development of utopian ideas. The representatives of *radical design* demonstrated that the self-conception of design can exist outside of the occupational profile shaped by commerce and service provision.
One of its main objectives lay in critically engaging with politics and society. Its most famous representatives included Superstudio, Studio65, and Alessandro Mendini, an artist, designer, architect, and author. His cross-disciplinary way of working with different people and groups constituted a typical feature of *radical design*.

056

Open Design Movement

The goal of the *open design movement* is to make products and systems – whether analog or digital – freely available to users. The movement sees free and open-source software (FOSS) as an important foundation. It is motivated by both charitable and commercial goals. The charitable arm is committed to driving public projects whose completion would otherwise be at risk due to a lack of resources (financial, material, expertise) or lack of commercial interest. The commercially motivated protagonists view the *open design movement* as an opportunity to develop pioneering technologies. They want their collaboration to take place across borders and companies and follow the copyleft principle, which makes license-free editing and further development of software and products possible.

056 ------ Superstudio, Studio 65

056.1 -------- Alessandro Mendini

Maker

The *open design movement* has an affinity with the *maker movement*. The latter originated in the USA and is founded on the classic do-it-yourself principle. It also became more prominent in Germany about 10 years ago, 057 particularly in connection with the newly developed method of 3D printing. Many academics and politicians believe that the *maker movement* harbors future potential. The editor-in-chief at the time of “Wired” magazine called the method of exchanging ideas, plans, and products – whether analog or digital – for free and without the need for a license as the “third industrial revolution,” while US president Barack Obama dubbed the USA the “nation of makers” in 2014. So-called “Fab Labs” organize exchange opportunities and workshops. By offering guidance on the do-it-yourself principle and providing expertise, they also help poorer regions around the world.

Eco-Design

Over the past decade, we have seen strong growth of public and critical awareness regarding the sustainability of products. Against this background, the significance of environmentally conscious design has also increased. Today, it is a matter of course to examine products for repairability, means of disposal, and their overall lifecycle. This also has consequences for design work, as an estimated 80% of a product’s environmental impacts and costs are determined by its design. A product should be material-efficient, made 058 of a suitable material, energy-efficient, low in harmful substances, durable, repairable, recyclable, logistics-friendly. Even if this mainly refers to product design, these principles can also be applied to communication design. Every reader should have answers to the mentioned requirements on hand when it comes to their own design and production processes.

The list of design trends and approaches is not exhaustive. I have focused on those that have thought and think beyond the development of purely technical aspects. The list shows that the subjective view of the world emits 059 energy and always has a speculative character – and that this in particular is the strength of design thinking.

057 ------ The Maker Movement
058 ------ History of Ecological Design, Kallipoliti
059 ------ Graphic Design: Now in Production, Blauvelt, Lupton

057.1 -------- hartz IV moebel.com, Le-Mentzel
057.2 -------- Fabrication laboratory (Fab Lab), Menichenelli et al.
057.3 -------- Social Design. Partizipation und Empowerment
058.1 -------- Planet B – 100 Ideen für eine Neue Welt, Bieber, Feireiss
058.2 -------- Kapitalistischer Realismus ohne Alternative? Fisher
058.3 -------- Caps Lock: How Capitalism Took Hold of Graphic Design, and How to Escape from it, Pater

1₺

The previous chapters presented different aspects that characterize and shape visual communication. From the designer's perspective, one question remains unanswered: How do we determine the standards of design quality? One crucial factor that motivates designers is the fact that their work results not only need to satisfy the protagonists of a form of visual communication, but also meet the quality demands of their own profession. These demands impose certain obligations on every design solution.

However, which criteria designers need to observe to produce good quality remains somewhat unclear. Designers have always searched for answers and will continue to do so. What constitutes good design? Do "objective" criteria exist? Does the target group's taste set the tone? Or the designer's taste? Is it permissible to use design to influence taste in an "educational" manner? How do we even define design?

Good Design – Influences of Aesthetic Perception

The term “aesthetics” appears time and again in the context of visual communication. It is considered the yardstick of quality for a design product. The role of aesthetics clearly carries great importance in the discussion about what makes for “good design.” Indications include countless statements from experienced designers on this topic over the last century. These often issue a demand for an aesthetic dimension, without which design is allegedly incomplete, but they remain vague. In addition, the use of the term in all kinds of suitable and unsuitable contexts leads to conceptual confusion. Against this background, entirely pragmatic questions arise: What exactly are “aesthetics,” how do we recognize them, and how do we create them?

Defining the term “aesthetics”

The longer one discusses the term, the more layers are added to its meaning. I think it helps to examine the relationship between “aesthetics” and “good design” from the pragmatic perspective of the designer, even if this might lead to the reproach of treating “aesthetics” with too little differentiation. However, at this point, it is not possible to elaborate on the history of the term and all the various interpretations and meanings it has held over the centuries. Because in addition to its colloquial use, “aesthetics” is also, and above all, a hard-to-grasp, continually reevaluated term that philosophers from Plato and Socrates through to Baumgarten, Hegel, Benjamin, and Adorno have grappled with. [060]

Here is a brief definition that captures the everyday use of the term: “Aesthetics” is the study of perception, or of sensual observation. Anything that stimulates our senses when we look at it is aesthetic: whether it is beautiful, ugly, pleasant, or unpleasant. [061] Regardless of its actual ambiguity, the term “aesthetic” is considered a synonym of “beautiful” and “attractive.” I will use these interpretations as the basis for my elaborations. Life scientists who study informational aesthetics proffer different causes for aesthetic sensations. For one, they claim that the way our brain processes information plays a crucial role: We perceive something as “beautiful” when it displays a manageable complexity, i.e., the right amount of stimulation to form patterns. Scientists who focus on evolutionary aesthetics have observed evolutionary psychological influences that are rooted in our genetic material, for example when it comes to judging shapes and colors. Neuroscientists, in turn, attribute the responsibility for the perceiving “beauty” to different areas of the brain, especially those that belong to the so-called “reward

060 ------ Definition of the term “Aesthetics”
061 ------ The History of Beauty, Eco
061.1 -------- Die Geschichte der Hässlichkeit, Eco

system." In any case, there must be reasons why humans find something "beautiful." Even the philosophers of antiquity assumed that these sensations are not conditioned in a "vacuum," but are instead based on the nature that surrounds us. And in fact, if we examine this aspect of "nature" in more detail, we will reach some conclusions on why we consider certain things "beautiful." 062

Aesthetics and the human body

This observation starts with the human species. Evolution designed the human body in a two-sided, symmetrical way. This makes complete sense when it comes to our extremities: The human body needs two legs of the same length to avoid stumbling and to move as effectively as possible; it needs two arms of the same length to operate flexibly and efficiently. The head, of which the body has only one, is also symmetrical – the nose divides the face into two equal halves. Now we could draw the conclusion that the more similarities the two facial halves share, the more attractive the face appears – i.e., symmetry as perfected beauty. However, experiments conducted by a photo artist support scientific findings claiming that symmetry does not, in fact, constitute a criterion for beauty. He took portraits of people and edited them by mirroring one half of the face to create perfect symmetry. 063 To his surprise, when comparing the original with the edited photo as part of his experiment, all observers found the asymmetrical portrait more attractive. A face's deviations give it individuality and personality. For our co-existence as a human race, the ability to assess these is essential. As a result, we can identify an initial finding: Humans associate "beauty" with usefulness. More proof exists for this finding, namely our body's proportions. Our lower body (i.e., our legs) are longer than the upper body. However, these proportions are not random, but have arisen based on the evolutionary necessity to establish the best method of covering ground on foot. After all, for thousands of years, it served as the sole means to get from A to B. If we compare the proportions of the lower body and upper body more closely, we can see that these approximately correspond to the golden ratio. This allegedly ideal ratio of upper to lower body reveals a manifested value judgment: Long legs have always been viewed as a beauty standard. Since they served a survival purpose, this implies a connection between usefulness and perceived beauty.

The golden ratio

The proportions of the golden ratio are prevalent throughout nature, appearing in animals as well as plants. The Greek mathematician Euclid turned his observations on nature into a mathematical principle. It stated that if the longer part of a stretch relates to the smaller part in the same way as the

062 ------ Hat Schönheit Regeln? Der Goldene Schnitt (Film)
063 ------ Experimenting with facial symmetry

larger part to the total stretch, the proportions of the golden ratio apply. If 064
you divide the larger by the smaller part, the result is always 1.618.[B 49, 50] This number plays an important role in nature. The fact that this mathematical principle of the golden ratio has found its way into the arts and architecture largely came down to the understanding of God that prevailed among the people at the time. They viewed nature – the determinant of the golden ratio – as the work of the gods. To pay homage to them, they constructed temples (the most famous examples include the Parthenon temple in Athens and the Pyramids of Gizeh) based on the proportions derived from nature. In the pre-modern period, the golden ratio was considered a "divine" proportion. From Leonardo da Vinci's Mona Lisa and Michelangelo's David through to Albrecht Dürer's self-portrait – the golden ratio has always defined proportions. Based on this understanding, only an artist who understood and was able to translate the divine regularity of nature could create work characterized by balance, clarity, and divine beauty.

The Fibonacci sequence

Nature also inspired another discovery: the Fibonacci sequence, developed 065
by the Italian mathematician Leonardo Fibonacci. He devised the Fibonacci sequence while conducting an experiment on the rabbit population. It states that the sum of two consecutive numbers always yields a new value, and that this principle repeats itself in an unending chain. This results in the following sequence of numbers: 1, 1, 2, 3, 5, 8, 13, 21, 34, 55, 89, 144 (and so on). Even today, the reason for this remains a mystery: because the numbers from this sequence appear most frequently in nature. For example, studies of cactus varieties revealed 13 left-turning and 8 right-turning spirals. Flowers have blossoms with 5, 8, or 13 petals. The calyx of a sunflower consists of 34 left-turning and 55 right-turning spiral arms – all Fibonacci numbers. The silver thistle's baskets are made up of hundreds of petals of the same shape, sticking to the base in baskets of different sizes. The blossoms in the smaller baskets are arranged in a 21-to-55 position, with larger number ratios reaching 34 to 89 and 55 to 144 – again, all Fibonacci numbers. From spruce cones to pineapple fruits – you will encounter the values of the Fibonacci sequence everywhere. And it should come as no surprise that a connection exists between the Fibonacci sequence and the golden ratio: If you divide a number from the sequence by its predecessor (for example, 55 divided by 34), the result is the value of the golden ratio: (1.617647 =) 1.618.

The pentagram

There is another phenomenon that bears the stamp of the golden ratio, stems from nature, and carries a special meaning: the pentagram, or five-pointed star. Living nature provides countless examples of this – from

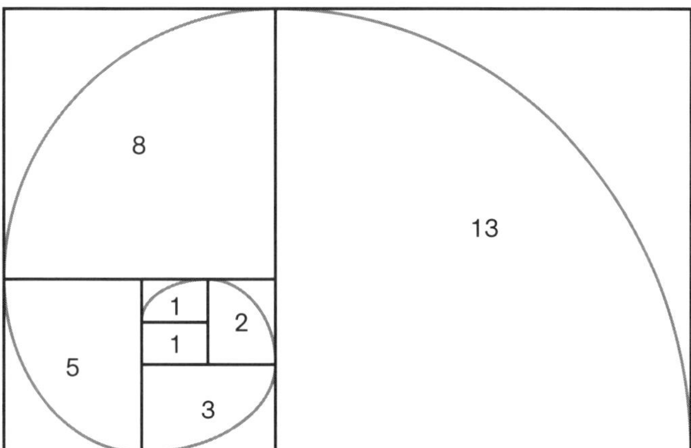

B 49
The golden ratio as a snail principle

C

A

B

B 50
The golden ratio as a principle of lengths: The ratio of the total length of C to partial length of A corresponds to the ratio of partial length A to partial length B.

starfish through to apple cores and the calyx of a hollyhock. Its symbolism is rooted in its inherent regenerative principle because it has no beginning or end.[B 51, 52] The pentagram even makes an appearance in human genetic material. The DNA model consists of two interwoven coils – the double helix. The distances between the spirals can be measured with a scanning electron microscope. And look at that: The smaller distance measures 13 angstroms (1 billionth of a meter), and the larger 21 angstroms – two Fibonacci numbers. The coils, twisted around each other, are arranged in the exact dimensions of the golden ratio. But there's more: Inside the structure, certain points on the coils are connected by a base bridge. If you were to shine a light down the tubes of a DNA model, it would cast a shadow in the form of a pentagram due to these overlapping base bridges.

What do symmetry and asymmetry, the golden ratio, the Fibonacci sequence, and the pentagram tell us? All these phenomena have a major impact on human perceptions because they form part of the world in which we live. Our environment shapes us: We internalize everything we perceive and assess it based on this stored image. From the color of the sky or of blood, the consistency of stones, or the sounds of the rain through to the sensation of warmth – the list of internalized impressions is long. It forms an intuitive foundation for imagining what we find pleasant and unpleasant, aesthetics, beauty, and its opposite. This is a universal insight into human perception. It also makes up the framework of human communication, both verbal and visual. The interplay of different cultures, religions, forms of society, philosophies, and arts gave rise to a range of globally differing interpretations and classifications of such intuitive experiences that have retained their distinctiveness until today. If we were to go into detail on these, we could fill an entire book (at least). That is why the rest of this section will focus on the development of quality standards for visual communication in Germany.

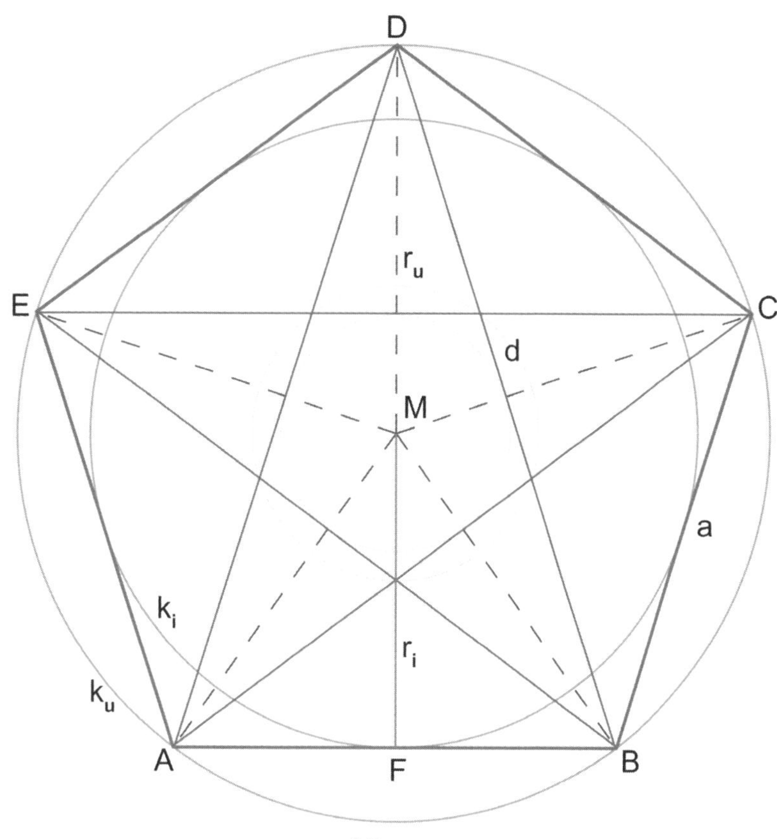

B 51
Geometric construction of the pentagram

B 52
The "Pentagramme de Faust" from Éliphas Lévi's *Dogme et rituel de la haute magie*

Good Design – A Brief History of the Criteria

From the early days of our profession – around the start of the 20th century – print workers, typesetters, and designers have debated the question of what makes design good. Their arguments spanned the described trends, findings from good use, and ideas on the societal role of design. Before I embark on a detour on these debates, I want to look back at the beginnings, when, following a technical revolution, visual communication started to influence human skills to a greater extent. Even back then, criteria for good design already existed.

From handwritten copies to book printing

Following the invention of movable lead letters by Johannes Gutenberg around 1450 and the accompanying possibility to technically reproduce texts, many standards began to emerge that proclaimed a suitable manner of producing visual communication (although the term itself was not coined until the 20th century). These standards defined the manual work of lead casters, typesetters, and printers. They were based on the viewing habits the work would cater to, the technical circumstances, and the economic framework conditions. Gutenberg's "42-line Bible" (created between 1452 and 1454) embodied these three aspects in an exemplary way, although this was not evident at first glance. The clergy, the almost-exclusive client for print products in the 15th century, was used to the writing style of the monks, who had carried out the laborious work of manually copying documents and books before the invention of lead letters. For economic reasons alone, it made sense for Johannes Gutenberg to quietly imitate this design – after all, a single manually produced copy came at a much higher cost than a copy created as part of a print run. Gutenberg put considerable effort into lending his lead-letter font the handwritten style of the monks: In the "42-line Bible," he used a total of 290 characters. Aside from the uppercase and lowercase alphabet, the font includes more than 92 abbreviations and 83 ligatures. On top of this, it contains numerous type variations – the letter "e" alone appears in 13 different versions.[B 53] 067
Gutenberg used the lead type font Textura. It closely resembled the handwritten styles with which the monks had written since the 13th century. Its characteristic traits included blackletter script that did without the curves of its predecessor fonts. Overall, the Textura letters were closely linked to one another, which enabled more letters to fit onto a line. Aside from catering to habits and economic considerations, Gutenberg's focus on the quality of handwritten precursors had another good reason: The monks' handwritten copies were masterpieces – in terms of the balance of the lines, line spacing,

067 ------ Gutenberg's 42-Line Bible and Textura, Krawietz, Hanebutt-Benz

B 53
Johannes Gutenberg not only used variants of individual letters, but also played with letters that were available as ligatures.

type area as well as the miniatures that embellished the starting letters (initials). Gutenberg even had the latter subsequently drawn into the lead-type books by hand to create one-of-a-kind features.

Fonts as a sign of national identity

Gutenberg's lead typeface was founded on the basic forms of Gothic minuscule, which had arisen from the Carolingian minuscule. Gothic minuscule served as the formal foundation of blackletter scripts. In addition to Textura, these include Schwabacher and Fraktur (15th/16th century) [B 54, 55]. Due to their frequent use in the German-speaking region, blackletter typefaces were considered "German" fonts; that said, this interpretation was never undisputed. The controversy revolving around which font most epitomized the German identity began with Martin Luther's translation of the bible in 1534, which was printed in the Schwabacher typeface. This also served to typographically distinguish the bible from the Roman versions. This example illustrates why typeface development diverged into two different paths during this time: the blackletter typefaces based on Gothic minuscule on the [068] one hand, and (primarily in southeastern Europe) the humanistic Antiqua on the other [B 56]. This parallel development lasted for about 400 years, always accompanied by sporadic discussions. In 1911, even the Reichstag addressed the matter of the "German font." The majority of parliamentarians viewed Fraktur as "German." It prevailed over the humanistic Antiqua style, preferred only by a minority. In this way, visual communication always embodied more than just a means to convey information. As it grew charged due to different intentions and values, it also influenced quality standards.

Functionalism as an expression of modernity

The debates revolving around the criteria for good design started to pick up speed in the 19th century. At the same speed with which industrialization was progressing and countless technical innovations first saw the light of day, the conditions and application options for visual communication were also evolving. Photography began to establish itself in the 19th century, revolutionizing the way humans portrayed the world thanks to its documentary, [069] technically objectifying aspirations. Rapid presses started to replace the long tradition of manually operated printing presses. These machines ran on steam and completed most of the printing process independently. New forms of writing emerged, such as the early Egyptienne fonts [B 57], for example, and the Grotesque fonts [B 58] towards the end of the century. These font developments arose as a result of changing economic demands (font alternatives required for the up-and-coming field of advertising, more robust letters for faster printing presses). The rapidly progressing industrialization brought about a large number of products and consumer offerings that

068 ------ Read + Play: Typografie ist evolutionär, Voelker
069 ------ Texte zur Theorie der Fotografie, Stiegler

068.1 -------- Read + Play. Einführung in die Typografie, Voelker
068.2 -------- Geschichte der Schrift, Haarmann
069.1 -------- Sehen. Das Bild der Welt in der Bilderwelt, Berger

Die Schwabacher ist eine Schrift aus der Gruppe der gebrochenen Schriften.

B 54
The blackletter font *Schwabacher*

Die Fraktur, von lateinisch fractura (Bruch), entstand in der Mitte des 16. Jahrhunderts.

B 55
The blackletter font *Fraktur*

Die Garamond basiert auf humanistischen Minuskeln. Sie ist eine Renaissance-Antiqua.

B 56
The Antiqua font *Garamond*

Die Egyptienne ist eine Schrift, bei der die Serifen betont sind.

B 57
The Egyptienne font *Rockwell*

Die Grotesk ist eine Schrift, bei der keine Serifen verwendet werden.

B 58
The Grotesk font *Akzidenz Grotesk*

began to compete with one another. The design profession was established, and designers began lending these products their unmistakable form and created advertising for them. This development took place concurrently with revolutionary events within society.

Industrialization was accompanied by exploitative working conditions, recurring economic crises, cramped living conditions, low life expectancy, and a hierarchical class society. Not only the socialist and communist parties spoke out against these conditions and led initial efforts in democratization (such as the 1848/1849 revolution in the German Confederation) – other non-party movements also expressed their dissatisfaction, examining the interplay between art, technology, and design. The first larger alliance emerged in the form of the Arts and Crafts movement in England, which redefined the relationship between art, society, and work, and in light of industrial work processes and their alienating character, made a case for a return to manual craft.
Art nouveau followed around the turn of the century (and spread to various European countries), opposing the prevailing historicism, but also the negative consequences of industrialization. At the same time, its protagonists researched new materials such as iron and concrete as well as new construction methods. Futurism (1909 – 1914, founded in Italy) rebelled against the bourgeois value system and viewed its underlying manifesto as a provocation. The movement saw itself as the avant-garde of a new, taboo-breaking culture that admired and glorified youth, violence, speed, and war. [070]
Dadaism, founded in Switzerland in 1916, argued against war, against bourgeois order, against any form of authority, and was associated with anarchistic and socialist ideas. [071]

In this phase before, during, and after World War I, the world was experiencing a transformation in many areas. Ideas of a new society emerged and were espoused by the major ideological movements of socialism and communism. In the first democracy on German soil, the Weimar Republic (1919 – 1933), they were the ones who fought for models of a better world with democratic and revisionist forces. As a result, the willingness and desperate need for new paths made its way into all parts of society, politics, and culture. In 1919, the Bauhaus art school was founded in Weimar. It aimed to merge art and craft in a programmatic way and thereby achieve what had been envisaged and addressed in many places in the preceding years. From today's perspective, Bauhaus can be described as the most influential educational facility of the 20th century. [072] It focused on the areas of architecture, art, and design. The avantgarde ideas it produced and taught are often mentioned in the same breath as modernism. Modernism comprises many

070 ------ Read + Play: Typografie ist politisch, Voelker
071 ------ Was ist der Dadaismus und was will er in Deutschland?
072 ------ Das Programm des staatlichen Bauhauses in Weimar, Gropius

trends in culture and society that were shaped by industrialization, enlightenment, and secularization. They shared the spirit of the "De Stijl" movement and Russian constructivism – whose protagonists were also all striving for a humane and just society through by interconnecting art, society, and work. Especially in the fields of architecture (dignified living) and product design (affordable products through serial production), the ideas of Bauhaus and those in its orbit – which were largely aligned with socialist ideals – became a reality. In the area of visual communication, pioneers led the way: In 1925, Jan Tschichold published his view of how political goals, social awakening, and visual communication should be connected under the title "elementare typographie." 073

Here is an extract from his ten-point manifesto:
"1. The new typography is functional. 2. The purpose of typography is to convey messages (for which it serves as the means). The message must appear in the briefest, simplest, most powerful form. (...)
8. Elementary design excludes the use of any ornamentation (including decorative lines). The use of lines and elementary shapes in general (squares, circles, triangles) must be justified within the overall construction. The decorative-artistic-speculative use of per se elementary shapes is not synonymous with elementary design."

In the same publication, László Moholy-Nagy praised the "typophoto": "(...) The clarity of reality in the everyday situation applies to all layers. Slowly, the hygiene of the visual, healthy aspects of what we see seeps through. (...) Typography is a message, representation of thoughts designed in print. Photography is the visual representation of what is optically tangible. Visually, the typophoto is the most precisely designed message. (...)" 074
In this optimistic mood, visual communication benefited from a revaluation: as the medium for information, but also for influence, both in regard to politics and aesthetics. The politically oriented, educational aspects of "modern" design as both a humanistic tool and measure of value provided a solution to the challenges of the times. Visual communication contributed with functional aesthetics. The term delineates a new understanding: The formal aesthetic principles no longer determine the beauty of a figure. This is a thing of the past. Contemporary beauty results from an object's functionality, at least that is the hope. The idea behind this: Design that feels obligated to visualize useful aspects and optimally supports functionality also produces "beauty." This notion of stepping back and integrating into the functionality of things and communication served as a guiding principle that started to catch on in the 1920s. In visual communication, many protagonists were formulating guidelines, design principles, and ideals that

073 ------ Elementare Typographie, Tschichold
074 ------ Typophoto, Moholy-Nagy

074.1 -------- Die Reklame, Stam, Lissitzky

extended into the diverse concerns of society. Paul Renner developed a constructed typeface, "Futura" [B 59]. Josef Albers designed a combination typeface 075 that reduced the number of available types to three [B 60]. The idea behind this: faster and simplified typesetting. Bauhaus propagated the use of lowercase letters, with the following reasoning: "we write everything in lowercase because it saves time. also: why 2 alphabets if one suffices? why write in uppercase when you cannot speak in uppercase?" Like many other new ideas, these did not always appeal to the mainstream. While some innovations would later celebrate global success (e.g., Futura), others disappeared back into their drawers (e.g., writing in lowercase or Albers' combination typeface). These examples show that inventors had to fight for their ideas. They saw themselves as avantgarde, and accordingly, the definitions regarding the requirements for good design were not negotiable. The criteria were morally and politically charged. They differentiated between "functional" and "ornamental," between "modern" and "historicizing," between "humanistic" 076 and "inhumane," between "socialist" and "capitalist" – in short: between "right" and "wrong."

Visual communication in times of National Socialism

When the Nazis came to power in 1933, the multi-layered aspirations for a humane and just society came to a brutal end. Emergency decrees, a so-called enabling act, bans on parties and organizing dictated everyday life. Political opponents were taken to concentration camps, tortured, and murdered. Jews were ostracized and systematically disenfranchised, and the objective of eliminating them started to take shape in the years that followed. Under the Nazis, the debate around the impact of good design gave way to a type of visual communication that was stipulated from above and shaped by ideology. It left no doubt about who was defining the only benchmark. The stipulations regarding the visual appearance of both the state bodies and the 077 NSDAP and its countless sub-organizations were strict and gradually began to extend to all visual communication under Nazi rule – starting with the symbols, flags, military designations through to movie propaganda, newspapers, magazines, posters, stationery, books, and font design. Especially the latter area revealed the extent to which the authorities governed even the tiniest details by enforcing rules on what they considered to be good design. It came as no surprise that the matter of the "German font" was revived after the Nazi takeover. Initially, the Nazis used both grotesque and Antiqua fonts, as demonstrated by numerous examples. However, due to their significance as a "national" identity trait, the blackletter typefaces eventually prevailed – the prospect of adopting a font type as the "national" one and thereby turning it into the unmistakable hallmark of the country's own visual communication was too tempting. The letters of blackletter typefaces were sim-

075 ------ Futura. Die Schrift, Eisele et al.
076 ------ Ornament und Verbrechen, Loos
077 ------ NSCI – Das visuelle Erscheinungsbild der Nationalsozialisten, Koop

075.1 -------- Herbert Bayers Universal-Schrift in ihrem historischen Kontext, Mills

B 59
Futura bold condensed **by Paul Renner**

B 60
Combination font **by Josef Albers**

The quick brown fox jumps over the lazy dog

Futura LT Book Regular

plified into so-called grotesque-gothic forms to give them a more modern look – after all, the Nazis already had slogans decrying the "dawn of a new era" at the ready. Instead of simplification, one could also speak of a process of coarsening the font style, which, in retrospect, demonstrated a nearly ghostly symbiosis with the communicated content. Typesetters referred to fonts such as Tannenberg as "high-boot grotesque" [B 61]. However, the preference for blackletter typefaces did not last for long. Against the background of Germany's presumed victory march in World War II – the war the country had instigated –, the Nazis opted for a typographic U-turn. To be able to communicate in occupied territories, Antiqua fonts proved more suitable than blackletter typefaces, which were more difficult for foreign eyes to decipher. These were unceremoniously declared "Jew letters" in 1941, their use prohibited, and the usage of Antiqua fonts ordered in their stead. This example demonstrates the political arbitrariness and the instrumentalization of visual communication for propaganda purposes. Many other little aspects ensured the backing of the Nazi system's ideological parameters in the area of design. There was no tolerance of visual communication that freed itself from the shackles of the system. Petty bourgeois administrators of the regime defined the criteria of good design, and their compliant henchmen enforced them.

The functionalism of the post-war era

After the end of World War II and liberation from the Nazis, a newly founded institution – the Ulm School of Design – revived the stances of progressive designers from the 1920s *(see also 050, 103.1)*. The educational impact of visual communication in the sense of an egalitarian, objective, humanistic, scientific influence became the focal point again. The idea was that filtering these values into society via visual communication would help prevent another catastrophe like the Nazi era and at the same time revive the Bauhaus ideals. With their holistic perspective, the protagonists of HfG Ulm [B 62, 63] made a significant contribution to revitalizing, continuing, and further developing the stances of modernism and thereby functionalism.
Against this background, in a sense as a sign of the zeitgeist in the years of reconstruction, another graphic style emerged in parallel, launching its victory march around the world in Switzerland: the "Swiss style." This soon-to-be international style also had its roots in the bustling years preceding World War II. It united rational strictness (achieved with a strikingly grid-oriented approach) with reduction and clearness. The rationality and clarity of design led to an unmistakable aesthetic that had its heyday in the 1950s and 1960s.

Die deutsche Schrift

B 61
The bold version of *Tannenberg*

B 62
The buildings of the *Ulm School of Design*, architect – Max Bill, 1955

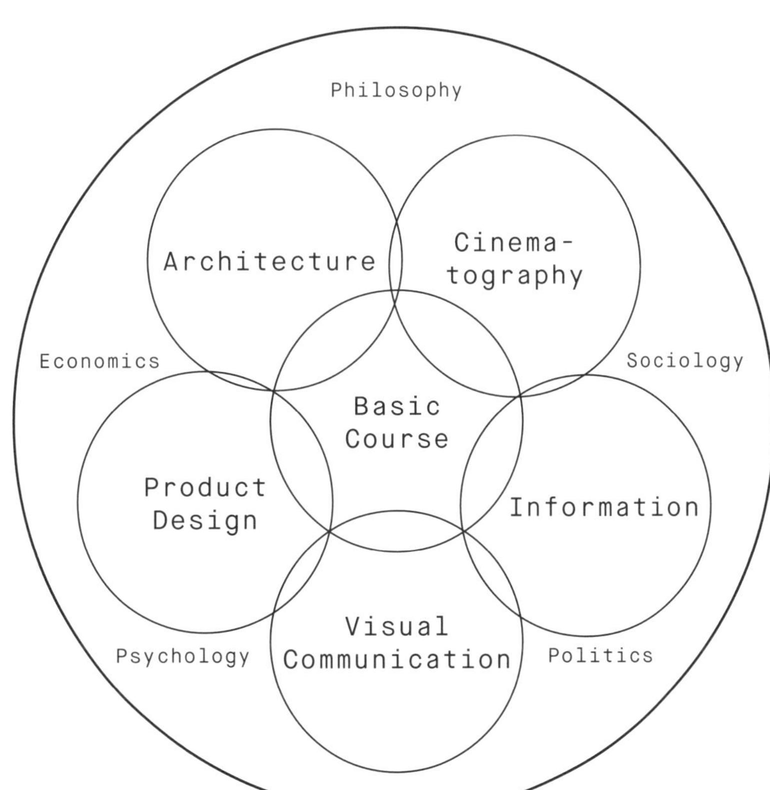

B 63
The teaching plan at the *Ulm School of Design*

079

With the Swiss style, functionalism gained a formal face in visual communication. Modernist protagonists such as the designer Anton Stankowski described the aesthetic dimension of "functional graphics" as follows: "(...) In the long term, both architecture and design (...) cannot make do without the functional aspect of aestheticism. Because it is never just about the thing itself, it is also always about the image you gain of the thing – and this image is largely determined by aesthetic qualities. But because graphic design essentially consists of conveying images of things, visualizing things, and even including the invisible in the image, it is obvious that aesthetics play a crucial role here. In addition to the signal effect, which allows us to quickly understand visual relationships, the harmonious overall effect carries the most significant meaning for a graphic solution. Aesthetics has a function, and if an object is lacking it, then it is incomplete (...)."
Some terms shimmer like gemstones in this quote: harmony, signal effect, quick understanding, functionality. And in the course of further implementations, design procedures are actually described that aim to help achieve good design, for example the maxims of "finding – simplifying – objectifying – humanizing." Concretely, this means: "Playing through all available formal, contextual, and functional options – as well as systematically simmering them down to a solution." The term "simplify" refers to the principle of "simple, yet strange," in the sense of unmistakableness. This is followed by a note on "the demand (...) for argumentation," meaning logic and seriousness. Stankowski understands "humanizing" to be the following: "(...) it can mean putting the visualization in relation to the human perceptive system and emotional life as well as the human processing conditions. This can be achieved through characteristics such as symmetry, proportion, or harmony – or by breaking with them (...)."*

A designer can only endorse these descriptions. Stankowski's text was published in a specialist book titled "Visuelle Kommunikation" ("Visual Communication") in the year 1987, which includes texts from other luminaries of the time (Otl, Aicher, Karl Duschek, and Hans Hillmann, to name a few) that dealt with various aspects of the discipline. Most of the text's statements make a claim to universal validity, as was common for the art of argumentation in the era of modernism. Abraham Moles, who composed the introduction, summed this up as follows: "(...) We have abstracted all of these rules from the informational theory of perception. They are founded on the simple idea that the graphic designer, layout artist, author of a road signal, that they are all addressing a specific average type of recipient who is educated to a certain level and finds themselves in everyday situations. This means that, by necessity, the rules have a static nature; they are also difficult or impossible to put into numbers. But that is not actually necessary: A graphic design-

*
"Visuelle Kommunikation," Anton Stankowski, Verlag Dietrich Reiner, 1989, p. 24

079 ------ Visuelle Kommunikation: Ein Design-Handbuch, Stankowski, Duschek

er is a man of practical experience. In particular, he demands maxims for his actions, ideas of certain conditions that he is not permitted to stray outside of, concrete orientations he must follow. He benefits from the knowledge that there are rules and that there is a science behind receiving messages that he applies, consciously or unconsciously (...)."

"The average type of recipient" – according to the quote, this is the kind of person that must be taken into account when making universally valid statements on what is "good" and "right" in design. Essentially, this is nothing to object to, because prototypical assessments are required to form a foundation. In addition, a culture's constant components offer reliable parameters that must be considered. However, the description lacks some detail on the modifications that are required to address target groups in the specific and suitable way that applies to each. And the years that followed (the publication of the book) would prove that rules and the science of receiving messages could be subject to completely different interpretations. That is why relativizations or reclassifications of such universally valid statements on visual communication were only a matter of time.

Thirteen years after the Stankowski's text was published, cultural scientist Dagmar Steffen wrote the following in "Das Jahrhundert des Design. [080] Geschichte und Zukunft der Dinge" ("The Century of Design: The History and Future of Things"):
"(...) 'Not one design for all, no, many designs for many people' – this maxim coined by the Kunstflug group characterizes – in a heavily abbreviated way – the break between design from the 1980s and 1990s and the decades of design that preceded it, shaped by functionalism. For one, the designers' image of users underwent a revision; and in addition, the ideas of the function that products fulfilled for users experienced a fundamental transformation. All in all, the values and guiding principles and their reflection through product semantics changed. For example, HfG Ulm alumna Gerda Müller-Krauspe remembered – at the same time continuing Walter Gropius' dictum on the similarity of all people's needs – that her generation had, in the 1960s, 'effortlessly projected their self-image onto their image of potential buyers.' They assumed that, after a few more educational attempts, they would soon learn to appreciate the irreproachably modern design of Braun, Knoll International, Zapf, or WMF; but by the mid-1970s at the latest, it became clear that this 'egalitarian fundamental approach had misjudged the social reality in Germany.' ... 'Design for everyone' – this ideal could no longer embody a generally binding objective, as the populace proved unamenable to the paternalistic attempts at educating them on the ethical and aesthetic value of 'good form.' On top of this, new political ideas, values, and

080 ------ Pluralistisch und allgegenwärtig: Design unter den Bedingungen der neunziger Jahre, Steffen

guiding principles were leading to changes in the social fabric of the prospering land of economic miracles; the traditional structural model of social hierarchies – which many had initially hoped would grow less distinct and turn into a 'leveled middle-class society' thanks to growing general prosperity – was overhauled as society splintered into different milieus and subcultures and was replaced by new target-group models devised by cultural sociologists (...)."

The functionalism conjured up by modernist representatives contained the world view of "right" and "wrong," linked with "paternalistic educational attempts" (Steffen) that strived to enforce this view. Along with the circumstance that functionalistic design became a trend, this contributed to a waning acceptance: Because with the "Swiss style," design-related functionalism increasingly shed its substantive justification and turned into a formal style that claimed to be suitable for all content and all target groups. It hereby broke with the core demand of modernism that had already been formulated at the end of the 19th century and initially referred to architecture, but later also to product design and visual communication: "The law of all organic and inorganic beings, all physical and metaphysical, all human and superhuman things, all real manifestations of the mind, the heart, and 081 the soul, states that life is recognizable in its expression that form always follows function," said the American architect Louis Sullivan in 1896. By this he meant that the form must be derived from its function, or that the form should allow us to draw conclusions on the function. Sullivan summed up this approach with the well-known remark: "Form follows function." 082 Strictly speaking, a style like the "Swiss style" could no longer meet this demand because it increasingly resorted to formal aesthetic decisions and was therefore intended for and applied to any content.

Good design in postmodernism

In the 1980s, the prevailing question was: What happens if the living conditions within a society change, democratic participation in decision-making becomes more of a matter of course, and the existing structures are called into question? This is exactly what had been happening in many (democratic) countries in the western world starting in the 1960s. Imagine the "Swiss typography" had remained the sole yardstick for "good" design. What does that make the psychedelic art posters from the 1960s? Bad design? And who would have made this judgment? It became clear that many different social groups with their own measures of value, preferences, and tastes were not only following their own life plans and goals, but also had their own ideas of what they considered "good" design (think of hippie culture, punk design, techno style, or other forms of visual communication

081 ------ Form follows function, Sullivan
082 ------ On the relationship between function and form

within various subcultures). The dilemma that arose due to the growing diversity in society reared its head through confrontations between old and young, traditions and new ideas, the establishment and underground movements, authority and rebelliousness. In communication design, it was just as impossible to uphold the strict formula of "Form follows function" in the sense of a defined measure of value as it was to uphold the "Swiss style" as THE benchmark for design quality. Nevertheless, young designers were subject to a barrage of strong criticism of their typographic "behavior" well into the 1990s. Even in 1989, Otl Aicher disputed the integrity of British designer Neville Brody, who had delighted his generation with his design of "Face" magazine. In relation to his design and font creations, he wrote: "It will always be the case that fonts will have to serve as a material for aesthetic structures (...). As long as you aren't required to read such fonts, that might work. But you can no longer call this typography." [B 64]
Not only subcultures were increasingly questioning modernist approaches in the 1980s. In many disciplines – literature, architecture, fashion, art, music, and also visual communication – viewpoints and forms of expression emerged that can be summarized under the term "postmodernism." *

Digital design is like painting, except the paint never dries.

B 64
FF Dirty Three **by Neville Brody, 1994**

*
There are different academic interpretations of when postmodernism started to rival modernism. From my perspective as a designer, the changes effected by postmodernism in visual communication date back to the late 1970s and 1980s.

For design, this meant: Any rules for "good" design that were deemed outdated were simply ignored. This led to a counterculture of creating, citing, copying, trying things out.
Adopting a clear political stance was not considered desirable; ideas on the societal role of design were replaced by ideas on self-portrayal and the appeal of decorative creations. The early 1990s also saw the bipolarity of the political blocs disappear (capitalism versus socialism) after the regime in Eastern Europe collapsed, replaced by the "victorious" ideology of capitalism. The design world responded to the focus on consumption and rising neoliberalism with attractive surfaces: They often became more important than the content. One very special tool made this widespread frenzy of formal trends possible: the Apple Macintosh. The technical standards in typography – once set through the interplay with the technical limitations of lead type and later phototype – were now viewed as an option that could be ignored depending on one's personal interpretation. Definitions of what constituted "good" design were increasingly evading the criteria that had dominated up until then. Visual communication had definitively become a matter of taste. [B 65, 66] An educational aesthetic of visual communication that influenced society – as envisioned by Max Bill, Jan Tschichold, or Otl Aicher – was a thing of the past. The "dogma" of modernism had been replaced by a wide array of perspectives, interests, and gestures that stood on equal footing.

Criteria of good design in post-postmodernism

If we look back now, it seems as if many postmodern attitudes have slowly become obsolete – irony, copying and citing, fetishizing graphic interfaces, the attitude of "anything goes." As difficult as it may be to sum up epochs in a few words or to narrow down and divide the respective time periods, it is possible to make out shifts in standards that signalize epochal transitions. Designating this new era that has started to replace postmodernism successively over the last 20 years is not an easy task, because there is not just one interpretation of how to evaluate the changes in culture, academia, politics, and also in communication. Here, I would like to pick up on the term "post-postmodernism," which occasionally appears in cultural discourse. It encompasses keywords such as trust, sincerity, sustainability, credibility, performance, honesty, equality, diversity, and dialog. And this return of certain values from the era of modernism, combined with the great variety of viewpoints, opinions, and interpretations opens up new perspectives when it comes to the question of "good" and "bad" design. Because the "new" old values also entail a serious search for plausible criteria to determine what could constitute good design today.

B 65
Design: John O'Callaghan, Ravensbourne College Chislehurst, UK

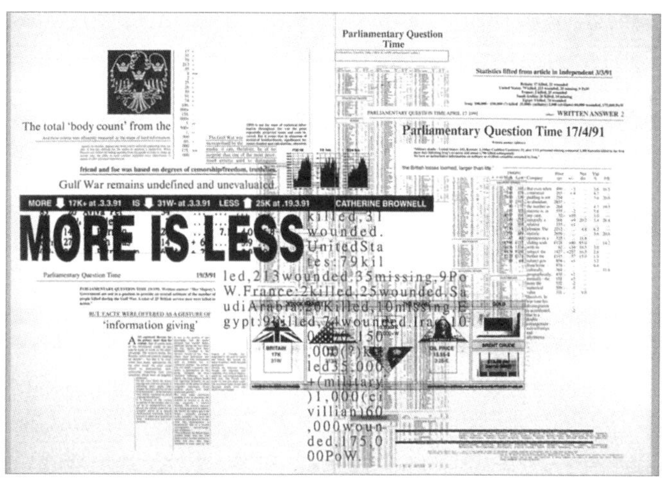

B 66
Design: John O'Callaghan, Ravensbourne College Chislehurst, UK

For this purpose, it helps to take a look at the fundamental aspects. For example, we could evaluate someone's work based on whether it presents a harmonious relationship between design and content. After all, it could be a sign of quality if a creation contains what it promises graphically. This would create an "aesthetic aura," to quote Anton Stankowski once more. He went into more detail on this, stating that: "(...) If we succeed in harmonizing form and function into an integrative solution, exactly this would constitute its aesthetic function. The function of aesthetics then lies in, one could also say, supporting the functionality of the depiction with the presentation format (...)." *

In practice, we can find excellent examples of this thesis. But the method has also produced disconcerting results: Are yellow-press magazines well designed? The private stories of celebrities, the trivialities decried as scandals from the world of royalty, the false reports, the bourgeois views – all of this is visualized in an accordingly banal manner. Or the tabloids: The gruff and loud design (at times with narrow text columns and holes in the justification, bold or compressed fonts, and so on) directly reflects their gruff, loud, and polemic content. Does this qualify tabloids to be nominated for a design award? Or pulp novels? [B 67] The examples all demonstrate a congruent relationship between content and design – "Form follows function," essentially. However, the "aesthetic aura" prognosticated for this case does not seem to come into being. The fact that form and content match is a first step, an important one. As we can see, this can be a trait of "good" design, but it does not have to be.

Another fundamental aspect might be helpful: the knowledge long harbored by typesetters – whose profession no longer exists. By this I mean: How does the human eye read, what is readable, what is legible, what does informative reading look like, what does linear or consultative reading look like, what hierarchies exist in reading layouts, what formats are comfortable, what font sizes are suitable for reading at a distance, and so on. To start with, a kind of preliminary sorting is helpful. It stems from Hans Peter Willberg and was first discussed in the book "Lesetypografie" ("Reading Typography," 1997): "(...) 'The one typography' does not exist. Typography is faced with a range of demands. Orientation typography must guide readers in the right direction in a parking garage or on a timetable; advertising typography aims to capture the reader's attention, and all means are acceptable to do so; design typography wants to forge new paths in an innovative, progressive, venturesome way; newspaper typography wants to get to the point as quickly as possible; magazine typography tempts readers to browse and linger; decoration typography wants to be beautiful – readability is not the key factor here, forms must be clearly structured; and it remains unclear

*
"Visuelle Kommunikation," Anton Stankowski, Verlag Dietrich Reiner, 1989, p. 25

B 67
Pulp fiction *A Family with a Heart*, Verlag Bastei Lübbe, Cologne, 2021

whether the small print on contractual forms is meant to be readable or is designed to be overlooked. Every task requires different methods. Universally valid rules cannot exist (...).” *(see 012)*

In the search for criteria of good design, the solution might therefore lie in addressing specific communication solutions and picturing the framework conditions. Here, we will generally find stipulations that arise from the sender's intention, the recipient's receptive behavior, and the medium used. And look at that, they do exist – the small, definitely concrete, and binding “rules” for good design. It looks like we must agree with Abraham Moles after all when he says that “rules exist and there is a science to receiving messages” – even though the term “science” seems a little lofty in my opinion and should perhaps be replaced by “findings.”
Here is an example from the discipline of typography, written by Jost Hochuli in the book “Das Detail in der Typografie”:
“(...) Like all other two-dimensional figures that our eye perceives, letters are also subject to optical laws. Therefore, we do not need measuring devices to evaluate their formal qualities, but instead solely the healthy human eye. That is why we do not want to call the following points, which must be taken into account when designing a font, optical illusions, but optical facts: 084
1. When they have the same height, a circle and a triangle appear smaller than a rectangle. To look like they share the same height, the points and curves must be pulled slightly above or below the head or base line.
2. When you geometrically cut a surface exactly in half, this results in a top half that visually appears larger than the bottom half. To create two visually equal halves, the horizontal divide must lie above the geometric one, at the so-called optical center.
3. If they have the same line width, a horizontal line appears wider than a vertical line. To create a visually balanced appearance with lines and horizontal bars that appear to have the same width, the horizontal line must be a little narrower. This not only applies to straight shapes, but also round ones – these need to be even wider at the widest horizontal spot than the corresponding verticals (...).”* B 68-71

Hochuli speaks of the “healthy human eye.” Of course, this does not just refer to its neurobiological functionality, but particularly the tendencies it has developed based on our visual experiences. This, in turn, is part of the human perception that comprises the sum of the process steps of “recording, selecting, processing, and interpreting” sensory information in its psychological and physiological definition. Our perception occurs in the listed sequence, so that we can adapt to the respective situations of our environment or to enable feedback on our own behavior. Because this process leads

*
“Das Detail in der Typografie,”
Jost Hochuli,
Niggli Verlag, 2005, p. 18

084 ------ Das Detail in der Typografie, Hochuli

084.1 -------- Bücher machen, Hochuli
084.2 -------- Graphic Grids in Everyday Design, Voelker

B 68
The circle (left) appears smaller than the rectangle, even though both have the same height. It must be slightly enlarged (right) to look as though it shares the rectangle's height.

B 69
The triangle (left) appears smaller than the rectangle, even though they have the same height. It must be slightly enlarged (right) to look as though it shares the rectangle's height.

a b

B 70
Dividing a rectangle into two equally sized parts allows the top part to appear larger (a). In order for them to look as though they are of the same size, the rectangle must be divided through the optical center (b).

B 71
When a horizontal and a vertical line share the same width, the horizontal line appears wider (c). In order for them to look like they are equally wide, the horizontal line must be slightly narrower (d).

to the construction of mental models of the world. Hochuli's example is one mosaic tile among countless others, from the areas of perception of images, general design foundations, or color theory, among others. Together, they 085 all form the canon that serves as the basis of any type of targeted design.

But here, we must also remember: Human perception changes due to perpetual learning processes. An experiment conducted by Gustav Theodor Fechner around 1860 illustrates this. He presented participants with rectan- 086 gles and asked them to choose the one they found the most appealing. The favorite matched the proportions of the golden ratio – a rectangle with the proportions of 5 to 8. [B 72, 73] We can assume that such formats were frequently used at the time, and the internalized sense of proportions acted as a guideline. However, it would be interesting to repeat this experiment today. The result might look completely different, since the variety of media and increased frequency of reading on screens has instilled different senses of proportion within humans. The various TV formats offer some proof of this: The screen ratio of 4:3, which was prevalent up until the 2000s and which still appears occasionally in an old movie, seems strangely foreign today. [B 74] We have grown too accustomed to the 16:9 format that is the standard now. [B 75] Accordingly, tendencies adopted through nature and socialization imprinted through manmade circumstances would constitute two different spheres of influence. And this raises the question of which current circumstances impact our perception and must therefore be incorporated into visual communication. [B 76]

Fechner, a doctor and physicist, presented a range of further principles on aesthetics, which he compiled in his book "Vorschule zur Ästhetik" ("Preschool for Aesthetics"). He illustrated the aspect of the "aesthetic association principle" with the following sentence: "We find an orange more visually appealing than a wooden ball painted to look like one." He meant that the "sensory eye" might not differentiate between the two objects – but the "cognitive eye" certainly would – due to the associative connections that are established in relation to the expected taste, scent, and country of origin (and its particular features, such as the climate, culture, people). According to Fechner, the impression gained through the "sensory eye" could be consistent with or stand in contrast to these associations. As a person grows older, the associative connections – which are nothing more than memories – can overlay the actual impression. The experiences and memories we accumulate in our lives make associative demands on new things. If the new thing behaves in a way that corresponds to the gathered experiences, we will perceive a feeling of harmony. However, if we witness a contradiction, we experience a sense of discomfort. Fechner's thesis matches the observations

085 ------ Kunst der Farbe, Itten
086 ------ Vorschule der Ästhetik, Fechner

B 72
The rectangle with the side ratio of 5 to 8

Tabelle über die Versuche mit 10 Rechtecken.

(V Seitenverhältniss, Z Zahl der Vorzugsurtheile, z Zahl der Verwerfungsurtheile, m. männlich, w. weiblich.)

V	Z		z		procent Z	
	m.	w.	m.	w.	m.	w.
$\frac{1}{1}$ □	6,25	4,0	36,67	31,5	2,74	3,36
$\frac{6}{5}$	0,5	0,33	28,8	19,5	0,22	0,27
$\frac{5}{4}$	7,0	0,0	14,5	8,5	3,07	0,00
$\frac{4}{3}$	4,5	4,0	5,0	1,0	1,97	3,36
$\frac{29}{20}$	13,33	13,5	2,0	1,0	5,85	11,35
$\frac{3}{2}$	50,91	20,5	1,0	0,0	22,33	17,22
$\frac{34}{21}$ ⊙	78,66	42,65	0,0	0,0	34,50	35,83
$\frac{23}{13}$	49,33	20,21	1,0	1,0	21,64	16,99
$\frac{2}{1}$	14,25	11,83	3,83	2,25	6,25	9,94
$\frac{5}{2}$	3,25	2,0	57,21	30,25	1,43	1,68
Summa	228	119	150	95	100,00	100,00

B 73
Table on tests with ten rectangles, with the goal of finding out which format appears particularly harmonious.

B 74
Screen format of 4 : 3

B 75
Screen format with a 16 : 9 ratio

B 76
Cell phone

on the expectations we set for certain media and their appearance, which I have already addressed several times.
As we can see, it is possible to approximate good design by closely observing the protagonists of a communication situation, their tendencies, and their perception experiences. But this excursion into history also shows that designers' attitudes influence the respective criteria. This combination of objective and subjective criteria constitutes an important trait of visual communication. The following descriptions will look at this aspect in more detail.

Good Design – Clichés and Differentiation

A few years ago, I was sitting with some students during a seminar. We were complaining about the state government's plans to relocate the university at which I was teaching at the time to a new building complex on the outskirts of town. We liked the location in the city center. Designers, we felt, needed a developed urban environment, whether to engage with the everyday visual language on different levels or shape the public sphere of communication with their own interventions.
Over the course of our conversation, we came up with reasons why it was necessary and logical for political decision-makers to let us stay in the city. The argument that the location of a design school has a positive impact on its immediate surroundings came up repeatedly. A survey conducted among residents and business owners had already revealed that the presence of students had a beneficial effect on the social and business climate. But our argumentation added another dimension: Sophisticated design, as taught and produced at a university, would "infect" (in whatever way) the immediate surroundings, leading to a better understanding of aesthetic quality among laypeople. In an ideal scenario, this high level of design would spread throughout the entire city, resulting in a greater understanding of aesthetic nuances among various social classes and increasing their willingness to accept something new. Other effects might include an increased tolerance of unfamiliar aspects, greater awareness of environmental matters, and sophisticated taste. After this, I left the university on foot and walked into the city center. And once again, it became clear to me that the university – from a creative perspective – existed in an insular state. Because visually, everyday life in the city gave no indication that we had any kind of influence on it: Few differentiated solutions, depending on the business area, and clichéd depictions dominated and still shape the cityscape today.

The taste of the masses versus design standards

With the observations described here, I want to point out an occupational conflict – that of how to respond to different tastes. We are familiar with the varying receptive and taste levels within society. There is no way around them, these different categories: In a similar vein, the world of literature produces sophisticated prose as well as pulp fiction. Music encompasses opposing poles such as 12-tone music and folk music; advertising comprises more or less subtle marketing but will also resort to the steamroller approach. The list goes on. Every category addresses its own target group and therefore looks different – but in general, a certain majority of the population has the prerogative of interpretation when it comes to defining what constitutes good taste. This is simply the result of the fact that design is measured by its degree of acceptance in everyday life: the higher the acceptance, the more successful it is. Sometimes it is not that easy determine whether this type of design is what the population demands or whether the mere existence of the "mainstream" evokes situations in which designers attempt to "anticipate" their wishes. But no matter how the standards develop: The taste of the masses exists, and it usually stands diametrically opposed to the experts' verdict on good design. But how does this discrepancy arise? Is it a matter of education? Is it elitist to appraise the taste of the masses critically from a designer's perspective? Do designers want to convince the world of better options, even though it is satisfied with what already exists? What arguments exist against allowing everything to look the way mainstream taste in society wants it to – from pulp fiction to tabloids, from car advertising to wine labels, from bank leaflets to hairdresser fonts?

These questions are difficult for designers to answer. I will illustrate why based on the seminar I have already mentioned. The task lay in explaining to laypeople what the profession of a communication designer entails and why their work is important. The lines of reasoning mainly revolved around functional aspects. Interestingly, the discussion initially focused on product design, claiming that the form of design makes the function of an object possible and visible. If this is not possible, for example in the case of electronic devices, where the housing "conceals" the function, the design would at least meet ergonomic requirements and thereby support the product's usability. In both cases, the best-possible relationship between purpose and usage creates an "aesthetic" dimension. It was interesting that this line of argumentation referenced traditional explanation patters of modernism – specifically, Sullivan's "form follows function." The postmodern motto of "anything goes," in contrast, delivered hardly any substantial supporting arguments. The question was: Could we transfer a similar opinion to communication design, which is actually intended to be the focal point of the

observation? At this point, all work groups drew on the specialist segment of "orientation systems," where the functional aspect of the design is dominant.
They also gave examples from typography, which focused on the readability and reading guidance of texts, enabled through professional design. Apparently, "functionality" serves as safe terrain in a discussion on what constitutes communication design and why it remains relevant in society. In a way, such arguments can be compared with other occupational groups in which predictable parameters form the basis of their work (for example, in medicine, engineering, or business).

But they do not suffice. Because communication design does not only cater to intended uses, but also to purposes of entertainment or advertising, or even purposes of deception (in political propaganda, for example); in short: There is a whole range of intentions that may appear in visual communication. But if other, difficult-to-measure levels exist, then the functional evaluation criteria lose importance, and the incalculable component of taste comes to the fore. Its infinite forms of expression relativize generally valid statements that are based solely on the congruence between content and form. Dealing with this insight in a clever way has always been a crucial matter in communication design. Nevertheless, some designers (even today, in "post-postmodern" times) would like to take on the role of design dictator in light of the "bad" taste exhibited by large parts of the population that dominates in visual communication.[B 77 – 81]

087

Product designer Dieter Rams, for one, opted to address his colleagues rather than the public (even back in the 1970s) with his theses on good design – and formulated a canon of values. In his "10 Thesen für gutes Design" ("10 Theses for Good Design"), he wrote the following under "Good design is aesthetic": "The aesthetic quality of a product is an integral aspect of its usability. After all, devices that we use daily shape our personal environment and impact our well-being. But something can only be aesthetic if it is well designed." Although he hits the nail on the head with this statement, it remains hard to concretize – or it would be if consumers were also allowed to have their say. Unfortunately, the judgments on what is "aesthetic" and what is "well designed" traditionally diverge. They are influenced by origin, socialization, level of education, and cultural background.
To understand what sets the oft criticized taste of the masses apart from the well-trained taste of a designer, it is worth taking a look at past and present discourses. The discussion around the topic of "kitsch" – a category that has penetrated all cultural areas in its triviality – illustrates the issue particularly well.

087 ------ Ten Principles for Good Design, Rams

087.1 -------- Less and More. The Design Ethos of Dieter Rams

rieker ANTISTRESS
12 | Slipper
49⁹⁹

Tamaris
13 | Stiefelette
69⁹⁹
11,12,13,16 Obermaterial
ECHTES LEDER
DUO-TEX
• Atmungsaktiv
• Wasser- und Kälteabweisend

Tamaris
16 | Hochfront-pumps
69⁹⁹

Tama
17 | Stiefel
59⁹⁹
ANTi shok
Schrittdämpfung um mehr als 50

Cheer®
15 | Stiefel
59⁹⁹
• Warmfutter

K KAUFANTRAG
(116,61)

Glasvasen
Eckig, in 6 verschiedenen Farben, Maße: ca. 15x4 cm
je 1 €

Glasvasen
Rund, in 6 verschiedenen Farben, Maße: ca. 18x7 cm
je 1,49

ECHTES LEDER
ECHTES LEDER

CHEF
MAS
• 8-Punkt
• 8 versch
Handbe
• Stärke u
• Stuhl un
• Art.-Nr.:

B 77 – B 81

From kitsch and high culture to CAMP

The way we determine what constitutes kitsch and how to deal with it has changed greatly over the last century – at least with regard to its role in art. Kitsch has been a topic of discussion here for a long time (examples: Pierre et Gilles, Jeff Koons) and has managed to secure its spot in the field of serious art. 088

For a long time, this was unimaginable. Well into the 20th century, so-called high culture and trivial culture – inherent to kitsch – formed two opposite poles on a vertical axis. It served as the yardstick for what could be deemed art (high culture) and what could not. These poles were linked with sociological classifications – educated citizens on the one side, the so-called lower (i.e., less educated) classes of the population on the other. American art critic Clement Greenberg embodied this education-related arrogance clearly when he compared a figuratively painted picture by pre-revolutionary Ilya Repin ("Barge Haulers on the Volga") with a picture by Pablo Picasso in an essay published in 1939 *. If we disregard the historic misrepresentation that pervades the essay (he indirectly and inaptly attributed Repin's picture to socialist realism), he outlines an interesting as well as judgmental difference regarding public reception of both works: He claims that Repin had already integrated the "reflective effect" into the picture [B 82], where the observer could enjoy it unthinkingly – for example, the uneducated farmer who would thus be able to consume art on a low level. Accordingly, he labels Repin's picture as kitsch (in the meantime, art history has disproved this evaluation). According to Greenberg, Repin paints the EFFECT, whereas Picasso paints the CAUSE. He suggests that Picasso's picture [B 83] triggers an interactive reception (see the picture, reflect on it, see it from a different perspective) that only an educated audience can take part in, which is why it represents the more meaningful form of reception. Regardless of the political undertones of the essay and its era-typical appraisals (that convey the American hubris of the 1930s), it is worth mentioning Greenberg at this point because he presents two reception models that play a role in visual communication: These revolve around the perceptions and impacts of "sophisticated" and "trivial" communication. More on this will follow shortly.

In the late 1970s, sociologist Pierre Bourdieu analyzed the "subtle differences" within society. In his opinion, "reflective taste" stands in contrast to "sensory taste," which easily rouses and appeals directly to the senses. Since education is considered a requirement for "reflective taste," and not everyone has access to the same kind of education, this leads to the establishment of social hierarchies – represented by the elites and their educational canon versus the masses and their seducible nature. 089 Bourdieu described what the view from above (from a cultivated status) revealed when he looked down (on the masses):

*
"Avantgarde und Kitsch," Clement Greenberg, from "Kitsch. Texte und Theorien," Reclam, 2007

088 ------ Kitsch. Texte und Theorien, Dettmar, Küpper
089 ------ Die feinen Unterschiede, Bourdieu

"(...) Rejection of everything simple, in the sense of easy, without depth, superficial, and cheap *(exists)* because it is deciphered effortlessly, requires little in terms of education, completely naturally leads to rejection of everything considered ethically or aesthetically easy that offers immediately accessible joys that are therefore decried as infantile and primitive (in contrast to the delayed pleasures of legitimate art) (...)."* Points of contact between the spheres of reflective and sensory taste, if they existed, also ran only from "top" to "bottom" in the past.

In her essay "Notes on Camp" (1964), American publicist Susan Sontag described the characteristics of "Camp," including theatricality, a penchant for the exaggerated and unnatural. But the cultural phenomenon of "Camp" – which has its place in all cultural areas and first emerged in the form of dandyism in the 1920s – merely toys with trivialities and flirts with their aesthetic appreciation. In the book "Kitsch, Texte und Theorien" ("Kitsch, Texts, and Theories"), this circumstance is discussed as follows:

090

"(...) Cultural scientist Franziska Roller (born in 1965) points out that especially turning towards kitsch with a wink allows the differences to prevail: 'Only those who know the rules can break them, can play with taboos of taste and creatively deal with the excesses of the consumer society. (...) Tackiness as an attitude only works if a loving distance is maintained towards the ostensible devotion to bad taste.' (...)" **

B 82
Ilya Repin, *Barge Haulers on the Volga*, 1872 – 1873

B 83
Pablo Picasso, *L'Aubade*, 1942

*
"Der Ekel vor dem Leichten," from "Die feinen Unterschiede," Pierre Bourdieu, Suhrkamp, 2021, p. 757 – p. 758

**
"Kitsch Art, Camp (...)," Ute Dettmar, Thomas Küpper, from "Kitsch. Texte und Theorien," Reclam, 2007, p. 280

A "one-way street" between high and trivial culture, from top to bottom, is apparent in all three examples. However, over the course of the last decade and leading up to today, it has been strongly relativized thanks to social changes (education, living conditions, etc.). The borders between milieus have grown more permeable, in part because they have consciously been made a topic of discussion – by writers such as Annie Ernaux, Didier Eribon, Saša Stanišić, or Kim de l'Horizon for example. They all focused on places of origin, education, and sense of belonging in relation to social inclusion. Nonetheless, high and trivial culture schemata have not disappeared. The hierarchy has turned into a side-by-side existence – at least on the surface.

"Differentiated" and "trivial" visual communication

If we wanted to transfer this analysis to the area of design, the equivalent pair of terms would be "differentiated" and "trivial" visual communication. Here too, the imaginary vertical axis of top and bottom has lost the meaning it held during the era of modernism. Most recently, it displays an openness towards all kinds of design – developed as a result of postmodern rule-breaking –, on the part of the audience as well as the designers. But while the growing awareness of educational elitism and social classification is a welcome and long-overdue development in the processes of creating and receiving art, the accompanying openness described above can lead to misunderstandings and shortcomings in design. Design deals with targeted communication using rhetorical tools that are powerful and that designers should be familiar with – but obviously do not necessarily need to be. The dilemma of communication design is that anyone can define its quality. This arbitrariness makes it possible for trivial solutions to spread, simply because they are obvious – and also accepted as successful by a majority. However, the prerogative to interpret the quality of design carries more weight within society compared to art because it shapes and regulates the way we interact with each other in everyday life. In the unfortunate case of a trivial approach, this means that clichés define life goals, prejudices replace judgments, indulging in impulses, such as voyeurism, satisfies archaic desires. The tendency to opt for clichés is not new and has accompanied humanity since its beginnings. Philosophers, sociologists, psychologists, theologists, and designers: They have all delved into the matter of differentiating reality again and again because they knew that life is multi-layered and that surfaces often conceal more complex backgrounds. However, some designers might ask themselves why they, of all people, must grapple with this phenomenon. After all, design is for the people, not the other way around. Designers need to communicate with those who are present and the intended recipients. They cannot simply "conjure up" the ideal design-savvy type. In addition, communication design is generally assigned the task of transporting content

quickly and in the least complicated way possible. It would certainly be tedious if we had to "work out" the content of a visual message first (as in the case of the Picasso picture), wouldn't it? However, we cannot simply cast aside the examination of the trivial, at least not if our goal essentially lies in creating "good" design in the sense of effective communication. Designer and author Anton Stankowski commented on this topic as follows:
"(...) A suitable method for increasing the – short-term – attention value as well as the 'retention value' – with a longer-term effect – is simply to omit a detail that the observer then needs to add in. The recipient registers the reconstructive effort required on their part as their own achievement. But they appear more likely to be able to store and incorporate into their own inventory the overall visual picture that required their contribution than when they simply consume an image without interacting with it. Not only does an obvious gap in the depiction make it easier for the observer to store the picture, but it also increases the interest in an evidently incomplete, but possibly completable creation from the start. Here, solving such a little quiz question is less significant than the fact that the painting even asks a question that tempts the observer to find an answer. (...)" *
The method described strikes a balance between design and the intention of visual communication and draws conclusions on the quality based on its successful effects (increasing the "attention value" and "retention value"). In contrast, trivial design, with its undifferentiated means – to show everything, often repeatedly highlighted – falls short of what design can achieve. In this case, "good design" means that it is pretty to look at.

The repertoire of design-specific modes of action is considerable, and amateur designers are generally unfamiliar with them. When they design something, this usually reflects what they already know. Unfortunately, the creators of trivial design are often also insufficiently trained designers; in this case, the allegation of unthinking actions is already a given. In any case, just consider what a house would look like if you, a construction layperson, had designed it yourself – and what would happen if you decided to hire a good architect instead. After examining all circumstances, they might advise you to travel the world or live in a bus or a tiny house, in a townhouse, in a rental apartment, or in a palace. And any advice would be given long before an initial draft is made, taking your lifestyle, location, budget, preferences, and needs into account.

*
**"Visualisierung," Anton Stankowski, from "Visuelle Kommunikation,"
Dietrich Reimer Verlag, 1989, p. 23**

091

Design means concept, design means responsibility

Sociologist Lucius Burckhardt put this perspective into concrete terms: To him, design means “concept,” not “form.” He asks himself whether the attitude of using design to make people happy can even be justified if it only tackles the surfaces. He gives the example of a typical uniform housing development in the USA, with houses constructed in a standardized pseudo-colonial style. An American sociologist asked why the resident of this development failed to notice the ugliness of their living environment. He discovered that they prioritized completely different aspects over the beauty or ugliness of the architecture and facilities: The housing development provided good connections to the highway, offered good schools, churches for all denominations, and a respectful neighborhood. Residents considered all these aspects important for a good life, the antithesis to their previous life, consisting of small apartments, long commutes, crammed subways, urban criminality, and so on. Against this background, it seems natural to overlook the design of a street sign or a house’s architecture. This suggests that observations should focus on the invisible rules of social processes. Burckhardt asks readers to recall the original definition of the term “design” (as “concept”). He presents a descriptive example relevant to the typical activities of designers: designing the exteriors of ticket machines for public transport. Based on traditional ideas, the design would contemplate usability, font type and size, informational hierarchies, and so on. Now Burckhardt asks the heretical question: “Have these boxes improved the environment of the old woman who is standing in front of them with two handbags, clammy fingers, and glasses that have fogged up in the cold? Would she not prefer to do away with all this design if she still had the option to buy her ticket inside the tram car? Would the best-possible design not abolish transport fees?”*

Design in the sense of developing a concept thus includes a deeper, social component and comes into play much earlier than most of us realize. This does not devalue the practical design process, but rather charges it with another sense of purpose because the designed surface should ideally be preceded by a holistic impulse. This means that, instead of – as initially mentioned – making a fuss about trivial design in everyday life, it would be more appropriate to opt for the social processes, which conclude with a first visible concept – whether good or trivial. But focusing on roles, relationships, and expectations comes with the prerequisite of an advanced design self-perception. Designers must understand that it is crucial for them to join a visual communication process early on if they want to create high-quality work. To put it bluntly, two prototypes of our profession are up for discussion:

* **“Design heißt Entwurf, nicht Gestalt!,” Lucius Burckhardt, 1970; from “Design & Politik. Texte zur gesellschaftlichen Relevanz gestalterischen Schaffens,” FB Gestaltung, FH Würzburg-Schweinfurt, Dr. Hans Höger, Dr. Kerstin Stutterheim (Eds.), p. 98 – 100**

A) designers as a service providers
They act as implementors of a commissioned task. Since they can neither ask questions regarding the content they need to communicate nor influence the framework conditions, they view themselves as a "cog in the machine," able to do nothing more than design in accordance with the stipulations. The client themselves generally presents the stipulations, which are based on their own taste or the successful products of competitors. This leaves no room for doubts that may arise, both concerning the content and the method of addressing the selected target group. Since the time budget is very limited, they unavoidably design "from the gut" and opt for tools that are easily accessible and from which they have compiled a design repertoire over time.

B) designers as advising creators
They find themselves confronted with jobs that explicitly entail the provision of their expertise in an advisory capacity. To start with, they discuss the communication intention with the client and analyze the receptive behavior of the chosen target group. This results in findings that might surprise the client, for example when it comes to the question of which medium would prove most suitable or which rhetorical/visual tool could have the biggest impact in transporting the content. They also work with a tight schedule, but one that takes the advisory and analytical stage into account.

Admittedly, the reality of the designer's everyday work sits somewhere in the middle – or might look more like one or the other variant depending on the client or work situation. But the two opposite poles of how a designer fulfills their role aim to make clear which circumstances harbor potential for good design, and which do not. However, regardless of the conditions that define a designer's everyday work, we can identify one specific aspect again and again: the designer's mindset. Their presence influences everything. In the "First Things First" manifesto from 2020, the initiators write on behalf of 1,600 signatories:
"We, the undersigned, are designers who have been raised in a world in which we put profit over people and the planet in an attempt to grease the wheels of capitalism and keep the machine running. Our time and energy are increasingly used to manufacture demand, to exploit populations, to extract resources, to fill landfills, to pollute the air, to promote colonization, and to propel our planet's sixth mass extinction. We have helped to create comfortable, happy lives for some of our species and allowed harm to others; our designs, at times, serve to exclude, eliminate, and discriminate. Many design teachers and professionals perpetuate this ideology; the markets reward it; a tide of imitations and "likes" reinforces it. Encouraged in this

direction, designers then apply their skills and imagination to sell fast fashion, fast cars, and fast food; disposable cups, bubble wrap, and unending amounts of single-use plastics; fidget spinners, microwave dinners, and nose hair trimmers. We market unhealthy body images and diets; products and apps that propagate social isolation and depression; the consumption of unbalanced food systems; we sell pills to pop, tiks to tok, and a scrolling feed that never stops… and then the desire to consume it all over again and again. Yes, commercial work has always paid the bills, but many designers have let it become, in large measure, what designers do. This, in turn, is how the world perceives design. Many of us have grown increasingly uncomfortable with this view of design. Because of this, we call for a massive change in what and how designers design. Climate change is critically entangled with class, race, and gender-based dominance, we can no longer push merely for sustainability, but must create new systems that undo and heal what's been done. (…)."* The manifesto I have quoted has two famous predecessors *(see 055, 055.1)*. All three manifestos focus on the role we play in how the world communicates. The mindsets expressed in this process form the meta level of the profession. These could be summarized as follows: Consciousness determines the creation, or to transfer the statement to the field of design: Reflective thinking determines the type and quality of design.

In light of this, I would like to return to my walk through the city center. Everyday design is as varied as humans are – beautiful, solid, boring, ugly, trivial, deep. We can lament this, but we cannot change it. Only in a dictatorship would it be possible to order (short-term) homogenous behaviors and visuality. But as history has shown, even force cannot permanently suppress the human urge to unfold our individuality. In addition, we must admit that triviality per se does not necessarily need to be a bad thing. While the presented contrast between "differentiated" and "trivial" design does exist, it is of course characterized by nuances and ambivalences. On the other hand: We designers can certainly succeed in influencing the taste of large swathes of the population and inspiring them to observe their environment in a differentiated way. Many examples from the past have proved this. Innovative design approaches often went hand in hand with social progress and transitions, sometimes associated with something programmatic (modernism), sometimes they were simply overdue and had a more intuitive character (postmodernism), sometimes they turn political again (F1rst Things F1irst 2020). But when design leaves traces in society, then it is worth thinking about the constant dripping that wears the stone. If these drops are called "emphatic and responsible design" – then all the better.

*
F1rst Things F1rst Manifesto 2020, see 055.2

PREMIUM GASHAPON
こちらの商品のご購入には
500
が必要です
BANDAI
POS
BANDAI NAMCO
01 COIN SLOT
02 ROTATE
the handle
360 degrees clockwise
03 TAKE OUT
BAN DAI
こちらの商品は500円玉が必要です。
後ろの両替機で100円玉から500円玉に両替できます。
This product requires a 500 yen coin.
You can exchange 100 yen coins into 500 yen coins at the nearby exchange machine.
1500円

This section of the book discusses the challenges that designers face in everyday life and beyond. On the one hand, these include the expectation of creating something new again and again, delivering something surprising, and conveying information in a convincing way. On the other hand, design is supposed to tie in with visual experiences and thereby take conventions into account. In short: Designers must navigate the field of tension between tried-and-tested methods and innovations.

Designers can update their own understanding of design, for example, through their own lines of thought, which are based on the latest observations and studies.

Finally, we will address a basic principle that serves as a recurrent theme throughout this book.

Tried-and-Tested and New Methods

"Preserving established aspects and trying something new – we believe that this is the foundation of the success of our collaboration so far, for which we would like to express our heartfelt thanks and wish you wonderful holidays with your loved ones."
(Internet find on the topic of Christmas wishes, 2023)

The banality of the statement "Preserving established aspects and trying something new…" is so overwhelming that I fear you might skip this chapter to avoid the threat of more platitudes of this kind. But don't worry: I will be delving into a topic of visual communication that professional designers grapple with on a daily basis. The struggle of catering to the viewing and communication habits of diverse target groups while at the same time satisfying their expectations by adding new stimuli demonstrates the dilemma inherent to communication design that professionals must overcome again and again. This makes our job special.

Tried-and-tested methods

Let us compare it to handcrafts, for example. The core idea and strength of this field lies in gathering experience and deriving tried-and-tested methods and approaches from this experience. Repeating nearly identical work steps when faced with different challenges is a virtue, both in terms of quality and from an economic perspective. Of course, new impulses, techniques, and findings emerge now and again. But the way professionals handle these new influences is marked by the desire to integrate them into traditional norms immediately and thereby – if suitable – incorporate them into the canon of proven practices. A similar approach applies in industry or retail. This mechanism is motivated by the definition of the term "work performance," which, in an economic context, refers to the work volume produced by a worker within their working hours as a work result with a certain work quality. However, the tried-and-tested aspect also – to put it another way – forms part of the "human DNA." Because humans feel the basic need to gain orientation by identifying patterns and comparing these to our own experiences. This presents the only option for us to find our way. In other words: We love order because it enables us to navigate our complex everyday life with its countless stimuli. Therefore, tried-and-tested objects, structures, and behavioral norms penetrate our day-to-day lives: We use closets to store clothing; our apartment features rooms with different functions; we live in houses designated by numbers and on roads with names to help us tell them apart; we make purchases at shops that offer various goods; these are located in cities that provide familiar infrastructures for culture, education, and work. As a result, we form part of a society and its countless norms that have shaped us from our earliest days and within which we can move safely. In short: Without tried-and-tested factors, we would be lost.

Of course, the work we accomplish within our professional field is also familiar with the standards of proven practices. Design processes must be calculable, the service performed must be proportionate to the effort it entails. Consequently, our line of work also features – wherever possible – standardized [092] approaches based on proven practices. They include work-related procedures as well as technical design and production processes. On top of this, the communication design degree course also imparts basic knowledge based on proven findings and includes handcraft-related elements, for example when it comes to the foundations of design, photography, typography, illustration, interactive media, or programming. Most readers will remember their obligatory foundation course (or are perhaps still in the middle of it), with its mandatory seminars that convey this basic knowledge. The internalized foundations give graduates the ability to recognize creative opportunities and space within which to perform design processes as well as detect their limitations.

But once you have outgrown this phase, the real challenges await. And these are multi-layered, sometimes expectable, but often not, and they always call for specific solutions. In other words: They demand the creation of something new, something that solves a specific problem, something that stands out from the competition, that produces new stimuli, opens up new perspectives, and sometimes even aims to encourage new ways of thinking. However, the new creation shouldn't be too unfamiliar – at the very least, the observer should be able to understand it in terms of its underlying intention and within the framework of the targeted circle within which the new aspect is designed to unfold its effect. As mundane as it may sound, "Preserving established aspects and trying something new...," this Christmas wish that I quoted at the start is, unfortunately, as banal as it is true.

So what is this new aspect, how do we classify it, and how do we deal with it? I would like to look at six approaches in more detail.

First: Something new emerges in the margins between intention and design

Let us take the following banal insight: We always create something new when a new communicative purpose takes shape. However, the resonating linearity of this statement is a little misleading. Perhaps the time-honored adage of "form follows function" has contaminated us too much – after all, it promises nothing more than that, in an ideal scenario, form results from

092 ------ Professional associations for designers

purpose and function. This statement originated in the field of architecture for good reason, and it has also come up in product design time and again. This is because, in both areas, the intended purpose of the rule is hardly negotiable: The most pressing task of an office high-rise is to function as such – so its purpose is unmistakable, and the design must meet this need. The same applies to a kitchen appliance. In both cases, usage stands at the top of the list of aspects that significantly influence the design. While the statement of "form follows function" represents a diction that is nearly impossible to fulfil, simply because there is only one function (and therefore never just *one* logical form), this changes nothing about the fact that this is a specific, pragmatic type of design – regardless of what stylistic, functional, and ideational secondary aspects are then integrated and help determine the design.

In visual communication, there are also purposes that prioritize function, for example guidance systems, certain website navigations, or manuals. In these cases, the same principles apply as for architecture and product design: The design is the result of prioritizations that arise from the respective conglomerate of purpose, functions, and usage requirements. But in visual communication, you will also find intentions that place enjoyment, diversion, misdirection, or aesthetic impulses front and center. Such intentions do not formulate purposes that aim to signalize an unmistakable use. This has consequences: Now it is no longer necessary for new content to become recognizable through a new design. Because the intention itself could lie in giving the content an "old" look, or vice versa. For example, a new party might resort to traditional graphic means for its election advertising in order to simulate experience and solidity. A newspaper might lean conservative, but lend its appearance a new, pioneering look to reach younger readers. Right-wing media in particularly tend to opt for traditional graphic elements to dispel reservations.

In these cases, the new aspects of visual communication might not present themselves through the novel depiction of content alone, but also in the way design interprets content. This might take place in an obvious manner, or it could be concealed. In the latter case, it does not suffice to scan the (designed) surface for new features. Moreover, we need to detect the degree of novelty through the relationship between content and form.

Second: Fashions give rise to new features

A Latin saying that dates back to antiquity goes as follows: Variatio delectat – variety captivates. In terms of visual communication, this means: Only that which contains enough diversity and versatility rouses our aesthetic sensibilities and keeps us interested. This does not refer to stimuli as a permanent principle, but as deviation within a defined order. If we take this as a basis, it comes as no surprise that the novel aspects are closely linked to the term "fashion." As a phenomenon, fashions are frequently subject to criticism. Many suspect them of constituting a formal event designed [093] to encourage sales as an economic principle. Furthermore, fashions are alleged to be the worthless counterpart to everything functional. In modernism, fashions were also stigmatized because they stood opposed to the ideas of a morally superior functionalism due to their fickle attitude as a fleeting phenomenon. On the other hand, fashions play a crucial role: They serve as historic memory. As a general rule, we can only grasp epochs of the past through the documented memory of the fashions that shaped societal life at the time. No matter the perspective from which we view fashions: They existed, they exist, and they will continue to exist. They act as an expression of human creativity, inventiveness, and the aspiration for individuality on the one hand, and the desire to belong to a group on the other hand. Since fashions replace one another, they build on each other – because their essence stems from their dissociation from one another. It simply makes sense for the idea of novelty to come into play here. What does this new aspect consist of? Fashions use style elements from previous fashions and enrich them with other contemporary elements. In other words, fashions represent and at the same time shape the zeitgeist. Needless to say, visual communication is always imbued with fashionable elements. The chapters on variable and era-relevant components have made this clear. But while the fashionable elements are always linked to communicative intentions, an independent formal existence develops that – when uncoupled from the content it is actually meant to visualize – often celebrates itself. This aspect of design crossing the line is necessary and important for sounding out and developing the scope of visual communication.

Third: Novel elements emerge by chance

At first glance, the terms "communication design" and "chance" appear completely unrelated. After all, design processes are characterized by the original meaning of the term: "designare = designate, determine, outline." It revolves around a practical, creative activity that includes planned anticipation of the final product. This does not seem to leave any space for chance. These processes are usually portrayed as "chance-free": They include analyzing the causal chain of "sender – message – recipient" and developing a communication concept. This preliminary work then serves as the foundation for all design-related decisions. When designers present their results, they consequently make sure that the conceptional preliminary work lets the design result appear logical. The majority of professional designers will wisely refrain from making statements such as, "...and then we happened to discover..." or "then we just tried out different things." Chance implies

093 ------ Das Neue und die Mode, Groys

something unpredictable and therefore does not make a suitable argument – it even comes across as a little shady, since from the layperson's perspective, it doesn't constitute the original (and billable) "service" provided by the designer if they simply stumble upon solutions. In short: From an external perspective, chance has a bad reputation in the field of design. But if you discuss the topic with other professionals, a very different view will emerge – i.e., when the focus shifts away from economic justification and towards reflecting on one's own way of working. Here, two things quickly become clear: Without chance, without the accompanying experiments, nobody will escape the endless loop of eternally recurring visual vocabulary. To phrase this in a more positive way: Chance discoveries, links, and forms have enriched every planned conceptional procedure and often opened up entirely [094] new paths. If chance plays such an innovative role in creative processes, it is a shame that we cannot incorporate it in a predictable manner. However, it is possible to resolve this paradox. While we cannot deduce chance in a rational way, we can create framework conditions that set the stage for chance and allow it to give rise to something "new," something unexpected. These conditions include curiosity, the courage to take risks through playfulness, non-judgmental thinking, and the desire to experiment. Let us take a look at art to illustrate what this means. Here, you will find countless creations in which intuitive actions are front and center within a planned artistic procedure. One of many examples: The American artist Jackson Pollock painted so-called "drips." The picture titled "Number 32" (1950) is a famous example. Black lines with drops form an abstract jumble created by chance, because Pollock only had limited control over the paint dripping onto the canvas from a stick. Without the parameters that underpin this way of working, this painting would be inconceivable. Setting "parameters" means nothing more than determining linear and non-linear actions, deciding on materials, defining formats – in summary, making many decisions that construct the framework for an experimental arrangement, which in turn consists of intuitive actions. While we don't work in the field of art, it would be great if we showed the courage to proceed in a similar way now and again in our profession. For most of the communication designers among us, it seems inconceivable to simply set the computer aside and turn to sketches, drawings, or collages for that same task. Designers will often object that they simply lack the time for this, and this is a valid point. But let's be honest: A lot of the time, it doesn't even occur to us. Ideas for new developments are hiding in plain sight: For one of their seminars, two students paid a freelancer based in Asia to complete a design task for them. The design they received then served as a source for their own new ideas. Even the typical parameters that workshops are subject to (limited time, specific topic, experimental workflows, such as a switch from digital to analog work and then

094 ------ Die Künste des Zufalls, Gendolla, Kamphusmann

094.1 -------- Definition of the term Generative Design

back) produce visibly new ideas. There are plenty of processes, you just need to allow for chance.

Fourth: New ideas emerge through cultural diversity

The genesis of Latin letters provides the most famous proof of this statement. You owe your ability to read this text to migrant workers in the Middle East, among others. 095 The story behind this statement goes as follows: In the 3rd millennium before Christ, the people in the Middle East made their living through agriculture and livestock breeding. They started to irrigate and cultivate the land along the rivers Nile, Jordan, Euphrates, and Tigris. This led to the formation of densely populated cities surrounded by fields. Over the course of this civilizational development, it became necessary to establish a simpler accounting system, for example to collect taxes, record the harvests, and document trade. This accounting system consisted of words that were represented by pictures. The term "barley," for one, was visualized with the simplified image of a barley ear and impressed into a still-soft clay tablet with a wedge. When a Sumerian saw the barley pictogram, they would associate it with the word "barley," which sounds something like "cheh" in Sumerian. This means that images were also used as phonetic symbols. Writers or administrators could also use the barley pictogram for other phonetic purposes. For example, if you say the Sumerian word for "beautiful" out loud, it is pronounced "chehga." The writer would use the barley pictogram for the first syllable. The "ga" sound in the second syllable means "milk." The writer would therefore draw the pictograms for barley and for milk. Together, they created the word "beautiful." The use of pictures as phonetic symbols is referred to as the Rebus principle. It was common in many other cultures, including in South America and China. Around the year 1905 (A.D.), in the Sarabit al-Chadim temple complex on the Sinai Peninsula, archaeologists discovered strange characters alongside Egyptian hieroglyphs (which they could easily read) etched into steles and rock faces. To begin with, the archaeologists were stumped. They knew that the place of worship was also a mine for excavating turquoise gems, and they knew that migrant workers from other regions of the Middle East regularly worked here. But they could not find an explanation for the characters that they were unable to attribute to any other written language and that looked like poorly drawn hieroglyphs to them. Over the course of their research, they determined two facts: The characters had been etched into stone around 1850 B.C., and presumably by migrant workers from the Canaan region (the area comprises southwestern Syria, Palestine, and Israel). Successful attempts to decipher the characters finally brought a fascinating fact to light that can be viewed as the cornerstone of the alphabet we use today: The workers from Canaan lived among the Egyptians in

095 ------ Vom Schreiben und Denken.
Die Saga der Schrift, Arte

Sarabit al-Chadim. They knew little of their hieroglyphic writing, especially when it came to the layered meanings of the characters. For example: In Egyptian, a square signifies "house;" it serves as a classifier for everything related to building structures, and it stands for the Egyptian sound "per." Now the migrant workers started using the square as a symbol for "house" in their own language. Their word for "house" was "beit." They further simplified the writing by drawing the house pictogram (the square) whenever they needed the letter B. In this way, they revolutionized the Rebus principle: The symbol no longer stands for a word, but merely for its initial sound. And now they could suddenly write anything with about 25 – 30 pictures. They developed what was presumably the world's first alphabet. What followed was simply a logical sequence of events: The migrant workers returned to Canaan, taking their writing system with them. Back home, they encountered Phoenician tradespeople, who spread the alphabet across the entire Mediterranean region. The Greeks continued to develop the alphabet, then the Romans adapted it. This little extract from the history of the written word shows that when different cultures encounter each other, this creates combinations of necessities and coincidences that literally allow new ideas to emerge.

Fifth: Novelty lies in the eye of the beholder

I will use another example to illustrate the importance of coming out of one's own shell, with its entrenched standards, to absorb new impulses. Once again, different cultural influences play an important role here. A bus route in a major Belgian city forms a circle and leads through many different districts. Similarly to London or New York (and in contrast to most major German cities), ethnic communities gather in these neighborhoods, bringing their imported traditions to life, celebrating and giving them visibility. The neighborhoods include a Chinese district, a Moroccan one, and a quarter in which residents' migrant roots stem from a former Belgian colony, today's Democratic Republic of the Congo. Next to these residential districts lies a gentrified quarter, housing fashion flagship stores, museums, galleries, and expensive restaurants. The visual language of this area is characterized by the handwriting of designers. Their visual communication offers all the elements that make up good graphic design:
It features a mixture of era-typical fonts, slick contrasting dimensions, harmonious color constellations, a visible grid orientation, all in a proven visual language with tangible computer-based origins. Polished surfaces made of anodized metal, aluminum, or glass serve as the substrate.
This forms a great contrast to the visual language of the other districts mentioned: In the gentrified quarter, you will encounter established and traditional elements, while the other areas produce unusual and attractive

impressions thanks to a mixture of self-made graphics and cultural idiosyncrasies. Here, visual communication is very clearly geared towards different receptive behaviors and subject to other quality measures. For anyone who doesn't belong to the target group, the design triggers both curiosity and the reflex to compare this design with their own, familiar visual language and evaluate it accordingly. This example is representative of many others we might come across in everyday life – if we just keep an eye out for them. They illustrate that novelty lies in the eye of the beholder if it deviates from familiar elements. Through the influence of foreign cultures, we find ourselves confronted with other perspectives; they expand our knowledge and unveil new directions. This means that an interest in the unknown brings about the opportunity to develop something new.

Sixth: New ideas are part of the job description

The work of a communication designer is strangely complex: While they develop concepts for visual communication, they are not only responsible for the design, but also the final implementation of these concepts. They must master and be able to depict all practical aspects of visual rhetoric, but also consider the role of design within a larger social framework. They need to work in an interdisciplinary manner, while also exhibiting very specialized knowledge. A communication designer moves between culture and kerning*, between societal problems and the search for the right color profile. Let's compare our profession with others, for example architecture: If we were to transfer the described fields of tension to the job profile of an architect, this would mean getting involved in urban planning and discussions on sustainable infrastructures and environmentally friendly construction as well as being able to design a building and then actually build it, from the foundation through to the roof, including heating systems, stairs, and windows. An unrealistic scenario, right? In their design dictionary "Wörterbuch Design" *(see 008)*, published in 2008, editors Michael Erlhoff and Tim Marshall wrote the following:
"(...) When it comes to social reality and business tasks, design is now expected to debate and tackle complicated problems – this has changed and expanded our understanding of design, giving the design process more of an exploratively conceptual, strategic, and comprehensive planning role and considerably more responsibility and influence (...)." In light of this wide range of required abilities, it is only natural that every designer finds their own niche. Some specialize in and primarily deal with the practical implementation of ideas, others almost exclusively focus on conceptions, while others search for challenges in participating in social processes. The possibility to concentrate on such different areas is both a blessing and a curse. Because in times like these, in which technical developments

*
Kerning refers to the process of defining the horizontal distance between letters. The distances are reduced or enlarged as needed for a finished font to prevent visual irregularities and ensure a harmonious typeface.

in areas such as artificial intelligence, augmented reality, virtual reality, participatory design, interaction design, program additions, and product changes are progressing at rapid speed, it is hardly possible to look up and grapple with questions tied to society's major developments. And yet we need to do both. We need to focus more on the question of whether we drift along with the changing conditions and requirements or take matters into our own hands. Designer, author, and design theoretician Steven McCarthy examined the self-perception of our profession in one of his publications. He came to the conclusion that many role models exist that demonstrate [096] an expanded understanding of design that extends beyond mere design practice: designers as visual journalists; designers as publishers; designers as curators; designers as collectors; designers as performers.
In all these roles, designers are on the threshold of or crossing the borders of a traditional understanding of design. The list could be expanded to include activities in the border area of art as well as research. All in all, the profession does not have a closed definition, meaning innovation is essentially inherent to communication design. Modifications, changes of perspective, and individual interpretations form part of the profession's DNA.

Uniformity and Diversity

The previous chapter made clear that we designers need to face the latest developments to find out what adequate visual design strategies should look like. In contrast to academics, who need to develop specific access to new findings within their area of expertise, we must take a different, sometimes intuitive, and definitely holistic approach. This is because communication designers operate at the intersections with other knowledge fields. Although we do need to keep an eye on our own specialist development, new fonts, new programs, new techniques, or new media do not give us sufficient information on how target groups think, what the state is of society as a whole, what causes which trends, and what visual/communication strategies could look like against this overall background. We rely on this combination of close observation and critical questioning, and thus the ability to see the bigger picture.
It is in the nature of things that such a procedure is individual and garners the suspicion of not delivering universally valid results. That is why we focus on the prevailing discourses. The many individual perspectives, the analyses, and the different specialist findings deliver the mosaic stones with which we can assemble the tendencies, expected developments, and existing trends into a bigger picture. What could a procedure like this look like? I'd like to give you an example.

096 ------ The designer as: Author, Producer, Artist, Entrepreneur, Curator & Collaborator, McCarthy

Uniformity of design

For some time now, I have observed a growing discrepancy between design options and a visual language that consists of recurring stylistic devices and – regardless of the content – appears nearly uniform in its restricted design. You are probably familiar with this phenomenon yourself – you stumble upon certain design styles, whether in customer magazines, flyers, journals, advertising, appearances – without giving too much thought to why these designs are often so similar. To find out whether this first impression withstands closer examination, I looked at the magazine sector in more detail, as it generally offers the greatest options for variety in design. Through random sampling and in preparation for a lecture on this topic, I analyzed magazines. They focused on varied themes such as politics, lifestyle, and philosophy. B 85 – 90 They confirmed my first impression. I found it hard to attribute the spreads to the right magazines, differentiated mainly by the headlines or picture contents, because all designers relied on similar graphic devices. To a certain degree, similar treatment of content comes down to the medium "magazine" – for example, in terms of the format, the multi-column text, the headlines, image sizes, and captions. On the other hand, a considerable requirement exists to present unmistakable graphic handwriting, especially

Lassen Sie sich coachen

Im Fokus:
Herausforderung Schulpsychologie

Was macht eigentlich ...

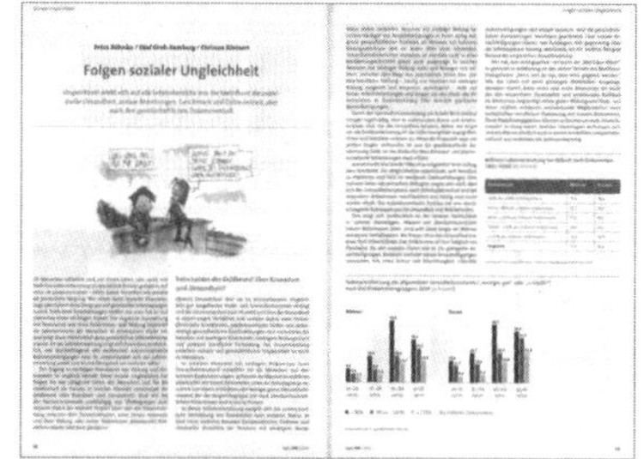
Folgen sozialer Ungleichheit

B 85 – B 90
Top row from left to right:
***Das Magazin* (customer magazine), *Flow* (lifestyle magazine),**
***Cicero* (politics magazine)**
Bottom row: *Psychologie heute* (magazine),
InStyle (women magazine), *Informationen zur politischen Bildung*
(magazine)

for comparable products that are possibly even geared towards the same target group. And I did come across outliers among the magazines within the segment I was examining, ones that certainly demonstrated individual stylistic devices. But most products appeared to follow more or less the same style guide. I kept looking around, this time in search of left-leaning and right-leaning products. Here, in these political spectrums, clear differences should become visible. However, even in this area, the risk of mistaking one magazine for another remained. [B 91, 92]
Of course, for a left-wing-right-wing comparison, alignment with mainstream design might be intentional. Nonetheless, the question remained: What was causing this lack of visual rhetoric?

No designer can elude the influence of current styles. This has always been the case. However, excessively following contemporary design trends (whether they are conservative or avant-garde) almost always leads to similar results. The quality of graphic work not only reveals itself on a superficial level, but also expresses itself in the ingenuity with which the content is staged visually/rhetorically. If this is the yardstick for design, variety emerges on its own.
The question is: What could be responsible for this inclination towards uniformity? If we look back at 1990s design with its wild individuality or the early hipster style of the 2010s, we can see that while non-conformist design did not align with the mainstream, it certainly could have influenced it, even if only partially and in specific thematic segments. Although a certain degree of uniformity crept into this non-conformity even back then, when a growing number of designers were starting to use the same style devices, all in all, visual communication still appeared to produce more variety.
We clearly owe the postulated homogeneity of the current visual language to era-typical circumstances. But what exactly are these?

First cause of uniformity: digitality

To start with, I discussed my observations with students and colleagues. At the same time, I conducted research on different levels. Gradually, indicators emerged that were worth considering as the cause of the lack of diversity – digitality, for one. The term denotes the condition of living in a digital culture, along with the intertwining of digital and analog realities. Here are a few related keywords:

“Artificial intelligence” (AI) – the term describes systems that resemble human qualities, such as logical thinking or creativity. AI is based on machine learning, which is capable of trawling through huge amounts of data. In design, AI can be used to create solutions and produce variants – based

GESELLSCHAFT

JONATHAN FRANZEN LIEGT FALSCH

Die aktuelle Klimapolitik hat viele Schwächen, aber gegen die Erderwärmung hilft nur Politik: Eine Erwiderung auf Franzens Meinung, das Paris-Abkommen sei »verloren«

52

TEXT: BERNHARD PÖTTER

53

B 91

***Futurzwei*, Berlin, 28/2024**

Gerechtigkeit für Pius XII.

VON ARTUR ABRAMOVYCH

Hier hören Sie das Schweigen des Papstes

B 92

***Cato*, Berlin, 3/2024**

on an impulse (e.g., a text) provided by the designer. With AI, algorithmic structures replace the variability of human creativity (and its irrational and subjective basis). 097

"Filter bubbles" – they prevent new, foreign impulses from getting through to us. This has consequences for design: Designers produce what is familiar to clients and customers. By sticking to this approach, they can stay "on the safe side." 098

"Scrounger mentality" – the importance of design is decreasing. People want it to cost as little as possible. After all: "Everyone can design" – at least if they know how to use layout programs. This attitude leads to laypeople at universities or public authorities, businesses, or publishing companies creating books, brochures, or even entire public appearances. This reduces the value of and the quality of design. Because ignorance of visual/rhetorical possibilities entices laypeople to copy familiar graphic examples without considering whether the design suits their content.

"The meaning of writing and fonts" – thanks to digital communication channels, we are writing more than ever before. Due to the high frequency with which we produce texts every day, formal criteria of the written word (grammar, spelling, typography) are losing their importance. This is rubbing off on everyday visual communication: It is produced with less care, errors are barely noticed.

"Globalization" – a design style shaped by western society that is spreading across the whole world – increasingly at the expense of regional particularities. The has led to a widespread reflex of always looking at what everyone else is doing first – and serves as a convenient shortcut in the process of generating ideas.

"Font aesthetics" – computer users have a growing number of license-free fonts (from Apple, Google, etc.) at their fingertips. In contrast to earlier system fonts, these exhibit a certain quality and are usable. The downside: This leads to a typical, repetitive aesthetic of neat but faceless typography.

"Sensory overload" – the flood of visual stimuli and the number of communication devices is changing our perception. Our attention spans are decreasing, as is our patience when it comes to finding the time to summon up more complex information or unusual relationships between content and form. This has resulted in two contradictory design trends: for one, a pleasing form of entertainment with moderate visual stimuli. The other

097 ------ Prinzip Mensch. Macht, Freiheit und Demokratie im Zeitalter der Künstlichen Intelligenz, Nemitz, Pfeffer
098 ------ The Filter Bubble, Pariser

097.1 – 097.7 -------- Artificial Intelligence (AI); Questions on Artificial Intelligence; Glossary of AI; ChatGPT, DALL-E, Stable Diffusion, Midjourney, Sora; Questions for ChatGPT 4.0; Artificial Intelligence put to the test – four forewords; Artificial Intelligence put to the test – a book cover aims to produce condensed content that attracts more attention. Both cases focus on generating short-lived stimuli.

Second cause of uniformity: the composition of society

To find out whether digitality is in any way connected to more recent behavioral phenomena within society, we looked at two scientific studies: the “18th Shell Youth Study” from 2019[099] and the “Trendstudie Jugend in Deutschland” (“Trend study of Germany’s youth”) from 2023. These studies constitute empirical surveys of adolescents and young adults between the ages of 12 and 25 for the Shell study and between the ages of 14 and 29 for the trend study. The research teams asked about their attitudes, values, habits, and social behavior. The value orientations from the 2019 Shell study that we considered most important form the basis of our assessments. We used random samples from the trend study to check whether these perspectives have changed significantly during this four-year period. The study from 2019 paints the following picture:

For the examined time period of 2019, young people demonstrated a pragmatic basic mindset. They are willing to align themselves with performance standards and want stable relationships in their personal surroundings. They are looking for a secure and independent place in society and adapt for this purpose. To a greater extent than in the past, many young people value a much more conscious lifestyle; they clearly and audibly articulate their demands for a sustainably developed environment and society. All groupings presented a number of commonalities, including increasing concern for the environmental future, a trend towards mutual respect and mindfulness in the way they lead their own lives, a strong sense of justice, and the urge to actively advocate for these matters. For nearly all young people, their family and social relationships serve as the most important value orientation by far. They consider them more important than “individual responsibility” (89%) and “independence” (83%), which play an important part during the coming-of-age period. Virtues such as respecting law and order (87%), being diligent and productive (81%), or striving for security (77%) have held high importance for about 20 years.
Young people also continue to view their relationship with their parents as exceptionally positive. Since 2002, the proportion of young people who have a positive relationship with their parents has steadily increased: four out of ten young people (42%) get along with their parents very well, half of them (50%) have a good relationship with them despite occasional disagreements. Their professional expectations have not changed over the last years. In this area, the need for security dominates. 93% of young people consider a secure workplace to be (very) important. When asked for their priorities, a secure

099 ------ 18. Shell Jugendstudie “Jugend 2019,” Albert et al.

workplace, the expectation of having enough free time alongside their job, and a high income topped the list. The creators of the study claim that pragmatism as a recurring keyword underpins all attitudes, values, habits, and social behavior.
The Internet is the preferred medium for the included age group in various ways. Young people use social media offerings and networking opportunities as well as the associated communication extensively. The attention economy that prevails here leads to higher pressure in terms of self-presentation and self-optimization. It provides a certain uniformity of standards regarding art, how to communicate, what values apply, and what fashions are up to date. All in all, the Internet is increasing the speed of communication. This goes hand in hand with the need for prioritization and clarity.

It would have been interesting to compare the results from the 2019 Shell Youth study with those of the latest Shell Youth study planned for 2023. Unfortunately, at the time of this book's publication (2024), these results were not available yet. A scientifically substantiated study from 2023, which was also designed by a renowned team of researchers (*"Trendstudie Jugend in Deutschland. Aktuelle Krisen belasten Jüngere starker als Ältere – ein Generationenkonflikt bleibt aus,"* Klaus Hurrelmann, Simon Schnetzer, and Kilian Hampel; english: *"Youth trend study in Germany. The current crises are affecting younger individuals more than older individuals – a generational conflict has failed to appear"*), has given us some more insight: The generation of 14- to 29-year-olds are particularly affected by the consequences of the climate crisis, the Covid pandemic, the war in Ukraine, and high inflation – 46% of participants suffered from stress, according to the researchers. At this point, we are unable to look at the details of the study more closely due to space constraints. However, many sentiments that the young generation is feeling can be summed up under a term coined by the study: "permanent-crisis mode."
It therefore does not come as a surprise that the value orientations (security, social ties, stable relationships) prevalent in the 2019 Shell Youth study remain important in 2023. These value orientations apply across generations, as indicated by the percentages throughout all age groups determined by the 2023 trend study.

Third cause of uniformity: the mega trend of "disambiguation"

I keep researching. Much of this has confirmed, in different ways, the consequences of digitization and the prevailing societal state that I had gleaned from previous sources and observations. This particularly applies to the tendency to disambiguate, which has penetrated all social and economic spheres and is already the norm in technology.

100

What does “disambiguation” mean? The term outlines a world in which nuances and ambivalences are unwanted; a world lacking tolerance of ambiguity and variety. We live in times of certainties and the yes/no principle, our daily lives in a capitalist economic order are measured by numbers that are then expressed in values. The focus lies on predictable work, measurable fitness, buying and selling, self-optimization, scheduling, the service-compensation ratio, workloads and ECTS points, quotas, algorithms – not to mention digital developments, such as self-driving cars or artificial intelligence. This mega trend is facilitated by humanity’s innate endeavor to attain certainty and create clarity. After all, order and predictability represent necessary components for us to gain an orientation and overview. The economic order in which we live, along with its intrinsic value system, has hit a nerve: We feel at ease when anything vague, anything ambiguous is eradicated and the world before us is clearly definable.

As it stands, it is hard to criticize this approach. But unfortunately – or rather, thankfully – humans are not as simple as the last sentences might lead us to believe. Just imagine if all art, all music, all literature, or all design were undeniably unambiguous. The protagonists of modernism occasionally attempted this: They defined a canon of standards which all cultural expressions, including design (but also art, music, and literature) were to follow in the sense of unambiguousness. As I pointed out in the different chapters of this book, a dictum on the optimal method for visual communication cannot be reconciled with real life. It even seems to be the case that any attempt at unambiguousness gives rise to vagueness. Simply think back on the simple formula of “form follows function” and the struggle to implement this reasonable formula with the same unequivocalness. For example, a chair should be built and also designed in such a way that it optimally supports its function of sitting – simply “form follows function.” However, a chair can have many other functions: as a representative object (in the entrance hall of an office building, where nobody will ever sit), as a kitchen chair for occasional use or an office chair for long-term sitting, as a chair on which you place your clothes at the end of the day, as an artistic object, as a chair for very tall or very short people, and so on. Here, the tastes of the chair’s targeted group of buyers have not even been taken into account yet, nor have the designer’s attitude and imaginativeness. So we would need to say that “form ought to follow functions,” as all of the listed functional possibilities, tastes, and prioritizations affect the design in different ways. But that would undo the nice unambiguousness of the original formulation *(see 082)*. However, on an unconscious level, humans sense that they need islands of clarity within the ocean of vagueness – but that the ocean must still form part of the equation. Because this is where we find the wealth of what we call culture. The depths of the ocean bring forth variety, subjectivity, ambivalence, and experimentation. In other words, society finds itself in an eternal struggle, with ambiguousness and variety battling the urge for clarity, whereby the latter heavily dominates our thinking, our actions, and our perceptions now. Two poles stand opposed: one comprising the economy, technology, politics, and everything associated with these, while the other pole encompasses culture and religion. The latter illustrates particularly well what kind of negative consequences can result from disambiguation. In the sphere of faith, which inherently bears the essence of uncertainty, unambiguousness leads to fundamentalism: Once all nuances, options for interpretation, and forms of reading are eliminated, only one view remains – the one truth, the purity of faith. We can observe the results of religious fundamentalism and its inhuman consequences around the world. In all areas in which it is purported as the measure of all things, unambiguousness is marked by fundamentalist traits.

But the mega trend is also giving rise to developments viewed as positive: In chapter C, I wrote about post-postmodernism and assigned it keywords such as trust, sincerity, sustainability, credibility, service, honesty, dialog. In a world of sensory and information overload, these terms are very obviously synonymous with unambiguousness – just as the famed term authenticity, which simply implies that the immediate appearance conforms with the content's actual meaning; that deception is precluded, and unambiguousness guaranteed. As we can see, disambiguating the world comes with pros and cons.

The way out of the dilemma

Back to communication design, which must operate on the battlefield between variety and unambiguousness. Unambiguousness is our friend, or so you would think: From guidance systems and manuals through to novels and many other media – we always strive to make our communication intention as clear as possible. However, as a goal, unambiguousness can tempt us into uniformity in design, which I have already criticized. Because many draw the false conclusion that fulfilling expectations (of what a magazine should look like, for example) in a clichéd way is unambiguous enough – a few little tweaks here and there, and the work is done. On a superficial level, this holds truth, as we can easily tell from the selected magazines and their spreads. But our task encompasses more than that. Any layperson even marginally interested in design can achieve uniformity. That doesn't require a design degree. Creating variety, on the other hand, makes up the core business of design. It arises when visual communication presents itself in its individuality.

This brings a (final) professional dilemma to light: Unambiguousness can lead to interchangeability and thereby the opposite of the intended effect. But when designers penetrate the core of our communication task and develop specific visual designs in this realm – in the spirit of visual rhetoric – variety will emerge on its own. Because particularities will appear that set it apart from other senders and their visual communication. The graphic options offered by the pallet of visual rhetoric become visible when we compare the so-called mainstream media with design created in cultural niches. Some might object to this kind of a comparison: Many customers would be overwhelmed by unusual design that deviates from familiar paths; designers usually lack the time for experiments; pointed designs are too daring, too wild, too calm, too serious, too nonserious, too who-knows-what-else. Sometimes this will apply, but it also constitutes a bit of self-censorship. There are plenty of examples of what clients might be willing to engage with if designers would only dare to show and cleverly present such ideas.

When unambiguousness leads to uniformity, then we are dealing with a misunderstanding of the meaning of unambiguousness in communication design: It remains a crucial goal in visual communication – but only with regard to the clarity of an intention. There cannot be unambiguousness in the sense of a linear design solution to be developed based on the content. I've already mentioned the example of designers who all received the same task and produced different results. The subjective interpretation of a communication situation demonstrates that variety is intrinsic to design. But if this is true, there is really no reason to hold back, to adopt the ideas of others, and to cater to an alleged perceptive consensus. In fact, the time has come for content-specific devices in design. This type of visual communication gives rise to new impulses, variety, innovation, and cultural enrichment.

My approach – researching, sampling, and analyzing – helped update my own design understanding. Every reader needs to decide for herself or himself whether to follow suit. The assessments may vary, but the findings I have described here will surely have a certain effect on most readers: You will inevitably check your own routines, form your own opinions, and in this way, grow alert.

Repoliticizing Design

Communication designers currently face a wide range of challenges. More than ever before, their skills are called for to communicate complex matters in an understandable manner or adapt visual communication for new digital media. Or when the focus revolves around important, socially relevant circumstances and developments. Due to their multidimensional nature, all of these topics greatly rely on differentiated and at the same time appealing visual communication. In light of these challenges, you could reproach many designers for not reflecting on their creations enough or at all. [101] This is a shortcoming, because designers are the ones who make consumer incentives, information, political intentions, and ethical/moral values visible and communicate them – whether in advertising, in the news, or in entertainment media. In addition, the discipline of design is closely intertwined with all aspects of human co-existence – in terms of gender, ethnicity, class, or culture. [102] The dynamics of these current topics ask for less design fulfillment through the formal aspects but demand more content-based positioning – not only in relation to visual communication, but also regarding the profession and personal everyday life.

If we glance into the past and the present, we can see that the relationship between society and communication design boasts a longstanding and eventful tradition – but also that its relevance in times of fake news, bots, and other mighty algorithm-based systems is growing, simply because visual communication, in its interface role between sender and recipient, is assuming an increasingly important role. That's why it is vital to have detailed knowledge of its modes of action, either to unmask and reveal its manipulative character or to design in a targeted and convincing manner ourselves. We can predict that innovations in the area of artificial intelligence will continue to change the work of communication designers.
For designers, the phrase "lifelong learning" is incredibly important, both with regard to technical aspects and in terms of ethics. Even now, assessing the authenticity and truth content of AI-manipulated visual and verbal information presents a nearly impossible challenge. This gives questions concerning what counts as "real" and "true" a whole new dimension. Even if the latest technological developments offer many exciting opportunities (at increasingly shorter intervals), designers must examine them critically. The topic will become relevant at the latest when they realize that many jobs and occupations in the field of design, including their own, are at risk, simply because layout programs and now also AI tools – used by non-designers – can deliver results more quickly and cheaply than designers ever could.

101 ------ Design's Delight, van Toorn
102 ------ Design Struggles: Intersecting Histories, Pedagogies, and Perspectives, Mareis, Paim

From the client side, many will be satisfied with a pretty, functional interface to communicate their own matters of interest. Laypeople are unfamiliar with all the conceptual and design principles of visual rhetoric that turn trivial into effective visual communication. It can be difficult to convey the fact that a design process takes time (and costs money). Designers must resist this pressure to justify their existence and instead meet these challenges proactively. For this reason, designers must expand their skills beyond design and communicate their competences and the quality standards of their profession on many levels. Designers operate as individuals. That's why design networks are particularly important: They promote the exchange of ideas and provide new impetus in terms of solidarity (as evidenced by countless conferences, workshops, and initiatives domestically and abroad). Creating such networks with colleagues can provide them with the latest industry expertise, strengthen their position during negotiations, and encourage them to reflect on their own actions.

Social engagement offers a good opportunity to link your own expertise with purposeful goals. This is not a new perspective – just think of the many holistic [103] design approaches that emerged throughout modernism. The rejection that characterized modernism and which led to postmodernism was based on many factors. But one aspect of modernist ideals that is hard to criticize is the fundamental belief that we must always view design within its relationship to society and derive design processes from this. If we set aside the (era-typical) stringency of the argumentation of the time, we are left with many ideas that still hold true today. The revival of holistic observations of terms of *justice*, *credibility*, *sustainability*, and *ethics* – in both society and design – is starting to replace the postmodern air of attractive superficiality (or has already done so). We will need to leave the labeling of our current era to the responsible academic fields. But it appears undisputable that this development must entail a repoliticization of communication design – and, to a certain degree, it already has.

For this reason, it is only logical that a basic theme runs through this specialist book. I have addressed it in the introduction, and it resonates throughout [104] the remaining chapters. The theme is "mindset." As described on numerous occasions, it constitutes an essential design factor. Mindset serves as the foundation for understanding visual communication, the basis for every objection, and the driving force behind creative work. By nature, it is political. It forms the basis for quality. Mindset sharpens our focus on all things new and empowers designers to shape the future of design. Mindset is emancipatory at its core. It helps designers correlate their own creative [105] work with the diverse processes that constantly keep our society on the

103 ------ Weltentwerfen – eine politische Designtheorie, von Borries
104 ------ Das RLF Manifest, von Borries
105 ------ Extra Bold: A Feminist, Inclusive, Anti-racist, Nonbinary Field Guide for Graphic Designers, Lupton et al.

103.1 -------- Die Welt als Entwurf, Aicher

move. Finally, mindset is not conceivable without assuming responsibility – and vice versa.

Against this background, here are a few very mundane suggestions for your everyday professional life: Every now and again, take a critical look at your pragmatism. Aspire to uphold your own ideals, even if you cannot always implement them in your daily working life. Continually research and question the structures that underpin society and express themselves in visual communication. Network with colleagues. Observe trends, fashions, and developments in society and in art. Avoid censoring yourself and boldly utilize the possibilities of visual rhetoric. Be a committed actor in the best sense of the word.

All of this will strengthen the feeling within you that called you to this profession or is leading you towards it: the desire to design and communicate with people.

E 1–3

Note on the reference information in E1:

Depicted below as an example: the titles of the references, the page number where they are originally found, and numbers with further references in chapter E2.

The abbreviations (eds.) for "editors" and (u.v) for "Ulysses Voelker" indicate self-written contributions.

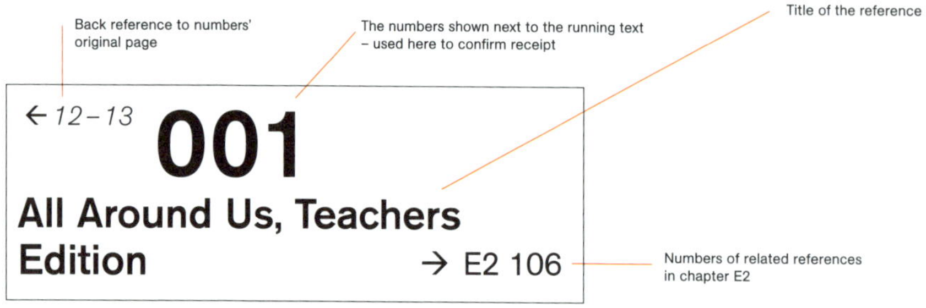

Back reference to numbers' original page

The numbers shown next to the running text – used here to confirm receipt

Title of the reference

← *12–13* **001**

All Around Us, Teachers Edition → E2 106

Numbers of related references in chapter E2

Sources, Specialist Texts, Books: 001 – 105

The references gathered here verify and complete the facts presented in chapters A–D.

← 12–13

001

All Around Us, Teachers Edition

→ E2 106

Bibliographic information:
"All Around Us – Teachers Edition"; Scott Foresman and co. (Eds.), USA, 1st edition, 1949;

Image source:
pages 38–39 in the book

These illustrations depict a harbor scene in 1949. What would a depiction of such a scene look like in today's world? These are a few of the changes that we would need to take into account:

Ships and general cargo: would be container vessels today.

Number of people: would be fewer thanks to advanced technologies.

Clothing: Today, a helmet and high-visibility vest are mandatory.

Propeller plane: replaced by jet planes; however, no-fly areas have been imposed above the city.

Blimp: no longer exists.

Horses and vehicles: These would be tractors and forklifts today.

Harbors: are usually located far outside of cities nowadays.

Warehouses at the harbor edge: now expensive lofts.

Ideally, a child-friendly depiction of a harbor contains a mixture of information and scope for children's imagination – back then as well as today. (eds.)

001.1

Definition of the term "Illustration"

→ E2 ––

Bibliographic information:
"Wörterbuch Design," Michael Erlhoff, Tim Marshall (Eds.); Birkhäuser Verlag, Basel, 2008;
ISBN 978-7643-7738-0 [in German]

This book contains in-depth discussions on the topic of "illustrating." The term stems from the Latin "illustrare" and is defined as "to make clear, to show clearly" by Merriam Webster. Communication design features many different areas of application in which facts are presented or commented on using images. Forms of illustration range from depictions of technical facts and idea sketches (storyboards) through to subjective artistic commentary, for example on literary texts. Special variants that have established their own genres include comics, graphic novels, and cartoons. In all cases, pictures help to "make clear or clearly demonstrate" something, or even present their own narrative. Illustrations can be designed in many different styles, for example as a sketch, painting, with letterpress and rotogravure techniques, or as a collage. Illustrators either work as independent visual narrators or as contractors for publishers, advertising agencies, or other clients. (eds.)

001.2

For Your Own Good

→ E2 107

Bibliographic information:
"For Your Own Good: Hidden Cruelty in Child-Rearing and the Roots of Violence," Alice Miller;
Farrar, Straus and Giroux, New York City, 1990;
ISBN 978-0374522698

Alice Miller (1923 – 2010) was a Polish-Swiss author and psychologist.

The book is a classic in the field of education: In "For Your Own Good: Hidden Cruelty in Child-Rearing and the Roots of Violence", Alice Miller uses three case examples (a drug addict, a political leader, a child murderer) to describe the consequences an upbringing can have. She says that a child's first years of life shape the rest of their life. Society bears witness to this in the form of encoded experiences: psychoses, crime, and drug addiction. Nonetheless, educative ideals have continuously and still are dominated by projections of good and evil, which originated in the medieval mindset. However, what children actually need is tolerance and sensitivity towards their emotions as well as a parental self-image that expresses itself by respecting the freedom of the other – as opposed to abstract educational considerations. (eds.)

← 12–13

002

Voyager freight to unknown recipients in space

→ E2 108

Text sources:
(1) https://de.wikipedia.org/wiki/Voyager_Golden_Record
(2) https://de.wikipedia.org/wiki/Carl_Sagan
(3) https://voyager.jpl.nasa.gov/golden-record/whats-on-the-record/images/

(All information: see sources)

001
001.1
001.2
002

Summary of sources (1) and (2):

The "Voyager Golden Records" are data plates with image and audio information and are on board the interstellar space probes Voyager 1 and Voyager 2, both of which launched in 1977. The data plates, containing 116 images and many different sounds, were created as a message, in the hopes that some intelligent, alien forms of life might be able to learn about humanity and its position in the universe. A diagram on the front explains the location of Earth and instructions on how to view and play the data sets. With an expected lifetime of 500 million years, the plates are designed to bear testimony to the fact that humans exist or once existed.
American scientist Carl Sagan (1934 – 1996) took on a leading role in developing the project. Jon Lomberg designed the plate. The information on the plate reflects humanity's state of knowledge in the year 1977.

In the meantime, "Voyager 2" has traveled more than 20 billion kilometers from the Earth, while "Voyager 1" is more than 23 billion kilometers away. Radio contact remains possible with both probes (as of 2022). Further information is available on the NASA website and in the book "The Politics of Design" by Ruben Pater. See entry 002.1 for further details. (eds.)

The list of other images on the data plate (according to source 3):

ʻ The sun, cells and cell division, anatomy 1–8, human reproductive organs, conception, fertilized egg, fetus, birth, father and daughter, group of children, family portrait, coastline, Snake River and Grand Tetons, sand dunes, Monument Valley, forest scene with mushrooms, leaf, fallen leaves, snowflake above Sequoia, tree with daffodils, flying insect with flowers, seashell (xancidae), dolphins, swarm of fish, tree toad, crocodile, eagle, watering hole, Jane Goodall and chimpanzees, bushman hunter, dancer from Bali, girl from the Andes, Thai construction worker, elephant, man with beard and glasses (Turkey), old man with dog and flowers, mountain climber, gymnast, cotton harvest, grape picker, underwater scene with divers and fish, cooking fish, Chinese dinner party, Wall of China, construction scene (Amish Country), house (New England), house's interior with artist and fire, Taj Mahal, English town (Oxford), Boston, Sydney Opera House, construction worker with a drill, inside of a factory, museum, Golden Gate Bridge, train, airport (Toronto), Antarctic expedition, sunset with birds, string quartet (Quartetto Italiano). ʻ

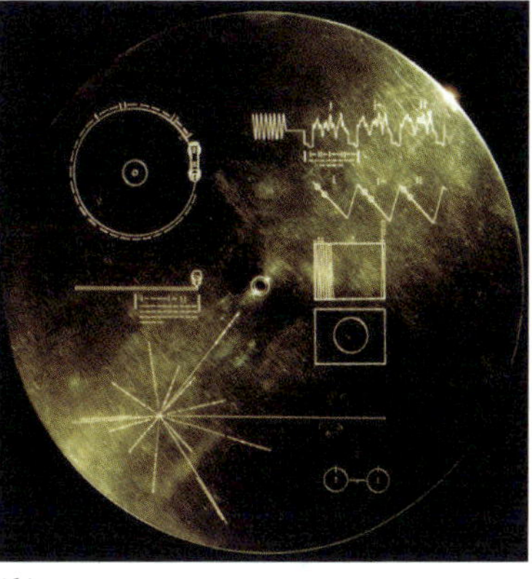

(1)

(2)

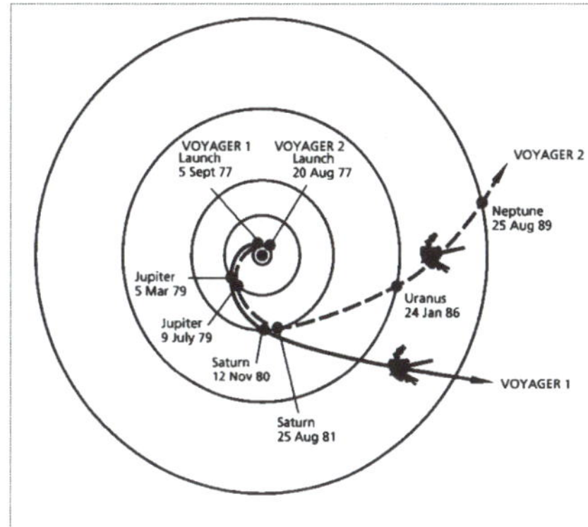

(3)

Image captions:

(1), (2)
The Voyager Golden Record

(3)
The trajectories of the Voyager probes

(4)
Attaching the record to the probe

(5)
Instructions for use

(6)
Selection of images on the data plate (next page)

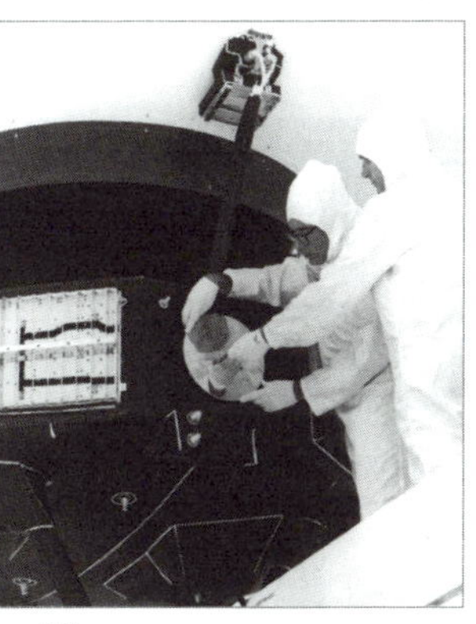

(4)

EXPLANATION OF RECORDING COVER DIAGRAM

THE DIAGRAMS BELOW
DEFINE THE VIDEO PORTION OF THE RECORDING

BINARY CODE DEFINING PROPER SPEED (3.6 seconds/ROTATION) TO TURN THE RECORD (|=BINARY 1, —= BINARY 0) EXPRESSED IN 0.70 × 10-9 seconds, THE TIME PERIOD ASSOCIATED WITH THE FUNDAMENTAL TRANSITION OF THE HYDROGEN ATOM

OUTLINE OF CARTRIDGE WITH STYLUS TO PLAY RECORD (FURNISHED ON SPACECRAFT)

PICTORIAL PLAN VIEW OF RECORD

ELEVATION VIEW OF CARTRIDGE

ELEVATION VIEW OF RECORD

PLAYING TIME, ONE SIDE = ~1 hour

GENERAL APPEARANCE OF WAVE FORM OF VIDEO SIGNALS FOUND ON THE RECORDING

BINARY CODE TELLS TIME OF THE SCAN (~8 msec)

SCAN TRIGGERING

VIDEO IMAGE FRAME SHOWING DIRECTION OF SCAN. BINARY CODE INDICATES TIME OF EACH SCAN SWEEP (512 VERTICAL LINES PER COMPLETE PICTURE)

IF PROPERLY DECODED, THE FIRST IMAGE WHICH WILL APPEAR IS A CIRCLE

THIS DIAGRAM DEFINES THE LOCATION OF OUR SUN UTILIZING 14 PULSARS OF KNOWN DIRECTIONS FROM OUR SUN. THE BINARY CODE DEFINES THE FREQUENCY OF THE PULSES.

THIS DIAGRAM ILLUSTRATES THE TWO LOWEST STATES OF THE HYDROGEN ATOM. THE VERTICAL LINES WITH THE DOTS INDICATE THE SPIN MOMENTS OF THE PROTON AND ELECTRON. THE TRANSITION TIME FROM ONE STATE TO THE OTHER PROVIDES THE FUNDAMENTAL CLOCK REFERENCE USED IN ALL THE COVER DIAGRAMS AND DECODED PICTURES.

(5)

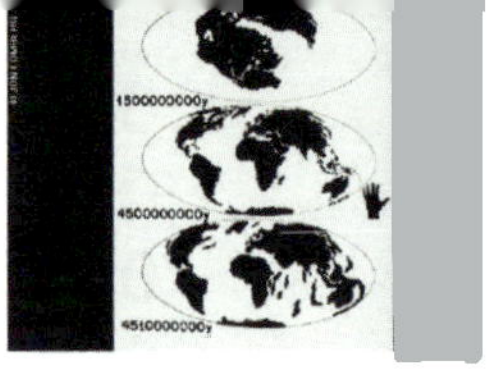

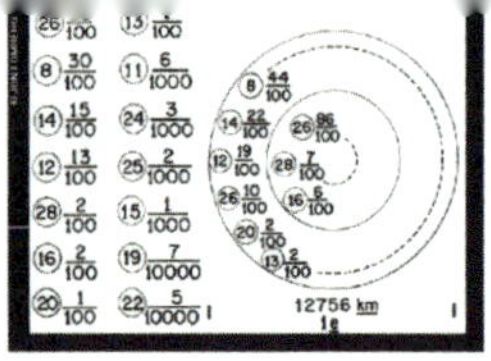

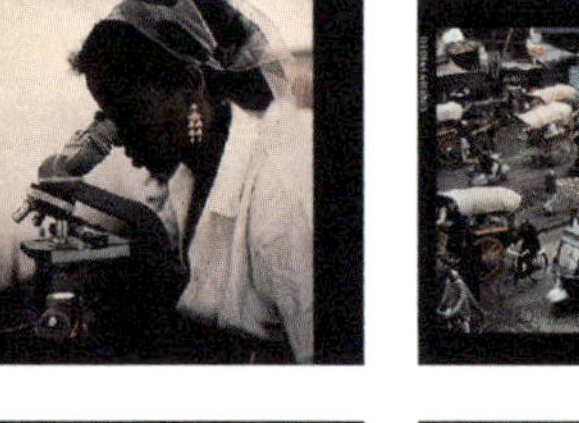
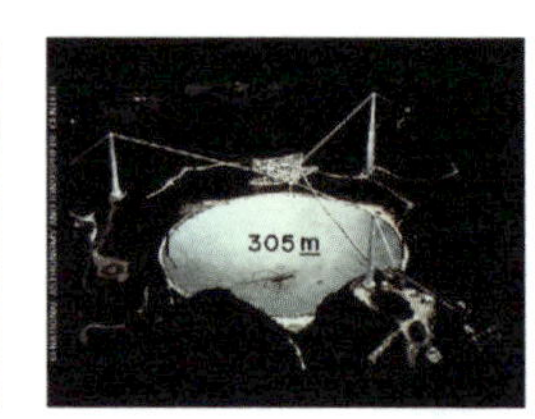

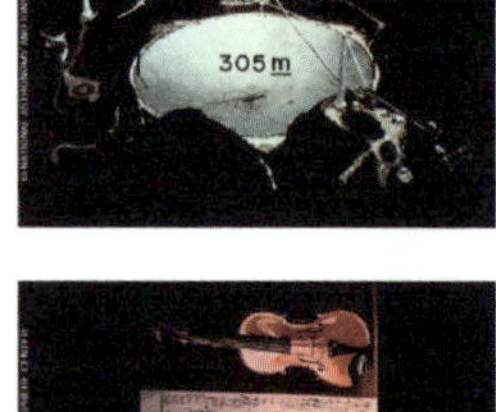
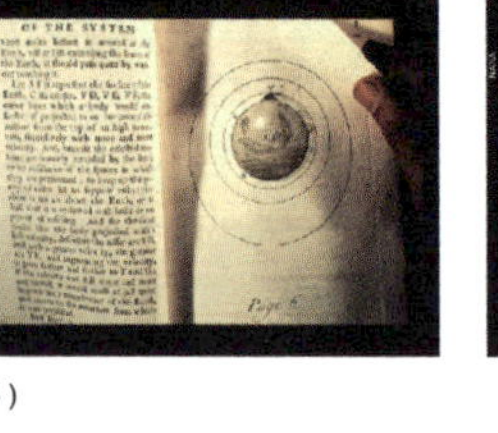

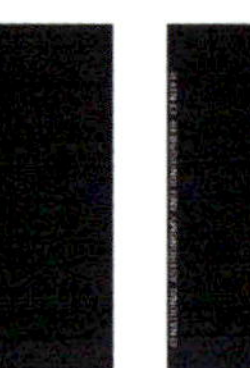

(6)

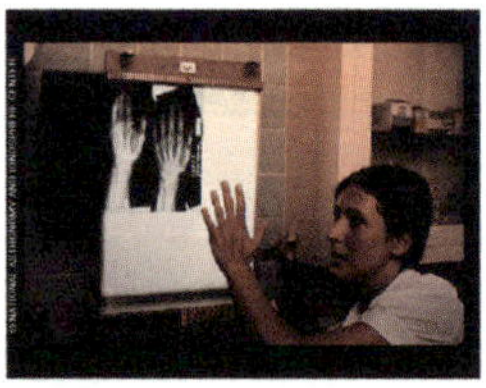

(1) https://upload.wikimedia.org/wikipedia/commons/5/56/The_Sounds_of_Earth_Record_Cover_-_GPN-2000-001978.jpg
(2) https://commons.wikimedia.org/wiki/File:The_Sounds_of_Earth_-_GPN-2000-001976.jpg
(3) https://voyager.jpl.nasa.gov/assets/images/galleries/interstellar_science.jpg
(4) https://upload.wikimedia.org/wikipedia/commons/5/5a/Record_is_attached_to_Voyager_1.jpg
(5) https://commons.wikimedia.org/wiki/File:Voyager_Golden_Record_Cover_Explanation.svg
(6) https://voyager.jpl.nasa.gov/golden-record/whats-on-the-record/images/#missing_images
(see sources)

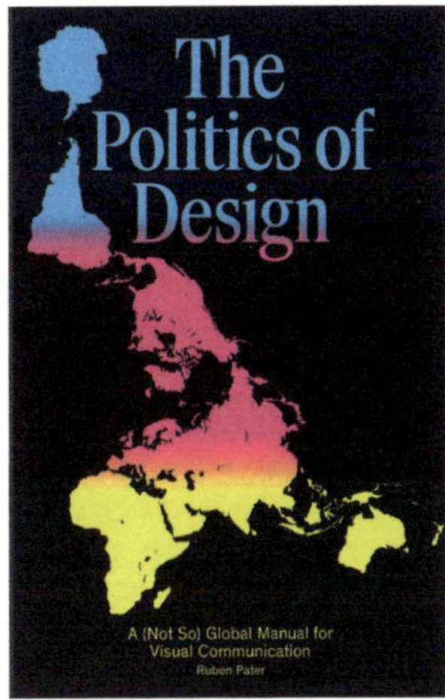

002.1

The Politics of Design

→ E2 109

Bibliographic information:
"The Politics of Design," Ruben Pater;
BIS Publishers, Amsterdam, 2016;
ISBN 978-90-6369-422-7

Text source:
page 141, line 01 – page 144, line 13
Image source:
front cover of the book

’(...) Can symbols communicate to alien civilisations? NASA tried it in 1972, when an engraved aluminium plaque was placed on the Pioneer spacecraft. Astronomer Carl Sagan designed a series of diagrams of the earths location, the spacecraft's itinerary, a hydrogen atom, and a drawing of a naked woman and man.
Carl Sagan was invited again by NASA in 1977 to create a message for the Voyager spacecraft. His team came up with a golden record that con-tained 116 images and a variety of sounds. A diagram on the front explained the earth's location and instructions on how to play the record. The diagrams, which are featured on the next page, could probably not even be deciphered by most humans today, and young people would not know how to use a record player. However, the idea was that alien civilizations could study it for decades, even centuries, before deciphering the message.

Warning Posthumans
Can symbols be used to warn future humans? Nuclear waste will remain radioactive for the next 24,000 years. In 1990, a group of scientists was put together to design warning signs for a nuclear waste facility in the New Mexico desert. Carl Sagan suggested to mark the site with a skull and bones. However, the meaning of the skull has changed significantly over centuries. The earliest skull and bones was a symbol of rebirth, and later it was a symbol for piracy.
Using only language was initially rejected for the same reason. The English language is around 1200 years old, but the English that was used then is incomprehensible to English speakers today. The team's advice was to use pictograms and warning messages in multiple languages. It was decided to build an information centre with eight-metre-high granite slabs inscribed in seven languages, with room left to add future languages.

Learning from Cave Paintings
Trying to communicate to aliens and future humans pushes the limits of our cognitive abilities. Artist Trevor Paglen makes a comparison with our attempts to understand the cave paintings in Lascaux in France: Cave paintings, or even things like pyramids or the Moai of Easter Island, are deeply strange artefacts to us – so strange, in fact, that some of the most popular shows on TV are about trying to 'uncover their mysteries'.
In fact, new mysteries are still being found in cave paintings. In 2010, paleoanthropologist Genevieve von Petzinger discovered reoccurring symbols that could indicate some sort of symbolic language. Similar basic symbols have been found in other caves, as far away as South Africa. (...)’

002.2

Long-term nuclear waste warning

→ E2 --

Text source:
https://en.wikipedia.org/wiki/Long-term_nuclear_waste_warning_messages
(see sources)

Image source:
https://en.wikipedia.org/wiki/Long-term_nuclear_waste_warning_messages#/media/
(see sources)

’Long-term nuclear waste warning messages are communication attempts intended to deter human intrusion at nuclear waste repositories in the far future, within or above the order of magnitude of 10,000 years. Nuclear semiotics is an interdisciplinary field of research, first done by the American Human Interference Task Force in 1981. A 1993 report from Sandia National Laboratories recommended that such messages be constructed at several levels of complexity.
They suggested that the sites should include foreboding physical features which would immediately convey to future visitors that the site was both man-made and dangerous, as well as providing pictographic information attempting to convey some details of the danger, and written explanations for those able to read it.

Message
A 1993 report from Sandia National Laboratories aimed to communicate a series of messages non-linguistically to any future visitors to a waste site. It gave the following wording as an example of what those messages should evoke:

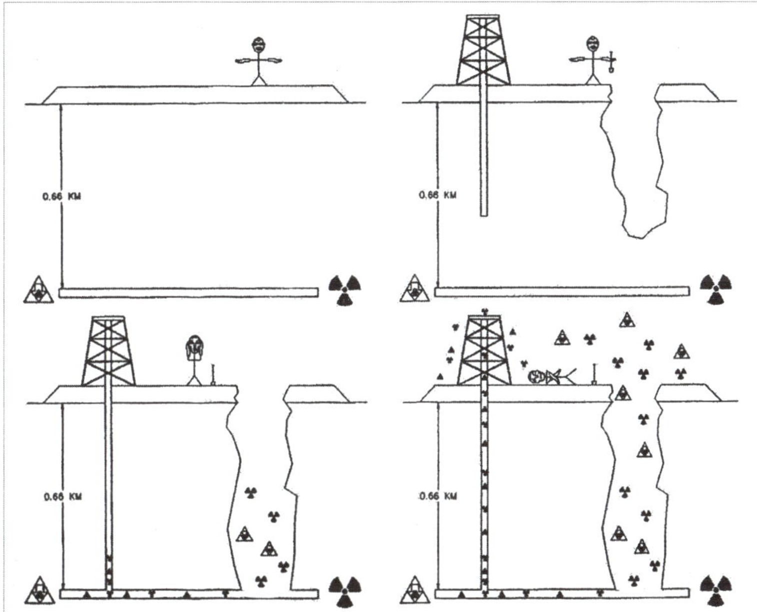

Pictogram for nuclear sites, US Department of Energy, 2004

– This place is a message ... and part of a system of messages ... pay attention to it!
– Sending this message was important to us. We considered ourselves to be a powerful culture.
– This place is not a place of honor ... no highly esteemed deed is commemorated here ... nothing valued is here.
– What is here was dangerous and repulsive to us. This message is a warning about danger.
– The danger is in a particular location ... it increases towards a center ... the center of danger is here ... of a particular size and shape, and below us.
– The danger is still present, in your time, as it was in ours.
– The danger is to the body, and it can kill.
– The form of the danger is an emanation of energy.
– The danger is unleashed only if you substantially disturb this place physically. This place is best shunned and left uninhabited.

The Sandia report further recommended that any such message should comprise four levels of increasing complexity:
1. Rudimentary information: "Something man-made is here".
2. Cautionary information: "Something man-made is here and it is dangerous".
3. Basic information: Tells what, why, when, where, who, and how.
4. Complex information: Highly detailed written records, tables, figures, graphs, maps and diagrams. (...)’

Bibliographic information:
"typography," Otl Aicher; Verlag Ernst & Sohn, 1st edition, 1988; Reprint, Verlag Hermann Schmidt, Mainz, 2005; [ENG/GER]
ISBN 3-87439-683-5

The adjacent text refers to a passage from the chapter titled "die ökonomie des auges" ("The economy of the eye"), page 128;

Otl Aicher (1922 – 1991) ranks among the most influential German designers in the Federal Republic of Germany. He co-founded the Ulm School of Design in the 1950s. He developed countless looks, including for the 1972 Olympic Games and Lufthansa. His font "Rotis" – named after his place of residence – was both famous and controversial in the early 1990s. He set a milestone with his book "typography," which offers an excellent description of his holistic approach to visual communication.
(eds.)

← 12–13

003

The Economy of the Eye

→ E2 ––

In the chapter "the economy of the eye" from his book "typography," Otl Aicher writes about the principles of human perception and behavior. He illustrates the extent to which these principles are subject to economic considerations by means of an everyday phenomenon: Every time there is freshly fallen snow, the footsteps left in the snow indicate that people do not necessarily opt for the path that is theoretically the shortest, but instead for the easiest. This phenomenon can be determined by the fact that they would go around even the slightest mound, meaning the trail would curve around the obstacle, even if this lengthened the path. Based on this behavior, he concludes that an "economic principle" controls our behavior. Aicher suggests that the eye is also subject to perceptive behavior based on this principle. He calls this "situational interest" and "quality of the offering." Design must respond to this. In particular, Aicher refers to typography, the task of which lies in finding adequate solutions to this phenomenon. (He writes using his individual style of exclusively lowercase letters): *"there are rules for writing, objective, social, and subjective. the rule that the eye only sees what it wants to see is a rule of subjective autonomy. the rule that one only reads what is offered well as reading material is objective. and the rule that one primarily determines credibility based on visual appearance, an aesthetic, is a culture humanity has acquired as a society. we find ourselves in a culture, and this culture provides us with the aesthetic criteria from which we choose."* (eds.)

003.1

Eye tracking

→ E2 ––

Text source:
https://de.wikipedia.org/wiki/Eye-Tracking
(see sources)

Image source:
https://de.wikipedia.org/wiki/Eye-Tracking#/media/
(see sources)

/ Eye tracking, which stems from the medical field of oculography, refers the recording of a person's eye movements, which primarily include fixations (points observed closely), saccades (rapid eye motions), and regressions. Eye trackers are devices and systems that record these movements and enable an analysis of these eye movements. The scientific method is used in neurosciences, perceptive, cognition, and advertising psychology, cognitive and clinical linguistics, for usability tests, in product design, and in reading research. Eye tracking data describe the time at which a person fixates on a specific point. During the analysis, the data is put into relation with the observed stimulus. In the area of usability, this allows for an analysis of which website elements a user has looked at, for how long, or when they first did so.

This process uses "areas of interest" (AOIs). AOIs are areas that are marked manually in the stimulus and then calculated for the different eye tracking measurements. (...)

To determine the measurement of "total dwell time," or fixation duration, the duration of the fixations is added up. This means that the total duration of observing an AOI is measured. Other measurements look at the time at which certain fixations occur. The measurement of "time to first fixation" identifies the time of the first fixation within an AOI. This reveals how long it took for the observer to look at a certain area for the first time. The measurements calculated based on AOIs can be conducted for the data of an individual test person as well as for the data of several test people. The results include average values for all test people.
With the AOI analysis, it is also possible to evaluate eye tracking data quantitatively. To name an example, this method is used to assess the distribution of attention within a stimulus, such as a website. But it is also particularly suitable for comparing eye tracking recordings in A/B tests, for example on different stimuli or to compare two groups of participants with one another.
(...) /

Screenshot of the Wikipedia page on "Visuelle Wahrnehmung" ("Visual Perception").

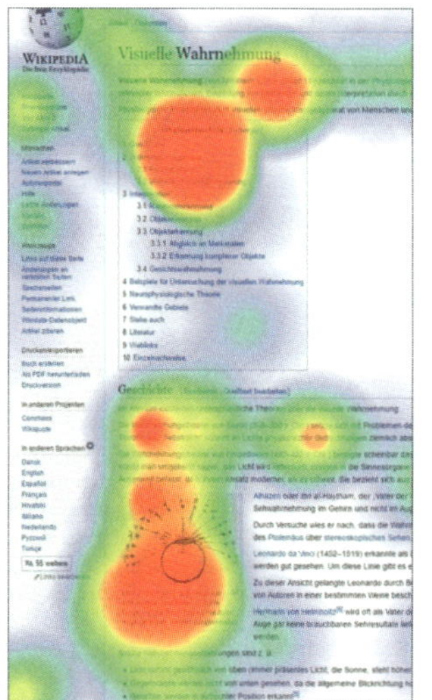

Heatmap, generated from the eye-tracking data from three test people.

Two areas of interest (AOIs) with the results for the measurement of "fixation duration" in seconds.

003.2

Die Entschlüsselung der Bilder

→ E2 110, 111

Bibliographic information:
"Die Entschlüsselung der Bilder – Methoden zur Erforschung visueller Kommunikation," Thomas Petersen, Clemens Schwender (Eds.); Herbert von Halem Verlag, Cologne, 2011; ISBN 978-3-86962-043-5
[in German]

The book describes a deficit in communication sciences, whose focus lies on analyzing the written, and perhaps also the spoken word. The authors suggest that the visual aspect is lacking. To counter this deficit, the authors primarily discuss the power of images. They present many different methods that focus on visual communication – such as analyzing content, reception, and impact. The descriptions of the most important procedures for exploring visual communication are directed at both students and researchers. (eds.)

← 14–15

004

The MAYA principle

→ E2 112, 112.1, 112.2, 112.3, 113

The MAYA principle is a tool from the field of psychology that is also used in marketing and advertising. MAYA is an acronym* and stand for: **Most Advanced Yet Acceptable**. French-American industrial designer Raymond Loewy established the principle in advertising. Attracting attention and curiosity constitute crucial goals in marketing. When something "new" appears on the market, it can achieve these goals. But this "new" product does not necessarily need to have a positive connotation. Something frightening or even deterring can also draw attention. The MAYA principle aims to unite both of these aspects: on the one hand, disrupting viewing habits, and on the other hand, irritating – but not in a negative sense. The motto is as follows: "Do something unusual, something new, but do not go as far straying into the realm of what is unacceptable." You can read more about what this means for communication design in chapter D1. The topic is titled: Tried-and-Tested Methods and New Aspects. (eds.)

* An acronym is an abbreviation made up of the first letters or syllables of several words or components of a compound.

004.1

The KISS principle

→ E2 ––

The KISS principle describes a solution strategy. The term KISS is an acronym*, it is composed of the words:
Keep it simple, stupid. This statement is not meant in a derogatory way, but instead offers positive encouragement to avoid making something complicated when a simple option exists.
This prompt is originally attributed to an American aircraft engineer who asked a group of colleagues to develop a jet engine that could be repaired by a regular mechanic with the simplest tools in the event of damage during wartime deployment. The KISS principle is viewed as an aspirational model in many disciplines, for example in the areas of the Internet, software development, and also design. The goal always lies in developing the simplest possible and most easily understandable solution. There are different versions of the KISS acronym, including "Keep it short and simple." This option is particularly popular in advertising and serves as a maxim for good marketing. "Keep it short and simple" is related to the acronym PEE (**Point, Evidence, Explain**). The latter is proffered as a recommendation for good writing at universities and schools in English-speaking countries.
(eds.)

* An acronym is an abbreviation made up of the first letters or syllables of several words or components of a compound.

← 14–15

005

Wie wirklich ist die Wirklichkeit?

→ E2 ––

Text source:
Transcript of an interview from 1997;
title of the interview: "Wirklichkeit und Wahrheit" ("Reality and Truth")
https://www.youtube.com/watch?v=5X2Gj6gIF-E
[in German]

Interviewer:
Prof. Dr. Martin Gertler

Paul Watzlawick (1921 – 2007) was an Austrian-American communication scientist, psychotherapist, philosopher, university professor, and author.

His academic work influenced psychotherapy as a whole. He wrote countless books, including "The Situation Is Hopeless, But Not Serious: The Pursuit of Unhappiness" and "Pragmatics of Human Communication." He is considered to be a representative of "radical constructivism."

Martin Gertler (M.G): How do you define reality and how do you define truth?

Paul Watzlawick (P. W): Well, you will have to tell me. Because I don't work with either term as a final, fully fledged concept. In the 1950s, I briefly lived in Bombay, where I was introduced to the Swamis – they were holy wise men who would have been diagnosed with schizophrenic catatonia in the Occident. So you see, it is a matter of perspective or definition. You might be familiar with the joke: What is the difference between an optimist and a pessimist? The answer is: The optimist says that a bottle is half full. The pessimist says that the same bottle is half empty. Who is right? And these contradictions, these opposites, this dispute regarding the right definition – that is the foundation of my work. By dealing with people who are struggling in life, who are suffering. One question here is how they see reality.

M.G: Then what is truth?

P. W: In my opinion, the term can only be used when people are part of the same construction of reality. Let me briefly explain what I mean by construction of reality. In our area of expertise, it is always assumed that there is a real reality, one of which those of a normal mental state and above all therapists are aware. And the people with a so-called mental illness have a warped perspective of this reality. Other disciplines have long abandoned this interpretation, which is no longer tenable. In modern epistemology, the task of science is to develop procedures that are effective for a very specific purpose. And this may very well mean that in five years' time, today's best way of dealing with the problem has been replaced by a better solution. But this certainly doesn't mean that the next one is true and this one is untrue.

M.G: But it is still based on what we know today. So essentially, something completely different would fall from the sky. Surely it isn't that arbitrary.

P. W: No, we need to be clear about this. In constructivism, which I am part of, we distinguish between two realities. The first reality is the one that our sensory organs convey to us. For example: I see a light, and the light is red. Let us put aside the fact that this is also the result of an incredibly complicated construction process in my central nervous system and that the sound "red" and the letters R-E-D are an invention, an ascription. You see, a small child with normal sight can, of course, also perceive a red light – and will do so. But the child doesn't necessarily know that the light means red. And certainly not that under certain circumstances, when a red light appears, this means that they may not cross the street. These are attributions to the so-called reality of the first order conveyed by my central nervous system. Inevitably, this leads to an attribution of meaning, purpose, and value. And this leaves absolutely no option to definitively determine who is right and who is wrong. That takes us back to the little joke: The pessimist says the bottle is half empty. The optimist says the same bottle – from the same reality of the first order – is half full. /

005.1

Visual Perception

→ E2 114, 115, 116, 116.1, 116.2

Bibliographic information:
"Visual Perception," Jürg Nänni;
Niggli Verlag, Salenstein, 2009; [ENG/GER]
ISBN 978-3-7212-0618-0

Image sources:
Front cover und image on the double pages: 20-21, 100-101

This comprehensive foundational work presents the most important phenomena and modes of action of visual perception. Countless examples demonstrate how easily seduced our brain and our eyes are. (eds.)

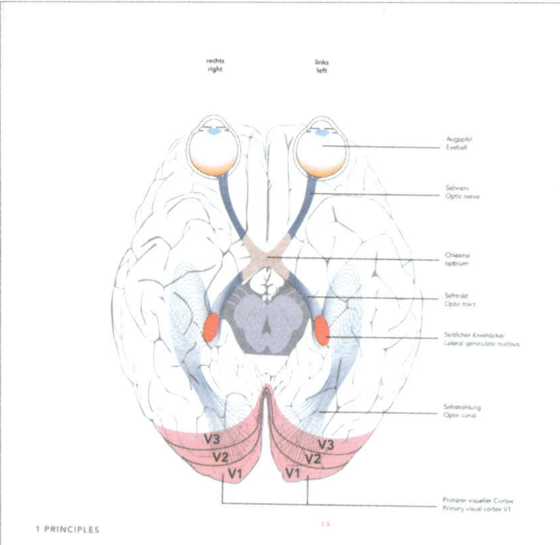

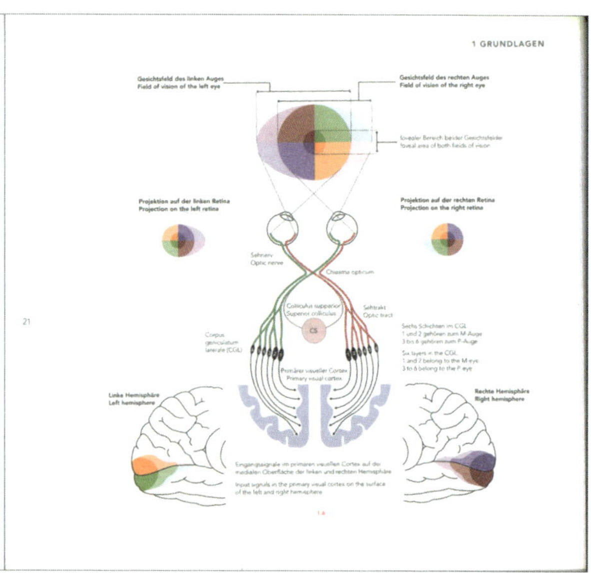

005.2

The Four Sides of a Message

→ E2 --

Bibliographic information:
"Structuring Design," Ulysses Voelker;
Niggli Verlag, Salenstein, 2020;
ISBN 978-3-7212-0994-5

Text source:
chapter "Stimulus, response and other phenomena,"
page 142, line 20 – page 143, line 03

005.1
005.2
006

This book introduces the principle of "the four sides of a message," developed by communication scientist Friedemann Schulz von Thun. It refers to verbal communication.

In my text, I describe the parallels with visual communication. (u.v)

'(...) There are four aspects that make up verbal communication –all take place at the same time:

1) the factual aspect (the communication of a fact),
2) the relationship aspect (the treatment of the fellow human being through the way of communication),
3) the self-revealing aspect (what does the way of communication say about yourself),
4) the appeal aspect (what do you want to achieve with communication).

Actually, all four aspects can be transferred to the design process – with the unbeatable advantage of being able to use them with a foresighted sense of proportion (in contrast to the complex simultaneity of all aspects of the spoken word). That means, however, that in every visual communication the questions of what is to be communicated, the relationship to the addressee, the own formative contribution and the effect to be obtained must be answered again. Although designers cannot avoid providing general answers to these questions (they do not communicate with individuals, but with target groups), such an analysis of the communication situation must precede every design assignment. What then follows can be called the graphic "coding" of a message: A whole series of visual and also haptic messages should be helpful to enable the recipient to understand the message correctly.
In communication psychology, every message is seen as a web of verbal and non-verbal messages. The sender therefore communicates on two levels. It does not only depend on what the sender says (on the verbal message level in the described "four-sided" way), but also on how it is commented non-verbally (on the meta level). (...) '

← 14–15

006

The world from different perspectives

→ E2 --

Image sources:
(1) Upside-down world map:
https://commons.wikimedia.org/wiki/File:World_map_geographical_(drab)
(see sources)

(2) Americanized world:
https://commons.wikimedia.org/wiki/Category:Global_maps_centered
(see sources)

As individuals, we take the depiction of our world for granted and rarely think about the fact that this view changes – depending on where in the world we are. We designers must be aware that the map section not only takes the specific location of potential observers into account, but is also based on cultural, religious, or political decisions – meaning the way some want us to view the world. It is not possible to depict the world "objectively." Making a claim to such an "objectivity" thus bears colonialist traits and disregards the perspectives of other cultures.
Another widespread idea is purely arbitrary: No scientific definition states that the north must be situated at the "top" and the south at the "bottom." Nonetheless, this perspective of "top = north" and "south = bottom" has prevailed for a substantial reason: pragmatism. From the start, it was easier to simply develop existing maps. And the first larger-scale maps already in circulation showed the north at the top. From a European perspective, east had actually been at the "top" during medieval times, since maps of the time were oriented towards the Holy City of Jerusalem (and the Orient). The term "Orient" stems from its historic usage in the context of maps. Since the Orient lay at the "top," maps had to be rotated; this was called "orienting a map." (eds.)

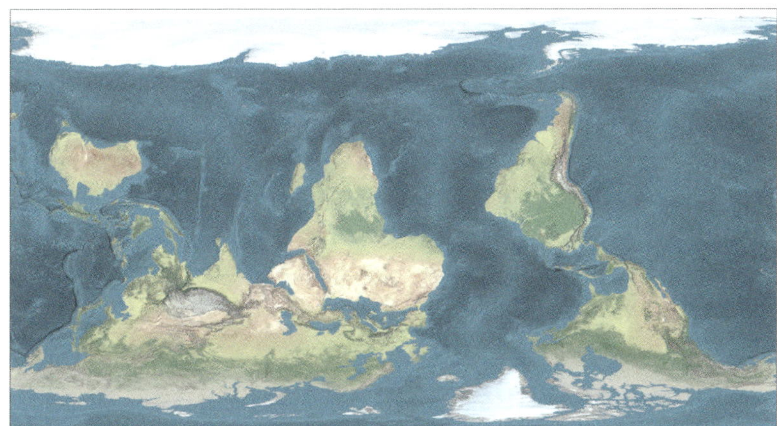

(1) This perspective exists:
The south sits at the top, the north at the bottom.

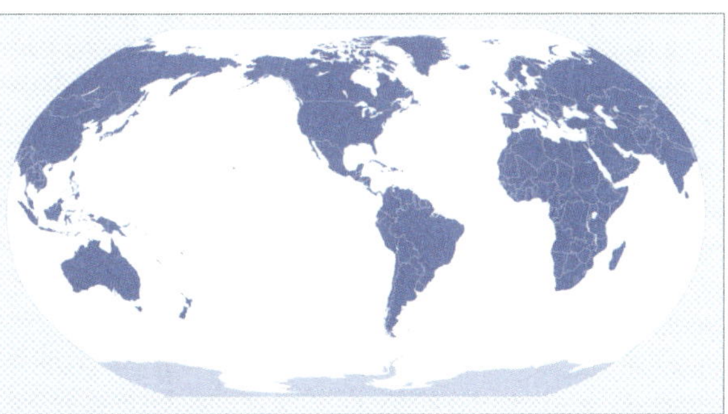

(2) The Americanized view of the world.

006.1

Shifts in Mapping. Maps as a Tool of Knowledge

→ E2 117

Bibliographic information:
"Shifts in Mapping. Maps as a Tool of Knowledge," Christine Schranz (ed.); Transcript Verlag, Bielefeld, 2021;
ISBN 978-3-8376-6041-8

Text sources:
(1) https://www.transcript-verlag.de/978-3-8376-6041-8/shifts-in-mapping (see sources)
(2) https://www.transcript-verlag.de/media/pdf/
(see sources)

(1) ' (...) Depicting the world, territory, and geopolitical realities involves a high degree of interpretation and imagination. It is never neutral. Cartography originated in ancient times to represent the world and to enable circulation, communication, and economic exchange. Today, IT companies are a driving force in this field and change our view of the world; how we communicate, navigate, and consume globally. Questions of privacy, authorship, and economic interests are highly relevant to cartography's practices. So how to deal with such powers and what is the critical role of cartography in it? How might a bottom-up perspective (and actions) in map-making change the conception of a geopolitical space? (...) '

(2) ' (...) The title of this publication "Shifts in Mapping. Maps as a Tool of Knowledge" began life as an online Symposium of the same name, which was organized by the FHNW Academy of Art and Design in Basel, Switzerland on January 20 and 21, 2021.
(...) The events aimed to shed light on our fascination with maps in order to highlight the tension between counter-maps and hegemonic top-down approaches of IT companies. With Web 2.0, and the possibility of generating one's own maps, the map is gaining enormous ground in terms of its importance as a knowledge tool. This aspect necessitated a focus on issues of democratization, access, and technology. (...) '

006.2

Alles so schön bunt hier – Ein Zeitalter der Vielfalt?

→ E2 ––

Bibliographic information:
"Die Vereindeutigung der Welt,"
Thomas Bauer; Reclam Verlag,
Ditzingen, 2018; [in German]
ISBN 978-3-15-019492-8
(see also reference 100)

In his book "Die Vereindeutigung der Welt," Thomas Bauer delves into Europe's cultural history and discovers that Europe had been one of the world's most monocultural regions for centuries. He suggests that this was not just due to geographical location – since Europe sits isolated on the western edge of Asia –, but also Christianization, which led to a religious homogenization. While many religions existed peacefully alongside one another in the premodern Orient, Europe had seen wars break out following comparably minor discrepancies in religious interpretations. A few examples include the Reformation and Counter-Reformation, the Inquisition, and the persecution of so-called heretics. In general, Judaism had merely been tolerated alongside Christianity in Europe, although the term tolerance should be used loosely – for centuries, Jews were victims of pogroms and were stigmatized and discriminated against even before the Holocaust. This formed a stark contrast to the proverbial tolerance along premodern trade routes that ran from the Far East to the Near East. Bauer goes into great detail on the diversity of people living alongside each other and works out that this diversity of religions and customs existing next to one another leads to an ambivalence and tolerance that, in principle, allows a rich culture to flourish.

I will quote Thomas Bauer once more in reference 100, in the context of disambiguation as a "counter-principle" to art and culture in general. (u.v)

← *16–17*

007

Addressing target groups, using the example of "All Around Us"

→ E2 ––

Bibliographic information:
"All Around Us," see 001

Image source:
(1) Original double page

(2), (3) design by Tobias Wenz;
(4), (5) design by Michael Schmitz

The first edition of the American schoolbook "All Around Us" (Teacher's edition) was published in 1949. The design catered to the average viewing and reading habits of educating adults at the time. We specialists assume we have sufficiently honed our eye to be able to assess the relationship between content and form. In this case – when looking at the book's textual introductory page –, this would mean: "a reputable look, appropriately unemotional, timeless from a typographic perspective." We often make judgments like these without adequately analyzing the relationship between the intention, sender, and recipient. If it seems suitable in terms of craftsmanship and does not step out of line, it must be fine. But is that always true? Can we accurately evaluate design without background knowledge? Or does our own taste play a bigger role than we think? The four examples on the next two pages aim to visualize the issue.
Because the envisaged target group also determines whether visual communication works well. (eds.)

006.1
006.2
007

CONTENTS

Copyright, 1944, by Scott, Foresman and Company
Printed in the United States of America

Introduction

Science in the Second Year of School

One of the *chief* duties of the school is to stimulate and guide the all-round growth of the pupil. A fundamental aim of an adequate science program is to stimulate and guide the pupil in a constantly growing understanding of the *forces*, elements, materials, and living things which, together, make up his everyday world.

There is an abundance of things to interest and challenge pupils—things to watch, things to investigate, things to do, and things to discuss. All the world lies before the child, to be explained and understood in its parts and, more important still, to be understood in the interrelationships of these parts.

So great is the diversity, as well as the extent, of the natural environment that an organized plan of presentation is essential if the pupils are to grasp not only facts but also relationships.

A course in science must present information in an efficient manner. It must insure the mastery of basic understandings. But, to be really effective, it must also foster the intellectual skills and abilities necessary for scientific thinking: the ability to observe accurately, the ability to perceive likenesses and differences, the ability to infer, the ability to generalize, and the ability to understand and use an oral science vocabulary. *All Around Us* and the *Teacher's Guidebook* have been carefully planned to promote the development of these skills.

A course in science may be considered successful only if it so affects the pupil that he maintains a true scientific attitude toward his total environment. Such an attitude leads to the development of accuracy in observation and report, intellectual honesty, open-mindedness, suspended judgment, and the ability to see relationships.

The purpose of *All Around Us* is to present examples from the environment that will lead the pupil to see relationships and help him organize his thinking. *All Around Us* is the second step in a program that helps the pupil to an understanding of the principles and laws of science.

Areas of Interest

In *All Around Us* four centers, or areas, of pupil interest—animals, getting work done, weather, and plants—provide a framework upon which the pupil organizes his knowledge. They also form a basis for further exploration. This broad plan of organization leads to systematic understandings rather than to massed, unrelated factual information. (For a detailed list of concepts presented in *All Around Us*, see the Index to Concepts, pages 78-80.)

The scientific content of these broad centers of interest in *All Around Us* has been determined by four types of analysis:

1. An analysis of environment to determine the problems of living that are dependent upon science for intelligent solution
2. An analysis of these problems to determine the principles and concepts of science that provide solutions
3. An analysis of the age and grade level of the child at which these principles and concepts may be developed experientially and scientifically
4. An analysis of these principles and concepts to provide the basic experiences upon which learning must be based

Little of the actual content of *All Around Us* is new or strange to the pupils, and gaps in the pupils' background can usually be filled in quickly and efficiently. For example, few of the animals discussed in the first unit are animals that the pupils have not seen, talked about, or heard about in stories. Consequently, the basic subject matter is usually familiar; and the manner of viewing the subject matter, making inferences, and generalizing from it, provides the new element. The pupil is guided in the organization of his information through comparing

(1)

This is the double page from the original. A solid presentation of typographic information to be read linearly.

But let us look at this from a different perspective. Who is the design geared towards? To 30-year-old parents in Berlin-Mitte? Or rather 50-year-old teachers at a problem school? What viewing habits and what kind of sense of respectability is it catering to? Is the design cool or inappropriate? And: Do your own taste and prejudices get in the way of your evaluation?

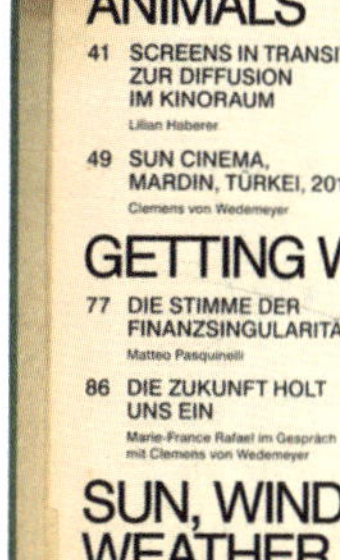

INTRODUCTION

ÜBER CLEMENS VON WEDEMEYERS FILME *BIG BUSINESS* UND *MUSTER*

Zoltán Kékesi

In *Occupation* (2002) von Clemens von Wedemeyer filmt ein Kamerateam die Versammlung einer größeren Menschenmenge. Wir sehen die Inszenierung einer Protestszene. Die „occupation" im Titel meint aber weniger diese Menschenansammlung und ihre Besetzung eines öffentlichen Ortes, sondern vielmehr den Apparat des Films und seine Art, ein Gelände und gesellschaftliches Geschehen für seine Zwecke zu vereinnahmen. In *Occupation* kommt die Produktion von Bildern des Protests beinahe einem Akt der Unterdrückung gleich: Das Erzeugen der Szene unterwirft Statisten einem hierarchischen Verhältnis des Inszeniertwerdens, das sich durch Sprache konstituiert und über Technologien des Sehens, Befehlens und Sichtbarmachens vermittelt. Von Scheinwerfern geblendet und unter dem Eindruck der Geräuschverstärkung agieren die Statisten als eine verwirrte, vom Filmapparat unter Kontrolle gehaltene Menschenmasse. *Occupation* ist ein Film über die Produktion eines Films und über das Filmemachen als Beruf, in dem beide Hauptbedeutungen des Wortes „occupation" – Beruf und Besatzung – zum Tragen kommen. Die Arbeit thematisiert das Film- oder Kunstschaffen als Beruf und darüber hinaus die Berufsausübung in ihrem Bezug zur Ausübung von Macht. Berufliche Arbeit bedingt und etabliert gesellschaftliche Verhältnisse, und *Occupation* handelt davon, dass diese Beziehungen Machtgefüge sind. Darüber hinaus „okkupieren" Filmbilder selbstverständlich auch unseren Geist, und in diesem Sinn erfasst das filmische Vereinnahmen gesellschaftlicher Beziehungen, so wie es in Clemens von Wedemeyers Werken vorgeführt wird, ebenso das Film- und Kunstpublikum. Seine neuere Arbeit *Muster* (2012) behandelt ebenso wie *Big Business* (2002) ausdrücklich solche Fragen von Widerstand und Macht, Film, Bild, Kunst und Beruf. Beide entstanden an Orten, die Schauplätze besonderer gesellschaftlicher Verhältnisse waren und sind. Was heißt es nun im jeweiligen Kontext, Filmbilder zu erzeugen, welche die Logik der „Okkupation" überwinden?

2002 drehte Clemens von Wedemeyer mit Strafgefangenen ein Remake von Stan Laurels und Oliver Hardys *Das große Geschäft* (1929). Die Kulisse der Neuverfilmung war ein „Idyll", das ihm die Haftanstalt Waldheim in Sachsen zur Verfügung stellte.

In ihrer klassischen Slapstick-Komödie spielen Laurel und Hardy zwei Christbaumverkäufer, die bei strahlendem Sonnenschein einem Vorstadtbewohner einen Tannenbaum andrehen wollen. Als der Mann ihnen eine Abfuhr erteilt, entwickelt sich eine Auseinandersetzung, an deren Ende das Haus des Mannes und das Auto der beiden Vertreter zertrümmert sind. Schauplatz der Neuverfilmung ist ein Gefängnis, in dem die Häftlinge als Teil der Verbüßung ihrer Strafe lebensgroße Häuser bauen, wieder abreißen und danach erneut aufbauen. Indem von Wedemeyer hier sein Remake dreht, lässt auch er die Häftlinge ein Haus bauen und wieder abreißen. Was bedeutet es, das an einem Ort zu tun, an dem Menschen einem Zwang zur Arbeit unterliegen? Die Entstehung des Films reproduziert den Gefängnisalltag der Häftlinge, macht aus dem Zwang aber das Erlebnis, eine Rolle zu spielen und am Dreh mitzuwirken. Strafgefangene stellen sowohl das Ensemble, als auch das Kamerateam. Ethisches Anliegen der Verfilmung von *Big Business* ist es einerseits, die Häftlinge zu unterstützen, die alltäglichen Zwänge zu überwinden und sich in einem schöpferischen Prozess zu entfalten. Andererseits erzeugt der Film Bilder, die sich mit dem Schauplatz und mit den von ihm hervorgebrachten und vorausgesetzten gesellschaftlichen Verhältnissen auseinandersetzen. Im Zuge des Remakes nehmen sowohl die klassische Komödie als auch ihre Neuinszenierung vielfältigere, neue Bedeutungen an.

Diese Neuverfilmung von *Das große Geschäft* ist eindeutig keine Komödie. Zerstörung, im Original wichtigste Quelle des Humors, wirkt hier schnell beklemmend. Das Unbehagen kommt zum Teil daher, dass das Haus, das für das

5

(2)

We can quickly conclude that the example on the right is not suitable as teaching material.
But if the design aims to trigger a debate on the topics of "fake news" and "tabloidization of content" by raising awareness of the power of design that exists around us among teachers and students, we might make a different judgment call.
The "cheap" design is almost too well-crafted and thus appears like an intellectual pastiche of "cheap" – at least for an experienced designer. But without any insider knowledge of the design, we are none the wiser.

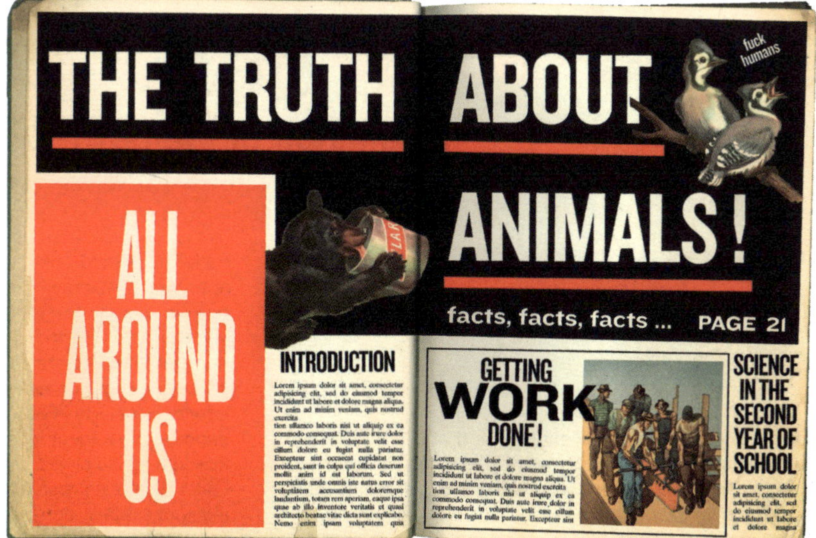

(3)

And what about this? The simplicity, combined with the volume, plus the colors of the sky and of blood: Could this be a textbook written by Christian fundamentalists?

(4)

This example illustrates the entire dilemma in which trendy design from the 2010s found itself: The target group of hipsters not only forgave everything, but also yearned for maximum allure (what might the receptive behavior look like today?).

To laypeople uninvolved in design, it appears to have been commissioned by a religious sect on drugs: wonderfully eerie – or just "pretty ugly."

Whether or not you agree with my evaluations: You can see the power of visual rhetoric. But you can also see that we must always also judge design quality based on the criteria of intention and impact.
(eds.)

(5)

← 18–19

008

Definition of the term "Design"

→ E2 ––

Bibliographic information for further details:
"Wörterbuch Design," Michael Erlhoff,
Tim Marshall (eds.); Birkhäuser Verlag, Basel, 2008;
[in German]
ISBN 978-3-7643-7738-0

Text source:
Summary of an extract from the entry on
"design" (authors: Michael Erlhoff, Tim Marshall)

In their dictionary entry, Michael Erlhoff and Tim Marshall emphasize that design is irrevocably involved in social processes. That is why precisely observing social reality forms a basic design requirement – this includes determining the developments, trends, and tendencies within society. But if this is the case, then design must also continuously re-establish itself and conduct qualitative research. An important approach that has emerged over the last decades entails a holistic view of design that extends beyond the mere focus on signs and composition.
Another finding states that design does not exist as an exclusive discipline, but instead constitutes a profession to which interdisciplinarity is essentially intrinsic. Design is hereby also criticizing the linear logic and one-sidedness of traditional academic disciplines. Design has the ability to convey, to make visible, it presents an integrative power and is therefore indispensable in complex social and economic processes.
(eds.)

← 18–19

009

Definition of the term “Rhetoric”

→ E2 ––

Rhetoric (from the Greek rhetor, or “orator”) is the art of speaking. Specifically, it refers to planned or intuitively developed techniques of effective speaking, with the goal of convincing the audience of a statement. Applied rhetoric provides the means to achieve this. It includes systems such as “the five production phases of a speech” (finding arguments, structuring the presentation, preparing the linguistic presentation, memorizing the presentation, giving the public presentation with the aid of verbal and non-verbal tools). There are also other descriptions of types of oration and parts of a speech. All of this information is based on the findings that have been acquired since Greek antiquity. Aside from applied rhetoric, the topic includes the theory of rhetoric, which analyzes the tools used to convince the audience. This means that a dual task is inherent to rhetoric – it is both oratory and an academic discipline. Detailed descriptions of the aspects of rhetoric mentioned here and many others are available on Wikipedia: https://en.wikipedia.org/wiki/Rhetoric and offer an introduction before delving into more in-depth specialist literature if desired. (eds.)

009.1

Declaration by Design: Rhetorik, Argument und Darstellung in der Designpraxis

→ E2 ––

Bibliographic information:
“Design als Rhetorik,” Gesche Joost, Arne Scheuermann (Eds.); Birkhäuser Verlag, Basel, 2008; [in German]
ISBN 978-3-7643-8345-9

Text source:
From the chapter: “Declaration by Design: Rhetorik, Argument und Darstellung in der Designpraxis (1985),” Richard Buchanan;
page 49, line 01 – page 50, line 09; continuing from page 51, line 24 – page 52, line 08;

The quoted original text underlines my arguments on pages 16 – 17. It features many footnotes that are not included here. I recommend reading the entire chapter in the original. (u.v)

/ Declaration by Design: Rhetoric, Argumentation, and Presentation in Design Practice (1985)

If there is one central topic in the science of design, then this is surely communication. Both directly and indirectly, communication and its related topics have started more discussions on design theory and practice than any others. And I am not only referring to graphic design, in which communication obviously plays a crucial role, and in which the concepts of classic rhetoric have in the meantime been applied and produced promising results, but also to design in the wider sense – ranging from industrial and product design to architecture and urban planning, and for which there is not overarching theory of rhetoric. It may not be apparent at first glance, but communication and rhetoric are unfolding a significant influence within this extended sphere on the way we understand things made for human usage. For example, let us look back at the numerous studies on design from the last decades in the fields of history, sociology, aesthetics, and the cultural sciences: While these were not explicitly rhetorical, they do venture into the area of rhetoric by touching on topics such as the influence of the designer and the design's impact on the group of consumers or society. These studies also address the core aspect of rhetoric when they delve into the design process itself, with the influence of the personal attitudes, values, or design philosophies of the respective designers or the way in which the social aspects of organization, management, and company culture define design. On top of this, if examinations of design aesthetics view form not only as a value in itself, but also as a tool for entertaining, teaching, and conveying information – or simply as a tool to produce the appearance required to achieve a desired effect –, then we can also call these studies rhetorical because they conceptualize design as a mediating authority between design and the intended audience. (…)

Design as rhetoric
Communication is commonly understood as a way in which a speaker prepares arguments and presents these using appropriate words and gestures, with the aim of convincing an audience. The aim lies in stirring up a certain belief in the audience, either regarding the past (in legal rhetoric, for example), the present (as in the rhetoric of a eulogy or ceremonial address), or the future (as in political rhetoric). The speaker delivers reasons to adopt a new stance or act in a new way. In this sense, we can designate rhetoric the form of art used to design society, influence the path of individuals and communities, and establish new behavioral patterns. In the wake of the rise of technology in the 20th century, it was discovered that humanmade objects could also hold the remarkable power to achieve something in this way: By having designers face an audience of potential users – whether with something as simple as a plow or a new type of hybrid seed, or something more complex, such as a lightbulb or a computer –, they directly influenced the actions of individuals and communities. They managed to alter views and ideals and shape society on a surprisingly fundamental level. This constitutes a previously unrecognized form of persuasion, a type of communication that has existed for a long time but was never fully understood, or examined from the viewpoint of human control, as had always been the case in rhetoric for communication in the area of language. (…) /

← 18–19

010

Visuell-verbale Rhetorik

→ E2 118, 118.1

Bibliographic information:
"Design als Rhetorik," Gesche Joost, Arne Scheuermann (Eds.); Birkhäuser Verlag, Basel, 2008; [in German]
ISBN 978-3-7643-8345-9

Text source: chapter "Visuell-verbale Rhetorik (1965, 2007)," Gui Bonsiepe; pages 31 – 33

Gui Bonsiepe (*1934) is a German designer and design theoretician. He taught at universities including the Ulm School of Design (1960–1968). The article quoted here gives examples that refer to the list of visual/verbal figures. The book is recommended for more in-depth reading on the topic. (eds.)

ʹ(...) The theorem from the 18th century states that rhetorical figures are merely decoration or added embellishments, and that simple, dehydrated information alone is what counts, allowing the recipient to absorb the information without the use of falsifying rhetorical figures. This theorem presumes that human communication is possible without rhetoric – which must be proven. Rhetoric-free, quasi aseptic communication leads to the breakdown of communication, to non-communication. For graphic designers, pure information is an abstraction anyway. The process of rhetorical infiltration already starts at the moment in which they design the information, making it tangible on a sensory level.

The linguistic background

For graphic design, it can be helpful to build a bridge between verbal rhetoric and visual rhetoric; because during the process of designing the information – an undefined, certainly problematic fundamental term –, the verbal and visual components unfold a reciprocal effect. One could formulate the hypothesis that visual communication cannot exist without a linguistic substrate. Visual communication is embedded in language and always takes place against a linguistic background – either explicitly or implicitly. Graphic design, on its part, unveils language in the retinal space as text, particularly typography.

Note on the catalog of visual/verbal figures

In the following, I will list a series of visual/verbal rhetorical figures originally defined in 1964 during a seminar at the former Ulm School of Design. This work, in turn, is founded on the semiotic articles of Tomás Maldonado, which are based on Peirce and Morris. Under the influence of French semiotics, which does not seem to exist for all contributions by Peirce and Morris, semiotics has verbalized itself and thereby lost a significant portion of its analytical potential. Maldonado writes: "Occasionally, certain histories of the semiotics of structuralist delineation convey the impression that only de Saussure and Hjemslev existed in the space that separates Peirce from Barthes and Greimas. This casts a shadow on the contributions to semiotics made by neo-positivism." This attempt, presumably the first, to systematically apply the conceptual distinctions of verbal rhetoric to the area of visual communication, and on top of this, to create new distinctions, remained an isolated undertaking. A rhetorical approach can still contribute to a deeper understanding of the phenomena with which designers grapple in their daily creative work.

List of visual/verbal figures:

ANALOGY
A verbal comparison is transferred to the visual area using semantically equivalent signs.

METONYMY
Verbally displayed content (meaning) is illustrated by means of other content with which a direct relationship exists, e.g., cause instead of effect, tool instead of result, creator instead of creation.

SYNECDOCHY
A part stands for the whole.

SPECIFICATION
A visual sign is accompanied by the minimal amount of text needed to make it understandable and narrow it down semantically. The name of the product's company is often used.

FUSION
A visual sign is integrated into a supersign due to its formal characteristics. The syntactic link suggests a semantic link.

PARALLELISM
Visual and verbal signs refer to the same object.

ASSOCIATIVE TRANSFER OR CONVEYANCE
One of a series of verbal signs is picked out to illustrate the ideas tied to it (associative context).

METAPHORICAL REVERSAL
The tension between the primary and secondary meaning is exploited in such a way that the visual signs illustrate the original meaning, take it literally, so to speak.

TYPOGRAM (OR ILLUSTRATIVE TYPOGRAPHY)
The meaning of a sequence of typographic signs is illustrated by the signs themselves. The text is essentially connected to typographic signs.

UNDERSTATEMENT
A verbally communicated understatement is illustrated visually.

EXAGGERATION
A meaning is visualized by means of signs, the content of which extends beyond the commonly seen dimensions.

VISUAL-VERBAL NEGATION
The meaning of a word sequence is illustrated using the visual opposite.

VISUAL-VERBAL COMPARISON
Two forms of content (meanings) are compared visually by means of verbal conveyance.

EXEMPLIFICATION
A verbally displayed meaning is illustrated in a visual way.

VISUAL LIST
Sequencing semantically linked picture elements creates the visual equivalent of a verbal list.ʹ

← 20–21

011

Die fünf metakommunikativen Axiome

→ E2 --

Bibliographic information:
"Read + Play," Ulysses Voelker; Verlag Hermann Schmidt Mainz, 2015;
ISBN 978-3-87439-868-8

Text source:
Page 128, 2nd column, line 06 – page 129, 1st column, line 21

I have summarized the five metacommunicative axioms by P. Watzlawick in the book "Read + Play – Einführung in die Typografie." (ed.)

In English available as:
"Pragmatics of Human Communication," Paul Watzlawick, Janet Beavin Bavelas, Don D. Jackson; W. W. Norton & Company, New York City, 2011;
ISBN 978-0393710595

ʹThe five metacommunication axioms*

In 1967, Paul Watzlawick, Janet H. Beavin and Don D. Jackson (Mental Research Institute Palo Alto, USA) examined human communication and summarized some of their findings in five axioms. These make up the following theoretical principles:

1) Since communication starts with the awareness of another person, it is impossible to refuse this communication, for example by not speaking and not gesticulating. Even "non-behavior" is a type of behavior. This brings us to the first metacommunication axiom:

"You cannot not communicate."

2) There are two levels of communication: content and relationship. The content level purely constitutes the flow of information, while the relationship level conveys how the sender wants the recipients to understand this information. The relationship level determines how the content is received. This leads to the second metacommunication axiom:

"Every instance of communication contains a content aspect and a relationship aspect, in such a manner that the latter determines the former and is therefore a metacommunication."

3) Communication is interaction. Every participant must provide an underlying structure for the exchange of messages. This is called the "punctuation of communication processes." This definition describes a triadic scheme, according to which "impulse – reaction – reinforcement" form a repetitive chain. This brings us to the third metacommunication axiom:

"The nature of a relationship is conditional on the punctuation of communication flows on the part of the partner."

4) Humans communicate on a digital and analog level. The digital level features a logical syntax, but it lacks the semantic aspect on the relationship level. Here, “digital” refers to the logic of “abstract” communication, for example when it uses words, numbers, or the alphabet. The analog level refers to relationships. It includes a semantic level, but is missing the syntax, the clear definition of the relationship between people. This brings us to the fourth metacommunication axiom:

“Human communication involves digital and analog modalities. Digital communication features a complex and varied logical syntax, but in the area of relationships, semantics are inadequate. In contrast, analog communication contains this semantic potential, but lacks the logical syntax required for clear communication.”

5) Interhuman communication is based on either equality or difference. The “symmetrical” and “complementary” aspects determine the type of interaction. We are dealing with a symmetrical relationship if differences are minimized. A complementary relationship results in hierarchical disparity. This brings us to the fifth metacommunication axiom:

“Interhuman communication flows are either symmetrical or complementary, depending on whether the relationship between the participants is based on equality or difference.”

* According to Merriam Webster, an axiom is rule or principle widely accepted as obviously true and not needing to be proved.

010
011
012
012.1

← 20–21

012

Different ways of reading

→ E2 ––

Bibliographic information:
“Lesetypografie,” Hans Peter Willberg,
Friedrich Forssman; Verlag Hermann Schmidt, Mainz, 1997;
[in German]
ISBN 978-3-87439-800-9

In this fundamental work, typographer, university professor, and author Hans Peter Willberg (1930–2003) describes the different types of reading. I have briefly summarized them here. (u.v)

1. Linear reading
The prototype for this type of reading is a novel. Absorbing the content in a linear way allows an individual to read without interruption and with the greatest possible reading comfort, as a novel generally contains a large amount of text.

2. Informative reading
Prototypes for this type of reading include newspapers, but also non-fiction books and guidebooks. Informative reading entails quickly moving, or even leaping, from one piece of information to the next. These texts are generally shorter, which makes them easier to absorb them.

3. Differentiating typography
Prototypes include scientific work. Here, readers prepare themselves for complex matters that are structured in a sensible way and by level of meaning. Differentiating typography is designed for experienced readers who are used to being guided by design nuances.

4. Typography for selective reading
Prototypes for this type of reading include all kinds of reference books, such as textbooks or cookbooks. This typographical offering for rather impatient readers is characterized by quick orientation and high reading comfort.

5. Typography for consulting reading
The classic prototype for this type of reading is the encyclopedia. Text entries tend to be short. Because of this, and due to the high number of entries in a publication, typographical measures such as particularly small fonts are acceptable.

6. Typography according to steps of meaning
Prototypes of this genre include publications in which the textual structure is particularly important. The spectrum ranges from books for new readers through to poetry collections.

7. Activating typography
Prototypes of this type of reading include magazines that aim to motivate readers to read actively. Activating typography is also used in advertising.

8. Orchestrated typography
This genre does not have a specific prototype; it is used in all kinds of artistic or onomatopoeic typography in which type and content form an expressive connection. (u.v)

012.1

Lesen – Ein interdisziplinäres Handbuch

→ E2 ––

Bibliographic information:
“Lesen – Ein interdisziplinäres Handbuch,”
Ursula Rautenberg, Ute Schneider (Eds.);
De Gruyter Verlag, Berlin, 2015; [in German]
ISBN: 978-3-11-027551-3

e-ISBN (PDF): 978-3-11-027553-7
e-ISBN (ePub): 978-3-11-038128-3

The manual is divided into four main chapters. The first chapter discusses research perspectives, methods, and theories. Representatives of different disciplines offer their insight here: cognitive neurosciences, cognitive psychology, artificial intelligence, communication sciences. The second chapter takes a closer look at the questions raised. It focuses on reading comprehension and linguistic perspectives. The third chapter is dedicated to the medium of books of the past and their development. A special contribution analyzes the media of newspapers and magazines. The manual concludes with a chapter that revolves around the challenges of the present – in the form of digital reading media.

With its mixture of theoretical penetration and practical focus, this manual represents a special contribution to all research questions revolving around the topic of reading. (eds.)

←24–25

013

Zeichen – Einführung in einen Begriff und seine Geschichte

→ E2 --

Bibliographic information:
"Zeichen. Einführung in einen Begriff und seine Geschichte," Umberto Eco; edition suhrkamp, Berlin, 1977;
[in German]
ISBN 978-3-518-10895-6

Umberto Eco (1932–2016) was an Italian writer, philosopher, and media scientist. He taught semiotics at the University of Bologna and composed countless publications on the theory and practice of signs, literature, art, and on the aesthetics of the Middle Ages. His novels brought him global fame (e.g., "The Name of the Rose"). (eds.)

In chapter B, I presented the example of Mr. Sigma, who needs to consult a doctor in Paris. Eco further elaborated on this example, stating that one should not succumb to the misconception that the wealth of signs that impact us in everyday life are specific to industrial civilization. Moreover, Mr. Sigma would still live in a universe of signs if he lived in an isolated rural area, for example. In this case, he would find more of these signs in nature, indicating whether or not it will rain soon, how ripe the fruit in his fields are, and whether they are infested with parasites. He could differentiate between poisonous and edible mushrooms and could most certainly interpret other natural phenomena. Because the isolated Mr. Sigma would have learned to "read" the signs of his rural environment. He would have internalized its prevailing interpretation systems that enable the decoding of natural data – which then turn into cultural data. But if this is the case, then it would be clear what a book on the term "signs" would need to focus on: "all signs." (u.v)

013.1

Scents of the City

→ E2 119, 120

Bibliographic information:
"Scents of the City,"
Isabel Naegele, Ruedi Baur;
Lars Müller Publishers,
Zurich, 2004;
ISBN 3-03778-012-6

Text source:
(1) Page 05, lines 1 – 4;

Image sources:
front cover, pages 18 – 19, 190 – 191, 254 – 255, 268 – 269

On the editors: Isabel Naegele is a designer, professor and head of the "Designlabor Gutenberg" research institute at Hochschule Mainz – University of Applied Sciences.

Ruedi Baur is a designer, professor and head of the "design2context" research institute at Zurich University of the Arts. (eds.)

(1) ′ "Scents of the City" is simply a collection of small samples and patterns from the great variety of public spaces in a city; it is the result of an obsession of many years, an obsession to collect things that, to us, visually denote a "city", the flavour of which is so difficult to describe with words. (...) ′

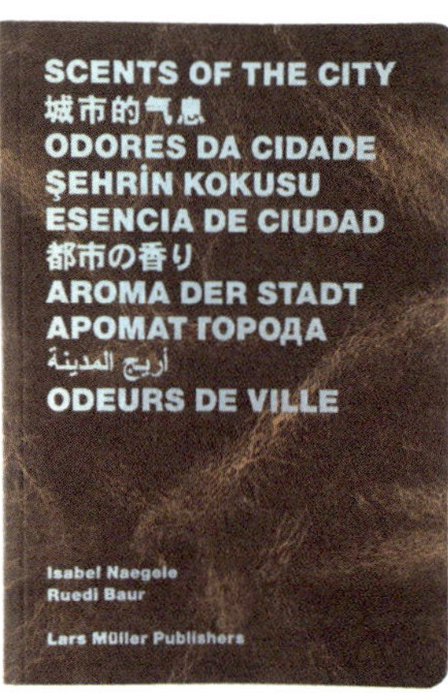

← 24–25

014

Einführung in die Semiotik

→ E2 --

Recommended book:
"Einführung in die Semiotik," Umberto Eco;
Verlag W. Fink UTB, Paderborn, 2002;
[in German]
ISBN 978-3-8252-0105-0

Information on the author: see reference 009

013
013.1
014
015

This book presents the basics of semiotics. Eco's exploration of culture as communication is considered the foundation of the entire field of humanities. Literary studies, sociology, philosophy, rhetoric, art, and advertising all rely on the insights of semiotics. Eco has the unparalleled ability to convey the study of semiotics in an understandable manner – despite the complexity of the subject. (eds.)

← 26–27

015

Otto Neurath – the Language of the Global Polis

→ E2 121, 121.1, 122, 123, 124

Bibliographic information:
"Otto Neurath – the Language of the Global Polis," Nader Vossoughian;
NAi Publishers, Rotterdam, 2008;
ISBN 978-90-5662-350-0

Image sources:
right: illustration of page 83

bottom:
illustration of page 68

Otto Neurath (1882–1945) was a pioneer in the history of the information age. He was a philosopher, sociologist, and urban planner. As co-founder of the Vienna Circle and the "Unity of Science" movement, as an employee of wide-ranging personalities such as Adolf Loos, Rudolf Carnap, Cornelis van Eesteren, Gerd Arntz, László Moholy-Nagy, and Le Corbusier, he played an important role in a range of disciplines, including architecture, philosophy, economy, urban development, and design. In this book, the author Nader Vossoughian presents him as a modernist theoretician who strived to promote participative and interactive approaches to social and urban planning.
Neurath's work is exemplary and raises the question of the extent to which we should take his commitment as an example when it comes to linking social, creative, and informative aspects and thereby viewing design in a holistic way. (eds.)

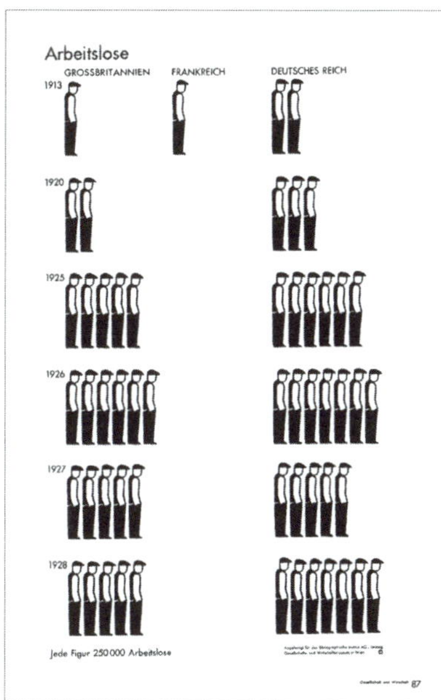

Wohndichte in Großstädten Bewohner auf 200 m² verbauter Fläche (Gebäudegrundstücke einschl. Strassen, ausschl. grosser Parkanlagen)

Einige Weltstädte

Die deutschen Großstädte über 400 000 Einwohner

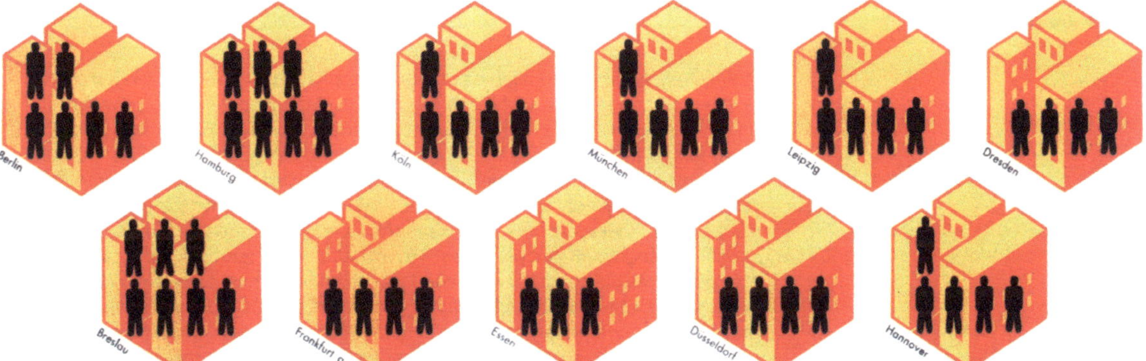

015.1

Die Transformierer – Entstehung und Prinzipien von Isotype

→ E2 125

Bibliographic information:
"Die Transformierer – Entstehung und Prinzipien von Isotype," Marie Neurath, Robin Kinross, Brian Switzer (Eds.); Niggli Verlag, Salenstein, 2017; [in German]
ISBN 978-3-7212-0950-1

Text sources:
(1) Publisher's text on the inside front cover;
(2) Page 128, line 6 – 34

Marie Neurath (1898–1986) was a German illustrator. Together with her husband Otto, she was responsible for devising the Isotype program.

(1) ʼ Isotype (= international system of typographic picture education) was developed in the 1920s by Viennese sociologist and philosopher Otto Neurath as a method for visualizing data and context. The educational goal lay in transforming complex matters into an intelligent and compressed form – that was easy to understand and interesting – by means of representational images and symbols. This volume, equipped with many illustrative examples, addresses the principles of Isotype, the task of 'transforming' – as was the contemporary term – and Marie Neurath, Otto Neurath's most important employee and companion. It focuses on an essay composed by Marie Neurath in 1986, shortly before her death, which has never been published in German. It gives the reader authentic insights into the processes of developing and designing Isotype diagrams and the work methods of Otto Neurath and his team, as well as its continuation after Neurath's death. In other articles, British typographer and publisher Robin Kinross writes about Marie Neurath, both as a person and as a significant figure in design history, and reflects on the legacy and future of Isotype in visual communication. ʼ

(2) ʼ (...) William Playfair (1759 – 1823) is generally considered to be the founding father of the graphic presentation of statistics. The Scotsman with a wide range of interests wrote a number of publications, most notably "The Commercial and Political Atlas" (1786) and "The Statistical Breviary" (1801). Allegedly, this was the first instance of using diagrams and other visualization options to display economic and social data. While Playfair was a lonesome precursor, two factors would later come together in the 19th century to enable the widespread use of graphic statistics: The growth of statistics as a tool to examine and learn and the increased use of pictures, made possible by new printing techniques, delivered entertainment and education for the emerging masses of readers. It therefore seems natural that graphic methods to present statistics were developed for every imaginable topic by the end of the 19th century. We can differentiate between two types of graphic statistics, both for the early period and (more clearly) for the more recent past and present: on the one hand, graphic presentations for statisticians, which help them analyze data, and on the other hand, infographics for a wider audience to make information understandable that is otherwise too extensive. Isotype clearly belongs to the second category: The goal of enabling widespread comprehensibility is based on the decision to use graphic symbols instead of non-iconic graphic means. (...) ʼ

015.2

Design von Frauen

→ E2 126

Bibliographic information:
"Design von Frauen," Charlotte Fiell, Clementine Fiell; Dumont Verlag, Cologne, 2019; [in German]
ISBN 978-3-8321-9967-8

Text source:
Back cover of the book

ʼ The most significant designers of the last 100 years. Ray Eames, Marianne Brandt, Coco Chanel, or Zaha Hadid – they and many other designers created the icons of design and architectural history. In over 100 brief profiles, this book discusses their life journeys and outlines the ways in which the innovative work of these women shaped their era and inspired the generations of designers that came after them. With pioneering designs from the fields of architecture, furniture, products, cars, graphics, textiles, and fashion design. ʼ

015.3

HerStories in Graphic Design: Dialogue, continuity, self-empowerment. Women graphic designers from 1880 until today

→ E2 ––

Bibliographic information:
"HerStories in Graphic Design: Dialogue, continuity, self-empowerment. Women graphic designers from 1880 until today," Gerda Breuer, Katja Lis (Eds.); Jovis Verlag, Berlin, 2023; [ENG/GER]
ISBN 978-3-8685-9773-8

Editor Gerda Breuer is a professor of art and design history (em.) and teaches at the University of Wuppertal.

Katja Lis (design) is an entrepreneur and co-founder of "DBF designbüro frankfurt."

Text source: publisher's blurb

ʼ The history of graphic design has been written largely without women. But if we take a look beneath the surface of this narrative, the influence they have had on the field's development from the very start becomes visible: Female graphic designers formed their own traditions, established dialogical references, served as role models for other women, set up networks, endeavored to empower themselves. Without simply wanting to add extraordinary women to the established narrative form, Gerda Breuer highlights the formats – women's collectives, workshops, and today's digital platforms – that women resorted to in order to make themselves visible. Not only renowned graphic designers such as Ljubow Popowa, Änne Koken, Ethel Reed, and Sarah Wyman Whitman played important roles here, but also completely unknown collectives. Breuer shows that their significant contributions were erased, devalued, ignored, or pushed into the background in the history of reception. In light of current challenges to the traditional canon, integrating these contributions into design history is long overdue. ʼ

← 26–27

016

Signs and Symbols

→ E2 127, 127.1, 127.2, 128

Bibliographic information:
"Signs and Symbols: Their Design and Meaning", Adrian Frutiger, Watson-Guptill, New York City, 1998, ISBN 978-0823048267

Adrian Frutiger (1928–2015) was a renowned Swiss font designer, designer, and author.

015.1
015.2
015.3
016
016.1
017

The book is a standard work that deals with the origin, usage, and meaning of signs. Countless images – including morphological tables – reveal the foundation of our cultural socialization. Adrian Frutiger, an internationally well-known font designer (who developed "Univers" and "Avenir," among others), takes us on a journey through history and opens our eyes to quite a few design details.

For example, he discusses the role of unprinted space in design, quoting Lao-Tse. The latter had discovered that the 16 rods (i.e., spokes) of a wheel are not all that make up the wheel. The clever division of the 15 gaps that create the wheel is crucial. He claims that the interior space, the empty space, has always played an important role in two-dimensional design. In this sense, graphic design presents parallels with architecture. This field also relies on the laws of material and space. Just like the alternative between black and white, between omitting and keeping, between material and space, represents one of the most significant factors for creativity in all artistic endeavors. (eds.)

016.1

Proust and the Squid

→ E2 128.1, 129, 130

Bibliographic information:
"Proust and the Squid: The Story and Science of the Reading Brain," Maryanne Wolf, Harper Perennial, 2008;
ISBN 978-0060933845

Available in German:
"Das lesende Gehirn," Maryanne Wolf; Spektrum Verlag, Heidelberg, 2009;
ISBN 978-3-8274-2747-2

Maryanne Wolf works as a professor in the field of child development at Tufts University (USA).

In her book, Maryanne Wolf examines the reciprocal effect between reading and writing abilities and between culture and civilization. According to her research, childhood learning processes and the circumstances that determine these processes shape an individual's lifelong further development. She writes that learning to read starts with telling or reading a story to a baby. A child's later reading success largely depends on how often this took place during the first five years of life. An invisible class society already starts to form during this early stage of life – divided into families that place great value on the spoken and written word, and those that cannot afford or do not want to. Studies have shown that the average middle-class child hears 32 million more spoken words in their environment than a child of the same age from an underprivileged background.
An understanding of the preliminary stages of reading can help remedy this social rift, since technologies are available that visualize the process of learning to read. This makes it clear that words learned from books play the most important part in training the brain. The repertoire of many five-year-old pre-school children includes around 10,000 words from books. A large part of these consist of morphological versions of word roots they have already learned.
A child learning the word "sail" will quickly and easily understand all forms derived from this word, such as "sailing" or "sailed" or "sailboat." But bigger vocabulary is not the only important factor. In fact, the syntax or grammatical structure in books is also crucial, even if it does not necessarily transfer into their everyday language. Expressions such as "Jenseits des Tales" ("across the valley") or "da sie kein Sonnenstrahl je berührte" ("since not a single ray of sun ever touched her") require quite a lot of flexibility. Few children under the age of five heard the word "da" as used in "da sie kein Sonnenstrahl je berührte," where it serves as a conjunction and in the grammatical function of "because." Children learn this meaning through context, according to Wolf. This enriches the syntactical, semantic, morphological, and pragmatic aspects of their language development.
(eds.)

← 28–29

017

Decodeunicode – Die Schriftzeichen der Welt

→ E2 131, 132, 133

Bibliographic information:
"Decodeunicode – Die Schriftzeichen der Welt," Johannes Bergerhausen, Siri Poarangan; Verlag Herman Schmidt, Mainz, 2011; [in German]
ISBN 978-3-87439-813-8

www.decodeunicode.org

Image sources:
(1) front cover of the book;
(2) screenshot from https://decodeunicode.org/en/u+03105 (see sources)

Johannes Bergerhausen (*1965) is a German professor, designer, and typographer. He teaches typography and book design at Hochschule Mainz – University of Applied Science. The Decodeunicode project, which he brought to life with designer Siri Poarangan, entailed visualizing all of the world's characters that were listed on Unicode. They have all been collected in this book (which was also published in Japanese) and on the website decodeunicode.org. (eds.)

(1)

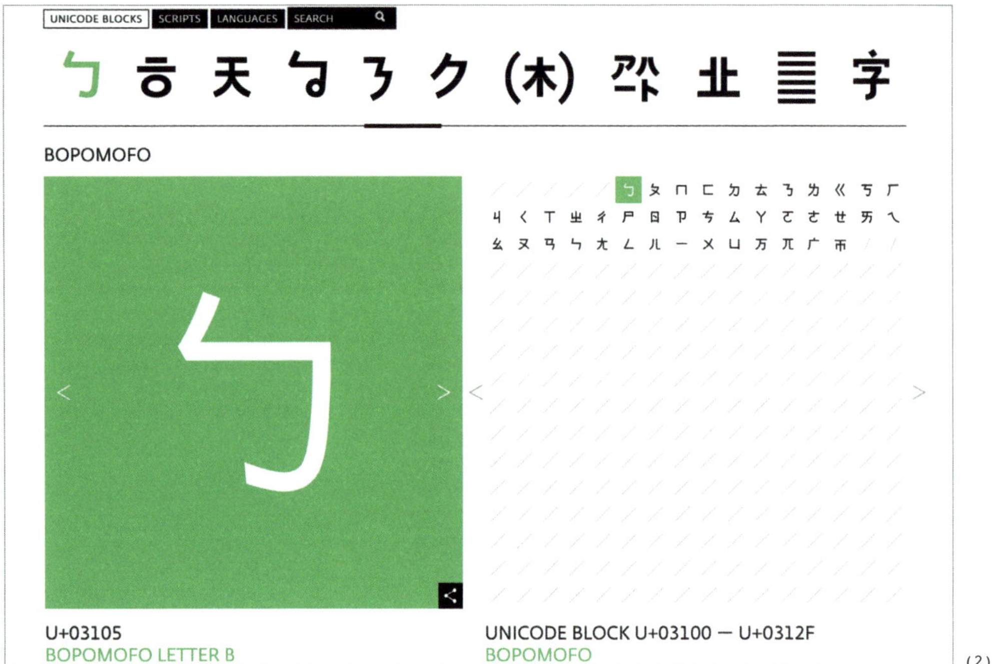

(2)

← 28–29

018

Detailtypografie

→ E2 ––

Bibliographic information:
"Detailtypografie," Friedrich Forssman, Ralf de Jong; Verlag Hermann Schmidt, Mainz, 2004; [in German]
ISBN: 978-3-87439-642-4

The book "Detailtypografie" compiles necessary knowledge for typesetters and therefore serves as a typographical reference work. It includes all orthotypographic information for the everyday work of communication designers. Countless entries ranging from "award" and "paragraph" through to "line break" and "finish" make up the tools for rules-conform use of type. (eds.)

← 30–31

019

Structuring Design

→ E2 ––

Bibliographic information:
(1) "Structuring Design," Ulysses Voelker; Niggli Verlag, Salenstein, 2019;
(EN) ISBN: 978-3-7212-0994-5

(2) "Ordnung in der Gestaltung," Ulysses Voelker; Niggli Verlag, Salenstein, 2018;
(DE) ISBN 978-3-7212-0995-2

(3) "グラフィックデザインにおける秩序と構築," Ulysses Voelker; BNN (Bug News Network), Tokyo, 2020;
(JP) ISBN: 978-4-8025-1172-8

(4) "Porzadek w projektowaniu.", Ulysses Voelker; D2D, Krakow, 2020;
(PL) ISBN: 978-83-950382-9-7

Text source: from the book's preface on page 04, lines 01 – 24

Image sources:
(1),(2),(3),(4): front cover of the respective country in which the book was published.

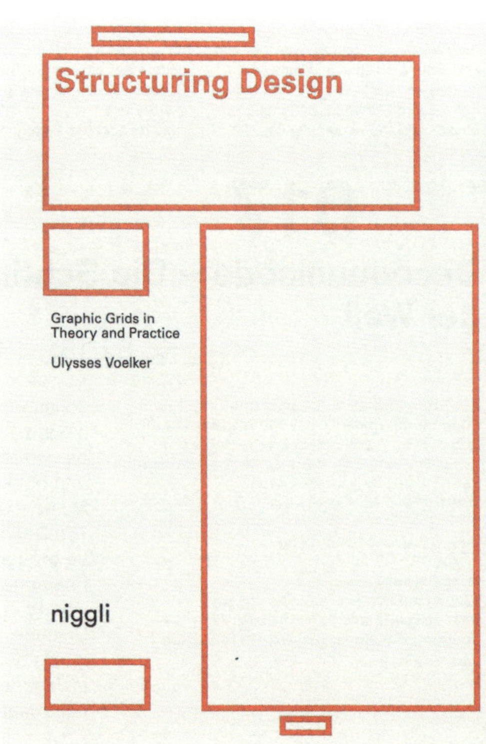

(1)

/ There are two legendary misinterpretations of the term "communication design" – the subject you are studying. The first is almost anecdotal: We contemplate the shape of telephones and smartphones. Very funny. The second interpretation is as popular as it is wrong: Many people think that our mission is to create attractive surfaces. Closer to the truth, but not good enough.
Our actions require much more than that and are therefore much more complex. Everything we do is about the "construction" of visual communication. "Visual communication" indicates the fact that there are people who want to communicate something nonverbally to other people. What these people want to say, to whom what is said should be addressed and in what way – are the topics we are dealing with. I must admit: Attractive surfaces are sometimes the issue, but not primarily. That depends very much on the communication intentions, the medium, and who finds what attractive at all. I was talking about "constructing" visual communication. But what does that mean? It means that, within the framework of the creative laws inherent in every medium, we arrange, systematize and create hierarchies for content, i.e. "stage" it. (...) /

This book deals with the design-related framework conditions within which we operate. It therefore comes as no surprise that one of the main topics focuses on design grids. (u.v)

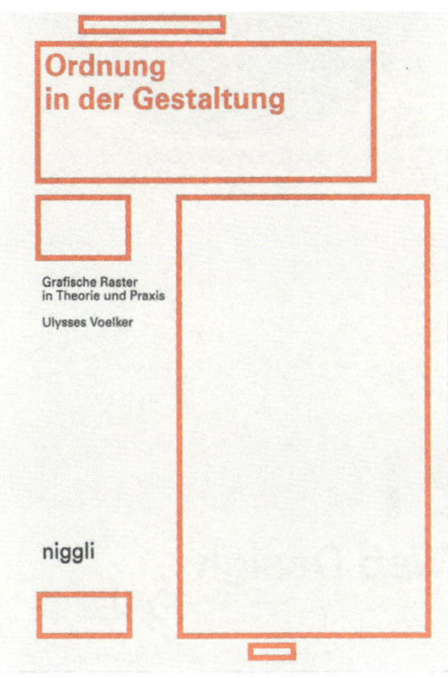

(2)

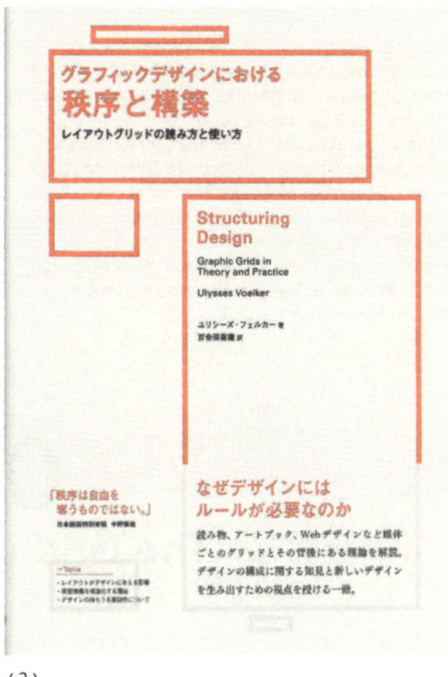

(3)

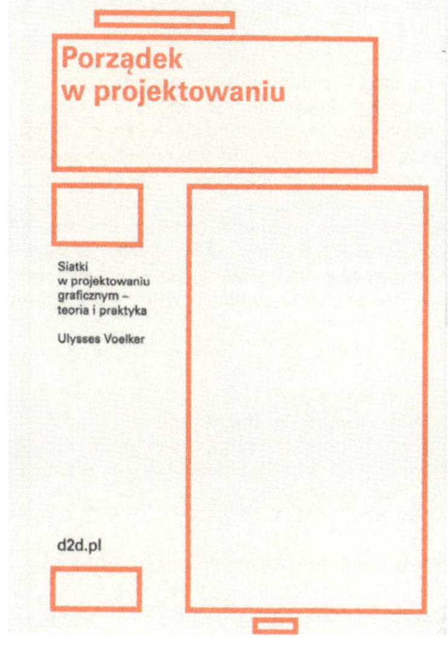

(4)

← 32 – 33

020

Orientierungssysteme und Signaletik. Führen – Finden – Fliehen

→ E2 134

Andreas Uebele has devoted over 20 years to the topic of "orientation systems and wayfinding." In his book, he investigates the ways in which systems and signs that serve purposes of orientation can be integrated into their spatial environment.
In an ideal scenario, orientation systems organically tie in with the architecture through which they guide people and are unmistakable in the best sense of the word. In extreme cases, they save lives.
In his book, he presents international examples, analyzes them, and adds detailed background information, ranging from the planning process and constructive details through to fonts, materials, and costs. The book is interesting for anyone working at the intersection between design and architecture. Andreas Uebele runs a design studio in Stuttgart (uebele.com) and teaches at the University of Applied Sciences Düsseldorf.

The adjacent book cover presents the relationship between space and surface in an effective way. By playing with our perception, it creates "retention effects," since the reader must do their part to decode the graphic (see also Anton Stankowski, pages 84 – 85). Because sometimes we need to take a close look to discover the terms "finden," "führen," and "fliehen" (find, guide, flee) within the labyrinth.
(eds.)

Bibliographic information:
"Orientierungssysteme und Signaletik," Andreas Uebele; Verlag Hermann Schmidt, Mainz, 2006; [in German]
ISBN 978-3874396745

Image source: front cover of the book

020.1

Visual Coexistence. Informationdesign and Typography in the Intercultural Field

→ E2 --

Bibliographic information:
"Visual Coexistence. Informationdesign and Typography in the Intercultural Field," Ruedi Baur, Ulrike Felsing, Civic City and HEAD Genève (Eds.); Lars Müller Publishers, Zurich, 2020;
ISBN 978-3-03778-613-0;

Image source: front cover of the book

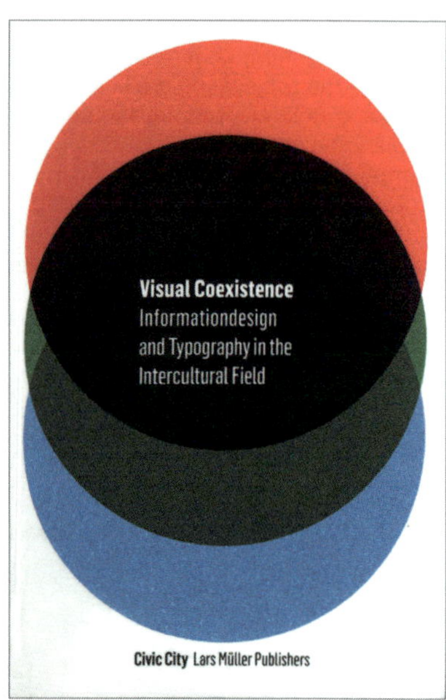

In a world of cultural diversity, designers are increasingly faced with tasks intended to respect the equality of cultures and that demand an interdisciplinary and intercultural approach to develop appropriate design solutions. That is why Ruedi Baur, Ulrike Felsing, and her team examined and analyzed visual communication from different cultural circles and devised the specific presentation principles. Their work is based on comprehensive design studies on the coexistence of Chinese and Latin as well as Arabic and Latin writing. Among other things, they focused on the conditions required not only to enable the coexistence of different scripts, but also to promote them through intercultural communication. The goal of the book "Visual Coexistence" and of many designers around the world increasingly lies in establishing a global understanding as well as preserving the wealth of languages and scripts.

A look at the front cover also proves interesting, as it demonstrates a strong signal character with its color fields. The graphic message is abstract yet clear, at least I can "read" the following (without considering the further meaning and color composition): Cultures are different and overlap at certain points, which is where something new arises. It is always worthwhile drawing conclusions based on a presumed briefing that may have preceded the design. Such deconstructions enrich one's own visual-rhetorical repertoire. (eds.)

← *32–33*

021

The Grid in Web Design

→ E2 --

Bibliographic information:
"Structuring Design. Graphic Grids in Theory and Practice," Ulysses Voelker; Niggli Verlag, Salenstein, 2019;
ISBN 978-3-7212-0994-5

Text source: page 86, lines 01 – 35

'Web design approaches are to a large extent determined by the technical conditions on which this medium is based. These – similar to our user behavior – are subject to constant change, which is very rapid, as can be seen by the growth of digital possibilities and the accompanying changes in our reading habits.
An example of this might be that it wasn't so long ago that web design only had to deal with the display options required for monitors whose size differed only slightly. The websites were inflexible: When the visible section became smaller, you had to scroll horizontally to make hidden content visible at the edge.

This uncomfortable state was soon addressed: In order to allow a grid-related adaptation to the different sizes, the layouts became "liquid". This means that as the screen width became narrower, the columns of the layout also became narrower (up to a tolerable size).
In the meantime, however, the number of devices on which websites could be accessed due to built-in browsers has increased. These should displayed without loss of information and comfort: on smartphones (portrait and landscape), on tablets (portrait and landscape), on laptops, on fixed monitors, and so on. With these requirements in mind, layouts had to be more than just "liquid". They have also become "adaptive": If the width of the layout changes, there are so-called "breakpoints" (i.e. display widths stored in the source code). If these breakpoints are exceeded or undercut, either by the end device itself or by narrowing the window, they trigger a change in the display defined in the source code. They therefore ensure that the layout changes by leaps and bounds after a phase of "liquid" narrowing – for example, when a three-column layout becomes two-column and then one-column after a certain width. This structural flexibility, consisting of "liquid" and "adaptive" control mechanisms, is called "responsive web design". (...)

← *32–33*

022

Stimulus and Response

→ E2 135

Bibliographic information:
"Structuring Design. Graphic Grids in Theory and Practice," Ulysses Voelker; Niggli Verlag, Salenstein, 2019;
ISBN 978-3-7212-0994-5

Text source:
Chapter "Stimulus, response and other phenomena," page 134, line 30 – page 136, line 17

The text source draws from the findings of communication psychologist Friedemann Schulz von Thun, which he compiled in a standard work:

"Mit einander reden 1," Friedemann Schulz von Thun;
Rowohlt Verlag, Hamburg, 2010;
ISBN 978-3499174896

'(...) If one looks around in everyday life, one comes across a first, proven communication psychological pattern: "Creating associations", a method that constitutes the essential part of advertising (together with "exemplary" and "benefit promising"). "Whether or not I move towards something or turn away from it depends strongly on the feelings the object triggers in me. The nature of the feelings in turn depends on the experiences I have made with them(...)" says the psychologist Schulz von Thun. As an example, he cites a child who received a shot from a doctor, a process that was painfully remembered by the child. A week later at the hairdresser's, the child begins to cry. The reason is that the white coat of the hairdresser reminds the child of the painful visit to the doctor (also a white coat). In communication psychology, according to Schulz von Thun, one speaks here of a "classical conditioning": certain feelings are triggered on the basis of earlier experiences of association. This is well known in advertising: it uses stimuli with positive connotations (natural landscape, good-looking and mostly young humans, beautiful weather, prosperity, health etc.) to create an association with products, which do not have necessarily something to do with the positive stimuli mentioned. If this “stimulus-response” model is transferred to design, it becomes clear that designers have much to gain if they can empa-thize with the associating experiences of the recipients of a visual message: Which cultural conventions generate which expectations? How serious, for example, must a book appear so that it can be recognized as such by a certain circle of readers and at the same time be distinguished from other literary genres? When and how does a website functionally and innovatively affect a defined target group? In all cases, it is a matter of generating a predicted response from certain addressees with a targeted stimulus.

Conditioning according to the stimulus-response pattern is based on the principle of “expression” and “effect”. In verbal communication, self-expression serves to communicate something to someone and to trigger a reaction from the other person. According to Schulz von Thun, “expression” and “effect” can be in balance with each other. As an example he cites a child who has injured itself and therefore screams (“expression”). The parents rush to help (“effect”). In this example, both components are in a harmonious relationship, because the expression of real pain has the desired appeal effect. But if the same child cries now, in memory of the achieved effect, with (conscious or unconscious) calculation also without serious cause, then it uses the tested “expression” to achieve an actually not appropriate “effect” – namely that the parents rush to it worriedly too. There is then no balance between “expression” and “effect” – the expression is corrupted for the sake of effect.
The example sounds almost banal in its obviousness, and yet the behavior to achieve an “effect” (whether appropriate or not, whether conscious or not) determines our daily lives. This is especially true for designers, because achieving “effect” with an “expression” is part of their core business. Therefore, it is worth asking: Where does the corruption of the “expression” of design begin in order to achieve “effect”? How can harmony be created between “expression” and “effect” in design?
And: Doesn't the diversity of people demand ever new forms of “expression” in order to create an individual “effect”?

If the latter were true, designers would have to have a large repertoire of creative expression. A consistent creative “style” could only be justified if one were to communicate comparable content to the same target group in the same continuous manner – this is true sometimes, but everyday graphic design usually is more diverse. “Differentiation” instead of “uniform mush” must therefore be the solution for design. (...)'

020.1
021
022
023
024

← 34–35

023

Definitions of the term “Taste”

→ E2 ––

Sources that we reference:
“Metzler Lexikon Ästhetik,” Achim Trebeß (ed.), entry „Geschmack“ by Frauke Annegret Kurbacher; Verlag J.B. Metzler, Stuttgart, 2006; [in German] ISBN 3-476-01913-6

https://de.wikipedia.org/wiki/Geschmack_(Kultur) (see sources)

The entry in “Metzler Lexikon Ästhetik” views taste, or sense of taste, as a reference to the person who perceives aesthetics and their aesthetic experience as the subject. Taste is based on a sensory-intellectual, critical, and cultivatable ability to perceive and differentiate. It either refers to the senses or the mind, but could be understood as a force that mediates between the two. The entry considers the potential similarity as well as the potential difference in taste as a basic problem, citing the expression that there is no accounting for taste. The crucial factor in discussing this question is whether it is assumed that taste is timeless or if the object to be judged as aesthetic varies historically in the same way that taste does and the conventions to which it refers.

If we take a look at Wikipedia, it is remarkable to note that on the article's homepage, at the time of researching in 2023, a warning appears regarding the potential absence of neutrality. The Wikipedia discussion page on this topic reveals different interpretations. The article itself defines taste as a cultural and aesthetic ideal that everyone should aspire to. Hans-Georg Gadamer is quoted, according to whom taste belongs to the humanistic guiding principles alongside education, judgment, and sensus communis (sanity and reason). The article then refers to different philosophers and their definition before it circles back to the core statement: “De gustibus non est disputandum” (There is no accounting for taste). The interpretations on the topic of taste move between the poles of aesthetics and morals. The sociological classification attributes a distinctive trait to taste, which differentiates between good (high) or bad (low) taste. According to Pierre Bourdieu, lifestyle and taste are tied to the social class to which an individual belongs. (eds.)

Sources we refer to:

https://en.wikipedia.org/wiki/Marketing (see sources)
https://en.wikipedia.org/wiki/Market_research (see sources)

← 36–37

024

On marketing. On market research

→ E2 136, 137, 138, 139, 140

The term **marketing** refers to the area of a company dedicated to presenting the company products or services to potential customers, with the goal of motivating them to make use of them. Since the start of the 21st century, marketing has formed part of holistic corporate management from a business standpoint, satisfying the needs and expectations of customers and other interest groups (stakeholders) with its market orientation. This holistic view has altered our understanding of marketing: Beyond the technique of influencing potential customers to encourage a purchase, the definition now extends to all facets of a company, including the leadership concept, management, personnel, but also procurement and production. In business administration, marketing is part of an overall corporate process. For details on the complex associated questions and theories, readers are advised to refer to specialist literature (Gabler Wirtschaftslexikon). The corresponding Wikipedia offers an initial overview (https://en.wikipedia.org/wiki/Marketing).

Market research constitutes one of the most important marketing tools. As a sub-discipline of empirical economic and social research, it works with different areas using different methods. This means it serves as a process based on scientific methods that objectively observes market activity as well as a company's environment in order to gain insights that, in turn, are incorporated into marketing decisions. Market research works in the form of the systematic collection, analysis, and interpretation of data related to the relevant markets of clients, with the goal of evaluating options to influence the market. In principle, the aim of market research – in whatever role and for whatever purpose it is used – lies in gathering data with a relevant value from which behavioral guidelines and strategies can be derived. For companies, the aim is always to optimize the sales strategy and thereby increase company profits. More information is available in specialist literature (such as the economic lexicon “Gabler Wirtschaftslexikon”) and on the Wikipedia page: https://en.wikipedia.org/wiki/Market_research. (eds.)

← 38–39

025

Typesetting

→ E2 ––

Text source:
https://en.wikipedia.org/wiki/Typesetting
(see sources)

ʼ (...) Typesetting is the composition of text for publication, display, or distribution by means of arranging physical type (or sort) in mechanical systems or glyphs in digital systems representing characters (letters and other symbols). Stored types are retrieved and ordered according to a language's orthography for visual display. Typesetting requires one or more fonts (which are widely but erroneously confused with and substituted for typefaces). One significant effect of typesetting was that authorship of works could be spotted more easily, making it difficult for copiers who have not gained permission.

During much of the letterpress era, movable type was composed by hand for each page by workers called compositors. A tray with many dividers, called a case, contained cast metal sorts, each with a single letter or symbol, but backwards (so they would print correctly). The compositor assembled these sorts into words, then lines, then pages of text, which were then bound tightly together by a frame, making up a form or page. If done correctly, all letters were of the same height, and a flat surface of type was created. The form was placed in a press and inked, and then printed (an impression made) on paper. Metal type read backwards, from right to left, and a key skill of the compositor was their ability to read this backwards text. Before computers were invented, and thus becoming computerized (or digital) typesetting, font sizes were changed by replacing the characters with a different size of type. In letterpress printing, individual letters and punctuation marks were cast on small metal blocks, known as "sorts," and then arranged to form the text for a page. The size of the type was determined by the size of the character on the face of the sort. A compositor would need to physically swap out the sorts for a different size to change the font size. During typesetting, individual sorts are picked from a type case with the right hand, and set from left to right into a composing stick held in the left hand, appearing to the typesetter as upside down. (...) ʼ

← 40–41

026

Phototypesetting

→ E2 ––

Text source:
https://en.wikipedia.org/wiki/Phototypesetting
(see sources)

ʼ (...) Phototypesetting is a method of setting type which uses photography to make columns of type on a scroll of photographic paper. It has been made obsolete by the popularity of the personal computer and desktop publishing which gave rise to digital typesetting.
The first phototypesetters quickly project light through a film negative of an individual character in a font, then through a lens that magnifies or reduces the size of the character onto photographic paper or film, which is collected on a spool in a light-proof canister. The paper or film is then fed into a processor, a machine that pulls the paper or film strip through two or three baths of chemicals, from which it emerges ready for paste-up or film make-up. Later phototypesetting machines used other methods, such as displaying a digitised character on a CRT screen. The results of this process are then transferred onto printing plates which are used in offset printing.
Phototypesetting offered numerous advantages over the metal type used in letterpress printing, including the lack of need to keep heavy metal type and matrices in stock, the ability to use a much wider range of fonts and graphics and to print them at any desired size, and faster page layout setting.

Background
Phototypesetting machines project characters onto film for offset printing. Prior to the advent of phototypesetting, mass-market typesetting typically employed hot metal typesetting – an improvement introduced in the late 19th century to the letterpress printing technique that offered greatly improved typesetting speed and efficiency compared to manual typesetting (where every sort had to be set by hand). The major advancement presented by phototypesetting over hot metal typesetting was the elimination of the metal type altogether which was not needed by the offset printing process. This cold-type technology could also be used in office environments where hot-metal machines (the Linotype, Intertype or Monotype) could not. The use of phototypesetting grew rapidly in the 1960s when software was developed to convert marked up copy, usually typed on paper tape, to the codes that controlled the phototypesetters. (...)
In retrospect, cold type paved the way for the vast range of modern digital fonts, with the lighter weight of equipment allowing far larger families than had been possible with metal type. However, modern designers have noted that compromises of cold type, such as altered designs, made the transition to digital when a better path might have been to return to the traditions of metal type. Adrian Frutiger, who in his early career redesigned many fonts for phototype, noted that "the fonts [I redrew] don't have any historical worth...to think of the sort of aberrations I had to produce in order to see a good result on Lumitype! V and W needed huge crotches in order to stay open. I nearly had to introduce serifs in order to prevent rounded-off corners – instead of a sans-serif the drafts were a bunch of misshapen sausages!" (...) ʼ

026.1

Weingart: My Way to Typography

→ E2 ––

Bibliographic information:
"My way to typography," Wolfgang Weingart; Lars Müller Publishers, Zurich 2000; [ENG/GER]
ISBN 3-907044-86-X

Text sources:
(1) Page 460, lines 05 – 07,
(2) Page 460, lines 23 – page 461, lines 10,
(3) Page 492, lines 20 – 30

Wolfgang Weingart (1941–2021) was a German typographer who worked and taught in Basel. His experiments with phototypesetting, which gradually replaced hot metal typesetting in the 1960s, are considered pioneering. (eds.)

(1) ʼ (...) In the middle of the seventies I finally finished with lead type for good an turned my attention toward transparent lithographic materials. (...) ʼ

(2) ʼ (...) My posters have two distinguishing characteristics: an irregular, wide border that holds the individual images together, framing the composite picture, and rough, fragmented dot screens. The low resolution of the screen reveals the photomechanical process, unseen in most reproductions that stimulate a smooth continuous tone: this is the interesting aspect of the posters' graphic quality. I discovered the effect by accident. Like the pixel of an electronic transmission, the dot of a photomechanical screen is invisible, yet essential, building unit of an entire process. When shifting and superimposing screen films with the copy camera, I recognized during certain movements, the intrinsic aesthetic quality of the dot. I invented a method to fabricate unlimited dot structures and patterns, a mother-father system, from two single standard screens: a twenty-percent line screen and a graduated gray tone screen. The layering of these textures developed into the trademark of my posters. (...) ʼ

(3) ʼ (...) Unlike type composition in lead, I did not have to rely on any outside manufacturing sources to realize my work with the film montage technique. From the sketch to press all aspects of the technical procedure required the same basic materials: film, developer, fix, a copy camera and ultimately, a metal printing plate. In comparison to letterpress, the photolithographic process was more flexible because of its simplicity. Freed from the constraints of standard sizes and positionable anywhere on the film in any orientation, typography became unlimited and my work was enriched by this technique. (...) ʼ

← 42–43

027

025
026
026.1
027

Technology’s influence on typography, updated 2024

→ E2 ––

(1)

(2)

Trend 01:
Kinetic typography

Kinetic typography refers to an animation technique. Letters, words, or word fragments illustrate a message in moving images in the form of an animated choreography. (eds.)

Image sources:
(1),(2) https://vimeo.com/301953910 (see sources)
Designer: Lucas Hesse (Hamburg)

(3)

Trend 02:
Multi-script font systems

More and more fonts are emerging whose repertoire includes adaptations for other font systems. One example of this is the Adelle Sans family. It exists as a slab serif font (Egyptienne) and as a monospaced version. Latin script supports pan-European, pan-African, and Vietnamese languages, covering around 400 languages in total. In addition, designers around the world have joined forces to design Arabic, Armenian, Chinese, Cyrillic, Devanagari, Greek, and Thai equivalents to Adelle Sans. Versions for Georgian, Hebrew, and Lao were released in 2021, followed by Bengali. The Korean variant appeared in 2023. (eds.)

Image source:
(3) Screenshot detail, from: https://www.type-together.com/2021-adelle-sans-multiscript (see sources)

Trend 03: Variable fonts

An “OpenType-Variable-Font” is a font file that behaves like several files. This technology comes with many advantages. A variable font is a single binary file with a highly compressed file size, meaning it requires little storage space and low web font bandwidth. As a result, it offers efficient packaging of embedded fonts, faster provision, and quicker loading of web fonts. The option of dynamically selecting user-defined instances within the space of design variations opens up new perspectives for new types of responsive typography that can adapt in order to depict dynamic content in the best possible way depending on the device, screen orientation, or even the reader’s reading distance.
The technology behind the variable fonts is officially called “OpenType Font Variations.” (eds.)

Image sources:
(4),(5) Screenshots, from:
https://v-fonts.com/ (see sources)

(4)

(5)

Trend 04: Variable fonts in corporate design

The example of the dynamic logo for "Amsteldok," created by the Netherlands-based agency VBAT (Amsterdam), demonstrates the potential that variable fonts harbor for the development of font systems in corporate design (see link on the right). After all, the trademark of variable fonts is the ability to export an infinite number of intermediate steps. For the corporate design of "Amsteldok" (a multi-purpose event venue in Amsterdam), the agency went one step further. Thanks to interactive tracking methods and mapping, the order and appearance of the logo changes in line with the heat sources recorded by a camera in the reception area. This means that every body contributes to the changing logo composition. (eds.)

Sample images below:
https://www.underconsideration.com/brandnew/archives/amsteldok_logo_variations.png

https://sites.wpp.com/wppedcream/2019/designand-branding/identity_and_branding_-_identity_design_medium_100s/amsteldok-a-wpp-campus

Trend 05: Alternative glyphs

These days, a set of glyphs offers more than just standard characters. Font designers are increasingly producing alternative glyphs to extend the pallet of typographic options. This enables the creation of specific typography-based visual identities. The major advantage of this: The alternative glyphs can be made available together with a font's usual set of glyphs as a single font file (as OpenType). The images below show two variants of the "Maxi Round" letter M by the type foundry abcdinamo. (eds.)

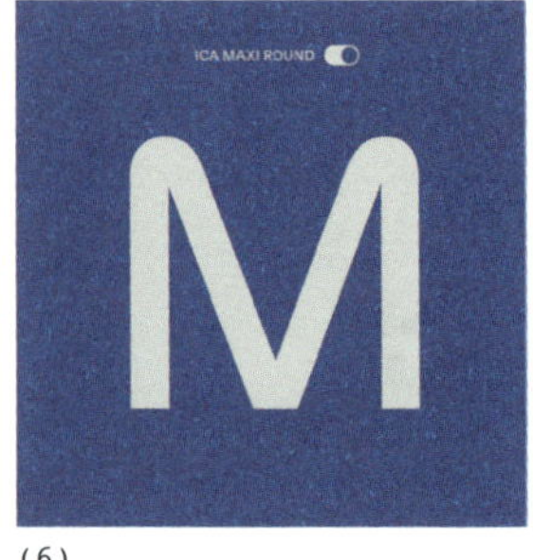

(6)

(7)

Image sources:
(6),(7) Screenshots from https://abcdinamo.com/custom/ica-london (see sources)

Trend 06: AI-generated fonts

Artificial intelligence has enabled a whole new breadth of variants in the area of font design. In this case, a user-friendly DCGAN (Deep Convolutional Generative Adversarial Network) is used. A "Generative Adversarial Network" stems from the image, video, and text area. It consists of two components trained through a contradictory process. The generator (also called "the artist") learns how to create images that appear "real," while the discriminator (called the "art critic") checks their authenticity. The continuous interplay of data creation and verification is an ongoing learning process for both components. The goal lies in increasingly approximating supposed authenticity.
GANs are also used in the area of fonts. One example is the "AI Font" created by the Viennese "Process Studios." The font was developed from a rudimentary collection of lines into a legible font in 500 steps. (eds.)

(8) AiFont Stufe 009

Latent Workspace

(9) Ai Font Stufe 427

Image sources:
(8),(9) Screenshots from https://aifont.process.studio/ (see sources)

Trend 07: 3D text rendering

Faster processors and the increased capacity of computer programs, paired with well-developed open-source programs, allow designers and type creators to craft objects (and also letters) that appear three-dimensional with minimal effort. In particular, the availability of tools such as DirectX and OpenGL had advanced and simplified the development and rendering of digital 3D elements. (eds.)

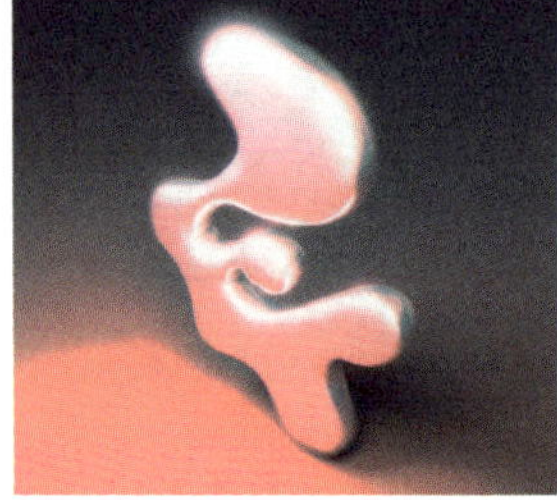

(10)

(11)

Image sources:
(10) Screenshot from: http://benjaminschupp.de/html/work.html
Designer: Benjamin Schupp, Mainz
(11) own graphic, Designer: M.Schmitz (see sources)

Current and future trends:

Documenting trends in technological developments in a book is really a fruitless endeavor – at least if you are claiming to report on the absolute state of the art. By the time this book is released, new trends, and perhaps even groundbreaking developments related to artificial intelligence, will have emerged. Nonetheless, keeping a snapshot of these can be helpful because it exemplifies the rapid speed at which technology develops. And meta trends are becoming visible – at the moment, we are seeing a trend towards more flexibility, made possible by AI and machine learning. Some developments will turn out to be gimmicks, while others will form an indispensable component of design. All in all, the transitions between font and image have grown more fluid over the last years. And positive developments have emerged in terms of ethics, as demonstrated by "Multiple Script Fonts": Aside from the envisaged wealth of variants, flexibility in typography also aims to garner respect towards non-western cultures. Twenty years ago, it was still assumed that everyone should be able to speak and read English. What was still a niche product back then has now become a company-wide management issue – harmonizing font styles in all global scripts. (eds.)

Bibliographic information:
„Max Bill: Typography, Advertising, Book Design," Max Bill; Niggli Verlag, Salenstein (ed.), 1999;[ENG/GER]
ISBN 3-7212-0341-0

Text source:
page 10, lines 01 – 21

Image sources:
from the book, (1) page 236 – catalog cover, 1945;
(2) page 218 – poster, 1932

Max Bill (1908–1994) was a Swiss architect and multi-talented artist (sculpture, industrial design, painting, graphics, typography). He served as the first rector of the Ulm School of Design from 1953 to 1956. Later, he taught at the University of Fine Arts Hamburg, among others. He wrote numerous books. Here, I am quoting from the catalog and showing two pieces of his work. His graphic language (diagonals, grid orientations, typography, composition) prove Max Bill to be one of the outstanding protagonists of modernism.(eds.)

← 44–45

028

Max Bill: Typography, Advertising, Book Design

→ E2 141, 142

ʹMax Bill was active in nearly every area of design. "Art" and "Design" were universal concepts for him, and in his work he lived out the tradition of the Bauhaus in this regard as well. Bill is known as a painter and as a sculptor, and less so as an architect. Consistent with his fidelity to the Bauhaus ideology, architecture was the highest league for him, although he himself was not able to realize many buildings as an architect. Although the architecture of Max Bill has enjoyed increased attention of late, his work is connected first and foremost with his sculptural works and his painting. Least known of all is that Bill earned his living in the early years almost exclusively by working in the areas of advertising, typography and book design. Yet already early on his commissions were concentrated around the architectural field. In the thirties Bill was called upon by the Zurich architects of the Modern for each and every propaganda objective related to the "Neues Bauen." He carried out the ideas of the "Wohnbedarf ideology" in type and image and he designed the outdoor signage for the urbanist Zett-Haus and for the Corso Varieté theatre. The present publication makes clear that much of what the Swiss avant-garde accomplished around 1930 with regard to habitation- and housing-reform, had been visualized for the public in the atelier "bill-zürich reklame." Compared to other European centers, this unique monopoly by one graphic designer lends a high documentary value to the commercial graphic work of Max Bill comprehensively published here for the first time. Max Bill was not one the creators of the "New Typography" – he was nearly a generation younger than El Lissitzky. He was, however, among those who consequently developed the "New Typography." (...)ʹ

(1)

(2)

Bibliographic information:
"Typography," Emil Ruder;
Niggli Verlag, Salenstein,
1967, 6th edition, 1996;
[ENG/GER]
ISBN 3-7212-0043-8

Text source:
from the introduction,
page 5, lines 24 – 36

Image source:
front cover of this book

Emil Ruder (1914–1970) was a Swiss typographer and teacher. He influenced generations of designers – not just in the German-speaking region – with his teachings, expert commentary, and books. The bilingual book "Typography" (eng/ger) is considered a standard work on design. The book's cover is also legendary, as it depicts the essence of typography – it portrays order and sensuality. (eds.)

← 46 – 47

029

Emil Ruder: Typography

→ E2 --

' (...) Typography work comes with two prerequisites: consideration for the acquired findings and an open-minded sense of new aspects. As is well known, reaching positions lead to self-satisfaction. That is why it is more necessary than ever before to develop experimental typography in such a way that the workshop turns into a laboratory and experimental facility to prevent typography from remaining stuck in its long known basic principles. The willingness to create lively and contemporary work must never wane; doubts and restlessness serve as good foundations to keep from slipping into the convenient path of least resistance. (...) '

Bibliographic information:
"Schweizer Grafik," Richard Hollis;
Verlag Birkhäuser, Basel, 2006;
[in German]
ISBN 978-3-7643-7267-5

Text source:
(1) Page 09, line 10 – page 10, line 03;
(2) Page 11, lines 15 – 43;

The book describes why the Swiss style – which emerged in the 1950s – achieved such global success and influence and depicts countless works from well-known graphic designers. (eds.)

← 46 – 47

030

Die Schweizer Grafik

→ E2 143, 143.1, 144, 144.1, 145, 145.1, 146, 147

(1) ' (...) At least three factors make up the Swiss style: The first is the country's positioning and its neutrality in the center of Europe. The second is the language. Northern Switzerland, which includes the two largest cities of Basel and Zurich, shares a language with Germany, where progressive ideas were proclaimed, attacked, and defended in the 1920s. The third factor is a combination of cultural phenomena. These include the Swiss interest in precision and craftsmanship, the greatly admired Swiss educational and practical vocational training system, the openness of Swiss museums, and the people's joy in a "graphical culture." The Swiss love flags, to name an example. Every city and every municipality has its own flag, as a reminder of the people's identity, even within the canton. The same applies to each of the 22 cantons of the Swiss Confederation. They also have crests, which appear on official documents, on advertising spaces in tram cars, or on uniforms. Today, the emblems and colors of the flags, derived from the battlefields of the Middle Ages, appear on festive occasions. All of these are designed in a markedly graphical manner. A heraldic element, careful attention to detail, the clear, fine, and creative font and typography, and a high printing standard have contributed to the attractiveness and efficiency of the Swiss business and industrial sectors. This is not only made clear by the technical and advertising brochures of large engineering plants and pharmaceutical countries, but also by the printed products of smaller companies, such as posters, leaflets, and timetables in the tourism industry. In terms of scope and variety, the country's printing industry was at its peak for the entire 20th century. The larger cities – Basel, Bern, Lausanne, and Geneva – still have their own large-format daily newspaper; Zurich even has two. The federal authorities are actively aware of the significance of graphic design. Switzerland was the first country in the world to have its citizens' passports professionally designed. A tender generally precedes public-sector printing contracts, for example for banknotes, postage stamps, or Swiss charitable institutions; the same applies to posters for national events – and the ministry of the interior has promoted the country's interest in design for many decades by selecting and exhibiting the "best posters of the year." (...) '

(2) ' (...) This book contains many references to constructivism and concrete art. Constructivism formed the foundation for many principles of the modern movement in architecture and design. The school of thought had emerged in Soviet Russia, parallel to the political

revolution; its influence spanned Central and Northern Europe. While it proclaimed its allegiance to the "unconditional fight against art," its draw stemmed from more of an aesthetic than political nature. This became clear through a very obvious preference for geometry – emphasizing the structure of an object –, the use of full-tone color surfaces, layouts with a diagonal axis, the asymmetrical arrangement principle, and the preference of photography over drawn depictions. Concrete art enriched the constructivist aesthetic with mathematical thinking. Many of its representatives were also graphic designers, so it made sense to incorporate, along with mathematics, a model for the geometrical arrangement of a space in two-dimensional design. The fact that constructivists worked with photography also had a great influence. Photography had set itself the goal of "objectivity," meaning the direct, impersonal recording of objects and events, a facet that pervades the entire book at hand. This interest and the avantgarde's insistence on typification and precision found their natural counterpart in the Swiss mentality. (...) ʹ

← 46–47

031

Grid Systems in Graphic Design

→ E2 148

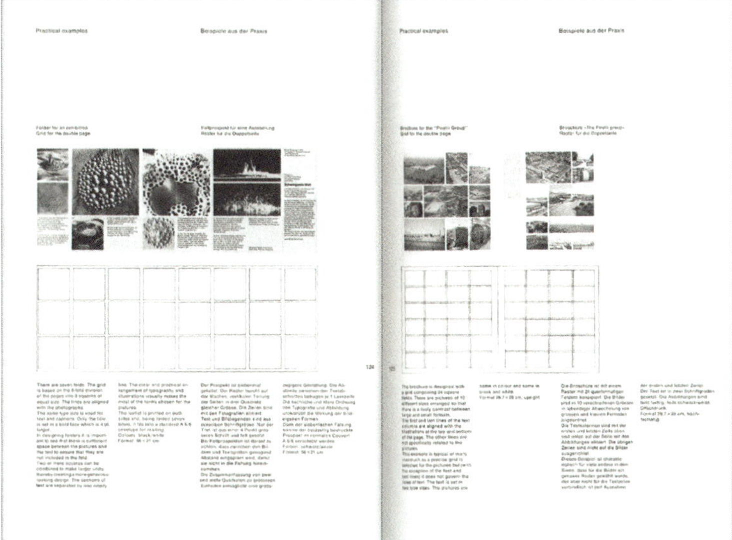

Bibliographic information:
"Grid systems in graphic design, a visual communication manual for graphic designers, typographers and three-dimensional designers," Josef Müller-Brockmann; Niggli Verlag, Salenstein, 1996; [ENG/GER]
ISBN 978-3-7212-0145-1

Text sources:
(1) Page 10, 1st column, lines 01 – 40;
(2) Page 13, 1st column, lines 16 – 27

Image sources:
front cover; pages 124 – 125

The book presented here is a classic in the area of graphic grids. There have been numerous editions since its first publication in 1981. Josef Müller-Brockmann (1914–1996) was an influential Swiss graphic designer, typographer, teacher, and author. (eds.)

(1) ʹ(...) The use of the grid as an ordering system is the expression of a certain mental attitude inasmuch as it shows that the designer conceives his work in terms that are constructive and oriented to the future. This is the expression of a professional ethos: the designer's work should have the clearly intelligible, objective, functional and aesthetic quality of mathematical thinking. His work should thus be a contribution to general culture and itself from part of it. Constructive design which is capable of analysis and reproduction can influence and enhance the taste of a society and the way it conceives forms and colors. Design which is objective, committed to the common weal, well composed and refined constitutes the basis of democratic behavior. Constructivist design means the conversion of design laws into practical solutions. Work done systematically and in accordance with strict formal principles makes those demands for directness, intelligibility and the integration of all factors which are also vital in sociopolitical life. Working with the grid system means submitting to laws of universal validity. The use of the grid system implies

- the will to systemize, to clarify
- the will to penetrate to the essentials, to concentrate
- the will to cultivate objectivity instead of subjectivity
- the will to rationalize the creative and technical production processes
- the will to integrate elements of color, form and material
- the will to achieve architectural dominion over surface and space
- the will to adopt a positive, forward-looking attitude
- the recognition of the importance of education and the effect of work devised in a constructive and creative spirit.

Every visual creative work is a manifestation of the character of the designer. It is a reflection of his knowledge, his ability, and his mentality. (...) ʹ

(2) ʹ(...) The reduction of the number of visual elements used and their incorporation in a grid system creates a sense of compact planning, intelligibility and clarity, and suggests orderliness of design. This orderliness lends added credibility to the information and induces confidence.
Information presented with clear and logically set out titles, subtitles, texts, illustrations and captions will not only be read more quickly and easily but the information will also be better understood and retained in the memory. This is a scientifically proved fact and the designer should bear it constantly in mind. (...) ʹ

Bibliographic information:
"Helvetica. Homage to a Typeface,"
Lars Müller, Lars Müller Publishers,
Zurich, 2002; ISBN 3-907044-87-8

Image sources:
front cover; double page from the unpaged book;

Text source:
from the introduction, pages 6 – 7

Author and publisher Lars Müller (*1955) deserves credit for documenting the font "Helvetica" and its meaningful as well as trivial locations of use around the world. As he phrases it so wonderfully in the book's preface, "Helvetica is the perfume of the city." (eds.)

ABCDEFGHIJKLMN
OPQRSTUVWXYZ

abcdefghijklmnop
qrstuvwxyz
ß äöü
1234567890 $&/!?%
"" ,;.-– ( ) § <> *'#

Helvetica Semibold, Max Miedinger, Switzerland
(Developed in 1957 as Neue Haas Grotesk and renamed Helvetica in 1960)

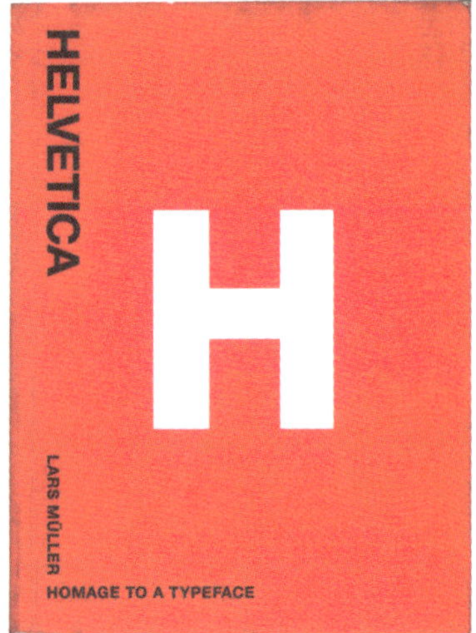

← 46–47

032

Helvetica – Homage to a Typeface

→ E2 ––

'(...) When it comes to typefaces I don't need variety. I remember as a child thinking that all cars were Volkswagens, that everybody smoked Gauloise, and that Sunday and chicken with french fries were inseparable. Here was one television channel and vacations were always in the same place. I didn't object that either. Helvetica was probably especially widespread in those days. All I can remember is the great big orange M of Migros, my family's favorite supermarket. It looked indescribably modern. From my later mentors Richard Paul Lohse and Josef Müller-Brockmann, I learned the rules and principles of matter-of-fact, functional design dedicated to content, and the quality of reduction and restriction. My preference for Helvetica was not a choice; it was a logical consequence.

Looking back, one can see that utopian intentions spurred the development of Swiss graphic design in the 50s and 60s. The undoubtedly modern and useful tools of design were meant to objectivize the aesthetic debate; people would make a better choice by means of honest, functional communication. The commercial game rules of this attitude were called information graphics. Akzidenz Grotesk was the typeface of the movement and the sign of recognition among like-minded people. The uniqueness of "Swiss Design" took shape in the design of posters and in corporate design for progressive companies. Success entailed reworking the tools of design, especially the range of typefaces, adapting them to the aesthetic Zeitgeist and to growing functional demands. Around 1957 new Grotesk typefaces came out on the market in rapid succession – Folio, Neue Haas Grotesk, Univers – their appearance more dispassionate and anonymous than that of their predecessor, Akzidenz Grotesk. Adrian Frutiger's Univers was the most independent. Its intelligent system of variations in weight and width, mapped out from the start, later also became the standard for Neue Helvetica. The Swiss Style spread swiftly and many countries adapted it to their own needs. In 1960 Neue Haas Groesk was renamed Helvetica (Latin for Swiss), a clever marketing ploy, for it ended up becoming synonymous with "Swiss Design". (...)'

Bibliographic information:
"Die Univers von Adrian Frutiger," Friedrich Friedl;
Verlag Form, Frankfurt/Main, 1998; [in German]
ISBN 3-931317-98-6

Image source: Univers 65 LT

Text source:
Page 21, line 23 – page 23, line 13

Friedrich Friedl (*1944) is a German typographer and university professor.

032.1

Die Univers von Adrian Frutiger

→ E2 ––

'(...) Adrian Frutiger's Univers was a font originally designated and designed for both hot metal and phototypesetting, in a coordinated font family of 21 fonts. For the first time in the history of fonts, these 21 alphabets were precisely designed as connected form systems. They were arranged so "compatibly" that when the fonts were mixed together, the shapes always looked like they stemmed from the same font family. This gave the typography undreamt of scope for distinguishment and contrasts, directly encouraging experiments and visualizations. When the new font was developed, it needed a name. Initially, Frutiger suggested Monde, then Europe. But as a result of Peignot's desire for international marketing, Frutiger landed on the name Universal, which Peignot then altered to Univers: a globally valid designation. Univers emerged during a third phase of developing sans-serif fonts – almost simultaneously with other successful alphabets: Helvetica (1957), Optima (1958), and Folio (1957). While Helvetica, for one, generally appeared modern, timeless, and neutral without any striking attributes (which also led to its great success), Univers exuded a factually cool elegance and rational competence. The initial considerations in implementing these systematized alphabets revolved around the problem

ABCDEFGHIJKLMN
OPQRSTUVWXYZ

abcdefghijklmnop
qrstuvwxyz
ß äöü
1234567890 $&/!?%
"" ,;.-– ( ) § <> *'#

Univers 65, Adrian Frutiger, Switzerland 1957

of the adequate and sensible width of the letter lines and their relationship with the white space. As a starting point for all alphabets, the font type was chosen that was intended for smooth typesetting and long pages of text: number 55. This font offered the most suitable ratio of black to white, of printed to non-printed parts, for the reading process. Following this, the same line width was used for all alphabets with numbers in the fifties. However, modifications were made regarding the gaps and inner spaces that lead to a semi-bold and bold image for narrow and slim fonts, and a lean look for wide fonts. This was maintained and designed consistently for all different widths. (...) /

032
032.1
032.2

032.2
Imitat und Original

→ E2 ––

Bibliographic information:
"Read + Play. Einführung in die Typografie," Ulysses Voelker; Verlag Hermann Schmidt, Mainz, 2015; [in German]
ISBN 978-3-87439-868-8

Text sources:
(1) Page 146, 1st column, line 01 – page 147, 2nd column, line 02

a a a a

Ich komme aus einem fernen Lande. Einst lebte dort ein friedliches und gottesfürchtiges Volk, das ein gütiger König regierte. Beraten wurde es von großen Gelehrten und kühnen Wissenschaftlern. Doch eines Tages kam ein edler Mann auf einem prächtigen Pferd daher geritten, den keiner je zuvor gesehen hatte.

Akzidenz Grotesk (Berthold)
7,1 pt / spacing 8,4 pt

Ich komme aus einem fernen Lande. Einst lebte dort ein friedliches und gottesfürchtiges Volk, das ein gütiger König regierte. Beraten wurde es von großen Gelehrten und kühnen Wissenschaftlern. Doch eines Tages kam ein edler Mann auf einem prächtigen Pferd daher geritten, den keiner je zuvor gesehen hatte.

Helvetica (Linotype)
6,5 pt / spacing 8,4 pt

Ich komme aus einem fernen Lande. Einst lebte dort ein friedliches und gottesfürchtiges Volk, das ein gütiger König regierte. Beraten wurde es von großen Gelehrten und kühnen Wissenschaftlern. Doch eines Tages kam ein edler Mann auf einem prächtigen Pferd daher geritten, den keiner je zuvor gesehen hatte.

Arial (Microsoft)
6,8 pt / spacing 8,4 pt

Ich komme aus einem fernen Lande. Einst lebte dort ein friedliches und gottesfürchtiges Volk, das ein gütiger König regierte. Beraten wurde es von großen Gelehrten und kühnen Wissenschaftlern. Doch eines Tages kam ein edler Mann auf einem prächtigen Pferd daher geritten, den keiner je zuvor gesehen hatte.

Univers (Linotype)
6,6 pt / spacing 8,4 pt

/ (1) Gutenberg's invention of movable lead letters enabled a multitude of different fonts that were designed and distributed over the centuries. Without being able to delve into the respective stylistic and functional influences, it must be stated that the topic of font design has always included offenses such as "copying." Designing a font that resembled existing fonts in its characteristic style and yet had a life of its own follows the entire history of fonts, and there is certainly nothing defamatory to it.

However, the question of why a new font was developed could bring quite a few stories to light that offer differing interpretations regarding their legitimacy: In 1957, Neue Haas Grotesk appeared, designed by Max Miedinger and released by the type foundry Haas'sche Schriftgießerei. It proclaims to be the answer to the commercially successful Akzidenz Grotesk (AG), distributed by its competitor H. Berthold. (...)
In 1960, Neue Haas'sche Grotesk is renamed to Helvetica for marketing reasons – reminiscent of the Swiss typography that is sweeping the world at the time. The proximity of Helvetica to "AG" is undisputed – it remains up to the observer to discover the aesthetic individuality of the respective font. In 1957, Adrian Frutiger designs Univers, the first font that is structured as a system. (...)
Arial follows in 1982, a Grotesk font designed to provide better readability on low-resolution screens. Allegedly, it surpasses Helvetica in this respect. Interestingly, the metrics of Arial correspond to those of Helvetica in a nearly identical manner. The company Monotype, who developed this font (design: Robin Nicholas, Patricia Saunders) for Microsoft, rejects all accusations of plagiarism. Microsoft has survived the accusations of plagiarism. (...) /

Segoe UI (Microsoft), 60 pt

abcd

Frutiger Next (Linotype), 60 pt

abcd

overlay of both fonts

Ich komme aus einem fernen Lande. Einst lebte dort ein friedliches und gottesfürchtiges Volk, das ein gütiger König regierte. Beraten wurde es von großen Gelehrten und kühnen Wissenschaftlern. Doch eines Tages kam ein edler Mann auf einem prächtigen Pferd daher geritten, den keiner je zuvor gesehen hatte.

Frutiger Next (Linotype/Monotype)

Ich komme aus einem fernen Lande. Einst lebte dort ein friedliches und gottesfürchtiges Volk, das ein gütiger König regierte. Beraten wurde es von großen Gelehrten und kühnen Wissenschaftlern. Doch eines Tages kam ein edler Mann auf einem prächtigen Pferd daher geritten, den keiner je zuvor gesehen hatte.

Segoe UI

After launching Windows Vista and Windows 7, Microsoft faced accusations of plagiarism again. The dispute was handled by the Office for Harmonization in the EU's internal market. In the 2000s, the former font distributor Linotype (now Monotype) objected to registration of the font as a community design. The company claimed that Segoe UI, developed by Microsoft as a system font, was identical to the Frutiger and Frutiger Next fonts distributed by Linotype (see image on the left), except for minimal differences. Microsoft defended itself, but in vain. Segoe UI's community design registration in the EU was declared void for having an "identical" typeface to Frutiger. (u.v)

Further details:
https://en.wikipedia.org/wiki/Segoe

032.3

Neue Schriften. New Typefaces

→ E2 149, 150, 151

Bibliographic information:
"Neue Schriften. New Typefaces,"
Naegele, Isabel, Petra Eisele,
Annette Ludwig (eds.);
Niggli Verlag, Salenstein, 2013;
[ENG/GER]
ISBN 978-3-7212-0892-4

Text source:
from the preface, page 13, 1. column,
line 40 – page 13, 2. column, line 17

Image sources:
(1) front cover of the book;
(2) pages 20 – 21; pages 114 – 115

Right: the font "HM Tilm,"
by Till Wiedeck, Timm Häneke

(1)

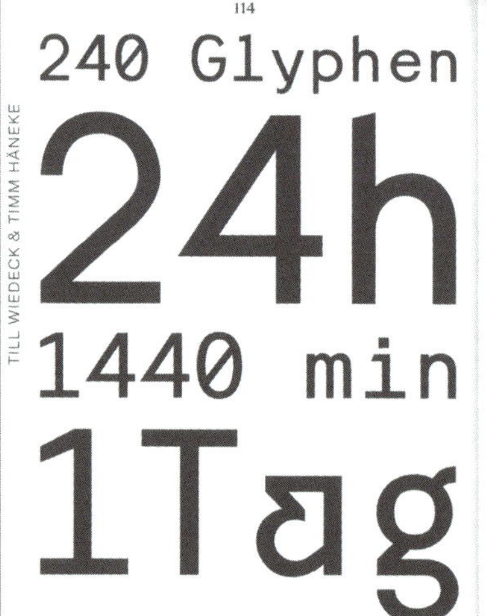

(2)

ʼ(...) In recent years, new software programmes and distribution channels have radically changed type design. This resulted in a vast increase of type production, but also a in a lot confusion. While in the 1970s just a few hundred new typefaces were published, today we can choose from tens of thousands of fonts – with upward tendency. This publication, however, shows that current type design is not a subject to random-ness or a fashionable "hype": from the rich international cosmos of typefaces it presents experimental type designs, based either on a spontaneous idea or the concept of an individually chosen design project. (...)
Seventy different type designs present an overview of current developments.

For the exhibition "Call for Type. Neue Schriften. New Typefaces." at the Gutenberg-Museum in Mainz twenty typefaces were chosen and expanded on in very personal reflections by their designers. (...)ʼ

← 46–47

033

Programme entwerfen

→ E2 --

Bibliographic information: "Karl Gerstner: Programme entwerfen," Lars Müller Publishers, Zurich, 2007; ISBN 978-3-03778-092-3

Also available in English: "Karl Gerstner: Designing Programs: Program as Typeface, Typography, Picture, Method," Lars Müller Publishers, Zurich, 2019; ISBN 978-3037785782

Text sources:
(1) from the preface, page 06, lines 05 – 30;
(2) page 13, 1st column, lines 01 – 2nd column, line 20

Karl Gerstner (1930–2017) was a Swiss graphic designer and an important representative of Swiss typography. As an advertiser, he made a name for himself with the GGK agency (Gerstner, Gredinger, Kutter). GGK operated in Switzerland and Germany and had branches in many other countries. His book "Programme entwerfen – statt Lösungen für Aufgaben Programme für Lösungen" ("Designing Programs – Programs for Solutions Instead of Solutions to Tasks") was first published by Niggli Verlag in 1964; a second edition followed in 1968. The edition presented here, from which I quoted from the preface, was published by Lars Müller Publishers in 2007. (eds.)

(1) ′ (...) After its publication in 1964, "Designing Programs" became an icon of a design belief that always viewed visual communication and design as an exact science. The systematic and rational examination forms the foundation of creative expression. The impression holds true that a growing group of followers adheres to this mindset to maintain their ability to act and judge in light of new technologies, but also trends and fashions. The theory of design has failed to support the fundamental transition towards digital thought patterns and design models with a solid superstructure. It is therefore all the more astonishing to realize that "Programme entwerfen" – written avant la letter – proves to be an exceptionally current thought pattern in the digital age. Neither the young initiators nor the author and the publisher are trying to pay their bibliophile respects to the original with this new edition. Moreover, they are insisting on the validity of the content and making a contribution to the theoretical design discourse, which has become increasingly cornered. Lars Müller. ′ (2007)

(2) ′ (...) Program as a lesson in thinking Programs for solutions instead of solutions to tasks – the subheading can also be understood as follows: Hardly any tasks have an absolute solution. The reason for this is that we cannot fully delimit the conditions. But there is always a group of solutions from which one can be selected as the best solution under certain circumstances. Describing the task forms part of the solution. This implies that we should not make creative decisions based on a feeling, but rather based on intellectual criteria. The more precise and complete it is, the more creative the work will be. The creative process is reduced to a choice. Designing means: selecting and linking elements. In this sense, design needs a method. The most suitable (that I am aware of) is the morphological method. (...) I call this scheme (...) the "morphological box" of the typogram. It contains the criteria – the parameters from top to bottom, the components in the left column, and the elements in the right – to be followed for designing word pictures, logos from letters. These are rough criteria, but they can be refined as needed as the work progresses.

Moreover: They are not only rough, but also indecisive. The component of "anything else" is the package that includes the remaining aspects, should it not be possible to cleanly break down the parameters. A lot of it is incomplete. But the process of designing the scheme yourself, of striving for perfection, makes up the work's substance. The method does not take away the effort, it merely shifts it to a different level.
Despite its shortcomings, this box contains several hundred solutions that emerge by blindly linking the components and elements. It acts as a kind of design machine. (...) ′

← 48–49

034

Psychedelische Kunst und Gestaltung der 60er Jahre. Die Hippie-Bewegung

→ E2 --

Bibliographic information: "Summer of Love. Psychedelische Kunst der 60er Jahre," Christoph Grunenberg (ed.); Hatje Cantz Verlag, Ostfildern, 2005; [in German] ISBN 3-7212-0341-0

Text sources:
(1) https://de.wikipedia.org/wiki/Hippie, 21.9.2021, 21:32 (see sources)

(2) From "Summer of Love": page 17, 2nd column, lines 16 – 45,3rd column, lines 18 – 47; page 18, 1st column, lines 16 – 21; 2nd column, lines 18 – 26

Image sources:
(1) https://commons.wikimedia.org/wiki/File:White_rabbit.JPG?uselang=de
(2) https://bit.ly/3LcNDxw (see sources)

′ (1) A hippie (also acidhead or flower child) refers to a member of the major countercultural youth movement that emerged in the USA in the 1960s. It centered around closeness to nature, criticism of consumerism, and a break with the common ideals and morals of the time, instead promoting a more peaceful and humane world. The hippie movement reached its sociopolitical peak in the peace movement against the Vietnam war, where it coined the motto "Make love, not war." Later, it split into alternative movements as well as a multitude of new subcultures and scenes, including the Goa and punk scenes. It greatly influenced the mindsets and actions of today's world, as it significantly promoted the sexual revolution, environmental protection, anti-racism, and the general dissolution of the authoritarian power structures within families and society that prevailed at the time. The style of the hippie movement also heavily influenced all aspects of mainstream culture, including fashion, film, and music (the most successful band in music history, for one, the Beatles). The movement that started in San Francisco questioned the middle-class ideals of prosperity, which it considered meaningless, and propagated an idea of life liberated from compulsions and bourgeois taboos. Compared to the protests of 1968 and the so-called "Gammler" (a derogatory term used in German-speaking countries), a stronger communal (self-realization) and sociopolitical concepts dominated here; the ideals of the movement partially overlapped. (...) The idea of a more humane and peaceful life was summed up with the keyword flower power, coined by American poet Allen Ginsberg in 1965 and often used synonymously with the hippie movement as a whole. Experimentally, these ideals were implemented in novel, often rural communes. By rejecting the existing social and political norms and values, the hippie culture picked up on certain approaches of the Beat Generation, which included William S. Burroughs, Neal Cassady, Charles Plymell, Jack Kerouac, and Allen Ginsberg. In the 1950s, the Beat Generation's nonconformism broached the topics of the peace movement, free love, drug use, and Far Eastern religions, and a reappraisal of fascism in Germany that extended all the way to the universities. Many observers claim that hallucinogenic drugs, particularly LSD, had a significant influence on the movement. Experiences from LSD trips made their way into the movement's culture, philosophy, and politics. After the substance was banned, its production shifted to underground laboratories. Countless pieces of music and films processed LSD experiences, and they also became a topic of discussion among the general public and in academia. (...) ′

'(2) (...) Some directly attributed the peak of certain art forms to revelations of LSD delirium. Leary himself said: „The LSD cult has already brought about revolutionary changes in American culture. When surveying this country's creative young musicians, it became clear that at least 80 percent of them systematically take psychedelic drugs. And this new psychedelic style didn't just add a new rhythm to modern music, but also brought new decoration to our discos, a new type of filming, a new kinetic visual art, a new literature, and it has started to compel us to review our philosophical and psychological way of thinking." On the one hand, they wanted to record the fascinating journeys into the depths of their consciousness, and on the other hand, they wanted to offer catalytic stimuli as a deeper and more expansive way of experiencing mind-altering drugs. Psychedelic drugs mainly manifest themselves visually, at least in the initial stages of a session, before they spread to other senses, such as tactile perception.

(1)

(2)

(...) Psychedelic art aims to record these fantastic visions, creatures, and landscapes. It is a visionary art in the tradition of Hieronymus Bosch, William Blake, the symbolism of the Fin de Siècle, surrealism, and certain forms of so-called outsider art. It opens the gates to new worlds, captures the flight of fantasy, and has a deeply mystical, religious character. In terms of style, psychedelic art is manifold, although most work displays a preference for the maximalist depiction of cosmological visions in formally complex, narcissistically abstract designs that are worked out into the tiniest detail. Op art, kinetic art, and light art delivered important impulses, but psychedelic artists rejected strict geometry and above all the restriction to black and white. One of the most important psychedelic painters is Isaac Abrams, who was drawn to painting through LSD. In works such as All Things Are One Thing from 1966, he combines a variety of floral, microorganic, and symbolic motifs into a lush Garden of Eden. (...) The abstract ornamentation with its oriental roots, the rediscovered decorative art of the Middle Ages, Art Nouveau, as well as the Victorian and Edwardian eras clearly served as the preferred stylistic devices. (...) Psychedelic art not only documented, visualized, and interpreted experiences of delirium, but also took on a role that artistic creations rarely hold: It serves as a sensory catalyst for fantastical, mind-altering visions and as a stimulus for creative work. (...)'

Further sources on the topic:
"Jugendkulturen in Deutschland 1950–1989," Klaus Farin, Verlag Bundeszentrale für politische Bildung, Reihe Zeitbilder, Bonn, 2006; ISBN 3-89331-671-X

One of the most important poster artists of the hippie movement is Victor Moscoso:
https://en.wikipedia.org/wiki/Victor_Moscoso

← 48–49

035

OZ, EAST VILLAGE OTHER, HOTCHA! The phenomenon of the underground press

→ E2 --

Bibliographic information:
"Protest. Eine Zukunftspraxis," Rogger, Basil, Jonas Voegeli, Ruedi Widmer, Museum für Gestaltung Zurich (eds.); Lars Müller Publishers, Zurich, 2018; [in German]
ISBN 978-3-03778-559-1

Text source: summary of a book section

The book section I am summarizing here first takes a look at Protestantism, as it was emerging around the same time as the printing press came into use. The authors describe how Protestants masterfully used the new communication options. By secretly copying publications, they were able to circumvent authoritarian censorship. Up to 4,000 copies were made of some of Martin Luther's pamphlets. Positions and counter-positions – the new possibilities served as the core tools of a propaganda and information war. As a result, it did not come as a surprise that both spiritual and secular powers were greatly interested in controlling the printed matter that made its way into the world. This interest extended to printed publications as well as the tools themselves, i.e., the printing presses. At the time, anyone who wanted to print without a printing license had to resort to clandestine means, for example fictitious printing places and publishers. Today, it is hard to say whether all of those involved identified as Protestants. However, due to their ecclesiastical, secular, or scientific counter-positions, they had taken a big risk – but one with which they were able to earn some money. According to the authors, from the middle of the 18th century, printed propaganda became a crucial method to fight for the rights of workers, lower social classes, and suppressed ethnic minorities. Well into the 20th century, access to printing presses remained one of the most significant tools for those involved in this fight. The fields of art and culture had joined the traditional political areas. Dada publications are worth mentioning here, which held both artistic and political aspirations. Not least because of this combination did reprisals stall the production processes again and again, thereby preventing regular releases of publications. During the Nazi era, underground publications constituted an important tool of resistance. This also applied to the Eastern Bloc states and dictatorships around the world. But according to the authors, counter-examples also existed, such as the propagandistic leaflets that were dropped over enemy territories during World War II. The text gives an excellent example that essentially served both sides: the Mao Tse-Tung's "Little Red Book." This publication, with countless printed editions and translations into many languages, was used as state propaganda (in China) but also as a tool for the underground resistance in other countries that were fighting for communism. Eventually, the post-war generation – forced to deal with the legacy of wars, genocide, and atomic bombing, as well as the subsequent wars – started to empower itself and use printing to their advantage. Many of the communities in urban areas contained groups that leaned left politically and were determined to communicate their visions of peaceful coexistence and other utopias – in addition, printed publications were easier to produce than ever before thanks to the process of photocopying. As a result, the 1960s saw a flood of do-it-yourself, self-published publications. This counterculture of the 1960s was eventually replaced by its successor: punk culture, which eclipsed everything that had come before it with its radicality and propelled magazine design into postmodernism overnight. The radical rejection of established politics was equally anarchistic and political. The establishment of desktop publishing also helped dissolve the boundaries of expressive possibilities and liberate production and distribution networks. According to the authors, this led to the loss of the exclusivity that was inherent to the underground press of the time. Today, everything is more accessible, everything is a niche that can be filled and cultured. What the next generation will do with this wealth of options remains open. Perhaps it will learn that it can be worth retaining the rights and power of disposition over one's own data. The technology to do so has been around for a while. (u.v)

← *48 – 49*

036

Free Press – Underground & Alternative Publications 1965 – 1975

→ E2 --

Bibliographic information:
"Free Press – Underground & Alternative Publications 1965 – 1975," Jean-François Bizot, Foreword by Barry Miles; Universe Publishing, New York, 2006;
ISBN 978-0-7893-1496-3

(1)

Image sources:
(1) front cover the book;
(2) "Berkeley Barb," USA, 1975

The book shows the way the alternative magazines produced by "Underground & Alternative Publications" influenced politics, culture, and thereby society in the 1960s and 1970s. This form of journalistic counterculture established its own structures – all publications were part of the "Underground Press Syndicate," founded in 1967, which was designed to freely exchange material. Its collaboration with artists was legendary: Robert Crumb, T.C. Boyle, and Art Spiegelman, to name just a few, published USA-wide with the Underground Press.

Aside from art and alternative fashion, the Underground Press primarily documented a lifestyle that strayed from the mainstream. Of course, this also included the famous triad of "sex, drugs, and rock'n'roll." Politically, the publications leaned left in their rejection of all parts of the establishment. This particularly became evident in the criticism of the Vietnam war, removal of taboos related to homosexuality, and questioning of traditional family structures. The magazines featured resounding names that referred to their production location: "The East Village Other," "The Berkeley Barb," "The Los Angeles Free Press," or "The San Francisco Oracle." Andy Warhol, with his magazine "Interview," was part of this movement. Other important protagonists included poet Allen Ginsberg and writer Lawrence Ferlinghetti, both of whom are considered founding fathers of the Beat Generation.

On the design:
The book's look (1) documents the graphic climate of the underground: slanting, seemingly carelessly arranged typography and an image that shows protagonists of this youth movement in their typical outfits. The cover of the "Berkeley Barb" (2) looks like a precursor of punk design: handwriting, Letraset letters, and typewriters make up the ingredients of a design that provided a counterpoint to the mainstream – resistance by design, essentially. (u.v)

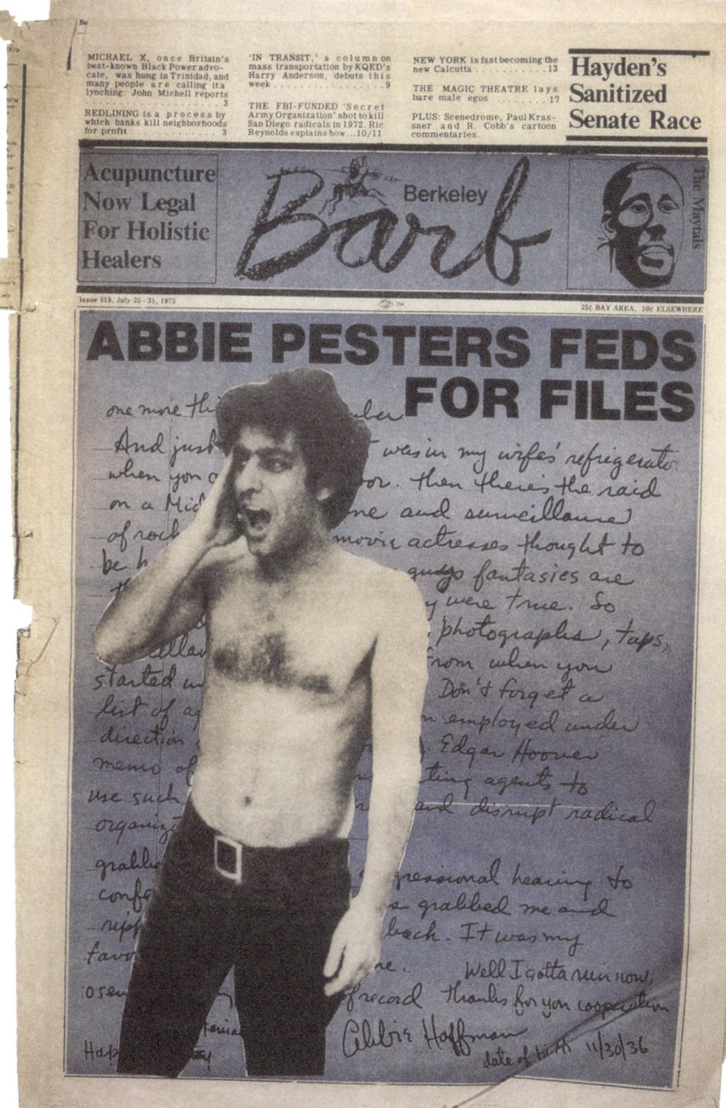

MICHAEL X, once Britain's best-known Black Power advocate, was hung in Trinidad, and many people are calling it a lynching. John Michell reports ... 3

REDLINING is a process by which banks kill neighborhoods for profit ... 3

'IN TRANSIT,' a column on mass transportation by KQED's Harry Anderson, debuts this week ... 9

THE FBI-FUNDED 'Secret Army Organization' shot to kill San Diego radicals in 1972. Ric Reynolds explains how ... 10/11

NEW YORK is fast becoming the new Calcutta ... 13

THE MAGIC THEATRE lays bare male egos ... 17

PLUS: Scenedrome, Paul Krassner and R. Cobb's cartoon commentaries.

Hayden's Sanitized Senate Race

Acupuncture Now Legal For Holistic Healers

Berkeley Barb

The Mayfairs

Issue 519, July 25 - 31, 1975

25¢ BAY AREA, 50¢ ELSEWHERE

ABBIE PESTERS FEDS FOR FILES

(2)

036.1

Under the Radar: Underground Zines and Self-Publications 1965 – 1975

→ E2 152

Bibliographic information:
"Under the Radar: Underground Zines and Self-Publications 1965–1975", Jan-Frederik Bandel, Annette Gilbert, Tania Prill (Eds.); Spector Books, Leipzig, 2019; ISBN 978-3-95905-104-0

Image source:
Double page 174/175;

With hindsight, the 1960s offered challenging framework conditions for designers – after all, computers did not exist yet, and reproducing graphic creations tended to be expensive. But these specific conditions led to a real furor of self-empowerment in design. The tools: hectographs, Rotaprint machines, typewriters, Letraset letters, handwriting, sketches, collages – in short, anything suitable for cheap reproduction was used. The limited methods available established a unique aesthetic of alternative graphics that, in combination with alternative content, was publicized through self-publishing. The book presented here introduces the scene – both in former West Germany and in an international context. One thing is certain: The "independent publishing" boom, with its risograph aesthetics, has prevailed for several years now – and has proud ancestors. (u.v)

Image sources:
Letraset and Mecanorma sheets that were and are in use.

← 48 – 49

037

Letraset letters

→ E2 153

"Letraset letters" refer to letters that were affixed to a sheet and could be transferred to a piece of paper placed beneath it by rubbing on it, for example with a pen or a special rubbing spoon. The name stems from the temporary market leader, the British company "Letraset." A number of other companies also offered this type of product, including "Mecanorma" or "Alfac specimen." This technique for visualizing type for layout purposes was particularly common before the rise of computers – so well into the 1980s – in graphic design, but also in engineering firms. The product range offered countless fonts in different sizes. Today, Letraset letters tend to be used for artistic purposes – or for media less suitable for printing (e.g., signs) and in cases that want to do without professional sheet lettering. (eds.)

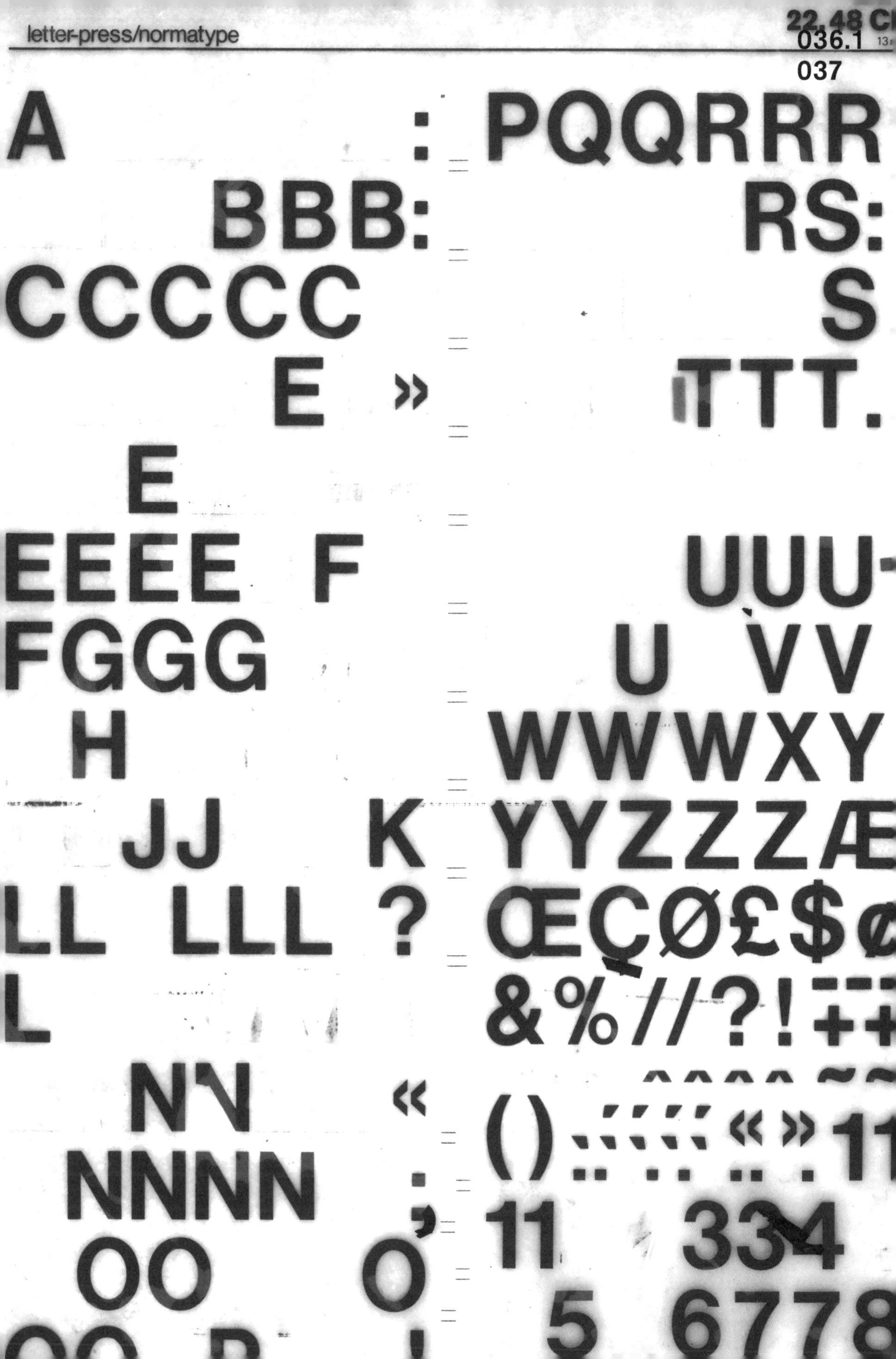

037.1

Rotaprint, Kleinoffset

→ E2 153

Text sources:
(1) https://de.wikipedia.org/wiki/Rotaprint
(see sources)

(2) https://de.wikipedia.org/wiki/Kleinoffset
(see sources)

(1) ʹThe printing press manufacturer Rotaprint was based in the former Berlin district of Wedding (today: Gesundbrunnen) and is considered a pioneer in mini offset printing. (...) ʹ

(2) ʹMini offset printing is a small-scale form of offset printing. Machines that offer this type of printing can create prints up to a format of DIN A3, which is a format of approximately 30 x 42 cm. This type of printing is frequently used for the production of book covers, forms, and commercial printing. A printing press can produce up to 15,000 prints per hour. That is why mini offset is used to produce small to medium-sized print runs of about 10,000 copies. The printing plates are made of a very thin, light metal. Instead of the metal plates common for offset printing, this method occasionally opts for paper or polyester sheets as print forms. The plates are produced either through copying or by direct lettering. (...)ʹ

← *50–51*

038

Verschwende deine Jugend

→ E2 ––

Bibliographic information:
"Verschwende deine Jugend," Jürgen Teipel;
Suhrkamp Verlag, Berlin, 2021; [in German]
ISBN 978-3-518-46318-5

Text source:
https://de.wikipedia.org/wiki/
Verschwende_Deine_Jugend (see sources)

ʹ"Verschwende Deine Jugend" is a book by Jürgen Teipel, published by Suhrkamp Verlag Frankfurt on October 17, 2001, with the subtitle "Ein Doku-Roman über den deutschen Punk und New Wave" ("A Documentary Novel About German Punk and New Wave"). In his novel, the author recorded about a hundred artists that were part of the music scene and thereby examined part of the rising youth culture of punk and the emergence of German-language punk music, New Wave, and Neue Deutsche Welle in the cities of Berlin, Hamburg, and Düsseldorf between 1976 and 1983. The title of the book is derived from the eponymous song by the Düsseldorf-based band DAF. The book starts with a four-page foreword by Jürgen Teipel. The author then divides the text into 28 chapters, chronologically arranges these into three parts, a prolog, and an epilog, and strings together – in his words – "a hundred different truths." Teipel clearly presents every anecdote as a single quote by inserting the name of the respective narrator beforehand in bold font. The either neither appears as an interrogator, nor does he provide commentary on the narratives. As conversations partners for the book, Teipel has exclusively chosen individuals from Berlin, Hamburg, and Düsseldorf. Almost all of them played in bands or moved in these kinds of social circles at the time. By compiling different, individual stories and perspectives that all share a common theme and are chronologically coordinated, he has created a retrospective study of the music scene of the time in the form of a social novel. The topics revolve around self-discovery and personality development, formation of political opinions, protests against the existing order, development of one's own sexuality, friendships and rifts, alcohol and drug use, and all influences on the young artists' creativity. Aside from the bands' practice rooms, the settings include the "Ratinger Hof" in Düsseldorf, "Markthalle" Hamburg, the "Rip Off" record shop, "Marktstube," and "Krawall 2000," as well as Berlin's "Dschungel," "Music Hall," and "SO36." The book also offers brief notes on every narrator's biography as well as a timeline of the events Teipel considers important to the plot, from the end of 1976 to July 1983. (...)ʹ

← *50–51*

039

Fucked up and Photocopied

→ E2 156

Bibliographic information:
"Fucked up + Photocopied: The Instant Art of the Punk Rock Movement," Turcotte, Bryan Ray, Christopher T. Miller; Gingko Press, Berkeley, 2002;
ISBN 1-58423-000-2

Image sources:
(1) flyer: Carl Swanberg, page 27,
(2) flyer: courtesy sis onet page, page 216

(1)

The book is a gem: countless flyers, posters, and stickers document the creativity, humor, irreverence, sensuality, and – despite the volume – the sense of design inherent to the punk aesthetic.

The two flyers shown here (1), (2) are taken from the book and underline this appraisal: As was the case with the Underground Press, the use of simple methods demonstrates the creators' self-empowerment. The motto: make collages, use glue, rub, steal. The result is design that reveals secure graphic handwriting in terms of proportions, spatial distribution, and arrangement.

In seminars, impromptu tasks on the punk aesthetic showed: creating order is comparatively simple. Daring to be adventurous, however, is difficult. Against this background, we should pay tribute to the makers of many punk artefacts. (u.v)

(2)

← 52–53

040

Macintosh computer

→ E2 154

'Created by the Californian company Apple, the Macintosh was the first microcomputer with a graphic user interface produced in higher quantities. The name is derived from the McIntosh apple variety; early on, users started to abbreviate the name to Mac. Today, Apple's personal computers officially bear this product name – in combinations such as MacBook, iMac, Mac mini, Mac Pro, etc. The name "Macintosh" is not even used internally anymore. "Mac" also formed part of the names of the range of operating systems used by the devices: Mac OS (until 2001) and Mac OS X (from 1999), which is now called macOS.

The first Mac was a successor of the technically similar, but commercially unsuccessful Apple Lisa – which cost USD 10,000. Apple cofounder Steve Jobs presented the Macintosh 128k on January 24, 1984. Just like its predecessor Lisa, the Macintosh was equipped with a graphic user interface and a mouse. The operating system was tailored to use with a mouse from the start and already featured concepts that were revolutionary at the time, such as the "waste basket," with which deleted files could be retrieved, the "desktop," drag and drop, the option to select texts or objects to change attributes, and a way to navigate the file system with the help of icons. Other fundamental concepts that intended to help users overcome their still widespread fear of computers included the undo function and the consistently standardized use of different user programs. Despite these innovations, Apple only sold small quantities of the new computer to begin with. Only with the successor models of the original Macintosh could Apple draw a larger user community that eventually reached a high overall market share. (...)'

```
Text source:
https://de.wikipedia.org/wiki/
Macintosh (see sources)

Image source:
https://upload.wikimedia.org/
wikipedia/commons/e/e3/Macintosh_
128k_transparency.png
(see sources)
```

This is the first Macintosh 128k, presented by Apple cofounder Steve Jobs on January 24, 1984. He revolutionized the world – and not just the world of visual communication.

Bibliographic information:
"5. Bundestreffen Forum Typografie 1988,"
Arbeitskreis Bremen (eds.); 1989;
[in German]

Text source:
From "Zum DTP-Vormittag," author:
Erik Spiekermann

040.1

5. Bundestreffen Forum Typografie 1988, Thema: Desktop Publishing (DTP)

→ E2 --

/ (...) It quickly became clear to us what topic we wanted to discuss, because it was obvious, it was controversial (especially among typesetters), and it had played a role in our firm for a while now: computers as a design tool, desktop typesetting, presentation aid. Under the oft quoted, though not accurate abbreviation of DTP, this electronic colleague had become a topic of discussion in the year before. It did not take long to find a keynote speaker for the event: Joachim Peters, management consultant, had just published a book titled "Desktop Publishing – was bringt's wirklich?" ("Desktop Publishing – What's It Really Good For?"), the publication of which was supported by Berthold AG – so it was no coincidence that the book put the new procedure in its place, but without attesting to the traditional producers of fonts and typesetting systems that the future belonged to them alone. The copies of the book that Berthold had provided us with were snapped up in no time. (...)
With many colorful, partly overwhelming slides, two graphic designers who had traveled in from London demonstrated the possibilities offered by programs such as Adobe Illustrator. (...)
Following Joachim Peters' provocative theses, the images from the future of our profession, and the proof visible in many places that – despite all the slogans in Apple's advertising and the new trade magazines published everywhere – a little more than just hot air had arisen regarding the topic of DTP, I, as the morning's moderator, had expected a lively discussion. And while there was a discussion, the topic was either too new or too hot – particularly the many typesetters in attendance, some of whom had vehemently opposed the participation of Forum Typographie in the DTP competition, largely remained silent. The rabbit was in full view of the snake. The topic will surely make another appearance at Forum Typographie, but by then we will all have a little more experience with the new tool, there will be more work on display, and finally, the typesetters, who have invested in their own Macs in the last months of the year 1988, in line with the motto, "you never know," can also have their say. /

Bibliographic information:
"Postmoderne," Eleanor Heartney;
Hatje Cantz Verlag, Ostfildern, 2002;
[in German]
ISBN 3-7757-1232-1

Text sources:
Page 06, line 01 – page 07, line 24;

← *52–53*

041

Postmoderne

→ E2 --

/ Similarly to the term of a god, who is everywhere and nowhere, that of postmodernism also stubbornly resists any definition. As a term that has been used to describe phenomena as wide-ranging as the Star Wars movies, the practice of digital sampling in rock music, election campaigns determined by television, and the fashion of Jean Paul Gaultier and Issey Miyake, postmodernism seems to penetrate all areas of our lives. And yet, outside of the limited world of academic disciplines dedicated to the study of culture, hardly anyone can say with certainty what exactly they think postmodernism is. Part of the problem arises from the name itself. The term postmodernism implies that it would be unthinkable without modernism. It can be understood as a reversal of modernist ideals, as a return to the state that preceded modernism. But regardless of whether the relationship is defined as parasitic, exploitative, symbiotic, or revolutionary, one thing is clear: Postmodernism cannot exist without modernism. And since the definition of modernism continues to be disputed, it comes as no surprise that the keenest proponents of postmodernism apparently cannot agree on what exactly it consists of. The extent of postmodernism's identity crisis can be gauged based on a few of the terms that are used to describe it. Defined as "skepticism towards meta-narratives," as "a crisis of cultural authority," or as the "transition from production to reproduction" and associated with words such as "decentered," "simulation," "schizophrenic," and "anti-aesthetic" in discussions, postmodernism seems to live a life devoid of substance and to be something that can only be defined as the negation of something else. Those who look at postmodernism in greater detail might find it resembles Narcissus' reflection in the water, which dissolves as soon as he reaches for it. Which, in turn, is a very postmodernism form of existence. Perhaps we can get a better handle on the problem if we observe a few situations that could be described as postmodern. Let us take the example of the Gulf War of 1991, where the army of journalists was excluded from the actual scenes of blood baths. Instead, we were only shown the material filmed by the air force itself with its target-recognition cameras. The result was a war that took place on the TV screen like a video game with surgical destructive blows against abstract targets. The foundation of the planned city of Celebration, near Orlando in Florida, provides a more idyllic example. The town, which is praised as an alternative to the American cities and suburbs plagued by crime, was created by and is managed by the Disney company. Falling back on the mythology of small-town America, on which Disney's movies and theme parks are based, Celebration offers the option to return to a friendlier, gentler time – a time that only ever existed on celluloid. As a third example,we could mention one of the most popular tourist attractions in France: the caves of Lascaux with their spectacular depictions of hunting scenes from the Stone Age. The fact that the actual caves have been closed to the public since 1963 and that today's visitors can only view reproductions of the caves and their paintings in a nearby quarry has by no means affected the appeal for the thousands of people who arrive every year. What makes these situations postmodern? All three are characterized by their distance from reality, the absence of which is barely even noticed. They hereby prove the postmodern thesis that our idea of the world is primarily based on conveyed images. They deliver proof of the view that we live under the spell of a mythology portrayed by the mass media, movies, and advertising. Since the "real" world on which such depictions are based was pulled from under our feet, we are falling into the rabbit hole of a postmodern wonderland. In this strange new world, works of art are being reborn as texts, history is unmasked as myth, the author dies, reality is discarded as an outdated convention, language rules, and ideology cloaks itself in the guise of truth. (...) /

← 52 – 53

042 The Graphic Language of Neville Brody

→ E2 155

Bibliographic information:
"The Graphic Language of Neville Brody," Neville Brody, Text and Captions by Jon Wozencroft; Verlag C.J. Bucher, Munich, Lucerne, 1988; ISBN 3-7658-0606-4

Image sources:
(1) front cover of the book,
(2) Pages 30 – 31

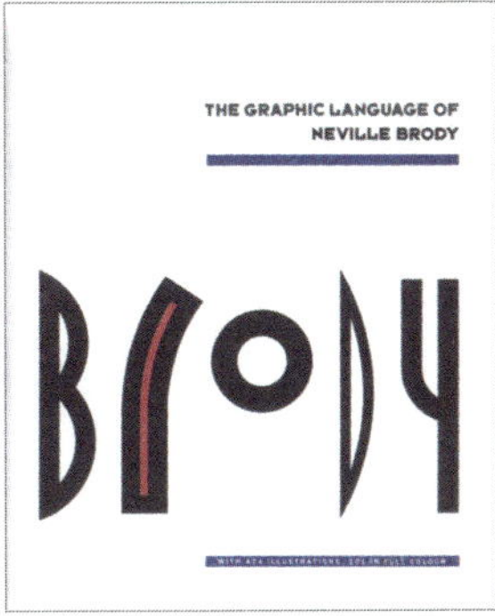

(1) 1988

Neville Brody (*1957) is a British graphic designer, typographer, and font designer.

He was the Art Director of the English magazines The Face Magazine (1981 – 1986), New Socialist (1986), and Arena (1987 – 1990).

Neville Brody is considered a radical innovator of typography. He was one of the first to use a computer as a design tool in the 1980s. He gained fame by breaking with the prevailing conventions in a targeted way. In 1990, Neville Brody founded the FontShop International in Berlin together with Joan and Erik Spiekermann.

He developed countless fonts himself, including Arcadia (1990), Industria (1990), Insignia (1990), FF Blur (1991), FF Gothic (1991), and FF Harlem (1991). (eds.)

(2) 1983 – 1986

(3) 1994

Bibliographic information:
"Die Grafik-Sprache des Neville Brody 2," Neville Brody, text by Jon Wozencroft; Bangert Verlag, Munich, 1994; [in German]
ISBN 3-925560-63-7

Image sources:
(3) front cover of the book,
(4) page 16 – 17

On his design:
The first book on Brody's work was published in Germany in 1988, the second followed in 1994. Both books serve as graphic documents of their time: Between 1983 and 1988, computer programs had already created certain graphic leeway. Brody's work – easy to recognize here on the cover of the book from 1988 and the double page – reflects these options as well as his tentative steps towards increasingly larger experiments. His fonts, logos, and magazine layouts became particularly well known. In the book published in 1994, readers can quickly discern the rapid development that took place between 1988 and 1994. And this did not just apply to the capacity of programs and computers, but also to the increasing experimental frenzy that – fueled by the climate of postmodernism – occasionally became artistically independent. In both books, one can virtually observe the emergence of a new convention – because in the 1990s, more and more of the work of other designers around the world started to look like "Brody" and offset pieces also started to spread in the mainstream. (u.v)

(4) 1992

042.1

Erik Spiekermann and Eckhard Jung, designer, teacher

→ E2 --

Eckhard Jung (*1944) is a German designer, typgrapher, and professor. He taught typography and visual communication at the University of the Arts Bremen until 2009. He studied under Abraham Moles and Otl Aicher, among others, at the Ulm School of Design. Alongside his teaching position, he ran the design studio "designgruppe jung" in the 1980s and 1990s, which gave many students – including myself – an opportunity to gain their first professional experience.

Erik Spiekermann (*1947) is a German designer, typographer, font designer, and author. He cofounded Metadesign in Berlin (1979). In 1989, Spiekermann – together with Joan, his wife at the time – launched Fontshop AG, one of the first mail-order businesses for computer fonts. In 1990, he founded the independent font foundry FSI FontShop International. Here, Spiekermann also published his own fonts, including modern classics such as FF Meta, FF Meta Serif, FF Info, and FF Unit.

In 2000, Erik Spiekermann left Metadesign. He then founded SpiekermannPartners (2007), followed by Eden-Spiekermann (2009).

https://de.wikipedia.org/wiki/Erik_Spiekermann

A personal note

In 1987, I started studying communication design at the University of the Arts Bremen. I left the university after completing my diploma in 1993. In the five and a half years studying, several aspects shaped me in such a way that, looking back, I can say that they served as important cornerstones of my later creative life.

It started with the professor of typography, Eckhard Jung, with whom I studied. He had graduated from the Ulm School of Design and was imbued with the social role of visual communication. He had a positive attitude and showed that communication design can and must consist of more than generating pretty surfaces and encouraging consumption (in this respect, he adopted the same stance as Professor Bernd Bexte, under whom I studied the subject of illustration). Jung's method of teaching combined the thoroughness of typographic expertise with the curiosity of penetrating content and developing an opinion on it. Over the course of my studies, he invited countless seasoned and young (at the time) experts who gave us insights into their mindsets and working methods: Gerard Unger, Hans-Rudolf Lutz, Jean Widmer, Alex Jordan, Anna Berkenbusch, Peter von Kornatzki, Roland Henss, Peter Rea, Franco Clivio, Wolfgang Weingart – and also Erik Spiekermann. The latter opened up doors to Holland: Spiekermann's famous international contacts enabled meetings with Gerd Dumbar, with Total Design, Hard Werken, Proforma, and many others. These teachings had an impact. Many graduates would later transition to teaching, just like I did: Tanja Prill, Viktor Malsy, Florian Pfeffer, Sven Völker, Robert Paulmann, or Daniel H. Bastian, to name just a few with whom I had studied (in parallel or at a different time) at the School of Design.

In addition to Eckhard Jung, Erik Spiekermann, who frequently visited the university in Bremen (as did Hand-Rudolf Lutz), also served as a role model. Like Jung and Lutz, he linked professional clarity with a liberal, multicultural, and still pugnacious spirit. We students were impressed by his insightful criticism of the "rotis" font (Otl Aicher) during a discussion with the design duo Baumann and Baumann, who preferred this font (this took place during the symposium "Positionen zur Gestaltung" ("Positions on Design") at the University of the Arts Bremen, 1993), or his commentary on Kurt Weidemann's redesign of the Deutsche Bahn logo in "Form" no. 144.

This is how I was inspired by the "Swiss kiss" of modernism and its design stringency (including a touch of Ulm) as well as a playful "Dutch touch" of experimental postmodernism. In this field of tension, Jung and his guest Spiekermann acted as transformers who knew how to convey the best of both worlds.

Spiekermann and his Berlin-based firm Metadesign took advantage of the technological opportunities offered by the new tool of computers in the late 1980s and early 1990s in a pioneering way. Unsurprisingly, this innovative environment also gave rise to the first digital font manufacturer in Germany, Fontshop. Cofounder Neville Brody played a crucial role in internationalizing the firm.

Finally, the project "Trends, Stile, Moden" ("Trends, Styles, Fashions") brought me closer to the intellectual and visual world of Erik Spiekermann. The seminar, conceived and led by Eckhard Jung in the fourth semester of my studies (1989), examined the visual language of well-known designers. As a trained carpenter (German: Zimmermann), I noticed Spiekermann's tendency to use all kinds of graphic bars, and I wrote a publication on this feature in which I analyzed his design method. The title of the book, published in 1992, is "Zimmermann meets Spiekermann."

Within the scope of this subjective retrospective, I struggled to decide on which pieces of work conclusively portrayed, in my opinion, Spiekermann's impact, as space is limited. I ultimately opted for "Hello, I am Erik", a review of his creative work in book form. In addition, I would like to show the postage stamps for the Dutch postal service, which demonstrate his conceptual refinement. Furthermore, his small publication titled "Ursache & Wirkung: Ein typografischer Roman" – first published in 1982, followed by a second publication in 1994 – is also worth mentioning, and still very current. In my first semester, this book, among others, helped alleviate my fear of typographic rules and augured the fun I would have working with fonts.

All other publications, writing, essays, commentary, engagements that Spiekermann has published so far are available on the Internet, as are his countless pieces of work and awards.

Ulysses Voelker, 2024

Eerste dag
van uitgifte ·
First day
of issue

Olympische
Spelen '92

Spiekermann designed postage stamps for the (formerly) design-conscious Dutch postal service. These were released in February 1992, the year of the Olympics. The task: to include the five sports of volleyball, track and field, rowing, speed skating, and field hockey on four stamps. The result: ingenious and optimistic (the arrangement, the proportions, the coloring, the typography). A typical Spiekermann.

← 52–53

043

David Carson. The End of Print

→ E2 --

Bibliographic information:
"David Carson. The End of Print," Lewis Blackwell;
Chronicle Books Llc,
San Francisco, 1995;
ISBN 978-0811811996

Image source:
Book cover

David Carson (*1956) is an American typographer, designer, teacher, and surfer. He founded David Carson Design Inc. (2007), based in Zurich.

Formerly a professional surfer, David Carson designed the layout of the "Beach Culture" surf magazine from 1989 to 1991. From 1992 to 1995, he worked as Art Director for the "Ray Gun" magazine. In 1995, he published his book "The End of Print," in which he introduced his magazine design. His work was polarizing because he always deemed the creative offering to be more important than the conveyance of readable information. Carson saw his work as an artistic composition to which he attributed its own informational value. In the postmodern 1990s, when the symbiosis of computer technology and formal surface aesthetics represented an ideal worth aspiring to, Carson garnered many followers among young designers, and within the younger generation in general. He received correspondingly severe criticism from many older designers. The conflict represented the replacement of the values that had been propagated by modernism in favor of an "anything goes" mentality. And that is why this ignorance of the allegedly irrefutable rules of the art of printing and typesetting felt like an emancipation from tradition to many ambitious designers. This internal debate within the field of design never reached mainstream design, although individual traces of Carson-inspired design found their way there.

Carson ranked among the most popular representatives of a generation of designers that produced further design firms in the 1980s and 1990s that displayed a similar style, including "Designers Republic," "Why Not Associates," "8vo," "Hard Werken," or "Emigre." Design universities such as the "Cranbrook Academy of Art" should be mentioned in this context, as should the designers Jonathan Barnbrook, Phil Baines, Neville Brody, Linda van Deursen, Edward Fella, April Greiman, Tibor Kalman, Jeffery Keedy, Max Kisman, Zuzana Licko, Armand Mevis, Phil Baines, Rudy VanderLans, and Jon Wozencroft.

The cover of the book "The End of Print" (left) offers a good example of the style of David Carson's design: Modified or independently designed fonts (with the frequent appearance of "eroded" letters), wide line spacing, large or also very small character spacing, image collages and overlays, neglect of the text's readability in favor of the layout's vividness – the book's cover makes a promise that the content keeps. (eds.)

Text sources:
(1) https://de.wikipedia.org/api/rest_v1/page/pdf/Emigre
(see sources)

(2) Ulysses Voelker

← 54–55

044

Emigre. Zuzana Licko, Rudy VanderLans

→ E2 ––

The design firm "Emigre" was founded in 1984 by Rudy VanderLans (Netherlands) and Zuzana Licko (former Czechoslovakia) in Berkeley, California, and alludes to the founders' emigration with its name.

(1) ′The approach for the business idea lay in offering the rapidly growing desktop publishing market – thanks to the launch of the Apple Macintosh – with its innovative experimental WYSIWYG screen and post-script fonts, an appealing design and the corresponding software. It was no accident that the company's foundation in 1984 coincided with the launch of the Macintosh. With their radical fonts, Licko and VanderLans, inspired by techno and underground culture, consciously turned away from the conventional standard fonts of traditional font manufacturers, such as ITC, Monotype, and Linotype, and instead searched for alternatives to the relatively expensive fonts of the emerging software company Adobe, where Licko had previously worked. Typographer Zuzana Licko was largely responsible for the fonts. She contributed her creative potential and also took responsibility for rendering the fonts on the computer. VanderLans, on the other hand, assumed the role of publisher and primarily took care of distributing the internal publication "Emigre Magazine," which served as a forum for innovative designs and designers, but was also a practical application example for and catalog of Licko's fonts. Alongside the magazine "Ray Gun" by American designer David Carson, the art print booklet soon became an insider tip in the Californian design scene and found acclaim on the European market too. In its 25 years of existence, the company published countless popular fonts, including some that have become design classics themselves, such as Triplex (Licko), Matrix (Licko), and Lunatix (Licko), or postmodern reminiscences of classic Bastard and serif fonts, such as Filosophia (Licko) or Vendetta (John Downer). With the increasingly inflationary distribution of so-called "shareware" or "freeware fonts," which accompanied the blurring of licenses through the market-leading companies in the area of graphics, Apple and Adobe, the initial boom of independent design firms also started to ebb. Following the epigonism on the graphic market, the charismatic-progressive "underdog nimbus" of "Emigre," David Carson, or Neville Brody's Research Studios in London, and many more, started to fade. (...) Twenty years after its first appearance, Emigre Magazine was discontinued after publication of issue no. 69 in 2005. Emigre Inc. still operates as an independent design company that distributes font software and various design products. (...)′

Hamburgefonts

Matrix Regular (Zuzana Licko)

Hamburgefonts

Triplex light (Zuzana Licko)

(2) "Matrix" and "Triplex" belonged to the canon of popular fonts used in the 1990s. They let layouts exude the zeitgeist – but especially in mainstream publications, they also served to make unexciting design more exciting. Many designers were inspired by the idea of designing fonts themselves instead of leaving this task up to venerable experts. In addition, fonts such as "Dogma" existed in all kinds of styles and interpretations. They were mainly suitable as display fonts, proving less useful for body text. Below is a magazine cutout that appears like font catalog. The graphic presentation (the loose arrangement, the lines, the font contrasts, the paper) simply left people wanting more. (u.v)

DOGMA

DDD

DOGMA

TYPI NON HABENT CLARITATEM INSITAM; EST USUS LEGENTIS IN IIS QUI FACIT EORUM CLARITATEM. INVESTIGATIONES DEMONSTRAVERUNT LECTORES LEGERE MELIUS QUOD II LEGUNT.

norman

INVESTIGATIONES

fine machinations

TYPI NON HABENT CLARITATEM INSITAM; EST USUS LEGENTIS IN IIS QUI FACIT EORUM CLARITATEM.

DOGMA OUTLINE

DD

Typi non habent claritatem insitam; EST USUS LEGENTIS IN IIS QUI FACIT EORUM CLARITATEM. 1234567890

Typi non habent

Double page spread 44/45 of "The Emigre Catalog" No. 02.0, 2001;

Font "Dogma", Zuzana Licko, ca. 1994

← 54–55

045

How to be Ugly, Michael Bierut

→ E2 ––

Published on "Designobserver.com" on November 11, 2007;
https://designobserver.com/feature/how-to-be-ugly/5867
(see sources)

Summary: Ulysses Voelker (quotes in italics)

Michael Bierut (*1957) is an American graphic designer, journalist, critic, and university professor.

In the fall of 2007, Michael Bierut published an article in the "Designobserver" that dealt with the design of the summer issue (no. 13) of the "032c" magazine. The responsible designer was Mike Meiré. Bierut began his text as follows:

I'm no purist when it comes to graphic design, and I thought I had seen it all. But that was before I saw Mike Meiré's redesign of German culture magazine "032c". Am I easily shocked? No. But with "032c", Meiré builds a whole publication around what I now realize is the last taboo in graphic design: the vertical and horizontal scaling of type. Dear God in heaven: at long last, is nothing sacred?

If you're unfamiliar with the work of Meiré und Meiré, you might just assume that "032c" was simply the output of a naive amateur.
But Mike Meiré is a great designer, and he's been responsible for some extraordinarily beautiful magazines, including the innovative business journal "brand eins" and its predecessor "Econy", both models of taste, precision and understatement. Meiré knows exactly what he's doing, and what he's doing with "032c" is telling

the world that we can take taste, precision and understatement...and shove them. (...)

Bierut stated that the style pendulum was swinging again. Ugliness was making a comeback on many levels. As proof, Bierut listed various design developments, not just in the area of magazines, but also in corporate design. He particularly highlighted the signet for the 2012 Summer Olympics, designed by the design firm Wolff Olins. This return of the ugly ("The ugly is back!") on many fronts did not constitute a phenomenon of isolated individual cases, according to Bierut, but had already become more than a trend and was approaching the dimensions of an epidemic stage. Bierut continued:

(...) "Ugly is back!" With these words, Patrick Burgoyne confirmed the diagnosis a few months ago in Creative Review, recalling the "mother of all rows" back in the early 90s that attended the publication in "Eye" of Steve Heller's now-legendary article "The Cult of the Ugly." As for this time around, Burgoyne asks, "are we witnessing a knee-jerk reaction to the slick sameness of so much design or a genuine cultural shift?" Whether reactionary spasm or irrevocable paradigm shift, if history is a guide, once the game is afoot, scores of designers will be eager to get with the program. Obviously, doing ugly work isn't difficult. The trick is to surround it with enough attitude so it will be properly perceived not as the product of everyday incompetence, but rather as evidence of one's attunement with the zeitgeist. (...)

Producing "ugly" design is more difficult than it seems. There can be different reasons to break rules. For one, a designer could claim that they were unaware of the rules and therefore could not follow them. David Carson made use of this argumentation himself, as did the Creative Director of the magazine "Super Super," Steve Slocombe, who had no formal design training. Unencumbered experimenting in the creative field, searching for new forms of expression, ignorance of the rules – these could all serve as exonerating reasons for those who established a "New Brutalism" in design. But not everyone is as unencumbered. The second reason for ugly design lies in resorting to differentiation, or otherness, as an intended purpose – which then sanctified all means. In his text, Bierut says:

If you can't ignore the rules, break them. "We have created something original in a world where it is increasingly difficult to make something different," announced Wolff Olins chairman Brian Boylan in the midst of the brouhaha surrounding the London 2012 launch. "I became a bit tired of all these look-a-like magazines," said Mike Meiré in Creative Review. "They're all made very professionally but I was looking for something more charismatic. I wanted to search for an interesting look that was beyond the mainstream. (...)

Absurdly, creating ugly design required great care; indeed, there was reason to suspect that more work goes into this than conventional graphic solutions. However, the creators considered it important to be aware of this intention. Otherwise, they could not lay claim to innovation for their envisioned image. Bierut knew that not everything new and shock-inducing could be condemned. This bore too great of a risk to out oneself as bourgeois. That said, he considered the possibility of ugly design actually generating innovation to be rather low. In most cases, "ugly design" was merely annoying.

← 54–55 **046**

Cult of the Ugly, Steven Heller

→ E2 ––

Published: in the design magazine "Eye," no. 9 vol. 3, 1993;
https://www.eyemagazine.com/feature/article/cult-of-the ugly

Summary: Ulysses Voelker (quotes in italics)

Steven Heller (*1950) is an American lecturer, author, and art director who focuses on topics and issues related to visual communication.

In 1993, the design magazine "eye" published an essay by Steven Heller with the title "Cult of the Ugly." His essay started with a description of a graphic fashion that inspired designers around to world to produce imitations and further developments in the 1990s. Heller illustrated the events from his perspective:

"Ask a toad what is beauty… He will answer that it is a female with two great round eyes coming out of her little head, a large flat mouth, a yellow belly and a brown back." (Voltaire, Philosophical Dictionary, 1794). Ask Paul Rand what is beauty and he will answer that "the separation of form and function, of concept and execution, is not likely to produce objects of aesthetic value". (Paul Rand: A Designer's Art, 1985). Then ask the same question of the Cranbrook Academy of Art students who created the ad hoc desktop publication Output (1992), and to judge by the evidence they might answer that beauty is chaos born of found letters layered on top of random patterns and shapes. Those who value functional simplicity would argue that the Cranbrook students' publication, like a toad's warts, is ugly. The difference is that unlike the toad, the Cranbrook students have deliberately given themselves the warts. "Output" is eight unbound pages of blips, type fragments, random words and other graphic minutiae purposefully given the serendipitous look of a printer's make-ready. The lack of any explanatory précis (and only this end note: "Upcoming Issues From: School of the Art Institute of Chicago [and] University of Texas") leaves the reader confused as to its purpose or meaning, though its form leads one to presume that it is intended as a design manifesto, another "experiment" in the current plethora of aesthetically questionable graphic output. Given the increase in graduate school programmes which provide both a laboratory setting and freedom from professional responsibility, the word experiment has come to justify a multitude of sins. (...)

Heller is certainly aware that, by its very nature, experimentation (not just in design) can be successful or can fail. However, he also defines attributes that are essential to experimenting: intelligence, instinct, and discipline. When viewing the work of graduate schools in the USA and Europe, he found that their results produced such a graphic ugliness that could only be explained by a lack of the three mentioned attributes. The dissolution of the previous criteria for what had been considered attractive and ugly in design was owed to the postmodern climate, which promoted the attack on conventional orders. In this way, ugliness was now becoming a cult. Heller also writes the following on the design publication "Output":

*(...) The ugly excesses – or Frankenstein's little monsters like "Output" – are often exhibited in public to promulgate "the new design discourse". In fact, they merely further the cause of ambiguity and ugliness. Since graduate school hothouses push their work into the real world, some of what is purely experimental is accepted by neophytes as a viable model, and students, being students, will inevitably misuse it.
Who can blame them if their mentors are doing so, too? (...)*

According to Steven Heller, experiments in design are the result of creative self-infatuation combined with affronts against typographic standards. Both contribute to the standardization of poor design:

(...) Common to all graphic designers practising in the current wave is the self-indulgence that informs some of the worst experimental fine art. But what ultimately derails much of this work is what critic Dugald Stermer calls "adults making kids" drawings. When Art Chantry uses naive or ugly design elements he transforms them into viable tools. Conversely, Jeffery Keedy's Lushus, a bawdy shove-it-in-your-face novelty typeface, is taken seriously by some and turns up on printed materials (such as the Dutch Best Book Designs cover) as an affront to, not a parody of, typographic standards. When the layered, vernacular look is practised in the extreme, whether with forethought or not, it simply contributes to the perpetuation of bad design.

The problem concerning the cult of ugliness was that the style had become independent so quickly. Worldwide imitation had led to a style without substance. Ugliness in itself was not objectionable – if it resulted in form that followed function. But ugliness as a virtue devalued what design was supposed to represent.

← *58–59*

047

Pretty Ugly Design

→ E2 --

Bibliographic information:
"Pretty Ugly Design – Visual Rebellion in Design," TwoPoints.Net (ed.); Gestalten Verlag, Berlin, 2012;
ISBN 978-3-89955-423-6

Image sources:
Two posters from University of Applied Sciences, Mainz, 2010

Many graphic works in the 2010s were characterized by a style that was described with terms such as "Pretty Ugly Design" or "Hipster Design." What this meant is described by back cover in the book "Pretty Ugly Design" as follows:

For hundreds of years new artistic styles have been established through aesthetic upheaval - as the initial repugnance for now seminal works such as Picasso's The Young Ladies of Avignon or Strawinsky's The Rite of Spring demonstrate. But while art was allowed to be ugly, design had to function. Trends in graphic design and visual communication were, until very recently, all variations on what was generally considered to be appealing. It is only in the last few years that those working in applied creative disciplines started to rebel. (...)

It remains to be seen whether "rebellion" is the right term for the festival of graphic opulence. But many new design approaches did emerge in those years. It engendered great variety and enriched the visual canon. As is always the case in communication design, there were fluctuations in quality – not just of a formal nature, but also with regard to understandability and contextual reference. The output produced around the world was so huge that websites like "trendlist.org" had to categorize the uploaded work (which not only served self-marketing purposes) by country. If we look at the parade of posters, flyers, and magazines, the attribute of "ugly" seems a little coquettish. The work was rarely ugly, perhaps just a little trivial in its continually recurring mix of styles. A lot of graphic work constituted personal tasks or served other private purposes. But plenty of commercial work also opted for this style. The clients often stemmed from the cultural area or needed this style to advertise products directed at young target groups. (u.v)

(1)

Cover of a student magazine from University of Applied Sciences, Mainz, Summer 2011;
Design: Michaela Kwier, Elliot Saalan

(2)

Poster for a presentation in the course "Conception and Design", title "Sensation", summer semester 2010;
Design: Naéj Reklov

047.1

Hipster – eine transatlantische Diskussion

→ E2 --

Bibliographic information:
"Hipster – eine transatlantische Diskussion,"
Mark Greif, Kathleen Ross, Dayna Tortorici, and Heinrich Geiselberger (Eds.); Suhrkamp Verlag, 2012;
[in German]
ISBN 978-3-518-06173-2

This book explores the phenomenon of hipsterdom that emerged in the 2010s and also infiltrated visual communication. The New Yorker cultural magazine "n+1" organized a conference on this topic. In 2010, the podium discussions and media reports were published, together with other essays responding to these contributions, in a publication titled "What was the Hipster?". The search for a definition of the term hipster proved difficult because, in contrast to all previously known subcultures, it was tricky to capture. Hipsters could not be defined by their social status, nor by specific professions. They also lacked an identifiable genre of music. The foreword of recommended books suggests that this resulted in "mostly intentional phenomenological definitions that list accessories by which hipsters can be identified (thick glasses, skinny jeans, bicycles without gears, etc.), or a non-descript definition." Hipsterdom, which originated in the southeast of New York, quickly spread around the world.
In 2011, men with full beards and flannel shirts could read the following sign in a shop window in the Berlin district of Neukölln, directed at them: "Sorry, no entry for hipsters from the USA. People who imitate American hipsters aren't welcome either." The book "Hipster. Eine transatlantische Diskussion" ("Hipster. A Transatlantic Discussion") brought the phenomenon into the present of 2012 and let journalists, authors, and academics have their say. For today's designers, it is interesting to observe how design reflects a sociological phenomenon. Because hipsterdom is the background noise against which "Pretty Ugly Design" had its heyday, and its impacts have left traces that are still visible in 2024. (eds.)

← 58–59

048

The Global Style – Modernist Typography after Postmodernism, Jeffery Keedy

→ E2 --

Bibliographic information:
"The Global Style – Modernist Typography after Postmodernism," Jefferey Keedy; Slanted Art Type, No.22; Slanted Publishers, Karlsruhe, 2013

Summary: Ulysses Voelker (quotes in italics)

Jefferey Keedy (*1957) is an American lecturer, designer, font designer, and author.

In his essay, Jeffery Keedy discusses the development of visual communication and the status quo at the time of publication, in 2013. He states that postmodern gestures have ebbed to make way for a return to modernism. Keedy recalls the International Style that grew out of the Swiss style of typography in the middle of the 20th century. This style had been tailored to commercial companies. Following postmodern trials and tribulations, a so-called Global Style was emerging now, but this time catering to cultural institutions. It could be observed in local museums and art galleries, and thanks to the Internet, it had spread much farther than the International Style had ever been able to. Keedy writes:

(...) For most graphic designers Modernism is not an unfinished project, it's an unending one. Where postmodern typography was a fragmented, de-centered, self-regulating (some might say self-defeating) system, for making meaning. The Global Style, like the International Style before it, is a prescriptive language of specific formal compositional rules that when followed will successfully convey a message while expressing a specific mood or emotional response. These rules that elicit the desired emotional response are what constitutes the style.
The emotional response that one has to the old International Style is that it is contemporary, sophisticated, cool, calm, and rigorously logical. And that is exactly how it's supposed to feel.
By contrast the Global Style looks new, but still familiar. In fact it radiates newness and very little else. Like the International Style before it, the Global Style is easy to assimilate and is obedient to the point of near transparency. On an emotional level it sublimates quotidian boredom into a contemporary expression of cool, ironic ennui. It is as if the lab-coat wearing designer/scientist of Unimark has been replaced by an App. (...)

According to Jeffery Keedy's view, the Global Style adopted many of the attributes that characterized the International Style:

(...) White space backgrounds, sans serif typefaces, minimalist asymmetrically balanced compositions with limited color palate. No extraneous decoration, ornament or complex patterns.
A love of simple geometric shapes. The one notable exception is the grid. It's not that the grid is no longer there it's that the grid is no longer visible or even detectable. It is embedded in the 0's and 1's and x and y coordinates of digital space. (...)

Grids played a particularly important role in the International Style. The division of surfaces, the positioning of typography within these, and the general use of a defined 2D surface gave the composition depth. The Global Style adopted many of the stylistic elements of the International Style, but the compositions were very different. Keedy argues:

(...) By contrast the Global style's typographic composition does not explicitly refer to the rectangle or object in which it exists, nor to anything in the real world. It may be on a poster or a book or website, but it is not an integral part of an object occupying a specific space or size. It could be a large poster that someone is holding in their studio or just a thumbnail JPEG of someone holding a poster. It makes no difference to the design. Because the design is not size, site, nor media specific. (...) Space in the Global Style is flat to the point of non-existence. Although there is almost always some layering of a tedious geometric shape on top of an insipid block of text, the effect is still one of simultaneity and flatness as the overlap is usually transparent.
The picture plane is not composed, it is just temporarily occupied. The hierarchy of forms is designed so that everything within the composition is of more or less equal unimportance. Some words go this way some go that way, here it is, easy to read, easy to look at, everything in place filling the page up nicely. (...)

The Global Style not only used aspects of the International Style, but also integrated elements of postmodernism. In this context, Keedy mentions a preference for the everyday, a "punk-inspired anti-aesthetic," and a focus on language. This blurring of the International Style's style canon demonstrated a certain arbitrariness. Obviously, the Global Style could do without references to the traditional findings of typography and composition. Keedy also suggests that the Global Style and its protagonists attempted to surround themselves with the aura of a theory, even though there was "hardly any tangible proof of a theory." All in all, Keedy is lacking a critical analysis of a style that almost appears like a style dictate due to its wide distribution. Postmodern designers would always have had to deal with the accusation of being self-infatuated with their aesthetic contortions and their computer tricks. This attitude did not apply to the representatives of the Global Style: Their self-infatuation was not aesthetic, but instead social. It was no longer about the different graphic media, but about the social media, which had the biggest impact on design. Presenting themselves with invented "projects" and disseminating them on blogs, Instagram, Tumblr, or Twitter raised the question of whether this still constituted design. After all, simply dabbling with design did not turn someone into a designer. Just as the act of cooking does not make someone a chef. Keedy concludes his critical appraisal of a superficial and simultaneously extremely successful style with the following sentences:

(...) The Global Style, like the International Style before it, will be with us for some time to come. It is the new normal, or base from which a multitude of stylistic iterations, and reactions will evolve. Every era and culture gets the style it deserves. What did we do to deserve that? Or maybe it's something we didn't do?

← 60–61

049

Definition of the term "Advertising"

→ E2 157, 158

Information on the topic of advertising:

"Wörterbuch Design," Michael Erlhoff, Tim Marshall (Eds.); Birkhäuser Verlag, 2008; [in German]
ISBN 978-3-7643-7738-0

https://en.wikipedia.org/wiki/Advertising

Advertising refers to all measures that serve to distribute information to the public or certain target groups. The purpose usually lies in communicating products and services offered by companies. However, as a rule, the goal is not just to increase sales, but also to maintain the associated brand and image. Advertising makes use of a range of methods that exert a targeted and conscious as well as unconscious influence. This includes impulse-arousing tools, stimulation, suggestions, or praise. But not only profit-oriented companies take advantage of advertising – it serves as a tool for any situation in which approval or other forms of support are considered necessary, for example in non-profit organizations or elections. Advertising uses all conceivable media for its purposes. The conceptional foundations are native to marketing and market research. Designers plan and implement advertising together with various advertising experts, such as copywriters and production specialists. Further information: see the adjacent sources. (eds.)

049.1

Texte zur Theorie der Werbung

→ E2 159

Bibliographic information:
"Texte zur Theorie der Werbung," Tilman Baumgärtel (ed.); Reclam Verlag, Ditzingen, 2018; [in German]
ISBN 978-3-15-019508-6

Text source:
(1) Page 11, line 27 – page 12, line 7

The book explores advertising in many different ways. It is a collection of important texts on the function and impact, on methods, history, aesthetics, and on criticism.
In the book's foreword, the author describes the significance of a collection of aspects related to the topic of advertising as follows (u.v):

(1) ' *(...) Therefore, the need for theories that promise to explain this elusive business is understandably great. Despite the eminent economic significance of advertising, the theoretical approaches that explore the field are by no means restricted to the area of economics or marketing. Advertising specifically works because it serves as a barometer and expression of the lifestyle of its time, reflects social and cultural trends, or in an ideal case, even shapes these for the purposes of the advertisers – this ranges from slogans that have become proverbial ("Impossible is nothing" or "Just do it") through to the design of elaborate "brand worlds," such as the flagship stores of fashion brands or VW's "Autostadt" in Wolfsburg. (...)* '

The book's table of contents:
The texts from chapter 1, "Ware und Marke" ("Goods and Brand") discuss the "Fetischcharakter der Ware" ("Commodity Fetishism," Karl Marx), "Die Gewinnung des öffentlichen Vertrauens" ("Gaining Public Trust," Hans Domizlaff), the topic of "market expansion" (Naomi Klein), and "Kritik der Warenästhetik" ("Criticism of Commodity Aesthetics," Wolfgang Fritz Haug).

Chapter 2, "Propaganda und ihr Publikum" ("Propaganda and Its Audience") talks about "Psychologie der Massen" ("Psychology of the Masses," Gustave Le Bon), "Die neue Propaganda" ("The New Propaganda," Edward Bernays), and "war propaganda." A final contribution to this chapter is titled "The Spectacular Achievements of Propaganda" (Noam Chomsky).

Chapter 3 of the book deals with "Methoden der Werbung" ("Advertising Methods"). The individual contributions are titled "Neununddreißigneunzig" ("Thirtynineninety," Frédéric Beigbeder), "Motivforschung und ihre Anwendung" ("Motivation Research and its Application," Ernest Dichter), "Reality in Advertising" (Rosser Reeves), "Advertising's 15 Basic Appeals" (Jib Fowles), and "Wie Werbung uns zu unseren Gunsten informiert" ("How Advertising Informs Us for Our Benefit," John E. Calfee). The chapter concludes with an article by the German Advertising Federation (ZAW) titled "Wettbewerb braucht Werbung" ("Competition Needs Advertising").
Chapter 4 then discusses "Die Ästhetik der Werbung" ("The Aesthetic of Advertising"). Karl Kraus provides his perspective in "Die Welt der Plakate" ("The World of Posters"), Walter Benjamin's "Passagen-Werk" has its say, and Michael Schirner offers insight into the hypothesis that "Werbung ist Kunst" ("Advertising is Art") in an interview.

Finally, chapter 5 of this book explores "Kritik an der Werbung" ("Criticism of Advertising"). It discusses "Abhängigkeitseffekt" ("The Dependence Effect," John Kenneth Galbraith) and "Die Frage der Moral" (the question of morality in "Hidden Persuaders," Vance Packard). Oliviero Toscani claims that "Die Werbung ist ein lächelndes Aas" ("Advertising is a Carrion that Smiles at Us"). "Culture Jamming" is mentioned (Mark Dery), Christiane Schmerl writes about "Werbung mit Frauenbildern: Bilder sind keine Frauen" ("Advertising with Female Images: Pictures are Not Women"). The book concludes with the article "Sex sells? Mit mir nicht!" ("Sex Sells? Not With Me!" by Terres des Femmes e.V., among others). (eds.)

← 60–61

050

Die Hochschule für Gestaltung, neun Stufen ihrer Entwicklung

→ E2 --

Bibliographic information:
"Die Hochschule für Gestaltung, neun Stufen ihrer Entwicklung," Otl Aicher; 1975 in Archithese, No.15, Niederteufen, 1975; [in German]

Source:
Text excerpt from pages 12 – 18

Former rector Otl Aicher describes the Ulm School of Design here. It existed from 1953 to 1968. The source text used only lowercase letters (a trademark of Otl Aicher's texts). The text excerpt translated here has adopted the use of lowercase letters.

' the ulm school of design celebrated impressive successive, rivaled by few other schools, in the ten years of its existence. its pedagogical concept has turned into a model. its products were pioneering for the future development of design.

a form of success that is almost even more significant than the results that were visible from the outside is the achievement of changing and developing its ideology every year, frequently in the midst of crisis. the school was always moving forwards thanks to permanent internal discussions. the organ of change was the pedagogical conference that often lasted for weeks, that established a new curriculum every year. the school management, which was in principle always a collective matter, also constituted a platform that promoted development and improvement.

the school was private, its funds were raised by inge aicher-scholl. it had to fight to secure its resources every year. this meant the school was unprotected and internal evolutions were carried outside too easily, especially when this came with personal consequences. for nearly the entire existence of the school of design, a type of public discussion about the school took place in the german media, whereby, according to the status of the press we received, substantive problems receded in favor of personnel stories. after all, the opponents and false friends of the school of design had no trouble stifling these.

nonetheless, the story of the internal development remains a thrilling chapter that deserves to be depicted beyond sketches one of these days. here is a brief summary of the most important stages.

first stage: the concept

considerable sociological rigorism à la veblen. no more art. the street is more important than the museum. the lead article more important than the art and literature section, also linguistically. creativity in the area of technique more important than in the studio. like zeischegg I am leaving the academy's sculpting class. we comprehend the quality of our society based on its products, its needs programs, and its communication.
first concept august 1947. concrete occasion the program of the adult education center. there are hardly any lecturers on the current problems of reconstruction. this adult education center gains significance to the extent that fritz winter and nonné Schmidt suggest, on behalf of former bauhaus affiliates, to have Bauhaus rise again in association with this adult education center. the program also includes sociology, political science, psychology as subjects. a novelty back then. drafting of texts as a design discipline on equal footing with graphic design, product design, or construction. a campus studio channel intended for this. contacts with hans werner richter and max. program is presented in 1949 by inge aicher-scholl to the american high commissioner mc cloy, who calls for donations to implement the project in the usa. prerequisite: german institution must cover half of the costs.

the pedagogical concept of not just enhancing design with teaching and research, but also expanding it with "development" (principle drafts up to prototypes), appears novel in the framework of the general discussion on university reform, especially for the burdened relationship between universities, art schools, and technical universities. zeischegg is working on the program for a research institute for product form. bill is working on construction plans.

second stage: planning and start

the initial building concept from bill. the plan to accommodate all institutions, student dormitories, workshops, and teaching rooms in one building is discarded. demarcation from its bauhaus ideals: no painting and sculpting class, no goldsmith workshop. art is understood to be design-irritating. nothing would be more dangerous than to use the graphic elements of concrete art in construction. there are merely methodical parallels.

bill first rector. he views the text department (information) as a verbal self-depiction of the school. his didactics more academy lessons. master-pupil ratio without fixed curriculum, albers and peterhans follow his call as guest lecturers. bill's design concept is still hierarchical: engineers and producers will be the executive organ of the designer. gugelot, maldonado are appointed fixed lecturers by bill.

third stage: curriculum

the younger lecturers urge for an evaluation of the design basics. gugelot and zeischegg are developing the program for the engineering sciences to be incorporated, maldonado the curriculum for information theory and methodical subjects as well as the foundation course.

the result is the ulm model: a design model supported by technology and science. the designer is no longer the overarching artist, but an equal partner in the decision-making process within industrial production. the last relics of a work federation for the applied arts are announced. material science and production technology replace global terms such suitable materials and faithfulness to the original.
curriculum: half theoretical subjects, half design work. aside from theoretical-scientific teaching and design practice, development groups will be set up (run by individual lecturers). demand: wherever possible, design hypotheses should be reviewed based on implemented designs that will move on to production. this brings experience based on feedback into the pedagogy. the development groups also help cover the school's operating costs with their proceeds. in 1957, bill leaves, two years after the school opened.

fourth stage: technological design

maldonado develops a foundational course with a large degree of quantifiable design steps. gugelot expands modular and system design, practical successes. bense alters the program for the information department. information-theoretical analyses. less practice-oriented. trouble finding lecturers for copywriting. requests to walser, andersch, arno schmidt. for a while, enzensberger teaches. the construction department with ohl exclusively explores prefabricated construction.
guest lecturer konrad wachsmann with extremely technology-oriented program. traditional architecture, also documented by le corbusier, is consciously negated in the teaching program. focus on elementary construction, joining technology, and production organization. modular arrangements.

ohl lays the foundations for an institute for industrialized construction. typography also as a set of rules and systems technology. more syntactic than semantic issues. emphasis on information systems rather than individual statements.

fifth stage: cybernetic design and positivism

methodological problems come to the fore: analyses, determination of factors, matrix, and diagrams. the design steps take on a life of their own and become more prominent than the result and its impact. stronger mathematization under rittel and preference of mathematically ascertainable processes. applied process and sequence research. under perrine, the perception is reduced to physiological problems based on ames demonstrations. also sociology unbiased as a statistical recording of processes. prognosis must stem from premises. design is formulated as a programming task for computer-controlled facilities. norbert wiener holds a lecture on the predictability of the weather.

information and aesthetics are measured in bits. demand for an unbiased, ideology-free university with a wide range of parallel teaching concepts, in line with the model of a natural sciences faculty.

sixth stage: value-based design

opposition against technocratic ideology. (zeischegg-aicher). objective and social value systems are demanded as factors of product evaluations. note on difference between natural science and social science causality. Sense, purpose, and form are not the end of determinable causal series, but subject to projective and final decisions. computer work is not discarded, but restricted to basics and partial aspects. design is like history, not inevitable, but made. consistency is only recognizable after the fact. design as morals bound by social developments. discussions on commercialism and market-oriented formalism. the school's design as long-term influence of the market instead of market orientation. reciprocal relationship between market offering and need program. confrontation between "scientists" and "craftspeople." theo pirker offers a still rare example of a design-oriented sociology in his seminar on office technology and office work. rittel and kesting leave the school.
seventh stage:

photography under christian staub turns to picture journalism and documentaries. this means the strengthening of old ambitions to push back the common aestheticism, as modern as it may be. clearer criteria for the semantic and syntactic relationship of communication. discovery of content. bonsiepe devises analysis models based on modern linguistics. kluge and reitz build a film institute without particular willingness to integrate into the other departments, supported by a new administration. this is developing into an autocratic organ and eyeing up a directorate structure. without success. the school will continue to be managed by the school.

eight stage: program design

individual tasks are replaced by complex programs that are processed throughout all departments under various aspects, in line with the suggestion of wirsing, schnaidt, and lindinger of the school complex. didactic division by project groups.

the student problems no longer revolve primarily around the school of design. they are brought in from the outside. call for one-third parity. at the same time public discussions about the school of design in the landtag. the ministry for culture demands fulfillment of conditions. planning intensity decreases along with discussions on constitutional matters. most important design tool the typewriter, relic of computer design. program replaces program design. out of fear of concepts and evaluable designs. These programs contain more and more empty phrases.

ninth stage: institute for environmental planning

to avoid the annual new procurement and securing of funds, nationalization of the school of design is put on the table. the idea is to connect it to stuttgart university. to perform this restructuring, the ministry for culture demands termination of all lecturers. a program is developed for an institute for environmental planning and new teaching staff are appointed. after a short period, it falters due to a lack of creative access. there are only formulaters, no planners and doers. one resorts to the misery of german universities that are content with cognitive departments without reviewing the knowledge on development and models through feedback. old dilemma between theory and practice. End of an attempt to no longer separate the two and view practice as a theory deliverer. along with the school of design, a pedagogical university model collapses. /

← 60–61 051

Text source:
https://en.wikipedia.org/wiki/Design_methods
(see sources)

Design Methods Movement

→ E2 --

/ Design methods are procedures, techniques, aids, or tools for designing. They offer a number of different kinds of activities that a designer might use within an overall design process. Conventional procedures of design, such as drawing, can be regarded as design methods, but since the 1950s new procedures have been developed that are more usually grouped together under the name of "design methods". What design methods have in common is that they "are attempts to make public the hitherto private thinking of designers; to externalise the design process". Design methodology is the broader study of method in design: the study of the principles, practices and procedures of designing.

Background
Design methods originated in new approaches to problem solving developed in the mid-20th Century, and also in response to industrialisation and mass-production, which changed the nature of designing. A "Conference on Systematic and Intuitive Methods in Engineering, Industrial Design, Architecture and Communications", held in London in 1962 is regarded as a key event marking the beginning of what became known within design studies as the "design methods movement", leading to the founding of the Design Research Society and influencing design education and practice. Leading figures in this movement in the UK were J. Christopher Jones at the University of Manchester and L. Bruce Archer at the Royal College of Art. The movement developed through further conferences on new design methods in the UK and USA in the 1960s. The first books on rational design methods, and on creative methods also appeared in this period. New approaches to design were developing at the same time in Germany, notably at the Ulm School of Design (Hochschule für Gestaltung–HfG Ulm) (1953–1968) under the leadership of Tomás Maldonado. Design teaching at Ulm integrated design with science (including social sciences) and introduced new fields of study such as cybernetics, systems theory and semiotics into design education. Bruce Archer also taught at Ulm, and another influential teacher was Horst Rittel. In 1963 Rittel moved to the School of Architecture at the University of California, Berkeley, where he helped found the Design Methods Group, a society focused on developing and promoting new methods especially in architecture and planning. At the end of the 1960s two influential, but quite different works were published: Herbert A. Simon's The Sciences of the Artificial and J. Christopher Jones's Design Methods.Simon proposed the "science of design" as "a body of intellectually tough, analytic, partly formalizable, partly empirical, teachable doctrine about the design process", whereas Jones catalogued a variety of approaches to design, both rational and creative, within a context of a broad, futures creating, systems view of design.
The 1970s saw some reaction against the rationality of design methods, notably from two of its pioneers, Christopher Alexander and J. Christopher Jones. Fundamental issues were

also raised by Rittel, who characterised design and planning problems as wicked problems, un-amenable to the techniques of science and engineering, which deal with "tame" problems. The criticisms turned some in the movement away from rationalised approaches to design problem solving and towards "argumentative", participatory processes in which designers worked in partnership with the problem stakeholders (clients, customers, users, the community). This led to participatory design, user centered design and the role of design thinking as a creative process in problem solving and innovation.
However, interest in systematic and rational design methods continued to develop strongly in engineering design during the 1980s; for example, through the Conference on Engineering Design series of The Design Society and the work of the Verein Deutscher Ingenieure association in Germany, and also in Japan, where the Japanese Society for the Science of Design had been established as early as 1954. Books on systematic engineering design methods were published in Germany and the UK. In the USA the American Society of Mechanical Engineers Design Engineering Division began a stream on design theory and methodology within its annual conferences. The interest in systematic, rational approaches to design has led to design science and design science (methodology) in engineering and computer science. (...)'

Text source:
"Experimente zu einer Theorie der Praxis. Historische Etappen der Designforschung in der Nachfolge des Bauhauses," Claudia Mareis, in kunsttexte.de, Themenheft 1: Kunst und Design, G. Jain (ed.), 2010. [in German]

Text source:
https://edoc.hu-berlin.de/bitstream/handle/18452/8019/mareis.pdf?sequence=1&isAllowed=y
Page 1, 2nd column, line 25 – page 3, 1st column, line 33
(see sources)

051.1

Das Design Methods Movement in den 1960er Jahren

→ E2 --

'(...) The beginnings of an organized design methodology can be dated relatively precisely if we take the first conference of design methods as its starting point, which took place in London in 1962.
The Design Methods Movement developed into an international, interdisciplinary movement in the 1960s, primarily operating in the Anglo-American region and with the goal of systematizing design processes. It strived to find methods with which the design processes, which were carried out more or less intuitively up until this point, could be recorded "rationally" and "objectively" and controlled efficiently. The hope was that both design education and the design profession would benefit from a systematic design methodology.
One of the fundamental premises of the movement stated that the design process in different disciplines – such as architecture, organizational planning, computer science, management, or engineering – shared a uniform pattern. Sydney Gregory called it "the design method." He defined design as *"a process the pattern of which is the same, whether it deals with the design of a new oil refinery, the construction of a character, or the writing of Dante's Divine Comedy"*. Accordingly, the term design was broadly formulated. In 1969, Herbert Simon postulated in his pioneering publication "The Sciences of the Artificial" that every person who turns an existing situation into a preferred situation is a designer. He hereby attempted to expand the social, but above all the scientific perception of design in a radical way. He wanted to move away from the understanding of design as a specialized, technical, or artistic activity and towards an interdisciplinary, future-oriented "science of the artificial," as a generalist manner of practical thinking, planning, decision-making, and acting in an environment whose most important feature is its artificiality.
From the start, the Design Methods Movement also differentiated between the approaches of designers and (natural) scientists. Simon wrote:
"The natural sciences are concerned with how things are [...], design on the other hand is concerned with how things ought to be".
Simon's approach should be understood within the context of rationalistic intelligence models in AI research of the 1960s – an area of research in which he himself took on a leading role. Furthermore, his idea of design as a synthetic (i.e., not analytical) field of activity reflected the virulent knowledge debate of the time – for example, the debate initiated by C. P. Snow on the "two cultures" of the humanities and natural sciences. Analogies to contemporary relevant cybernetic knowledge models also cannot be discounted. Specifically, this can be observed in situations where the synthetic potential of cybernetics is accentuated as both "teaching and technique" of insight and action and thereby promises to overcome the divide between the "two cultures" of academia. The idea of defining design in an expanded sense as an interdisciplinary, generalist activity still determines the contextual and methodical debates in design research today – even though the definition of design frequently oscillates in an undecided way between "designing as a process in general" and "designing as practiced by professional designers." The Design Methods Movement faltered after just a few years, at least partly due to substantial internal criticism. This criticism found fault in the excessive, one-sided systematization and rationalization of design processes as well as the increasing distance from design methodology and design practice. The postulated procedure of method-based design work had, according to John Christopher Jones, only led to design being viewed as a completely rational, objectifiable process, while at the same time the question of the importance of intuition and creativity in design processes was blocked out:
"The language used to describe designing became more and more abstract. The words lost touch with how it feels to be a designer and how it feels to inhabit the systems being designed". Critics took issue with the increasing "demystification" of design by means of the forced systematization and rationalization of its practices. The protagonists of the Design Methods Movement did succeed in blurring the discipline's boundaries under the shared umbrella definition of the term. But the boundaries that came to light within design, between its scopes of "theory" and "practice" deepened and perpetuated themselves noticeably. Even

today, this dichotomy structures the dominating culture of discussion in design research and its core topics. There is a clear call for proximity to practice and practical relevance in design research. Recently, the "Research through Design" method labeled a "project-led" form of design research that is both scientifically proven and aims to be productive for design practice. But in addition to undisputed advantages, the envisaged practical orientation also had its problematic side. Clive Dilnot has diagnosed a hegemony of design practice for design research, accompanied by a simultaneous lack of academic attention: *"Design not only suffers from a general unwillingness of the culture to grant it the status of an activity worth studying and defining [but of] an unwillingness shared by design practitioners who want design defined merely in terms of what designers do"*. Paradoxically, from the design perspective, a lack of a theoretical and scientific body is criticized, while an academic "foreign infiltration" is also feared. (...) /

← 60 – 61

052

Design Thinking

→ E2 ––

Design Thinking describes an approach (not a method) to solving problems and developing ideas in (visual) communication processes. Design Thinking is founded on consideration of various disciplines that work together, initially by raising questions on a conceptional level and then formulating answers. Aside from the creative spaces that emerge through this collaboration, the core components include profitability and feasibility. In a nutshell, it revolves around three essential aspects: benefit, practicability, and marketability. There are different procedural models for how this should take place. Roughly summarized, the process steps result in the following idea: The interdisciplinary group must first develop a common understanding of the problem at hand. To gain an understanding, they need to observe the overall situation. This includes recording and analyzing the customers' wishes and ideas. Against this background, the group develops its own stance on the problem and initiates brainstorming processes. The result is drawn up as a prototype and tested. The core elements of this process step are the desire for feedback, flexibility, critical ability, and the customer's satisfaction. (eds.)

Other sources of information:
https://en.wikipedia.org/wiki/Design_thinking

Book recommendation:
"Design Thinking," Gavin Ambrose, Paul Harris; AVA Publishing, 2010; ISBN 978-2940411177

← 62 – 63

053

Speculative Everything

→ E2 160

Bibliographic information:
"Speculative Everything," Anthony Dunne, Fiona Raby; MIT Press, Cambridge, London, 2013;
ISBN 978-0-262-01984-2

Text source: page VI, lines 01 – 25;

"Dunne & Raby" is the name of a design studio in London and New York City. It consists of Anthony Dunne and Fiona Raby.

Anthony Dunne (*1964) is a professor and head of the "Design Interactions Programme" at the Royal College of Art (RCA) in London.

Fiona Raby (*1963) is a professor for industrial design (id2) at the University of Applied Sciences in Vienna and teaches "Design Interactions" at the RCA, London.

/ Speculative Everything began as a list we created a few years ago called A/B, a sort of manifesto. In it, we juxtaposed design as it is usually understood with the kind of design we found ourselves doing. B was not intended to replace A but to simply add another dimension, something to compare it to and facilitate discussion. Ideally, C, D, E, and many others would follow. This book unpacks the B bit of the list, making connections between usually disparate ideas, locating them within an expanded notion of contemporary design practice, and establishing some historical links. It is not a straightforward survey, anthology of essays, or monograph but offers a very specific view of design based on several years of experimentation, teaching, and reflection. We use examples from our own practice, student and graduate work from the Royal College of Art, and other projects from fine art, design, architecture, cinema, and photography. In researching this book we also surveyed literature from futurology, cinematic and literary fiction, political theory, and the philosophy of technology. The ideas in this book move from a general setting out of what conceptual design is, through its use as a critical medium for exploring the implications of new developments in science and technology, to the aesthetics of crafting speculative designs. It ends by zooming out to explore the idea of "speculative everything" and design as a catalyst for social dreaming.

Speculative Everything is an intentionally eclectic and idiosyncratic journey through an emerging cultural landscape of ideas, ideals, and approaches. We hope designers interested in doing more than making technology easy to use, sexy, and consumable will find this book enjoyable, stimulating and inspiring. /

← 64–65

054

Victor Papanek, The Politics of Design

→ E2 ––

Bibliographic information:
"Victor Papanek, The Politics of Design," Mateo Kries, Amelie Klein, Alson J. Clarke (Eds.); Vitra Design Museum and Victor Papanek Foundation, Weil am Rhein, 2018; [in German]
ISBN 978-3-945852-25-5

Text sources:
(1) Text from the front inside cover of the book "The Politics of Design";
(2) Text excerpt (author: Amelie Klein), page 15, line 01 – page 16, line 35

Victor Papanek (1923–1998) was an influential pioneer of a design that put social and ecological aspects front and center. Starting in the 1960s, Papanek increasingly propagated a critical understanding of design. His stance went hand in hand with many progressive movements that were searching for new values at the time. In 1971, his book "Design for the Real World" was first published. It has been translated into 20 languages. (eds.)

/ (1) "Victor Papanek: The Politics of Design" offers a comprehensive overview of the work of the designer, author, and activist Victor J. Papanek. It examines his main work, the polemic publication "Design for the Real World" from 1971, as well as his designs and his engagement for social minorities, the so-called Third World, and the considerate use of natural resources. The book documents countless photographs, objects, artistic work and designs, drawings, letters, and other materials that are hereby published for the first time. Papanek's close communication with contemporaries such as Richard Buckminster Fuller, George Nelson, and Marshall McLuhan is also explored. The book is supplemented with the pieces of work from Tomás Saraceno, Catherine Sarah Young, Gabriel Ann Maher, Thomas Thwaites, and Forensic Architecture, as well as Flui Coletivo and Questtonó, among others. This contemporary work shows: Papanek's interpretation of design as a tool for societal change is more current than ever before and still shapes today's debates on social design, critical design, and Design Thinking. With contributions from Alison J. Clarke, Amelie Klein, Jan Boelen, Felicity Scott, Jamer Hunt, Cameron Tonkinwise, and others. /

/ (2) The book and the exhibition "Victor Papanek: The Politics of Design" are dedicated to one of the most important design thinkers of the 20th century, his core teachings, and the question of how we can translate these into the 21st century. "I view design as a tool for political change," the Austro-American said on Swedish television in 1970, and he never tired of repeating this message throughout his lifetime. Papanek spoke of design for minorities – which, when viewed as a whole, are not actually minorities –, of the designer's social, moral, and ethical responsibility, of environmental sustainability, of processes and systems that must be considered as design, of the consumer society and waste, and of all of our insatiable greed for new things. In short: He spoke of the societal and thereby political implications of what designers do, while on the surface, they are focusing on the formal or functional aspects of their work, matters of user friendliness, or the marketability of a design. Design is a highly political concept, as Papanek repeated in a lecture in 1990 – 20 years after the interview on Swedish TV: "Design is never silent. Design always impacts society, the environment, and ecology." This is the most important message that Victor Papanek wanted to share with his contemporaries and everyone who came after him. He was not the only one determined to spread this insight. This book and the eponymous exhibition want to convey the same message. Papanek was part of a larger movement that also took the field of design into account when it came to the social upheaval that radically changed the USA and Europe in the 1960s and 1970s. Without a doubt, he was one of the first to join this movement, but his thinking was certainly also heavily shaped by others. He was strongly influenced by Richard Buckminster Fuller, the great architect, designer, and visionary who was Papanek's friend and mentor for decades. Buck's image of "Spaceship Earth," in which everything is connected to everything, is based on an understanding of the world that much of Papanek's writing reflects. Other important protagonists from 20th century theory and practice have also left visible traces in Papanek's thinking: cultural theoretician Bernard Rudofsky, for one, with his criticism of modernism and penchant for folkloric design; or designer George Nelson, who presented furious criticism of American post-war politics and the consumer society in his TV lecture "How to Kill People: A Problem of Design;" media theoretician Marshall McLuhan in terms of the power of TV and video, the new media of the time; as well as architect Richard Neutra, who, like Buckminster Fuller, was already contemplating the formability of the world in a way that benefited the environment and sustainability; and finally, Frank Lloyd Wright, who had already recognized the reciprocal effects between society, the environment, and architecture in the 1920s.
Victor Papanek was therefore not the first or only one to formulate such thoughts, but what rightly propelled him to the top in design history was his ability to compile his views into a 350-page book in a compact, polemical, impactful, and understandable manner. "Design for the Real World" is unquestionably one of the most important books of design history. It has been translated into over 20 languages and, since its first publication in Swedish in 1970 and the first US edition from 1971, has always been available in English (with the exception of a brief moment in the summer of 2018, when the shop of the Vitra Design Museum stocked up for the upcoming exhibition titled "Victor Papanek: The Politics of Design"). "The book has become a bible for anyone who wants to bring about social change through design," Alice Twemlow writes in this publication, adding that "Every generation of young designers rediscovers his mantras, as if they hold a timeless validity. The hands of the book's clock continue to point to 'one minute to midnight'." "Design for the Real World" brings a sense of meaning to a profession that – then as now – is stuck in a deep crisis of purpose.
Another table, another chair, another soap dish for a Swedish furniture company – for many designers, this no longer represents an aspirational professional perspective in times of refugee crises and millions of tons of plastic waste in the oceans. "Design can and must become an opportunity for young people to help change society" – this is Papanek's main mantra. (...) /

054.1

Design for the Real World

→ E2 ––

Bibliographic information:
"Design for the Real World," Victor Papanek; Thames & Hudson Ltd, London, Reprint 2020;
ISBN 978-0-500-29533-5

Text sources:
(1) The book's back cover;
(2) Page 03, line 1 – page 04, line 18

/ (1) (...) Victor Papanek's lively and instructive guide shows how design can reduce pollution, overcrowding, starvation, obsolescence and other modern ills. He leads us away from "fetish objects for a wasteful society" towards a new age of morally and environmentally responsible design. (...) /

/ (2) 1. What is Design?
A Definition of the Function Complex
"The wheel's hub holds thirty spokes. Utility depends on the hole through the hub. The potter's clay forms a vessel. It is the space within that serves. A house is built with solid walls. The nothingness of window and door alone renders it usable. That which exists may be transformed. What is nonexistent has boundless uses. (LAO-TSE)"

All men are designers. All that we do, almost all the time, is design, for design is basic to all human activity. The planning and patterning of any act toward a desired, forseeable end constitutes the design process. Any attempt to separate design, to make it a thing-by-itself, works counter to the fact that design is the primary underlying matrix of life. Design is composing an epic poem, executing a mural, painting a masterpiece, writing

a concerto. But design is also cleaning and reorganizing a desk drawer, pulling an impacted tooth, baking an apple pie, choosing sides for a backlot baseball game, and educating a child.
"Design is the conscious and intuitive effort to impose meaningful order." It is only in recent years that to add the phrase "and intuitive" seemed crucial to my definition of design. Consciousness implies intellectualization, cerebration, research, and analysis. The sensing/feeling part of the creative process was missing from my original definition. Unfortunately intuition itself is difficult to define as a process or ability. Nonetheless it affects design in a profound way. For through intuitive insight we bring into play impressions, ideas, and thoughts we have unknowingly collected on a subconscious, unconscious, or preconscious level. The "how" of intuitive reasoning in design doesn't readily yield to analysis but can be explained by example. Watson and Crick intuitively felt that the underlying structure of the DNA chain would express itself most elegantly through a spiral. Beginning with this intuition, they began their research. Their instinctive precognition paid off: a spiral it is! (...)/

← 64–65

055

First Things First Manifesto, 1964

→ E2 161, 162, 163

Text sources:
(1) Project description: https://bit.ly/3JNi1g1, (see sources)
(2) Manifesto: http://www.designishistory.com/1960/first-things-first/ (see sources)

(1) The First Things First manifesto was written 29 November 1963 and published in 1964 by Ken Garland. It was backed by over 400 graphic designers and artists and also received the backing of Tony Benn, radical left-wing MP and activist, who published it in its entirety in The Guardian newspaper. Reacting against a rich and affluent Britain of the 1960s, it tried to re-radicalize a design industry which the signatories felt had become lazy and uncritical. Drawing on ideas shared by critical theory, the Frankfurt School, and the counter-culture of the time, it explicitly reaffirmed the belief that design is not a neutral, value-free process. It rallied against the consumerist culture that was purely concerned with buying and selling things and tried to highlight a Humanist dimension to graphic design theory. It was later updated and republished with a new group of signatories as the First Things First 2000 manifesto.

Undersigners:
Edward Wright, Geoffrey White, William Slack, Caroline Rawlence, Ian McLaren, Sam Lambert, Ivor Kamlish, Gerald Jones, Bernard Higton, Brian Grimbly, John Garner, Ken Garland, Anthony Froshaug, Robin Flor, Germano Facetti, Ivan Dodd, Harriet Crowder, Anthony Clift, Gerry Cinamon, Robert Chapman, Ray Carpenter, Ken Briggs

(2)/ We, the undersigned, are graphic designers, photographers and students who have been brought up in a world in which the techniques and apparatus of advertising have persistently been presented to us as the most lucrative, effective and desirable means of using our talents. We have been bombarded with publications devoted to this belief, applauding the work of those who have flogged their skill and imagination to sell such tings as:
cat food, stomach powders, detergent, hair restorer, striped toothpaste, aftershave lotion, slimming diets, fattening diets, deodorants, fizzy water, cigarettes, roll-ons, pull-ons, and slip-ons.

By far the greatest time and effort of those working in the advertising industry are wasted on these trivial purposes, which contribute little or nothing to our national prosperity.
In common with an increasing number of the general public, we have reached a saturation point at which the high pitched scream of consumer selling is no more than sheer noise. We think that there are other things more worth using our skill and experience on. There are signs for streets and buildings, books and periodicals, catalogues, instructional manuals, industrial photography, educational aids, films, television features, scientific and industrial publications and all the other media through which we promote our trade, our education, our culture and our greater awareness of the world.

We do not advocate the abolition of high pressure consumer advertising: this is not feasible. Nor do we want to take any of the fun out of life. But we are proposing a reversal of priorities in favour of the more useful and more lasting forms of communication. We hope that our society will tire of gimmick merchants, status salesmen and hidden persuaders, and that the prior call on our skills will be for worthwhile purposes. With this in mind, we propose to share our experience and opinions, and to make them available to collegues, students and others who may be interested./

055.1

First Things First Manifesto, 2000

→ E2 ––

Text sources:
(1) Project description: https://en.wikipedia.org/wiki/First_Things_First_2000_manifesto
(2) Manifesto: https://bit.ly/3n74uGp (see sources)

(1)/ The First Things First 2000 manifesto, launched by Adbusters magazine in 1999, was an updated version of the earlier First Things First manifesto written and published in 1964 by Ken Garland, a British designer. The 2000 manifesto was signed by a group of 33 figures from the international graphic design community, many of them well known, and simultaneously published in Adbusters (Canada), Emigre (Issue 51) and AIGA Journal of Graphic Design (United States), Eye magazine no. 33 vol. 8, Autumn 1999, Blueprint (Britain) and Items (Netherlands). The manifesto was subsequently published in many other magazines and books around the world, sometimes in translation. Its aim was to generate discussion about the graphic design profession's priorities in the design press and at design schools. Some designers welcomed this attempt to reopen the debate, while others rejected the manifesto. The question of value-free design has been continually contested in the graphic design community between those who are concerned about the need for values in design and those who believe it should be value-free. Those who believe that design can be free from values reject the idea that graphic designers should concern themselves with underlying political questions. Those who are concerned about values believe that designers should be critical and take a stand in their choice of work, for instance by not promoting industries and products perceived to be harmful. Examples of projects that might be classified as unacceptable include many forms of advertising and designs for cigarette manufacturers, arms companies and so on. Adbusters has been a significant outlet for these ideas, especially in its commitment to detournement and culture jamming. ′

Jonathan Barnbrook
Tibor Kalman
Ellen Lupton
Katherine McCoy
Rick Poynor
Abbott Miller
Lucienne Roberts
Jan van Toorn
Rudy VanderLans
Bob Wilkinson
Nick Bell
Jeffery Keedy
Zuzana Licko
Armand Mevis
Andrew Howard
Jessica Helfand
Milton Glaser
Andrew Blauvelt
Hans Bockting
Irma Boom
Sheila Levrant de Bretteville
Max Bruinsma
Sian Cook
Linda van Deursen
Chris Dixon
William Drenttel
Gert Dumbar
Simon Esterson
Vince Frost
Ken Garland
Erik Spiekermann

and
various designers

(2) ′ First Things First manifesto 2000

We, the undersigned, are graphic designers, art directors and visual communicators who have been raised in a world in which the techniques and apparatus of advertising have persistently been presented to us as the most lucrative, effective and desirable use of our talents. Many design teachers and mentors promote this belief; the market rewards it; a tide of books and publications reinforces it.
Encouraged in this direction, designers then apply their skill and imagination to sell dog biscuits, designer coffee, diamonds, detergents, hair gel, cigarettes, credit cards, sneakers, butt toners, light beer and heavy-duty recreational vehicles. Commercial work has always paid the bills, but many graphic designers have now let it become, in large measure, what graphic designers do. This, in turn, is how the world perceives design. The profession's time and energy is used up manufacturing demand for things that are inessential at best.
Many of us have grown increasingly uncomfortable with this view of design. Designers who devote their efforts primarily to advertising, marketing and brand development are supporting, and implicitly endorsing, a mental environment so saturated with commercial messages that it is changing the very way citizen-consumers speak, think, feel, respond and interact. To some extent we are all helping draft a reductive and immeasurably harmful code of public discourse.
There are pursuits more worthy of our problem-solving skills. Unprecedented environmental, social and cultural crises demand our attention. Many cultural interventions, social marketing campaigns, books, magazines, exhibitions, educational tools, television programmes, films, charitable causes and other information design projects urgently require our expertise and help. We propose a reversal of priorities in favour of more useful, lasting and democratic forms of communication – a mindshift away from product marketing and toward the exploration and production of a new kind of meaning. The scope of debate is shrinking; it must expand. Consumerism is running uncontested; it must be challenged by other perspectives expressed, in part, through the visual languages and resources of design.
In 1964, 22 visual communicators signed the original call for our skills to be put to worthwhile use. With the explosive growth of global commercial culture, their message has only grown more urgent. Today, we renew their manifesto in expectation that no more decades will pass before it is taken to heart. ′

055.2
First Things First Manifesto, 2020

Text source:
Manifesto and project description:
https://www.firstthingsfirst2020.org/
(see sources)

→ E2 ––

′ Updated 2020, text co-written by Marc O'Brien, Namita Dharia, Ben Gaydos, with the help of Sarah Harrison, Julia Yezbick, Karen Stein Shanley, Rachel Cellinese, and Rich Binell.

This manifesto is a living document. Help us rewrite the manifesto by adding your voice. We believe the First Things First Manifesto should reflect collective thoughts on what the world needs and where design plays a role within that world.

We, the undersigned, are designers who have been raised in a world in which we put profit over people and the planet in an attempt to grease the wheels of capitalism and keep the machine running. Our time and energy are increasingly used to manufacture demand, to exploit populations, to extract resources, to fill landfills, to pollute the air, to promote colonization, and to propel our planet's sixth mass extinction. We have helped to create comfortable, happy lives for some of our species and allowed harm to others; our designs, at times, serve to exclude, eliminate, and discriminate.
Many design teachers and professionals perpetuate this ideology; the markets reward it; a tide of imitations and "likes" reinforces it. Encouraged in this direction, designers then apply their skills and imagination to sell fast fashion, fast cars, and fast food; disposable cups, bubble wrap, and unending amounts of single-use plastics; fidget spinners, microwave dinners, and nose hair trimmers. We market unhealthy body images and diets; products and apps that propagate social isolation and depression; the consumption of unbalanced food systems; we sell pills to pop, tiks to tok, and a scrolling feed that never stops… and then the desire to consume it all over again and again. Yes, commercial work has always paid the bills, but many designers have let it become, in large measure, what designers do. This, in turn, is how the world perceives design.
Many of us have grown increasingly uncomfortable with this view of design. Because of this, we call for a massive change in what and how designers design. Climate change is critically entangled with class, race, and gender-based dominance, we can no longer push merely for sustainability, but must create new systems that undo and heal what's been done. What We Must Do:

– We must challenge and examine the histories, processes, and ethics of design and develop new creative skills, resources, collaborations, and languages of design.

– We must support community-based efforts to advance and promote justice, healing, co-existence, and mutual respect.
– We must understand that we are not outside of nature; we are a part of a complex system and our actions must reflect that knowledge.
– We must reverse our profession's priorities in favor of more inclusive, empathetic, and engaged forms of action — a mind-shift that goes beyond sustainability — towards regeneration, exploration, and co-creation of a non-exploitative, non-appropriative set of social-environmental relations.
– We must commit to reconnecting design, manufacturing, distribution, and use of the things we design to the Earth, and all of its inhabitants.
– We must direct our skills for the betterment of humanity towards a more ecological civilization.

We believe all of these principles should be integrated into multidisciplinary design education. We acknowledge the complex and varied nature of designing, which has many possible uses and outcomes.

We do not want to take any of the fun out of life. But we are proposing a reversal of priorities in favor of more useful, generative, and equitable forms of design. In 1964, 22 visual communicators, young and old, signed the original call for our abilities to be valued. In 1999, 33 designers and commentators signed an updated version of First Things First published in magazines around the world, and the document attracted hundreds of signatures online.
In 2014 – on the 50th anniversary of the manifesto – over 1600 designers across the world renewed their commitment to the manifesto.
With the ongoing destruction of essential living systems on our planet, this message has only grown more urgent. As we celebrate the 50th anniversary of Earth Day, we renew the previous manifestos with a greater sense of urgency as we see the compounded effects of our climate crisis unfold before us. It is imperative that we take climate action now. ′

← 64 – 65

056

Superstudio, Studio 65

→ E2 ––

Image source:
Scan of the original; the displayed book on "Superstudio" is out of print. Visual research via the Internet is recommended.

In 1966, six architects (Peter Frassinelli, Alessandro Magris, Roberto Magris, Adolfo Natalini, Alessandro Poli, Cristiano Toraldo di Francia) founded the Superstudio. It focused on architecture and industrial design. In 1966 and 1967, their designs on the "Twelve Ideal Cities" were exhibited in Pistoia and Modena. In 1972, the Museum of Modern Art in New York City displayed this work as part of its exhibition titled "Italy, the New Domestic Landscape." (eds.)

Bibliographic information:
"SuperDesign: Italian Radical Design 1965–75," Maria Cristina Didero; The Monacelli Press, New York, 2017; ISBN 978-1-58093-495-4

Text source:
https://en.wikipedia.org/wiki/Studio_65 (see sources)

Image source:
https://www.monacellipress.com/book/superdesign/

′ Studio 65 (Studiosessanta5) is an Italian architecture studio. It was founded in 1965 in Turin as an avantgarde experimental collective of architects, designers, poets and artists. Its founders were Franco Audrito, Roberta Garosci, Enzo Bertone, Paolo Morello, and Paolo Rondelli. Studio 65 played an important role in the Radical movement in Italian design in 1960 – 70s. Some of the most famous products designed by them is the Bocca sofa and Capitello chair. Other notable pro-jects include the Leonardo sofa, which became one of the icons of the Radical Design movement, interior design of the Casa Canella apartment, the Palladian Villa, as well as the Barbarella night club. (...)

Other members of the Radical design movement from Turin were Piero Gatti-Cesare Paolini-Franco Teodoro, LIBIDARCH, Ceretti-Derossi-Rosso, Guido Drocco, Franco Mello, and Piero Gilardi. Towards the end of the seventies the collective broke up and Audrito and Sampanitou - keeping the name Studio 65 - started an Architectural and design activity base in Arab countries, in parallel with a work of re-edition, rediscovery and contamination of some of the most iconic pieces of their production and creation of unique pieces, often produced in collaboration with iconic Made in Italy companies such as Gufram and Savio Firmino. Currently the firm has offices in Turin, Jeddah, Riyad and Bali. ′

Alessandro Mendini

→ E2 --

Text source:
Shortened version of the entry
https://de.wikipedia.org/wiki/Alessandro_Mendini
(see sources)

Image source:
https://upload.wikimedia.org/wikipedia/commons/1/13Alessandro_Mendini_Poltrona_di_Proust_Studio_Alchimia_1979_ (see sources)

ʼAlessandro Mendini (1931 – 2019) was an Italian designer and architect. He played an important role in the development of design in Italy and held the position of editor-in-chief or publisher of the magazines Casabella, Modo, and Domus alongside his artistic career. (…) Mendini was a trendsetter whose work tried to connect art, architecture, and design. Together with other Italian designers, he developed “Banal Design,” which reinterpreted everyday objects by adding color, patterns, and small shapes. Mendini called this process “redesign.” Around 1978, he concentrated on redesigning seating furniture. His starting materials included classics such as the “Wassily” armchair by Marcel Breuer, the “699 Superleggera” by Gio Pont, or the Thonet chair, plus cheap used furniture from the past decades or historicizing pieces of unknown origin, which resulted in the “Kandissi” sofa and the well-known “Proust” armchair (based on the Louis Seize style). (…)ʼ

Proust Armchair (1978)

← 66 – 67

057

The Maker Movement

→ E2 --

Further information:
https://en.wikipedia.org/wiki/Maker_culture

The “Maker Movement,” also called “Maker Culture,” is a subcultural phenomenon that emerged in the USA. Makers are viewed as the protagonists of a new DIY movement. They use existing objects and materials they already have at hand to create something new by means of modern techniques. The focus lies on the effort of solving a technical problem with one’s own devices, without relying on pricey solutions offered by third-party providers. Makers drew the attention of a wider audience through the use of 3D printers in the 2010s, with which they produced spare parts or entire devices themselves. Aside from a technical curiosity, many makers are also interested in artistic procedures and the development of alternatives to commercial products. A few names that originated in the Maker Movement have made their way into everyday use, for example “hacker spaces,” “FabLabs,” and “makerspaces.” The latter two terms describe open workshops in which members can use jointly acquired equipment that would be unaffordable for individuals. In addition, these spaces serve to exchange information and experiences. A general declared belief in openness, accessibility, transparency, diversity, and open licenses characterize the mindset of this movement. (eds.)

057.1

hartzIVmoebel.com, build more buy less

→ E2 --

Bibliographic information:
“hartzIVmoebel.com, build more, buy Less,” Van Bo Le-Mentzel (ed.); Hatje Cantz Verlag, Ostfildern, 2018; [ENG/GER]
ISBN 978-3-7757-3395-3

Text source:
From the foreword, page 05, line 08 – 21; line 30 – page 7, line 01 – 07;

Image sources:
(1) Pages 40 – 41,
(2) Pages 42 – 43

ʼWelcome!
(…) I am the inventor of Hartz-IV furniture. This is a novel principle for operating a furniture manufacturing company. Entirely without a factory and capital. With this do-it-yourself project, I am giving thousands the opportunity to work without creating overproduction. DIY is the solution. Even though nobody is paid, everyone is highly motivated. Following the furniture, there will now be a book. In line with the same principle: designing together, not alone. Normally, an author comes up with a text, looks for a publisher, which then finds readers. As a rule, a book is only printed once everything is completed. Here, everything is different. I’ve started with sales. I’ve found companions among the so-called supporters who want to help write this book. This book was created through the crowd. This is what I call the thousands of supporters of the Hartz-IV furniture project. This is a social DIY project that I started in 2010. (…) The crowd consists of people who are unemployed and employed, the young and old, the healthy and sick, theoreticians and practitioners, conservatives and visionaries. In an elevator, we would all turn away from each other. But what unites us is our mindset: constructing instead of consuming (build more, buy less). Do you like this attitude? Then join the crowd, because together we can achieve something big. For example, building new furniture or taking over the world… (…)ʼ

(1)

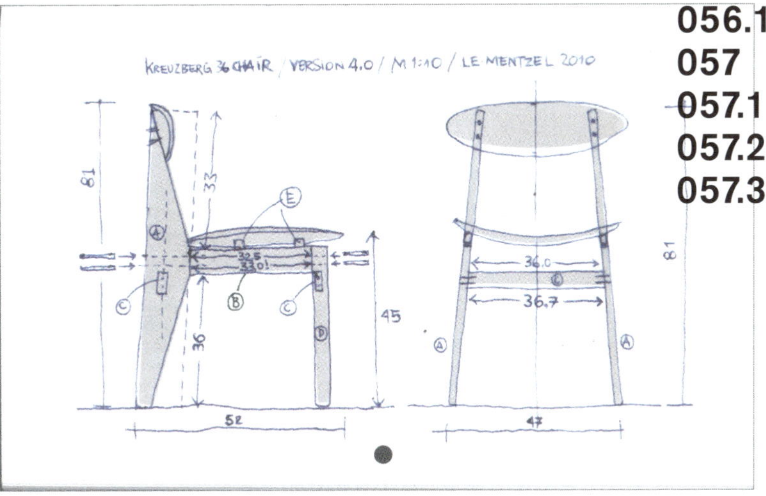

(2)

057.2

Fabrication Laboratory (Fab Lab) – Revolution Field Manual

→ E2 164, 165, 165.1, 166, 167

Bibliographic information:
"Fab Lab – Revolution Field Manual,"
Massimo Menichinelli (ed.);
Niggli Verlag, Salenstein, 2017;
ISBN 978-3-7212-0965-5

Text source: from the book's back cover;

Image source: the book's front cover

ʼA Fab Lab (short for fabrication laboratory) is simultaneously a workshop and a laboratory, equipped with computer-controlled tools like laser cutters, CNC milling machines and 3D printers. A global network of Fab Labs gives teams and individuals access to digital high-tech fabrication technologies. The Fab Lab movement is founded on the groundbreaking idea of enabling almost everybody to make almost everything, almost everywhere.

The book opens with various authors sharing in-sight on topics including the emergence of Fab Labs, the philosophy behind them, and their commercial aspects, as well as the techniques, methods and processes used. Following this, a real-world example is presented, looking at the creative and technical processes of one project undertaken at Fablab Amsterdam. In the second half of the book, 27 note-worthy projects and products are featured in the Fab Gallery, demonstrating the full diversity of possibilities that Fab Labs offer. (...)ʼ

057.3

Social Design. Partizipation und Empowerment

→ E2 --

Bibliographic information:
"Social Design. Partizipation und Empowerment,"
Museum für Gestaltung (ed.); Lars Müller Publishers, 2018;
[in German]
ISBN 978-3-03778-571-3

Text sources:
(1) Text from the back cover; (2) from "Geschichte und Gegenwart," author Angeli Sachs, page 21, lines 01 – 18

(1)ʼSocial design is design for society and with society. On the basis of dialog and participation, social design confronts the imbalance regarding resources, means of production, and future prospects, and strives for a new, equitable exchange between individuals, civil society, the state, and the economy. 25 international projects from different disciplines are demonstrating current solution approaches, putting the redesign of social systems, living and working conditions up for discussion, and thereby enabling a debate on their possibilities and contradictions.ʼ

(2)ʼSocial design as design for society and with society is not a recent invention. But the topic is current because the globally operating economics of growth and the associated consequences for people and the environment are causing trouble for societies or even pushing them to the limits of their existential means. Anyone who is not in this situation yet is worried about the future, and for good reason. It is growing evermore clear that the imbalance with regard to resources, means of production, education, and future prospects makes up a considerable part of the problem. That is why, as has also been the case in past times of crisis – and in contrast to the tendencies towards increasing nationalization and isolation – the development of a liberal-minded social culture and the redesign of social systems, living and work environments that take the world as a whole into account, must be discussed. Architects, designers, craftspeople, and engineers have always played an important role in designing such a social culture. (...)ʼ

Text source:
(1) https://oxfordre.com/environmentalscience/view/
(see sources)

← 66 – 67

058

History of Ecological Design

→ E2 --

Ecological design (also called sustainable design or eco design) refers to the approach of taking environmental aspects (sustainability, service life, reusability) into account when designing products, architecture, and other services. When ecological design was first developed, it primarily focused on incorporating environmental factors into the design process. Over time, this approach gradually began to affect the role of the product: its varied relationships with ecological, economic, social, and cultural areas. By incorporating life cycle models through energy and material flows, ecological design was also linked with the new interdisciplinary field of industrial ecology. In industrial ecology, models simulate the natural ecosystem to develop new approaches for the conception of environmental and technical matters. Ecological design encompasses a complex realm in which political, financial, technical, and social issues correlate with environmental questions. Further research of this vast field is recommended. (eds.)

(1) ′ History of Ecological Design; (Author: Lydia Kallipoliti, 2018), Summary
The term ecological design was coined in a 1996 book by Sim van der Ryn and Stewart Cowan, in which the authors argued for a seamless integration of human activities with natural processes to minimize destructive environmental impact. Following their cautionary statements, William McDonough and Michael Braungart published in 2002 their manifesto book From Cradle to Cradle, which proposed a circular political economy to replace the linear logic of "cradle to grave." These books have been foundational in architecture and design discussions on sustainability and establishing the technical dimension, as well as the logic, of efficiency, optimization, and evolutionary competition in environmental debates. From Cradle to Cradle evolved into a production model implemented by a number of companies, organizations, and governments around the world, and it also has become a registered trademark and a product certification.
Popularized recently, these developments imply a very short history for the growing field of ecological design. However, their accounts hark as far back as Ernst Haeckel's definition of the field of ecology in 1866 as an integral link between living organisms and their surroundings (Generelle Morphologie der Organismen, 1866); and Henry David Thoreau's famous 1854 manual for self-reliance and living in proximity with natural surroundings, in the cabin that he built at Walden Pond, Massachusetts (Walden; or, Life in the Woods, 1854). Since World War II, contrary to the position of ecological design as a call to fit harmoniously within the natural world, there has been a growing interest in a form of synthetic naturalism, (Closed Worlds; The Rise and Fall of Dirty Physiology, 2015), where the laws of nature and metabolism are displaced from the domain of wilderness to the domain of cities, buildings, and objects. With the rising awareness of what John McHale called disturbances in the planetary reservoir (The Future of the Future, 1969), the field of ecological design has signified not only the integration of the designed object or space in the natural world, but also the reproduction of the natural world in design principles and tools through technological mediation. This idea of architecture and design producing nature paralleled what Buckminster Fuller, John McHale, and Ian McHarg, among others, referred to as world planning; that is, to understand ecological design as the design of the planet itself as much as the design of an object, building, or territory. Unlike van der Ryn and Cowan's argumentation, which focused on a deep appreciation for nature's equilibrium, ecological design might commence with the synthetic replication of natural systems. These conflicting positions reflect only a small fraction of the ubiquitous terms used to describe the field of ecological design, including green, sustain, alternative, resilient, self-sufficient, organic, and biotechnical. In the context of this study, this paper will argue that ecological design starts with the reconceptualization of the world as a complex system of flows rather than a discrete compilation of objects, which visual artist and theorist György Kepes has described as one of the fundamental reorientations of the 20th century (Art and Ecological Consciousness, 1972). (...) ′

058.1

Planet B – 100 Ideen für eine Neue Welt

→ E2 --

Bibliographic information:
"Planet B – 100 Ideen für eine Neue Welt," Alain Bieber, Lukas Feireiss (eds.); Verlag der Buchhandlung Walther König, Cologne, 2016;
ISBN 978-3-86335-944-7

Text source:
the book's back cover

′ How will we live in the future? What does the world of tomorrow look like? What will we wear? What will we eat? What will we fight for? The publication at hand is an eclectic collection of different ideas for a new world – a Planet B.

Plan A has failed; the time has come to work on plan B. In this book, the most visionary global artists, designers, architects, writers, and future researchers present their political, poetic,cosmic, humorous, and radical ideas for a new world. With contributions from Rachel Armstrong, Nelly Ben Hayoun, Ernst Bloch, Steward Brand, Brad Downey, Kevin Kelly, Ray Kurzweil, Chus Martinez, Niklas Maak, Lucy McRae, Philippe Rahm, raumlaborberlin, Tomás Saraceno, Space Caviar, Jakob Tigges, Friedrich von Borries, and many more. ′

058.2

Kapitalistischer Realismus ohne Alternative?

→ E2 --

Bibliographic information:
"Kapitalistischer Realismus ohne Alternative?", Mark Fisher; VSA-Verlag, Hamburg, 2013; [in German]
ISBN 978-3-89965-421-9

Also available in English: "Capitalist Realism: Is there no Alternative?" Mark Fisher, Zer0 Books, 2022;
ISBN 978-1803414300

Text sources:
(1) Excerpt from the back cover text;
(2) Page 10, line 27 – page 12, line 09, lines 14 – 17

(1) ′ (...) Why is it easier to imagine the end of the world than the end of capitalism? After 1989, capitalism presented itself as the only realistic political and economic system. As Margaret Thatcher summed it up, "There is no alternative." Any knowledge that things could be different is long gone. British cultural theoretician Mark Fisher (1968 – 2017) analyzed the effects of this "capitalist realism" on our work, our mental well-being, the organization of our schools, and the pop culture that surrounds us, from gangster rap to reality TV. And he asks an important question: Is it possible to imagine an alternative to capitalism that does not represent a step back to the discredited models of state control? In the epilog of the German-language edition, he asks what consequences the financial crisis of 2008 and the Occupy protests had for capitalist realism. ′

(2) ʼ(...) The power of "capitalist realism" is partly derived from the way capitalism subsumes and consumes all prior history. This is one of the effects of his "equivalence system" that assigns all cultural objects – whether these are religious icons, pornography, or an edition of "Capital" – a monetary value. If you walk through the British Museum and see the objects that have been torn from their living environment and hoarded as if they were on board of a "Predator" spaceship, this gives you a powerful idea of how this process works. By transforming practices and rituals into purely aesthetic objects, the world views of past cultures are objectively ironized and turned into "artefacts." Capitalist realism is therefore not just a certain type of realism; rather, it resembles realism in itself. Marx and Engels themselves had already commented on this in their "Communist Manifesto": "(Capital) has drowned the holy shiver of pious rapture, of chivalrous excitement, of bourgeois melancholy in the ice-cold water of egotistical calculation. It has dissolved personal dignity into an exchange value and put an unscrupulous freedom of trade in place of the countless documented and vested freedoms. In other words, it has replaced religious and political illusions of veiled exploitation with open, unabashed, direct, barren exploitation." (Marx/Engels 1972: 464f.)
Capitalism is what remains when the rituals or elaborate symbolic worlds of all belief systems have collapsed, and only the observer-consumer wanders through the ruins and relics. But this shift from belief to aesthetics, from engagement to viewership, is generally described as one of the benefits of capitalist realism. By claiming to have – as Alain Badiou put it – "liberated us from the deadly abstractions" inspired by "ideologies of the past," (Badiou/Cox/Whalen, 2001), capitalist realism presents itself as a shield that protects us from the dangers inherent to belief. An ironic, distanced stance, typical of postmodern capitalism, will allegedly immunize us against the temptations of fanaticism. Lowering our expectations, we are told, is a small price to pay to ensure our protection against terror and totalitarianism. "We live in a contradictory state," says Badiou: "A brutal status quo, unequal to the highest extent – because every form of existence is valued only on the basis of money – is presented to us as an ideal. To justify their own conservatism, partisans of the established order cannot truly describe this state as 'ideal' or 'wonderful'. Instead, they have decided simply to call all other states 'terrible'. Of course, we do not live under the conditions of pure goodness, they say. But we should be happy that we do not live under the conditions of evil. Our democracy is not perfect. But it is better than the bloody dictatorships. Capitalism may be unjust. But it is not criminal like Stalinism. (...)" The "realism" described here works along the lines of the dampened perspective of depression, believing that any positive condition and any hope are dangerous illusions. (...)ʼ

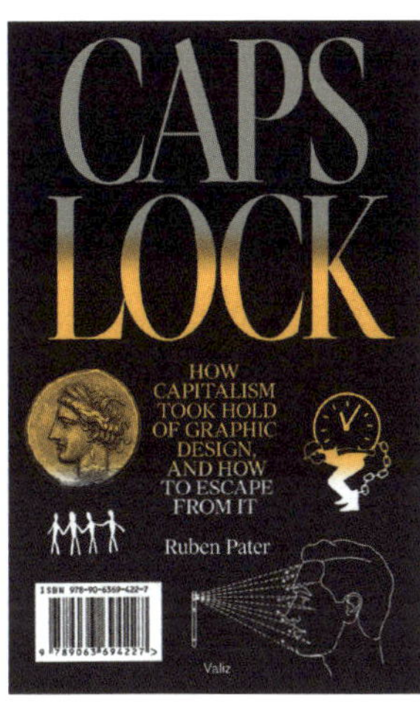

058.3

Caps Lock: How Capitalism Took Hold of Graphic Design, and How to Escape from it

→ E2 --

Bibliographic information:
"Caps Lock: How Capitalism Took Hold of Graphic Design, and How to Escape from It," Ruben Pater; Valiz Publishers, Amsterdam, 2021;
ISBN 978-9-4920-9581-7

Text source: https://valiz.nl/en/publications/caps-lock.html
(see sources)

Image sources: the book's front cover; pages 108 – 109

Ruben Pater (*1977) is a Dutch designer. As an author, he examines visual communication and its role in society (see also 002.1)

ʼCapitalism could not exist without the coins, notes, documents, graphics, interfaces, branding and advertisements; artefacts that have been (partly) created by graphic designers. Even anti-consumerist strategies such as social design and speculative design are being appropriated within capitalist societies to serve economic growth. It seems that design is locked in a system of exploitation and profit, a cycle that fosters inequality and the depletion of natural resources.
CAPS LOCK uses clear language and striking visual examples to show how graphic design and capitalism are inextricably linked. The book contains many case studies of designed objects related to capitalist societies and cultures, and also examines how the education and professional practice of (graphic) designers supports the market economy and how design practice is caught within that very system.
The content of CAPS LOCK is structured in chapters with titles of professions that designers can occupy (such as Educator; Engineer, Hacker, Futurist, Activist, etc.). These titles respond to the importance of not just how designers make work, but also how they perform daily economic and social roles. Each chapter is divided into coherent articles in which diverse examples of objects and design practices are relayed. The book also features examples of radical design collectives, that work towards alternatives between design, community and reciprocity.ʼ

GET OFF MY PROPERTY!

Owning land is for many families an important step to ensure future wealth. In feudal times, only a handful of wealthy families owned all the land, while the rest had to pay tribute or rent. Being born into nobility meant that you could live off the taxes for the rest of your life—free money for generations to come. That sounds like ancient history, but research found that in the UK, less than 1 percent of the population today still owns 66 percent of the land. Most of whom are the same dukes, barons, and earls who have owned it for centuries.[32] Maps of land ownership still reveal a history of inequality. For example in Colombia, 0.4 percent of the population owns 61 percent of the land.

The End of the Commons

One of capitalism's chief architects, Adam Smith, believed that property, together with markets and money, was the foundation on which human society was built.[33] Land ownership is perhaps not as self-evident as he made it seem. Throughout history and across cultures, we find many different forms of land use, such as land stewardship and common land. Many cultures do not believe land should be owned since it belongs to all living beings, human and non-human alike. The notion of land ownership suggests that the owners can do with it as they please, without taking the ecological value, or the cultural value, into account. Cutting up land and selling it as 'property' piece by piece has not only led to inequality but also to the unrestrained extraction of natural resources, leading to the climate crisis we are faced with today. Regarding land as property was central to the beginning of capitalism.

Lands in medieval Europe were owned by feudal lords. Part of a lord's estate (manor) was land for shared use, called the common land, or 'commons'. Peasants could have cattle graze there or grow

The Designer as Engineer 109

← 66–67

059

Graphic Design: Now in Production

→ E2 ––

Bibliographic information:
"Graphic Design: Now in Production," Andrew Blauvelt, Ellen Lupton, Walker Art Center (eds.), Minneapolis, 2014; ISBN 978-0-935640-98-4

Text source:
book description on the back cover

ʼWith more than 250 Artists and some 1.400 images, this ambitious catalogue and exibition survey the vibrant landscape of graphic designers who have seized the means of production and are rewriting the nature of contemporary design practise. Charting a rich vein of activity that cuts across wildly diverse fields, Graphic Design: Now in Production chronicles the postmillenial scene of all-access design tools and self-publishing systems, the open-source nature of creative production, and the entrepreneurial spirit of the designer turned producer. Part operating manual, part academic reader, and part sourcebook, the catalogue features writings by some of the field's major thinkers, including Åbäke, Ian Albinson, Peter Bil'ak, Andrew Blauvelt, Rob Giampietro, James Goggin, Peter Hall, Steven Heller, Jeremy Leslie, Ellen Lupton, Ben Radatz, Michael Rock, Dmitri Siegel, Daniel van der Velden, Armin Vit and Bryony Gomez-Palacio, and Lorraine Wild. Freely mixing writing styles, from personal rants to the collective speak of Wikipedia, the book touches upon hundreds of topics. Picking up where the design authorship debates of the 1990s left off, this catalogue examines the evolution of graphic design in an expanded field of practise. It considers myriad issues, such as the changing nature of reading and writing, self-publishing and clientless design, the persistence of the poster and the book in a screen-based culture, the designer's voice in the age of crowdsourcing, the visualization of journalism, the ubiquity of branding, and the democratization of design tools and software. Sprinkled throughout are numerous bits – factoids, expanations, and tangents – exploring everything from fake Apple stores to Adobe DPS, Ghanaian coffins to cultural analytics, Scriptographer to heraldry.ʼ

← 70–71

060

Definition of the term "Aesthetics"

→ E2 168, 169, 170

Text source:
https://en.wikipedia.org/wiki/Aesthetics (see sources)

ʼAesthetics (also spelled esthetics) is the branch of philosophy concerned with the nature of beauty and the nature of taste; and functions as the philosophy of art. Aesthetics examines the philosophy of aesthetic value, which is determined by critical judgements of artistic taste; thus, the function of aesthetics is the "critical reflection on art, culture and nature".
Aesthetics studies natural and artificial sources of experiences and how people form a judgement about those sources of experience. It considers what happens in our minds when we engage with objects or environments such as viewing visual art, listening to music, reading poetry, experiencing a play, watching a fashion show, movie, sports or exploring various aspects of nature.

The philosophy of art specifically studies how artists imagine, create, and perform works of art, as well as how people use, enjoy, and criticize art. Aesthetics considers why people like some works of art and not others, as well as how art can affect our moods and our beliefs. Both aesthetics and the philosophy of art try to find answers to what exactly is art and what makes good art.

Aesthetics and the philosophy of art
Some distinguish aesthetics from the philosophy of art, claiming that the former is the study of beauty and taste while the latter is the study of works of art. But aesthetics typically considers questions of beauty as well as of art. It examines topics such as art works, aesthetic experience, and aesthetic judgement.

Aesthetic experience refers to the sensory contemplation or appreciation of an object (not necessarily a work of art), while artistic judgement refers to the recognition, appreciation or criticism of art in general or a specific work of art. In the words of one philosopher, "Philosophy of art is about art. Aesthetics is about many things – including art. But it is also about our experience of breathtaking landscapes or the pattern of shadows on the wall opposite your office." (...) ʼ

← 70–71

061

The History of Beauty

→ E2 ––

Bibliographic information:
"History of Beauty," Umberto Eco, Alastair McEwen; Rizzoli, New York, 2004;
ISBN 978-0847826469

In his book "History of Beauty," Umberto Eco discusses the category of "beauty" and demonstrates that and how the standards, perspectives, and values have changed again and again over time. His descriptions range from antiquity to the present day and are accompanied by countless texts from literature and philosophy. (eds.)

061.1

Die Geschichte der Hässlichkeit

→ E2 ––

Bibliographic information:
"Die Geschichte der Hässlichkeit," Umberto Eco; Carl Hanser Verlag, Munich, 2007; [in German]
ISBN 978-3-446-20939-5

Text source: book blurb
English edition: "On ugliness," Umberto Eco

ʼThe history of ugliness compiles a panopticon: from horror in Greek antiquity through to the ugliness of industry, from hell and the devil to witches and satanists, from the grotesque to obscenity, from the apocalypse to modern kitsch. Umberto Eco and his employee have assembled an overwhelming wealth of four-tone images from the areas of painting, film, and photography, from sculpture and architecture and quotes from literature and philosophy, thereby showing us the fascinating dark side of the beauty in which western culture likes to bask.ʼ

The film can be accessed on YouTube at the following address: https://www.youtube.com/watch?v=7Zxc-22Vd9VQ (see sources)

← 70–71

062

Hat Schönheit Regeln? Der Goldene Schnitt (Film)

→ E2 171, 172, 173

The 15-minute film from broadcaster Bayerischer Rundfunk explains where in nature we can find regularities that humans have extolled as principles of beauty. The film presents astonishing relationships. Furthermore, it is fascinating to discover all the different areas in which the golden ratio, the Fibonacci sequence, and the pentagram play a role: The spectrum ranges from petal arrangements through to DNA. The film shows the extent to which these relationship parameters shape our perceptions. (eds.)

← 70–71

063

Experimenting with facial symmetry

→ E2 --

Text source:
https://mymodernmet.com/eray-eren-asymmetry/
(see sources)

Image source:
(1, 2) own photographs;

Countless examinations and experiments have been conducted on facial symmetry. We, Ulysses Voelker and Michael Schmitz, also decided to manipulate a picture of each of us (see pictures 1 and 2).
We were inspired by the work of the artist Eray Eren. His procedure is described in the following. The text is taken from the website (see text source), where he also presents his work. (eds.)

'Turkish photographer Eray Eren takes faces and presents them as triptychs – each panel representing a standard, forward-facing portrait (left photo) along with two additional images that split the original face down the middle and form a mirrored version of the left half of the subject's actual face (middle photo) and another one of the right side (right photo). The project, titled Asymmetry, explores the asymmetry in faces and just how different one would look, were they to have symmetrical faces that mimicked either side.

The series, first brought to our attention by Eren himself, offers a very visual look at both beauty and the genetic materials that make up one's physical appearance. Each person has multiple factors to their face alone that are not balanced on both sides, yet it's that imbalance that skews from perfect symmetry that makes them look the way they do. The adjacent portraits prove that symmetry transforms the human face enough to look like a completely different person.'

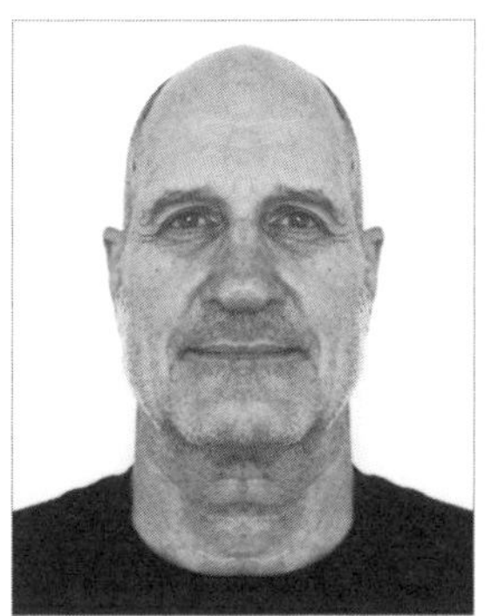

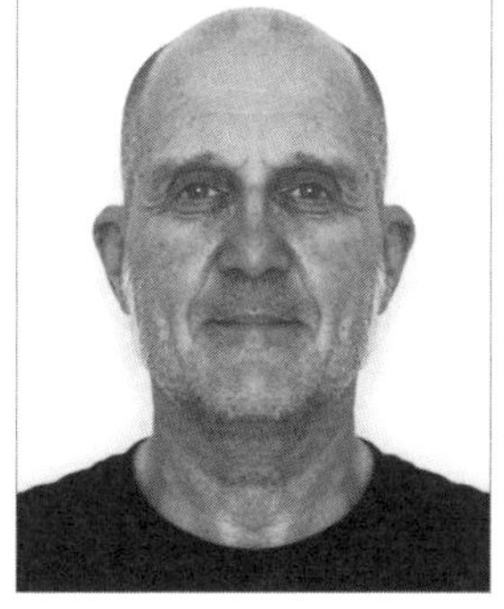

(1) Ulysses Voelker

(2) Michael Schmitz

← 72–73

064

The Golden Ratio

→ E2 174, 175

The so-called “golden ratio” (from the Latin “sectio aurea” or “proportio divina,” the divine proportion) refers to an ideal proportionality. It applies in the following scenario: If you divide a line in two in such a way that the longer part (a) relates to the shorter part (b) in the same manner as the overall line (a+b) to the longer part (a) – in both cases, the ratio has a value of 1.618 (see figure on the right).

These ideal proportions were discovered in nature back in antiquity, in the time of Euclid. For centuries, they were considered the ultimate benchmark in art and architecture. (eds.)

Detailed information:
https://en.wikipedia.org/wiki/Golden_ratio

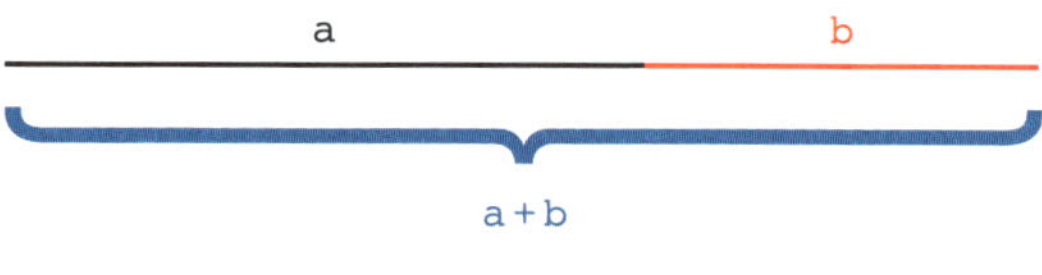

$\frac{a+b}{a}$ corresponds to $\frac{a}{b}$ = 1,618

← 72–73

065

The Fibonacci Sequence

→ E2 --

The so-called Fibonacci sequence refers to proportionalities discovered in nature. Leonardo Fibonacci described this phenomenon (which was known back in antiquity) after encountering it while observing the growth of a rabbit population in 1202.

The Fibonacci numbers form an infinite sequence of natural numbers in which every number represents the sum of the two previous numbers. The sequence starts as follows:

0, 1, 1, 2, 3, 5, 8, 13, 21, 34, 55 … and so on. Examinations have shown that the Fibonacci sequence appears in nature in many different ways and represents growth patterns. (eds.)

Detailed information:
https://en.wikipedia.org/wiki/Fibonacci_sequence

Figure below:
Tile pattern of (black) squares, the edge lengths of which correspond to the Fibonacci sequence.

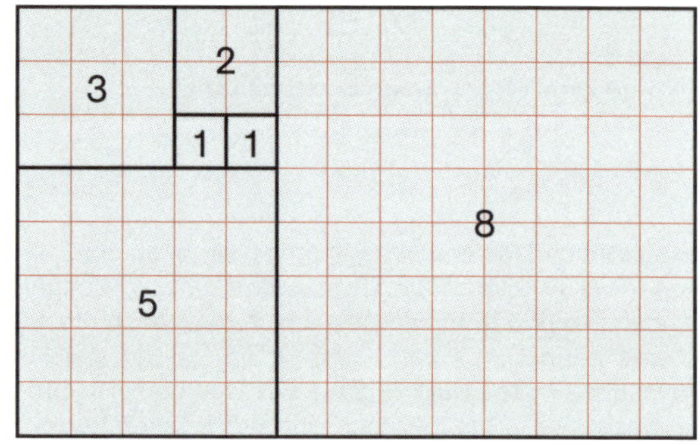

← 74–75

066

The Pentagram

→ E2 176

The term pentagram stems from the ancient Greek (“pénte” for “five” and “gramm” for “line, stroke”). It refers to the shape of a five-pointed star. The pentagram held a symbolic meaning for thousands of years. In Mesopotamia, it served as a symbol of “divinity” around the year 3,000 B.C. Pythagoras viewed the pentagram as a sign of health. In the Middle Ages, the pentagram was also called “druid foot” and “druid star.”

The five-pointed star was considered a symbol to banish evil. The construction of the pentagram includes the proportions of the golden ratio. Since it can be drawn without putting down the pen, finishing where it started, the pentagram is also considered a symbol for the circle of life. (eds.)

Detailed information:
https://en.wikipedia.org/wiki/Pentagram

The pentagram also contains the golden ratio:

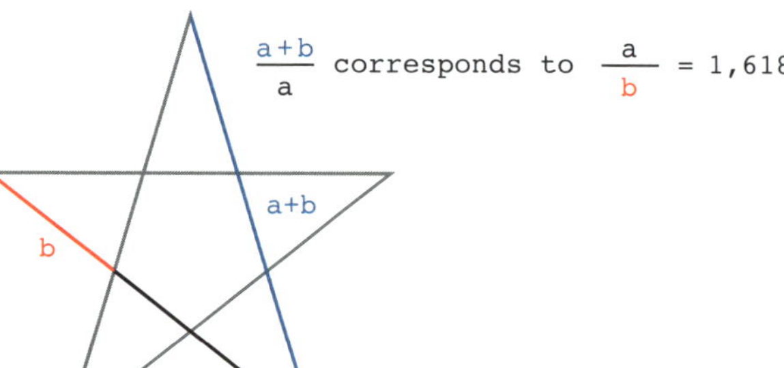

$\frac{a+b}{a}$ corresponds to $\frac{a}{b}$ = 1,618

066.1

Altpersische Numerologie – die Zahl 5

→ E2 --

Bibliographic information:
“Altpersische Numerologie,”
Arman Sahihi; Ariston
Verlag, Geneva, 1992;
[in German]
ISBN 3-7205-1717-9

Text sources:
Page 30, lines 01 – 17,
page 31, lines 29 – 30

‘5. The number of the carefree one. The number of the lively one. The number of disorder. The existing orders are questioned. Life is viewed with cheerfulness. The number of fingers on one hand, toes on one foot. The number of sepals on a rose. The number of elements in Ancient Persia: earth, water, fire, light, air. Composed of the male three and the female two. Inseparable in its connection, close to perfection when added together. Magical as a symbol of the connection between man and woman. Sensual in regard to the natural shape of petals. Frequently mysterious in its depiction. The five fingers on the raised hand, warding off threats. The five arms of the starfish, an old sign of the oracle. Five is the ultimate life-affirming number. (…)
Five carries special meaning as the oracle number. It embodies the magical element. (…)’

← 76 – 77

067

Gutenberg's 42-Line Bible and Textura

→ E2 177, 178

Bibliographic information:
"Gutenberg – Aventur und Kunst. Vom Geheimunternehmen zur ersten Medienrevolution," Stadt Mainz (ed.), Peter Krawietz (Man.), Dr. Eva-Maria Hanebutt-Benz (Konz.), 2000; [in German]
ISBN 3-87439-507-3

Sources:
(1) Page 196, 2nd column, lines 28 – 41
(2) Page 197, 1st column, line 38 – 2nd column, line 19
(3) Page 197, 2nd column, line 28 – page 198, 1st column, line 8

Illustrative material available at:
https://de.wikipedia.org/wiki/Gutenberg-Bibel

The quotes stem from the catalog for the exhibition organized by the city of Mainz in 2000 on the occasion of Johannes Gutenberg's 600th birthday. (u.v)

(1) ′(...) B42 and Its Types
In contrast to the comprehensive innovations for book production that accompanied Gutenberg's invention on a technical and logical level, the product of this media revolution appears astonishingly traditional. Earlier book printing had actually never tried to confront the manuscript. Moreover, it viewed itself as a perfected form of this manuscript and therefore maintained an unbroken continuity, not only in terms of aesthetics, but also content. Just like the scribes, incunabulum printing used handwriting as templates, in the case of B42 this would have been a version of the Parisian Vulgate. (...)′

′(2) (...) Gutenberg printed his Latin bible in two columns with 42 lines each (with the exception of a few pages with 40 or 41 lines) – hence the designation B42. He chose the typeface "Textura," a representative book typeface that does not attempt to deny its origins from the medieval manuscript tradition. Gutenberg's Textura is characterized by a dense typeface in which the individual letters appear to be interwoven; an impression created by the absence of any rounding and that reinforces the print in its regularity. Even an "o" consists of individual lines that sit across from each other at an angle. In addition, the size of the letters and the spaces between them are proportional. The distances between, v, o, and s in the word "vos" are larger than those between the v and I in the word "vidit." Such a procedure is also derived from the repertoire of medieval scribes, as is the use of ligatures (connecting individual letters such as the "d" and "e" in the word "de") or abbreviations. For example, the symbol that resembles the number 9 represents the Latin ending "us," while a horizontal line denotes the absence of the following letter. (...)′

′(3)(...) Not only his own skills, but also the type material available to him played an important role in producing high-quality work. That is why Gutenberg had 290 different characters (figures) cut and poured für his B42, 47 of which were uppercase letters, 63 lowercase letters, 92 abbreviations, 83 ligatures, and 5 punctuation marks. Ligatures and abbreviations made it easier to maintain the correct line length. However, a scribe can hardly accomplish a truly vertical edge of the right column, as demonstrated by the red handwritten parts of the text of B42, whereas printing with movable metal typeface enabled precise vertical line endings for the columns. Because while the scribe needs to arrange the line in advance and cannot alter anything that has already been written, typesetting allows for any number of corrections. If the typesetter is dissatisfied with the line division, they can undo it and reassemble it. That is why the abbreviations in book printing are actually superfluous and disappear at the end of the 15th century, like many obsolete habits adopted from the manuscript. But at the early stage of B42, they primarily still point to the close intellectual and aesthetic relationship between handwriting and typesetting. (...)′

← 78 – 79

068

Read + Play: Typografie ist evolutionär

→ E2 ––

Bibliographic information:
"Read + Play. Einführung in die Typografie," Ulysses Voelker; Verlag Hermann Schmidt Mainz, 2015; [in German]
ISBN 978-3-87439-868-8

Text source:
Page 15, line 08 – page 19, line 26;

Image source:
https://de.wikipedia.org/wiki/Gutenberg-Bibel#/media/
(see sources)

′(...) The writing system we use nowadays has its origin in the Phoenician characters. Following its development over the centuries, we can follow the change from pictograms via abstract signs (graphemes) right down to our letters of today. Around 900 BC, the Phoenician writing – hitherto only based on consonants – was adopted by the Greeks and completed by adding vowels. The result was geometrically orientated form of writing with capital letters. The Romans adapted and completed the Greek monumental form, and around 100 BC created the chisselled Capitals Monumentalis (again, an alphabet consisting of capitals only). Like the Greek model, the Capitalis was not a very practical form of writing. Its geometrical static meant that it could only be drawn (or chisselled), but it was not suitable for fluent writing. However, the letter shapes of this representative form of writing were the graphic base dominating the written communication in everyday life.

The writing tools, the material used for writing on and the speed of which people wanted to read and write, all this influenced the shapes of the letters. The development of such a utilitarian script took its course from the unical (a handwritten interpretation of the Capitalis) via the semi unical (with very pronounced ascenders and descenders) up to the proportions of the three-level letters we know nowadays, with their typical ascenders, x-height and descenders. During the reign of Charlemagne (approx. AD 800) they received the form which is largely the form we use today, the so-called Carolingian minuscule.

Up to the 15th century, the Gothic minuscule, which evolved from the Carolingian minuscule, was the dominating book type in Europe. In German-speaking areas, the very severe Gothic Textura dominated, particularly in liturgical texts, while in southern Europe the softer Rotunda prevailed. The Renaissance, beginning in the 14th century, then had a lasting influence on the further development of our script, because in northern Italy a variant became established which distressed from the aesthetics of the Gothic minuscule: the Humanistic minuscule. This shows some special features, thanks to the art of the humanists. In their desire to recreate the spirit of antiquity, they rediscovered the Roman Capitalis and signed it to the alphabet of the late Carolingian minuscule, because they erroneously assumed that this has been the script of the ancient Romans. From the Monumental script of antiquity and the script of the monks they created a new alphabet, which formed the basis of our present-day characters.

It cannot be a coincidence that this creative age of the Renaissance also brought forth another epoch-making development: around 1450 Johannes Gutenberg of Mainz invented the printing press with movable lead type. Up to that time, written documents were unique items. If a copy was needed, this was copied from the original. The invention of movable type revolutionised communication and rang in a „Democratization of knowledge", since in the course of the following centuries the printing of ever larger editions gave more and more people access to information.

Johannes Gutenberg took the Gothic minuscule, which was the dominating script in his home country, as the basis for his lead type. This was very much orientated along the handwritten ductus of the monks and first of all tried to conceal its technical

The Gutenberg Bible (page cutout)

origin: thus, there are still many variants of single letters and ligatures (connected pairs) to be found in the printed version of the Gothic Textura, which was not only needed for a well-balanced justification, but were meant to convey an impression of handwritten individuality. During the initial development of printing with movable lead type, the ideal was to achieve as great a similarity to handwriting as possible – a difficult undertaking, because in the end the repetition of type resulted only in rigid imitations of handwritten texts. Later so-called Broken type developed in the tradition of the Gothic minuscule, like the Schwabach (15th century) and the multifaceted Fracture (16th century). The latter was one of the most commonly used types in the German speaking areas and in Northern Europe right into the first decades of the 20th century, until it was forbidden by the Nazis in 1941.

The Humanistic miniscule of the beginning 15th century was, on the other hand, mostly used in the Romance languages of southern Europe. It established a style called Antiqua and which – in contrast to Gutenberg's Gothic-orientated lead type – established a new aesthetic in the field of print. The single letters no longer disguised their consistent form and abandoned their ligatures. Through the visual commitment to the ordering principle of the lead type, the typeface radiated distance and objectiveness, which was lacking in the individuality of hand writing (and in the lead script imitating it).

However, in the Venetian as well as the French Renaissance Antiqua the influence of the writing tool upon the form of the single letter was still visible. Over time, the script design for lead type diverged more and more from the model for a script written with the quill. The Baroque Antiqua (16th century) appeared simpler and more robust, and the classicist Antiqua of the 18th century had totally lost the "handwritten ductus". In Classicism, things came full circle: the print media were assigned the representative character which had already served to distinguish their model, the Capitalis Monumentalis of antiquity. This had consequences, because as far as readability was concerned, the static, contrasting typeface did not stand comparison with its predecessors.

The development of scripts throughout the centuries was always subject to two influences: on the one hand they were shaped by the requirements of everyday use, on the other hand they were at all times regarded as an expression of stately and clerical power and representation. The scripts developed during the Renaissance, the Baroque and

Hamburgefonts

Bembo (French Renaissance-Antiqua)

Hamburgefonts

Times (Baroque-Antiqua)

Hamburgefonts

Bodoni (Classicist Antiqua)

Hamburgefonts

Akzidenz Grotesk (Grotesk font)

Hamburgefonts

Rockwell (Egytienne font)

Classicism are to a great extent still in use today. Their features are still the basis of many type designs, and for the designer it is part of his basic knowledge to know them.

The stylistic eras changed, but the lead type technique was in use almost unchanged until the Sixties of the 20th century. Even the sociological, economical and technical developments of the 19th century, which during industrialization influenced the development of typefaces, could not change this. Because industrial production suddenly resulted in products competing with each other, therefore they had to meet the challenges of the market. So they had to be advertised. Advertising, however, had to be loud, space-saving and yet conspicuous. For this, the available range of typefaces was not sufficient. There followed the so-called Sans serif types (called Gothic types in America) which got their name from their appearance, which had been unknown up to then: they had no serifs. At the same time, the Egyptienne fonts developed, with letters that featured rather robust serifs. (...)'

068.1

Read + Play. Einführung in die Typografie

→ E2 --

Bibliographic information:
"Read + Play. Einführung in die Typografie," Ulysses Voelker;
Verlag Hermann Schmidt Mainz, 2015;
[in German]
ISBN 978-3-87439-868-8

Text sources: page 06, line 01 – page07, line 20

The book serves to help readers navigate the jungle of typographic specialist knowledge.

More than a hundred book recommendations and links are linked to texts that deal with all relevant aspects of typography.

'(...) The relevance of the subject of typography becomes clear over the course of a degree program (at the latest). It becomes apparent that typography is a core subject of visual communication. Because typography means nothing more than dealing with language put down in writing, which dominates our everyday lives and represents one of most important sources of information. Whether in the form of a book, magazine, as part of signage, as information on the Internet, as a package insert, or as timetable information: They all contain combinations of letters that form words,

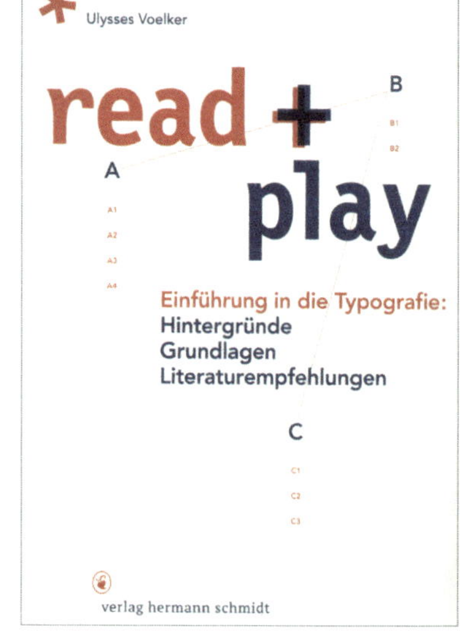

and whose arrangements on surfaces convey content. This finding is easy for laypeople to understand, as is the fact that the use of characters made human civilization possible in the first place. Aspiring designers will therefore find themselves privy to a subject whose relevance they had underestimated and whose content seems unexpectedly complex. Because all information on the subject belongs to a greater context: The history of typography is always also the history of communication and production methods. Typography was and is always a reflection of the dominant political and cultural conditions.
To the present day, typography is both written communication and a design style. (…) A degree program is short, the list of skills to be acquired tends to be long. Books and expert literature on all specializations are available for typographic education. The selection will not make it easy for you: Some specialist books repeat each other's content, others portray outdated opinions, and some reflect the latest debates. There is an endless selection of strange opinions and standard works. Some books have a scientific/theoretical character, others simply show pretty typography. "Read + Play" will help you find your way in this sea of information. (...) /

068.2

Geschichte der Schrift

→ E2 --

Bibliographic information:
"Geschichte der Schrift," Harald Haarmann; Verlag C. H. Beck, Munich, 2011; [in German]
ISBN 978-3-406-47998-4

Text sources:
Page 10, line 18 – page 11, line 14, line 19 – 26; page 12, line 01 – page 14, line 10

Image sources:
(1) The English version of the contract, page 12;
(2) The Delawares' contract version, page 13;

(see sources)

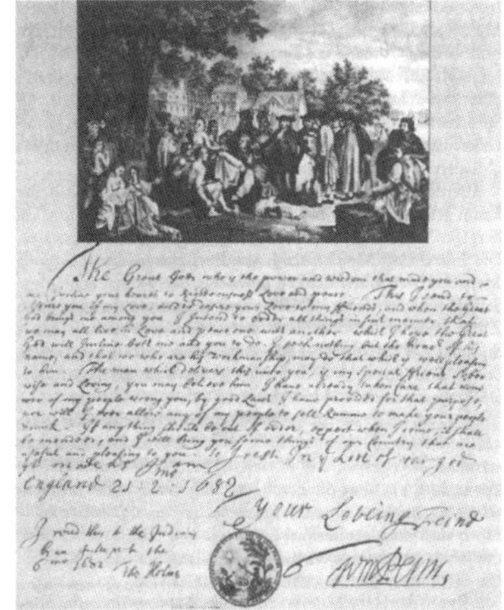

(1)
The English version of the contract between William Penn and the Delawares from the year 1682.

/ (...) In an environment of literacy, where illiteracy is a side note, there is hardly any reason to contemplate alternative models of society that function without writing. The situation looks different in developing countries, where literacy is a privilege reserved for the social, economic, and political elite, while illiteracy constitutes a characteristic of the living conditions of broad levels of the population. But what this world, despite its literacy gap, shares with the developed states and their generally available textuality, is the unavoidable civilizational ideal of written culture. However, there are many cultures that still exist without the use of writing: in the rain forests of Brazil, Venezuela, and Colombia, in the Sahel region of Africa, in the Malaysian jungle, in the inaccessible mountain valleys of Papua New Guinea, and in the outback of the Australian continent. Modern cultures without writing exist in small populations whose language is only spoken by a few hundred or thousand individuals. The existence of many of these small populations is endangered, and their cultures are at risk of declining in the wake of global assimilation pressure. However, there are also small populations whose existence is hardly threatened. This applies to the approximately 900 Etoro in the mountainous inland area of Papua New Guinea's Bosavi region. The Etoro are masters of traditional lifestyles that prove to us text-oriented humans that culture without writing is still functional. (...)

Europeans believe they are witnessing "primitiveness" in places that do not use writing. But if we take a closer look, we will have to admit, with astonishment, that a wide range of skills and techniques are required to organize life within a village community without the achievements of industrial society. The Etoro provide a good example of how a traditional culture with roots dating back thousands of years has remained functional to the present day in harmony with the natural environment. (...)

The inventiveness of people in traditional cultures for recording information for reuse without writing, but with visual means, is impressive. The cultural history of the native North Americans offers particularly interesting examples of mnemonics that use visual methods and oral transmission of texts in a symbiotic interrelationship. One of countless examples in colonial history that illustrates the major cultural contrast between the world of textuality and the world of visual-oral mnemonics is the contract that William Penn negotiated with the Delaware natives in 1682 concerning the acquisition of lands in the region that would later be named Pennsylvania in his honor. Penn composed a corresponding text in English. The piece of paper with the image and blacklines on it had little meaning for the Native Americans participating in the negotiation. To record the memorable event of concluding the contract, the Delawares produced their own version of the contract. This document, in turn, meant little to the white people – to them, it simply contained three belts with decorative patterns. (...) They consisted

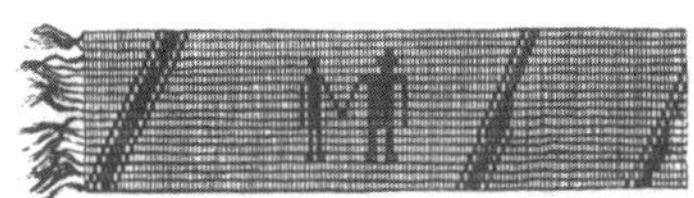

(2)
The Delawares' contract version.

of several strings tied together and strung with oval discs with colorful seashells. On the first "wampum" of the contract with Penn, the contractual partners are depicted in the form of embroidered figures. The geometric motifs on the other two belts symbolize mountains and river courses. (...) /

← 78–79

069

Texte zur Theorie der Fotografie

→ E2 179

Bibliographic information:
"Texte zur Theorie der Fotografie," Bernd Stiegler (ed.); Reclam Verlag, Ditzingen, 2018; [in German]
ISBN 978-3-15-018708-1

Text source:
Page 21, line 01 – page 23, line 08

It might be a little surprising that "photography" is mentioned only briefly in the text on page 76 of this book. After all, it undisputedly plays a major role in visual communication. It shares the fate of other subfields that also have their very own function in visual communication and to which genre-typical discussions, perspectives, schools of thought, traditions, and techniques are also inherent. The fact that we can only cite initial theoretical/historical approaches of these subfields and point to related sources is simply due to the limited scope of the book.

But with the book "Texte zur Theorie der Fotografie" ("Texts on the Theory of Photography"), we are quoting a wonderful option for introductory reading that conveys an initial understanding of how complex, interesting, socially relevant, and changeable photography is (beyond all practical experience with the camera). The book has six chapters that contain many different contributions. Here are the chapter titles:

1 Photography and What is Real
2 Photography and Indexicality
3 Photography and Art
4 Photography and Perception
5 Photography and Society
6 Photography in the Digital Age

(eds.)

/ Photography and What is Real – Introduction

Photography is the technical medium of realism. This legacy is unique to photography and continues to determine our image of photography. To the present day, it has been unable to free itself from it. This "realism" of photography is conveyed medially, in an idiosyncratic manner, and is visualized and reflected in the pictures. In photographs, that which is understood as reality becomes visible: Photographs construct forms of an assumed reality of what is visible. To take this thesis even further: Photographs are medial constructions of reality. Photography is a visual materialization of certain concepts of reality in images. This is the continuity, but at the same time also the difference between the various forms that photography can take and has taken in a protean way, and the application fields that it has conquered so far. And this is also the meaning of photography – in both senses of the word: the meaning that is attributed to photography culturally, historically, epistemologically, and aesthetically, and the meaning that these pictures carry. Photographs are performative of reality, of medially conveyed reality. In different times, these take very different and sometimes mutually exclusive shapes: Sharpness vs. blurring, art vs. science, document vs. staging, analog vs. digital pictures – as some classic basic distinctions – or CCTV, advertising photos, smartphone snapshots and montages – as highly different image types – are respectively different strategies that allocate a certain form of relationship to reality, construction of reality, and interpretation of reality. The recent changes that photography has undergone in different medial contexts, and the ontological doubt that digitization brought with it, have not changed anything about this. Photographs continue to be visual reflections of reality, are conveyed medially, and represent realism concentrated in images – even if reality is radically constructed and sometimes consists of nothing but image material generated on and edited on the computer. Even then, photography is a visual abbreviation of a certain concept of reality that can also be, and occasionally has been, understood as a radical construction. This "principle of realism" of photography accounts for its referential and reflexive character. Photography's "meaning of meaning" lies in producing and distributing design forms of reality. This allows certain forms of interpretation to circulate and condense themselves in pictures. The history of photography is a historical sedimentation of such conceptions of reality that seek to link the subjectivity of perception with the alleged objectivity of "nature's pencil" (Talbot), as photography has been dubbed for good reason. Photographs are index fossils of historical constructions of reality. The history of photography is therefore not only a complex story of different interpretations of reality, but also a story of perception. Photography owes its meaning to this special feature that no other technical medium can claim for itself in this way. Even if there has been talk of the apparent end of photography, or at least of the photographic age, for a few decades now, these prophecies of doom fail to realize that the ontology of the photographic images is determined less by its materiality and more by its ability and function to make reality as a construction visible in the picture and record this in the picture, spread it, and thereby ensure its circulation. This constitutes its meaning and its socio-cultural relevance and task. Through photographs, we medially assure ourselves of the reality, the actuality in which we live and that we view as our reality. (...) /

069.1

Sehen. Das Bild der Welt in der Bilderwelt

→ E2 ––

Bibliographic information:
"Sehen. Das Bild der Welt in der Bilderwelt," John Berger et al.; Fischer Verlag, Frankfurt/Main, 2016; [in German]
ISBN 978-3596036776

Text source:
From the edition published by Rowohlt Verlag, 1996, ISBN 3-499-16868-5: page 08, line 01 – page 10, line 06

Also available in English: "Ways of Seeing". John Berger (1926–2017) was a British art critic and writer. (eds.)

/ (...) Our means of perception is influenced by our knowledge or our faith. In the Middle Ages, for example, when humans believed in the real existence of hell, the sight of fire must have held a different meaning than it does today. The idea of hell at this time was shaped by the sight of fire that burned everything to ashes and the experience of the pain caused by a burn. And with lovers, the sight of their beloved partner can be one of such totality that can – for a limited time – be achieved only in the act of love itself, but otherwise neither by words nor embraces. This complex optical perception, that words can never live up to, is therefore more than a mechanical reaction to certain optical stimuli. (This would merely refer to the physical visual process on the eye's retina.) Seeing also means selecting. We only see, or only perceive, what we observe. This selection shifts what we have observed into our area. This does not necessarily need to be the close range of our arms. If we touch something, we form a relationship with it. (Close your eyes, walk around the room, and discover that our sense of touch is comparable to a static, restricted way of seeing.) We never see only an object for itself, but moreover perceive the relationship between things and ourselves. Our gaze is always active, constantly moving, constantly focused on things around us, and thereby determines what is present to us. Soon after we can see, we become aware that we can also be seen. The gaze of others connects with ours and thereby makes it fully believable that we are part of the visible world. For example, if we see a mountain before us, we would need to assume that we can also be seen from there. This reciprocal character of seeing and being seen is more comprehensive than a spoken dialog, which is often characterized by the attempt to translate visual perception into language, to explain either literally or figuratively how we "see" and find out how others "see." This book explores pictures produced by humans. A picture is an imitated or reproduced view; it is an appearance or a complex of appearances that is removed from the time and place of its original current appearance and has been conserved – for moments or centuries. Every picture embodies a certain way of seeing, even a photographic image. Photographs are not, as is often assumed, merely mechanical recordings. If we take a close look at a photograph, we might understand that the photographer has chosen this specific view from an infinitely large number of options. (...) ⁄

Bibliographic information:
"Read + Play. Einführung in die Typografie,"
Ulysses Voelker; Verlag Hermann Schmidt Mainz, 2015;
[in German]
ISBN 978-3-87439-868-8

Text source:
Page 29, line 01 – page 37, line 10

← 80–81

070

Read + Play: Typografie ist politisch

→ E2 180

⁄ Some developments at the beginning and towards the middle of the 20th century serve as an exemplary demonstration of the interaction between developments in society and typography. The industrialization at the end of the 19th century brought with it a permanent change within the societies of industrial nations. This is not the place to amplify on all the political, cultural and economic components. We need to remember, though, that there were artistic movements springing up with the intention to emancipate themselves, distance themselves from tradition and to postulate new values. This started around 1900 with Art Nouveau, a movement which established itself mainly in Germany, Austria, France, Belgium and England (under different names). Art Nouveau was an open challenge to artistic historism and classicism. It saw its ideal as the symbiosis between art and industrial production. One of its main protagonists was the Belgian artist Henry van de Verde, a painter, architect and theoretician who contributed significantly to the movement from the turn of the century until the Thirties. As early as 1894 he coined the phrase: "An object which benefits only a single person is as good as useless, and in the society of the future only that will be of value which is of use to everybody."
With this position he anticipated an attitude which many artists adopted during the first decades of the 20th century. The Werkbund, founded by industrialists, architects and artists in 1907 was an important forum for this. One of the topics under discussion here was the replacement of handcraft (and the unique objects it produced) by serialised products (and their prototype). Typograph saw the advent of the geometric Art Nouveau, which declared the shapes circle, triangle, square to be the basis of its new canon of forms. The aim was a new style of rational conception and of pure forms, governed by their function.

Apart from Art Nouveau it was the movement of Filippo Tomas Marinetti in the second decade of the 20th century, which exemplarily mirrored the Zeitgeist of those years. This, too, was a settling up with established values and views. His founding manifesto in 1909 not only euphorically declared the start of a new era; it also glorified speed, violence and provocation. Point 7 of this founding manifesto read: "Only in struggle is there any beauty left. A piece of art lacking aggression in character cannot be a masterpiece."
Futurism influenced all art forms. Its protagonists swayed between communist, anarchist and fascist positions. In tendency nationalistic and misogynous, it spread before the World War I – simultaneously with cubism and the trend towards abstraction – throughout many parts of Europe and as far as Japan. The experiments in literature also had consequences for typography: the methods of collage and montage represented an unheard-of break with conventions and had a lasting influence on visual communication in the 20th century.

Halfway through World War I, there appeared a new form of artistic expression, which was a strong reaction to the political and sociological climate (and the war, of course). It was called Dada and radically questioned the prevailing conceptions of law and order. Influenced by the experiments of the Futurists, here the stylistic centre was also the collage, supplemented by many experiments with phonetic ways of writing, poetry and sound. After World War I, while Germany underwent a phase of political and economic orientation and was searching for a new order of values, Dada gained in dynamism. Lectures, posters and flyers as visual transport media. Because of its political attitude, its artistic diversity and its individual radicalism, Dada is regarded as a milestone in typography. Most Dadaist artists (among others Hugo Ball, Raoul Hausmann, Hannah Höch, Kurt Schwitters) were united in their critical stance towards any kind of order (they did, indeed, flirt with anarchistic ideas). At the same time, another discussion gained in momentum, which had been started by the Werkbund and was increasingly influenced by Russian Constructivism (here, mainly El Lissitzki), about the relationship between art and technology – two genres which had up to then been strictly separated – and its influence on society. The ideology of constructivism (which needs to be seen against the background of Bolshevik Russia) was summed up as follows: only by linking those two apparently opposite poles can we make a significant contribution towards a truly humane and just life. Architecture, seen as the supreme discipline, was meant to form an alliance with other art forms like painting and sculpture, and even wide-ranging, with advertising and typography. In addition, one hoped to reap the benefits of the industrial developments of the time, in particular serial production (but also developments like e.g. steel construction), which one would use as a general blessing for mankind (and not just for profit.) The interaction of technology, art and industry would result in new ethical and aesthetic standards for the benefit of society. The Bauhaus, a new art school founded in 1919, tried to give those avant-garde positions a home. At the Bauhaus, however, the emphasis of teaching was about the individual and its intuitive relationship with his surroundings. Those "expressionistic" approaches, which were publicised, among others, by the Bauhaus teacher Johannes Itten, were predominant during the first years. The reputation of the Bauhaus as a world famous institution in the modern era was due to the influence of the De Stijl movement, which Theo van Doesburg brought from the Netherlands in 1923. Now the focus moved more towards the sociological dimension of the artist's work, and the idea of constructivism took over from the "expressionistic" Bauhaus. Before it was closed down by the Nazis in 1933, teachers like Walter Gropius, Wassily Kandinsky, Paul Klee, Hannes Meyer, Ludwig Mies van der Rohe, Lázló Moholy-Nagy and others developed a curriculum which tried to combine handcraft, technology and art. Their emphasis was on creative education in combination with guidance on social responsibility. In typography, the Bauhaus questioned quite an number of things: in his Kombinationsschrift 3 (Combination type 3), Josef Albers experimented with a canon of fonts which only new three basic forms. The aim was a speeding up and optimizing of the type setting process. The Bauhaus demanded that written German should be reduced to lower-case letters only. The reasoning was printed at the bottom of the Bauhaus letterheads: "we use lower case only, because it saves time. Why 2 alphabets if one serves the same purpose? why use capitals if we can't speak in capitals?" The suggestions to simplify and thereby internationalize written German ranged from the demand to do away with the ‚ph' in words like alphabet, typography and photography and replace it with an ‚f', to the suggestion to abandon the established spelling in favor of phonetic spelling. Làzlò Moholy-Nagy invoked the new symbiosis between typography and photography and declared the typo photo to be the modern form of communication, because in his opinion it carried the visually most exact message. These examples demonstrate the struggles to implement political visions through a symbiosis of technology and artistic expression. Full of enthusiasm, Moholy-Nagy wrote: "The definiteness of that which is real in the everyday situation is there for all classes. Slowly the hygiene of the visual, the wholesomeness of what we see is seeping through." (...) ⁄

Footnotes on the quotes are listed in the book that is quoted here, but are omitted here due to lack of space.

← *80–81*

071

Was ist der Dadaismus und was will er in Deutschland?

→ E2 181

Bibliographic information:
"Das Lachen DADAs – Die Berliner Dadaisten und ihre Aktionen," Hanne Bergius, from the series "Werkbund-Archiv," Werkbund-Archiv; Verlag Anabas (ed.), Wetzlar, 1989; [in German]
ISBN 3-87038-141-8

Text source:
Translation of the image on page 40

⁄ I What is Dadaism and what is its purpose in Germany?

Dadaism demands
1. the international revolutionary union of all creative and intellectual people around the entire world on the foundation of radical communism.
2. the introduction of progressive unemployment through comprehensive mechanization of every activity. Only through unemployment can the individual gain the opportunity to ascertain the truth of life and finally grow used to experiencing.
3. the immediate expropriation of assets (socialization) and communist nourishing of all, as well as the establishment of light and garden cities that belong to the general public to help people develop freedom.

II The central council stands up for:

a) daily public feeding of all creative and intellectual people at Potsdamer Platz (Berlin).

b) the obligation for all intellectuals and teachers to adopt the Dadaistic dogmas.

c) the most brutal fight against all schools of thought of so-called intellectual workers (Hiller, Adler), against their concealed bourgeois attitude and against expressionism and post-classical education as represented by the Sturm.

d) the immediate establishment of a state-run art gallery and the revocation of ownership terms in new art (expressionism), the ownership term is fully eliminated in the supraindividual movement of Dadaism, which liberates all people.

e) the introduction of a simultaneous poem as a communist state prayer.

f) approval for churches to perform bruitist simultaneous and Dadaistic poems.

g) the establishment of a Dadaistic advisory board in every city with more than 50,000 inhabitants to redesign the way of living.

h) immediate completion of a large-scale Dadaistic propaganda project with 150 circuses to enlighten the proletariat.

i) control of all laws and regulations through the Dadaistic central council of global revolution.

k) immediate regulation of all sexual relationships in the international Dadaistic sense by establishing a Dadaistic gender council.

The Dadaistic revolutionary central council,
German group: Hausmann, Huelsenbeck, Golyscheff
Head office: Charlottenburg, Kantstraße 118.
Declarations of membership are accepted here. ⁄

← 80–81

072

Das Programm des staatlichen Bauhauses in Weimar

→ E2 182

Bibliographic information:
"Das Bauhaus-Manifest (1919)," Walter Gropius, from Hans M. Winger: Das Bauhaus 1919 – 1933. Weimar, Dessau, Berlin und die Nachfolge in Chicago seit 1937; Bramsche, Cologne, 1968; [in German]

Text source: page 39 – 41

' Staatliches Bauhaus in Weimar emerged through a union of the former Grand-Ducal Saxon Art School and the former Grand-Ducal Saxon Applied Art School, along with the new addition of an architecture department.

The goals of Bauhaus
Bauhaus aspires to gather together all artistic creative work as a union, to reunite all arts and crafts disciplines – sculpting, painting, applied arts, and handicrafts – into a new art of building as its inextricable components. The final, if more distant, goal of Bauhaus is the unified work of art – large-scale construction – which dissolves the border between monumental and decorative art. Bauhaus wants to train architects, painters, and sculptors of all levels to become proficient craftspeople or independently creative artists in line with their abilities and to establish a working group of leading and upcoming artists who know how to design buildings in their entirety in a unified way and with a similar mindset.

Basic principles of Bauhaus
Art is created beyond all methods, it is in itself not teachable. But what can be taught is the craft. Architects, painters, sculptors are craftspeople in the original sense of the word, which is why Bauhaus demands thorough craft training for all students in workshops and test and activity areas as an essential foundation. Our own workshops should gradually be expanded, training contracts concluded with external workshops.

The school is the servant of the workshop, one day it will rise with it. That is why Bauhaus does not have teachers and students, but instead masters, fellows, and apprentices. The teaching method arises from the nature of the workshop:

Organic design developed through craftsmanship. Avoidance of everything rigid in favor of creativity; freedom of individuality, but strict studies.

In keeping with the guilds, master and fellow trials before the Bauhaus council of masters or before external masters.

Students assist with their masters' work. Contracts also assigned to students.

Joint planning of comprehensive utopian building designs – folk and ritual structures – with ambitious goals. Collaboration of all masters and students – architects, painters, sculptors … on these designs with the goal of creating harmony within all structures and parts belonging to the building.
Constant contact with the country's trade and industry leaders. Contact with public life, with the people, through exhibitions and other events.

New attempts in exhibitions to solve the problem of displaying images and plastics in the architectural space.
Maintain friendly contact between masters and students outside of work; including theater, lectures, poetry, music, costume parties. Establishment of a ceremonial at these gatherings.

Teaching scope
Bauhaus teachings encompass all practical and scientific areas of artistic work.
a) architecture,
b) painting,
c) sculpting,
including all craft-related branches. Students receive craftsmanship (1) as well as drawing-painting (2), and scientific-theoretical (3) training.

1. Craft training – whether in our own workshops, which will be gradually enhanced, or external ones acquired through a training contract – covers:

a) sculptors, stonemasons, stucco masons, wood carvers, ceramicists, plaster casters,
b) blacksmiths, metalworkers, molders, turners,
c) carpenters,
d) decorative painters, glass painters, mosaic artists, enamel specialists,
e) etchers, wood engravers, lithographers, art printers, engravers,
f) weavers.

Craft training forms the foundation of the Bauhaus teachings. Every student should learn a craft.

2. Drawing and painting training covers:

a) free sketching from memory and imagination,
b) drawing, painting based on heads, nudes, and animals,
c) drawing and painting landscapes, figures, plants, and still lifes,
d) composing,
e) producing murals, panel paintings, and picture shrines,
f) designing ornaments,
g) letters,
h) construction and projection designs,
i) designing outside, garden, and interior architecture,
k) designing furniture and commodities

3. The scientific-theoretical training covers:

a) art history – not presented in the sense of style history, but on relevant insights into historical methods and techniques,
b) materials science,
c) anatomy – based on a living model
d) physical and chemical color theory
e) rational painting methods,
f) basic terms of accounting, contract conclusions, tenders,
g) generally interesting individual lectures on all areas of art and science.

Teaching arrangement
Training is divided into three courses of studies:
I. Course for apprentices,
II. Course for fellows,
III. Course for young masters.
The individual courses will be designed at the discretion of the individual masters within the framework of a general program and work assignment plan that will be redesigned every semester. To offer students a varied, comprehensive, and artistic training program, the work assignment plan will be scheduled in such a way that every aspiring architect, painter, or sculptor can also participate in a part of the other courses.

Admissions
Admission is open to any respectable person, without consideration of age and gender, whose prior education is deemed sufficient by the Bauhaus master council, and so far as there is enough space. The apprenticeship premium amounts to 180 Marks per year (the goal is to eliminate this fee as the Bauhaus income increases). In addition, a one-time admission fee of 20 Marks will be due. Foreign students pay double the amount. Queries should be submitted to the secretariat of the Staatliches Bauhaus in Weimar.

APRIL 1919, The Head of Staatliches Bauhaus in Weimar,

Walter Gropius '

← 80–81

073

Elementare Typographie, Ivan Tschichold

→ E2 183

Bibliographic information:
"Elementare Typographie," Jan Tschichold, from the eponymous special issue of "typografische mitteilungen" from October 1925, a "zeitschrift des bildungsverbandes der deutschen buchdrucker leipzig;"
reprint: Verlag Hermann Schmidt Mainz, 1986; [in German]
ISBN 3-87439-129-9

Text source: special issue – pages 198 – 200
(facsimile, the orthography of the original was adopted, the orthotypography was not)

Jan Tschichold (1902–1974) was a German typographer, font designer, calligrapher, poster designer, teacher, and author. In this special issue, Tschichold (who had recently given himself the first name of "Ivan" to express his connection to Russian constructivism) describes the basic principles of a new typography.

' 1. The new typography is functional.

2. The function of every typography is to convey a message (the means of which it represents). The message must appear in the briefest, most simple and emphatic form possible.

3. To make typography subservient to social purposes, the internal (content-arranging) and external (correlating the

means of typography) organization of the materials used is required.

4. Internal organization is the restriction to the elementary means of typography: typeface, numbers, signs, letter case lines, and the typesetting machine. In today's world, which is focused on optics, the elementary means of the new typography also includes the exact image: photography. The elementary typeface is any variation of the Grotesk font: lean – semi-bold – bold – narrow to broad. Fonts that belong to certain styles or bear a limited national character (Gothic, Fraktur, Church Slavonic) are not designed in an elementary way and partly restrict the ability to communicate on an international level.

The medieval Antiqua is the type that most people are familiar with today. In the (consecutive) Werksatz, it still has the advantage of better readability compared to many Grotesk fonts, even though it was not designed in an elementary manner. As long as an elementary form readable in Werksatz has not been developed, it is advisable to opt for an impersonal, objective, discreet form of the medieval Antiqua (i.e., one that reveals a temporal or personal character to the smallest extent possible) over Grotesk.

The exclusive use of the lowercase alphabet, which omitted all uppercase letters, would lead to extraordinary savings – a form of spelling recommended by all innovators as our writing of the future. See the book "Sprache und Schrift" ("Language and Writing") by Dr. Porstmann, Beute-Verlag, G.m.b.H., Berlin SW 19, Beuthstrasse 8. Price 5.25 Marks. our writing loses nothing through the use of lowercase letters, but it becomes easier to read, easier to learn, much more economic. why use two signs, A and a, for single sound? one sound, one sign. why two alphabets for a word, why twice the number of signs when half would achieve the same thing?

The logical structure of the printed work is designed in a visually perceptible way with the use of starkly different degrees and forms, without consideration of the previous aesthetic factors. Both the unprinted parts of the paper and the printed forms serve as design resources.

5. External organization is the design of the stark contrasts (simultaneity) through the use of contrasting forms, degrees, widths (the value of which must be justified for the content) and the correlation of these positive (colored) formal values with the negative (white) formal values of the unprinted paper.

6. Elementary typographic design is the creation of a logical and visual relationship between the letters, words, clauses stipulated by the task at hand.

7. To increase the forcefulness, the sensational aspect of the new typography, vertical and slanted line directions can also be used, including as a means for internal organization.

8. Elementary design excludes the use of any ornaments (including ornamental lines, such as semi-bold lines). The use of lines and fundamentally elementary forms (squares, circles, triangles) must be justified in the overall construction. The decorative, handicraft, speculative use of fundamentally elementary forms is not the same thing as elementary design.

9. For the arrangement of the new typography, the standardized (DIN) paper formats stipulated by the German Institute for Standardization should be used in the future, as these enable an organization of printing that encompasses all typographic designs. (Literature: Dr. Porstmann, "Die Dinformate und ihre Einführung in die Praxis" (The DIN Formats and Their Introduction into Practical Use"), Selbstverlag Dinorm, Berlin NW 7, Sommerstrasse 4a. 3.00 Mark) In particular, the DIN A 4 format (210 to 297 mm) should be used for all business and other letters. The business letter itself has also been standardized: DIN 676, business letter, to be purchased directly from Beth-Verlag, G.m.b.H., Berlin SW 19, Beuthstrasse 8, 0.40 Marks. The DIN sheet "Paper formats" has the number 476. – The DIN formats have been introduced recently. This issue is only a piece of work for which a DIN format was consciously used.

10. Elementary design is also never absolute or final in typography, as the term elementary design inevitably changes along with the change of the elements (through inventions that create new elements of typographic design, such as photography). /

← 80–81

074

Typophoto, László Moholy-Nagy

→ E2 184, 184.1, 184.2, 184.3

Bibliographic information:
"Typophoto," László Moholy-Nagy, from the special issue "elementare typographie" from "typografische mitteilungen" from October 1925, a "zeitschrift des bildungsverbandes der deutschen buchdrucker leipzig," reprint: Verlag Hermann Schmidt Mainz, 1986;
[in German]
ISBN 3-87439-129-9

Text source: from the special issue pages 202 – 204 (facsimile)

László Moholy-Nagy (1895–1946) was a Hungarian-American painter, photographer, stage designer, and typographer. He taught at Bauhaus from 1923 to 1928. After his emigration (enforced by the Nazi rule), which brought him to the USA following a detour, he initially founded the New Bauhaus in Chicago and, after its closure in the late 1930s, the School of Design. (eds.)

/ TYPO-PHOTO

It was not merely curiosity, not merely economic considerations, but a deep human interest in the global events, the strong desire to be switched on in every moment and every situation, that led to the incredible dissemination of the news service, of typography, of film, and radio. The artist's design work, the scientist's experiments, the salesperson's calculations, those of today's politicians, everything that moves, everything that forms, is tied into the common ground of interacting occurrences. A person's actions in the moment always also have a long-term impact. The technician holds the machine in his hand: satisfaction of present needs. But essentially far more: He is the founder of a new social stratification, paving the way for the future. The work of the printer (and any other designer), which still does not receive enough attention today, has such a long-term impact: international communication along with its implications. The printer's work is part of the foundation on which the NEW WORLD is constructed. The strict, clear work of the organization is the intellectual consequence that brings all elements of human creation into a synthesis (a sensible context): play instinct, sympathy, inventions, economic necessities in an interrelationship. One person invents printing with movable letters, another invents photography, while a third invents the grid process of the cliché, a fourth the electrotyping, light printing, the celluloid cliché hardened with light. These people will beat each other to death, they have not yet understood how they live, why they live. Politicians fail to notice that the earth is a union – but they invent the telehor, the television; one can look into one's fellow human's heart tomorrow, be everywhere and still be alone. People print millions of illustrated books, newspapers, magazines. The clarity of what is real in everyday situations applies to all classes. Slowly, the hygiene of the visual, the healthy part of what is seen seeps through. What is typography? What is photography? Typography is a message, depiction of thoughts designed in print. Photography is the visual depiction of what can be captured optically. The typophoto is the message presented in a visually accurate way. Every era has its own visual mindset. Our era is that of film, of neon signs, of the simultaneity of sensorily perceptible events. (...) /

074.1

Die Reklame, Mart Stam, El Lissitzky

→ E2 --

Bibliographic information:
"Die Reklame," Mart Stam,
El Lissitzky, from the special issue "elementare typographie" from "typografische mitteilungen" from October 1925, a "zeitschrift des bildungsverbandes der deutschen buchdrucker leipzig; "reprint: Verlag Hermann Schmidt Mainz, 1986; [in German]
ISBN 3-87439-129-9

Text source: special issue
pages 206 – 207

Mart Stam (1899–1986) was a Dutch architect and designer. El Lissitzky (1890–1941) was an important graphic designer, typographer, architect, and photographer of the Russian avant-garde. With his diverse work and pleas, El Lissitzky made a major contribution to the implementation of constructivist ideas.

/ In today's community system, advertising has become a necessity, a consequence of competition. Advertising impacts its audience with its message – more so through propaganda – and even more so through suggestion. Purposeful advertising also requires a clear understanding of the material at hand, particularly psychological insight.

THE POSTER

a) Naming the commodity.
The message is conveyed through text. The dynamic expression of the words used must be clearly developed. All secondary matters should be omitted. An understanding of the audience guarantees that observers remember brief sayings and names, whereas an abundance of words only does harm. You will know where to place the text, how to distribute it across the poster's surface, as soon as you have accounted for the reading process and how the text is read; whether the text is even read, or whether words, names, or brands are merely recognized. The color and form serve to make the text readable, and they must do so in the right way, i.e., abandoning readability for the sake of color is a mistake, abandoning readability for the sake of form is a mistake. Any charming line, any daintiness and color nuances are completely foreign to the purpose of advertising and can only do harm.

b) Displaying the commodity.
It should be noted that modern people (particularly in big cities) are flooded with labels and posters; for this reason, it is highly advisable to show the commodity instead of naming it. Alongside the poster with the informative text, a completely different form which opts for display.
Solely the photographic depiction of the advertised object itself, or its impact, or both, fill the entire surface of the poster. The object bears the name of the company or brand, and with its graphicness alone it silently commits itself to the memory of passersby. For this purpose, a photomechanical reproduction, equipped with a striking signet, should be given preference over any more or less drawn or painted image. Here, advertising and artistic approaches work too.

PRECISENESS OVER
BLURRING,
REALITY OVER
IMITATION.

In these two ways:

1. the utmost organization of the readable text, the color, and the form to functional force,

2. the photomechanical reproduction of the object (...) will develop the modern poster. For modern advertising and for modern designers, the individual element (of the artist's "individual stroke") is completely meaningless. The flourishes of rococo calligraphies are very dainty, but the "Standard Typewriter" font is clearer and therefore more convincing. The growing collective understanding of elementary means is more valuable than individualistic randomness. The circumstances of modern life provide the artist with a tremendous amount of material from which they are tasked with designing a new variety using their imagination.

That is why modern poster art will make use of the developing technical options, both in typography and reproduction. /

← 82–83

075

Futura. Die Schrift

→ E2 185

Bibliographic information:
"Futura. Die Schrift," Petra Eisele, Annette Ludwig, Isabel Naegele (eds.); Verlag Hermann Schmidt, Gutenberg Museum Mainz, Institut Designlabor Gutenberg/Hochschule Mainz, 2016; [in German]
ISBN 978-3-87439-893-0

Source:
From "die Sterne der klassischen Schriften verblassen – von der klassischen Antiqua zur Modernen Grotesk," Petra Eisele; page 53, 1st column, start – 2nd column, line 41; page 54, 2nd column, line 19 – 29

The book tells the development story of the "Futura" font in the 1920s, introduces its creator Paul Renner, and outlines the cultural and political surrounding circumstances that influenced the emergence and appearance of this font. The book documents the design climate of the times in Germany in an exemplary way.

About the editors:
Petra Eisele (*1966) is a professor of design history and theory and the author of many books. She teaches at Hochschule Mainz: University of Applied Science.

Annette Ludwig (*1963) is an art historian, university professor, and held the role of director of the Gutenberg-Museum Main until 2022.

Isabel Naegele (*1962) is a designer, specialist author, professor of communication design and head of the research institute Designlabor Gutenberg at Hochschule Mainz: University of Applied Science.

The book is also available in English: "Futura. The Typeface," Laurence King Publishing, 2017

/ (...) Grotesk fonts had already been developed in Germany in the 19th century; however, their overall proportions were inspired by bold Antiqua fonts and not especially well regarded, particularly because they were clearly characterized by the aesthetic of 19th century industrialization. Looking back, Renner wrote:

When I designed this font (i.e., Futura, P.E.), the term Grotesk font had not entered my vocabulary yet; (...) As someone who had become known for their work on typefaces for attractive books, Grotesk constituted a proletarian font family without renowned ancestors, suitable for newspaper ads; but what book artist would have seen an artistic task in the typographic design of an ad back then? Nothing was further from my mind than wanting to design a Grotesk font. No, my starting point had been the roman Kapitale.

How did it come to a positive re-evaluation in Germany of the Grotesk font, considered qualitatively inferior up until then, which eventually led to it being propagated by avantgarde designers? What inspired Renner to broach the topic of Grotesk fonts?

Like many of Renner's progressive contemporaries, he felt that he could achieve the greatest possible objectivity of a letter by using the basic shapes (circle, square, and triangle) as the foundation. The return to the basic shapes and colors illustrates the attempt to return to the origins of design. The goal lay in throwing historical ballast overboard and recreating design from scratch by focusing on abstract forms. As a result, the preoccupation with basic geometric shapes at the start of the 20th century formed an essential foundation of progressive art and design education. Viennese writing educator Rudolf von Larisch, for one, had traced the shape of the letters back to the circle, line, triangle, and rectangle, Adolf Hölzel had established elementary design laws for art and examined the circle, square, and triangle – a tradition that his student Johannes Itten would continue at Bauhaus. In his publication "Concerning the Spiritual in Art" from 1912, Vasily Kandinsky had described geometric shapes such as the square, circle, triangle, rhombus, or trapezoid as purely abstract essences and "equal citizens of the abstract realm." In his teachings at Bauhaus, he systematized and concretized these art theory considerations and assigned a specific basic color to the circle, square, and triangle: The dynamic triangle was yellow, the static square red, and the calm circle blue. Subsequently, the pairing of these three basic shapes and colors became the leitmotif and recognizable theme of Bauhaus. From a typography-specific historical perspective, Walter Porstmann's publication "Sprache und

The quick brown fox jumps over the lazy dog

THE QUICK BROWN FOX JUMPS OVER THE LAZY DOG

1234567890 ;:?!()&""

Schrift" ("Language and Writing") is also informative. In the 1920s, it had demanded an even more far-reaching "simplification of signs":

all attempts at new fonts and shorthands are based on line combinations. the last unit of bars, just like those of any geometric figure and all forms of art, is the simple stroke, the line, straight or arced. (...)

The actual problem that Renner encountered while developing Futura therefore consisted of designing the lowercase letters from the formed capital letters derived from the roman Kapital font. Therefore, the actual innovation of Futura is that lowercase and uppercase letters consistently follow a standardized elementary design vocabulary. Futura thereby met the time's demands for a radical reduction in form to extend to type design. (...)'

075.1

Herbert Bayers Universal-Schrift in ihrem historischen Kontext

→ E2 186

Bibliographic information:
"Dreieck, Quadrat und Kreis. Bauhaus und Design-Theorie heute," Ellen Lupton, J. Abbott Miller (eds.);
Birkhäuser Verlag, Basel, 1994; [in German]
ISBN 3-7643-2984-X

Text source:
From "Herbert Bayers Universal-Schrift in ihrem historischen Kontext," Mike Mills; page 38, lines 01 – 39, page 41, line 01 – 11, line 17 – 22

' With the downfall of the German Reich in World War I, the legitimacy of 19th century culture suffered bankruptcy. Many Germans felt that they had to start over. Progressive designers, such as those with ties to Bauhaus, demanded a new way of thinking about seeing and the function of the visible environment. They argued that design should no longer serve to reflect and support a hierarchical society. Sibyl Moholy-Nagy, a representative of the Bauhaus approach, explained that "a new visual value system" needed to be established in order to spit in the face of "the harmonious image" that "had concealed decay, betrayal, and exploitation." Many Bauhaus members believed in a future built on "universal" laws of reason that had disentangled itself from the constraints of the traditional culture.

Herbert Bayer was a Bauhaus student from 1921 to 1923; in 1925, Walter Gropius asked him to teach the class on typography and printing. Bayer played a crucial role in developing a "new typography" that used sans-serif font, strong lines, and systematizing grids to achieve a clean and logical composition. Bayer hoped to overcome the transient moods of culture by basing his designs on timeless, objective laws. Considerations on style and self-presentation were subordinate to the "purity" of geometry and the demands of function. This method culminated in Bayer's attempt to design a font with such "essential" letter shapes that it could be considered universal. The "Universal font" that Bayer created in 1925 represents a reduction of roman typeface on simple geometric shapes. To Bayer, the roman typeface letters were the basic form from which all subsequent styles had developed. (...)

Contemporary designers such as Josef Albers and Paul Renner agreed with Bayer's advocacy for a "rationalized" typographic construction. Albers' Stencil (1925) (i.e., Kombination font, ed.) is built on few shapes and gives the font an evenness and simplicity cleansed of subjective intentions, which Albers believed was the "essential" core of writing. The original design of Renner's Futura (1928) was based on shapes created with a compass, T-square, and bracket. (...)

universal only existed in lowercase letters. bayer argued that language was unaware of uppercase letters and that these were therefore no longer needed in typography. this kind of alphabet was much easier for children to learn and allowed for more efficient writing. the absence of capital letters would reduce the printing press' need for space, the typesetting time, and the overall costs. (...)'

universal
abcdefghijklmnopqrstuvwxyz

← 82–83

076

Ornament und Verbrechen

→ E2 187, 188, 189, 190

Bibliographic information:
"Trotzdem. Gesammelte Schriften 1900–1930," Adolf Loos, Adolf Opel (Eds.); unaltered reprint of the first edition from 1931; Braumüller Verlag, Vienna, 1982; [in German]

The text is available at:
https://de.wikisource.org/wiki/Ornament_und_Verbrechen

Adolf Loos (1870–1933) was an Austrian architect, cultural writer, and architectural critic. He is considered one of the pioneers of modern architecture. (eds.)

In 1908, Adolf Loos composed a harsh polemic against any form of ornamentation. His criticism extended to all areas of life, from architecture and art through to the shape of prepared food. In his eyes, ornamentation is backwards, degenerated, and inappropriately expensive in its production, whereas clear, unornamented shapes not only represent the aesthetic of the future, but also demonstrate the appropriately affordable form of production. His occasionally discriminating polemic must be judged against the historical background at its time of publication. (eds.)

← 82–83

077

NSCI – Das visuelle Erscheinungsbild der Nationalsozialisten, 1920 – 1945

→ E2 191

Bibliographic information:
"NSCI-Das visuelle Erscheinungsbild der Nationalsozialisten 1920–1945," Andreas Koop, Verlag Hermann Schmidt, Mainz, 2008; [in German]
ISBN 978-3-87439-768-1

Text source: page 30, line 31 – page 31, line 42

Victor Klemperer (1881–1960) was a German literary scholar, Romance philologist, and politician. He was a Holocaust survivor and ranks among the most important chroniclers of the Imperial Era, the Weimar Republic, the Nazi era, and the GDR.

'(...)
Signs and words with new meaning. "The Third Reich has coined the fewest words in its language in a self-creative way, perhaps, or probably even none at all. In many respects, the Nazi language refers to foreignness, adopts most other terms from pre-Hitler Germans." Even if it is hard to imagine creating a new language, a new form of expression, this remark refers to an "instinctive" reuse of terms and associated connotations. With the unique feature that "word values and word frequencies" turn it into "common knowledge." Klemperer states: The party confiscated "what once belonged to an individual or a tiny group" and forced it to "serve its terrible system" and covered the entire country with it. Klemperer saw language "turned into the carrier of poison" and "the most effective, (...) public, and secret advertising material." As already described, this brutalization of language did not consist of new creations, but instead of reinterpretations and appropriations of familiar words. The word "German," for example, and its meaning were now charged with a new value and used in new contexts. The same occurred with other words, such as work, fight, power, which now entered language use with growing forcefulness. That said, a more extreme version of the process described by Victor Klemperer does not exist in design. This analogy becomes blatantly obvious not only in terms of its writing, but also the symbols: The central symbol of German National Socialism, the swastika, had already been used many decades earlier by the "Völkisch movement;" another, similarly striking icon, the "SS" sign, has existed as runic insignia from time immemorial. Even the color red was stolen from political opponents. In terms of fonts (at least until 1941), "blackletter" fonts – the term "Fraktur" was not popular due to its Latin origins –, especially the "Gothic" and "Schwabacher" fonts were highly popular – at least typefaces from the 15th and 16th centuries.

Nominalization and uppercase type
In Klemperer's opinion, nominalization is another aspect of his specific "LTI." He writes: "There was a celebration at the grave of the "Rathenau eliminators." How much disregard, how much amorality or emphasized master morality does this nominalization harbor, this method of elevating murder to a profession." Is it not possible to view uppercase type as a typographically corresponding habit for this formation of nouns? It also had a boom, though understandably not with blackletter typefaces, but otherwise in many different media and applications. Combined with Antiqua fonts and repeatedly placed on the central axis, it quickly acquires a rather authoritarian effect. (...)'

← 84–85

078

Typography and Civil Liberties

→ E2 ––

Bibliographic information:
"typography," Otl Aicher; Verlag Ernst & Sohn, Lüdenscheid, 1988; [ENG/GER]
ISBN 3-433-02090-6
Information on the author: 003

Text source:
Chapter "typography and civil liberties," page 69, 2nd column, lines 28 – 40; page 69, 2nd column, line 47 – page 70, 4th column, line 03. Lowercase letters and orthography have been adopted from the original text.

From Aicher's point of view, design decisions always incorporate political statements. Design and stance are therefore inextricably linked. (eds.)

'(...) It would clearly be unfair to modern proponents to accuse everyone who uses capitals, either for initial letters or as a general style, of having leanings towards imperious domination. That would be a case of not seeing the forest from the trees. But any typographer interested in understanding underlying writing and printing traits, i.e. the deep structures of what he actually does, must recognize script and typography as a socio-cultural activity defined by politics. (...)
The typographer is a homo politicus. On one level, even the decision on whether to use justified or unjustified type constitutes a choice between order and freedom. Only if you're for law and order do you centre your text. Opting, consciously or otherwise, for a central axis makes you an advocate of "order", of symmetrical political "like-mindedness". Typographers are no more exempt from declaring where they stand than anyone else. What ever one does, be it of an aesthetic or a social nature, is not done in a cultural vacuum.

Culture, society and history embrace us all, as does politics. A given typographer may be a man who wishes to drift with prevailing trends. But his actions are no less political for that. He can doctor or dress up information, or he can stick to its factual content. He can ensure that we are not deceived or misled. He knows that most non-oral information reaches us via print. Consequently, he can go for either maximum information or maximum effect. That makes his work political. It forces him to think about the political objectives that writing serves, the political structures that have been organized and perpetuated through the agency of writing systems. There are writing systems that function as showcases. And social behaviour nowadays is primarily demonstrative. We show off. We go one better. But is there also a typography of communication, for the transmission of socially neutral ideas? Is there, as it were, a republican typography? If there is, then it has to be typography as communication and not as ostentatious showcase. (...) ʼ

← 86–87 **079**

Visuelle Kommunikation: Ein Design-Handbuch

→ E2 192

Bibliographic information:
"Visuelle Kommunikation: ein Design-Handbuch," Anton Stankowski, Karl Duschek (eds.), foreword by Otl Aicher, introduction by Abraham Moles; Dietrich Reimer Verlag, Berlin, 1989; [in German]
ISBN 3-496-01061-4

Text source:
From the foreword "visuelle kommunikation – versuch einer abgrenzung," Otl Aicher: page 08, lines 01 – 11

This design manual – published in 1989 – offers an excellent introduction to the profession. The editors Anton Stankowski (1906–1998) and Karl Duschek (1947–2011) were renowned designers themselves. They managed to convince leading experts in various specialist areas to submit contributions. Due to its contextual density and competence, this fundamental work – despite being over thirty years old – is highly recommended.
Here, Otl Aicher illustrates a pioneering paradigm shift that took place at the former Ulm School of Design. (eds.)

ʼto begin with, we need to ask the question: what exactly is visual communication? is visual communication identical to graphics or graphic design? obviously not. graphics refers to a concept, the activity of a graphic designer. visual communication is the exchange of information between two people, a sender and a receiver, whereby the receiver can always take on the role of the sender. visual communication is a pictorial message in a communication process. linking graphics with a social process is new. and back in ulm, it took a lot of effort to no longer understand graphics as applied art, but instead as the optimization of interpersonal or social communication. (...) ʼ

← 86–87 **080**

Pluralistisch und allgegenwärtig: Design unter den Bedingungen der neunziger Jahre

→ E2 ––

Bibliographic information:
"Das Jahrhundert des Design, Geschichte und Zukunft der Dinge," Wolfgang Schepers, Peter Schmitt (eds.), Verlag Anabas, Wetzlar, 2000; [in German]
ISBN 978-3870383220

Text source:
from "Pluralistisch und allgegenwärtig. Design unter den Bedingungen der neunziger Jahre," Dagmar Steffen, page 52, 1st column, line 21 – page 53, 2nd column, line 31; page 59, 1st column, line 10 – 32

Dagmar Steffen is a researcher and lecturer at Lucerne University of Applied Sciences and Arts. Her work focuses on product semantics and design theories.

Dagmar Steffen describes the stylistic plurality of the 1990s, her background, and the new design stances that inevitably accompanied change:

ʼ(...) The traditional structural model of social classes – which, it had initially been hoped, would grow closer to one another in a "leveled middle-class society" as a result of generally increasing prosperity – was overhauled following the fragmentation of society into different environments and subcultures and was replaced by the new target-group models of cultural sociologists. For example, around 1979, the Sinus Institute in Heidelberg developed the approach – still used today – of researching living environments. According to this approach, we can no longer only describe target groups based on conventional demographic traits such as age, education, income, etc., but also by social milieu and substantive criteria such as respective value orientation, future expectations, lifestyles, and the corresponding everyday aesthetic preferences and tastes. It is easy to see, for example, that in the so-called "traditional bourgeois milieu," which is characterized by values such as performance of one's duty, order, discipline, and protection of one's achievements, a conventional, tasteful aesthetic dominates, while in the "status-oriented milieu," which considers social advancement and demonstrable success to be central purposes in life, values a prestige-demanding consumption style and status symbols, and the "postmodern milieu," that strives for unhindered development of one's own personality and sensual experiences, opts for a narcissistic self-presentation through consumption. A patchwork-style coexistence of value structures, lifestyles, and everyday aesthetic orientations has emerged that is constantly in flow due to societal and social changes (transformation of the world of work, increase in higher education degrees, adopting values from other milieus, etc.) and has further differentiated itself and drifted apart over the years. But sociologists, psychologists, and market researchers are not only revising the image that designers devised of social reality. Their critical eyes also picked up on the fact that users not only expected commodities to fulfil a practical, useful function. The understanding – shaped by functionalistic thinking and long prevailing in design circles – that products, in the words of Fritz Eichler, should be viewed as "discreet, silent helpers and servants" that remained in the background inconspicuously, also proved to be far from true to reality. Instead of offering merely an instrumental use, products should also take on an expressive and communicative function in the prospering urban society filled with single people; because in contrast to closed structures, the protagonists in more anonymous, metropolitan work and acquaintance markets are forced to first gain an impression of their counterpart based on their external attributes and habitus. Clothes and accessories, cars, furniture, and sports products – all of these things are therefore chosen partly based on the extent to which they – or more precisely: their product semantics – are suitable for signalizing their affiliation with a certain social group, a social milieu, to highlight their self-image, and consolidate their own identity. It is clear that this type of "self-definition" generally cannot be achieved with the help of objects that fall into the category of the initially described "conventional design," but instead requires semantically differentiated products, such as the "Porsche 911, bomber jacket, Birkenstock shoes, Levis 501, Louis Vuitton suitcase, Rolex Dayton, Apollinaris, and nowadays also a lemon press (Juicy Salif) by Philippe Starck for Alessi." The need for symbolic differentiation is growing, and the „designer as the interpreter of social sensitivities in the form of adequate hardware" is more in demand than ever before. Of course, the question we need to ask is based on which parameters the current stylistic jungle could be mapped. Certainly, the "big" company and brand names make up a constant of order: Porsche, Daimler Benz, or VW; Levis or Jil Sander; Rolex or Swatch. Products from these brands inherit tradition, they feature a precise brand image, are collectively charged with stories and events and are associated with certain types of people, lifestyle groups, and scenes. In short, they represent a dedicated mindset and offer customers an identification model. For design, this comes with the task of "brand management": Designers need to develop products in an innovative way, but at the same time, they need to be recognizable as typical descendants of their brand family.

At the same time, the multitude of more or less rapidly blossoming and withering partial styles offer orientation, primarily in the area of interior design. This refers to the different stylistic directions or looks ranging from the "oak rustic look" and the "romantic farmhouse look" through to design-relevant trends. While in the exhibition "Design heute" in the late 1980s, Volker Fischer diagnosed that the most important trend designs, such as as "High Tech," "Trans-High Tech," "Alchimia/Memphis," "Postmodernism," "Minimalism," and "Archetypes," would almost fully cover the appearance of present-day design, today's stylistic spectrum has clearly shifted. As the main trends of the nineties, we could list "Author design," "New Simplicity," "Retro design," "inFUNtiles design," and "New decors," although with these kinds of terms, the diverse reality always comes across a little one-dimensionally. What is unmistakable is that semantics of these style trends essentially display the currently prevailing values and guiding principles as well as the sociocultural and economic conditions in a seismographic way. (...)

(...) All in all, the nineties are characterized by a stylistic plurality that should be revocable in the foreseeable future. Because in contrast to the preceding decades, it is based on mutual acceptance of the protagonists. Of course, such contrary design positions also existed alongside each other in the sixties and seventies – for example, "good form" and the Braun design on one side and the influences of pop art, the visions of Luigi Colani, or radical design, developed by Italian groups, on the other. But the doctrine represented by German design institutions and universities at the time was undoubtedly highly monolithic. Here, good design was simply equated with "good form," and any deviators were not met with tolerance, but instead denounced as "stylists" and "hairdressers." But those times are over. (...) /

← 88–89

081

Form follows function

→ E2 ––

Text source:
Sullivan, Louis H.; The tall office building artistically considered; Lippincott's Magazine, March 1896

https://ocw.mit.edu/courses/architecture/4-205-analysis-of-contemporary-architecture-fall-2009/readings/MIT4_205F09_Sullivan.pdf (see sources)

"Form follows function" – quoted hundreds of times, but hardly anyone knows the origins and context of this quotation. This passage, which includes the famous phrase, is extracted from the text that can be read in full at the link above.

The author, Louis H. Sullivan (1856–1924), was an American architect.

/ Whether it be the sweeping eagle in his flight, or the open apple-blossom, the toiling workhorse, the blithe swan, the branching oak, the winding stream at its base, the drifting clouds, over all the coursing sun, "form ever follows function", and this is the law. Where function does not change form does not change. The granite rocks, the ever-brooding hills, remain for ages; the lightning lives, comes into shape, and dies in a twinkling.

It is the pervading law of all things organic and inorganic, of all things physical and metaphysical, of all things human and all things superhuman, of all true manifestations of the head, of the heart, of the soul, that the life is recognizable in its expression, that form ever follows function. "This is the law." /

← 88–89

082

On the relationship between function and form

→ E2 --

Bibliographic information:
"Gestaltung – Zur Ästhetik des Brauchbaren,"
Andreas Dorschel, Universitätsverlag C. Winter,
Heidelberg, 2002; [in German]
ISBN 3-8253-1254-2

The book consists of 86 sections. It highlights aspects of the relationship between function and form in design and reflects on debates around the topic. Important insights can be derived from this for communication design. That is why I will summarize a few points here. On top of this, I recommend that you read the book. (u.v)

We talk about civilization when the point is not just to do something, but also how to do something. An example: eating. If it were just a matter of satisfying hunger, you could tear off a raw piece of meat and gobble it down. A civilizing moment occurs when you do not simply think about filling your stomach, but about how you eat. This is where reciprocal effects begin. For example, how you eat is determined by the shape of the silverware that is available. And vice versa: The shape of the silverware is determined by the idea of how you should eat the food. All design processes are integrated into these interactions. However, in cases when not just the WHAT counts, but also HOW, efficiency cannot be the exhaustive criterion for design. An aesthetic dimension of any kind is added to practicality. This in turn means that form is not simply and solely determined by function. It is appropriate to think about these reciprocal effects. Modernism, which gave rise to functionalism, was not questioned by postmodernism (PM), but merely rejected. There was no substantive engagement with the positions of modernism, which had revolutionized the past century; design became pure fashion in PM. The book presented here aims to carry out a constructive examination of the positions of modernism – in so-called post-post-modern times – retroactively.

Dorschel begins by stating that an object of utility only becomes one when it is used. It is not defined by its appearance. Take a fountain pen, for example: It only reveals what it is when I write with it. But I can only write because I have learned to do so. For someone who is unfamiliar with writing, the function and therefore the meaning of a fountain pen may be unknown. People's habits turn everyday objects into what they are: Rules of behavior are constitutive for them.

What is the relationship between the shape of an object and its purpose? Louis Sullivan defined a relationship based on necessity. He speaks of a "necessary relationship between function and form." There are two patterns for this relationship: causal and logical. Natural causality refers to the principle of "cause and effect" in physical processes. The logical interpretation refers to the relationship between the premise and the conclusion. While causality in nature (growth, reproduction) can be calculated in advance, there is no such compelling causality in design, because different forms can fulfill the same or similar functions. Example: eating with "tools" – knives and forks are suitable forms for this, as are chopsticks. The answer to the statement "form follows function" is therefore: There are functionally equivalent objects that differ greatly from one another. This leads to the realization that, in reality, function is based on form, because a new form generates a different use. And the use depends on the respective need. However, the purpose of an object is only realized when it is used. Humans come across a form and must figure out how to deal with it. They can use the object for its intended purpose, but they can also misuse it. Example: Some people use paper clips to clean their fingernails.
The logical interpretation of the sentence "form follows function" allows for deviations – in contrast to the causal interpretation. It allows for the justification of the knife/fork as well as the chopsticks. The only premise in the evaluation is the purpose.

For consequential relationships, as those implied in the relationship between function and form, the premise and the consequence must be of the same type. Example: the chair. To begin with, it is nothing more than a seat. The seat corresponds to the human buttocks. Since every person is built differently, parameters must be found that make a chair design appear suitable for as many people as possible. The discipline of anthropometry determines numerical values for this purpose. Ergonomists work with the term percentile. It helps to set upper and lower limits. The 5th and 95th percentiles are most commonly used - anything beyond these values is not taken into account. The aim is to design a suitable chair for as many people as possible. Now there are a number of other functions that need to be considered: as a dining chair, as a desk chair, for higher sitting, for low sitting, tense or dignified sitting, etc. In other words, there is no one true interpretation of function in design, but a multitude – better or worse perhaps, but in any case, not the only possible one. In addition, there is something that, according to doctrinaire functionalist thinking, would be a misappropriation, but could also be described as the discovery of purpose: The chair can be used for gymnastics exercises, it can offer height to change light bulbs, it can hold laundry and act as a drying rack. Now one could argue that a chair is primarily designed for sitting. But in reality, not all chairs are made for sitting or are purchased for this purpose. A chair can also simply fill a corner of a room or serve as a representative piece. Conversely, you do not need a chair in order to sit. You can simply sit on the floor, as is customary in many cultures.

The term "function" is therefore ambiguous: On the one hand, it signifies something like a task, i.e., a conceived, targeted purpose. On the other hand, the term refers to something that works. Both interpretations must be kept separate, because there can be technically functioning things that are useless. Functionalism combines both interpretations, which is a flaw. Something that technically fulfills its purpose is called functional. The functional aspect in turn contains the unfulfilled claim of the most humanitarian concerns. We should move away from substituting one interpretation with another, or conflating the two. Instead, we should use the terms "purpose" and "technology." However, technology not only plays a role in the construction of everyday objects, but also in their manufacture. For thousands of years, design and production stemmed from a single source, the craftsman. Today, production processes are largely industrialized. The term design can be used for both craftsmanship and industrial production. In both cases, however, the available technologies do not restrict the form of the products. This does not result in designs that are necessarily defined by the technology used. But what must be taken into account are technical framework conditions. However, just because something needs to be taken into account does not mean that it also ensures a defined determination. In this respect, functionalism symbolizes technical necessities, it is not a logical consequence of technology. The liberation from ornamentation is therefore an aesthetic decision. The elevation of basic geometric shapes (cones, spheres, cylinders, pyramids) to the most beautiful forms does not arise from a functional necessity, but is part of an aesthetic conception of design in which simplicity (in the worst case, monotony) is elevated to a principle. According to Le Corbusier, what is "tangible" and "unambiguous" is beautiful. This view stands in contrast to the principle of pre-modernism, according to which variety delights – the motto was "variatio delectat." It is precisely the deviation from simple geometric figures that creates an irresistible aesthetic appeal – not as a permanent principle, but as a deviation within a defined calmness. The name of the game is: boredom and confusion. If this were not the case and if the purism of functionalism were right, then no music more beautiful than the sound of the tuning fork would exist. To sum up: Only that which harbors enough variety and ambiguity arouses and holds our aesthetic interest.

If we look at the previous argumentation, we can see that neither the purpose nor the technique nor the materials determine the form with a compelling necessity. If this were the case, there would be no need for design, as the result would already be a foregone conclusion. Rather, the purpose, the technique and the materials are "coefficients of friction" that influence the form. Form emerges through the confrontation with them. This results in a new definition: The form should correspond to the criteria mentioned. The appellative character of this definition calls into question the necessity according to natural law based on which form results from function. This turns the phrase "form follows function" into a moral postulate, which should actually read "form ought to follow function." This moral approach is the trademark of functionalism: Adolf Loos categorizes ornamentation as a "crime" and thus makes a moral assessment – because, of course, it cannot be prosecuted under criminal law. For Le Corbusier, architecture is a question of ethics. For Gropius, it even constituted an "ethical necessity." Natural law thereby becomes an obligation.

The moral interpretation of creative design processes offers an advantage for the designer. Because regardless of styles and fashions, they only ever have to cater to the good. Evil is and remains excluded. What sounds simple is actually complicated. Because assuming that functionality describes the appropriateness of the relationship between means and purposes, there are two evaluation possibilities that function separately from each other: one relates to the pure relationship between purposes and means, and the other is defined by evaluating the purpose in moral thinking. Whether a product is good for a purpose and whether the purpose itself is good are two different things. Example: weapons.

Strictly speaking, both formulas – "form follows function" and "form ought to follow function" – cannot offer instructions for design activity. Because in the situation of practical design, the designer needs to weigh up numerous needs, purposes, wishes, and other requirements against each other. It will hardly be possible to balance these numerous aspects in such a way as to arrive at a practicable and feasible conclusion that can only look one way and not another. Some prioritizations will have to be made in advance in which some aspects are favored and some disadvantaged. The extent to which this happens is not a question of logic, morality, or natural law, but of arbitrariness. (u.v)

← *90–91*

083

Post-Postmodernism

→ E2 ––

`This article serves to briefly mention the cultural context of contemporary design.`

Many sociologists and cultural theoreticians consider it nearly impossible to describe exactly what era we are living in and how it differs from the preceding eras. This is partly due to the fluent transitions; however, other current reasons include society's diversity and the resulting lack of a central perspective, making homogenous observation and categorization more difficult. Nonetheless, the present offers a number of indications that tempt opinions and lead to discussions on whether we are still in the postmodern era or have already entered a new one, and if the latter applies, how much "postmodernism" it still contains.

Looking at past eras, descriptions are naturally easier to come by. If we wanted to briefly describe their development in the last century, this would start with modernism. Its most important characteristics included: a radical aesthetic, abstract art, technical experimentation, a perspective that tried to interconnect art, science, technology, and society, a reflexivity that believed in progress, and finally, a kind of "educational" humanism. The book at hand examines these features and their influences on design in different places – as well as the characteristics of the following era, postmodernism. As the name reveals, this era emancipated itself from its predecessor. This entailed flinging accusations at modernism and its perspectives that were considered dogmatic as well as unfulfilled promises. Postmodernism made its way into the various cultural fields at different times, presumably from the end of World War II, according to some cultural theoreticians. In any case, it is first recognizable in communication design in the 1970s, when postmodern traits became visible and then started to consolidate: Ironizing, playing with styles and citations, anti-utopian aspects – and above all, the negation of a "grand narrative" in western culture, as propagated by modernism (see also 041 and 070). The characteristic feature of a multidimensional nature of "narratives" and their simultaneousness presumably constitutes the biggest differentiating factor from modernism. Because with the growing diversity, the narrative principle from a central perspective, which had prevailed in modernism and had been deemed "patriarchal," naturally lost its authority. A few indicators allow us to assume that we have surpassed postmodernism – or at least its superficial attitudes: Postmodern ironizing has given way to an existential seriousness, future-oriented thinking is replacing the famous postmodern arbitrariness of "anything goes," terms like authenticity – used in postmodern times to describe individual qualities – are now becoming guiding principles in social discourses along with credibility, sustainability, gender equality, and morality, and for several years, have been illustrating an underlying mood that sets itself apart from the carefreeness and postmodern self-presentation, particularly in the 1990s. With regard to courses of action, the vague feeling of a "lack of alternatives" took the place of carefreeness – both in terms of ecology and the economy (see also "Capitalist Realism with no Alternative?," 058.2).
In the microcosm of communication design, the described indications and traces of modified values and perspectives are detectable (as demonstrated in various passages of the book). From communication design's point of view, the name borne by this cultural phase we are currently in and when it started do not play a significant role – in the cultural discourse, it has been dubbed "Trans-postmodernism" (Epstein), "Post-postmodernism" (Turner), or "Postmillenialism" (Gans).

In any case, the era is still pervaded by its predecessors, meaning we cannot speak of a radical break, a key event, or a complete rejection or reversal of values. However, recurring feedback shows fairly precisely how the respectively prevailing cultural backgrounds influence and shape visual communication.
To follow up on further reflections, it is advisable to peruse the work and discussions of sociologists such as Armin Nassehi and Hartmut Rosa or philosophers such as Boris Groys. (u.v)

← 94 – 95

084

Das Detail in der Typografie

→ E2 --

Bibliographic information:
"Das Detail in der Typografie," Jost Hochuli;
Niggli Verlag, 2005; [in German]
ISBN 978-3-7212-0547-2
Available in English as "Detail in typography."

Quotation source:
chapter "Der Buchstabe," page 18, line 32 –
page 20, line 03;

Author Jost Hochuli (*1933) is a Swiss graphic designer and book designer. (eds.)

083
084
084.1
084.2

In his book, Hochuli describes the aspects that need to be taken into account for detailed typography – his explanations discuss the reading process itself, followed by expert information on letters, words, lines, and points of view regarding the appeal of fonts. The adjacent quote is characteristic of the book. (eds.)

ʼ (...) 4. When curves come across straight lines or other curves or two diagonals meet, and as long as no corrections take place, this results in knots that disfigure the letters and give the typesetting pattern a blotchy appearance.
5. Small font sizes must be proportionally wider than larger ones. This is a visual requirement that is essential for optimal readability. (We can observe the same phenomenon in our own handwriting: The larger we write, the slimmer the proportions of the individual letters become, and vice versa). The former punch cutters took this into account. (...)ʼ

084.1

Bücher machen

→ E2 --

Bibliographic information:
"Bücher machen," Jost Hochuli; Agfa Compugraphic,
Wilmington (Mass.) USA, 1989; [in German]

Text source:
page 12, line 01 – page 13, line 20

Hochuli published this book in 1989, when controversies between the interpretations of modernism and postmodern airs were accumulating. Hochuli participated in the debate, but more from a book artist's perspective. The dig at Otl Aicher's book "typographie" from 1988 can be found at the end of the text. (eds.)

ʼ (...) The dispute between followers of "symmetrical" typography and proponents of "asymmetrical" typography, which erupted in the 1920s as a result of the New Typography and which has been ongoing for decades, has abated in the past years. Only obstinate ideologs will continue to deny that both design styles have their advantages (and disadvantages) and that, depending on the type of book, one or the other may be better suitable, or that the solution might even include a mixture of both principles.
Defaming symmetric typography in general and in an undifferentiated way as an expression of antidemocratic, hierarchical power structures is nonsense. Bilateral symmetry is ubiquitous in nature and the environment: It exists in the human body as well as in the animal and plant kingdoms and in minerology. Folk art and anonymous craft have always made use of it. It is true that profane and intellectual hierarchies have opted for axialsymmetrical forms in all eras, and it is also true that in book typography, we hardly ever find traditional solutions without a title arrangement on the central axis. But the simple reversal of this statement, that design along the central axis is traditional and expression of hierarchical thinking, is not true. Symmetry as such is – ideologically – value-free. In general, it is advisable to refrain from taking the terms "symmetrical" and "asymmetrical" all too literally in typography. In so-called asymmetrical layouts, type areas and page numbers tend to be symmetrical; in so-called asymmetrical layouts, the subtitles are often positioned to the side, and indentations and break lines result in a more or less asymmetrical image of the double pages. Ultimately, the two terms only refer to the arrangement of main, section, and chapter titles. Unless one uses them in place of the adjectives "traditional" and "contemporary," in which case they admittedly imply more.

Function and functionalism
In architecture, the discussion around function and functionalism dates back to more than a hundred years ago. In typography, it gained ground around 1920, but focused exclusively on the question of "symmetry or asymmetry." Asymmetrical typography is often referred to as functionalist. This implies a logically ordered, transparent and therefore well-functioning typography. Despite any claims to the contrary, functionalism is essentially nothing more than a style, and it often relates to function the way classicism does to classic: it simply pretends. Asymmetrical typography "can" work well, it certainly does not need to just because it is asymmetrical.
Example: A bilingual non-fiction book on typography that wants to be read, not looked at; almost square, 278 x 295 mm; printed on heavy, ultra-white, matt-coated paper that is hard on the eyes; with 256 pages, a weight of 1.95 kg; asymmetrical typography, larger amounts of text in narrow columns, ragged margin, consistent use of lowercase letters; a lot of white space and many images with a purely informative purpose, meaning they have no separate value and could therefore have been produced in a smaller format. Functionalist? Yes. Functional, i.e., fulfilling its function in the best-possible way, easy to read? No.ʼ

084.2

Graphic Grids in Everyday Design

→ E2 --

Bibliographic information:
"Structuring Design. Graphic Grids in Theory and Practice,"
Ulysses Voelker; Niggli Verlag, Salenstein, 2018;
ISBN 978-3-7212-0994-5

Text source:
Page 10, line 02 – page 12, line 08

Image source:
(1) Double page magazine grid, pages 64 – 65;
(2) Double page newspaper grid, pages 78 – 79

ʼ (...) A grid organizes graphic elements on a surface – images, text columns, colored areas, and so on. It defines their positions and sizes as well as the edge distances, and in this way structures the entire graphic design with a "blueprint" consisting of a grid of lines. The grid can be simple or multipart – depending on the requirements. A novel consists of not

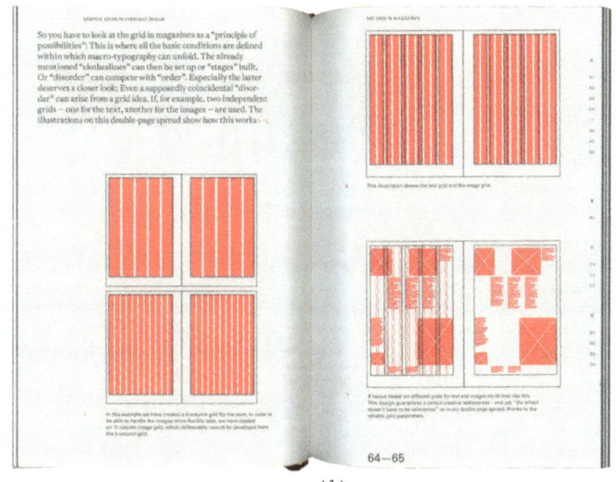

So you have to look at the grid in magazines as a "principle of possibilities": This is where all the basic conditions are defined within which macro-typography can unfold. The already mentioned "clotheslines" can then be set up or "stages" built. Or "disorder" can compete with "order". Especially the latter deserves a closer look: Even a supposedly coincidental "disorder" can arise from a grid idea. If, for example, two independent grids – one for the text, another for the images – are used. The illustrations on this double-page spread show how this works.

64—65

(1)

much more than a long text block, while the page of a newspaper consists of a large number of articles, which in turn are divided into headings, texts, images and captions. It follows logically that the grid of a book is rather simple, the grid of a newspaper rather multi-part. The “construction style” of the grid is determined by the content requirements.

Before the grid can divide content (simple or multi-part), it must be decided how large the area in which the content is organized should be on a page: You have to define a type area. This is surrounded by margins – the result is an area within the area. The edge distances are handled differently from medium to medium. Divisions are made within the type area surrounded by edge distances. The area is divided into vertical columns. The number of columns is freely selectable and depends on the content and the medium. The columns are separated by so-called column spacing. The area is also – a necessity for some media – divided in the vertical:
This results in equal-sized modules, which are formed from a multiple of the line spacing. Possible image sizes can be derived from them. In addition, images and/or texts can be aligned with them. There. That defines a grid. It doesn't get much more complicated from here on. Yet it gets more detailed. Because there are very different contents. They each require an obvious medium, which the designer then chooses (in coordination with the sender) – this can be a novel in book form, a magazine, an encyclopedia, a website, a newspaper or an atlas, to name just a few examples.

Each medium awakens a certain reading expectation through its design. Each reading expectation is followed by a certain reading behavior. The grid is partly responsible for ensuring that content; expectation and behavior correspond with each other. This is absolutely necessary because we are all rather conservative when it comes to reading: A newspaper that doesn't look like one is not even taken at hand; a novel that has four columns on each page annoys us and is put aside. (...) ′

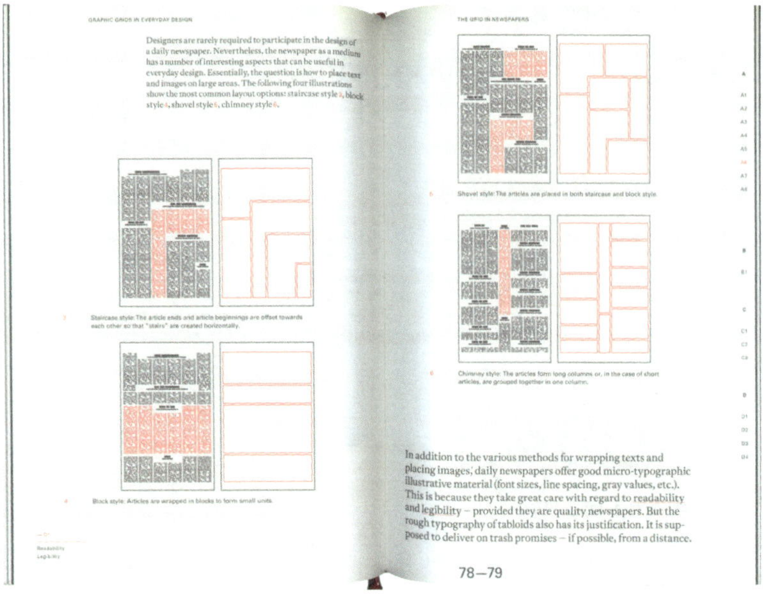

(2)

← 96–97

085

Kunst der Farbe

→ E2 193, 194, 195

(a)

(b)

(a)
The yellow square appears larger on white than on black.

(b)
The red square appears smaller on white than on black.

Bibliographic information:
“Kunst der Farbe,” Johannes Itten;
Christopherus Verlag
in Christian Verlag GmbH, Munich,
2021; [in German]
ISBN 978-3-86230-161-4

Text source:
Chapter “Farbwirklichkeit und Farbwirkung”: page 17, 1st column, line 01 – page 18, 1st column, line 14

Johannes Itten (1888–1967) was a Swiss art educator, art theoretician, painter, and master at Bauhaus in Weimar, where he taught from 1919 to 1923. Itten developed a theory of form and color. His teaching at Bauhaus resulted in a theory of color types. On top of this, he examined the interplay of shapes and colors and the resulting effect. (eds.)

′ (...) Color reality refers to the physico-chemically definable and analyzable pigment of the color, the dye. This receives its human content and meaning through the color perception that takes place in the eye and brain. However, the eye and mind can only arrive at clear perceptions through comparisons or contrasts.
A color can only be given its meaning through its relationship to a non-color such as black, white, gray, or to a second or several colors. In contrast to the physico-chemical reality of color, the perception of color is color perception is its psycho-physical reality.
I call this psycho-physical reality of color the color effect. Color reality and color effect are only identical when harmonious sounds are in place. In all other cases, the reality of color simultaneously achieves a changed, new effect. A few examples

will prove this. It is well known that a white square on a black background appears larger than a black square of the same size on a white background. The whiteness radiates beyond the boundary, while the black contracts. A light gray square on a white background appears dark, and the same light gray square on a black background appears light. Fig. a shows a yellow square on black and white. Yellow on white appears darker than white and has a delicate, subtle warmth. On black, yellow has the strongest brightness and a cold, aggressive, expressive character. Fig. b shows a red square on black and white. Red on white appears very dark and its luminosity is difficult to accentuate. In contrast, red on a black background glows like radiant warmth.
If we paint a blue square on black and white, blue on white comes across as deep darkness. The surrounding white square appears brighter than in the experiment with yellow. On black, the blue takes on a light character and the color as such emits a deep glow. If we paint a gray square on ice blue and reddish orange, the gray looks reddish on ice blue, while the same gray looks bluish on reddish orange. The difference is very clear when both compositions are viewed simultaneously. If color reality and color effect are not the same, we have a disharmonious, dynamically expressive, unreal, and floating expression. The fact that material realities and colors can be transformed into unreal vibrations gives the artist the opportunity to express the unspeakable. (...) ⁄

← 96–97

086

Vorschule der Ästhetik

→ E2 196, 197, 198

Bibliographic information:
"Vorschule der Ästhetik," Gustav Theodor Fechner, tredition, Hamburg, 2012; [in German]
ISBN 978-3-8424-8959-2

Text source:
Chapter "Ästhetisches Assoziationsprinzip": page 102, line 26 – page 104, line 27

Gustav Theodor Fechner (1801–1887) was a German physician, medic, and natural philosopher. His book "Vorschule der Ästhetik" consists of a series of essays. It was published in 1876. (eds.)

⁄ (...) Perhaps the most beautiful of all fruit, or, if you consider the term beautiful too much, the most appealing to the eye, must be the orange. In the past, this applied even more so than today, when it was displayed on all store counters and was served as dessert at almost every lunch table: because anything's appeal wanes the more frequently it appears. However, I do remember the almost romantic attraction that the sight of this fruit used to have for me, and even now, I don't think any other could surpass its appearance.

What is so appealing about its appearance? Of course, everyone first thinks of her beautiful pure golden color and pure curves. And certainly, there is much to this; perhaps one might even think that this is the only reason. Yes, what else could it be? But if the reader were to ask in this way, this would serve as proof that our principle does not apply to it, or if they were to notice anything else, it would certainly fall under the principle. So let us consider for a moment whether the entire charm of this fruit's appearance really lies in its beautiful golden color and pure roundness!

I would say no; because why would we otherwise not appreciate a yellow over-varnished wooden ball as much as an orange, when we know that it is a wooden ball, not an orange? Yes, in spite of the fact that the orange has a rough skin and that roughness is generally less pleasing than smoothness, as is proven by comparing different wooden balls, and in accordance with a principle discussed earlier, we still prefer the rough orange to the varnished wooden ball.
This cannot be due to a preference for the pleasantness of form and color in itself; in this respect the two objects are equal, or might even give the wooden ball the edge. The advantage of the orange can only lie in the fact that we see an orange, but not a wooden ball in it, that we link the meaning of the orange to its shape and color. The meaning of the orange, however, partly comes down to its form and color, but by no means just that; rather, in the totality of what it is and does, especially in relation to us. If only form and color are directly discernible to the senses, then memory adds the rest; not individually, but as an overall impression, it carries it into the sensory impression; hereby enriches it, fills it in, so to speak; we could call this the spiritual color that joins the sensory one, or the associated impression that ties in with one's own or direct impression. And therein lies the fact that the orange appears more beautiful to us than the yellow wooden ball. Indeed, does the person who observes an orange see only a round, yellow spot in it? With the sensual eye, yes: but spiritually, they see an object of delightful aroma, refreshing taste, growing on a beautiful tree, in a beautiful country, under a warm sky: essentially, they see the whole of Italy, the country to which we have always been drawn by a romantic longing. The spiritual color is comprised of the memory of all this, with which the sensual one is beautifully glazed: While the person who sees a yellow wooden ball sees only dry wood behind the round, yellow spot, which is turned in the woodturner's workshop and varnished by the painter. In both cases, the impression resulting from the memory associates itself so directly with the perception, merges so completely with it, determines its character as fully as if it were a component of the perception itself. That is why, of course, we may easily be inclined to perceive it as a thing in itself, and only by comparison, like the one we have just made, can we discover that it is not. (...) ⁄

← 100–101

087

Ten Principles for Good Design

→ E2 199

Text source:
"Ten Principles for Good Design," Dieter Rams, accessed via: http://www.vitsoe.com/us/about/good-design (see sources)

Dieter Rams (*1932) is a German industrial designer. He is considered a representative of modernism, and the principles of "clarity of form," "material equity," and "functionality" take shape in his designs. Already back in the 1960s, he started to develop theses for good design. They culminated in his "10 Principles for Good Design." Dieter Rams gained global fame with his design for the German company Braun, which developed and sold electric devices. The minimalism and formal aesthetic of his products continue to serve as role models for current designs. (eds.)

⁄ **1 Good design is innovative**
The possibilities for innovation are not, by any means, exhausted. Technological development is always offering new opportunities for innovative design. But innovative design always develops in tandem with innovative technology, and can never be an end in itself.

2 Good design makes a product useful
A product is bought to be used. It has to satisfy certain criteria, not only functional, but also psychological and aesthetic. Good design emphasizes the usefulness of a product whilst disregarding anything that could possibly detract from it.

3 Good design is aesthetic
The aesthetic quality of a product is integral to its usefulness because products we use every day affect our person and our well-being. But only well-executed objects can be beautiful.

4 Good design makes a product understandable
It clarifies the product's structure. Better still, it can make the product talk. At best, it is self-explanatory.

5 Good design is unobtrusive
Products fulfilling a purpose are like tools. They are neither decorative objects nor works of art. Their design should therefore be both neutral and restrained, to leave room for the user's self-expression.

6 Good design is honest
It does not make a product more innovative, powerful or valuable than it really is. It does not attempt to manipulate the consumer with promises that cannot be kept.

7 Good design is long-lasting
It avoids being fashionable and therefore never appears antiquated. Unlike fashionable design, it lasts many years – even in today's throwaway society.

8 Good design is thorough down to the last detail
Nothing must be arbitrary or left to chance. Care and accuracy in the design process show respect towards the user.

9 Good design is environmentally-friendly
Design makes an important contribution to the preservation of the environment. It conserves resources and minimizes physical and visual pollution throughout the lifecycle of the product.

10 Good design is as little design as possible
Less, but better – because it concentrates on the essential aspects, and the products are not burdened with non-essentials.

Back to purity, back to simplicity. ′

087.1

Less and More. The Design Ethos of Dieter Rams

→ E2 ––

Bibliographic information:
"Less and More. The Design Ethos of Dieter Rams," Keiko Ueki-Polet, Klaus Klemp (eds.), Die Gestalten Verlag, Berlin, 2010; [ENG/GER]
ISBN 978-3-89955-277-5

Text source:
from the chapter "Funktion und Form: Dieter Rams und Yanagi Soetsu," author Hitoshi Yamamura:
page 709, line 35 – page 711, line 31;
page 713, line 11 – line 31

Between January 2009 and September 2010, an exhibition cycle took place dedicated to the work of Dieter Rams and making stops at the following locations: Suntory Museum, Osaka, Fuchu Art Museum, Tokyo, the Design Museum, London, Museum für angewandte Kunst, Frankfurt am Main. The passage is taken from the book published on this occasion. Author Yamamura goes into detail on Dieter Rams' stance, which can be derived from his theses. (eds.)

′ After reading Rams' *Weniger, aber besser* (Less but better, 1995), and looking at photographs of products that he has designed, it is clear that Rams is an intellectual designer with the meticulousness of a craftsman. A stoic and austere aesthetic and critical reasoning have been incorporated into his many designs such as radios, audio equipment, projectors, lighters, shavers and furniture. No conspicuous colors feature in any of Rams' products, which are generally achromatic, functional and gentle in shape and look as though they would feel good to hold. Much of Rams' work is designed to be a tool to be used. In his "Ten Commandments of Good Design", conceived by Rams and listed at the beginning of this catalogue, Rams presents the following as representing good design:

1. Good design is innovative.
2. Good design makes a product useful.
3. Good design is aesthetic.
4. Good design helps us to understand a product.
5. Good design is unobtrusive.
6. Good design is honest.
7. Good design is durable.
8. Good design is consequent to the last detail.
9. Good design is concerned with the environment.
10. Good design is as little design as possible.

These Ten Commandments that could be human ideals are evidence of the ethics behind Rams' philosophy and the extent to which he puts himself into the position of the user. For a designer with a strong sense of responsibility, the relationship between the product and the user represents the relationship between the self and the user. At the end of Ten Commandments, Rams added the words "Back to purity, back to simplicity!" This can be interpreted as an attempt on the part of Rams, who lived through late 20s century post-Modernism, to reappraise modern design by returning to its roots. This is because Rams found the arbitrariness, fickleness and decorativeness of post-Modern design intolerable. In this section, which discusses „function and beauty" as it applies to Rams, I shall first examine „function". The second, fourth and seventh commandments are clearly related to service ability or usability in the broad sense. Rams gives the following explanation for the second commandment – „good design makes a product useful". The product is bought in order to be used. It must serve a defined purpose – in both primary and additional functions. The most important task of design is to optimize the utility of a product.

„(…) I shall now discuss „beauty". The third of Rams' Ten Commandments is „good design is aesthetic", which he explains as follows: „The aesthetic quality of a product – and the fascination it inspires – is an integral part of the products utility. Without doubt, it is uncomfortable and tiring to have to put up with products which are confusing, that get on your nerves, which you are unable to relate to. However, it has always been a hard task to argue about aesthetic quality. For tow reasons: first it is difficult to talk about anything visual since words have a different meaning for different people. Secondly, aesthetic quality deals with details, subtle shades, harmony and the equilibrium of a whole variety of visual elements. A good eye is required, schooled by years and years of experience, in order to be able to draw the right conclusions.

Although the beauty of a product is one element of usability for Rams, beauty also has a special importance. Although there is a clear order in function and beauty – usability first, and beauty second – aesthetic quality can not be easily explained in words, and similarly, a debate about aesthetic quality amongst colleagues will not easily result in a conclusion. Beauty may be one element of design, but it is also essential to design. What is the ideal color and shape for optimizing the function and purpose of the product? It may be impossible for all one's colleagues to come to an agreement, or to come up with an answer to this question. When this question is examined through Rams' product designs and furniture designs to date, however an aesthetic unique to Rams emerges, as mentioned earlier. The features of this aesthetic are outstanding texture, craftsmanship with a focus on functionality and simple, geometric and clear form. (…) ′

Bibliographic information:
"Kitsch. Texte und Theorien,"
Ute Dettmar, Thomas Küpper (Eds.);
Reclam Verlag, Berlin, 2007;
[in German]
ISBN 978-3-15-018476-9

Text source:
Page 10, line 25 – page 11, line 07;
Page 11, line 19 – page 12, line 20

This book offers an in-depth examination of the various aspects of kitsch. The text passage from the editors' introduction describes the blurring of boundaries between kitsch and so-called high culture. (eds.)

← 102 – 103

088

Kitsch. Texte und Theorien

→ E2 --

087.1
088
089

′ (...) The fact that the general approach to kitsch has noticeably relaxed, new access options have opened up, and once frowned upon objects are crossing the borders of the milieus in which they once were primarily found, must be viewed against the background of a more comprehensive social change: the trend towards "deverticalization" of the sociocultural space as described by Gerhard Schulze. Well into the 20th century, high culture and trivial culture – with the associated objects, the meanings and social classes attributed to both – represented two clearly opposed positions within the sociocultural sphere, structured vertically, along an axis from top to bottom. Kitsch was warded off by high culture as the threatening other and degraded as the counter term to art. (...) Thanks to educational expansion, better standards of living, the spread of consumer and popular culture, these cultural spheres started to shift. According to Schulze, the clear hierarchical order was replaced by aesthetic pluralization and a mostly peaceful coexistence of different lifestyles. Neither aesthetic pattern of experience can now make an exclusive and binding claim to hegemony and normative validity beyond its own milieu: "A climate of indifference and contemptibility with a shrug prevails between the milieus, unregulated and hierarchical due to comprehensive semantics of up and down." (Classical) educational claims, such as the high estimation of a canon of art and literature have lost their bindingness. Now these aspects, which were considered irreconcilable for a long time, can come together in the experience-oriented sociocultural practice: "Proximity to the high culture scheme in our society does not simultaneously mean distance from the trivial scheme. Although the disdain for kitsch and the petty bourgeoisie remains in subgroups, it is not strong enough to form a clear opposition between the high culture and trivial culture schemes. The borders are growing porous, opportunities to combine and integrate aesthetic forms are emerging that were once separated into legitimate and illegitimate culture and constituted subtle differences. Signs, like those of kitsch that were connected to the petty bourgeoisie since the late 19th century, no longer clearly point to a social status and thus must be reevaluated in every specific context. (...) ′

← 102 – 103

089

Die feinen Unterschiede. Die Kritik der gesellschaftlichen Urteilskraft

→ E2 --

Bibliographic information:
"Die feinen Unterschiede. Die Kritik der gesellschaftlichen Urteilskraft," Pierre Bourdieu; Suhrkamp Verlag, Berlin, 1979; [in German]
ISBN 978-3-518-28258-8

Text sources:
From the chapter "Der Ekel vor dem Leichten":
(1) page 757, line 17 – page 758, line 27;
(2) page 760, line 18 – 29

Pierre Bourdieu (1930–2002) belonged to the most influential sociologists of the second half of the 20th century. He wrote numerous books and taught at the "École des Hautes Études en Sciences Sociales" (EHESS), Paris, among other universities.

The cited texts concretize my arguments from page 101. (u.v)

(1) ′ (...) At the risk of ostensibly falling prey to the "easy", i.e. "superficial effects" branded by "pure taste," it could be demonstrated that the entire language of aesthetics is caught up in a fundamental rejection of simplicity, this word understood in all the connotations attached to it by bourgeois ethics and aesthetics, that "pure taste," by its very nature purely negative, is based on a physical aversion, on disgust (it "makes you sick," "induces nausea") towards everything "easy," "superficial," "affable" in music and writing, but also "frivolous" in relation to a woman's manners, for example. The rejection of everything easy in the sense of "simple," "without depth," "superficial," and "cheap" because its deciphering is effortless and "costs" little in terms of education, leads quite naturally to the rejection of everything easy in the ethical or aesthetic sense, which offers immediately accessible pleasures and is therefore decried as "infantile" or "primitive" (in contrast to the deferred pleasures of legitimate art). "Easy," "pleasing effects": This is used to characterize the garish elegance of a certain journalistic style as well as the overly sought-after and obtrusive appeal of so-called "light" music or certain performances of classical music (so that a music critic can denounce the "vulgar sensuality" as well as the "qualityless orientalism" that turn that interpretation of the "Dance of the Seven Veils" from "Salomé" by Richard Strauss into "coffeehouse music"). As can already be seen from the words intended to expose them - "easy" and "effortless," of course, but also "frivolous", "thoughtless," "garish," "superficial," and "lurid," or from the register of oral gratifications, "tawdry," "insipid," "disgusting" –, the "vulgar" works are not only to a certain extent an insult to the sophistication of the connoisseur, an affront to the "difficult" audience, who find it almost incomprehensible that someone dares to present them with such "superficial" and "shallow" things (artists, especially conductors, are benevolently said to have respect for themselves and the audience); their methods of seduction, usually rejected as "base," "degrading," "humiliating," arouse discomfort and aversion in the spectator and listener, who sees himself treated as if he were the first to come along, whom one tries to trick with the charms of glamor and trash, whom one invites to regress to elementary, primitive levels of pleasure, partly to the passive satisfactions of the infantile taste for soft and sweet things, partly to the quasi-animal taste of the sexual instinct. (...) ′

(2) ′ (...) No other aspect of popular spectacle – from Punch and Judy shows, circuses and the suburban cinema of yesteryear to catch and soccer – stands in such stark contrast to bourgeois entertainment as that of audience participation: non-stop, loud (shouting, whistling), and sometimes in a direct manner (people storming the field or the stage), in one case, it is sporadic, distant, highly ritualized (with the obligatory applause, the mandatory expressions of approval at the end), sometimes even completely silent (at concerts in churches) in the other. Only jazz seems to confuse this pattern: A bourgeois spectacle that simply mimes the popular character, the signs of participation (snapping fingers and tapping along to the beat with one's feet) are reduced to the mere silent gesture (at least in free jazz). (...) ′

← 102–103

090

Anmerkungen zu Camp

→ E2 ––

Bibliographic information:
"Kitsch. Texte und Theorien,"
Ute Dettmar, Thomas Küpper (Eds.),
Reclam Verlag, Berlin, 2007;
[in German]
ISBN 978-3-15-018476-9

Text source:
From the chapter "Anmerkungen zu Camp," Susan Sontag; excerpt from ten theses presented here: page 285, line 24 – page 286, line 13; page 287, line 15 – page 288, line 08, continuing on line 17 – 22

Primary source:
"Notes on Camp," Susan Sontag, in Penguin Modern: 29, 1964;
ISBN 978-0-241-33970-1

Susan Sontag (1933–2004) was an American publicist, writer, and director. She gained fame with her countless interventions in favor of human rights. She also distinguished herself as a critic of social circumstances in the USA. In her essay, Sontag defined "camp" based on eighty-five points. She dedicated her "Notes on Camp" to Oscar Wilde. This was no coincidence – she viewed camp as a phenomenon that was culturally closely interwoven with dandyism and homosexuality. (eds.)

/(...) 1. To start very generally: Camp is a certain mode of aestheticism. It is one way of seeing the world as an aesthetic phenomenon. That way, the way of Camp, is not in terms of beauty, but in terms of the degree of artifice, of stylization.
2. To emphasize style is to slight content, or to introduce an attitude which is neutral with respect to content. It goes without saying that the Camp sensibility is disengaged, depoliticized – or at least apolitical.
3. Not only is there a Camp vision, a Camp way of looking at things. Camp is as well a quality discoverable in objects and the behavior of persons. There are "campy" movies, clothes, furniture, popular sons, novels, people, buildings... This distinction is important. True, the Camp eye has the power to transform experience. But not everything can be seen as Camp. It's not all in the eye of the beholder. (...)
6. There is a sense in which it is correct to say: "It's too good to be Camp." Or "too important," not marginal enough. (...) Many examples of Camp are things which, from a "serious" point of view, are either bad art or kitsch. Not all, though. Not only is Camp not necessarily bad art, but some art which can be approached as Camp (...) merits the most serious admiration and study. (...)
7. All Camp objects, and persons, contain a large element of artifice. Nothing in nature can be campy... Rural Camp is still man-made, and most campy objects are urban. (...)
8. Camp is a vision of the world in terms of style – but a particular kind of style. It is the love of the exaggerated, the "off," of things-being-what-they-are-not. (...)
9. As a taste in persons, Camp responds particularly to the markedly attenuated and to the strongly exaggerated. The androgyne is certainly one of the great images of Camp sensibility. (...) Allied to the Camp taste for the androgynous is something that seems quite different but isn't: a relish for the exaggeration of sexual characteristics and personality mannerisms. (...)
10. Camp sees everything in quotation marks. It's not a lamp, but a "lamp"; not a woman, but a "woman." To perceive Camp in objects and persons is to understand Being-as-Playing-a-Role. It is the farthest extension, in sensibility, of the metaphor of life as theater. (...)/

← 106–107

091

Design heißt Entwurf, nicht Gestalt!

→ E2 200

Bibliographic information:
"Design? Umwelt wird in Frage gestellt," Der Themenkreis im IDZ Berlin (ed.), Berlin, 1970.
[in German]

Text source:
"Design heißt Entwurf, nicht Gestalt," Lucius Burckhardt; page 30, line 01 – page 32, line 04

In 1970, the Internationales Designzentrum Berlin sent three questions to sociologists, architects, urban planners, design theoreticians, economists, philosophers, designers, and other experts. The questions were the following:
How should we design the environment for it to deserve the designation of a humane environment? What role does design play in this?
In your opinion, could the discipline you represent contribute to resolving these issues?
They received 56 responses and compiled these in a book. The result was an impressive collection of contributions that shows the breadth of the spectrum of responses and the reflective way in which design was discussed in the 1970s.
Hasn't the time come to repeat this? (eds.)

Lucius Burckhardt (1925–2003) was a Swiss national economist and sociologist. He taught at the Ulm School of Design in 1959 and lectured at the ETH Zurich in the years that followed. From 1972 to 1997, he held a professorship for Socioeconomics of Urban Systems in the department of Architecture, Urban and Landscape Design at the University of Kassel.

/The belief that design could produce a more humane world is one of the fundamental misconceptions of the pioneers of the modern movement. Only a small part of people's environments is visible and the subject of formal design; a far greater part consists of organizational and institutional factors. Changing these is a political task.

In light of the endless suburb of Levittown with its identical little houses designed in the pseudo-colonial style, American sociologist Herbert J. Gans asked himself whether the clients of Levitt & Sons did not notice the ugliness of this way of living. He discovered that the environment of these buyers consisted of completely different factors than the beauty of ugliness of buildings and facilities: Their environment encompasses a respectful society, good schools for their children, access to the church from their respective denomination, the joy of ownership and the option to rebuild, a safe slip road to the highway and their place of work; the environment they had left behind included fear of dismissal, a socially discriminating neighborhood, poor company for their children, schools that did not pave the way to universities. This is the kind of environment people in the constraints of life experience; only once he has succeeded in enabling his son to study at the School of Design will he teach his father during the university vacation that Levittown was poorly planned and that his parents' house was designed in an impossible style. Perhaps his father might respond that the name of a humane environment is earned by a place where residents can live without fears, without exploitation, without external supervision; an environment that everyone can choose and help design, in which nobody is subject to design terror, not even that of "good design." Ethnological museums try to teach visitors about the culture of foreign peoples based on objects; a spear, a canoe, and a musical instrument from a certain tribe are on display, for example. Let us imagine that a foreign people wanted to get to know our culture, and we sent them a kettle, poultry shears, a sewing machine, and a hair dryer. We need to admit it: These are the kinds of exhibitions for "good design."

This modern design met its death with the invention of semiconductor technology, at the latest. While up to World War II, it was still believable that technology would find its way back to an organic morphology that would express the device's purpose as clearly as pliers or a coffee pot, we can see today that identical elements (certain transistorized aggregates) result in different devices depending on their arrangement: a box full of wires and batteries could either be a musical device or a computer. The difference lies in the internal organization, figuratively speaking in the "software." Under these circumstances, design only holds a function to improve our environment insofar as it refers back to the original meaning of the word: design = concept, not form. The primary goal is not to design the device based on its form, but its potential use, its applicability, its usability in different areas, its non-usability for chicanery and regression. I am thinking of a typical traditional designer task: ticket machines for the tram are being set up on the roadsides; dashing boxes with previously award-winning signets and an elegant electronic buzzing sound. Have these boxes improved the environment of the old woman who is standing in front of one with two handbags, clammy fingers, and glasses that have fogged up in the cold? Would she not gladly do without all this design if she could continue to buy her ticket inside the tram car? Would the very best design not eliminate transport fees? The discipline that I hope to represent teaches us that it isn't the object that takes center stage… "but the people," most want to add. Wrong: The building blocks of the environment are neither people nor things, but the invisible rules of the social process, whether we call them roles or relationships or behavioral expectations or anything else. Only the minutest part of our visible environment is designed by designers. Even the visible parts primarily receive or change their looks due to the impact of productive forces. Let us consider a weekend drive that takes us through a picturesque pre-alpine landscape. This landscape is neither the product of refined designers nor the blind impact of nature; rather, it is maintained by farmers who cut the grass, plant fruit trees, keep the hedges in check. If the agricultural means of production changes, so does the landscape. Or let us think of a popular city center with its stores and old and new buildings: It is neither built by urban planners nor "organically grown," but instead represents a snapshot of the impact of economic circumstances and speculative forces, political power structures, and cherished shopping habits. Preserving or improving these environments in a controlled way would certainly barely take place through design, but rather by influencing social conditions.

This is what my discipline teaches: The environment is the product of interaction, which takes place between the involved protagonists, meaning between planners, authorities, owners, and residents, or between designers and users and fellow human beings, or in the learning process of the individual who is learning to keep reinterpreting their own environment. ⁄

← 112–113

092

Professional associations for designers

→ E2 ––

Text sources:
(1) https://de.wikipedia.org/wiki/Allianz_deutscher_Designer
(2) https://de.wikipedia.org/wiki/Berufsverband_Kommunikationsdesign
(3) https://de.wikipedia.org/wiki/Deutscher_Designer_Club
(see sources for all entries)

See also: http://www.designlinks.de/verbaende/

(1) ⁄ The **Allianz deutscher Designer e. V.** (Alliance of German Designers, AGD) is a German association and professional organization consisting of self-employed designers from all disciplines that addresses economic, legal, and tax questions within the profession. In 1976, the Arbeitskreis arbeitnehmerähnlicher Grafik-Designer AGD was founded in Bremen and now has 2,600 members in 15 regional groups. The association was based in Braunschweig until December 31, 2016, and has now moved to Berlin. (…) The AGD is a founding member of Deutscher Designtag (German Design Day) and represents the (sub-)sector represented by it in the German Cultural Council. The AGD actively participates in the development of the legal framework of design practice. (…) The remuneration contract for design services (VTV Design) that the AGD negotiated with the SDSt (Selbstständige Designstudios e. V., "Independent Design Studios"), among others, has been considered a standard work for the creative industry since 1977 as well as a reference on the appropriate remuneration of services for contractors. (…) ⁄

(2) ⁄ The **Berufsverband Kommunikationsdesign** (Professional Association for Communication Design, BDG) was founded on May 3, 1919, by Max Hertwig, Jupp Wiertz, and Hans Meyer, among others, as the Bund der Deutschen Gebrauchsgraphiker and is thereby the first German professional association for this profession. In 1968, the BDG was renamed to Bund Deutscher Grafik-Designer to reflect the evolving professional title of its members together with the changes to the occupational profile. In 2009, the BDG changed its name to Berufsverband Kommunikationsdesign to indicate gender equality. (…) ⁄

(3) ⁄ The **Deutsche Designer Club** (German Designer Club, DDC) is an association that promotes "Good Design" and "Good Designers" in the German-speaking region. (…) The association was founded in 1989 by Tassilo von Grolman, Lothar Erdmann, Olaf Leu, Gerd A. Müller (†), Christian Steguweit, Joachim Stenger, and Hans Welling (†), with the goal of promoting "good design." It claims that design not only has an "artistic" value, but also acts as a driving force of economic success. The association connects different design disciplines and promotes interdisciplinary communication. The goal lies in improving the quality of design together with clients and training facilities for designers. The DDC organizes an annual competition and publishes specialist publications. ⁄

International Design-Associations
American Institute of Graphic Arts (AIGA), Design Management Institute, Boston (DMI) International Council of Design (ico-D), Interaction Design Association (IxDA), Int. Society of Typographic Designers (ISTD), Swiss Design Association (SDA), User Experience Professionals Association (UXPA),

and many more.

← 114–115

093

Das Neue und die Mode

→ E2 ––

Bibliographic information:
"Über das Neue. Versuch einer Kulturökonomie," Boris Groys; Fischer Verlag, Frankfurt a. Main, 2002;
[in German]
ISBN 3-596-14433-7

Text source: from the chapter "Das Neue und die Mode," page 45, line 01 – page 47, line 21

Fashion is an everyday phenomenon that is a regular topic of discussion, but whose cultural significance we are hardly aware of. This text passage offers a first insight.

Boris Groys (*1947) is a philosopher, art critic, and media theoretician. From 1994, he taught at the Karlsruhe University of Arts and Design as a professor of fine arts, philosophy, and media theory.
Since 2005, he has been working as a professor at the Faculty of Arts and Science at New York University. (eds.)

′(...) New developments usually appear as trends in history. In general, trends are subject to more radical judgments than simply aspiring to create something new. This judgment often takes the form of a disparaging remark: "Oh, that's just a trend." This means that the respective cultural phenomenon has no historical longevity, that it has a fleeting nature and will soon be replaced by a new trend. Trends should actually be condemned if you believe that the only duty of thought is to preserve a truth revealed in the past in an unchanged way. Trends should also be condemned if you believe that the goal of thought lies in uncovering a new universal truth that could fully determine the future. Trends are radically anti-utopian and anti-totalitarian, as their constant evolution proves that the future is not predictable, cannot evade historical change, and that there are no universal truths that can fully determine the future. That is why trends were condemned in ancient times, and modernism condemns them too. Even in the postmodern ideology of our time, which proclaims a new era of pluralistic otherness, trends are still subject to judgment: If all people only partly differ from one another and are still all the same, then trends harm this ostensible equality by highlighting some aspect of difference among all the partial differences as more important and valuable.
Despite all judgments, trends have heavily shaped intellectual and artistic life throughout all eras. What's more: The system of historic memory on which all theoretical and artistic production is based follows trends, as it particularly preserves trends of the time or would-be trends if new intellectual and artistic trends emerged. Therefore, contrary to widespread opinion, today's trends have the highest chances of being preserved in the future – not as an eternal truth, but as a permanently preserved characteristic of a certain era. New developments primarily function as trends in history, since trends are the designation for radical historicity – not the type of historicity that is addressed within a certain theoretical discourse, but the historicity of the discourses that want to discuss what is historical. Every theory of history is always at risk of losing the trait of novelty and being forgotten by history. What is the point of a theory of historicity if not a single library wants to store the book in which it is described? And what is the point of a theory of desire that nobody desires to read and study because it is no longer fashionable?
In his era, Wyndham Lewis rightly pointed out that pressure to be fashionable has replaced the former pressure to be traditional in modernism. New cultural trends do not indicate a victory of individual liberty, but instead create new – although smaller and temporary – homogeneities, social codes, certain behavioral patterns, and a new corresponding group conformism.
This description is of course accurate, but it only means that fashion creates a value disparity that clearly differentiates between "ours" and "others": individual differences are defined as particularly valuable and crucial at the expense of others.
In this way, fashion enables an elitist mindset within society, a value hierarchy, and a system of criteria whose validity is recognized within the framework of a certain group. This temporary set of values allows for the steady continuation of old value hierarchies in new forms as well as the cultural criticism that uses the same arguments against the elitist fashions that were once used against established traditions.
New developments and fashions can therefore be understood as something that resists both the modern utopia of identity and the postmodern utopia of otherness. Newness is more valuable than mere difference, it claims a social meaning and wants to represent the truth for its time. Newness demands to be preserved for the future by the mechanisms of cultural memory. But at the same time, newness does not raise a claim to absolute meaning, truthfulness, and universality; what's more, it does not want this universality, as it fears for its historical originality. The focus on newness, which today's civilization basically lives for, excludes the factors of oneness, identicalness, and general validity, but it also does not mean capriciousness, arbitrariness, and a lack of orientation. Newness is a rare occurrence. Entering something into historic memory is a difficult task, and nothing guarantees that one will master it. Newness never emerges passively and automatically when a past culture is forgotten and through the internal orientation towards a hidden reality, towards what has always been, or vice versa, from amorality, avarice, or increased ambition. Moreover, newness is the result of certain cultural economic strategies for reassessing the values that require knowledge of real cultural mechanisms and their functional principles. It presupposes that we can estimate the value attributed to the difference in tradition, the old, the existing in every concrete era, which is why this difference has the opportunity to enter the system of the cultural memory. (...)′

← 116–117

094

Die Künste des Zufalls

→ E2 201

Bibliographic information:
"Die Künste des Zufalls," Peter Gendolla, Thomas Kamphusmann (Eds.), Suhrkamp Verlag, Berlin, 1999;
[in German]
ISBN 978-3-518-29032-3

Text sources:
(1) from "Das Modell der nichtintentionalen Werkgenese," Holger Schulze:"4'33"" (1952), page 96, line 08 – page 98, line 10
(2) from "Aleatorik wird Mainstream: Remixästhetik und die lakonische Moderne," page 116, line 02 – 14; line 27 (footnote) – page 117, line 20

The book examines the varied forms and strategies of chance within art. Some of these strategies have also been adopted by communication design – keyword: generative design. The example given here (1) discusses a piece of work by John Cage (1912–1992), one of the globally most successful composers of the 20th century. His work is shaped by conditions that have integrated factors of chance or are based on them. Example (2) addresses chance in communication design. (eds.)

(1) ′Most of you will associate the name John Cage with his supposedly silent composition. Titled "4'33"," this piece is composed for piano and premiered on August 29, 1952, in Woodstock. David Tudor, Cage's longstanding friend and collaborator, played the score. It consists of a single sheet of music divided into three parts of different lengths: 33" – 2'40" – 1'20". At the premier, David Tudor closed the keyboard cover before each of these sections and only opened it again after they had finished. Because the full text of the score is as follows:

I
Tacet
II
Tacet
III
Tacet

During the entire performance, the pianist touched neither the white nor black keys, nor the pedals, producing nothing that could constitute piano music in any sense, perhaps aside from the heavily muted whiff of moving the keyboard cover. That said, it would be premature to conclude that the concert audience had not heard any music. Despite all of this, a form of music had been performed by the end of this piece. After all, the audience could still hear the breathing of everyone present in the concert hall, perhaps also noises from outside, such as swaying trees, pedestrians with dogs, children playing, or a slight wind movement, maybe also quiet conversations conducted in the hallway in front of the door. And the particularly impatient audience members will certainly not have refrained from clearing their throat in a self-important way, nervously switching their leg and hand positions, and inevitably, whispering and rustling paper. On the surface, there appears to be no connection between a piece like the Roaratoria, in which all kinds of noises and musical pieces sound all at once, and a piece like "4'33"" – in which no music had actually been performed, but the audience heard only random ambient noises. But the connection stems precisely from this unintentio-

nal sequence of randomly combined background noises. Because both pieces very obviously emphasize the sound of their surroundings and present this sound as music, either live or as a recording. For the silent piece, these are the sounds of a fully filled concert hall and its immediate surroundings, while the Roaratorio makes use of the randomly dispersed noises in Joyce's Wake. Decades later, Cage still has the following to say on "4'33"":
"I think my best composition, or at least the one I like best, is the silent piece. It has three movements, and none of these movements include a single sound. I wanted to liberate my work from my tendencies and aversions, since I believe that music shouldn't depend on the emotions and thoughts of the composer.
I believed and hoped that I could give other people the sense that the sounds of their environment create a kind of music that is far more interesting than the music you hear in a concert hall."
We can observe one aspect again and again in the strikingly different works composed by Cage since the 1940s and 1950s: He never wants to make his own intentions for the composition and his message audible and bring these to the fore; moreover, he wants to present the sounds or expressions of an environment, another work, or the expressive possibilities of a form of art rather than already completed music. But to keep his own intentions in terms of the message on the sidelines to the greatest extent possible, Cage uses two procedures that are typical for the non-intentional genesis of aleatoric music in general. (...) /

The following text discusses the German techno magazine "Frontpage," which existed from 1989 to 1997. (eds.)

(2) / (...) There was an attempt to use layout techniques in such a way that seems to contradict all rules of reader-friendliness and directing attention. For example, within a single article, the elements of running text, graphics, headline, captions, and photographs are distributed in a completely unsystematic way, photographs and fonts are distorted and edited beyond recognition, or overlayed in so many layers that they result in a rather fascinating texture and anything but a functional page layout. But the procedures used here only become transparent and analyzable when they are viewed as a popularized variant of aleatory. (...) After a relatively short period, (...) the layout principles and fonts of "Frontpage" had grown so popular that other lifestyle magazines that wanted to target a larger audience very carefully started to adopt the latest innovations of "Frontpage," usually for a one-year period, though in a more moderate way to meet the criteria of reader-friendliness. And solely to avoid getting lost among all the popular applications of their own successful innovations, Frontpage was forced to carry out a complete redesign every fall, with new fonts, new anti-layout techniques, and new anti-structures. And it also released a CD-ROM with the new font types. Copying these typographies was also promoted as free design marketing, as spreading an aleatoric selection field that had only become possible through digitization, through random mixes and combinations, visual sampling and remixes of random selection areas based on random procedures with random patterns. But this open publication of own sources and permanent self-transformation is typical of remixing in general, which is characterized by an extremely high processing speed. The procedure of processing – innovation – overproduction and processing new influences accelerated rapidly in the first half of the 1990s, since the products were easy to create on a computer and publish in clubs, and could receive immediate feedback. But since this was now taking place on all levels, for record production, cover design, design revivals, new samples, and sound editing, this area of pop culture turned into a prime example of what systems theory would call a "hot system." (...) /

Note (eds.):
In music, art, and literature, aleatory refers to the use of operations that lead to a largely random result. (see also Wikipedia)

093
094
094.1
095

094.1

Definition of the term "Generative Design"

→ E2 --

Generative design refers to a design method in the areas of art and design. Its main feature is that it uses an algorithm (usually in the form of a computer program) to achieve a design result (e.g., an image, sound, animation, architectural model, or other graphic creations) – and thereby does away with the conventional work steps of a design process. Generative design differs from computer art or generative art, which have existed for a longer period of time, in that it revolves around tasks for communication design, but also architecture and various engineering disciplines. In communication design, generative design can be used in many different areas: for developing and depicting informational graphics or for flexible looks, for example. In architecture, generative design is used to shape structures and models. In technical product development, generative design appears in all areas regarding optimization, the pallet ranges from the selection of materials through to production processes. It can help generate new approaches that traditional methods might not have identified. In 2022, OpenAI launched Point-E software, which enabled the generation of 3D models on the basis of text entries for the first time. The growing simplicity of development environments is increasing the significance of generative design. (eds.)

Further information:
https://en.wikipedia.org/wiki/Generative_design

← *116–117*

095

Vom Schreiben und Denken. Die Saga der Schrift

→ E2 --

"Vom Schreiben und Denken. Die Saga der Schrift" (3 parts); Arte Film documentary from November 21, 2020

Text source:
https://www.youtube.com/watch?v=sQy-Q_psTJ0
(see sources)

/ A bull with its head turned and a wave of water: Over thousands of years, simple images developed into a writing system that we consider a natural part of our world today. Back then, pictures gave rise to characters, which then turned into the first letters. The bull's head turned into the letter A, the wave of water is an M today. But what lies behind this story of our writing systems, which spans thousands of years? And how did the letters develop over this period? / (Text: Arte)

The three-part documentary "Vom Schreiben und Denken. Die Saga der Schrift," broadcast by ARTE on November 21, 2020, got to the bottom of these questions. (eds.)

← 120–121

096

The Designer as: Author, Producer, Artist, Entrepreneur, Curator & Collaborator

→ E2 --

Bibliographic information: "The Designer as: Author, Producer, Artist, Entrepreneur, Curator & Collaborator," Steven McCarthy; BIS Publishers, Amsterdam, 2013; ISBN 978-90-6369-292-6

Text source: Text on the back cover;

In his book from 2013, Steven McCarthy describes the fields that the designer's profession covers today. Over six chapters, he illustrates the roles that are listed in the book's title. (eds.)

/ "The designer as ...: Author, Producer, Activist, Entrepreneur, Curator and Collaborator: New models for Communication" by Steven McCarthy promises to take the reader on a stimulating tour of the many ways that graphic designers have extended their field. Formerly "hired guns" simply providing a professional service, to now embracing issues of social, cultural, political and economic importance. This book tells the story of how designers currently seek opportunities to meld form and content, and function and meaning in their work. The book's six chapters – amply-illustrated and energetically designed by Martin Venezky – are devoted to: concept and history; writing, type and text; advocacy and social activism; design for art's sake; entrepreneurism and economy; and community design; authorship, to give professionals and design students alike a sense of the possibilities for an expanded definition of design. Explanatory, analytical, crtitical, and inspirational, "The designer as..." is essential for inquiring and creative minds. /

← 124–125

097

Prinzip Mensch. Macht, Freiheit und Demokratie im Zeitalter der Künstlichen Intelligenz

→ E2 202

Bibliographic information: "Prinzip Mensch. Macht, Freiheit und Demokratie im Zeitalter der Künstlichen Intelligenz," Paul Nemitz, Matthias Pfeffer; Verlag J. H. W. Dietz, Bonn, 2020; [in German] ISBN 978-3-8012-0565-2
See also: prinzipmensch.eu

Text sources:
(1) the text from the back cover;
(2) page 15, line 06 – page 17, line 05

The discussions on artificial intelligence and information on the latest developments usually revolve around technical capabilities and the associated, growing possibilities of manipulation. This book delivers an important social and political classification. (eds.)

(1) / Human or algorithm – who decides our future in the age of artificial intelligence? The digital corporations of Silicon Valley already harbor an overwhelming amount of power. They tempt us into a trap of convenience and undermine individual freedom, the constitutional state, and democracy. Artificial intelligence further increases the concentration of technological and economic power into the hands of these companies. Paul Nemitz, Principal Adviser of the EU Commission and member of the Federal Government's Data Ethics Commission, and Matthias Peffer, philosopher, TV journalist, and producer, show how to ward off this threat to democracy and freedom through politics in Germany and Europe.

Their book is a self-affirmation of the sources and necessities of freedom and democracy in the age of increasing technological power. It invites us to contribute to the design of new binding and democratically established rules for social networks, Internet platforms, and artificial intelligence and conveys the necessary knowledge on technologies, corporate strategies, and current political debates to do so. /

(2) / (...) Analyzing AI requires a holistic view of the business models of these digital technologies and of the power they wield today. We are firmly convinced that the rise of technology and the accompanying power of control and manipulation will lead to need to reflect on the "principle of humanity," on the fact that humans can take advantage of this technology, that they are in control of it, and that a humane future determined by humans remains possible. For this reason, this book opts for a twofold approach to the complex issue:

1. To start with, we will focus our analysis on power: the link between the different digital technologies in the hands of the companies that rule the Internet and the state. Due to the rapid speed of technological development, it unfolds its own dynamic that challenges democratic processes.

2. Then we will suggest self-assurance in the way we think about freedom and democracy. Philosophy can play a part here if it recognizes that while the age of entrenched world views may have met its irreversible end, its retreat into specialism and strict scientific character would reveal exactly what Jürgen Habermas refers to as its essential core: its "proprium," namely its contribution to the "rational clarification of our understanding of ourselves and the world." It therefore should hold onto the "holistic connection to our need for orientation." Today, we need orientation.
Because technology, economic and political power are entering into an increasingly tighter symbiosis. Digital technology knows more about humans and the world than they do about themselves. We are giving it more and more decision-making power. Both are leading to a huge asymmetry of knowledge and power in relation to humans and machines. These developments are gradually sidelining the classic operative and decision-making models of democratic societies. This means we need to pose the question of who wields technological power in a new way. Who will make decisions in the future? Shoshana Zuboff takes this question one step further: "Who decides who makes decisions?"
The power to shape processes through technology is experiencing fundamental changes. This is a real stress test for the basic intellectual and cultural conceptions on which modern societies are built. And it is unavoidable. Since we are already experiencing the second stage of the "digital revolution" in light of current upheavals caused by AI and quantum computers, it is worth looking back to the beginnings of the digital age – to understand and learn why the great hopes it harbored largely remain unfulfilled. In this second revolutionary phase we are currently in, we can no longer afford to make mistakes such as those we made in the early days of digital technology and the global Internet. Technology and knowledge seem to be positively exploding. Some point to an exponential development.
In the near future, this could take a turn towards a completely new – uncontrollable – quality. What stands in the way of this development are the consciously decelerated processes of deliberative democracies. They are decelerated because experience has shown how important it is for democracies to incorporate reflection and discussions on matters that involve humans exercising power before solidifying the formation of an opinion and decisions. One consequence of this insight also affects the division of power. If technology creates facts and if it develops at a faster pace than democracies make decisions, does this mean that technology easily wins this hare-and-tortoise game? Will technology even have its own developmental logic that eventually grows immune to democratic control? Currently, technology is creating facts at such a speed that the question of power could be decided in its favor solely based on this factor. We believe that the questions of who will rule in the future and who will make decisions must be asked today. If we want to answer it in line with democracy, we need to start a discussion between the representatives of technology and democracy.
We know that we stand on the shoulders of giants: Immanuel Kant, Jürgen Habermas, and, yes, also Edward Snowden, without whose courage the world might never have known the extent to which the mightiest surveillance machines ever conceived by mankind are already observing and manipulating us today. (...) /

097.1
Artificial Intelligence (AI)

→ E2 --

Text source:
https://en.wikipedia.org/wiki/Artificial_intelligence
(see sources)

' Artificial intelligence (AI), in its broadest sense, is intelligence exhibited by machines, particularly computer systems, as opposed to the natural intelligence of living beings. It is a field of research in computer science that develops and studies methods and software which enable machines to perceive their environment and uses learning and intelligence to take actions that maximize their chances of achieving defined goals. Such machines may be called AIs. AI technology is widely used throughout industry, government, and science. Some high-profile applications include advanced web search engines (e.g., Google Search); recommendation systems (used by YouTube, Amazon and Netflix); interacting via human speech (e.g., Google Assistant, Siri, and Alexa); autonomous vehicles (e.g., Waymo); generative and creative tools (e.g., Chat GPT and AI art); and superhuman play and analysis in strategy games (e.g., chess and Go). However, many AI applications are not perceived as AI: "A lot of cutting edge AI has filtered into general applications, often without being called AI because once something becomes useful enough and common enough it's not labeled AI anymore."
Alan Turing was the first person to conduct substantial research in the field that he called machine intelligence. Artificial intelligence was founded as an academic discipline in 1956.
The field went through multiple cycles of optimism, followed by periods of disappointment and loss of funding, known as AI winter. Funding and interest vastly increased after 2012 when deep learning surpassed all previous AI techniques, and after 2017 with the transformer architecture. This led to the AI boom of the early 2020s, with companies, universities, and laboratories overwhelmingly based in the United States pioneering significant advances in artificial intelligence. (...) '

097.2
Questions on Artificial Intelligence

→ E2 --

Recommended book:
"Atlas of AI – Power, Politics, and the Planetary Costs of Artificial Intelligence," Kate Crawford; Yale University Press, 2022; ISBN 978-0300264630

Image source:
(1) front cover of "Atlas of AI"

Questions for Florian Jenett, professor of media informatics at Hochschule Mainz (on February 14, 2024);

F. Jenett is a member and project coordinator of the research project KITeGG ("Making AI comprehensible and tangible: connecting technology and society through design"). Five German universities are conducting research on integrating AI into design teaching. More information is available at: https://gestaltung.ai. The initiative is supported and funded by the Federal Ministry of Education and Research (BMBF) and the states of Baden-Wuerttemberg, Hesse, North Rhine-Westphalia, and Rhineland-Palatinate.

What does artificial intelligence (AI) mean to you?

F. J.: There really isn't just one definition of AI. The term encompasses many different aspects, and unfortunately now also includes a lot of marketing and myth. What we usually mean when we're talking about "AI" is "machine learning" (ML). If we take the example of "ChatGPT," this already consists of many versions (GPT-3.5-Turbo, GPT-4, etc.), packaged into a user interface or ports and working with filters and system prompts in the background. In fact, this isn't related to the technological core of AI – this is simply a function that turns input into output. The special feature of this is its development process. Conventional software functions are optimized by humans (e.g., by rewriting codes), while in machine learning, an additional software takes care of this. The "second digital revolution" is using the automation of the first and applying it to itself.

AI is developing at a rapid pace. Do you have any tips on sources of reliable quality to help you stay up to date?

To be honest, I find myself confronted with the same question again and again: Where can I get up-to-date, and above all, reliable knowledge on the latest AI developments? Since we are dealing with an extremely fast-paced field, my current strategy is to combine slow and fast food. On the one hand, I read quite a lot on the topic (books, articles), and on the other hand, I try to capture the latest information and the zeitgeist through a stream of short messages (on X/Twitter) that keeps increasing in speed. In addition, I consider a practical interaction with the topic to be extremely important.
I think many aspects only become understandable when you actually experience them. In the beginning (around 2018), this meant trying out different models and tools on cloud services (e.g., Google Colab), today, I work on our own infrastructure and platforms such as Hugging Face (https://hugging-face.co/). At the moment, I'm excited by the development that more and more AI models can run on very small computers (e.g., Ollama, llama.cpp) or in a browser (e.g., transformers.js, diffusers.js). This provides plenty of scope for experiments.

Can you recommend any glossaries that give an initial overview of terms that are relevant to AI?

F. J.: My go-to glossary is usually one made by Google: "Machine Learning Glossary" (https://developers.google.com/machine-learning/glossary). There are others that also try to describe the terms in a less technical manner, for example Dezeen (dezeen.com). I think many of these glossaries offer a good overview of the core terms of the technology. However, aspects such as ethics, data, transparency, etc. tend to be underrepresented. We've developed our own glossary for our publication ("Unlearn AI," issue 1, 2024) as part of the KITeGG project (https://gestaltung.ai), which is also available online (https://unlearn.gestaltung.ai/).

What is the situation concerning control and transparency of AI?

F. J.: In my opinion, transparency is one of the most important aspects. It's still alarming to see how advanced proprietary models such as OpenAI's GPT are compared to open models. In light of the societal impacts, I think we need to establish some kind of balance between corporate interests and the common good. Transparency and access constitute important factors here. And I don't just mean technical aspects (architecture, data, etc.), but also information on resource usage and business practice, for example when outsourcing data cleaning. Another factor could be to introduce clear international rules on what data may be used. My current impression of the AI community is that there is a strong tendency to avoid (more) dependencies on major companies. I haven't seen this much openness to sharing data and codes as displayed by the AI community anywhere else in the last 20 years. When research articles are published without the associated code and data, for example, this is almost a flaw now. This openness has made a whole range of projects possible (AUTOMATIC1111, ComfyUI, etc.) which are in turn making the technology more accessible to broader circles, for example in design.

In its newsletter from the start of 2024, VG Bild-Kunst wrote: *"Politically, the year 2023 was – in terms of copyright – shaped entirely by the big issue of generative artificial intelligence. Never before has the culture sector faced such a major challenge. Because this is very clearly a disruptive technology that will replace the work of many creative artists."*
Can you describe where you – in relation to the profession of communication design – see and expect the biggest changes?

F. J.: To start with, the areas that I would attribute to production will change, such as image processing, the pre-print stage, and so on. As a result, conventional tools (Photoshop and co.) will be developed and new ones will emerge. This will essentially continue the development that started with the introduction of desktop publishing, as there will be more and more new systems and tools to resort to. Even though communication design, like many other design areas, has always been conflated with its tools and a certain technology generation, I think that the increasing focus on production is the wrong way forward. You can't achieve good design solely by masterfully operating software. The technology shift therefore always also provides the opportunity to return to the original qualities of design. Presumably, the way we communicate will also change drastically over the coming years – thanks to AI, content can be processed, created, and consumed much faster. So far, changes like these have always been accompanied by an adaptation and further differentiation of the profile of communication design. And that's the good news: There are more and more occupational profiles and tasks for designers. Along with the new work profiles and modified tools, the work processes will also change. My previous experience has shown that the new work processes based on data and language suit designers very well as interfaces.

What are the major advantages of AI?

F. J.: Implicit learning. Machine learning can record and apply patterns that we would presumably struggle to formulate clearly. Instead of clear formulas (algorithms, recipes), we can use "experience" in the form of sample data for the purpose of development. This comes with major advantages in production and for the result.

What are the major disadvantages of AI?

F. J.: Probably implicit learning as well, as this means that subliminal patterns (such as discrimination) feed into the systems too. Other disadvantages include the tremendous need for resources (energy, materials, problematic working conditions) and the dependence on data. I can recommend the book "Atlas of AI – Power, Politics, and the Planetary Costs of Artificial Intelligence" by Kate Crawford for further details on the topic.

The big players that we know of in AI are primarily based in the USA. Does a western hegemony exist in terms of the data sets, filters, and value standards? And are there competing models in China, Russia, or India that work with other cultural definitions?

F. J.: I would say that the powerful are clearly dominant. Just because we do not know of or discuss major AI systems from Russia, China, or India, this doesn't mean that they don't exist. AI development relies on a few factors: expertise, data, and resources. Assuming that western countries have entered this territory alone… that's a western point of view. But fundamentally, I agree with the concern that AI development is restricted to those who have the means to do so. Other developments are more encouraging: In the meantime, it's possible to compress large language models to such an extent that they can run on small computers like the RaspberryPI (approx. €50). It could be operated with solar energy and make AI usable without Internet access. We need more of this.

Artificial intelligence lives off data. The larger the amount it can use, the better it gets. Are there currently options for protecting the copyright of one's own work and preventing free access via databases?

F. J.: I don't believe in technical solutions here. The only way to protect your data is not to publish it. But that completely contradicts the nature of communication design. Nonetheless, setting rules and adapting copyright to the new circumstances is necessary. But for me, this begs the question of whether communication designers will still want to protect their own work in this way.
After all, sharing data, codes, and posting designs without protective measures has become part of everyday life in design, and essentially a necessity to gain visibility.

The new tools are also enabling laypeople to design all kinds of media, edit images, and write texts. What consequences does this have for the profession of communication design?

F. J.: Ideally, this development will follow the same path as that of templates and clip art. To make good design, you need someone with design experience. Because it isn't about using tools, but about evaluations and decisions. We shouldn't strive for less.

You teach media informatics and digital design in communication design at the Hochschule Mainz. Has AI noticeably changed the way you teach and the way students work?

F. J.: In its basic structure, teaching itself hasn't changed that much. But the application possibilities of AI are playing an increasingly important role. This is because tools such as Chat GPT or Dall-E are very helpful – whether for honing concepts, expanding brainstorming, or developing mood boards. But this also means: AI only gives answers that are as clever as the question that was asked. And those who receive the answer must be able to decipher whether it contains nonsense or offers a smart approach. This might be

(1) "Atlas of AI"

the biggest task of universities: to convey that knowledge, analysis, and reflection are now, more than ever before, the key qualifications of their profession. For students, the main challenge lies in recognizing that growing technical simplification of the aspect of craft must go hand in hand with enhanced intellectualization.

In light of the many open questions in relation to AI, do we need to rethink and discuss professional ethics?

F. J.: In my opinion, we need to look back to the distant past. In modernism, we at least saw the attempt to pursue a humanist approach in design and thereby incorporate an ethical component. In postmodernism, these approaches were lost. Nowadays, as societal and cultural sensitization play a major role, aspects of ethics, equality, decolonization, and gender issues are part of the agenda. It is telling that all big AI players have their own ethics departments. But it is also telling that this is taking place against the background of retaining sovereignty in interpretation. Every debate on this that arises through society can restrict the business model and revenue. On top of this, AI corporations themselves often don't seem to know exactly what impacts their products can have. OpenAI, for one, commented on their idea for their AI model as follows at the start of 2024:
"We'll be engaging policymakers, educators and artists around the world to understand their concerns and to identify positive use cases for this new technology. Despite extensive research and testing, we cannot predict all of the beneficial ways people will use our technology, nor all the ways people will abuse it. That's why we believe that learning from real-world use is a critical component of creating and releasing increasingly safe AI systems over time." (Source: OpenAI.com, February 16, 2024, 6:44 p.m.) Dilemmas like these show: Yes, we do need to have a debate on ethical aspects – and not just in communication design.

You started a big research project on the topic of artificial intelligence with your colleagues. Please explain what you're examining.

F. J.: In the research project KITeGG ("Making AI comprehensible and tangible: connecting technology and society through design," 2021 – 2025), we are researching and testing the use of AI in teaching at five design schools. These include HfG Offenbach, HfG Schwäbisch Gmünd, Hochschule Trier, KISD in Cologne, and us, Hochschule Mainz, as the project lead. Currently (mid-2024), we are about halfway through. In the first year, we mostly laid the foundations: hired employees, created and appointed professorships, set up AI labs, installed a GPU infrastructure, conceptualized, designed, and launched a teaching-learning platform, and tested teaching formats. In addition, we started our six-monthly symposiums. On the teaching side, we have been running courses since the 2022 winter semester, two in the area of theory and two practical design courses at each location. This amounts to a total of 120 course and workshop offerings over the course of the project.
When we wrote the proposal, we had no idea that AI would go through the roof only a year later. So we were very lucky with the timing. This has led to different effects that we are now trying to capture. The topic has arrived among students, and we don't need to put nearly as much effort into advertising it or laying the foundations as we had assumed. In addition, other teaching staff members have also shown a lot of interest, and we spend a lot of time transferring AI to other specialist contexts and demonstrating tools in mini workshops, but also making opportunities and challenges visible.
My personal teaching experience has been very positive; I have just led two AI courses in the last semester. At the beginning, the students are often very lost due to the many possibilities. But this changes quickly, as soon as they discover that they can interact with AI systems by using examples and data. Even though we need to offer support now and again, the students are, in my opinion, making greater leaps in these courses than they were able to in code-based courses in the past. This is a good incentive for now, but it also means that we need to start with different course goals for teaching.

To gain an idea of how we connect teaching and research in this project, it's worth taking a look at the following symposiums that we have organized over the past two years:

https://hiddenlayers.de/ (KISD Cologne)
https://www.correlationsforum.de/ (HfG Offenbach)
https://reshapeforum.hfg-gmuend.de/ (HfG Schwäbisch Gmünd)
https://kind-lab.de/transform2023/ (Hochschule Trier)

097.3
Glossary of AI

→ E2 --

Text source:
https://www.dezeen.com
(see sources)

"Dezeen.com" is an online magazine for architecture, interiors, and design based in London (GB). It was established in 2006 and was bought by the Danish media company JP/Politikens Hus in 2021. In the issue from June 20, 2023, Nat Parker presents the "The Dezeen guide to AI," which we have cited here. The full guide is available at https://www.dezeen.com/2023/06/20/ai-guide-aitopia/.

Florian Jenett recommends two additional glossaries on AI: https://developers.google.com/machine-learning/glossary and https://unlearn.gestaltung.ai/

Machine learning
Machine learning is when computers use experience to improve their performance. It underpins most of the advanced capabilities of AI systems. Rather than humans programming computers with specific step-by-step instructions on how to complete a task, in machine learning a human provides the AI with data and asks it to achieve a certain outcome via an algorithm.
Through a process of ultra-fast trial and error, the AI can very quickly start to spot patterns – including those that humans may not be able to identify – and use them to make predictions about what is likely to help it achieve the desired outcome. (...)

Deep learning
Deep learning is a specific type of machine learning used in the most powerful AI systems. It imitates how the human brain works using artificial neural networks (explained below), allowing the AI to learn highly complex patterns in data. While machine-learning systems are able to get better at tasks they've been trained on when presented with previously unseen data, deep learning enables computers to learn to do things they were never trained for. (...)

Neural networks
Neural networks are found in the human brain. They are a series of neurons connected to each other that exchange information, strengthening their connections as they do so and enabling us to learn.
Advanced AI systems use artificial neural networks that mimic these structures, processing data through layers of interconnected artificial neurons to become better at making predictions.

Narrow AI
Sometimes called weak AI, narrow AI refers to AI systems that are only able to complete specific tasks, such as automative driving or image recognition. They may perform these tasks much better than humans, but cannot apply their intelligence to different problems and situations.
All AI systems currently in existence are "narrow AI."

Artificial general intelligence
The definition of artificial general intelligence (AGI) is a matter of debate among experts, but at the most basic level it typically refers to a computer being able to perform any intellectual task that a human can. Such a computer would likely be able to perform these tasks much faster and better than a human would be able to, meaning that the emergence of AGI could have enormous implications for society. Ian Hogarth, co-author of the annual State of AI Report, calls it "God-like AI": "A superintelligent computer that learns and develops autonomously, that understands its environment without the need for supervision and that can transform the world around it."

It is often what people are talking about when they discuss the dangers of AI, worrying that AGI could lead to humans becoming obsolete or even extinct. (...)

Superintelligence
In his influential 2014 book "Superintelligence: Paths, Dangers, Strategies", philosopher Nick Bostrom defined superintellgence as "any intellect that greatly exceeds the cognitive performance of humans in virtually all domains of interest". Some researchers predict that superintelligence would emerge shortly after the advent of AGI, but others are doubtful it will ever become a reality.
If a superintelligent AGI were to be created, there are concerns over whether humans would be able to control it. Bostrom and University of California, Berkeley professor Stuart Russell have warned that even giving a superintelligent AGI an ostensibly sensible, straightforward task could have unexpected and devastating results.
"If we put the wrong objective into a superintelligent machine, we create a conflict that we are bound to lose," he said in a 2021 lecture. *"The machine stops at nothing to achieve the specified objective."* (...)

Alignment
In the context of AI, alignment refers to attempts to make sure that systems have goals that match human values, in order to reduce the risk they could harm us. Currently, it often involves ensuring that AI chatbots do not engage in harmful content.
However, creating computers with truly human ethics is very difficult and there is not yet scientific consensus on how this would work, even in theory. (...)

Singularity
A term borrowed from mathematics, singularity is the hypothetical point in the future at which technology has advanced to the point where it is uncontrollable and irreversible.
Some consider the emergence of an AGI more intelligent than humans and able to self-improve to be the most likely moment of singularity.
A popular interpretation of the theory holds that after this point, technology would enter a period of rapid, exponential, self-perpetuating advancements that are difficult to comprehend, with humans usurped as the dominant beings on Earth.

Generative AI
Generative AI systems are those that can create different types of content, including images, text, videos, music, voice audio and code. They are trained on large reams of data, and by the process of machine learning are able to then extrapolate to produce new data.
Examples include text-to-image generators such as DALL-E 2, Midjourney and Stable Diffusion, in which users input a text prompt and the model quickly produces a corresponding image. Chatbots such as OpenAI's ChatGPT and Google's Bard are also forms of generative AI.
The emergence of these easy-to-use tools over the past two years have dramatically increased interest in generative AI. The technology has the potential to boost productivity in a wide range of industries, including architecture and design. Zaha Hadid Architects principal Patrik Schumacher recently revealed that the firm is using text-to-image generators to come up with early designs for projects.
However, commentators have also expressed concerns about the potential for generative AI to spread misinformation, both inadvertently and maliciously. The most advanced version of Midjourney is capable of producing near-photorealistic but completely fabricated images.
In addition, the technology can be susceptible to biases and stigma embedded within training data.
Others have suggested its ability to mimic existing media so convincingly could have major implications for copyright holders.

Large language models
Large language models (LLMs) are AI systems that use deep learning to understand language. An example is Generative Pre-trained Transformer, which powers ChatGPT.
LLMs are trained on enormous quantities of data to become very good at recognising language patterns, like a highly advanced form of predictive text. (...)

Hallucinations
LLM chatbots are prone to stating falsehoods – whether getting facts wrong or making things up entirely.
In the industry, these episodes are called hallucinations, though some argue that this term makes AI systems seem more human-like than they really are.

Their tendency to generate casual and convincing mistruths remains a major shortcoming for LLMs like ChatGPT. "No one in the field has yet solved the hallucination problems," Google CEO Sundar Pichai recently said in an interview.

097.4

ChatGPT, DALL-E, Stable Diffusion, Midjourney, Sora

→ E2 --

Text sources:
(1) https://en.wikipedia.org/wiki/ChatGPT
(2) https://en.wikipedia.org/wiki/DALL-E
(3) https://en.wikipedia.org/wiki/Stable_Diffusion
(4) https://en.wikipedia.org/wiki/Midjourney
(5) https://openai.com/sora
(see sources)

097.3
097.4
097.5

'(1) **ChatGPT** is a chatbot and virtual assistant developed by OpenAI and launched on November 30, 2022. Based on large language models (LLMs), it enables users to refine and steer a conversation towards a desired length, format, style, level of detail, and language. Successive user prompts and replies are considered at each conversation stage as context. (...)'

'(2) **DALL·E**, DALL·E 2, and DALL·E 3 are text-to-image models developed by OpenAI using deep learning methodologies to generate digital images from natural language descriptions known as "prompts". (...) The first generative pre-trained transformer (GPT) model was initially developed by OpenAI in 2018, using a Transformer architecture. The first iteration, GPT-1, was scaled up to produce GPT-2 in 2019; in 2020, it was scaled up again to produce GPT-3, with 175 billion parameters.
(...) DALL·E's model is a multimodal implementation of GPT-3 with 12 billion parameters which "swaps text for pixels," trained on text–image pairs from the Internet. In detail, the input to the Transformer model is a sequence of tokenized image caption followed by tokenized image patches.
(...) DALL·E 2 uses 3.5 billion parameters, a smaller number than its predecessor. DALL·E 2 uses a diffusion model conditioned on CLIP image embeddings, which, during inference, are generated from CLIP text embeddings by a prior model. (...) The models released were trained on a dataset "WebImage-Text," containing 400 million pairs of image-captions. The total number of words is similar to WebText, which contains about 40 GB of text.'

'(3) **Stable Diffusion** is a deep learning, text-to-image model released in 2022 based on diffusion techniques. It is considered to be a part of the ongoing artificial intelligence boom.
It is primarily used to generate detailed images conditioned on text descriptions, though it can also be applied to other tasks such as inpainting, outpainting, and generating image-to-image translations guided by a text prompt. Its development involved researchers from the CompVis Group at Ludwig Maximilian University of Munich and Runway with a computational donation from Stability and training data from non-profit organizations.
Stable Diffusion is a latent diffusion model, a kind of deep generative artificial neural network. Its code and model weights have been released publicly, and it can run on most consumer hardware equipped with a modest GPU with at least 4 GB VRAM. This marked a departure from previous proprietary text-to-image models such as DALL-E and Midjourney which were accessible only via cloud services.'

'(4) **Midjourney** is a generative artificial intelligence program and service (...) [It] generates images from natural language descriptions, called prompts, similar to OpenAI's DALL-E and Stability AI's Stable Diffusion. It is one of the technologies of the AI boom. It is primarily used to generate detailed images conditioned on text descriptions, though it can also be applied to other tasks such as inpainting, outpainting, and generating image-to-image translations guided by a text prompt. (...) The Stable Diffusion model supports the ability to generate new images from scratch through the use of a text prompt describing elements to be included or omitted from the output.'

'(5) **Sora** is an AI model that can create realistic and imaginative scenes from text instructions. (...) Sora can generate videos up to a minute long while maintaining visual quality and adherence to the user's prompt. (...) Sora is able to generate complex scenes with multiple characters, specific types of motion, and accurate details of the subject and background. The model understands not only what the user has asked for in the prompt, but also how those things exist in the physical world. (...)'

097.5

Questions for ChatGPT 4.0

→ E2 --

For test purposes, we asked ChatGPT 4.0 a few questions. We have included the answers here – without correcting any mistakes or abbreviating the texts.

An overview of the questions:

A – What does the future look like for the profession of communication design? (plus follow-up questions)

B – What is effective communication and what is culturally relevant design?

C – How would you describe AI in communication design if you were the harshest critic of AI?

D – Are there different artificial intelligence systems around the world that use very different data pools and therefore postulate different values and standards?

E – How can attempts to globally standardize AI design standards avoid eliminating the regional peculiarities of different cultures?

F – What sources are you using for your responses?

Concerns: artificial intelligence in communication design.

We asked ChatGPT 4.0 some questions on June 6, 2024:

Hello ChatGPT

The profession of communication design is undergoing radical changes: artificial intelligence, bots, fake news, social media, the overwhelming flood of information, amateurish design due to easily accessible graphic tools, efficiency and cost pressure, the speed of processes, but also the competition in the area of design, sometimes precarious working conditions – all of this is putting pressure on communication designers, leaving them hardly any time to think about their own actions. More so than ever before, the circumstances call for reflection, comprehensive education, and thinking beyond the confines of one's own profession.

A – What does the future look like for the profession of communication design?

ChatGPT: The future of the communication design profession, amidst the swirling currents of technological advancement and societal change, appears poised for a period of significant evolution and, perhaps, revolution. The challenges you've outlined—ranging from artificial intelligence to the deluge of information and the democratization of design tools—do indeed place considerable pressure on professionals in the field. However, these challenges also offer opportunities for growth, innovation, and the redefinition of what it means to be a communication designer. Here's a look into the future of the profession, considering the forces at play:

1. Integration of Artificial Intelligence
AI and machine learning technologies are becoming increasingly sophisticated, capable of performing tasks ranging from content creation to data analysis. For communication designers, this means an opportunity to harness AI for creativity, efficiency, and personalization at scale. AI could become a collaborator, aiding in the generation of ideas, automating routine tasks, and providing insights into audience preferences. However, this also necessitates designers to develop skills in working alongside AI, understanding its capabilities, and critically evaluating its output.

2. Emphasis on Critical Thinking and Ethical Design
The rise of fake news and the ethical implications of design decisions in shaping public opinion and behavior underscore the importance of critical thinking and ethical considerations in communication design. Professionals will need to cultivate a deep understanding of the societal impact of their work, embracing roles that go beyond aesthetics to include ethical stewardship and advocacy for responsible design practices.

3. Adaptation to Rapid Technological Changes
With the speed at which new technologies are developed and adopted, staying abreast of the latest tools, platforms, and media formats will be crucial. Continuous learning and adaptability will become key professional traits, enabling designers to leverage new mediums (such as augmented reality, virtual reality, and interactive web elements) for innovative communication strategies.

4. Expanding the Skill Set
The boundaries between disciplines are becoming increasingly blurred. Communication designers will benefit from broadening their skill sets to include areas such as user experience (UX) design, data visualization, coding, and digital marketing. This interdisciplinary approach will allow designers to offer more holistic solutions and work effectively in cross-functional teams.

5. Navigating the Gig Economy
The prevalence of freelance and contract work in the creative industries is likely to continue, if not increase. This presents challenges in terms of job security and working conditions but also offers flexibility and the opportunity for designers to work on a diverse range of projects. Professional success in this context will require strong personal branding, networking, and business skills in addition to design talent.

6. Fostering a Reflective Practice
Given the pressures and pace of the modern design environment, carving out time for reflection and critical assessment of one's work will be vital. This reflective practice can lead to more thoughtful and impactful designs and help professionals navigate ethical dilemmas and societal responsibilities.

Questions about points 1 and 2:

to 1
Will the need for communication designers decrease?

ChatGPT: Given the rapid advancements in artificial intelligence and automation, it's natural to wonder if the need for communication designers will decrease. However, the reality is more nuanced and suggests not a decrease in need but an evolution of the role itself. Here are several reasons why communication designers are likely to remain in demand, albeit with shifting responsibilities and skill sets: Human Creativity and Empathy, Strategic Thinking, Ethical and Cultural Sensitivity, Adaptation to New Technologies and Media, Personalization and Customization, Interdisciplinary Collaboration, Evolving with AI.
In summary, while the tools and methods of communication design will undoubtedly evolve, the need for skilled, creative, and strategic designers is likely to remain strong. The profession will continue to require human insight, creativity, and strategic thinking, even as it integrates new technologies and adapts to changing landscapes.

to 2
How do communication designers adapt their skills?

ChatGPT: Adapting to the rapidly changing landscape of communication design requires designers to continuously evolve their skill sets and approaches. Here are strategies and areas of focus that can help communication designers stay relevant and excel in their field:

1. Continuous Learning and Skill Development
– Technical Skills: Stay updated with the latest design software, tools, and platforms. This includes traditional design software as well as new tools powered by AI and machine learning.
– Digital Literacy: Gain proficiency in web design, coding (HTML/CSS, JavaScript), and understanding of digital platforms to create more interactive and engaging designs.
– Data Skills: Learn the basics of data analysis and visualization to communicate complex information effectively and make data-driven design decisions.

2. Embracing Interdisciplinary Knowledge
– Marketing and Branding: Understanding principles of marketing and branding can help designers create more strategic and impactful designs that align with business goals.
– User Experience (UX) and User Interface (UI) Design: Acquire skills in UX/UI design to enhance the usability and appeal of digital products, focusing on creating a seamless user experience.
– Storytelling and Content Creation: Develop storytelling skills to craft compelling narratives around brands or messages, enhancing emotional engagement through design.

3. Developing Soft Skills
– Critical Thinking and Problem-Solving: Strengthen the ability to analyze challenges from multiple angles and devise creative solutions.
– Communication and Collaboration: Enhance communication skills to articulate design concepts clearly and work effectively in multidisciplinary teams.
– Adaptability and Resilience: Cultivate flexibility in adapting to new challenges and resilience in the face of setbacks or rapid changes.

4. Engaging with Ethical and Sustainable Design
– Ethical Considerations: Educate oneself on the ethical implications of design decisions, focusing on creating responsible and inclusive content.
– Sustainability: Integrate sustainable

practices into the design process, considering the environmental impact of materials and digital footprint.

5. Leveraging AI and Automation
– Co-creation with AI: Learn to use AI as a collaborative tool for generating ideas, automating repetitive tasks, and enhancing creativity.
– Critical Evaluation of AI Outputs: Develop the skill to critically assess and refine AI-generated designs, ensuring they meet high standards of quality and creativity.

6. Building a Personal Brand and Network
– Online Presence: Establish a strong online presence through a portfolio website and social media to showcase your work and attract opportunities.
– Networking: Engage with the design community, participate in forums, attend workshops, and connect with peers and mentors for learning and collaboration opportunities.

7. Exploring Niche Areas
– Identify emerging niches within communication design where you can specialize, such as AR/VR design, motion graphics, or social media content creation. Specializing can set you apart in a crowded market.

By focusing on these strategies, communication designers can not only adapt to the changing landscape but also position themselves as valuable assets in the industry, ready to tackle current challenges and capitalize on new opportunities.

B – What is effective communication and what is cultural relevant design?

ChatGPT: Effective communication and culturally relevant design are closely intertwined concepts that focus on ensuring messages and designs resonate appropriately with diverse audiences. Here's a detailed look at both:

1. Effective Communication
Effective communication, as previously outlined, involves the clear, concise, and accurate exchange of information, ensuring that all parties involved understand the message as intended. Key components include:

– *Clarity:* Using straightforward and unambiguous language.

– *Active Listening:* Fully engaging with the speaker and providing feedback.

– *Empathy:* Understanding and respecting the perspectives and emotions of others.

– *Non-Verbal Communication:* Employing appropriate body language, eye contact, and facial expressions.

– *Consistency:* Aligning verbal and non-verbal messages.

– *Feedback:* Offering and accepting constructive criticism.

– *Adaptability:* Modifying communication styles to suit different audiences.

– *Confidence:* Communicating assertively and positively.

– *Respect and Open-Mindedness:* Valuing others' opinions and being open to new ideas.

– *Technical Proficiency:* Using communication tools effectively.

2. Culturally Relevant Design
Culturally relevant design involves creating products, services, or messages that are meaningful and appropriate for specific cultural contexts. This requires a deep understanding of the cultural norms, values, and expectations of the target audience. Key components include:

– *Cultural Awareness:*
Understanding the cultural background, values, and traditions of the target audience. Being aware of cultural sensitivities and taboos.

– *Inclusivity:*
Designing for a diverse audience, considering factors such as race, ethnicity, gender, age, and ability. Ensuring representation and avoiding stereotypes.

– *Localization:*
Adapting content to fit the local language, idioms, symbols, and conventions.
Considering local customs, holidays, and historical contexts.

– *Visual Design:*
Using culturally appropriate colors, fonts, images, and symbols. Ensuring that design elements are meaningful and respectful to the target culture.

– *User Research:*
Conducting thorough research to understand the needs, preferences, and behaviors of the target audience.
Engaging with community members and stakeholders in the design process.

– *Accessibility:*
Making designs accessible to people with different abilities and backgrounds.
Ensuring that designs meet local accessibility standards and guidelines.

– *Communication Styles:*
Adapting communication styles to match cultural norms (e.g., direct vs. indirect communication).
Considering cultural preferences for verbal and non-verbal communication.

By combining effective communication strategies with culturally relevant design principles, designers can create products and messages that are not only clear and engaging but also respectful and resonant with diverse audiences.

C – How would you describe artificial intelligence in communication design if you were the harshest critic of artificial intelligence?

ChatGPT: If I were to channel the perspective of the harshest critic of artificial intelligence in communication design, the critique might unfold as follows:

Artificial intelligence, for all its touted efficiencies and capabilities, represents a double-edged sword in the realm of communication design. At its core, it threatens the very essence of creativity and personal touch that defines the field. AI, with its algorithms and data-driven processes, introduces a mechanized, formulaic approach to design, stripping away the nuanced, human element that is fundamental to truly resonant and meaningful communication.

Critics argue that AI, in its relentless pursuit of optimization and automation, undermines the creative process. It reduces design to a series of predictable patterns and templates, eroding the space for experimentation, intuition, and serendipity. The personalized, crafted approach that designers bring to their work is overshadowed by AI-generated content, which, while efficient, lacks the depth, context, and empathy that only a human designer can impart.

Furthermore, the increasing reliance on AI tools commodifies creativity, pushing designers towards a homogeneous aesthetic that caters to algorithmic preferences rather than human emotions and experiences. This shift not only dilutes the diversity and richness of design but also fosters a culture where quantity trumps quality, and where the value of design is measured by metrics rather than impact.

Moreover, the advent of AI in communication design raises pressing ethical concerns. The ease with which AI can generate convincing imagery and text blurs the lines between authenticity and fabrication, contributing to the proliferation of misinformation and eroding public trust. The opaque nature of AI algorithms also poses questions about bias, accountability, and the erosion of privacy, as personal data becomes a commodity in the quest for tailored content.

In this light, the harshest critics of AI in communication design caution against an uncritical embrace of technology, urging professionals to consider the long-term implications of surrendering the creative process to machines. They advocate for a return to principles that prioritize human insight, ethical responsibility, and the cultivation of a diverse, vibrant design culture that champions authenticity over efficiency.

Ultimately, the debate over AI in communication design reflects broader questions about the role of technology in society and the values we seek to uphold in our creative endeavors. As such, it demands a thoughtful, nuanced discussion that weighs the benefits of innovation against the preservation of the human essence that lies at the heart of true creativity.

D – Are there different artificial intelligence systems around the world that use very different data pools and therefore postulate different values and standards? I think of India, or China or Russia. We wonder whether the Western standard of artificial intelligence doesn't only affect a minority of the world's population.

ChatGPT: Yes, artificial intelligence (AI) systems around the world can indeed be based on very different data pools and consequently reflect and reinforce different values, standards, and biases. The divergence in AI development and application across different geopolitical regions—such as India, China, Russia, and Western countries—stems from a variety of factors, including cultural norms, government policies, economic priorities, and technological infrastructures. This diversity in AI systems raises important questions about the universality of the standards and values they embed and propagate.

Cultural and Ethical Norms
Each society has its own set of cultural norms and ethical values, which can influence the type of data collected and how AI systems are trained and deployed. For example, what is considered ethical or acceptable in one country may not be so in another. This divergence can lead to AI systems that, even when addressing similar problems, prioritize and operationalize outcomes in very different ways.

Government Policies and Surveillance
Government policies significantly impact the development of AI. In some countries, governments have adopted AI technologies for surveillance and control, prioritizing datasets and algorithms that enhance these capabilities. For instance, China's approach to AI includes extensive use of surveillance technologies, heavily influenced by government directives and control mechanisms. This is in contrast to some Western democracies where, despite surveillance technologies being in use, there might be more stringent regulations regarding privacy and individual rights.

Economic Priorities
Economic factors also play a crucial role. In countries where certain industries dominate, AI development may prioritize data and applications relevant to those sectors. For example, an economy focused on manufacturing might develop AI systems optimized for industrial automation and efficiency, while countries leading in digital services might prioritize AI in consumer tech and personalization algorithms.

Technological Infrastructure and Access
The availability of technological infrastructure and the general population's access to technology can influence the development of AI. In regions with limited access to the internet or advanced technology, AI development may lag or focus on solving basic infrastructural challenges, contrasting with regions where digital technology is ubiquitous, and AI can be applied to a wider range of advanced and consumer-focused applications.

Ethical and Social Implications
The variation in AI systems across the globe underscores the need for a nuanced understanding of AI ethics and governance that respects cultural diversity while striving for standards that protect fundamental human rights. The Western model of AI, often driven by commercial interests and a specific set of ethical standards, indeed affects a minority of the world's population. This recognition has led to calls for more inclusive approaches to AI governance that consider a broader spectrum of ethical frameworks and societal needs.

The global landscape of AI is a patchwork of approaches, reflecting the diversity of human values and societal structures. This diversity challenges the notion of a one-size-fits-all AI ethic or standard, highlighting the importance of international collaboration in creating AI systems that respect and enhance human dignity and rights worldwide.

E – How can attempts to globally standardize AI design standards avoid eliminating the regional peculiarities of different cultures?

ChatGPT: Balancing the goal of globally standardizing AI design standards with the preservation of regional cultural peculiarities is a nuanced challenge. This endeavor requires a multi-faceted approach that prioritizes inclusivity, adaptability, and ethical considerations. Here's how this balance might be achieved:

1. *Inclusive Standard Setting:* Include diverse stakeholders in the standard-setting process. This means not only multinational corporations but also representatives from various regions, cultures, and sectors, including those from developing countries, indigenous communities, and underrepresented groups. Their input can ensure that standards are not overly prescriptive and leave room for regional adaptation.

2. *Cultural Sensitivity and Adaptability:* Develop standards that are sensitive to cultural differences. This could involve creating flexible guidelines that can be adapted to suit local needs and preferences. For instance, AI applications could be designed to accommodate multiple languages, cultural norms, and ethical values right from their inception.

3. *Ethical Guidelines:* Implement ethical guidelines that respect cultural diversity. These guidelines should promote respect for human rights, privacy, and the protection of cultural heritage and knowledge. They should discourage the use of AI in ways that could lead to cultural homogenization or the erosion of cultural identities.

4. *Decentralized Development:* Encourage decentralized AI development models. This involves supporting local AI ecosystems around the world to develop technologies that reflect and serve their unique cultural contexts. This could be facilitated through investment, knowledge exchange, and collaboration at both the regional and global levels.

5. *Cultural Competence in AI:* Incorporate cultural competence into AI design and development. AI systems should be capable of understanding and interacting with users in culturally appropriate ways. This requires incorporating cultural knowledge into AI training data

and algorithms, as well as testing AI systems in diverse cultural settings.

6. Global Standards with Local Flexibility: Design global standards that specify the core principles and objectives (e.g., safety, transparency, accountability) but allow for local variations in implementation. This approach recognizes the universal aspects of AI ethics and functionality while respecting the nuances of local contexts.

7. Continuous Dialogue and Revision: Establish mechanisms for ongoing dialogue and the periodic revision of standards. As cultures evolve and new insights emerge, standards must be revisited and revised to reflect these changes. This process should remain open and inclusive, ensuring that diverse voices are heard and incorporated.

8. Education and Capacity Building: Support education and capacity-building initiatives to raise awareness about the importance of cultural diversity in AI. This can help cultivate a generation of AI developers and policymakers who are attuned to the cultural implications of their work.

Achieving a balance between global standardization and the preservation of cultural peculiarities requires a commitment to diversity, equity, and inclusion at all stages of AI development. It's a dynamic process that necessitates continuous engagement with cultural contexts and a willingness to adapt and evolve over time.

F – What sources are you using for your responses?

ChatGPT:
I use a variety of sources to provide accurate and up-to-date information in my responses. These sources include:

– OpenAI Training Data: This includes a mix of licensed data, data created by human trainers, and publicly available data. This broad training helps me provide responses based on general knowledge and common information.

– Real-time Browsing: For current events, recent developments, or specific queries, I can use the browsing tool to search the internet and access the latest information from reliable and authoritative websites.

– Scholarly Articles and Publications: For more in-depth and specialized information, I refer to academic journals, scientific publications, and other scholarly sources.

– Government and Organizational Websites: Information from official government or reputable organizations' websites is used to provide accurate and authoritative data, especially for policy, legal, or health-related queries.

– News Outlets: Reputable news websites and sources provide current events and news information.
– User-Provided Links: If a user provides a specific link, I can open it directly to gather information from that source.

When using the browsing tool, I cite the sources directly in my responses to ensure transparency and credibility. If you have a specific topic or need information from a particular type of source, feel free to let me know!

Result of the interview:

Beforehand, we tested the free version (3.5) and the paid version (4.0) of ChatGPT. The latter delivered more detailed and useful answers. We fed ChatGPT 4.0 information on the current framework conditions of the design profession and asked about the future development.
ChatGPT answered appropriately and offered plenty of practical action models. In terms of content, the responses correspond with our research as well as the conclusions we drew from it, and partly extend beyond these.
The answers reveal a liberal, ethically sensible "mindset" tailored to work efficiency that reflects certain stances of current societal debates within the western hemisphere (e.g., stances on diversity, on social responsibility, or on sustainability). Chat GPT was extremely customer-oriented: very fast, clearly structured and confident in the text and style in both German and English.

That said, the answer we received to the question of what sources ChatGPT uses was sobering. Rather, the presented knowledge is based on training data (which naturally has an expiry date when it comes to currency). Furthermore, additional options for gathering information are described, including online research. The outlined options are of a general nature and do not cite any verifiable sources. This lack of transparency must be criticized, as it makes it difficult to verify the answers' correctness and offers many possibilities for manipulation.

Conclusion: ChatGPT can be a helpful tool, even for dedicated specialist issues like ours – especially for those who are familiar with the respective topic. For laypeople, the tool can be enticing because it conveys the impression of providing "objective" information and offering a shortcut for acquiring knowledge. In fact, ChatGPT cannot replace the effort of checking the credibility of statements and referring to other sources. Students should be aware of this. (u.v)

097.6
Artificial Intelligence put to the test – four forewords

→ E2 ––

ChatGPT is a tool that imitates human communication. It also claims to know a lot. The consequence: If it offers content that is well and convincingly phrased, the reader will tend to believe it. However, AI cannot think in a logical way, but is trained to recognize patterns. The following test shows that we need to proceed with caution: ChatGPT generated texts for different prompts with less and less plausible content. You can read them yourself.

You will discover that AI can be helpful as well as useless. The reason for this ambivalence is obvious: The more you know before you ask, the better you'll be able to filter out useful information. If you ask stupid questions, you'll get stupid answers. The quality of the questions and expectations are therefore crucial. This finding isn't as banal as one might think, as AI can make a lot of things simpler and thereby tempts users to choose the easy option. AI might lead users to believe that they don't need to think as much. However, it actually requires more effort to emancipate themselves from the technology and use it correctly.
The fourth foreword addresses the "thought" structure of AI that was mentioned at the start: Here, our absurd claims were treated as facts. What a shame. We (somewhat naively) hoped that ChatGPT would be skeptical of their plausibility based on data reconciliation. (eds.)

Foreword 1
We asked ChatGPT 4.0 some questions on June 7, 2024;

Prompt:
Write a foreword that is based on the following book description and directed at students: *The profession of communication design is in a state of upheaval: Artificial intelligence, an excessive flood of information, amateur design due to easily accessible graphics tools, efficiency and cost pressure – all of this is putting pressure communication designers, with the result that they hardly have any time to think about their own actions.*

ChatGPT:

ʼDear Students,

Welcome to the dynamic world of communication design, a field that is constantly evolving and presents you with diverse challenges. In a time when artificial intelligence is redefining creative endeavors, information is overwhelming us, and digital tools allow everyone to become a designer, you are at the start of an exciting journey.
This book is intended to serve as a compass to help you navigate through the complex challenges and incredible opportunities of your field. It provides insights into the latest trends, technologies, and the changing role of designers in society. Now more than ever, it is important to look beyond the obvious, reflect critically, and act creatively.
We invite you to use this book not only as a study resource but as a catalyst to think about your own role and responsibility as a designer. It is meant to encourage you to push boundaries, question conventional paths, and actively participate in shaping the future of communication design. May your time studying not only serve to acquire knowledge but also to develop your unique voice in the choir of creative designers. This book is a starting point from which you can explore, understand, and ultimately co-create the world of design. Here's to an inspiring journey filled with discoveries and success!

Best wishes, [The Author]ʼ

Foreword 2
We asked ChatGPT 4.0 some questions on June 7, 2024;

Prompt:
Write a foreword that is based on the following book description and directed at students: *Everything is in a state of upheaval these days, with the exception of communication design. Design has always been and continues to be a human issue – even if the tools, in this case programs and computing power, keep getting better.*

ChatGPT:

ʼDear Students,

In a world of rapid change, one thing remains constant: communication design is an art deeply rooted in human creativity. Technologies evolve, but the core of design—ideas, emotions, stories—remains unchanged. This book is a reminder that despite advanced tools, you are the true creators.

You will learn how to master modern technologies while understanding the significance and impact of your work. It's about finding a balance between using machines and preserving the human essence in design. Achieving this balance is your task as future designers.

We hope this book inspires you to unleash your creativity and create works that are both aesthetically impressive and profound. May your journey through design studies and beyond be marked by continual discovery and the pursuit of meaning.

Wishing you success and inspiration on your path.

Best wishes,
[The Author] ʼ

Foreword 3
We asked ChatGPT 4.0 some questions on June 7, 2024;

Prompt:
Write a foreword that is based on the following book description and directed at students: *Communication design is returning to analog times. Analyses revealed that digital tools have measurably decreased the design quality and conceptual approaches. The future of design revolves around scissors, cutters, glue, typometers, and drawing boards.*

ChatGPT:

ʼDear Students,

We live in an era where digital technology dominates our understanding of design. However, recent findings suggest that the future of communication design may require a return to analog principles. Digital tools, as efficient as they may be, have, according to our evaluations, compromised the quality and depth of our designs. It is time to reassess the value of traditional techniques. In this book, we explore why scissors, cutters, glue, typometers, and drafting boards are more than just nostalgic tools. They are the foundation of a profound, tactile understanding of design, which is often lost in the digital world. These tools force us to work more slowly and foster an intimacy with the material that is hard to achieve in digital designs. Our goal is not to discard digital design but to find a harmony between digital and analog methods. This balance allows for a new level of creativity and originality in your work. We encourage you to think beyond the screen and embrace the physical dimension of design.

This book serves as a guide to rediscover and integrate the forgotten skills of analog design. It is an invitation to expand the boundaries of your creative expression and to utilize the diversity of tools available to you.

May this book inspire you to develop your own design language that encompasses both the depth of traditional techniques and the limitless possibilities of digital methods. The future of communication design is in your hands—shape it wisely.

Best wishes for your creative journey,
[The Author] ′

Foreword 4
We asked ChatGPT 4.0 some questions on June 7, 2024;

Prompt:
Write a foreword that is based on the following book description and directed at students:

The development predicted by Gutenberg and John Lennon has come to pass: We are experiencing a shortage of words. This heralds a steady decline for communication design. As the dictum by Karl Marx goes: Buttercup, poppy, forget-me-not, these three grew in a garden plot.

ChatGPT:

′ Dear Students,

As you embark on your educational journey through this book, you are invited to explore an unusual yet increasingly pressing issue that affects us all— a shortage of words. This concept might seem abstract at first, akin to running out of air to breathe or water to drink. Yet, as this book reveals, the prediction by visionaries like Gutenberg and John Lennon about a constrained linguistic landscape has indeed materialized, presenting unique challenges and opportunities in the field of communication design.

In "The Final Word," you are called to navigate this new terrain where words, once abundant and taken for granted, have become precious commodities. This scarcity impacts how we communicate, connect, and understand each other, underscoring the critical role that creativity and innovation must now play in our interactions.

Karl Marx, in an often overlooked aspect of his work, hinted at the symbolic power of simplicity through his poetic words: "Buttercup, poppy, forget-me-not, these three grew in a garden plot." This line, emblematic of the themes you will encounter, suggests that beauty and meaning can flourish even in constraint. It encourages you to find depth in simplicity, urging a reevaluation of how complex ideas can be conveyed with limited verbal resources.

As students of communication, design, literature, or any discipline that relies on the articulation of thought, you are on the frontline of this new reality. This book does not merely aim to describe a crisis but intends to equip you with the skills to thrive within it. You will learn to craft messages that are not only effective but also resonate deeply, using fewer words to convey broader, more profound messages.

This journey will challenge you to think critically about the role of language in society and your personal expression. It will ask you to innovate, to find new paths through uncharted lexical landscapes, and ultimately, to contribute to the evolving dialogue on what it means to communicate meaningfully in an age of word scarcity.

Welcome to a thought-provoking exploration of language and its limits. May you find both inspiration and practical guidance in these pages.

Sincerely,

[The Author] ′

097.7

Artificial Intelligence put to the test – a book cover

→ E2 --

We tested different tools from the platform Hugging Face (https://huggingface.co/). Since we weren't satisfied with the results, we asked ChatGPT 4.0 some questions with its integrated Dall-E tool. Its designs are pictured here.

Artificial intelligence became known to the wider public through deceptively realistic manipulated images. It also didn't disappoint in our tests of various tools when it came to generating a few oddities. The language-image model worked well here.

At the moment, we cannot say the same about solutions for prompts that relate to typography and layouts. At the time of our tests, all AI offerings struggled to integrate typography into its layouts without errors. For the task of generating a book cover with the title "The Power of Communication Design," ChatGPT 4.0 with its integrated image tool Dall-E seemed most capable. We will present three results from a number of additional attempts that we cannot show here due to space restrictions.
Admittedly, the prompts were challenging due to the demand to "Design in the style of…" Such demands require that the AI is sufficiently trained. As expected, ChatGPT fulfilled the tasks well sometimes, and less so other times.

The conclusion of our experiment: AI cannot (yet) design like humans. This particularly applies to the aspect of tension between printed and non-printed areas, dealing with a lot of white space, and playing with typographic elements. It is certainly possible to use the suggested layouts to gain ideas – but they will not replace a designer's own work. Our dialog with AI regarding a book cover did not exceed the standards of a somewhat superficial game of ping pong, as can be seen by the prompts. The designs must be evaluated against this background.

The main thing our use of artificial intelligence showed were the many options that are already available. Significant developments are only a matter of time, or are continually in progress.
But AI also showed us that – not only regarding the book cover experiment – such a powerful innovation needs savvy users. Clear ideas of the concept, the ability to formulate clear prompts, and design expertise are necessary – then AI can be helpful. (eds.)

On the next page, you will see three book covers based on our prompts.

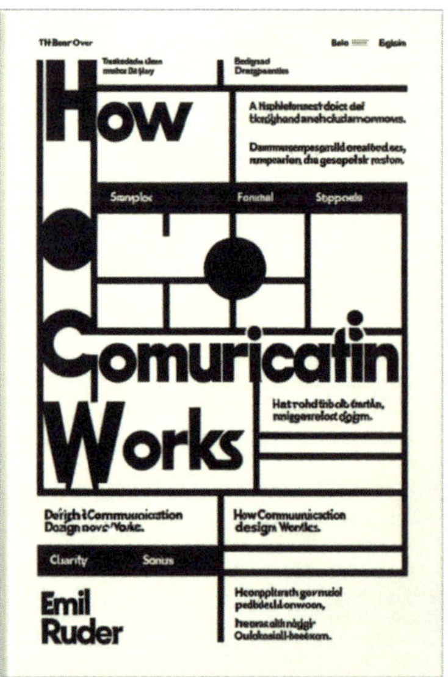

Source:
ChatGPT 4.0, https://chat.openai.com/, June 7, 2024.

Prompt:
Please create the cover of a textbook titled “How Communication Design Works” in the style of Emil Ruder.

Response from ChatGPT 4.0:
Here is the cover for the textbook “How Communication Design Works,” designed in the style of Emil Ruder. The design emphasizes a clear, functional approach with a focus on typography and a grid-based layout, fully in line with Ruder’s principles of the Swiss graphic design tradition.

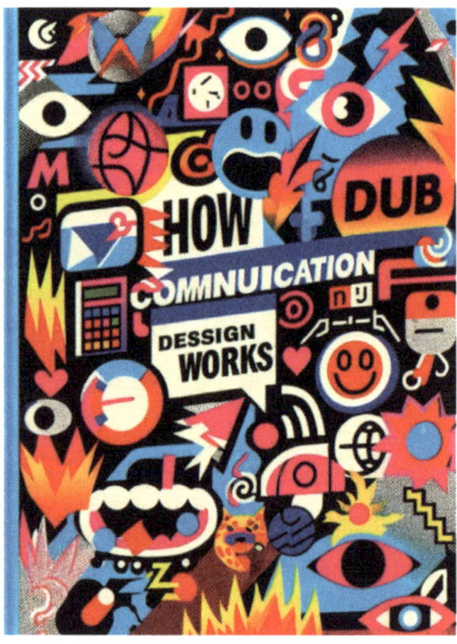

Source:
ChatGPT 4.0, https://chat.openai.com/, June 7, 2024.

Prompt:
Please create the cover of a textbook titled “How Communication Design Works” in the wild style of the 1990s, attributable to Post-Modernism. Terms like “avant-garde, breaking visual habits, unconventional” and “playful” should be represented.

Response from ChatGPT 4.0:
Here is the book cover, designed in the wild, postmodern style of the 1990s for “How Communication Design Works.” It displays avant-garde, unconventional, and playful elements that are typical for this era.

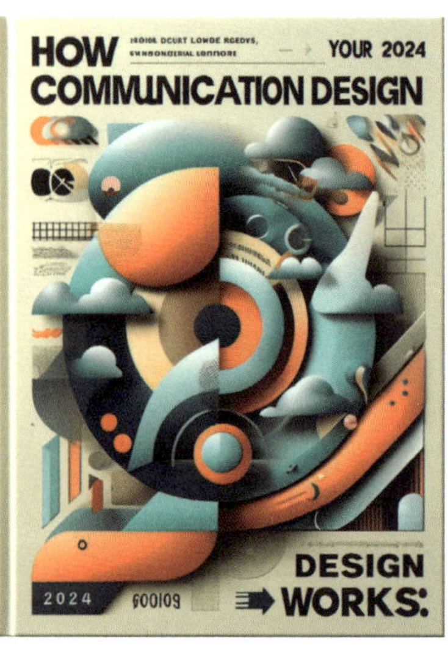

Source:
ChatGPT 4.0, https://chat.openai.com/, June 7, 2024.

Prompt:
Please create the cover of a textbook titled “How Communication Design Works” in the avant-garde style of 2024, which appears modern and incorporates the current trends in cover and book design.

Response from ChatGPT 4.0:
Here is the book cover for “How Communication Design Works” in the avant-garde style of 2024. It features a lively and modern design that reflects current trends.

← 124–125

098

The Filter Bubble. What the internet is hiding from you

→ E2 --

Bibliographic information:
"The Filter Bubble. What the internet is hiding from you," Eli Pariser; Penguin Books, London, 2011;
ISBN 978-0241954522

Text source: page 01, line 01 – page 03, line 16

097.7
098
099

/ Few people noticed the post that appeared on Google's corporate blog on December 4, 2009. It didn't beg for attention – no sweeping pronouncements, no Silicon Valley hype, just a few paragraphs of text sandwiched between a weekly roundup of top search terms and an update about Google's finance software. Not everyone missed it. Search engine blogger Danny Sullivan pores over the items on Google's blog looking for clues about where the monolith is headed next, and to him, the post was a big deal. In fact, he wrote later that day, it was "the biggest change that has ever happened in search engines." For Danny, the headline said it all: "Personalized search for everyone."

Starting that morning, Google would use fifty-seven signals – everything from where you were logging in from to what browser you were using to what you had searched for before – to make guesses about who you were and what kinds of sites you'd like. Even if you were logged out, it would customize its results, showing you the pages it predicted you were most likely to click on. Most of us assume that when we google a term, we all see the same results—the ones that the company's famous Page Rank algorithm suggests are the most authoritative based on other pages' links. But since December 2009, this is no longer true. Now you get the result that Google's algorithm suggests is best for you in particular – and someone else may see something entirely different.

In other words, there is no standard Google anymore. It's not hard to see this difference in action. In the spring of 2010, while the remains of the Deepwater Horizon oil rig were spewing crude oil into the Gulf of Mexico, I asked two friends to search for the term "BP". They're pretty similar – educated white left-leaning women who live in the Northeast. But the results they saw were quite different. One of my friends saw investment information about BP. The other saw news. For one, the first page of results contained links about the oil spill; for the other, there was nothing about it except for a promotional ad from BP. Even the number of results returned by Google differed – about 180 million results for one friend and 139 million for the other. If the results were that different for these two progressive East Coast women, imagine how different they would be for my friends and, say, an elderly Republican in Texas (or, for that matter, a businessman in Japan).

With Google personalized for everyone, the query "stem cells" might produce diametrically opposed results for scientists who support stem cell research and activists who oppose it. "Proof of climate change" might turn up different results for an environmental activist and an oil company executive. In polls, a huge majority of us assume search engines are unbiased. But that may be just because they're increasingly biased to share our own views. More and more, your computer monitor is a kind of one-way mirror, reflecting your own interests while algorithmic observers watch what you click. Google's announcement marked the turning point of an important but nearly invisible revolution in how we consume information. You could say that on December 4, 2009, the era of personalization began. (...) /

← 124–125

099

18. Shell Jugendstudie "Jugend 2019"

→ E2 --

Bibliographic information:
"18. Shell Jugendstudie Jugend 2019. Eine Generation meldet sich zu Wort." Shell Deutschland Holding (ed.), concept and coordination: Mathias Albert, Klaus Hurrelmann, Gudrun Quenzel, Kantar; Beltz Verlag, Weinheim, 2019; [in German]
ISBN 978-3-407-83195-8

Text sources:
from pages 13, 14, 15, 16, 18, 19, 20, 25, 27, 29, 30

The following passages are taken from the summary at the beginning of the study, which precedes the in-depth analyses. They provide initial insights and depict the characteristic style as well as a few sample findings from the study. To gain a more differentiated understanding, I recommend reading the full publication. The subsequent study will be published in 2024/2025. (u.v)

/ (...) A pragmatic basic orientation continues to be characteristic of Germany's youth. As already described in the last Shell Youth study, young people are still willing to follow performance standards to a high degree, while at the same time expressing a desire for stable social relationships in their personal environment. In their individual search for a secure place in society, they are adapting to the circumstances in such a way that they can take advantage of opportunities that come along. (...) / Page 13

/ **The Internet as the most important source of political information**
The majority of young people go online to learn more about political topics. Most frequently, they use news websites or news portals (20%), many also refer to social media offerings, i.e., relevant sources of information in social networks, messenger apps (14%), or YouTube (9%). 23% list television as a source of information, 15% listen to the radio, and another 15% read conventional print media, but the Internet and social media have now overtaken classic media for targeted searches for political information. However, they still trust the classic media more than the others. The majority considers the information provided by the news broadcast on ARD or ZDF as trustworthy. (...) In contrast, approximately every other young person deems YouTube less or not trustworthy. For Facebook, this number rises to two out of three young people who distrust the information provided there. And only a minority trusts Twitter [X]. (...) /
Page 14

/ **Environmental and climate protection are greatly impacting young people**
While up until 2010, young people's main problems revolved around the economic situation and the rise in poverty as well as fear of unemployment or failing to find an apprenticeship, this has changed considerably in the meantime. Currently, nearly three out of four young people list pollution as the main problem that scares them, followed by fear of terrorist attacks (66%) and climate change (65%). In contrast, just over half of young people included the economic situation and rising poverty, while only slightly over a third fear losing employment or failing to find an apprenticeship. (...) / Page 15

/ **All in all, young people view German as socially just**
With 59%, the majority of young people are convinced that, overall, Germany operates fairly. When the question is differentiated a little more, 79% agree that everyone has the opportunity to educate themselves in accordance with their skills and talents in Germany. (...) But the lower the participant's social class of origin, the lower the proportion of those who agree with this statement. (...) / Page 15

/ **EU signifies opportunity, prosperity, cultural diversity, and peace**
Most young people do not view the EU as a risk, but as an opportunity, and therefore do not question it. Every other young person rates the EU as positive (43%) or very positive (7%). (...) / Page 15

/ **Between cosmopolitanism and affinity to populism**
As a general rule, populist argumentation patterns have also proven to be compatible with young people,

but important differences are evident: The majority of young people (57%) emphasizes that they approve of Germany accepting a large number of refugees. However, an even bigger majority (68%) agrees with the statement: "In Germany, you can't say anything negative about foreigners without being called a racist." Apparently, the argumentation pattern covers a widespread feeling that it isn't possible to express certain things without being morally chastised based on subjective perception. (...)′ Page 16

′ **Tolerance remains a trademark**
A vast majority of young people in Germany continues to be tolerant of other lifestyles, minorities, and social groups. (...)′ Page 18

′ **Satisfaction with democracy has clearly risen for young people in the east**
A large majority of young people in Germany consider democracy to be the norm as a form of government. Specifically, nearly four out of five young people (77%) are somewhat or very satisfied with the current state of democracy in Germany – this value has been rising for many years. (...)′ Page 18

′ **Young people's personal engagement is wavering and appears to be declining slightly**
The proportion of young people who indicated that they engage in social or political matters or simply to help others held at a percentage between 33% and 40% for a long time. However, more and more boys and girls stated that they do not engage in any activities of this kind, and the number of those who do so at least occasionally has declined. (...)′ Page 19

′ **Optimistic outlook**
58% of young people have an optimistic outlook on their own future, 37% have a mixed outlook (sometimes positive, sometimes negative), and only 5% have a rather dismal outlook. The proportion of optimistic young people has therefore decreased slightly compared to 2015 (61%), and the trend of increasing optimism that could be observed in 2006 has not continued, although the overall level remains comparably high. (...)′ Page 20

′ **Value orientations: family and relationships remain the main points of orientation for their own way of life**
"Family" and "social relationships" are by far the most important value orientations that nearly all young people want to have guaranteed; even more important than "individual responsibility" (89%), and "independence" (83%), which represent special development tasks in the transition to adulthood, particularly in adolescence. The focus on virtues such as respecting law and order (87%), being diligent and productive (81%), or striving for security (77%) have also remained at the same levels since 2002. (...)′ Page 20

′ **Relationships with parents remain exceptionally positive**
Since 2002, the proportion of young people who have a positive relationship with their parents has increased steadily: Four out of ten young people (42%) get along very well with their parents, half of them (50%) have a good relationship despite occasional disagreements. (...)′ Page 20

′ **Professional expectations prove to be very stable – security continues to be the main priority**
When it comes to professional expectations, the need for security continues to dominate. 93% consider secure employment to be (very) important. (...)′ Page 27

′ **Secure job, enough free time, and a high income are priorities**
(...) The study revealed that job security, the expectation of having enough free time outside of work, and a high income have high priority. This mindset also appears very pragmatic. (...)′ Page 29

′ **Ways of accessing the Internet and duration of Internet usage**
70% of young people primarily use their smartphones to access the Internet. On an average day, they estimate that they spend about 3.7 hours online. (...) Most of this time is spent on communication: 96% visit social networks (messenger services or social networks) at least once a day. (...) ′ Page 30

′ **Concerns and insecurities**
When asked for their opinions on the Internet and social networks, concerns and insecurities dominate: 60% don't like that they, as Internet users, are part of a business model and corporations such as Facebook or Google earn money with their users' data. Just as many (61%) fear they have no control over the data they leave behind online. The majority of young people agree that the Internet contains hate speech (58%) or fake news (51%). There is slightly less fear of missing out while not being online all the time. 40% think that they need to be on social networks to find out what others are doing, and 38% indicated that they would lose half their life if they misplaced their smartphone. (...)′ Page 30

← *126–127*

100

Die Vereindeutigung der Welt

→ E2 203

Bibliographic information:
"Die Vereindeutigung der Welt. Über den Verlust an Mehrdeutigkeit und Vielfalt," Thomas Bauer;
Reclam Verlag, Ditzingen, 2018;
[in German]
ISBN 978-3-15-019492-8

Text sources:
(1) Text on the back cover;
(2) Page 13, lines 01 – 16;
(3) Page 45, line 05 – page 46, line 11

Thomas Bauer (*1961) is a professor of Islamic and Arabic studies at the University of Münster. His research topics span cultural history, historical anthropology, tolerance of ambiguity, and the history of classical Arabian literature and rhetoric.

′(1) What do the loss of diversity in apple varieties, the way politicians and actors appear on talk shows, pigeonhole thinking, egalitarian racism, religious fundamentalism, and the art and music market have in common? They all represent the reduction of diversity, repression of the inappropriate. An alleged "authenticity" is increasingly appearing in its stead: It is no longer about "what," but only about "how." Thomas Bauer examines this fatal tendency to suppress variety in meaning and depicts the consequences that would accompany a continued path of disambiguation.′

′(2) The German word for "ambiguity" is less common than the English or French equivalent – "ambiguity" and "ambiguité" are part of everyday language. But the German word is also essential, specifically as a term for all phenomena of ambivalence, distinctiveness, and vagueness with which people are confronted all the time. Sometimes it helps to differentiate between vagueness and ambiguity. For our purposes, however, this is not necessary, since both indicate that multiple interpretations can be attributed to a sign or circumstance, whether because the sign or circumstance is not clear enough (vagueness) or because the sign or circumstances point to several meanings at the same time (ambiguity in the strict sense). We will therefore use "ambiguity" as a general term in the following. (...)′

′(3) (...) Modernism did not constitute a movement towards greater tolerance of ambiguity in music – and this was also not the case in art. "Purity" also became a leitmotif here. The concept of purity had already represented a central topic for Adolf Loos (1870 – 1933), the pioneer of modern architecture. In his (extremely racist) pamphlet "Ornament und Verbrechen" ("Ornament and Crime"), Loos wrote the following in 1908: "evolution of culture is equivalent to removing ornamentation from commodities (...) soon the city's streets will gleam like white walls!" Suprematists, futurists, and many other branches of modernism – another fundamentalist move – accompanied the ideologies of improving the world and alternatingly produced political manifestos and works of art. On the path to purity, one task lay in "filtering out of the specific effects of a form of art everything that could possibly also be borrowed from the medium of a different form of art – or lent to the medium of a different form of art."

This would "cleanse the individual arts and help them find the guarantee for their quality measures and independence in their purity," as Greenberg characterized "modernist painting" in 1960. However, this made an interaction between the arts impossible: Natural fusion developed into "near hostility," according to Jürgen Weber. On their way to purity, the individual arts not only needed to be "liberated" – not just from each other, but also in themselves. As a result, architecture was "liberated" from ornamentation, art from tradition as a whole, music from tonality, poetry from alleged mandatory forms, color from shape and shape from color, and of course, painting and plastic from representationalism, and finally from meaning. Or, as Greenberg elaborates: "The pure artistic or abstract qualities of a work of art are the only valid ones." This also eliminated meaning from art. What remained was a fundamentalist insistence of possessing the one truth. In Europe and the USA, "abstract purism consolidated into a school, a dogma, a credo." (...)/

100.1
Vereindeutigen vs. Übersetzen

→ E2 ––

Bibliographic information:
"Wie können wir den Schaden maximieren? Gestaltung trotz Komplexität," Christoph Rodatz, Pierre Smolarski (Eds.), transcript Verlag, Bielefeld, 2021; [in German]
ISBN 978-3-8376-5784-5

Source:
From the chapter "Vereindeutigen vs. Übersetzen," Ingo Offermanns:
page 188, line 18 – page 189, line 23; page 190, line 01 – page 191, line 01; page 191, line 14 – page 192, line 09; page 192, line 11 – page 193, line 14; page 193, line 30 – page 194, line 28; Accompanying text: (u.v)

In his contribution to the book "Wie können wir den Schaden maximieren? Gestaltung trotz Komplexität," Ingo Offermanns picks up on various aspects that are inherent to visual communication. I would like to discuss and cite some of them here. I recommend reading the full article.

In "Vereindeutigen vs. Übersetzen," Ingo Offermanns postulates that many deem the current role of (graphic) design to consist of promoting the capitalist growth mantra and eradicating aspects of unpredictability, foreignness, and ambiguity in the process. He does not consider this surprising in a system that declares "productivity to be the highest virtue." Consequently, he says, all visual communication tools suitable for advertising and seduction are at the forefront of these activities. According to Offermanns, on a superficial level, it is hard to object to the professional use of visual language. But if we take a closer look at visual communications, this paints a different picture: We must keep in mind who is commissioning these advertising and seduction activities as well as how they relate to societal concerns. Content translations – and that's all that visual communication is – always incorporate all aspects of rhetoric: logos (the level of argumentation), pathos (the level of emotions), and ethos (the level of morality). Offermanns:

/(...) This not only entails conveying in a functional (literal) way, but developing and implementing translations within and between societies from which a responsibility arises that cannot be grasped with the logic of standardized work processes (sensation, omnipresence, volume, trend, exclusivity, readability). Translations are always also interpretations, as they attempt to bring foreign emblems to society and society to these emblems through speech and contradiction, through exploration, analysis, criticism, and invention, as outlined by writer and translator Karl Dedecius in his book *On Translating*. (...)/

Offermanns references architect and design theoretician Friedrich von Borries (see also 103, 104), who attributes

Ingo Offermanns (*1972) is a German designer. He teaches at the University of Fine Arts Hamburg as a professor of graphic design. (u.v)

"political, meaning critical and interventionist potential" to design, which arises from a "field of tension that is intrinsic to design – between rootedness in social and economic everyday life, speculative production of desires, and artistic imagination." Offermanns speaks of the "possibility to be different" and its inherent aspects of criticism and resistance. But when he takes a look at design practice, he discovers:

/(...) Contemporary graphic design often seems less contradictory to me. If I look at a multitude of design forums (festivals, biennials, symposia, awards, blogs), I end up seeing individual exhibitions, in a similar vein to trade fair shows, which rarely involve questioning, analysis, or criticism, but rather displays of power within a profession using polished staging techniques. I get the impression that the forces of production of desires and imagination are primarily geared towards self-design, driven by fears of deficits and failure, i.e., personal survival in the everyday economy, rather than the possibility of being different in terms of individual and societal striving. Above all, forces are mobilized to achieve attention, individuation, and demand for designers and clients in a competitive way instead of – in terms of graphic design – breaking up positions speculatively in the translation, and finding experiments in dialog instead of a monological exchange of blows. Translation aims for a dynamic and not precisely identifiable in-between. It is dialogical and deals with the distance, not the difference, between various parties to establish commonalities, maintain the parties' tension, and at the same time interactively break open their positions and bring them closer together. (...)/

In Offermanns' opinion, this "in between" stands in contrast to the "logic of efficiency and exploitation" of a globalized capitalist system. He continues:

/(...) In contrast, advertising primarily targets classificatory disambiguation to achieve exclusivity with the help of a brand (or a visual identity) and turn (alleged) needs into demand. Here, exclusivity feeds from variations of similar factors instead of heterogeneous diversity to satisfy the logic of efficiency and use of globalized capitalism. In the predatory competition for attention, sensation, omnipresence, volume, trend, exclusivity, and readability are its references – all of them calculable factors –, and its goal lies in manipulatively producing emotions. This may also be a form of conveyance, but conveyance in the form of a one-way street without wrong turns. Since the history of graphic design is closely linked to the establishment of today's economic principles, this begs the question of to what extent graphic design can even appropriate the field of tension described by von Borries and Geiger. After all, graphic design is a creative discipline that largely depends on (commercial) contracts, primarily works with the (precise) linguistic statements of others, is always embedded into (verbal) language, and whose artefacts can only be appropriated by its users to a far lesser degree than those of fashion or architecture, for example. In addition, let's not deceive ourselves: The purpose of (visual) rhetoric lies in the efficient use of seductive heuristics in order to shape attitudes and influence actions. Nonetheless, persuasion presupposes options. And this is where I see the potential for a stronger tendency towards the possibility of being different: Designing does not mean following alleged inevitabilities, but exploring, perceiving, and disclosing options. It means sounding out (communicative) scopes from the perspective of different authors and making them permeable – whereby the designer also becomes the author through the translation and/or interpretation. (…) ⁄

The "authorship" that Offermans describes here is based on analytical thinking, on the knowledge of all aspects of visual rhetoric, and above all, also on a mindset. He continues: ⁄ (…) Graphic designers analyze the narrative of the statement they receive, take stock of their narrative potential, and accentuate certain aspects of the statement or give them a character to make them accessible and permeable, and thereby activate the in-between of the fundamental contextual impulse, client, designer, and fourth parties. If we assume that contents are potentially diverse in our differentiated and interconnected world, we should also assume that the just described procedure will bring about equally diverse (visual) expressions. After all, the translation – as mentioned at the start – should transport the foreign emblems to society with the voice (and authorship) of the designer and transport society to this emblem. In this sense, translation does not mean forcing foreign aspects onto familiar ones, it does not mean assimilation, nor focusing on similarity, but rather the search for commonalities and adding tension to the respective unique aspect. However, if I take a look at the (western-style) visual uniformity, observable around the world, of commercial as well as hipster mainstream in graphic design, I ask myself how many designers really strive to fulfil this ambition. Moreover, what can be observed is the endeavor to either synthesize a uniform visual language – at least one that works imperatively and universally for a period or a generation – or retreat into a hermetically subjectivistic or identity-related in an escapist way. But where does that leave the awareness of plurality, porousness, of the simultaneousness of the non-simultaneous – that which harbors the potential to give rise global interconnection? Where does this leave resonance, exploration, multilingualism, ambiguity, and nuance? This leads to the impression that designers yield to the pressures of economic everyday life rather than giving themselves the opportunity to develop a polyglot translation intelligence that emphasizes diversity, variety, and polyphony in dialog. (…) ⁄

Bibliographic information:
"Design's Delight," Jan van Toorn,
nai010 publishers, Rotterdam, 2006;
ISBN 978-90-6450-522-5

Text source:
page 27, line 01 – page 28, line 53

Jan van Toorn (1932–2020) was a Dutch graphic designer. In the 1980s, he started teaching at the Gerrit Rietveld Academie, Amsterdam, and at the Jan Van Eyck Academie in Maastricht. In his book, he tries to draw attention back to the societal role of design. (eds.)

← 130–131

101 Design's Delight

→ E2 ––

⁄ This essay deals with thinking as a designer of visual communication – with thinking as a method of understanding my own action and role as an expert in the socio-cultural context. In other words I see my personal and professional activity in relation to social reality, in relation to the smaller and larger contexts of human activity. My thinking should be operational in this: a con-struct of notions and arguments which enables me – as a person, as a social being and as a professional – to deal with the complexitiy of the world we live in. Against the background of the libertarian-socialist worldview of the historical avant garde, with which I feel a close affinity, this thinking should first and foremost be understood as an ongoing attempt to deal imaginatively with the conflict between tradition and innovation, related to the collective interest in the sense of social emancipation and human survival. This orientation towards social and public goals is needed more than ever now that the disciplines of practical intellectuals have affiliated to such an extent with the power of money, bureaucracy and the media, whose solutions for the social, economic and ecological crisis are far from convincing.
For us, as designers, architects, televisionmakers et cetera, to escape from this entanglement with institutional interests – which wish to set priorities in such a way as to reflect their private interests – it is important to formulate a concept and strategies which once more make action for the public concern possible. Communication is largely formed by unreasoned action. Therefore the formation of a concept which strives for a more independent forming of opinions, requires besides the analysis of the existing production relations an unceasing reflection on that empirical experience. In this way it will be possible, admidst the shifting and opposing corporate interests – and at the same time being dependent upon them – to develop politico-cultural criteria and strategies which will open new space for professional action in the media. Action starting from a non-authoritarian attitude towards the public and not concealing its own mediating role. Design, I think, has not received the attention needed to understand its present social position. Despite the enormous dissemination of information, the complex factors of institutional power which definitely contribute to its production have mostly been ignored. Nor has contemporary design been related to the theoretical developments in other spheres of cultural production, and critical thinking about economy and media. Because our living environment has been intrumentalised by a wide variety of institutional interests, the con-

sumer has become dependent upon an encreasing denseness of comunicative networks, the strategic aims of which remain as obscure as possible. Design is inevitably connected with these developments of modern (post)industrial society. It plays an essential role in the organisation of production and stimulates the distribution of this production by articulating the form of goods and messages.
Through its relationships with the organized interests of the economy, the state and the media, design also contributes to the cultural staging which intervenes with all aspects of social and cultural life. Designers and other professional mediators have proved, unfortunately, to be unable to stay out of this ongoing process of colonisation of the media and have found themselves incapable of renegotiating an attitude which is related to the benefit of all. As a result, the image of reality they produce consists of no more than a myriad of individual side tracks, reduced to mere form and stereotypical content. Because designers and intellectuals fail to reflect critically upon the conditions und which their own action comes about, their mediating role between private and public interest has been lost. The visual language of graphic or other design…originally intended as an emancipating force – has been replaced by the forms of expression of advertising and public relations. In the media, problems of public nature are increasingly veiled by a multiform spectacle, the public interest formulated by the language of marketing.
According to Abraham Moles, the role of the designer does not so much exist in making "new" objects which serve as structural elements of an immaterial culture, but in creating an absolutely stable environment. Before introducing anything new, the designer must first protect the status quo; only after that does it become possible for the individual to participate spontaneously and without much effort in the seductive immaterial nature of the present world. (…) ʼ

Bibliographic information:
"Design Struggles: Intersecting Histories, Pedagogies, and Perspectives," Claudia Mareis, Nina Paim (eds.); Valiz, Amsterdam, 2021;
ISBN 978-9492095886

Text source: book description on the back cover

← 130 – 131

102

Design Struggles: Intersecting Histories, Pedagogies, and Perspectives

→ E2 204

ʼ *Design Struggles* critically assesses the complicity of design in creating, perpetuating, and reinforcing social, political, and environmental problems both today and in the past.
The book proposes to brush the discipline against the grain, by problematizing Western notions of design, fostering situated, decolonial, and queer-feminist modes of disciplinary self-critique. In order to reimagine design as an unbound, ambiguous, and unfinished practice, this publication gathers a diverse array of perspectives, ranging from social and cultural theory, design history, design activism, sociology, and anthropology, to critical and political studies, with a focus on looking at design through the intersections of gender, race, ethnicity, culture, class, and beyond.
It combines robust scholarly insights with engaging and accessible modes of conveyance and storytelling by bringing together an urgent and expansive array of voices and views from those engaged in struggles with, against, or around the design field.
– With accessible and engaging stories about examples of intersectional, transformative approaches to design.
– An indispensable source book and sounding board for creative makers, designers, artists, architects and educators. ʼ

← 130 – 131

103

Weltentwerfen – eine politische Designtheorie

→ E2 --

Bibliographic information:
"Weltentwerfen – Eine politische Designtheorie," Friedrich von Borries;
edition suhrkamp, 2017; [in German]
ISBN 978-3-518-12734-6

Source: page 119, line 01 – page 123, line 23

Friedrich von Borries (*1974) teaches at the University of Fine Arts Hamburg as a professor of design theory. He wrote additional books on the relationship between design and society (see also 104). (eds.)

ʼ (…) **6. The world is the subject and result of design.** Design changes the world it encounters, it is the subject of design. Therefore, the world is not just found, but also made. We are thrust into a world that we design because we live in it. Here, the relationship between what we find and what we change is increasingly shifting towards what we change. Today, humanity is considered the driving force of geological development. To take this one step further, we could even say that the world we perceive today and the Earth's surface as we observe it today are human-made. Chemist and Nobel Prize winner Paul Crutzen (*1933) therefore suggested at the start of the 21st century that the present geological era should be designated the "Anthropocene," an era defined by humans.

6.1 Designing the world is an inevitability. In the Anthropocene, the world is both the subject and the result of design. It is inevitable that design will impact the whole world. The natural living environment is no longer the sole condition of being human, rather humans are also a condition of the natural living environment. This reversal demands a new understanding of politics and design.

6.2 The world is changing and has no borders. The world that is the subject and object of design is not an unchangeable entity. The world is changing. In some respects, the world is getting bigger, and in others, it is getting smaller. On the one hand, the globe is shrinking into a global village, as media theoretician Marshall McLuhan (1911 – 1980) put it; on the other hand, the world wide web is inflating into an independent and infinite virtual space. In the early days of humanity, the world of humans' imagination still constituted the tangible and therefore very limited living environment. But the idea of the world changed, the understanding of the world spatially expanded over the centuries. First, the world became a disc, then a ball, then the solar system, and finally, the universe that comprises many planetary systems. Today, the world has exploded into the virtual space, which knows no boundaries, a space of opportunity that consistently regenerates itself. The world has no boundaries because humans, as the expansive beings in their history, are continually extending the respective boundaries of the world – meaning the boundaries of what was perceptible and imaginable as the world. Today, the world forms part of outer space, exploitation of which is being researched and developed, but also the virtual space that overlaps with the physical space. Aside from space, expansion also affects time. The factors that already apply to humanity's physical environment certainly also apply to this broadening world. Virtual worlds are spaces conceived or created by humans. The conditions to which these expansions are subject to have also been drawn up by humans. A world that changes continually is designable.

6.3 Designing the world is a moral duty. The modern era has left the world – in part through design – in a state in which humanity's livelihood is at risk; terms such as global warming, scarcity of resources, global migration, etc. are only rough keywords that characterize the symptoms of the comprehensive devastation of the world through the existing economic system. According to social psychologist Harald Welzer (*1958), there are only two ways to escape this state: either "by disaster" or "by design" (Sommer/Welzer 2014, p. 27 ff). Here, we have two opposing strategies. "By disaster" means waiting until the existing system collapses and building something new from the ruins, while "by design" means transforming the existing system into a new one in advance, i.e., preventatively, by means of targeted and methodical actions. This kind of transformational design refers to the whole world. That is why, based on a progressive understanding of responsibility, designing the world is a moral duty.

6.4. Every designer can decide whether they want to participate actively in the design process or submit to the will of others.
The self-perception of many designers, which has emerged along with growing prosperity in the western hemisphere since World War II, is that of a service provider – they do not see themselves as self-assured and responsible designers. Usually, the designer serves as an agent whose creativity is used to represent or legitimize the intentions of others. This restriction is – at least, when it comes to personal decisions, in the relatively free societies of western democracies – a self-incapacitation, and every designer must decide for themselves whether they can answer for this.

6.4.1 Every designer is responsible for what they design. A critical analysis of their own practice forms the foundation for this decision. On both the major and minor level, the designer is a demiurge who determines the conditions of our lives with what they design. They change the world in which we live. Designers are not always aware of the reach of their own actions and the resulting responsibility, even though the problem of the irresponsible creator was already conceived in the early modern period (e.g., in 1818 with the figure of Viktor Frankenstein). To be able to act in a responsible way, the designer must be aware of the societal significance (including the economic, ecological, and social consequences) of their actions. Because they are responsible for what they design.

6.4.2 Designing means putting up aesthetic resistance. When making the decision of whether – and how – a designer wants to act in a "designing" "submissive" way in the present climate, they must take the framework conditions of the respective society in which they are operating into account. Submissive forces also dominate life in western states. Anyone who wants to take advantage of what is generally termed prosperity and success in this society must submit to the economic logic of the present. Designing therefore also means resisting – as a designer, with aesthetic, meaning sensually tangible methods that are also political. (...) /

103.1

Die Welt als Entwurf

→ E2 205

Bibliographic information:
"Die Welt als Entwurf," Otl Aicher,
Verlag Ernst & Sohn, Berlin, 1991;
[in German]
ISBN 3-433-02185-6

Aicher advocates for a design approach that relates thinking and doing to one another. As in some of his other compositions, he views design action as a holistic process that must incorporate social and ecological effects. Against this background, he addresses various questions in his essays. In this book from 1991, published shortly before his death, he campaigns against the superficiality of the postmodern zeitgeist that prevailed at this time. "design relates to the cultural state of an era, the time, the world. today's world is defined by its design state. today's civilization is made by man and also subject to him. The quality of designs is the quality of the world," Aicher once said; this quote is taken from a foreword by Wolfgang Jean Stock. (eds.)

← 130–131

104

Das RLF Manifest "SHOW YOU ARE NOT AFRAID."

→ E2 ––

Bibliographic information:
"RLF, Das richtige Leben im falschen," Friedrich von Borries; Suhrkamp Verlag, Berlin, 2013;
[in German]
ISBN: 978-3-518-46443-4

Text source:
https://www.friedrichvonborries.de/de/projekte/rlf-manifest (see sources)

/ 5 bullet points on the criticism of total capitalism
SHOW YOU ARE NOT AFRAID.

1. FIGHT AGAINST YOURSELF.

Today's capitalism is total. It is comprehensive and omnipresent. It has taken possession of our thoughts and feelings. We have internalized the logic of the system. The way we design our life, the way we establish our interpersonal relationships and dream up our own future is shaped by the logic of accumulation, profit maximization, and growth. We are afflicted with Stockholm syndrome; we have learned to love that which destroys us. Not only are we part of the global capitalist system, but capitalism is part of us. Fighting it also means fighting a part of ourselves: a part of our identity, our thinking, our desires. A fight against capitalism is a fight against our own being. Fight against yourself.

2. USE THE SYSTEM.

The current state of capitalism knows nothing outside of itself. It does not recognize any alternatives. Criticism against today's capitalism cannot occur from the secure standpoint of an alleged outside. It operates from a standpoint within the system. Criticism is not independent, but participatory. All previous criticism of capitalism was received by the system itself and misused as a motor for innovation. If criticism does not want to serve the further development and refinement of capitalism, it must appropriate the means, tools, methods of the subject it wants to criticize. Criticism must occur from within the system itself. Use the system. Force your own internalizations to the outside. Infiltrate the media, instrumentalize its power of dissemination. Misuse the logic of marketing and the aesthetics of surfaces to create new, opposing desires. Affirmation as a critical strategy. Establish capitalist companies, stock companies to market criticism. Act as a double agent. Sell false ideals. Earn profits. Speculate and thereby increase your profits. Uncover the perversions of capitalism by generating them yourself. Breed the greed on which the monster will suffocate.

3. CREATE FREE SPACES BETWEEN REALITY AND FICTION.

Western capitalism likes to boast about the freedom it claims to grant. Art as a space to think differently serves as its poster child. Here, everything can be thought, claimed, done. It holds the task of aestheticizing the living environment and at the same time criticizing society. Art is the space of fiction that turns into reality, in which all possibilities may be thought of or at least symbolically tested. At the same time, no other social space is as economized and subject to the relentless laws of the market as that of art. This field of tension opens up free spaces. Use art as a cape of invisibility. Use art as legitimation. Work with paradoxes. Think in black and white. Offer ambiguousness to evade capture by the algorithms. Elaborate irritation. Invent stories and identities. Let fiction turn into reality and fictionalize reality. Because art allows you to live what is otherwise forbidden. Use the free spaces that emerge between reality and fiction.

4. INTERVENE IN YOUR REALITY

The omnipotence of globality, its corporations, and its economic power let the individual and their actions appear powerless. At the same, demanded individualism leads to further isolation that makes us feel even more powerless. Only Superman can change something, I can't. This feeling of powerlessness is part of the current governance mechanism. Resist these implications of helplessness. Change your reality. Don't wait for the big moment, the big solution, the ultimate truth. Switch to the mode of permanent intervention. Intervene in your environment. You will find fellow combatants. Because nobody is happy in a system that cannibalizes itself. Protest and resistance can only become global if they exist locally everywhere in the world. Hack the source codes in your field of action. Become a smuggler who transports the ideas of otherness, the spirit of resistance, to places where nobody expects them. Become a radical opportunist, a double agent. Organize an invisible cell that awakens at the right moment.

5. THERE IS NO REAL LIFE IN THE WRONG ONE.

The fight against capitalism is the fight against yourself. But the fight against yourself is also the basic demand of capitalism. Because in order to maintain the growth spiral, the system is indoctrinating us with dissatisfaction. I am not good enough. I can do it better. Just do it. I need to optimize myself. Not only competition with everyone else, but also competition with myself. Become who you are meant to be. Identity as a brand message, individuality as a competitive edge. Fighting against yourself is not only the prerequisite for overcoming the capitalism within us, but also the mantra of capitalism itself. The right life of capitalism is the sum of the empty promises of advertising. The dream of the right life implants an image of inadequacy within us. Because the dream of the right life is part of the suppression machine. There is no right life in the wrong one. Refuse optimization, but don't give up in defeat. Fight against what is wrong.ʼ

← *130–131*

105

Extra Bold: A Feminist, Inclusive, Anti-racist, Nonbinary Field Guide for Graphic Designers

→ E2 ––

Bibliographic information:
"Extra Bold – a feminist inclusive anti-racist nonbinary field guide for graphic designers," Ellen Lupton, Farah Kafei, Jennifer Tobias, Josh A. Halstead, Kaleena Sales, Leslie Xia, Valentina Vergara (Eds.); Princeton Architectural Press, New York, 2021; ISBN 978-61689-918-9

Text sources:
(1) Page 06, line 07 – 12;
(2) page 09, line 01 – 15

(1) ʼ(...) Extra Bold explores power structures and how to navigate them. Essay link theories about feminism, racism, diability, and binary thinking to real people and practices. Type specimens, biographies, and interviews showcase the ideas of people marginalized by sexism, racism, ableism, and other systems of exclusion. (...)ʼ
(2) ʼ Creating a more just world requires struggle and debate. Over time, securing rights for some people has ended up excluding others. Graphic designers produce representations of society, and help create access to information and ideas. But who gets to be represented, and who gets access?
Eurocentric principles of modern design were conceived as egalitarian tools of social progress, yet they served to suppress differences among people across the globe. Indeed, alternative viewpoints and methodologies flurish outside the norms of Western design theory. Inclusive design is created by people with varied identities, backgrounds, and abilities.ʼ

Notes on the reference information in E2:

Sample pictured below:
The titles of the references, their origin numbers (from E1), and the number of the following reference (in E3).

The abbreviations (eds.) for "editors" and (u.v) for "Ulysses Voelker" indicate self-written contributions.

Reference to the origin of the entry (E 001) and reference to another entry (E 206).

The current reference number

Title of the reference

E 001 ←
→ E 206 **106 Behavioral communication and its cultural influences**

Supplements: 106 – 205

This chapter presents references, pictures, and books that offer a deeper insight into the aspects addressed here.

E 2

E 001 ←
→ E 206

106 Behavioral communication and its cultural influences

Bibliographic information:
"An Ideal Boy – Charts from India",
Sirish Rao, V. Geetha,
Gita Wolf, dewi lewis publishing, 2001;
ISBN 1-89935-83-3

Text source:
The following text (1) stems from the book "An Ideal Boy," page 07, 1st column, lines 16 – 26; page 08, 2nd column, lines 01 – 12; lines 21 – 26; page 10, 1st column, lines 13 – 25;

Image source: poster;
Mahesh Arts, P.BOX No. 42, SIVAKASI - 626 123 (INDIA)

Illustrations expand on how the world is or should be seen. The image and the quoted text reveal the Indian view of the world. (eds.)

(1) '(...) Charts address the two basic pedagogical axes of the Indian educational system: the need for facts, and the need for moral instruction. In both cases, pupils across age groups (from five to fourteen) must organise information into simple, tabular formats. Chart publishers – sometimes assisted by teachers – respond to this, taking their cues from actual examination questions. The varied and sometimes puzzling categories of people, places, animals, birds, objects, human behaviour, activities and habits, are all part of a repertoire of knowledge made easy.
(...)
In a largely non-literate society, the visual takes on a certain potency. But there is no easy slot into which chart art fits, and it seems to incorporate elements of several popular art forms simultaneously.
There are certainly several aspects here that would fit into Western theories of kitsch. Charts simulate knowledge for easy consumption, much as kitsch objects simulate the aesthetic experience without actually having to struggle with it. Mass-produced, derivative, and clearly not original they also draw information and visual input from a variety of sources, making generous use of ideal homes, sweet children and buxom women.
(...)
Ironically though almost all these artists are nameless. The typical chart artist is usually a self-taught commercial artist, whose work includes magazine illustration, signboards, calendars, or cinema hoardings. Charts tend to rank low in this scale of urban graphic art, perhaps because they have neither the visibility nor the flamboyance of other street forms.
(...)
Generally, artists are more concerned with successful narrative than realistic depiction, and visual codes are read as a language that signifies, rather than represents. It is a dialogue between given models and an active imagination that comes closest to defining the art of the charts. Artists play with form almost as a matter of course, some more generous with the play impulse than others. The art communicates because it uses stereotypes so effectively. Yet it simultaneously allows an imaginative space for individual rendering. As form, this translates into an interesting and complex tension between the stock image and the fantasy of the creator. '

E 001.2 ←
→ E 207

107 Kinder brauchen Märchen

Bibliographic information:
"Kinder brauchen Märchen," Bruno Bettelheim, dtv, 2020; (in German)
ISBN 978-3-423-35028-0

Text sources: (1) text from page 02, (2) page 93, lines 21 – 41;
Available in English: "The Uses of Enchantement" (Alfred A. Knopf, Inc., New York)

(1) '"Kinder brauchen Märchen" is a plea to accept children as they are and give them what they need. The problem of finding purpose in one's one life over and over again, a problem that both adults and children have, is a common theme that runs through the book. It therefore isn't just a call to tell children fairy tales, but has also become a "fairy tale book" for adults …

The first part centers around the child … The second part analyzes core statements of individual fairy tales and fairy-tale groups … "If a story aims to captivate a child," writes Bettelheim, "it must entertain them and pique their curiosity. But to enrich their life, it must stimulate their imagination and help them develop their intelligence and understand their emotions. It must be tailored to their fears and longings, address their struggles, and at the same time offer solutions to their problems. In short: It must refer to all aspects of personality." As Bettelheim proves, fairy tales meet all these requirements. (...) '

(2) '(...) In "Brother and Sister," the following happens: "Brother took his sister by the hand and said: Come, let us go into the big wide world together" to escape a home in which hadn't spent a single good hour since the death of their mother. "They wandered across meadows, fields, and stones all day, and when it rained, the sister said: God and our hearts, they cry together!" In this and many other fairy tales, being driven out of one's home represents the necessity of finding oneself. Self-realization demands that one leaves the surroundings of one's home – a desperate, painful experience with many psychological threats. The development process is unavoidable; the pain it causes expresses itself in the children's unhappiness due to being forced to leave their home. As is always the case in fairy tales, the psychological dangers are symbolized by the challenges the hero must overcome on their journey. In this story, the brother embodies the essentially inseparable unit, while the sister, as the symbol of motherly care for those who have been removed from their home, is the savior. In the child's mind, the fairy tale leaves no doubt that the characters must endure the pain and take risky measures to establish their personal identity: But despite all fears, the happy ending is out of the question. Not every child can or wants to inherit a kingdom, but the

child that understands the fairy tale's message and appropriates it will find the true home of their self; they become the ruler of this great realm that is at their service because they understand themself. (...) ' Bruno Bettelheim (1903 – 1990) was born in Vienna, emigrated to the USA in 1939, and worked as a professor of educational sciences, psychology, and psychiatry at the University of Chicago. He is also one of the most famous child psychologists. He has published numerous books on child education. (eds.)

E 002 ←
→ E 208

108 Patches for Space Missions

These patches for space missions cater to the archaic desire for adventures and aim to fuel patriotism. The scientific, economic, and political/military dimensions and interests that enabled the missions do not form part of the communication goal. (eds.)

(1) https://upload.wikimedia.org/wikipedia/commons/9/9f/STS-102_Patch.svg
(2) https://upload.wikimedia.org/wikipedia/commons/7/70/Enterprise_1977_Approach_and_Landing_Test_mission_patch.png
(3) https://upload.wikimedia.org/wikipedia/commons/thumb/2/2b/ISS_Yearlong_mission_patch.png/640px-ISS_Yearlong_mission_patch.png
(4) https://commons.wikimedia.org/wiki/File:Soyuz-TMA-01M-Mission-Patch.svg
(5) https://commons.wikimedia.org/wiki/File:Apollo_14-insignia.png
(6) https://commons.wikimedia.org/wiki/File:Soyuz36patch.svg
(7) https://commons.wikimedia.org/wiki/File:Skylab1-Patch.png
(8) https://commons.wikimedia.org/wiki/File:Skylab3-Patch.png
(all information: see sources)

1 The STS-102 crew insignia depicts the International Space Station as it looked when Space Shuttle Discovery was docked, 01-2001.

2 The official patch for the Approach and Landing Tests flown by the Space Shuttle Enterprise during 1977.

3 Patch for a yearlong mission. American Scott Kelly and Russian Mikhail Kornienko were slated to stay a year on the International Space Station.

4 Imitation of the official logo of the Soyuz TMA-01M mission. The patch is based on the drawing by Alexander Turovsky of Michurinsk, Russia.

5 This is the Apollo 14 crew patch designed by astronauts Alan B. Shepard Jr., commander; Stuart A. Roosa, command module pilot; and Edgar D. Mitchell, lunar module pilot.

6 The official patch of the Soyuz 36 space mission.

7 This is the emblem for the first manned Skylab mission. It was a mission of 28 days. Skylab was an experimental space station consisting of a 100-ton laboratory complex in which medical, scientific and technological experiments were performed in Earth orbit.

8 This is the emblem for the third manned Skylab mission. It was a mission of 84 days. Skylab was an experimental space station consisting of a 100-ton laboratory complex in which medical, scientific and technological experiments were performed in Earth orbit.

E 002.1 ←
→ E 209

109 Stop Signs in various cultural circles

Image source:
https://de.wikipedia.org/wiki/Stoppschild (see sources)

Recommended website:
https://en.wikipedia.org/wiki/Stop_sign

The octagonal stop sign, as we know it in Europe, is used in many traffic systems around the world – although with differing labeling. Due to its characteristic shape, it can easily be recognized without any knowledge of the respective country's alphabet and language. However, today's standardized appearance did not always exist. In the USA, for example, different shapes and colors were used (from around 1915): Initially, signs were white with black lettering, followed by yellow signs with black lettering from 1924 to 1954. Today, the English word "STOP" is common around the world, but versions in other languages also exist, for example in Canada, Turkey, South America, and Asia. The octagonal sign has been included in the Unicode standard, where you can find it under: octagonal sign U+1F6D1, in the category of traffic and card symbols. (eds.)

Germany (before 1937)

Germany (1938-1953 for FRG/1956 for GDR)

Finland (1957-1971)

Greece

Italy (1959–1990)

Romania (1957-1961)

United Kingdom (1965-1975)

Sweden (1951-1976)

United States (before 1954)

Ethiopia

Libya

Zambia

North Korea

Japan (1950-1960)

Japan (1960-1963)

Thailand

Australia (1940-1956)

Pakistan

Vietnam (1955-1975)

South Africa

Costa Rica, El Salvador, Guatemala, Honduras, Mexico, Nicaragua, Panama

Cuba

Mainland China

Egypt, Libya, Morocco, Saudi Arabia, Sudan

Ethiopia

France, Ireland, Portugal, Spain

Tunisia

Hong Kong SAR China

Iran, Afghanistan

Israel, Palestine

India (Punjabi areas)

Japan

Laos

Turkey

Malaysia

Mongolia

Myanmar

Nigeria

North Korea

Province of Quebec, Canada

Vietnam

Russia

South Africa

South Korea

Taiwan

Thailand

Tonga

E 003.2 ←
→ E 210

110 Bilder, die lügen; Exchanging the "Flag Iwo Jima" image

Bibliographic information:
"Bilder, die lügen," Haus der Geschichte der Bundesrepublik Deutschland (Ed.) Bouvier Verlag, 2000; (in German)
ISBN 3-416-02902-X

Image sources:
(a), (b): https://de.wikipedia.org/wiki/Raising_the_Flag_on_Iwo_Jima
(see sources)

Text sources:
(1) https://de.wikipedia.org/wiki/X_für_U_–_Bilder,_die_lügen
(see sources)
(2) eds.

(1) ' "X für U – Bilder, die lügen" ("X for U – Images that Lie") is a traveling exhibition curated by the Haus der Geschichte der Bundesrepublik Deutschland Foundation in cooperation with the Federal Agency for Civic Education. Jürgen Reiche came up with the idea and concept. The exhibition focuses on the objectivity of pictures and illustrates the basic pattern of manipulation of and with pictures. In an "Alphabet of Lies," around 300 objects depict the breadth of the topic. The name of the exhibition plays with the German saying "ein X für ein U vormachen," which means to deceive someone. The exhibition received a lot of media coverage. (...) '

(2) In World War II, US forces stormed the embattled Japanese island of Iwo Jima. Four days after the invasion, a troop of soldiers raised a provisional American flag on Mount Suribachi. War photographer Lou Lowery captured the process on camera (a). However, the battalion commander on the island's beach felt that the flag was too small, so a second troop was sent up to replace it with a larger one. War photographer Joe Rosenthal captured this process on camera (b). Those involved did not consider the photo to be particularly spectacular, but it was still sent to Washington. There, the propaganda department recognized the potential of this iconic image, and it made its way across the world. Its highly symbolic significance turned it into one of the most reproduced pictures of all time. The battles for the island cost the lives of 6,821 US soldiers and 18,000 Japanese soldiers. (eds.)

(a)

(b)

E 003.2 ←
→ E 211

111 Top Secret. Bilder aus den Archiven der Staatssicherheit

Bibliographic information:
"Top Secret. Bilder aus den Archiven der Staatssicherheit,"
Simon Menner, Verlag Hatje Cantz, 2014; (in German)
ISBN 978-3-7757-3620-6

Image sources:
(1,2) https://de.wikipedia.org/wiki/Ministerium_für_Staatssicherheit;
(see sources)

The recommended book "Top Secret" presents pictures from the archives of the GDR's Ministry for State Security – from "western tourist" disguises through to conspirative sign language. The pictures shown here depict the following:

(1) a high-performance shoulder-mounted camera for filming from a great distance;
(2) a box with magnetic Sennheiser MM26 microphones owned by the Ministry for State Security. The company Sennheiser (FRG) did not deliver to the Stasi; instead, they purchased them on the free market. (eds.)

(1)

(2)
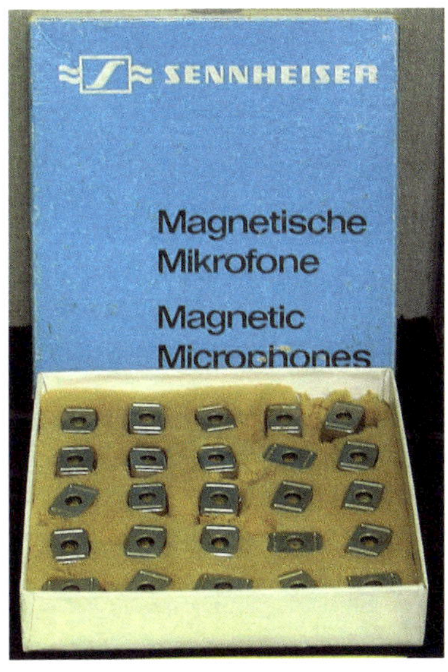

E 004 ←
→ E 212

112 Principles for setting up a supermarket

Image source: Michael Schmitz;
Further sources of information: consumer advice centers, materials for schools

A supermarket is set up in accordance with certain principles. Their goal lies in increasing consumption. What is sold as a service for customers is essentially a huge package of promotional measures: where goods are placed, routes through the store, the climate, and the lighting. Of course, it's convenient to find certain goods in the same place every time, no matter what supermarket you visit. Dairy products are positioned in the back of the store because customers often head straight for these so-called "fast movers." The idea is therefore to guide customers past as many shelves as possible. Fruit and vegetables, on the other hand, await by the supermarket entrance, have special lighting, and aim to create the impression of a "paradise of freshness." As we know: Fresh produce ensures frequency. Frozen goods and chilled drinks are placed near the cash register, since the customer likes to add these to their shopping cart at the end – to make sure their temperature remains low for as long as possible. And the temperature in general: Supermarkets consistently maintain a temperature of 19 degrees. It was revealed that customers grow more sluggish at higher temperatures. At lower temperatures, customers feel a little chilly and want to get their shopping done quickly. In both cases, this negatively affects revenue. Ideally, supermarket managers want customers to use a shopping cart rather than a basket because the cart looks empty if it only contains a few items, thereby encouraging shoppers to add a few things they weren't originally planning on buying. There is a whole range of additional measures that aim to provide the customer with as much convenience as possible, for example by placing coffee, creamer, jam, and sugar close to one another, as these all fall under the category of breakfast items. Brand products (which have a higher trade margin) are positioned at eye level (140 – 180 cm) or a little lower, in the so-called "reachable zone." Low-priced items can be found in the lower or higher zone. Candy is placed in the cash register zone, where parents are forced to wait with their children – which isn't an easy task for children. Here, they like to grab so-called "pester power items." They are joined by high-price goods such as cigarettes and batteries, so that the cashiers can keep an eye on these. Sales in the cash register zone make up about 5% of the total revenue – while taking up only about 1.5% of store space. Other measures are tailored to emotional responses in customers: music (72 bass beats per minute are ideal), pallets (they give the impression that the products placed on them are cheap), and finally, the route through the supermarket. Scientists discovered that customers prefer to walk through the store in a clockwise direction. Supermarkets that guide customers counterclockwise achieve a higher revenue. Consequently, most entrances are located on the right. All promotional measures rely on the fact that two thirds of customers make purchasing decisions based on emotions. (eds.)

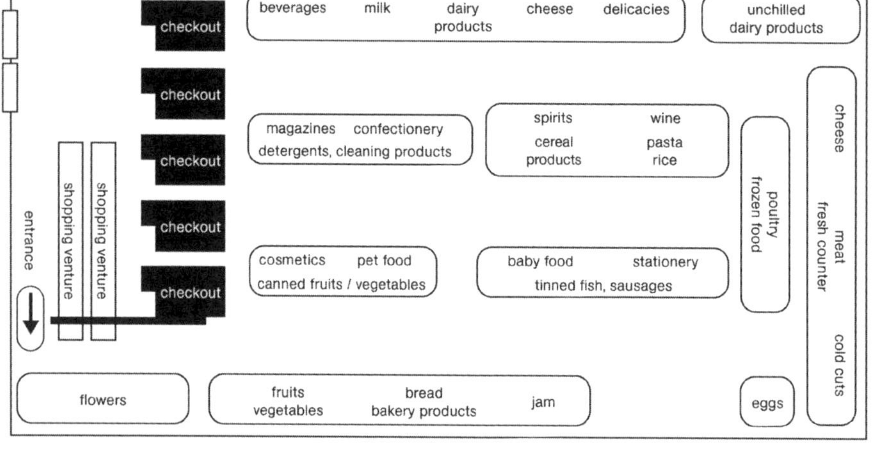

The average wayfinding system through a supermarket runs counterclockwise and places goods in accordance with clever principles.

E 004 ←
→ E 212

112.1 Focus on children in the advertising industry

The industry tries to motivate children to purchase products in a number of different ways. Three- to six-year-olds are particularly good at noticing jingles, but cannot identify them as such, just as they cannot perceive advertising as such. On top of this, the prefrontal cortex, i.e., the part of the brain responsible for rationally evaluating advantages and disadvantages, is not fully developed in children. The limbic system, however, develops early – it is home to the emotional center. It makes decisions instinctively and categorizes them as "good" or "bad." Using this method, humans have been able to master many attacks and life-threating situations from the beginning of time. Today, advertising exploits these reflexes with a tool called "neuromarketing," which targets both children and adults. This is treacherous for children: They are exposed to a flood of brand messages that aim to generate needs and disguise disadvantages of products. The respective products are often too sweet or too fatty, but still praised as healthy, for example by extolling an "extra portion of milk" or "bone-strengthening calcium." This is made worse by the food industry's efforts to make their way into schools. This takes place by means of sponsoring (cheap deliveries to school cafeterias, sports equipment purchases, etc.) and teaching materials that are provided for free. Addressing children directly has proved worthwhile for the industry. These industry practices as well as the advertising business have come under fire by consumer advisers for a long time. A (very) small partial success: As of 2021, the advertising industry wants to eliminate advertising targeted at children – but as a voluntary self-restriction. In Germany, food advertising directed at children is regulated by the State Treaty on Youth Media Protection. This is also supplemented by the rules of conduct set by the German Advertising Standards Council. The German Advertising Standards Council's code of conduct is approved and adopted by the German Advertising Federation. (eds.)

E 004 ←
→ E 212

112.2 Advertising psychology researches purchasing behavior

There is a phenomenon in advertising psychology called "choice overload." This term describes the problem that can arise if consumers are confronted with too many options when choosing a product or service. Research teams created different decision-making scenarios, for example the choice of a vacation location, phone plan, or type of jam. For the jam experiment, some customers were offered six different varieties and others twenty-four varieties. Only 3% of testers presented with the wide-ranging offering of twenty-four varieties made a purchase. In contrast, of those customers offered just six different varieties, 30% made a purchase. This purchasing behavior and the reluctance exhibited when faced with a large selection is attributed to the phenomenon of "choice overload." This reaction is based on different factors: time pressure, too many or too complicated comparisons, but also other individual behavioral traits. The advertising industry therefore must take into account that "too many alternatives impede the decision-making process." In visual communication, the method of "less is more" is paramount to ensure clarity.
Further information is available in the literature listed on the website https://en.wikipedia.org/wiki/Overchoice. (eds.)

E 004 ←
→ E 212

112.3 Compulsive buying promotes antisocial tendencies

Text-source:
https://de.wikipedia.org/wiki/Kaufzwang (see sources)

/ Compulsive buying ("oniomania" in technical terminology), also known as shopping addiction or pathological buying, is a type of psychological disorder in consumers that expresses itself through compulsive, episodic purchasing of goods. Similarly to pathological games or the compulsion to work, compulsive buying is not considered a separate disease, but rather falls under the category of physical dependencies or obsessive-compulsive disorders, sometimes also impulse-control disorders.

History

According to Max Nordau, the term "oniomania" was coined by the French physician Valentin Magnan in 1892 in his psychiatric lectures. Magnan describes compulsive buying as a symptom of degeneration. In his book "Entartung" (1892, published in English with the title "Degeneration"), Nordau outlines similar ideas: "The collecting mania of our contemporaries, the process of cramming apartments with useless junk (...) appears in a whole new light when we know that Magnan has discovered an irresistible urge to purchase pointless stuff in individuals afflicted with degeneration. (...) Unlike paralytics, those who suffer from oniomania (...) neither purchase significant amounts of one and the same object, nor are they indifferent to the price. But they cannot pass clutter without feeling the urge buy it." German psychiatrist Emil Kraepelin included the term in his textbook in 1909.

Expression

For a psychiatric diagnosis, what counts is that the goal does not lie in owning goods, but in liberating oneself from an imperative urge by means of the purchasing act itself. The shopping addict is usually aware of the senselessness of their actions; in this respect, compulsive buying differs from consumerism. Exerting willpower ("getting a grip on oneself") won't help. If the affected individual is prevented from making the purchase, they generally experience withdrawal symptoms, for example in the form of vegetative agitation. Usually, they have a preference for a specific product group (e.g., shoes). The objects, far more of which are purchased than needed, are often stored in their apartment in their original packaging or even thrown away. Frequently, those afflicted have comorbid psychological disorders, especially depression, anxiety, binge-eating disorder, and compulsive hoarding. Many patients also display compulsive, evasive, depressive, or emotionally unstable personality traits. (...) /

E 004 ←
→ E 213

113

Maslow's Hierarchy of Needs

Information source: https://de.wikipedia.org/wiki/Maslowsche_Bed%C3%BCrfnishierarchie (see sources)

The following text is a summary of more extensive information on Wikipedia.
Graphics: Michael Schmitz, Ulysses Voelker

Maslow's hierarchy of needs is visualized as a type of pyramid. It illustrates a sociopsychological model developed by American psychologist Abraham Maslow (1908 – 1970). Maslow is considered one of the most important pioneers of humanistic psychology, which pursues the goals of mental health and human self-realization within the framework of a holistic concept.
The pyramid depicts a hierarchical structure of human needs and motivations. Thanks to the simplicity of the graphic depiction, the model became well known to a far-reaching audience.

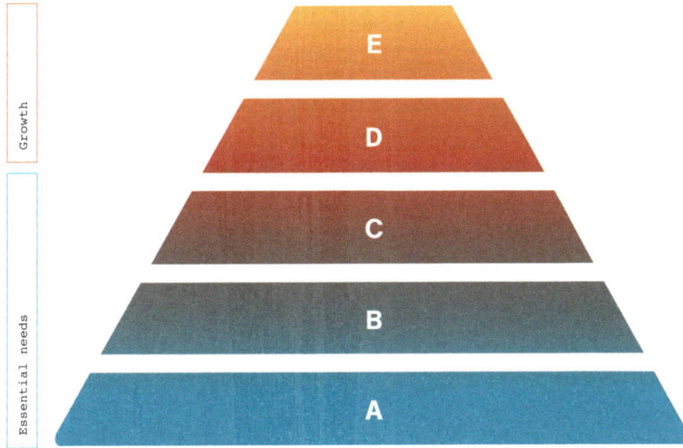

The Principle

The needs hierarchy illustrates content-related motivations. It also describes when and according to which laws certain motives determine human behavior. Inevitably, such an observation leads to a ranking of needs that need to be met.
For example, elements such as water and air are more important to human existence than consumer goods. Maslow defined five categories, from the most basic needs of human existence to highly developed needs. The principle: When a need isn't satisfied, a person takes action and tries to influence the circumstances. As their satisfaction grows, they start to lose this motivational drive. The five categories developed by Maslow are as follows.

A
Physiological needs

Here, Maslow (1943) includes all basic needs for preserving human life, such as air, water, food, sleep, reproduction, homeostasis (e.g., hut, weather protection). He differentiates these from a group of elementary needs (minerals, hormones, vitamins, etc.) that the body regulates itself.

B
Safety needs

Once the physiological needs have been met sufficiently, a new range of needs appears: safety needs (such as physical and emotional security, basic material provision, work, apartment, family, health). Maslow states that it is better to examine children when it comes to researching safety needs. Their reactions to being treated roughly (suddenly being let go) or unusual sensory stimulation (flashing lights, sudden noise) are unadulterated – unlike adults, who have often learned through socialization not to show fear or lack of security. In the history of his time, Maslow considered safety needs to be largely fulfilled. He therefore deemed another examination and direct observation of this needs category sensible, or even at all possible, for neurotic individuals or economic and social outsiders. In the broader sense, he says that the search for security and stability, but also the human preference of the familiar over the unfamiliar, is present. In addition, striving for security at least partly triggers the creation of religions and scientific world views: Humans also strive for security in the sense that they want to explain every phenomenon and uncover connections.

C
Social needs

Once the first two categories are largely satisfied, humans experience a strong longing for social relationships (motive of connection). This includes family, friendships, group affiliation or a sense of belonging, communication, social exchange, community, mutual support, relationships, affection, love, and sexual intimacy. The absence of friends, of a loved person, a life partner, or children will act as a strong motivator to overcome this gap or recreate a non-frustrating situation. At the same time, they will try to fulfil a certain role or secure a spot in a social group. (...)

D
Individual needs

Under individual needs, Maslow includes trust, appreciation, self-affirmation, success, freedom, and independence. Here, Maslow tries to differentiate once more between two subcategories:
– the desire for (mental/physical) strength, success, independence, and freedom,
– the desire for respect, prestige, appreciation, esteem, and importance, i.e., a passive component of our self-respect that only other people can fulfil for us.

E
Self-realization

According to Maslow, once the needs from the previous categories are met, a new, different dissatisfaction arises, expressing itself through the need for self-actualization. This refers to the individual's aspiration to unfold their talents and creativity and further themselves based on their own abilities. Naturally, the individuals themselves must decide what this means to them (good athlete, good mother, good manager, good salesperson). In 1970, Maslow estimated that 2% of the global population had reached this level of needs.

→

Extension 1970

Maslow continued to develop his model shortly before his death in 1970. An excerpt from Wikipedia states:

' (...) The top level of the new pyramid is "transcendence," meaning a dimension that stretches beyond the individual self or something that lies outside of the observable system. This extension reflects Maslow's journey from humanistic to transpersonal psychology. Although the year 1970 is often indicated, the old version of the pyramid, which includes self-realization at the top instead of transcendence, frequently appears in literature. He also expanded the pyramid by the two levels of aesthetic and cognitive needs, which he ranked above the individual needs. (...) '

This results in the following eight-level pyramid

A Physiological needs
B Safety needs
C Social needs (motive of connection)
D Individual needs
E Cognitive needs
F Aesthetic needs
G Self-realization
H Transcendence

Dynamic or static depiction

The graphic depiction of the needs hierarchy as a rigid pyramid does not stem from A. Maslow; it was an interpretation and most likely published by Charles McDermid in 1960.
Moreover, Maslow pointed out that the static depiction of a pyramid could give the wrong impression that the individual levels must be fully satisfied before the subsequent needs arise.
In fact, research showed that a satisfaction level of 70% or less was sufficient to make room for a subsequent need. A dynamic presentation of the needs hierarchy, as pictured on the right, was used to try to do justice to this ambivalence.
(u.v)

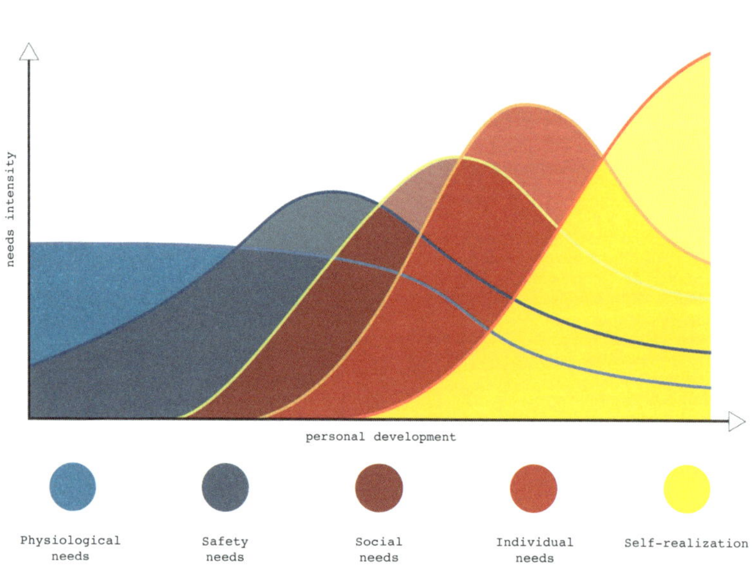

E 005.1 ←
→ E 214

114

Dazzle Camouflage, Flecktarn

Text sources:
(A) Dazzle Camouflage, https://de.wikipedia.org/wiki/Dazzle_camouflage
(B) Flecktarn, https://de.wikipedia.org/wiki/Flecktarn

Image sources:
(1) https://commons.wikimedia.org/wiki/File:Mauretania_with_dazzle_camouflage_bringing_troops_home_from_Europe.jpg
(2) https://de.wikipedia.org/wiki/Flecktarn#/media/Datei:Flecktarn.jpg
(3) https://bit.ly/3y5EgN2
(4) https://de.wikipedia.org/wiki/Flecktarn#/media/Datei:OCP_SW2.jpg
(5) https://de.wikipedia.org/wiki/Flecktarn#/media/Datei:CADPAT_digital_camouflage_pattern_(Temperate_Woodland_variant).jpg
(all information: see sources)

(1)

(A) ' *Dazzle camouflage*, or *dazzle painting*, sometimes also called razzle dazzle in the USA, refers to a series of methods for painting ships (and other vehicles) in a way that would deceive the opponent. The Royal Navy and the United States Navy particularly used this method during World War I, and to a lesser extent in World War II. This painting consisted of complex patterns of geometric shapes that alternated in contrasting colors. The idea is attributed to British marine painter Norman Wilkinson. Mostly referred to as dazzle camouflage or dazzle painting, the American term razzle dazzle was rather colloquial and does not appear in the US forces' official documents.
(...)
While the shapes used in actual camouflage aim to conceal a target object to the best extent possible, dazzle painting had a different purpose. It aimed to make it difficult for the enemy to discern the size, direction, and speed of a ship (or another object). In 1919, Norman Wilkinson explained that the goal lay in confusing the enemy concerning a ship's course, which meant they adopted a worse attack position. (...) Technological progress ended the discussion on dazzle. Increasingly effective air reconnaissance and the development of radar technology made it easier for the enemy to locate and assess a ship. (...) '

(B) ' *Flecktarn* is an internationally used camouflage pattern in which colored, irregular spots or dots are arranged on a ground color. The principle was developed in different variants around 1935 by Johann Georg Otto Schick on behalf the Waffen-SS. Similar patterns are still used around the world today. (...) '

Examples of current Flecktarn patterns:
(2) Bundeswehr (Germany)
(3) People's Army Vietnam
(4) US Army
(5) Canadian Army

(2)

(3)

(4)

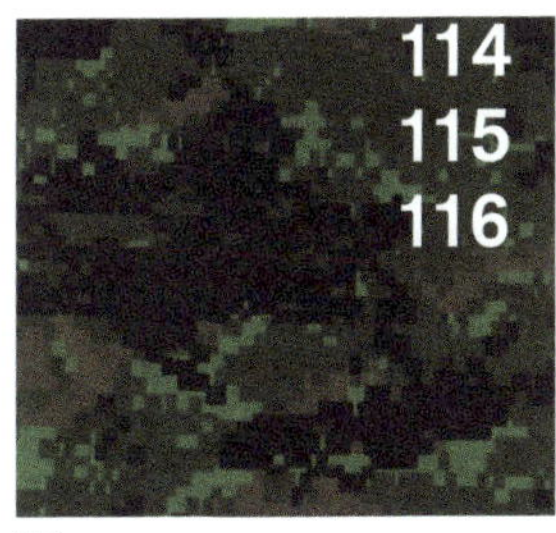
(5)

E 005.1 ←
→ E 215

115

Typography is culture

Image sources: Ulysses Voelker

Our everyday lives are shaped by all kinds of visual messages, often of varying typographic quality. Designers should get over this. Sometimes these amateurish typographic efforts are the ones that spawn random and appealing oddities, as demonstrated by the example of a gas station in the Belgian town of Ghent. After all, diversity in visual communication is also a sign of cultural vitality. Through-and-through standardization of design expressions (in the sense of "compliant" or "good" typography) would run counter to human nature and would hardly be democratically enforceable. In fact, the opposite applies: The coincidences of semi-professional design in the world's everyday cultures actually serve as a source of inspiration. They expand the visual canon into which and with which we have settled over the years. Nevertheless, the fundamental regularities on which visual communication is based naturally represent the norm. But that is exactly why deviations from this norm rouse our curiosity. (u.v)

From a designer's perspective, this car wash offering (opening hours on the left, facade front on the right) does not inspire confidence. However, the bizarreness of the design has a peculiar appeal. Because of or despite the design, this is a thriving business.

This does give designers something to think about. (u.v)

E 005.1 ←
→ E 216

116

Braille

Text source: https://www.dbsv.org/wie-die-braille-schrift-funktioniert.html (see sources)
From the website of the "German Federation of the Blind and Partially Sighted"

Image source: https://de.wikipedia.org/wiki/Brailleschrift (see sources)

ʼ(...) Six dots in two vertical lines of 3 dots each arranged next to one another, and thereby easy to identify by touch, make up the basic shape. Imagine an egg carton with 6 eggs. We can now assign numbers to the eggs (or dots). Dot 1 is at the top left, dot 2 beneath it, and dot 3 at the bottom. Dot 4 sits at the top right, below which is 5, and finally, dot 6 at the bottom right. Braille letters consist exclusively of combinations of these dots: Dot 1 on its own signifies the letter "a," dots 1 + 2 indicate "b," dots 1 + 4 mean "c" (...)

A 6-dot cell, like the one used in Braille, enables 63 dot combinations. This means that we need to use our dots sparingly. One way to achieve this is to do without separate signs for capital letters. As a result, we use only lower-case letters in Braille, and this does not cause any issues. Of course, we can depict capital letters: To do so, we use auxiliary characters that indicate, for example, that the next letter was capitalized in the original text. We take a similar approach to numbers. For the numbers 1 through 10, we use the letters "a" to "j." We add the so-called "number sign" before the first digit, which indicates that the following characters signify a sequence of numbers, not letters. (...)ʼ

1	a	b	c	d	e	f	g	h	i	j
2	k	l	m	n	o	p	q	r	s	t
3	u	v	x	y	z	&	%	[	ß	st
4	au	eu	ei	ch	sch	`	^	ü	ö	w

Letters from the Latin alphabet, depicted in the Braille system.

E 005.1 ←
→ E 216

116.1

Braille in the unicode system

Image source:
https://decodeunicode.org/en/u+02874
(see sources)

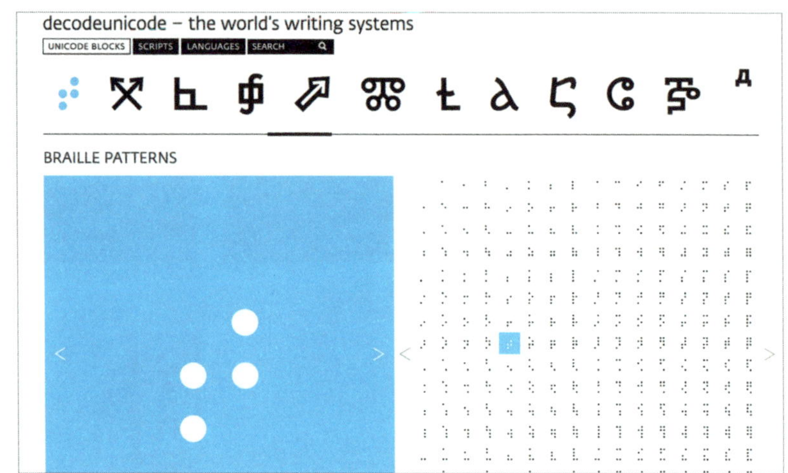

Braille in the Unicode System.

E 005.1 ←
→ E 216

116.2

Dialog im Dunkeln, Dialog Museum

Text source:
https://de.wikipedia.org/wiki/Dialog_im_Dunkeln (see sources)

/ *"Dialog im Dunkeln" ("Dialog in the Dark")* is a social franchise product from Dialogue Social Enterprise GmbH (DSE), alongside "Dialog im Stillen" ("Dialog in Silence") and "Dialog mit der Zeit" ("Dialog with Time"), and was originally conceived by Andreas Heinecke. With the goal of giving sighted people an insight into the everyday life of blind people and enabling them to meet on equal footing, the exhibition has already traveled to more than 30 countries and over 130 cities since it was founded in 1988, reaching more than 9 million visitors. In addition, the exhibitions created approximately 9,000 job opportunities for the blind and partially sighted. Blind people guide groups of visitors through the completely darkened exhibition. Here, they experience reconstructed everyday situations, such as a park, an urban landscape, or a bar, including scents, wind, temperatures, sounds, and textures. The concept also entails a role reversal, in which blind people guide the visitors, who are removed from their familiar perception routines. (...)
"Dialog im Dunkeln" has existed in Hamburg since 2000. It started with state funding and a limited duration but was then permanently established as a company (Dialogue Social Enterprise GmbH). About 90,000 visitors view the exhibition every year. Alongside the exhibition, Dialoghaus Hamburg also houses a workshop center for darkness workshops and the dialog exhibition *"Dialog im Stillen"* (*"Dialog in Silence"*). The Dialogmuseum can be found in Frankfurt. It was founded in 2005 and, in addition to the exhibition, offers darkness workshops as well as various events. Another permanent Dialog im Dunkeln exhibition can be found in Vienna, also offering Dinner in the Dark and other events. A similar museum, "muZIEum," is situated just across the border in Nijmegen (NL).

Additional permanent exhibitions can be found in (...) Turkey, South Korea, Hong Kong, India, Australia, China, Thailand, Japan, Malaysia, Italy, Mexico, Russia, and Argentina. /

E 006.1 ←
→ E 217

117

Marshall Islands stick charts

Recommended website:
https://en.wikipedia.org/wiki/Marshall_Islands_stick_chart
(see sources)

Image sources:
(1) https://upload.wikimedia.org/wikipedia/commons/b/bf/Micronesian_navigational_chart.jpg
(2) https://upload.wikimedia.org/wikipedia/commons/f/f1/%C3%9Cberseemuseum_Bremen_2009_063a.jpg
(see sources)

The Marshall Islands stick charts are very special navigational documents. Marshallese cartographers were the first to chart ocean swell patterns. Their unique design used seashells, sticks, and threads to depict islands, waves, and ocean swell patterns. Inhabitants of the Marshall Islands in the Pacific created and used these maps. Instead of taking them out to sea, the respective skippers memorized them. The knowledge was passed on from generation to generation, and only a few skilled people were privy to it. The depictions of waves and currents were particularly important because the inhabitants traveled from island to island by canoe. The course of the waves and the way they changed before they reached land was of existential significance to these small boats. The nautical charts were crafted individually and never intended to be understood universally. That is why every map had its own look that outsiders could not easily interpret and use. This method of creating nautical charts fell out of use after the end of World War II and was replaced by modern navigation technologies. (eds.)

Further information:
see the recommended website.

(1)

A navigation map of the Marshall Islands, which is on display at the Berkeley Art Museum and the Pacific Film Archive. It's made of wood, sennite fibers and cowrie shells.

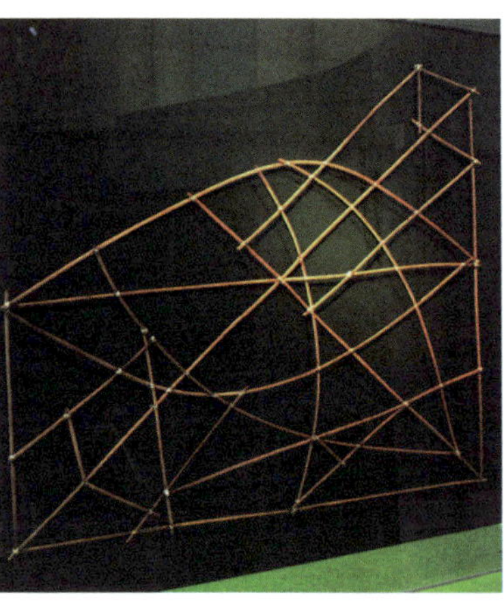

(2)

Stick chart in the Überseemuseum Bremen.

E 010 ←
→ E 218

118

Punkt und Linie zu Fläche

Bibliographic information:
"Punkt und Linie zu Fläche," Vasily Kandinsky, Benteli Verlag Bern, 1964; [in German] ISBN 978-3-7165-0182-5
Available in English as "Point and Line to Plane."
Text sources:
page 14, lines 13 – 19; page 17, lines 15 – 23; page 18, lines 19 – 20; page 21, lines 01 – 16

In 1926, the book "Punkt und Linie zu Fläche" (English title: "Point and Line to Plane") was published by Verlag Albert Langen, Munich, as volume 9 of the "bauhaus-bücher" – edited by Walter Gropius and Laszló Moholy-Nagy. In 1955, 1959, and 1963, revised editions followed, including an introduction by Max Bill. These were published by Benteli Verlag, Bern. Simply the participation of renowned protagonists of modernism exemplifies the significance of Kandinsky's examinations and reflections.
He viewed the book as a continuation of his work "Concerning the Spiritual in Art." The subtitle of "Punkt und Linie zu Fläche" translates to "a contribution to the analysis of pictorial elements," thereby referring to the fundamental observations on general questions of design. These formed part of Kandinsky's teachings at Bauhaus.

The following quotes from the book demonstrate the motivation to develop a new science of art:
/ (...) In terms of analytical examinations, painting strangely takes on a special position compared to other arts. Architecture, for example, which is by nature tied to practical purposes, had to include certain scientific knowledge from the start. Music (...) has had its own theory for a long time. (...) /

When it comes to painting, Kandinsky defines the following:
/ (...) The research that needs to be made the foundation of the new science – the science of art – has two goals and emerges based on two necessities:
1. the necessity of the science in general, which freely grows from a thirst for knowledge that is inexpedient or lies outside the function: the "pure" science, and 2. the necessity to balance the creative powers, which can be categorized in two schematic parts – intuition and calculation: the "practical" science (...). /

At the start of his analysis, he defines the "artistic elements" that form components of works of art. He differentiates between "basic elements," which, whether intentionally or not, must be separate from so-called "auxiliary elements." After clarifying these terms, he begins his analysis with the following sentence:
/ (...) Here, we need to start with the primordial element of painting – the dot. (...) /

He continues:
/ (...) The geometric dot is an invisible being. It must therefore be defined as an immaterial being. When we consider it as material, a dot equals a zero. But this zero conceals different qualities that are "human." In our mind, this zero – the geometric dot – is linked with the greatest scarcity, i.e., the greatest restraint, but one that speaks. Therefore, the geometric dot is in our mind the highest and most individual "connection of silence and speaking." That is why the geometric dot has primarily found its material form in writing – it belongs to language and means silence. In flowing speech,
the dot is the symbol 116.1
of an interruption, of
non-being (negative 116.2
element), and at the
same time, it is a bridge
from one form of being 117
to another (positive
element). In writing, this 118
is its "inner meaning."
(...) / 118.1

Kandinsky not only describes the role that the basic elements of dot, line, and plane play in painting as well as music and graphics, but also links his findings to philosophical questions.

At this point, it is also worth mentioning the publication "Pedagogical Sketchbook" by Paul Klee. It was published as volume 2 of the "bauhaus-bücher" series in 1925 and formed the foundation for Klee's "Elementarunterricht" ("Elementary Instruction") at Bauhaus. (u.v)

E 010 ←
→ E 218

118.1

Das grafische Zeichen. Kommunikation und Irritation

Matthias Götz, author and professor of design theory, composed the chapter "Das grafische Zeichen. Kommunikation und Irritation" ("The Graphic Character. Communication and Irritation") in his book "Visuelle Kommunikation" ("Visual Communication," published in 1989 by Anton Stankowski and Karl Duschek, see also 079, 192).

In his introduction, he refers to the use of the term "character," which has a different meaning in visual communication than in communication theory, as the former area pursues practical goals and thereby generates aspects that are theoretically not intended. In communication theory, every "character" is ideal if its signal transmission runs without interruption. However, in the area of visual communication, aspects of irritation could intentionally be used, for example to generate greater attention or distinction. For this reason, Götz developed a theoretical approach in his book that was based on the framework conditions of visual communication.

In the subchapter "Das grafische Zeichen. Kommunikation und Störung," Götz writes:
/ (...) Graphically, an exemplary function is inherent to the character. It reduces visual complexities to representationally acceptable measures, and it does so for reasons of communication. The term "graphics" traditionally contains both components: Any form of "graphics" is essentially a "drawing," and any form of "graphics" is designed to be reproduced. (...)
Semiotically, any random object can be treated as a character; graphically, only the "discreet" character counts. Together with the "reduction feature," as it is known in model theory, the graphic character acquires a quality that can be given a communication theory term, but is used in another, narrower meaning: the quality of the signal element. While from an information theory perspective, the signal is viewed as a sign carrier and the character as the signal content, the graphic character requires the signal element without specifically separating content and form, character carrier and character asset. Moreover, a signal element is already a defining feature of the graphic character. (...) /

Bibliographic information:
"Visuelle Kommunikation: ein Design-Handbuch," Anton Stankowski, Karl Duschek (Eds.); Dietrich Reimer Verlag, Berlin, 1989; [in German] ISBN 3-496-01061-4

Text sources:
Page 55, lines 01 – 05, lines 17 – 27, lines 31 – 38; page 56, lines 06 – 19, lines 33 – 37

Götz points out once more that communication theory terms cannot simply be transferred to graphic characters, but they can be helpful:
/ (...) Usually, communication is still understood to imply only "successful communication" in the narrower sense that everything that disturbs the seamless transmission of a "message" is excluded from the scope of the theory as anti-communicative and the term "disruption" is consequently treated in a one-dimensional way with regard to communication theory, but not the differentiation that would be necessary to capture aesthetic communication as well. (...)

(...) The clarity that the technical communication strives to achieve regarding the subject matter to be conveyed is, graphically speaking, already questionable before the actual communication takes place, namely when it comes to the intention, but this is where the most successful designs are realized through decided undecidability. In terms of graphics, irritation is sometimes at least as important as the arbitrarily coded message is not. This graphic undecidability of course does not refer to the ambiguous drawing or the diffuse appearance that makes recognition difficult, but rather the indeterminable "message" that stands between at least two possible interpretations. We do not need to go as far MacLuhan did and call the medium the message; it suffices to point out that the coding method often helps determine the message, and with regards to graphics, this is markedly the case. (...) /

Götz points out that (mathematical) communication theory already extended beyond the technical aspect early on. He cites Warren Weaver, who defined three levels:
1. the technical level: How can we transmit characters?
2. the semantic level: How do the transmitted characters correspond to the intended meaning?
3. the efficiency level: How strongly do the characters affect the (desired) behavior?

Here, Matthias Götz sums up:
/ (...) One can also apply the terminology of three semiotic "dimensions," as introduced by Charles Morris, to this breakdown: These are the syntactic (1), semantic (2), and pragmatic (3) dimensions, whereby syntactics refers to the relationship between characters, semantics refers to the relationship of the character to its object, and pragmatics refers to the relationship of the character to the recipient's disposition. (...) /

This brief summary aims to pique your interest in the book, which is certainly worth reading. The author divided his book into further subchapters: *Unterscheidung, Identität und Identifikation* (Differentiation Identity, and Identification), *Die Kategorien Raum und Zeit* (The Categories of Time and Space), *Das singuläre Zeichen* (The Singular Sign), *Das Systemzeichen* (The System Character), and *Sinnfärbung, Ästhetik, Skepsis* (Coloring of Purpose, Aesthetics, Skepticism). (u.v)

E 013.1 ←
→ E 219

119

Apolitical murals

More information about Doel:
https://en.wikipedia.org/wiki/Doel

Image sources:
Ulysses Voelker, 2010

Doel is a village in the Belgian province of East Flanders. It sits on the left bank of the Scheldt and is home to one of Belgium's three nuclear power plants. In the 1960s, Doel became known due to the plans to expand Antwerp's harbor. Over the course of this expansion, Doel was to be given up. There were countless incentives for residents to leave the village. Only a few people persevered in the midst of abandoned houses. In 2022, a political shift took place as a result of a court decision. Not only can Doel continue to exist, but it will also be rebuilt and repaired. A solution for the necessary harbor expansion has also been found.

During the many years in which the village stood completely empty, a kind of lawless space emerged that encouraged artists to take over the houses. The village developed into a unique place that featured a large number of paintings and illustrative interactions with the buildings. However, the murals – with a few exceptions – neither refer to the protests of the few remaining residents, nor to the issue itself. The many, usually illustrative innovations largely present themselves as art for the sake of art. (u.v)

The “Northern Ireland conflict” refers to a civil-war-like dispute between two population groups in Northern Ireland.
These are:

Protestants, mostly descendants of English and Scottish immigrants, who want to remain part of the United Kingdom of Great Britain and Northern Ireland as unionists or loyalists, and Catholics, republicans who advocate for a united Ireland, meaning secession from Great Britain and a union of Northern Ireland and the Republic of Ireland.

Due to legitimation by British politics, the Protestants had and still have a power advantage, which has manifested itself on a cultural, social, and economic level. The conflict between these two groups dominated Northern Irish and British politics between 1969 and 1998. The capital of Belfast formed the battle ground and saw bloody confrontations. It is still marked by these today. A “peace line” divides the city: In West Belfast (west of the “West Link” motorway), a wall (plus barbed wire) separates the areas of Falls Road (where Catholic republicans live) from Shankill Road (where Protestant unionists live). Propagandistic murals can be seen in both the Falls and Shankill quarters. They commemorate fallen comrades, depict calls to battle, mark territories, and remember those who are in prison. At the same time, they serve as a kind of record of conflict, which is currently dormant, but still unresolved. In 1998, the Good Friday Agreement ended the armed conflict for the time being.

The current Brexit developments are endangering the fragile peace and have reignited the old conflict of whether Northern Ireland belongs to Great Britain or should be reunited with Ireland. (u.v)

E 013.1 ←
→ E 220

120
Political murals

More information about the Northern Ireland conflict:
https://en.wikipedia.org/wiki/The_Troubles
https://en.wikipedia.org/wiki/Provisional_Irish_Republican_Army
https://en.wikipedia.org/wiki/Ulster_Volunteer_Force

Image sources:
Ulysses Voelker, 2019/2022

E 015 ←
→ E 221

121 Visual Codes (1): Sign Language

Image source:
The German sign-language alphabet with umlauts and special characters – provided by the Landesverband Bayern der Gehörlosen e. V. (Bavarian state association for the deaf)
https://commons.wikimedia.org/wiki/File:Deutsche_Fingeralphabet.jpg
(see sources)

Recommended website:
https://en.wikipedia.org/wiki/Sign_language
https://www.lvby.de/

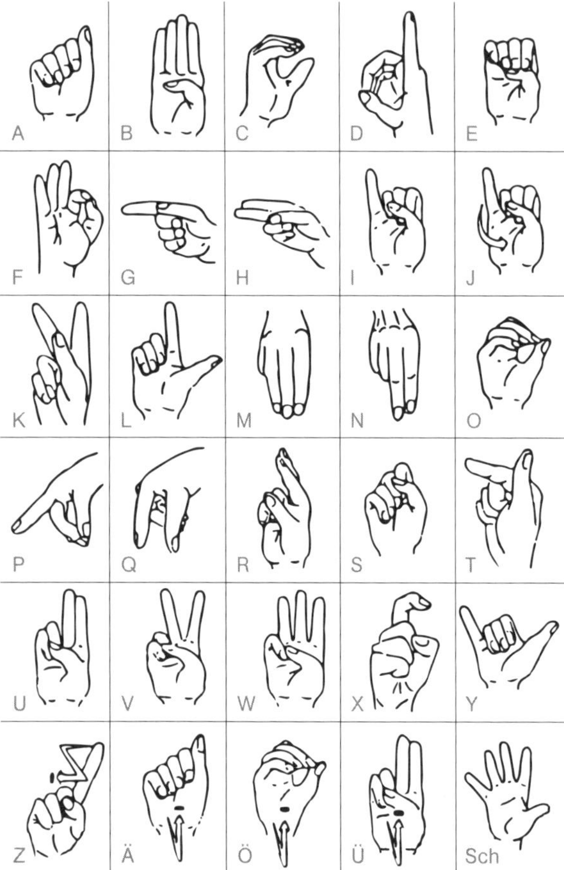

Sign language is a form of communication from and for non-hearing and hard-of-hearing individuals. Communication is based on a combination of different visually perceptible methods: gestures, facial expressions, soundless speaking (where mouth movements form words). To communicate with gestures, a set visual vocabulary was developed (see image), making it possible to translate Latin letters. The use of the mentioned means of expression allows individuals to formulate words, sentences, and sequences of sentence. This means that sign language is a fully developed natural language on par with spoken language in its complexity. (eds.)

E 015 ←
→ E 221

121.1 Visual Codes (2): SignWriting

Image source:
https://www.delegs.de/gebaerdenschrift
(see sources)

Text source:
https://de.wikipedia.org/wiki/Geb%C3%A4rdenschrift#SignWriting
(see sources)

More information about sign language characters:
https://unicode.org/charts/PDF/U1D800.pdf

′ (...) *SignWriting*, also known as *Sutton SignWriting*, is a script that was developed to depict sign language in a visual way. Valerie Sutton invented it in the 1970s, enabling exact recordings of sign language in written form. In contrast to the finger alphabet, which only pictures letters, *SignWriting* can express movements, facial expressions, body postures, and spatial relationships – all of which are important components of sign language. (...) ′

Sign language is comprised of the following elements:

[a] There are symbols for every hand shape.
[b] Hand pictograms visualize the position of the arms and hands.
[c] Symbols depict the hand movements.
[d] Facial diagrams illustrate the mouth positions.

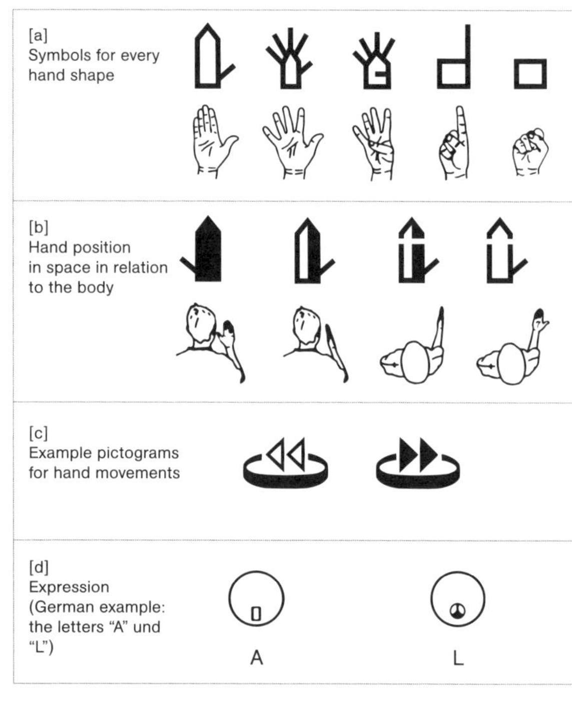

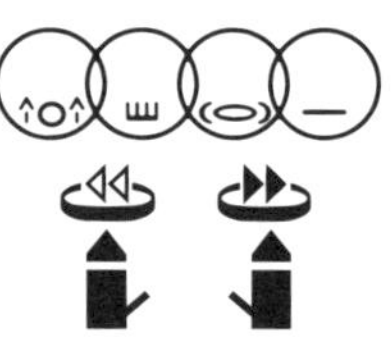

The word "schwimmen" (swimming) is made up of the characters shown here.
The transformation from the Latin term to sign language is shown in the example below.

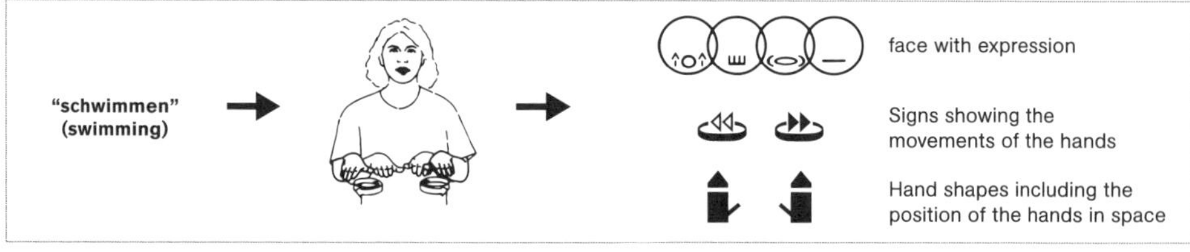

Word to be represented in the Latin alphabet

Movement to Word in Sign Language

Structure of sign writing

E 015 ←
→ E 221

122 Visual Codes (3): The flag alphabet

Text source:
https://en.wikipedia.org/wiki/International_maritime_signal_flags
Image source:
https://en.wikipedia.org/wiki/International_maritime_signal_flags
(see sources)

ʻ (...) International maritime signal flags are various flags used to communicate with ships. The principal system of flags and associated codes is the International Code of Signals. Various navies have flag systems with additional flags and codes, and other flags are used in special uses, or have historical significance.

Usage
There are various methods by which the flags can be used as signals:
– A series of flags can spell out a message, each flag representing a letter.
– Individual flags have specific and standard meanings; for example, diving support vessels raise the "A" flag indicating their inability to move from their current location because they have a diver underwater and to warn other vessels to keep clear to avoid endangering the diver(s) with their propellers.
– One or more flags form a code word whose meaning can be looked up in a code book held by both parties. An example is the Popham numeric code used at the Battle of Trafalgar.
– In yacht racing and dinghy racing, flags have other meanings; for example, the P flag is used as the "preparatory" flag to indicate an imminent start, and the S flag means "shortened course". (...) ʻ

Letter / radio name	Flag	Blazon	ICS meanir
A Alfa		Swallowtailed, per pale argent and azure	"I have a diver down; k speed."
B Bravo		Swallowtailed, gules	"I am taking in or disch dangerous goods." (Ori Navy specifically for military explosives.)
C Charlie		Azure, a fess gules fimbriated argent	"Affirmative."[a][b]
D Delta		Or, a Spanish fess azure	"Keep clear of me; I am maneuvering with difficulty."[b]
E Echo		Per fess azure and gules	"I am altering my course to starboard."[b]
F Foxtrot		Argent, a lozenge throughout gules	"I am disabled; communicate with me."[c]
G Golf		Paly of six or and azure	"I require a pilot." By fishing vessels near fishing grounds: "I am hauling nets."
H Hotel		Per pale argent and gules	"I have a pilot on board."[b]
I India		Or, a pellet	"I am altering my course to port."[b]

The international Flag Alphabet
(Excerpt from the Wikipedia page)

E 015 ←
→ E 221

123 Visual Codes (4): Elemente eines Zeichens

Bibliographic information:
"Der Mensch und seine Zeichen," Adrian Frutiger, marixverlag, Wiesbaden, 2006; [in German]
ISBN 978-3-865-39907-6

Image and text source from chapter "Elemente eines Zeichens:" page 22, line 01 – page 23, line 34;

ʻ (...) The observer's behavior towards a figure is very complex. To learn to understand the reception process, one must restrict oneself to one scheme from the start – the structure that is simple enough to offer the biggest chance of capturing the origin. This is why the first morphological table was set up, consisting of only one square with a cross in the middle to avoid all "parasitic" or "anecdotal" influences. The scheme is built on three verticals and three horizontals that, when laid over one another, alternatingly cross, touch, and enhance each other. From a mathematical perspective, these six lines can express 40 variants (7 x 7).

We refer to this process as exploiting a program, essentially searching for all possibilities provided by a given structure.

When observing the table, the reader will first recognize that very simple characters emerge at the top left in A1 and grow denser towards the bottom right, concluding with the full G7 character. In the middle of sheet, we can see the cross D4, the clear encounter of the vertical with the horizontal line. This central position indicates the intersection or separation point, which extends out in all four directions.
The cross is the most abstract sign, it takes up the least amount of surface space, as it does not have an interior space; the angles are not recognized as inner sides of the space, since the crossing lines do not give the impression of a "corner." Crossing means "striking through" rather than "drawing."
Square C3 presents a complete contrast to the cross. This character particularly stands out when observing the entire sheet; its interior surface appears white, the enclosed surface has an active meaning, but also secludes it from the rest of the paper's surface. Most people who observe a closed square like to identify with it: The square is the primitive expression of an object, of property, of housing. Based on these first two observations, we can determine that the characters without enclosed surfaces evoke rather abstract sensations, whereas closed, circumscribed surfaces trigger memories of objects. (...) ʻ

"Morphological Table 1", from "Der Mensch und seine Zeichen", Adrian Frutiger.

E 015 ←
→ E 222

124 Visual communication using the example of the "pictogram"

Image sources: Ulysses Voelker

Some pictograms lead an inconspicuous but at the same time meaningful life. We usually need them in urgent situations and uncomplainingly accept the way they are designed, as long as they lead to the goal. This applies to the pictograms for toilets. But this little partial segment of visual communication also reflects the whole bandwidth of human creativity – which must in turn provide the answers to many questions.

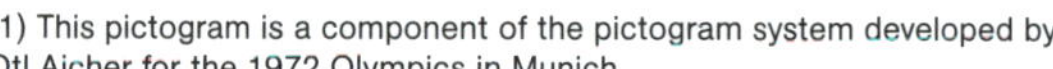

(1) This pictogram is a component of the pictogram system developed by Otl Aicher for the 1972 Olympics in Munich.
(2) This image aims to communicate "Toilets for women and men," without displaying (supposedly) gender-specific traits.
(3) This is a sign for toilets for non-binary people.
(4) This information is not barrier-free because people who are unfamiliar with the Latin alphabet cannot understand it. However, the ash tray makes a universal statement.
These four examples, some more and some less successful, demonstrate how even small forms of visual communication contain many needs, lines of conflict, and aesthetic considerations:
reduction in favor of clarity, consideration of gender debates, accessibility – and aesthetics as a sign of seriousness and as a sign of a promised service. (u.v)

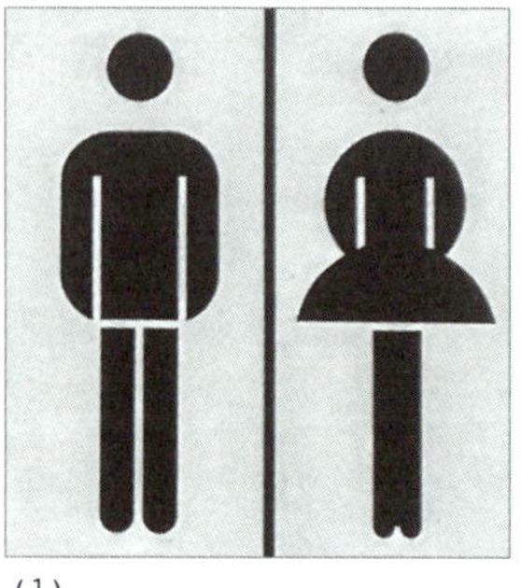
(1)

(2)

(3)

(4)

E 015.1 ←
→ E 223

125 Die XX. Olympiade München 1972: Richtlinien und Normen für die visuelle Gestaltung

Bibliographic information:
Reprint, Niggli Verlag, 2019; [in German]
ISBN 978-3-7212-0999-0

Text source:
Preface by Erik Spiekermann, booklet, page 04, lines 14 – 42

′ (...) We designers know that good results not only depend on us, but also – and perhaps primarily – on a client who knows how much freedom they are offering the designers and what guidelines they need to give. In 1972, the following conditions were in place:
Willi Daume as the client and Otl Aicher as the leader of a team consisting largely of students recruited from the Ulm School of Design, whose abilities he was familiar with. Nearly 50 years ago, such a design system was formalized: It featured content-related and formal rules, defined basic elements, completed images, grid sheets, and other tools. In combination, they ensured that even the tiniest printed material – the sign completed at the last minute, patches on jackets, seat numbers in the stadium – worked within the context and complemented each other to produce an appearance that not only looked uniform, but also exuded the same spirit across all media and locations. Manuals like the one at hand are no longer needed. However, we have bought the flexibility of digital documentations by giving up control. In this scenario, entropy determines the results because the common denominator grows smaller the more complex the system is. Today, this documentation seems like a bright light from an analog past in which design elements could stand out before all eyes because the creators knew what the result was to look like. (...) ′

E 015.2 ←
→ E 224

126 About diversity and antidiscrimination at FU Berlin

Text source:
https://www.fu-berlin.de/en/sites/diversity/antidiskriminierung/index.html (see sources)

/ **Diversity**
"Diversity" refers to our ability and readiness to acknowledge and value the many interlinked differences and commonalities between groups of people, and to dismantle barriers that prevent people from being able to participate equally in society. Antidiscrimination is thus an inherent aspect of our understanding of diversity here at Freie Universität Berlin.

Freie Universität Berlin considers it a core responsibility to acknowledge and to promote diversity and to self-critically identify, reflect on, and remove exclusionary practices and structures. This requires an awareness of the power structures at play. We strive to foster equitable participation and a learning and working environment that values all members of the university. In order to achieve our overarching objectives we have developed and documented a Diversity Strategy and Action Plan in which our objectives are translated into concrete outcomes and measures.

This website provides a wide range of information about the topic of diversity and (anti)discrimination and about relevant concepts, structures, goals, resources and activities at the Freie Universtität. (...)

Taking a Stand Against Hate and Exclusion, Standing Up for Diversity and Anti-Racism
Racist violence and discrimination are deeply embedded in our society – and exclusion fueled by racism even happens at institutions of higher education like ours. Freie Universität Berlin acknowledges that racism is a societal issue that doesn't simply stop where our campus begins. We are strongly opposed to racism in all its forms and manifestations. That is why we are reaffirming our stance as a firmly anti-racist institution on International Day for the Elimination of Racial Discrimination – which takes place every March 21 – as well as on every other day of the year.

At Freie Universität Berlin we strive to reflect upon systemic racism at our institution and aim to dismantle racial discrimination, especially through the measures outlined in the Diversity Strategy and Action Plan 2021–2023. Not only that, but we want to take specific measures to confront discrimination on the basis of ethnic origin, racism, and anti-Semitic assumptions, as well as discrimination that can be considered intersectional. Every diversity measure we put in place must be anti-racist in nature.

We already offer support services at Freie Universität Berlin where instances of racist discrimination can be addressed. The BIPoC Office at ASTA, for example, offers counseling for black students and other students of color, while employees who want to file a complaint regarding racial discrimination on the job can reach out to the Complaint Center for Employees. However, we know that this is not enough. That is why Freie Universität Berlin is committed to creating working structures that put in place counseling for students and employees that they can turn to if they encounter racial discrimination or other types of discrimination as well as services to investigate such incidents. (...) /

E 016 ←
→ E 225

127 Lexicon der Tatoeages van Aarsgewei tot Zwitserland

Bibliographic information:
Lexicon der Tatoeages van Aarsgewei tot Zwitserland,
Henk Schiffmacher; Uitgevereij Carrera, 2008; [In Dutch]
ISBN 978-90-4880119-0

Tattoo artist, collector, and author Henk Schiffmacher (Amsterdam) has compiled a comprehensive lexicon. Listed from A – Z, the book includes "facts, technical terms, anecdotes, powerful stories, crazy details, and an endless parade of heroes and bad guys from the world of tattoos," as the curator of the Amsterdam Tropical Museum has put it on the back cover. The extended title "Vom Arschgeweih bis zur Schweiz" ("From tramp stamps to Switzerland") says it all. (eds.)

E 016 ←
→ E 226

127.1 Tattoos as cult and identification model

Image sources: (1) Image: Thomas Klefisch, 2018; (2) Tattoo artist: Ulysses Voelker, 1984

(1)

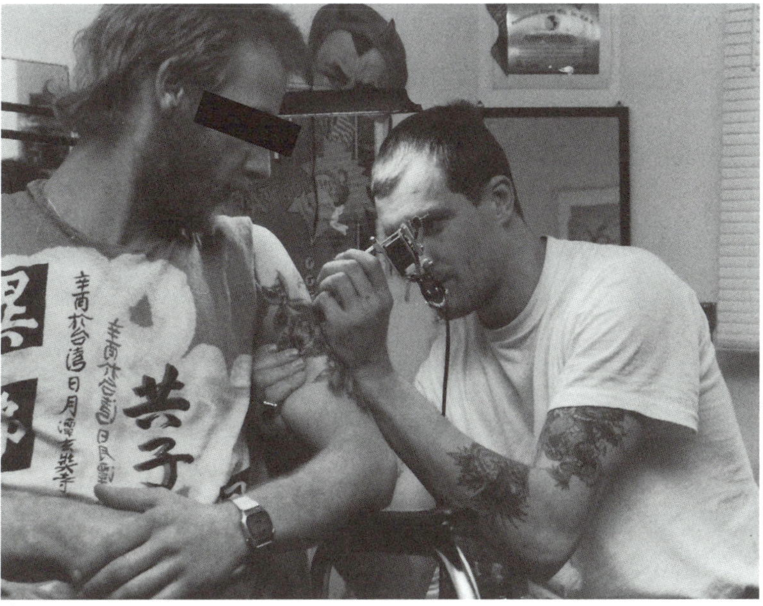

(2)

The book “Forever – The New Tattoo” shows the work of tattoo artists who embarked on new paths beyond the mainstream and presented new styles. It features a broad spectrum of contemporary tattoo art, ranging from traditional interpretations through to the latest fashion trends. Forever was published in 2012. Five years later, the volume “Forever More – The New Tattoo” followed. The work depicted here illustrates the development of styles as well as the increasingly high level of craftsmanship. (eds.)

E 016 ←
→ E 226

127.2 Forever – The New Tattoo; Forever More – The New Tattoo

Bibliographic information:
(1) “Forever – The New Tattoo,” Gestalten Verlag & Floyd Schulze, 2012;
ISBN: 978-3-89955-442-7
(2) “Forever More – The New Tattoo,” Hannah Graves & Gestalten Verlag, 2017;
ISBN: 978-3-89955-926-2

E 016 ←
→ E 226

128 The artistic font “AK Shavcat”

Image source:
“Die Lügen des Kapitalismus,” two-tone screen print,
825 × 450 mm, 8th edition, 2019;
Font design and designer: Ulysses Voelker
More work is available at: ulyssesvoelker.com

The font “AK Shavcat” emerged in light of the question concerning the impact that fonts have on observers as a purely formal event. Such a process occurs when the informational aspect is – at least superficially – extinguished by the use of a new and not instantly decipherable alphabet. The adjacent image offers a taste of this. The digitized version of the font is depicted below. (u.v)

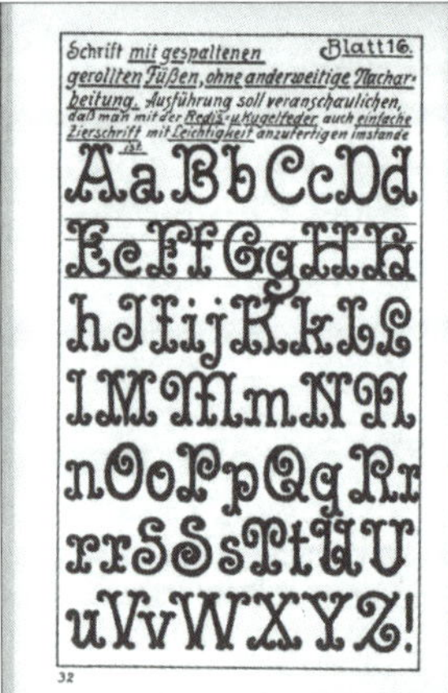

Schrift mit gespaltenen gerollten Füßen, ohne anderweitige Nacharbeitung. Ausführung soll veranschaulichen, daß man mit der Redis- u. Kugelfeder auch einfache Zierschrift mit Leichtigkeit anzufertigen imstande ist. Blatt 16.

Aa Bb Cc Dd
Ee Ff Gg Hh
hJ Ii j Kk L l
l M m N n
n O o P p Q q R r
r s S s T t U u
u V v W X Y Z !

32

Anwendungen: Blatt 17.

Dieselmotore.
Turbinenbau.
Schiffsmaschine.
Fabrikanlagen.
Bebauungsplan
Ausverkauf.

Für Haupttitel sind geeignet obige Schriften ausgezeichnet, weil die leichte Herstellungsart auch „viel Zeit und Geld erspart.“ Auch für Warenhaus, Geschäfte empfiehlt man diese Schrift auf's beste.

Wenn der Wortlaut augenfällig, trotzdem sei er doch gefällig mit der Feder hingeschrieben, -wie man schreibt, steht im Belieben

Wie die Aufschrift auch mag lauten, ob für Handwerk, Praxis, Bauten, ob für Schulen, ob für's Haus, immer kenne man sich aus, daß das Wortbild sei indessen auch dem Zwecke anzumessen.“

„Ist der Zweck erreicht ?!“ Alsdann hat man selbst auch Freude dran.

33.

E 016.1 ←
→ E 227

128.1 Handgeschriebene Schriften

Bibliographic information:
“Handgeschriebene Schriften – Schriftenvorlagen für einfache und leicht auszuführende Beschriftungen,” author: Franz Endreß, year of original publication unknown, Verlag Hermann Schmidt, Mainz, 2022; [in German]
ISBN 978-3-87439-691-2

Image source:
Double page from the booklet’s interior

The 64-page booklet has compiled 46 different handwritings. This is a reprint of a publication first published around 1905. It was printed at a time when graphic designers still had to demonstrate drawing skills – beyond the various tools we use today. (eds.)

E 016.1 ←
→ E 227

129 Designing Type

Bibliographic information:
"Designing Type", Karen Cheng; Yale University Press, Yale, 2020;
ISBN 978-0300249927

The book discusses microtypography and examines the question of what makes up and should make up the anatomy of letters. It outlines what font designers must do to create a harmonious typeface and guarantee good readability. Author Karen Cheng is a typeface designer herself and teaches this subject at the University of Washington in Seattle (USA). (eds.)

E 016.1 ←
→ E 228

130 Digital Cuneiform

Bibliographic information:
"Digitale Keilschrift – 1.063 Glyphen der ältesten Schriftsysteme der Welt," Johannes Bergerhausen; Verlag Hermann Schmidt, Mainz, 2014;
[ENG/GER]
ISBN 978-3-87439-861-9

Image source:
The unnumbered double page with the Unicode symbols U+1202D–U+1202E

As part of a research project, Johannes Bergerhausen, typographer, author, and professor (HS Mainz), delved into cuneiform, the dominant script for over three thousand years. Countless cuneiform tablets have been found and are now stored in museums and research institutions. Bergerhausen has now digitized this script for the first time and included it in his project Decodeunicode (decodeunicode.com).

The design work has also been documented as a book. In this way, cuneiform, along with all its fascinating facets, has been made available to a wider audience. (eds.)

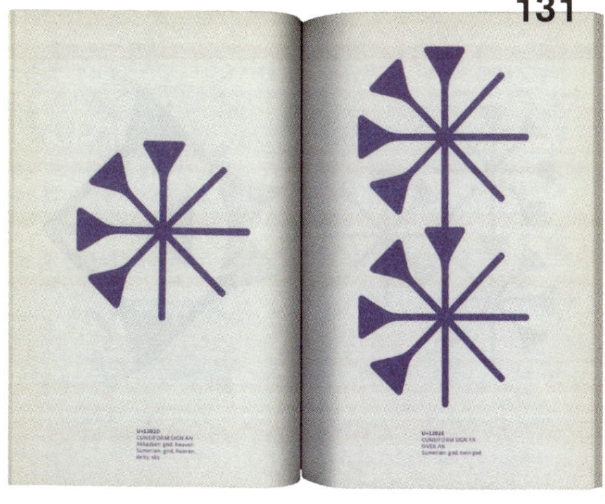

บ้านเมือง
เริ่มต้น · ครบเครื่อง เรื่องข่าว www.banmuang.co.th

ตลาดบ้าน ที่ดิน รถยนต์ หน้า 21-23

ศาลยกฟ้อง
'ดวงเฉลิม' รอดคุก
คดีดังฆ่าดาบยิ้มหลักฐานอ่อน
อธิบดีศาลอาญาไม่สนกระแส

เสียเม้งปฏิเสธ
ผู้พันคดียิงน้อง
ชี้ปมถูกล้างหนี้

รัฐ-ไอทีวีสงบศึกสัมปทานฉาว

จูบปากกันชื่นมื่น
ก่อนปรับผังใหม่

ตามเจอแล้ว
ปืนทหารพัน4ที่ถูกปล้น
'โกวิท' ยึดคืน
'นัจมุดดีน' กบดาน
ทรท.ตั้งทนายช่วย

2คู่4ศพ
นัดตาย
เกย์โหด
เฒ่าหึง
ปืนถล่ม

โอกาสเดียวที่เราให้ได้

E 017 ←
→ E 229

131 Globally valid media "laws"

The medium pictured here, in a script that is foreign to Europeans, signalizes that it is most likely a newspaper.

The structure of the layout resembles what is typical of newspapers in Europe and other locations. The visual impression feeds the suspicion that media "laws" – in terms of the way information is structure – are similar around the world, regardless of the glyphs and the reading direction. (eds.)

E 017 ←
→ E 230

132 The Voynich Manuscript

Image and text source:
https://de.wikipedia.org/wiki/Voynich-Manuskript (see sources)

' (...) The Voynich manuscript (named after Wilfrid Michael Voynich, who acquired the manuscript in 1912) is a handwritten medieval piece of writing that was owned by Rudolf II, among others. It has been held by the *Beinecke Rare Book and Manuscript Library* at Yale University since 1969, with the signature MS 408. The manuscript is composed in an unknown script. Over time, many approaches to decipher the manuscript have been suggested, but so far none of these approaches have stood up to specialist examinations, and it remains unclear whether the text actually conveys any meaningful content. Images included in the manuscript suggest botanical, anatomical, and astronomical topics and were drawn with care, but due to the lack of context, the content of the illustrations is also ultimately just speculation. (...)

Text and alphabet

The design of the text itself does not seem unusual: It was written from left to right (discernible based on the somewhat more irregular right margin); the individual letters are separated from one another via small gaps; the text is arranged into "words" through larger gaps, and a kind of paragraph structure can be recognized in longer text sequences. The handwriting style appears fluid, as if the writer were practiced in the language and script of their manuscript, in contrast to the usual uncertainties that are visible when "tracing" the characters of an unknown script. The lack of corrections indicates that a template of the text existed that the writer copied. According to analyses conducted by Prescott Currier in the 1970s, two or more writers and writing styles are discernible. More recent analyses question the correctness of this observation. Another handwriting expert who examined the manuscript could only detect one hand. (...) '

E 017 ←
→ E 231

133 Cryptography

Image source:
(1) https://books.google.at/books?id=iW85AAAAcAAJ&printsec=frontcover&dq=Schreibekunst&hl=de&sa=X&ei=69MyUuSNIaq40QWY1YCQDA#v=onepage&q&f=false (see sources)

Recommended website: https://en.wikipedia.org/wiki/Cryptography

Cryptography deals with encrypting information, and as such forms part of the knowledge field of cryptology. "Secret writing" has always been a subject of communicative procedures, and so it simply makes sense that cryptology has long become a "subfield of information technology that focuses on the development and evaluation of procedures for encrypting secret data" (Duden). One of the main requirements of digital communication is that it works securely and without vulnerabilities. Whenever encrypted communication is used, it goes hand in hand with attempts to penetrate these secure systems. The specialist field that concentrates on this is cryptoanalysis. (eds.)

Double pages from:
Tacheagraphia, Christian Friedrich Geßner, 1743

44 Französische Abkürzungen.

Figur.	Bedeutet	Figur.	Bedeutet
S. M.	Sa Majesté	S. oder St.	Saint
V. A. S.	votre Altesse Serenissime	Ste	Sainte
		les des	les dites
V. E.	votre Excellence	Sus dt	sus dit
S. M. I.	Sa Majesté Imperiale	Sus d. e.	Sus dite
		Sus d. s.	Sus dits
L. H. P.	leurs hautes puissances	Sus d. es.	Sus dites
		1e	premiere
S. S.	Sa Sainte	2e	deuxime
V. S.	votre Sancté	3e	troisieme
led.	ledit	4e	quatrieme
lad. e	ladite		

STEGANOGRAPHIA
oder vielmehr
CRYPTOGRAPHIA,
oder
Geheim Schreibe-Kunst.

Dieses ist eine Wissenschaft seine Meynung heimlich und ohne allen Verdacht, durch Ziffern, Buchstaben oder Quadrat-Figuren, wie folgende Alphabete zeigen, einem andern davon Wissenschaft habenden zu entdecken.

Man bezeichne erstlich die Buchstaben des Alphabets mit den Zahlen nach ihrer Ordnung also:

1, 2, 3, 4, 5, 6, 7, 8, 9, 10, 11, 12, 13, 14, 15,
a, b, c, d, e, f, g, h, i, k, l, m, n, p, q.
16, 17, 18, 19, 20, 21, 22, 23, 0
r, s, t, u, w, x, y, z, o

Den Buchstab o tractirt man wie in der Arithmetica numeroso; die null, weil diese, wie der Buchstabe o äuserlich aussiehet.

Noch

Geheim Schreibe-Kunst. 45

Noch ein Schema.

A B C ch D E F G H I K L M N
O oo P Ph Pf R S Sch Sk T th U od. W X Z

Auf eine andere Art.
Geheime Briefe zu schreiben, und deren Auflösung:

a b c d e f
g h i k l m
n o p q r s
t u x W y z

Diese Quadraten kan man, nach erforderender Ordnung der Buchstaben, eine rechte Vierung, oder aber in ein- und andern Abrisse gewisser Bauwercken an statt der Fenster anbringen. Wer alsdenn solche Schrift lesen will, der nehme aus dem Brief oder Riß, eine viereckichte, in vier kleine Cubos abgetheilte Figur nach der andern heraus, mercke mit Fleiß auf den Unterscheid der würfflichten Schat-

46 Geheim Schreibe-Kunst.

Schattirungen und Puncte, und suche dergleichen Figuren im vorstehenden Alphabeth, und schreibe die darunter stehende Buchstaben auf, so wird ihm das Geheimniß nicht können verborgen bleiben.

Noch eine andre Art.

Diese Art, geheim zu schreiben, kommt mit vorhergehenden überein, und diese ist das Fundament, woraus auch die vorige hergeleitet wird, der gröste Unterscheid ist, daß jene Quadraten in 4 kleine Cubus abgetheilet, hier aber die Quadrätgen, aus welchen der Brief bestehet, vermittelst der Diagonal-Linien durch lauter dreyeckichte Schattierungen gemachet ist, wie folgende Figuren zeigen.

a b c d e f g h
i k l m n o p q
r s t u w x y z

Diese Anleitung und Alphabeth einen künstlichen Brief aus lauter viereckichten durch mannigfaltige Durchschnitte und Schattierung von einander unterschiedene Felder, zu formiren, ist zur geheimen Correspondenz zu gebrauchen, wie von dem vorigen gemeldet worden: denn, wenn man das Verborgene aus dem Tunckeln hervor suchen will, so nimmt man ein Quadrätgen nach dem andern, giebt wohl Achtung, wie dasselbige durchschnitten und schattiret ist, suchet dergleichen in vorstehenden Alphabeth und schreibet den darunter stehenden Buchstaben auf, so kan man den Innhalt des Briefes dadurch errathen.

Wie

Geheime Schreibe-Kunst. 47

Wie man einen heimlichen Brief schreiben soll, in welchen die natürlichen Buchstaben des Geheimnisses unverändert behalten, und nach der Reihe in gewisse Wörter versetzet worden.

Exempel eines solchen Briefs der auf solche Manier ausgearbeitet ist, und darbey Anleitung gegeben wird, wie man das Geheimniß daraus lesen soll.

Mein Herr!

Gestern empfing Herr Eberhard das Indianische Elfenbein, so er nach Augspurg befördert. Es nehmen der Niederländer ihre Commercien hier täglich ab, und soferne der erschreckliche Mars hier abermal Unruh sollte erwecken, dürffte unsere Wohlfarth ihren Rückgang suchen: Triffts Spanien oder Niederland, so triffts uns mit. Bey den Engelländern ist noch Lermen: Es bedeutet einen neuen Krieg, ob mercket man es nicht. rc.

In diesen Schreiben ist folgendes Geheimniß enthalten: Gehe diesen Abend nicht aus dem Hause, du wirst umb dein Leben kommen. Wer solches lesen will, der nehme nur von jeden Worte den ersten Buchstaben, und setze sie nach der Reihe zusammen so wird ers finden.

Ferner:

Einen Brief da der erste Buchstabe, damit der Brief sich anfängt, und hernach alle die ersten Buchstaben die auf ein Comma, Colon, Punctum, oder andere Distinctiones folgen, gelten müssen; z. E.

Mon-

E 020 ←
→ E 232

134 Communication design and subjectivity

Image sources:
Ulysses Voelker; (1) 2019; (2) 2020; (3) 2021

Since the beginnings of their profession, designers have always harbored the desire to determine once and for all what form of graphic depiction is the right one. Not only informational, but above all the aesthetic quality would be measured based on this standard. As we know, it still has not been possible to turn this pipe dream of universally valid criteria into reality. The examples below show that many influences (socializations, viewing habits, mentalities) help shape design to a considerable extent. In any case, they communicate their contents effortlessly in their environment. Finding out what good design is therefore remains a vital subject for designers. But beware of easy answers.
(1) In Ireland, the sheep is recognized instantly; (2) Active and still casual: wheelchair users in France; (3) "The chart of the foot reflective zones" opts for a particularly vivid graphicness. We recommend that readers keep their own archive of such examples – even if just to capture the world's variety. (u.v)

(1)

(2)

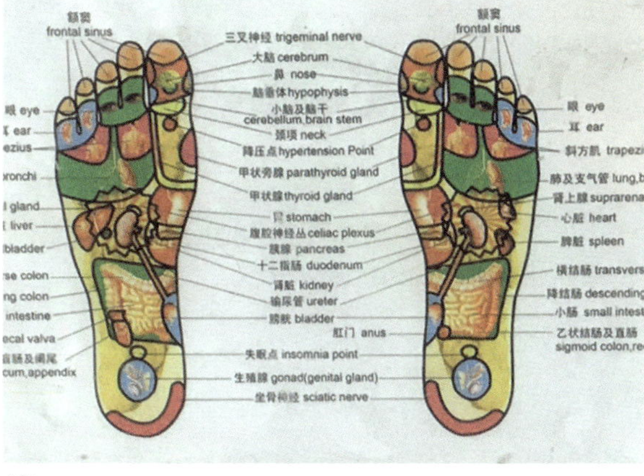

(3)

E 022 ←
→ E 233

135 How Real Is Real? Confusion, Disinformation, Communication

Bibliographic information:
"How Real Is Real? Confusion, Disinformation, Communication,"
Paul Watzlawick; Random House Inc, New York City, 1977;
ISBN 978-0-3947-2256-6

Watzlawick's book revolves around a central thesis: Reality is the result of communication. The thesis contradicts the generally accepted opinion that reality "exists," while the task of communication is to describe and share it. But if reality is the product of communication, then it is also clear that there is not one, but countless realities. The book discusses different levels of the thesis, including the phenomenon of "power of the group," which has a considerable influence on the evaluation of reality. An experiment reveals what lies behind this. The structure and procedure were as follows: Two boards were shown to groups of seven to nine students. Board 1 contained a vertical line, while board 2 pictured three vertical lines of different lengths. Psychologist Prof. Asch explained to the participants that they needed to identify the line on board 2 that had the same length as the line on board 1.

Board Nr. 1

Board Nr. 2

Watzlawick described what happened next. To start with, the participants were asked for their answers in the order in which they were seated. Everyone in the first round of questioning indicated the same line on board 2 that matched the length of the line on board 1. Now a second, identical pair of boards was shown – with an equally unanimous result. Something unexpected happened in the third round: Deviating from everyone else, one participant had reached a different conclusion. This caused quite a lot of irritation on his part. In the following round, the voting result repeated itself, which led to incredulous astonishment due to the difference in opinion. Over the course of the next rounds, the dissenter grew increasingly insecure and started to distrust his own perception. What the insecure participant couldn't know: All other students had been instructed to give the wrong answer from a certain point onward. The participant, who was the only one who gave the right answer again and again, therefore either had to disagree with the unanimous perception – or distrust his own. According to Watzlawick, the most astonishing aspect of this experiment was the result: 36.8% of the participants submitted to the group's incorrect judgment and revised their own, correct assessment.

Findings like these are very significant for visual communication. They support the thesis stating that design is a construction of reality that shapes intentions and expectations and therefore must largely be classified as subjective. The manipulative power that arises from this circumstance requires a high degree of responsibility, and designers must be aware of this. (u.v)

E 024 ←
→ E 234

136 Adbuster Media Foundation

Recommended websites:
https://www.adbusters.org/
https://en.wikipedia.org/wiki/Adbusters

Adbusters is a shortened version of the term advertisement busters. The Adbuster Media Foundation is a non-profit organization that has dedicated itself to criticism of consumption. It was founded in Canada in 1989 by Kalle Lasn and Bill Schmalz. The official agenda of Adbusters, which also publishes an eponymous magazine, states that it is a network including artists, students, pedagogs, entrepreneurs, and many other participants that is pursuing the goal of changing the lifestyle and living conditions in the 21st century. In particular, it aims to break down the dominance of consumption and thereby also the influence of advertising.
"Adbusters" magazine is ad-free and – after its initial focus on advertising – also discusses social and other political topics. It addresses an international audience. The Adbusters Media Foundation has ties with similar organizations in Europe and Asia. (eds.)

E 024 ←
→ E 235

137 Guerrilla marketing

Image source:
https://de.wikipedia.org/wiki/Guerilla-Marketing#/media/Datei:-Sixt1DSC_1153.jpg (see sources)

Recommended website:
https://en.wikipedia.org/wiki/Guerrilla_marketing

Guerrilla marketing is a term that describes marketing strategies and measures that deviate from the norm. The term was coined in the 1980s. Even though it draws on the political definition of a certain type of warfare that includes tactics that are difficult to calculate, the term is not related to consumer criticism or other political content. Moreover, guerrilla marketing aims to surprise using unusual, sometimes rebellious actions – in line with the goal of raising profits. Different versions of guerrilla marketing are used in advertising: viral marketing, ambient marketing, or ambush marketing. (eds.)

E 024 ←
→ E 235

138 The Yes Men, Guerrilla communication

Recommended websites:
https://en.wikipedia.org/wiki/The_Yes_Men
https://en.wikipedia.org/wiki/Barbie_Liberation_Organization
https://en.wikipedia.org/wiki/Culture_jamming

"The Yes Men" are a duo involved in guerrilla communication and culture jamming. It consists of science fiction author and professor Jaques Servin (USA) and professor of media art Igor Vamos (USA). Both are responsible for many actions with which they unveiled the business practices and unethical goals of international corporations and institutions using satirical methods (e.g., exaggerated demands, alleged confessions, etc.) – in such a believable way that their authenticity was not immediately called into question. For example, they faked the World Health Organization's website (WHO) and announced its dissolution due to ethical reasons, or they apologized for wars of aggression on behalf of the White House.
The duo gained fame under their pseudonyms Andy Bichlbaum (Servin) and Mike Bonanno (Vamos). One of their first actions in the 1990s consisted of swapping the speech modules of Barbie dolls and talking GI Joe dolls. Then they smuggled the manipulated dolls back into stores. At the same time, they published an explanation on behalf of the "Barbie Liberation Organization."

"The Yes Men" have filmed several movies that gained international popularity: "The Yes Men" (2003), "The Yes Men Fix the World" (2009), and "The Yes Men Are Revolting" (2014). (eds.)

E 024 ←
→ E 235

139 Dries Depoorter, The Lookout, 2021 – 2024

Recommended website:
https://driesdepoorter.be/thelookout/
https://driesdepoorter.be/jaywalkingframes/

Dries Depoorter is an artist from Belgium. He focuses on artificial intelligence and topics related to social media and camera surveillance in public spaces. The project "The Lookout" (2021 – 2024) is illustrative of his work. At the core of this work lies the manipulation of unprotected surveillance cameras using a Playstation controller. The installation shows what 1,500 CCTV cameras broadcast in real time. Depoorter gained access to the cameras in question because they either weren't password-protected or protected by an easy-to-guess password. Now the controller, which forms part of the installation, allows the viewer to target and manipulate a camera anywhere in the world, for example by swiveling the camera, tilting it, or zooming in. Visitors are asked to take pictures with the cameras. Another one of Depoorter's projects is called "Jaywalking Frames" (2018 – 2024). He also used unprotected surveillance cameras for this. In this case, the cameras photograph people around the world who cross the street when the traffic light is red. Special software makes this work possible. The pictures of traffic offenders can be purchased – for a price in the amount of the fine that would be due in the respective country. The proceeds go to an artist.

Dries Depoorter is in demand around the world and represented in many global exhibitions. He also gives lectures. (eds.)

E 024 ←
→ E 235

140 Werbekodex des Deutschen Werberats

Text source:
https://www.werberat.de/content/leitfaden-zum-werbekodex-des-deutschen-werberats
(see sources)

/ (...) **Guideline on the advertising code of the German Advertising Standards Council**

The jurisdiction of the Advertising Standards Council spans all media and applies to all forms of commercial communication – online and offline. It includes classic advertising, for example on television, on posters, in newspapers or magazines, on the radio, at the movie theatre, but also Internet/mobile advertising, advertising in social networks, sponsoring measures, or advertising at a point of sale. The German Advertising Standards Council is not responsible for the advertising of political parties, churches, foundations, associations, or non-government organizations. If a complaint refers to a potential breach of law (as opposed to the violation of the voluntary advertising codes), the Advertising Standards Council will forward the case to the institutions that have the right to bring proceedings or will inform the complainant to whom they can turn. As guide rails, the Advertising Standards Council's code of conduct (advertising code) is already helping to prevent transgressions in advertising design. The basic rules for commercial communication as well as special codes of conduct also form the basis for decisions made by the Advertising Standards Council concerning individual advertising measures. The Advertising Standards Council's rules of procedure and its working principles guarantee a standardized and just procedure for the involved complainants and companies. Based on fictitious examples (...) regarding the individual policies, we explain how the Advertising Standards Council positions itself on certain topics. These also show "classics" of the advertising landscape that are decided by the committee in regular intervals. (...) /

E 028 ←
→ E 236

141 Der Typografiestreit der Moderne – Max Bill kontra Jan Tschichold

Bibliographic information:
"Der Typografiestreit der Moderne – Max Bill kontra Jan Tschichold,"
Hans Rudolf Bosshard; Niggli Verlag, Salenstein, 2012; [in German]
ISBN 978-3-7212-0833-7

Image and text source:
https://www.niggli.ch/Produkt/der-typografiestreit-der-moderne/ (see sources)

/ As soon as we are dealing with aesthetics – meaning things that cannot be ascertained with certainty – different, even controversial stances are unavoidable. Again and again, exponents of typography have expressed their opinions on the suitability of fonts, the use of ornaments, or the optimal type area. Hans Rudolf Bosshard names a few historic examples – from Bodoni and Bertuch through to Morris and Morison – before he focuses on the so-called "typography dispute of modernism" from 1946 between Max Bill and Jan Tschichold. Even back then, the dispute caused emotions to run high – and it still generates a lot of interest today, not just in the German, but also the Anglo-Saxon language area.

The dispute was triggered by a lecture by Tschichold titled "Konstanten der Typografie" ("Constants of Typography"), in which he renounced the formerly practiced and theoretically championed "new typography" and declared a return to traditional typography an attack on modernism. Both accused each other (from opposing positions and completely unjustifiably) of adopting a National Socialist aesthetic. The intense exchange, described here in detail for the first time, took place in the "Schweizer Typographischen Mitteilungen." /

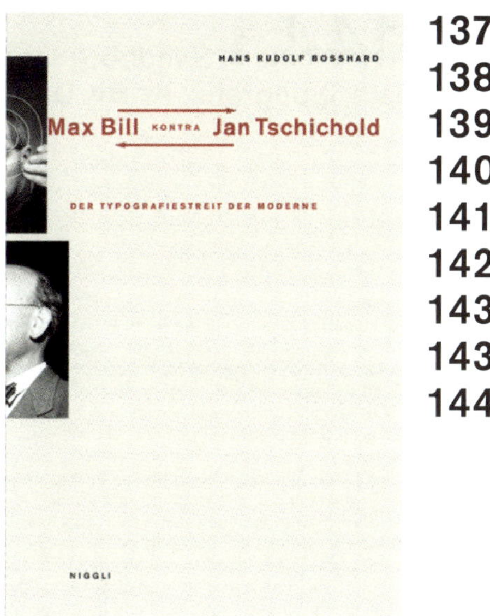

E 028 ←
→ E 237

142 Richard Paul Lohse – Konstruktive Gebrauchsgrafik

Bibliographic information:
"Richard Paul Lohse – Konstruktive Gebrauchsgrafik," Richard Paul Lohse-Stiftung (Ed.), Zurich, Verlag Hatje Cantz, 1999;
[in German]
ISBN 978-3-7757-0767-1

Recommended website:
https://www.hatjecantz.de/richard-paul-lohse-808-0.html

Richard Paul Lohse (1902 – 1988) is an important representative of modernism and Swiss typography. In addition, Lohse is considered a pioneer of constructive-systematic art. As a graphic designer, he made an important contribution to the history of constructive commercial graphics. The recommended book shows work produced between the 1930s and 1960s. It depicts the diverse relationships between politics and graphic aesthetics that particularly shaped the period after World War II. Essays highlight and explain this important phase of modernism. The book, which is structured as a catalog of works, shows all applied work for the first time. (eds.)

E 030 ←
→ E 238

143 Ausbildung in typografischer Gestaltung

Bibliographic information:
"Ausbildung in typografischer Gestaltung," Hans-Rudolf Lutz, Verlag Hans-Rudolf Lutz, Zurich, 1987; [in German]

Recommended website:
http://lutz-verlag.ch/ausbildung-in-typografischer-gestaltung/

Hans-Rudolf Lutz (1939 – 1998) was an important Swiss typographer and teacher. In the 1960s, he worked in Paris for a time before he founded a studio in Zurich. Particularly in the postmodern years of the 1980s and 1990s, he managed the balancing act between the dogmatic demands of modernism and the experimental explorations of design possibilities. If one could accuse of Lutz of following any dogmas at all, it would be in the form of his humanist/political mindset and his care and meticulousness in typographical matters. Lutz collected pictures of everyday typography around the world and created stage sets for a rock band he was part of.

E 030 ←
→ E 238

143.1 Typoundso

Bibliographic information:
"Typoundso," Hans-Rudolf Lutz, Verlag Hans-Rudolf Lutz, Zurich, 1997;
[in German]

Empfohlene Websites:
(1) http://lutz-verlag.ch/typoundso/,
(2) http://lutz-verlag.ch/about/

On top of this, he founded a publishing house that produced both of the books recommended here. They present assignments for students, explain backgrounds – and open up the cosmos of an exemplary design mindset. All of his work and his teaching puts an emphasis on the relationship between society and visual communication. (u.v)

E 030 ←
→ E 239

144 False Flat: Why Dutch Design is so Good

Bibliographic information:
"False Flat: Why Dutch Design is so Good," Aaron Betsky, Adam Eeuwens, Phaidon Press, 2004;
ISBN 9780714840697

Recommended website:
https://www.abebooks.com/9780714840697/False-Flat-Why-Dutch-Design-0714840696/plp

In many ways, Dutch design from the last 30 years can be viewed as exemplary. It has always aspired to incorporate the individual desire for freedom and creativity into communal visual communication. As is the case for some self-praise, (a little bit of) hubris and justified pride go hand in hand in the book. Dutch designers created unique solutions that combined courage and skill. But it is also true that the Dutch business sense quickly knew how to turn this into a brand. Hardly any other nation understood how to market a style that achieved global success and is linked to a presumed mentality (that said, Switzerland could also be named in this context). The recommended book from 2004 shows the ways in which the Dutch and their graphic, architectural, and other design work stood out. It was designed by the renowned Irma Boom. (eds.)

E 030 ←
→ E 239

144.1 Sandberg Instituut, Werkplaats Typografie, KABK Den Haag

Text sources:
(1) https://sandberg.nl/about;
(2) https://www.artez.nl/en/courses/master/werkplaats-typografie;
(3) https://www.kabk.nl/en/about/mission-statement

Recommended websites:
(1) https://sandberg.nl;
(2) https://www.werkplaatstypografie.org/;
(3) https://www.kabk.nl/

(1) **Sandberg Instituut**

/ (...) As the postgraduate programme of the Gerrit Rietveld Academie Amsterdam, the Sandberg Instituut offers Master Programmes in Fine Arts, Interior Architecture and Design. The five Main Departments aim to deepen the practices of artists, designers and critics. In addition, the Temporary Programmes reflect on specific urgencies in society and the arts, and the Hosted Programmes focus on collaboration with other institutes.

Main Departments

Sandberg Instituut's Main Departments are Critical Studies, Design, The Dirty Art Department, Fine Arts and Studio for Immediate Spaces. An average of only twenty students per programme allows each course to be flexible and open to initiatives from students and third parties. The course directors, who are prominent artists, designers, theorists and curators with international practices, invite tutors and guests who are able to challenge the students to critically reflect on their profession, their work and their progress. The Sandberg Instituut is open to candidates from many different backgrounds. We require a valid Bachelor degree in a field relevant to the programme you are applying for, as well as proof of proficiency in the English language. (...) /

(2) **Werkplaats Typografie**

/ Werkplaats Typografie is a two-year experimental Master's programme in graphic design. It functions as a research environment wherein participants define the content, aims and conditions of their international independent design practice, and develop their artistic, visual, discursive and practical qualities. Being part of a questioning community, they learn how to interact with their ambitions and skills, positioning themselves in the field while pushing its limits. (...) /

(3) **KABK Den Haag**

/ (...) *Mission Statement*

The Royal Academy of Art, The Hague (KABK) educates students to become independent and self-aware artists and designers with investigative mindsets and unique visual and conceptual abilities. They are able to produce authentic and in-depth creative work that advances their chosen disciplines and contributes to the wellbeing of society as a whole.

Vision

The Royal Academy of Art, The Hague (KABK) is founded on a vision of educational excellence. In our culturally diverse academy, the commitment, passion, and curiosity of our students and staff come together in a respectful and tolerant learning environment. Our intensive, structured and small-scale curriculum revolves around experimentation and personal guidance. We provide students with a significant degree of freedom to shape their interests and personal ambitions. We value skill and disciplinary expertise as well as interdisciplinary practice. We encourage innovation through collaboration and facilitate critical reflection on the ever-changing roles of artists and designers in our societies. Our graduates have the capacity to become leaders in their fields, produce outstanding creative work, and dare to disturb. They are able to innovate, collaborate, and generate new knowledge. We inspire our students to question how art and design shape contemporary societies and contribute to cultural, economic, and social well-being in a global context. We look outwards from the academy, interacting with the communities of The Hague, the Netherlands, and beyond, and aim to contribute to an inclusive debate on issues relevant to art, culture, and society. /

E 030 ←
→ E 240

145 DDC Wettbewerb 2023: "Was ist gut" – Kriterien

Text source:
https://www.ddc.de/de/wettbewerb/was-ist-gut-2023/infos.php
(see sources)

Design competitions play an important role in the working life of many designers. Some view them as a yardstick by which good design is measured. They hope that winning an award will help them climb the career ladder. Others categorically reject participating because many competitions require a high financial contribution on the part of the designer if they win an award. Whether recognition of achievements or daylight robbery: We can only find an answer by examining the individual competitions. Competitions have started to change their focus over the last years. One example of this is DDC, which has combined critical questions with competition for a while now. In 2023, it published the following competition description (eds.):

/ *Call for a competition for value-based design*

The only way to find new and innovative answers is to ask questions that haven't been asked before. WHAT IS GOOD? is one of these questions. This novel design award initiated a process that we are determined to build on this year. We are focusing on what designers do best: create. But what exactly are we creating when we design spaces, products, communication, and processes? We establish value/s. (...) We can only confront these times of change, shifts, and transformation through critical questioning – and this also includes questioning existing matters, ourselves, and our work. Or to be more precise: How do we design valuing content that doesn't remain neutral in communication? How do we design value-adding things that can empower others? And how do we design value-based living environments in which values can no longer be ignored?

This design award is different.

We are looking for realized, professional, and conceptional projects or ideas that you've always wanted to pursue because they're good and important. They can be small or big. They can be implemented "following all the rules of art," they can be wacky or realistic. What's important is that they strive to make the world a better place. Because we believe that designers can make an important contribution to this goal. And since WHAT IS GOOD? is different, there won't be a traditional jury – instead, participants will meet, discuss, and crown the winners. (...) DDC WHAT IS GOOD 2023 is geared towards agencies, designers, and students of all disciplines as well as design enthusiasts, charitable institutions, NGOs, freelancers, and companies – in short, everyone. (...) The evaluations won't be subject to the traditional criteria. Factors that have the potential to change society could be more important than pure aesthetics or craftsmanship-related criteria. The effect of change could be more important than perfection. Projects should revolve around value-oriented design and creation. The focal point: value/s through which the project replaces prevailing circumstances and processes and promotes a social, democratic, and environmentally friendly future. (...) /

E 030 ←
→ E 241

145.1 German Sustainability Award Design 2024 – Criteria

Text source:
https://www.nachhaltigkeitspreis.de/en/design-en (see sources)

Another example of a change in competition focus is the German Sustainability Award. The competition was paused in 2023 and relaunched in 2024. Here is an excerpt of the description (eds.):

/ Sustainable design provides answers to the most pressing challenges of our time and changes the way of life - users are able to choose sustainability and contribute to transformation. In the foreseeable future, products and services that enable this, will establish themselves.

The German Sustainability Award Design recognizes the best solutions in all segments.

By design we do not refer solely to the design of physical products, but the development of any conceivable product, system or service. Ideally the development starts with the question of how the result can achieve the greatest possible positive effect for sustainability, and the design and realization are inspired by this.

The GSA Design wants to motivate and give good examples a tailwind for their success. The GSA Design can make sustainable design more successful and thus more effective. /

E 030 ←
→ E 242

146 Symbolism and use of the White and Red Cross

Text sources:
(1) https://de.wikipedia.org/wiki/Fahne_und_Wappen_der_Schweiz
(2) https://de.wikipedia.org/wiki/Griechisches_Kreuz
(3) https://de.wikipedia.org/wiki/Fahne_und_Wappen_der_Schweiz
(all information: see sources)

144.1
145
145.1
146
147

(1) ' The Swiss flag and Switzerland's coat of arms contain an upright, free-standing white Greek cross on a red background – the Swiss cross. (...) '

(2) ' The Greek cross is a cross with four equally long sides, connected via right angles. Numerous other forms of the cross have been derived from it (Jerusalem cross, German cross, cross potent, sun cross, cross pattée, Occitan cross, Swiss cross, and more). In a specific context, it is referred to as the beam cross.

The Greek cross was used in a wide range of contexts. An early form is the Mithras cross that served as the symbol of Sol Invictus (= undefeated sun) during the time of Constantine the Great. In Scandinavia, it represented the Christian symbol on picture and rune stones. The Greek cross appears in the national coat of arms of Greece, Malta, and on the flag of Switzerland, among others. (...)

The cross can be modified as a common figure in heraldry, such as the German cross. For example, in some historic forms of Greece's national coat of arms, the lengths of the vertical and horizontal arms of the cross are connected at a ratio of 7:6. (...) '

(3) ' The colorful counterpart to the Swiss cross is the red cross on a white background. The Red Cross organization chose this symbol as its mark and sign of protection in honor of its founder Henry Dunant and his home country. (...) '

E 030 ←
→ E 243

147 The German Federal States' Coats of Arms

Image sources:
https://de.wikipedia.org/wiki/Flaggen_und_Wappen_der_L%C3%A4nder_der_Bundesrepublik_Deutschland (see sources)

Text sources: Ulysses Voelker
(1) Quote about Schleswig Holstein – https://www.deutschlandfunkkultur.de/schleswig-holsteins-wappen-eine-geschichte-voller-wirrungen-100.html

If a designer were tasked with creating a (colorful) sovereign coat of arms with an integrated image of an animal, then the following presents a few initial considerations that seem befitting in terms of the illustration:

a) Due to the sovereign and symbolic character, a neutral and abstracting character is recommended;
b) if a (scalable) format is planned, the image should not be too detailed, as it might come in a small size;
c) the illustration of the animal must present its typical physical form;

Against this background, if we look at the coats of arms of the German federal states, we would evaluate them rather differently. For example, imagine how you would justify the facial expressions of some animals in front of a large group if you were responsible for these. I am showing five of the depicted coats of arms (Baden-Wuerttemberg, Bavaria, Bremen, Hamburg, Mecklenburg-Western Pomerania) in the smallest display sizes, while eleven coats of arms have a standard size (meaning they are scalable). My critique consciously omits the tradition of heraldry, as the aim is to hone the designer's eye – and encourage them to ask questions.

Mecklenburg-Western Pomerania:
The bull is sticking its tongue out at the observer, while the mythical creature's eyes are nearly closed. Due to the exaggerated facial expression, the illustrations look like they belong in a comic book.

Conclusion: comical.

Saarland:
This animal also gives a disheveled impression. The graphic functionality suffers from too much detail.

Conclusion: comical.

Berlin:
The reduced depiction appears succinct.
But: The positioning of the mouth and the eyes gives the bear a panicked look.

Conclusion: comical.

Brandenburg:
The cartoon-like line lends the bird a tousled look, while the yellow support lines in the wings look like comic arms.

Conclusion: comical.

Saxony-Anhalt:
The positioning of the eyes and mouth gives the impression that the bear is low-spirited, depressed. The act of balancing on the wall strengthens the impression of a tortured creature.

Conclusion: comical.

Rhineland-Palatinate, North Rhine-Westphalia, Thuringia, Lower Saxony: animal depictions, arranged from "too detailed" to "graphically succinct" (from left to right).

With one exception (Schleswig-Holstein, pictured on the opposite page), all animals are looking to the left.
The reason: Coats of arms originated during a time when they were primarily placed on shields. These were worn on the left arm. This way, the animal was looking at the opponent (see adjacent diagram).

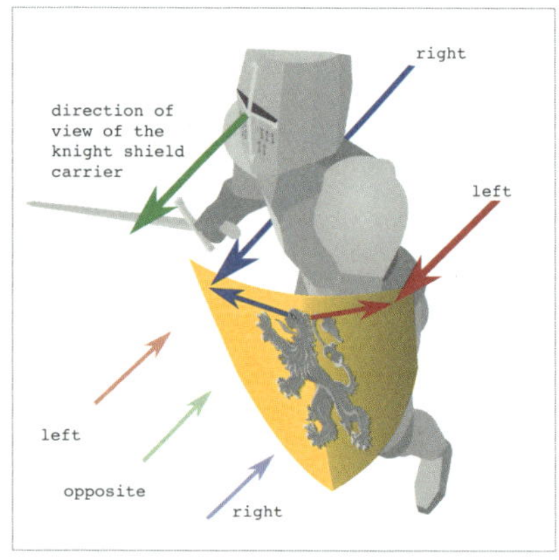

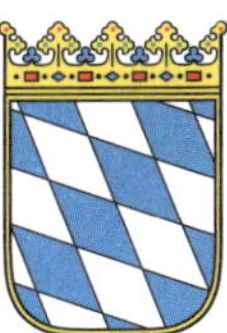

Four coats of arms omit the animals entirely.
From left to right: Saxony, Bavaria, Hamburg, Bremen.

Hesse:
The heraldic animal features less detail but still exudes a traditional appearance. In its gesture and proportions, the lion corresponds to the traditions of the past. The facial expression is neutral.

Conclusion: The coat of arms fulfills high functional demands (good long-distance effect, succinctness).

Schleswig-Holstein:
The only coat of arms on which the heraldic animal is looking to the right. The explanation:
' The Schleswig lions stem from the Danish royal coat of arms. (...) For hundreds of years, Schleswig formed part of the Kingdom of Denmark. And the lions stand to the left, seemingly moving to the edge of the coat of arms. Then the U-turn. From 1891, they stand on the right, facing the center of the coat of arms. The following anecdote often makes the rounds: After the German-Danish war, Otto von Bismarck ordered that the lions should look to the nettle leaf. After all, it would be unseemly to show the other part of the country one's rear end. (...) '
Source: see (1)

Conclusion: Today, the lions depict the generally familiar dynamic of left to right; despite its minimalist appearance, its style looks traditional; the abstract nettle leaf gives the coat of arms a modern look.

Baden-Wuerttemberg:
The combination of tradition (crown and animal) and functionality (long-distance effect) is a trademark of this coat of arms. The animals are well-proportioned, graphically simplified, their facial expression is neutral to predator-like.

Conclusion: The coat of arms fulfills high functional demands (good long-distance effect, succinctness).

Summary:
Coats of arms with strange details are lovable and arise from early forms of depiction and ancient interpretations. It is nice that such artefacts are still in use. Closer observation of German states' coats of arms also reveals a sense of humor that is not usually attributed to us Germans. The desperate Berlin bear makes us laugh, as do the anarchistic animals of Mecklenburg-Western Pomerania.

On the other hand, such an assessment doesn't help us much in everyday design life. The designer tasked with designing a coat of arms must take numerous application possibilities into account – both analog and digital.

The examples from Hesse, Schleswig-Holstein, and Baden-Wuerttemberg show that it is possible to manage the balancing act between tradition and modern succinctness. (u.v)

E 031 ←
→ E 244

148 Josef Müller-Brockmann. Ein Pionier der Schweizer Grafik

Bibliographic information:
"Josef Müller-Brockmann. Ein Pionier der Schweizer Grafik",
Lars Müller; Lars Müller Publishers, Baden, 2001; [in German]
ISBN 978-3907078594

Josef Müller-Brockmann (1914 – 1996) was a Swiss graphic designer, typographer, and author. He taught in Zurich and temporarily (1963) worked at the Ulm School of Design. Müller-Brockmann was not just a practician, but also a theoretician who contributed to the foundations of Swiss typography with his implementations. He viewed the profession of graphic designers in a holistic way: Aside from conceptual and design skills, designers should have technical, business, and cultural competences. In addition, graphic design work was too closely connected to the different facets of social concerns, in his opinion. The recommended book introduces Josef Müller-Brockmann as a pioneer of Swiss graphic design. In particular, his posters are still highly important today in terms of graphics because their style appears timeless. The book also includes work from the areas of corporate design and exhibition design. (eds.)

E 032.3 ←
→ E 245

149 The "Opendyslexic" font

The font presented here is called "OpenDyslexic" and was developed to simplify the reading process for dyslexics. Even though the impact of this free font (and other comparable dyslexia fonts) is scientifically disputed, attempts to aid the reading process by modifying fonts contribute to dyslexia research. Various studies conducted with "Open-dyslexie" and comparable fonts reveal that they did not lead to any significant improvements in the reading flow. However, it was also discovered that fonts could be helpful for some reading issues. Organizations for affected individuals, such as the "British Dyslexia Association," recommend "simple, evenly distributed sans-serif fonts" such as Arial, Comic Sans, Verdana, or Trebuchet MS instead of specific dyslexia fonts. (eds.)

Image sources:
https://de.wikipedia.org/wiki/OpenDyslexic#/media/Datei:OpenDyslexic3Regular-sample.svg
(see sources)

Recommended websites:
https://en.wikipedia.org/wiki/OpenDyslexic
https://de.wikipedia.org/wiki/European_Dyslexia_Association
https://de.wikipedia.org/wiki/Bundesverband_Legasthenie_und_Dyskalkulie

The Quick Brown
Fox Jumps Over
The Lazy Dog
g

abcdefghijklmnopqrstuvwxyz0123456789[](){}/\<>?

The quick brown fox jumps over the lazy dog
1234567890,.;:!?&%$()

E 032.3 ←
→ E 245

150 "Ryman Eco" font

Website: https://www.rymaneco.com/

The font presented here, "Ryman Eco," was designed with the intention of reducing the use of printing ink. As is visible here, the letters are constructed of lines that generate white spaces between each other. When depicted in a common reading size, the white spaces are hardly or not at all discernible. This lets the typeface appear like a conventionally constructed font. If you enlarge the letters, this results in graphically interesting textures. Dan Rhatigan created the font in 2014. The number of glyphs is reduced (signs for breaks and superscripts are missing, among others), as this is where technology reaches its limits. (eds.)

E 032.3 ←
→ E 246

151 Font development for documenta 15

Websites:
https://www.stanhema.com/en/podium/custom-typeface-for-documenta-fifteen
https://en.wikipedia.org/wiki/Documenta_fifteen

The font shown here was designed for documenta 15. The aim was to mirror the collective idea of the documenta concept, its processualism, and its internationality in the font. For this purpose, the font designers also formed a collective, consisting of André van Rueth (stanhema, Berlin), the Indonesian design studio Studio 4oo2, and Fabian Maier-Bode. (eds.)

ABCD
EFGHIJK
LMN
OPQRST
UVWXYZ
0123456789
.,:;-&?!@€$/%<>•&§¡}{¿-*[\]_""„

Tupamaros (Uruguay)
The Tupamaros, short for Movimiento de Liberación Nacional – Tupamaros (MLN-T, National Liberation Movement – Tupamaros) were a Communist guerilla movement in Uruguay established by trade unions and active as an underground movement from 1963 to the 1970s. Since 1985, they have operated as a political party. (...)
Source: https://de.wikipedia.org/wiki/Movimiento_de_Liberaci%C3%B3n_Nacional_%E2%80%93_Tupamaros (see sources)

E 036.1 ←
→ E 247

152 Liberation movements

Image sources:
Detailed information – see captions;

Website:
https://en.wikipedia.org/wiki/Liberation_movement

Generally speaking, liberation movements are resistance groups that organize their own military. They first emerged in colonial times, when the fight for national independence against colonial rulers erupted. Liberation movement battles also oppose other circumstances, such as the general political suppression in dictatorships or economic exploitation and social injustice. Liberation movements may also arise through the manifestation of separatist motivations – for example, when individual population groups fight for territory, or when fundamentalists pursue religious goals. To begin with, typical features of liberation movements include widely different forms of open or hidden peaceful resistance. These can then escalate into a hidden battle using guerilla tactics that often lead to open liberation wars. Liberation movements always fight against more or less powerful authorities, so communication plays a crucial role. This includes compelling names and graphic signs that promise high recognizability. (eds.)

The “National Liberation Front of South Vietnam,” NFB for short – (...) (Việt cộng in Vietnamese), was a guerilla organization that led an armed resistance against the government and the USA’s armed forces, who supported the government, in South Vietnam during the Vietnam War. (...)
Source: https://de.wikipedia.org/wiki/Nationale_Front_f%C3%BCr_die_Befreiung_S%C3%BCdvietnams (see sources)

E 037 ←
→ E 248

153 Manual typesetting for children

Image source:
Stamp Letters from the fund of Ulysses Voelker;

Stamp letters, designed as children’s toys, can also be interesting for designers. The aesthetic of the analog aspect and the “faultiness” of the printed image create an authenticity that is hard to duplicate digitally. Furthermore, analog work is beneficial for anyone who otherwise spends their days creating digital designs. (eds.)

ANALOG IST
RAU UND FEHLERHAFT
REIZVOLL

American Computer 286-A (1986)

E 040 ←
→ E 249

154 Computers and their designs 1979 – 1986

Image sources:
(1) https://upload.wikimedia.org/wikipedia/commons/f/f2/American_286-A.jpg
(2) https://commons.wikimedia.org/wiki/File:Intellec-MDS-80--Museum-Enter-6094735.jpg
(all information: see sources)

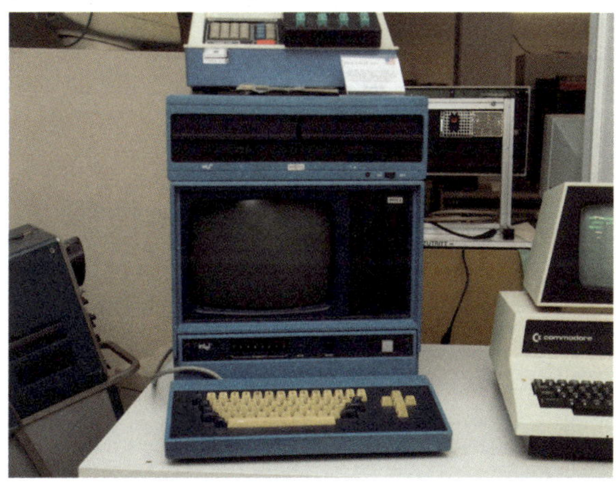

Intel MDS80 (1983)

E 042 ←
→ E 250

155 Anarchie der Zeichen

Bibliographic information:
"Anarchie der Zeichen," Rick Poynor; Birkhäuser Verlag, Basel, 2003; [ENG/GER] ISBN 9-783764-304492;

Websites:
https://en.wikipedia.org/wiki/Rick_Poynor#Career
https://designobserver.com

Rick Poynor is a British author who focuses on the topics of design, cultural criticism, and visual communication. He was the editor of the "eye" design magazine (1990 – 1997) and coordinated the *First Things First manifesto* with others in 2000. He founded the "designobserver" website, on which many prominent critics of current topics have their say, including Michael Bierut, Jessica Helfand, and Steven Heller.

Rick Poynor's book "Anarchie der Zeichen" discusses graphic design from the 1980s and 1990s – the time in which postmodernism fully established itself in visual communication. The book presents various works and structures them based on different aspects: origins, deconstruction, appropriation, technology, authorship, and opposition. Poynor provides a substantiated overview. The book is essential for learning about how societal developments, cultural trends, and the (at the time) new technique of computer-based design shaped visual communication. The lines of conflict are also addressed, for example when representatives of modernism criticized the disappearance of any design rulebooks. For today's designers, this book serves as both a source of inspiration and information. (eds.)

E 039 ←
→ E 251

156 The Risograph

Image source:
Fanzine "Let's Fetz," Workshop University of Applied Sciences Mainz, 2011;

Websites:
https://en.wikipedia.org/wiki/Risograph;
https://www.riso.co.jp/english/

The risograph was used for a printing process that resembles screen printing due to its color-separated procedure. The device was developed by the Japanese company Riso. Originally, the risograph was intended for work in administrations and schools, where it was used as an affordable and quick method to reproduce documents. Over time, the risograph gave way to faster, cheaper, and higher-quality reproduction machines that could print all colors at the same time – meaning they did without the exchange of color cartridges, which was required for the risograph. Nonetheless, artists and designers still appreciate the device, as its printed creations offer a very specific aesthetic that others cannot achieve. On top of this, the risograph is comparably environmentally friendly, as the color is put to the paper without chemicals and thermal effects.
The risograph also scores points with its low running costs. A potential downside is that it can only be used with uncoated paper and the drying process for the printed paper takes a long time. Further information, particularly on the device's technique: see the websites. (eds.)

The fanzine "Let's fetz" was produced in 2011 on the Risograph in a small edition in two colors.

E 049 ←
→ E 252

157 Art Directors Club Germany

Image source:
https://de.wikipedia.org/wiki/Art_Directors_Club#/media/Datei:ADC_Logo_2018.png (see sources)

Website: https://www.adc.de

According to its own description, the Art Directors Club is "an independent association with the goal of finding and promoting excellent creative communication." The club views itself neither as a federation nor as an organization that wants to generate revenue. Its members work in all kinds of professions related to visual communication (design, film and sound, advertising). Professionals in the area of communication in space (interior design) and those who work in research and teaching can also become members. It isn't possible to join the ADC on one's own initiative. Instead, candidates must be nominated by at least one member before they can start the admissions procedure. The ADC is located in Berlin and run by an executive committee together with a 13-person presidium. (eds.)

E 049 ←
→ E 253

158 Sinus Milieus

Text sources:
(1) https://de.wikipedia.org/wiki/Sinus-Milieus (see sources)
(2) https://www.sinus-institut.de/sinus-milieus/sinus-milieus-deutschland (see sources)

(1) '"Sinus-Milieus" is a protected brand name under which the societal and target-group typology of the Sinus Institute is marketed. This division into milieus was developed at the end of the 1970s and ranked among the most significant approaches in target-group research in Germany in 2007 according to the trade magazine "media & marketing." The categorization of the Sinus milieus has been criticized by various scientists.
(...)
In the social sciences, milieus are defined as groups of like-minded people with similar basic values and principles concerning their lifestyles, characterized by increased internal communication and isolation from other groups. The Sinus milieu model follows the sociological lifestyle interpretation that was developed in the mid-1980s in the area of academic inequality research. It makes the following assumption: Equal socioeconomic living conditions produce obviously unequal lifestyles and living environments. Accordingly, the differences in lifestyles are much more significant for people's everyday reality

than the differences of socioeconomic living conditions. Social affiliation is therefore largely defined on the basis of the shared mentalities of socio-culturally homogeneous subgroups (milieus).
However, social milieus do not make the consideration of social class redundant. A radical "decoupling" of objective and subjective living conditions, meaning social class and social milieus, is hardly propagated anymore today. Rather, we start with the context of milieu affiliation and social situation – specifically, upper class, middle class, and lower class milieus. (...)
Since the early 1980s, companies and agencies as well as ministries, political parties, non-governmental organizations, foundations, associations, and academia have used the Sinus milieus for a range of questions concerning strategic planning, brand and communication strategies, and even product development and product management. (...)
As of the late 1980s, the Sinus milieu model has also been incorporated into the major market media studies and TV and consumer panels, as well as being picked up on in academic research. Measuring the audience rating of TV channels in Germany, Austria, and Switzerland is also linked to the Sinus milieus as a standard today, meaning all test viewers are classified accordingly and the channels offer respective evaluations. (...) ʼ

(2) ʼ An overview of the Sinus milieus as defined by the Sinus Institute

Conservative, upper class milieu
The old structurally conservative elite: classic responsibility and success ethic as well as a claim to exclusivity and status; desire for order and balance; self-image as a pillar of postmodern arbitrariness; erosion of leadership role in society.

Traditional milieu
The older generation that loves security and order: stuck in the petty bourgeois world or traditional workers' culture; undemanding adaptation to necessities; increasing acceptance of the new sustainability standard; self-image of righteous little people.

Nostalgic, bourgeois milieu
The harmony-oriented (lower) middle class: desire for secure conditions and appropriate status; self-image as the middle of society, but a growing feeling of being overwhelmed and fear of social decline; sense of loss of acquired rules and certainties; longing for the old days.

Post-material milieu
Engaged, confident educated elite with post-material roots. Self-determination and development as well as focus on the common good; advocates of post-growth, sustainability, non-discriminatory conditions and diversity; self-image as the societal corrective.

Precarious milieu
The lower class striving for orientation and participation: belonging to and keeping up with the living standards of the wider middle class – but accumulation of social disadvantages and exclusion; feeling of being left behind, bitterness, and resentment; self-image as robust and tenacious.

Adaptive, pragmatic middle class
The modern mainstream: willing to adapt and motivated, but also harboring the desire for fun and entertainment; strong need for anchoring and a sense of belonging; growing dissatisfaction and uncertainty due to societal developments; self-image of a flexible pragmatic.

Consuming, hedonistic milieu
The (lower) middle class focused on consumption and entertainment: having fun in the here and now; self-image of the cool lifestyle mainstream; strong craving for recognition; professional adaptation vs. free-time escapism; increasingly irritated by the dictate of sustainability and political correctness.

Milieu of performers
The efficiency-oriented and performance elite that is optimistic about progress: global economic and liberal way of thinking; macrosocial perspective based on individual responsibility; self-image of style and consumer pioneers; high technical and digital affinity.

Expeditive milieu
The ambitious, creative bohème: urban, hip, digital, cosmopolitan, and interconnected; searching for new borders and unconventional experiences, solutions, and success; strong self-presentation skills, self-image of the postmodern elite.

Neo-ecological milieu
The drivers of global transformation: optimism and new-era mentality along with strong problem awareness regarding planetary challenges; open to new value syntheses: disruption and pragmatism, success and sustainability, party and protest; self-image of progressive realists; environmentally friendly and climate-conscious lifestyle. ʼ

E 049.1 ←
→ E 254

159 All-American Ads, 1950s

Bibliographic information:
"All-American Ads," Jim Heimann (Ed.); Taschen Verlag, 2001; [in German]
ISBN 3-8228-1158-0

This book presents advertising for all kinds of products and services from 1950s USA. The campaigns and visual stylistic devices not only give insight into the offerings and consumer incentives, but also take you on a journey through time and into a different world – in which babies suggested their mothers should smoke a cigarette to relax and atomic bomb explosions in the Nevada desert tried to make a trip to Las Vegas more appealing. The victory march of capitalism that was touted in the USA of the 1950s (including the Communist witch hunt of the McCarthy era), the accompanying idea of infinite possibilities, and faith in technology served as role models for the western world. (eds.)

E 053 ←
→ E 255

160 Motivation + Aktion

Bibliographic information:
Motivation+Aktion, Michael Schmitz; self-published, Hochschule Mainz, 2016; [in German]

Image source: pages 204 – 205;
Text source: excerpt from the preface, page 06, lines 16 – 41

Recommended website: https://studiomichaelschmitz.eu

ʼ (...) The following pages are intended to be more than just a guidebook that motivates readers to draw attention to the societal problems of their own surroundings in a creative way. This publication aims to help overcome the feeling of powerlessness towards society's big problems by means of concrete questions and directives. This publication wants to pique the reader's curiosity to discover their surroundings for themselves and intervene on a political level. A complete, universal project cannot be expected here. Rather, this work represents an incentive for activism in the public space. A work that should be shared and could motivate other people to take new actions.

It is consciously left up to the readers of this work to continue to elaborate on the presented ideas that the mentioned question of how to contribute to our society (if possible) tries to answer in a definitive way. ʼ

**»We believe that abstraction, a movement away from realism but towards reality, is the ultimate form of engagement.
We believe that to focus on the physical dimensions of design, to create a piece of design as a functional entity, as an object in itself, is the most social and political act a designer can perform.**

That's why we believe in color and form, type and spacing, paper and ink, space and time, object and function and, most of all, context and concept«.
Experimental Jetset

E 055 ←
→ E 256

161 The Oslo Manifesto

Text source:
https://designmanifestos.org/wp-content/uploads/2020/04/the-oslo-manifesto_english-.pdf
https://designmanifestos.org/

/ **The SDGs are a Design Brief for the 21st Century**
On 25 September 2015, when the 193 Member States of the United Nations approved the 2030 Agenda and the 17 Sustainable Development Goals, (SDGs) they also created the world's most demanding design brief. The SDGs are "universal": this means they apply to every nation, every sector, every business, every profession, including design and architecture.
The SDGs are about "integration": this means they demand a new emphasis on a systemic approach that does not sacrifice environmental and social considerations to economic gain, but rather seeks for true synergies and solutions that benefit people, nature, and prosperity. Finally, the SDGs are about "transformation": this means they challenge us to rethink the way we live, to rebuild all the systems that are degrading ecological and human health – and to make our world sustainable. In sum, the SDGs are the ultimate design and architecture challenge: how do we create, and recreate, a world that achieves all 17 of the visionary goals that have now been agreed to by all the world's nations? And how do we achieve this by the year 2030?
The designers, architects, and creative professionals of the world have been handed a special and enormous responsibility, given to them by the 193 heads of state. They must imagine and bring to life the design elements of a new, sustainable world – quickly.

The Oslo Manifesto
Designers and architects are challenged to consider the following /17 questions, whenever they initiate a new project, design a new product, or accept a new commission:
/01
How can this design contribute to the goal of ending poverty in all its forms, everywhere?
/02
How can this design contribute to ending hunger and encouraging the transition to sustainable agriculture?
/03
How can this design help ensure healthy lives and well-being for all at all ages?
/04
How can this design support quality education and lifelong learning?
/05
How can this design advance gender equality and the empowerment of women and girls?
/06
How can this design help ensure the sustainable management of water and universal access to sanitation?
/07
How can this design contribute to a sustainable energy transition?
/08
How can this design promote decent work for all?
/09
How can this design advance sustainable industrialization and innovation, especially in those places that do not have access to modern industry?
/10
How can this design help to reduce inequality within and among countries?
/11
How can this design make our cities more inclusive, safe, resilient, and sustainable?
/12
How can this design transform production and consumption patterns, to make them more sustainable?
/13
How can this design be part of the urgent action that is needed to combat climate change and its impacts?
/14
How can this design be part of caring for our oceans and seas?
/15
How can this design help to protect and restore ecosystems and preserve biodiversity?
/16
How can this design contribute to the development peaceful, inclusive, and just societies?
/17
How can this design advance the global partnership needed to achieve all of these goals?

A Call to Action ... for a Sustainable Century
Everyone in the global design and architecture community has a role to play. This new, universal design brief is going to be with us for a long, long time. The SDGs have the year 2030 as their target. But the ideas, solutions, buildings and surroundings envisioned by designers and architects will last far longer. And it will not always be possible to evaluate the success of a design – in terms of the degree to which it meets these new global criteria, and answers these 17 questions – at its inception.
Designers and architects will need to continuously review and evaluate the impact of their designs, sometimes decades after they were first conceived. Designers and architects who accept this new responsibility are essentially making a life-long commitment to bring a sense of care for the whole world to every design project they undertake, and to a process of life-long learning about what designs do, or do not, contribute to "Transforming Our World: The 2030 Agenda for Sustainable Development."

Making the Commitment
By signing this document, we who work as designers and architects, employ designers and/or architects, or in any way use, have connection with or organize the professions of design and architecture, are declaring that we accept this "commission" from the global community.

We adopt the 2030 Agenda as a new design brief for the creation of a sustainable world. We commit to considering all 17 of the Sustainable Development Goals in every project or review or commission we undertake. We commit to promoting the universal adoption of the SDGs by others in our profession, by our clients – and by the generation of designers and architects coming after us. /

E 055 ←
→ E 256

162 The Last Whole Earth Catalog, 1972

Bibliographic information:
The Last Whole Earth Catalog, USA, 1971

Image sources:
(1) the front cover of the catalog; (2) detail from page 351;
(3) excerpt from 003; (4) page 52/53; (5) page 154/155

Text sources:
(A) https://de.wikipedia.org/wiki/Whole_Earth_Catalog; (see sources)
(B) Texts from page 002 of the catalog

(A) / The Whole Earth Catalog was an American counterculture magazine and product catalog. It was published between 1968 and 1972 (...) The catalog featured essays and articles, but primarily concentrated on product evaluations. Its main focus lay on self-sufficiency, ecology, alternative pedagogy, DIY, and holism. (...)
The catalog shaped and spread many approaches that are associated with the 1960s and 1970s today, such as counterculture and the environmental movement. Later issues influenced the 1970s to 1990s. Steve Jobs, the founder of Apple Inc., referred to the catalog as his generation's bible and as an analog predecessor of online search engines like Google. He quoted the catalog's call to "Stay hungry, stay foolish." /

(B) / Function

The WHOLE EARTH CATALOG functions as an evaluation and access device. With it, the user should know better what is worth getting and where and how to do the getting.
An item is listed in the CATALOG if it is deemed:
1) Useful as a tool,
2) Relevant to independent education,
3) High quality or low cost,
4) Easily available by mail.
CATALOG listings are continually revised according to the experience and suggestions of CATALOG users and staff.

Purpose

We are as gods and might as well get good at it. So far remotely done power and glory – – as via government, big business, formal education, church – – has succeeded to point where gross defects obscure actual gains.
In response to this dilemma and to these gains a realm of intimate, personal power is developing – – power of the individual to conduct his own education, find his own inspiration, shape his own environment, and share his adventure with whoever is interested. Tools that aid this process are sought and promoted by the WHOLE EARTH CATALOG.
This issue of the CATALOG is the last. We encourage others to initiate similar services to fill the vacuum in the economy we stumbled into and are stepping out of. We don't see how using our name or copy can aid

(1)

originality, so they're not available, for love or money. Ideas we've had and evaluations we've made are free for recycling.

Preparation of the CATALOG was done on an IBM Selectric Composer and Polaroid MP-3 Camera.
Printing by: Nowels Publications, Menlo Park, California
Deven Lithographers, Inc., Long Island City, New York

For credits and How to Make a WHOLE EARTH CATALOG AND TRUCK STORE, see p. 434.
1st Printing June 1971 – 200 000.

(Rental: $110)

(Rental: $65)

Cool Hand Luke (Rental $65.00)

(2)

(3)

Understanding Whole Systems

Buckminster Fuller

The insights of Buckminster Fuller initiated this catalog.

Among his books listed here, **Utopia or Oblivion** *is now probably the most direct introduction. It's a collection of his talks and papers from 1964 to 1967, at a bargain price.* **An Operating Manual for Spaceship Earth** *is his most recent, and succinct, statement.* **Nine Chains to the Moon** *is early, and openly metaphysical.* **The Untitled Epic of Industrialization** *is lyrical and strong.* **Ideas and Integrities** *is his most autobiographical, and perhaps the most self-contained of his books.* **No More Secondhand God** *is the most generalized, leading into the geometry of thought.*

People who beef about Fuller mainly complain about his repetition––the same ideas again and again, it's embarrassing, also illuminating, because the same notions take on different contexts. Fuller's lectures have a raga quality of rich nonlinear endless improvisation full of convergent surprises.

Some are put off by his language, which makes demands on your head like suddenly discovering an extra engine in your car––if you don't let it drive you faster, it'll drag you. Fuller won't wait. He spent two years silent after illusory language got him in trouble, and he returned to human communication with a redesigned instrument.

–SB

Operating Manual for Spaceship Earth
Buckminster Fuller
1969; 133pp.

$1.25 postpaid

from:
Pocket Books, Inc.
1 W. 39th St.
New York, N.Y. 10018

or WHOLE EARTH CATALOG

To comprehend this total scheme we note that long ago a man went through the woods, as you may have done, and I certainly have, trying to find the shortest way through the woods in a given direction. He found trees fallen across his path. He climbed over those crisscrossed trees and suddenly found himself poised on a tree that was slowly teetering. It happened to be lying across another great tree, and the other end of the tree on which he found himself teetering lay under a third great fallen tree. As he teetered he saw the third big tree lifting. It seemed impossible to him. He went over and tried using his own muscles to lift that great tree. He couldn't budge it. Then he climbed back atop the first smaller tree, purposefully teetering it, and surely enough it again elevated the larger tree. I'm certain that the first man who found such a tree thought that it was a magic tree, and may have dragged it home and erected it as man's first totem. It was probably a long time before he learned that any stout tree would do, and thus extracted the concept of the generalized principle of leverage out of all his earlier successive special-case experiences with such accidental discoveries.

•

To begin our position-fixing aboard our Spaceship Earth we must first acknowledge that the abundance of immediately consumable, obviously desirable or utterly essential resources have been sufficient until now to allow us to carry on despite our ignorance. Being eventually exhaustible and spoilable, they have been adequate only up to this critical moment. This cushion-for-error of humanity's survival and growth up to now was apparently provided just as a bird inside of the egg is provided with liquid nutriment to develop it to a certain point. But then by design the nutriment is exhausted at just the time when the chick is large enough to be able to locomote on its own legs. And so as the chick pecks at the shell seeking more nutriment it inadvertently breaks open the shell.

•

A new, physically uncomprised, metaphysical initiative of unbiased integrity could unify the world. It could and probably will be provided by the utterly impersonal problem solutions of the

Craftool

More than other craft suppliers, this outfit has whole-system supplies. A spinning wheel as well as looms. Various hand presses. A whole paper-making mill ($3,650). And the best line we've seen of beginning kits. —SB

[Suggested by Julia Brand and Cynthia Mathews]

Catalog

$1.00

from:
The Craftool Company
1 Industrial Road
Woodbridge, New Jersey 07075

Woodworking/Craft Kit $79.95 ✦
Gem Stone/Tumbling & Jewelry Making Kit $24.95
Batik/Fabric Dyeing Kit $24.95
Bookbinder's Repair Kit $14.95
Clay Modeling & Sculpture Kit $24.95
Woodcarving & Sculpture Kit $34.95
Graphic Arts/Etching & Block Printing Kit $49.95
Jewelry Making Kit $59.95
Stone/Sculpture Kit $34.95
Printing Press/Outfit $99.95

The ART PRESS
$159.50

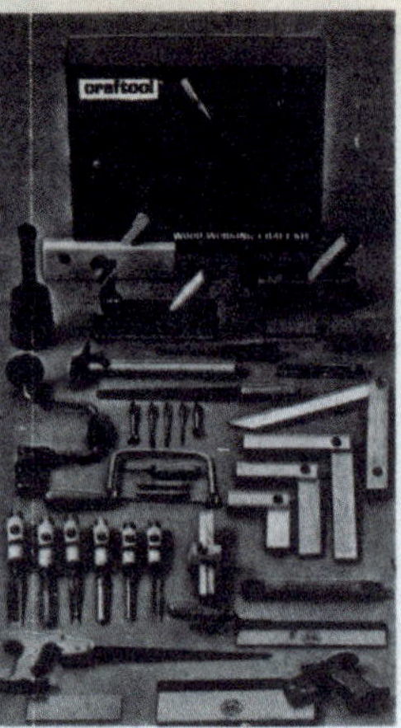

CRAFTOOL COMPLETE BOOKBINDING OUTFIT

All the basic equipment and tools necessary for the bookbinding craftsman.

Standing Press 1450-8	Shears	Drills
Stitching Frame 1380-8	Needles	Nipper
Lying Press 1560-AZ	Backing Hammer	Glue Brush
Book Saw	Hand Drill	Bone Folder
Book on "Bookbinding"	2 Knives	Wax

No. 28008 — Complete with laminated top bench 24" x 48" x 32" high $248.00

No. 2801-LB — Tools and equipment only — less bench and top $215.00

Sax Art Supplies

Big catalog, sort of school oriented, wide range of ar craft supplies.

[Suggested by Karen Shu

Catalog

$1.00

from:
Sax Arts & Crafts
207 N. Milwaukee St.
Milwaukee, Wisconsin 53202

BATIK FORMULA WAX
Special formula wax.
No. 12738. . . . . . . $1.
10 or more lbs. . . . . 1.
50 or more lbs. . . . . 1.

STONEWARE CLAY CONES 4–8.
A true stoneware clay, when fired at the recommended temperature of Cones 4 to 8 bisque, is a warm buff peppered throughout with dark specks. Interesting textures. Amaco High Fire Glaze recommended for this stoneware body. Specify No. 48-M (Moist) or No. 48-D (Dry).

5 lbs. $1.00
50 lbs. $6.50

5158

5159

Arts & Crafts

This catalog looks like it's more for the school trade. Good prices on a wide range of tools and materials. —SB

[Suggested by Mrs. W. B. Mohin]

Catalog

free

from:
CCM: Arts & Crafts, Inc.
321 Park Avenue
Baltimore, Maryland 21201

CONTENTS

List of Major Classifications

MOULAGE

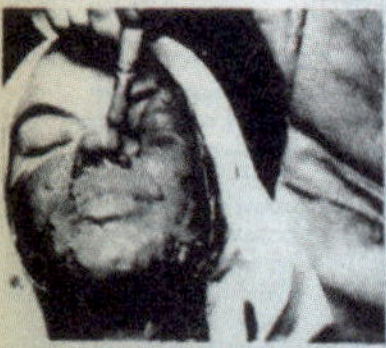

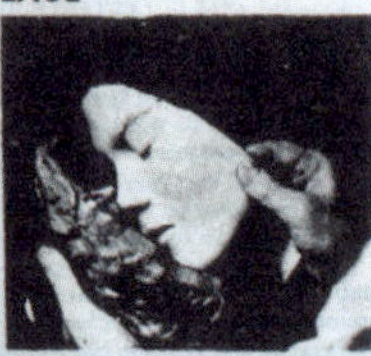

A mold material for taking impressions from life—for reproducing valued antiques when an ancient patina must be preserved, too delicate to submit to being molded in plaster, rubber or gelatine. Moulage will not adhere to anything—molds can be made on human hair or the most delicate skin. Apply warm with brush and palette knife. Captures minutest details. Reuse it approximately 150 times. Complete instructions helps beginners succeed on first project.
No. 7678 Moulage, per 2 lb. can..................................**$4.95**

Art Consultants

Stuff for sculpture and ceramics. —SB

Catalog

free

from:
Art Consultants
97 Saint Marks Pl.
New York, N.Y. 10009

$1.50 ea.

Hand Forged Stone Carving Chisels

Professional tools forged of finest steel, tempered for marble, limestone, sandstone. Sculpture House craftsmen know how to forge and temper cutting edges that last and last; for this reason professional carvers purchase Sculpture House tools exclusively. Order by number.

#BAZ Basic Carving Set Tools Nos. 1, 6, 9, 11, 13 plus H-17 Hammer $9.50

#1AZ Complete Set of 15 Tools plus H-20 .... 23.95

Average Length 8 inches

D-A MONZINI

1 quart (including hardener) ....
1 gallon (including hardener) ...
5 gallons (including hardener) ...

D-A MONZINI FILLER
For adding to D-A MONZINI w thicker consistency is desired and tial build-up.

1 lb. package ....
5 lb. package ....

GENUINE PULVERIZED BRONZE
For fusing to final surface of D-A ZINI or other material.

1 lb. can ....
5 lb. can ....
10 lb. can ....

12 FOOT DOLPHIN MADE WITH D-A MONZINI

Handcraft House

A western Canada supplier. Leclere looms, Indian spinners, procion dyes, oils, brushes, books. —SB

Northwest Handcraft House Ltd.
110 West Esplanade
North Vancouver, B.C.
Canada

CIBALAN DYES FOR WOOL

Blue 8G (Turquoise) all prices for 1 oz.	.65
Blue BRL	.90
Brilliant Blue GL	.95
Kiton Red B2R (HOt Pink)	.55
Red 2 GL	.80
Brilliant Red BL	1.00

Craft Tool Plans

You do not seem to hit the pattern sources, I suppose your reade don't really need these detailed plans like my readers do. But on example will suffice perhaps——For $2 one can secure a detailed, dimensioned plan to build a 4-harness, 6-treadle jack loom. Patte Catalog No. 396 and it includes a materials list. Order from Mr. Rockler, Craftplans, 8011 Lewis Road, Minneapolis, Minnesota 55427. A catalog showing the plans he has patterns for is availab for 25 cents, same address. He includes three types of spinning wheels and a sundial packet as well as the more usual jig-sawn jiggers and clocks and more or less standard subjects like bars of little interest to Whole Earth people. But for a catalog of plans I'd put Craft Patterns Studio, Elmhurst, Illinois 60126 first on th list——they have more in greater variety and though their catalog is more (50 cents the last time I heard from them) their plans are generally cheaper.

Lura LaBarge
Newton, New Jersey

[Step]-by-Step Craft Series

[Th]e, low-priced series of introductory craft books. [Each] one has a thorough list of relevant periodicals, [book]s, material suppliers, and schools which give courses [in th]e subject. It's an intelligent way to begin——light, [quic]k, and real.
—SB

[Suggested by Jan McClain]

[Step-]by-Step Jewelry
[Thom]as Gentille
[1968]; 96 pp.
[$2.]50 postpaid

[Step-]by-Step Weaving
[Nell] Znamierowski
[1967]; 96 pp.
[$2.]50 postpaid

Step-by-Step Macramé
Mary Walker Phillips
1970; 80 pp.
$2.50 postpaid

Step-by-Step Printmaking
Erwin Schachner
1970; 80 pp.
$2.50 postpaid

from:
Golden Press Division
Western Publishing Co., Inc.
850 Third Avenue
New York, N. Y. 10022

or WHOLE EARTH CATALOG

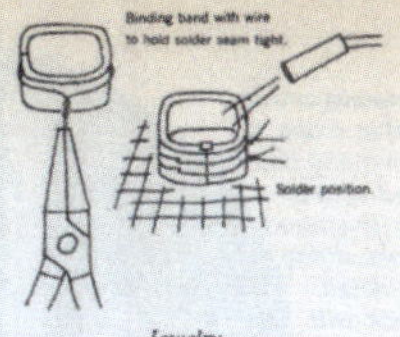

Jewelry

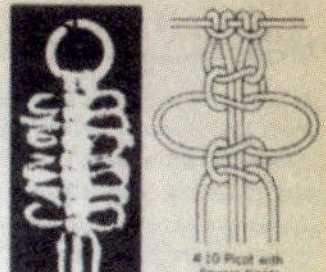

Macramé

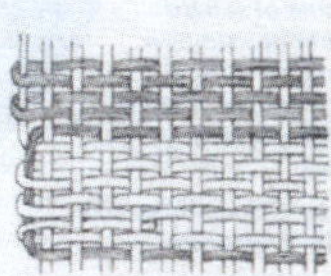

Weaving

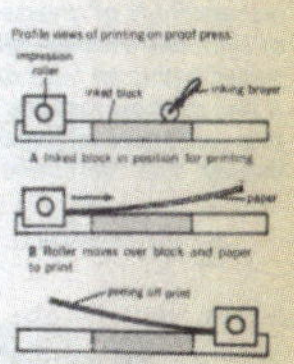

Printmaking

[C]raft

[An exce]llent catalog of tools and materials for jewelry work [and e]nameling. Also stained glass.
—SB

[Catal]og
[Free]0

[Allcra]ft Tool & Supply Co.
[215 Pa]rk Ave.
[Hicks]ville, N.Y. 11801

	No.	
○	108	○
○	112	○
○	124	▯
○	143	▭
▽	208	△
○	164	▽
▽	169	○
▭	170	○
○	16	○

1H-16 HOME WORKSHOP OR SCHOOL GRADE
Available in styles 5, 6, 7, 10, 17, 101, 181, 126, 108, 112, 208, 16. $1.75 each

E4-469
MORTARS AND PESTLES for grinding enamels to a consistency for painting and special effects.
a. Wedgewood 3½" dia. $5.15
b. Wedgewood 4" " $5.55
c. Wedgewood 5" " $6.45

3A-1 Chasing Tools
$14.00 Set of 25

$2.55
FORMING HAMMER - 4-1/8", flat face 1", round face 1" - 3/4 lb.

E4-753
BROKEN GLASS ASSORTMENT
Random sized pieces ranging up to approximately 3" x 2". Each assortment contains 12 or more colors. $1.50 2 lb. box

$149.50
Shown with 3-jaw Chuck

[Dixo]n Tools & Supplies

[A bea]utifully engraved hard cover catalog of splendid [jewele]r's and engraver's tools. (See also p. 142.)
—SB

[William] Dixon, Inc.
[Carlsta]dt, New Jersey 07072

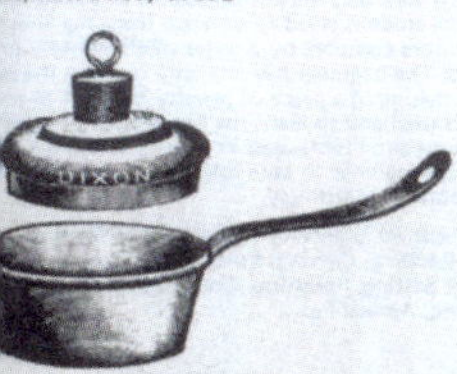

Fig. 156-2
COPPER BOILING CUP
[... dia]meter by 1" height; furnished with [an]d without cover.
[No. 1] With Cover No. 2 Without Cover

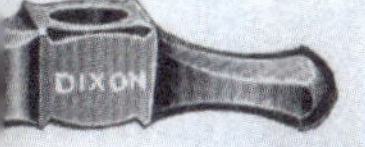

No. 15, ¾" Face $2.35

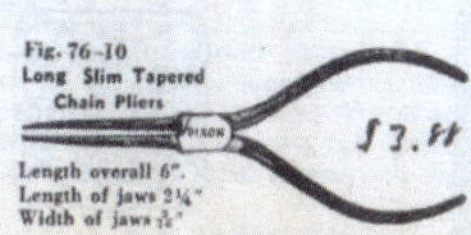

Fig. 76-10
Long Slim Tapered Chain Pliers
$3.84
Length overall 6".
Length of jaws 2¼"
Width of jaws $\frac{3}{32}$"
A fine plier for reaching difficult places. Jaws make it adaptable for electronics.

Otto Frei

Jeweler's and engraver's supplies.
—SB

Otto Frei-Jules Borel Inc.
Box 796
Oakland, CA 94612

PEER MAGNIFIERS
Imported high quality magnifiers with specially corrected lenses that give good distortion free viewing.

No.	Style	Working Distance	Power	Price
22-011	Doublet	1"	10X	$5.10
22-016	Coddington	¼"	15X	6.00

ANTI-RUST SOAP
Prevents rust caused by perspiration from your hands. Simply wash hands twice daily using this soap.

No.	Description	Each
52-771	Cake	$0.90

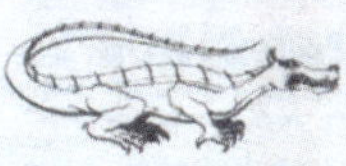

GOING THROUGH CHANGES

The I Ching was what was happening. Estelle took three pennies out of her bag, handed them to D.R., then turned back to her book. The way she did it, the way she fished in her bag for the coins and handed them to him as if he was collecting for the Heart Fund or something, infuriated D.R. He came close to throwing the coins right in her face. His next impulse was to jerk the book out of her hand and fling it across the room.

Fuck it! he yelled inside his mind. Fuck it!

In the bedroom with the door shut D.R. took his place on the mattress again and worked at cooling his mind with some of the breathing exercises the Greek had taught him. He tried to do alternate nostril breathing but he was so stirred up he didn't have enough patience to hold his breath for sixteen counts. Bellows breathing was easier. Huffing and puffing, doing them in sets of twenty, then twenty-five and finally thirty-five, D.R. stoned himself on breathing, his mind joined him on the mattress and at last he felt cool enough to toss the coins.

He didn't feel that way long. The first goddamn throw came up fucking Stagnation and he didn't want to read about it. He knew it was a sin not to accept the reading but he didn't give a shit. He threw the coins again. It came up Adversity and Weariness. He threw them again. It was The Estranged this time. Opposites. Fuck opposites. He threw them again. It was Ku, Decay, with changes in the third, fifth and sixth nines which gave him Abysmal, The Abyss. Fuck it. It was Eddie's I Ching, it was Eddie's room, fuck it, Eddie's dead, and Divine Right threw the book across the room, then burst into the living room and told Estelle to get off her ass, they were going to the Western Union office.

Estelle looked up at D.R., half expecting to be afraid. But she wasn't. She got up and went out with him, but she definitely wasn't afraid.

E 055 ←
→ E 257

163 Anonymous: Rules of the Internet

Bibliographic information of the recommended book:
"Texte zur Theorie des Internets," Tilman Baumgärtel (Ed.); Reclam Verlag, Ditzingen, 2017; [in German]
ISBN 978-3-15-019476-8

Text sources: (1) Ulysses Voelker; (2) https://rulesoftheinternet.com/ (see sources)

Website:
https://en.wikipedia.org/wiki/Anonymous_(hacker_group)

(1) The group "Anonymous" comprises a worldwide network of participants and has neither a consistent political philosophy nor a central chain of command. Anonymous gained fame with high-publicity hacks and attacks on networks and websites of institutions and companies. These activities didn't just take place online, but were often accompanied by actions in the public sphere. One of its trademarks was the Guy Hawkes mask, borrowed from the movie "V for Vendetta." The loose structure of this hacker network is both a strength and a weakness – because aside from the flexibility and de-centrality, another characteristic of Anonymous is that its statements strongly fluctuate in terms of impact direction, coherence, and rhetoric. The "Rules of the Internet," which have been attributed to Anonymous, reflect this vagueness inherent to this organization, since every Internet user can modify them as they please. The "Rules" represent a network-typical mixture of political ambitions and nonsense demands and have a fluid character. (u.v)

' **Rules of the Internet**

1. Do not talk about /b/.
2. Do NOT talk about /b/.
3. We are Anonymous.
4. Anonymous is legion.
5. Anonymous never forgives.
6. Anonymous can be a horrible senseless, uncaring monster.
7. Anonymous is still able to deliver.
8. There are no real rules about posting.
9. There are no real rules about moderation either – enjoy your ban.
10. If you enjoy any rival sites – DON'T.
11. All your carefully picked arguments can easily be ignored.
12. Anything you say can and will be used against you.
13. Anything you say can be turned into something else – fixed.
14. Do not argue with trolls – it means that they win.
15. The harder you try the harder you will fail.
16. If you fail in epic proportions, it may just become a winning failure.
17. Every win fails eventually.
18. Everything that can be labeled can be hated.
19. The more you hate it the stronger it gets.
20. Nothing is to be taken seriously.
21. Original content ist original only for a few seconds before getting old.
22. Copypasta is made to ruin every last bit of originality.
23. Copypasta is made to ruin every last bit of originality.
24. Every repost is always a repost of a repost.
25. Relation to the original topic decreases with every single post.
26. Any topic can easily be turned into something totally unrelated.
27. Always question a person's sexual preferences without any real reason.
28. Always question a person's gender – just in case it's really a man.
29. In the internet all girls are men and all kids are undercover FBI agents.
30. There are no girls on the internet.
31. TITS or GTFO – the choice is yours.
32. You must have pictures to prove your statements.
33. Lurk more – it's never enough.
34. There is porn of it, no exceptions.
35. If no porn is found at the moment, it will be made.
36. There will always be even more fucked up shit than what you just saw.
37. You can not divide by zero (just because the calculator says so).
38. No real limits of any kind apply here – not even the sky.
39. CAPSLOCK IS CRUISE CONTROL FOR COOL.
40. EVEN WITH CRUISE CONTROL YOU STILL HAVE TO STEER.
41. Desu isn't funny. Seriously guys. It's worse than Chuck Norris jokes.
42. Nothing is sacred.
43. The more beautiful und pure a thing is – the more satisfying it is to corrupt it.
44. Even one positive comment about Japanese things can make you a weaboo.
45. When one sees a lion, one must get into the car.
46. There is always furry porn of it.
47. The pool is always closed. '

E 057.2 ←
→ E 258

164 3D printing projects

Image source:
https://en.wikipedia.org/wiki/Liberator_%28gun%29#/media/File:DDLiberator2.3.jpg
(see sources)

Websites:
https://en.wikipedia.org/wiki/3D_printing
https://en.wikipedia.org/wiki/Cody_Wilson
https://www.sueddeutsche.de/politik/halle-attentat-3d-drucker-waffe-1.4988996

3D printing (also called additive manufacturing) is a production process that can create three-dimensional objects. These are built layer by layer with selectable raw materials (solid or liquid). The process is controlled via a computer. In the early days of the technology, the choice of material was restricted to plastics, but in the meantime, the use of ceramics, specially prepared metals, or carbon materials is also feasible. The application possibilities of 3D printers have grown continually over the last years. Now they are not only used in model construction, but in almost all production areas – to create models, medical prostheses, patterns, tools, and prototypes. Interesting projects are described on the Internet – including bridges, bicycles, and houses. 3D printing has also established itself in the world of art, particularly to create sculptures and reliefs.

However, the use of 3D printers is not conflict-free, which is due to the choice of the object to be printed and the creators themselves.

In 2013, for example, the 3D-printed weapon produced by American Cody Wilson caused a stir – he made the blueprints available on the Internet for free. Weapon detectors could not identify the weapon. Wilson considers himself a "Libertarian" and "crypto anarchist." In 2012, he founded "Defense Distributed" with the goal of freely distributing weapon blueprints. Initially, the American authorities allowed him to do so. As a result, the blueprints were downloaded 100,000 times. Although they have been banned in the meantime, the plans can still be accessed online and used to produce weapons.

A Neo-Nazi in Halle (Germany) achieved a sad kind of fame in 2019 when he tried to storm the local synagogue with homemade weapons. After failing at this attempt, he shot two people outside of the place of worship. Beforehand, the perpetrator had not only spread Nazi propaganda on the Internet, but also delivered instructions for building weapons.

In the meantime, the discussion on ethical and legislative guidelines to keep this technology in check form part of the political discourse. These efforts stand in contrast to the all-in-all honorable ground rules of the *Maker movement*, whose principles include sharing blueprints and all kinds of expertise. It will be difficult to draw ethical and legislative lines that divide the online world into good and evil. (u.v)

The "Liberator" gun from the 3D printer

E 057.2 ←
→ E 259

165 Sharing economy

Text source:
https://wirtschaftslexikon.gabler.de/definition/sharing-economy-53876/version-384536 (see sources)

I have taken the definition from Gabler's online lexicon and briefly summarized it here. I recommend reading the full version. (u.v)

ʹ(...) General
The term "sharing economy" (or "shared economy") refers to the systematic lending of objects and mutual provision of objects, rooms, and spaces, particularly through private individuals or interest groups. The term "share economy" is used synonymously or – in addition to the original definition by Martin Weitzman – means sharing information and knowledge.

Goals and characteristics
According to the idea of the economy of sharing, those asking for an object should not make it their own, but only use, inhabit, and cultivate it temporarily. Of course, the prerequisite of this is usually the property of a provider. The focus lies on collaborative consumption. The goods change owners, for as long as they are usable or available. The owner is generally responsible for maintenance.

Platforms
Electronic platforms and social networks allow users to reach a wide market, offer and respond at short notice, and achieve optimal usage and capacity. Some platforms focus on apartment and land sharing, while others offer variants such as book and jewelry sharing. Exchange or donation platforms also form part of the ever-growing landscape. Using social media functions, users can rate demanders and providers and thereby sanction vandalism and misuse.

Criticism and outlook
From an economic perspective, the economy of sharing is viewed critically, but also used productively. For example, car sharing is very popular in some countries and operated by cooperatives and companies. In addition, private cars are being converted into public taxis, and drivers and passengers find each other via apps. Criticism is directed at the users – as primarily those who have access to the virtual world are the ones who can also access the sharing economy, which, using the terms of informational ethics, leads to a digital divide, or digital or informational injustice. If we take a look at the intermediaries, it is striking that these can shake up entire industries with their platforms alone, without owning their apartments, vehicles, content, etc. This "platform capitalism" (Sascha Lobo) can be picked up by informational and business ethics. One positive aspect is that these platforms protect the environment and encourage more conscious and social consumption. The sharing economy experiences a boost in times of crisis; at the same time, it serves as an expression of the experience and hedonist society. (...)ʹ

E 057.2 ←
→ E 259

165.1 Local sharing platforms

Recommended Website: https://nextdoor.com/#neighbors

Countless sharing platforms exist today. Some have established themselves and – like Airbnb or uber – have matured into market-leading company constructs. Others are consciously focused on regional circumstances and aim to serve the community. Inserting a list at this point would be prohibited based on the dynamic that prevails in the sharing sector alone. New, interesting, and innovative solutions are constantly emerging, while others simply disappear. Many examples that can be researched on the Internet show how sharing platforms present themselves, what goals they are often pursuing, and how they combine digital communication with analog requirements – these range from neighborhood assistance to repair cafes. The impacts of neighborly interactions should not be underestimated. They reduce loneliness in old age, lead to new friendships, and help people recycle – not to mention save money.
One example is the commercial network nebenan.de, which, as a local platform, aims to replace what once existed in the form of a marketplace or local café – places to meet and help each other (nebenan.de is majority owned by Hubert Burda Media). While users can take advantage of the sharing platform for free, critics warn that they might be paying for it with their data (which the platform could sell).

Those who are suspicious of commercial neighborhood platforms will surely find others in their local region. (eds.)

E 057.2 ←
→ E 259

166 Internet Archive

Text source:
https://archive.org/about/ (see sources)

Further information: https://blog.archive.org/2023/12/15/internet-archive-defends-digital-rights-for-libraries

ʹAbout the Internet Archive
The Internet Archive, a 501(c)(3) non-profit, is building a digital library of Internet sites and other cultural artifacts in digital form. Like a paper library, we provide free access to researchers, historians, scholars, people with print disabilities, and the general public. Our mission is to provide Universal Access to All Knowledge.
We began in 1996 by archiving the Internet itself, a medium that was just beginning to grow in use. (...)

As our web archive grew, so did our commitment to providing digital versions of other published works. Today (2024/1) our archive contains:
- 735 billion web pages
- 41 million books and texts
- 14,7 million audio recordings (including 240,000 live concerts)
- 8,4 million videos (including 2,4 million Television News programs)
- 4,4 million images
- 890,000 software programs

Anyone with a free account can upload media to the Internet Archive. We work with thousands of partners globally to save copies of their work into special collections.

Because we are a library, we pay special attention to books. Not everyone has access to a public or academic library with a good collection, so to provide universal access we need to provide digital versions of books. We began a program to digitize books in 2005 and today we scan 4,000 books per day in 18 locations around the world. Books published prior to 1927 are available for download, and hundreds of thousands of modern books can be borrowed through our Open Library site. One of the Internet Archive's missions is to serve people who have difficulty interacting with physical books, so most of our digitized books are available to people with print disabilities (learn about access here). Like the Internet, television is also an ephemeral medium.
We began archiving television programs in late 2000, and our first public TV project was an archive of TV news surrounding the events of September 11, 2001. In 2009 we began to make selected U.S. television news broadcasts searchable by captions in our TV News Archive. This service allows researchers and the public to use television as a citable and sharable reference. (...)ʹ

E 057.2 ←
→ E 259

167 Texte zur Theorie des Internets

Bibliographic information:
"Texte zur Theorie des Internets", Tilman Baumgärtel (ed.);
Reclam Verlag, Ditzingen, 2017; [in German]
ISBN 978-3-15-019476-8

Life without the Internet is unimaginable these days, especially for those who work in professions like design. In the early days of the Internet, many hoped that it would (finally) provide a space for authority-free communication. This hope is long gone and has given way to the realization that goals of monopolies and manipulation are most certainly on the agenda anywhere one can make money and exert political influence. While the character of the Internet has changed over the course of its existence and this focus on process essentially forms part of its DNA, we interact on social media platforms, acquire information, and present ourselves – without taking a step back and consciously observing what reflexes we are actually following and which smart analyses might give us food for thought. The recommended book "Texte zur Theorie des Internets" ("Texts on the Theory of the Internet") might be of help here.
It features a collection of articles on the topic of the Internet. The collection is divided into the chapters *Programme und Manifeste* (Programs and Manifestos), *Gesellschaft und Philosophie* (Society and Philosophy), *Ökonomie* (Economy), *Politik* (Politics), *Psychologie* (Psychology), and *Kunst und Kultur* (Art and Culture). The authors discuss hacker ethics, collective intelligence, the attention economy, post privacy, memes and big data, Internet art, and Post-Internet art, to name a few keywords.
According to Tilman Baumgärtel, the book's editor, the book gives "the most important voices" a platform. (eds.)

E 060 ←
→ E 260

168 Ästhetisches Denken

Bibliographic information:
"Ästhetisches Denken," Wolfgang Welsch, Reclam Verlag, Ditzingen, 2010; [in German]
ISBN 978-3-15-019472-0

Text source:
page 231, line 05 – page 232, line 23

Wolfgang Welsch (*1946) is a German philosopher who published numerous contributions on postmodern aesthetics and their cultural role. The following quote stems from a collection of essays first published in 1990 and was taken from a revised and extended 8th edition (2017). His outlook on the consequences of postmodernism in connection with the pending problems is astonishingly accurate. (eds.)

ʼ (...) 3. Outlook
I believe that our present time will be determined by two major trends in the foreseeable future: postmodernism and ecological challenges. And I also think that design can become the intersection between these two trends. This certainly calls for an expanded definition of design, which I will address again at the end. Today, we can recognize that all human activity – from the "designs" of big politics to family life, and from our traffic systems through to fleeting gestures and momentary perceptions – includes elements of design. The scope of design is not exhausted by the object design, but already starts with the establishment of living conditions and shaping of forms of behavior. From a postmodern perspective, all of these conscious and unconscious forms of production and behavior will require redesign. The transitional period in which we live is the time of redesign on all levels. In addition, the ecological challenges also necessitate a restructuring of all or our living conditions, ranging from global economic and political problems through to the most personal living circumstances. An expanded design becomes eminently significant for this redesign.
That is why a convergence exists between the postmodern cultural demands and the ecological challenges. The global ecological tasks can only be resolved in the broader sense by means of a new design: with a different design of the economy, international relations, the individual relationship with nature. The postmodern shift away from ideas of control, centrality, and anthropocentrism and the postmodern focus on external consequences of actions are congruent with such demands of ecology. The transition from object design to framework design, as proposed by postmodernism, also corresponds with the demands of ecology. And the assignment of design is now increasingly shifting to framework design (which modernism had focused on). We must – on both a postmodern and ecological level – change the framework conditions of our living conditions.
In the sense of this expanded definition of design, the 21st century could be a century of design – while the 20th century was a century of art. ʼ

E 060 ←
→ E 260

169 Pierre & Gilles

Bibliographic information:
"Pierre et Gilles," Taschen Verlag, 1993; [in German]
ISBN 3-8228-9377-3

Image source: the book's front cover

Recommended websites:
https://en.wikipedia.org/wiki/Pierre_et_Gilles
https://de-de.facebook.com/PierreetGillesPageOfficielle/photos/

"Pierre et Gilles" is the name of a homosexual artist couple consisting of Pierre Commoy (*1950) and Gilles Blanchard (*1953) from France. The two photographers rose to fame with their complex studio portraits. With costumes and plastic backgrounds, they created settings critics considered to be kitsch, in both a positive and negative sense. This type of exaggerated presentation is the duo's trademark. Despite or perhaps because of this, the duo has photographed numerous celebrities from the areas of culture, fashion, and pop: for example, Marc Almond, Catherine Deneuve, Serge Gainsbourg, Jean Paul Gaultier, Nina Hagen, Madonna, Siouxsie Sioux, and Paloma Picasso. (...) Stagings of Catholic saints and of children complete their comprehensive body of work. To see for yourself what sets the duo's work apart from the trivial kitsch of roaring stags and embroidery of fiery Andalusians, I recommend taking a look at their work. I believe that *Pierre et Gilles* create a very unique symbiosis of sensibility and theatricality with their photographic work, which often, though not always, elicits amusement as well as deep emotions.
Further information: see the recommended website and particularly the catalogs that show their work. (eds.)

E 060 ←
→ E 260

170 Kitsch! oder: Warum der schlechte Geschmack der eigentlich gute ist

Bibliographic information:
"Kitsch. Texte und Theorien," Uwe Dettmar, Thomas Küpper (Ed.), Reclam Verlag, Ditzingen, 2007; [in German]
ISBN 978-3-15-018476-9

The text refers to a contribution by Konrad Liesmann in the above book

The book "Kitsch. Texte und Theorien" ("Kitsch. Texts and Theories") contains an article by the philosopher Konrad Liesmann (*1953). Titled "Kitsch! oder: Warum der schlechte Geschmack eigentlich der gute ist" ("Kitsch! Or: Why Bad Taste is Actually Good"), the author's contribution discusses his considerations on whether kitsch can be accepted as advanced art. In a somewhat exaggerated way, he claims that, at the latest since Jeff Koons, we have known that kitsch is now avantgarde itself. What counted as kitsch for a long time now forms the peak of aesthetic consciousness. All forms in which kitsch expressed itself, whether rhyming heart with art or creating beseeching angels, were not only absolved from the accusations of mass betrayal, but on the contrary, represent discerning progress. Anyone who hadn't understood this should be considered an incorrigible cultural pessimist and had merely failed to comprehend that poor taste is actually good taste. Art and kitsch coincided in post-postmodernism, according to his analysis in the cited essay from 2002. But if this were the case, then kitsch had changed its meaning: It stopped being an object of public accessibility. Instead, it was up to the expert to decide what art is acceptable and what is out of the question. The ambivalence that arises through the ennoblement of kitsch has consequences, as every avantgarde artist would from now on have to expect that any of their work created by falling back on the techniques of kitsch would be made obsolete by reality or has already become obsolete. In this context, Liessmann mentions the work "Madonna" by the artist duo Pierre et Gilles in order to deduce that an admirer of this work might demonstrate even more expertise if, instead of turning to Pierre et Gilles, they drove straight to Mariazell and purchased a real kitsch Madonna there. Of course, if the original kitsch culture is declared art, an artist would run into the risk of their own kitsch art being downgraded to cheap plagiarism. That is why, in most cases, kitsch is used in art as an ironic and thereby critical citation. But this indirect distancing from kitsch is probably not even necessary, as the "uninhibitedly affirmative kitsch aesthetic of artists such as Pierre et Gilles or Jeff Koons" shows – after all, it seems questionable that their work should be deemed unsuccessful due to a lack or ironic distance. Moreover, precisely the act of forgoing irony could allow the principle of kitsch to unfold its aesthetic potency in art to begin with. Against this background, it is time for an aesthetic re-evaluation of the phenomenon of kitsch. (u.v)

E 062 ←
→ E 261

171 The Barbie doll as a beauty ideal

Image sources: (private images)
(1) © Mattel INC, 1966, Hongkong; (2) © Mattel INC, 1995, China;
(3) © Mattel INC, 1999, China; (4) © Mattel INC, 2010, China;
(5) © Mattel INC, 2015, China; (6) https://commons.wikimedia.org/wiki/File:Barbie_Logo.svg, (see sources)

All Barbies are equal, one might assume. But this is not the case. Aside from the changing clothes and hairstyles, the faces have also transformed. The history of the Barbie doll starts in the 1950s. Ever since, it has served as a seismograph of developments in fashion and society.

More information on the discussions around the figure's proportionality, its controversial status as a role model, and questions on diversity: https://en.wikipedia.org/wiki/Barbie (eds.)

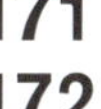

(1) 1966

(2) 1995

(3) 1999

(4) 2010

(5) 2015

Barbie

(6)

The Barbie logo is designed in a way that meets the clichéd idea of lettering for female target groups. This begs the question of what came first – conditioning through design or the female desire for soft shapes and the color pink, which the design follows. In any case, Mattel had no idea that the "Barbie" movie (2023) would link the doll with emancipatory aspects.

E 062 ←
→ E 261

172 BIG JIM as a beauty ideal

Image source (photo: private):
Advertisement from the 1970s, published in a comic book

As is well known, Barbie has a male counterpart – her boyfriend Ken. Market analyses from the 1970s revealed the potential for "more masculine" men. The result is BIG JIM, whose arms could perform various functions (flexing his bicep, gripping hand, "karate" hand). The advertising language and the design target a male audience. This also raises the question of why the figure was successful – whether through conditioning by means of a visual appeal (bearded, well-built men, the logo) or the needs of boys satisfied through the design.

It would be worth taking a more in-depth look at which gender clichés are reproduced on today's toy market and how these have changed since the 1970s. (eds.)

More details on BIG JIM are available at:
https://en.wikipedia.org/wiki/Big_Jim_(toy_line)

BIG JIM
Jungs aufgepaßt!
jetzt mit
NEU!
Festhalthand
Die Abenteuerfigur für Jungen
Brandneu, brandheiß, Jungs!
Achtet auf die neuen
Big Jim Packungen.
Big Jim und seine Freunde
haben jetzt Hände, die alles
richtig festhalten können.
Und nicht vergessen!
Nur Big Jim und seine
Freunde können
1. Karate schlagen
2. Bizeps anschwellen lassen
3. Muskelband sprengen.
BIG JIM
BIG JEFF
BIG JACK
DR. STEEL
FOR AGES OVER 3
BIG JOSH
MATTEL

E 062 ←
→ E 261

173 Schöne Hunde

Bibliographic information:
"Schöne Hunde," Käte Knaur, Marga Ruperti; Albert Müller Verlag, Rüschlikon, Zurich, 1953; [in German]

Image source:
the book's front cover

This cover raises a number of questions that are discussed in "how communication design works":

Is design good if it meets the expectations of the target group? Is unintended kitsch more objectionable than intended kitsch (see reference 170)? Does the typography match the image? Are the colors well chosen? If we view the cover critically – then what would adequate design need to look like?

These questions aren't that easy to answer. At least not if one wants to fulfil the expectations of a dog-loving clientele while at the same time delivering "good" design that lies outside the bounds of kitsch and cliché.

In any case, this scenario takes us into the depths of everyday design – where designers face real challenges. (u.v)

E 064 ←
→ E 262

174 The Grid in Novels

Bibliographic information:
"Structuring Design", Ulysses Voelker, Niggli Verlag, 2019;
ISBN 978-3-7212-0994-5

Text source:
Ulysses Voelker, pages 16 – 17

Image sources:
Graphics by Michael Schmitz, Ulysses Voelker

/ The large illustration shows a type area constructed according to the principle of the golden ratio (see the black dotted lines). The margins are created automatically here.

The ten small illustrations show step by step how the type area was constructed as a double-page spread format.

The type area design according to the golden ratio is rare nowadays, as it produces very large margins, which means an uneconomical use of space.
Nevertheless, the margin proportions (narrowest in the gutter and then dynamically widening above, outside and below) are still applied. /

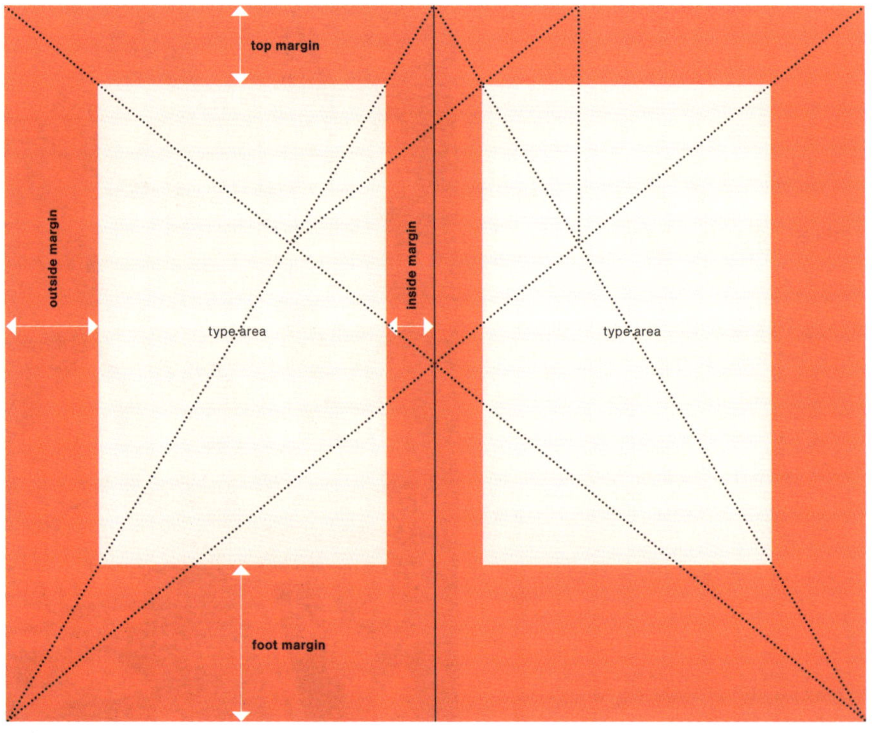

aspect ratio of individual page 1:1.618

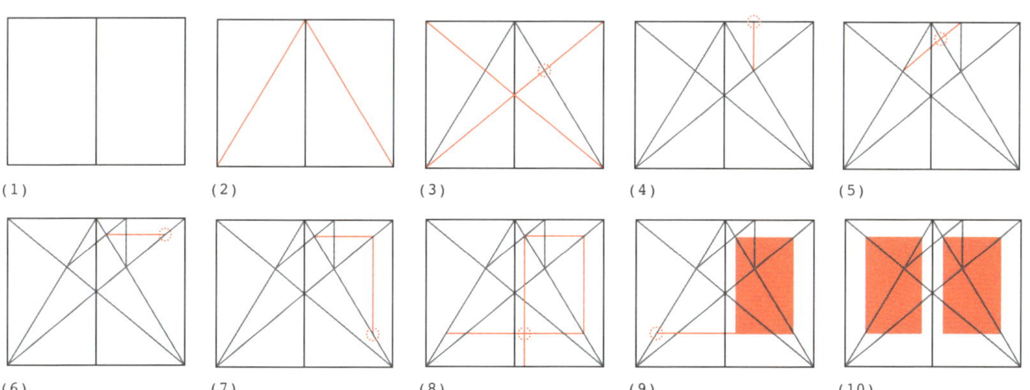

E 064 ←
→ E 262

175 Radiolaria

Text source:
https://de.m.wikipedia.org/wiki/Strahlentierchen (see sources)

Image sources:
(1) – (2): "Kunstformen der Natur," Ernst Haeckel, 1862

(1) https://upload.wikimedia.org/wikipedia/commons/c/c2/Haeckel_Spyroidea.jpg (see sources)
(2) https://upload.wikimedia.org/wikipedia/commons/d/d3/The_royal_natural_history_%281893%29_%2814778597471%29.jpg (see sources)

/ Radiolaria, or radiozoa (radiolaria, Lat. radiolus "little ray"), are a form of single-cell organisms with an opal endoskeleton (silicon dioxide, SiO2) that belong to the eucaryotes.

Radiolaria have cytoplasmic extensions (axopodia) supported from the inside with thin, rigid spikes made of silicon dioxide and microtubule bundles consisting of proteins. The silicon dioxide supports radially extend from the endoskeleton, which also consists of silicon dioxide, made up of a spherical, perforated capsule or several of such capsules concentrically arranged.

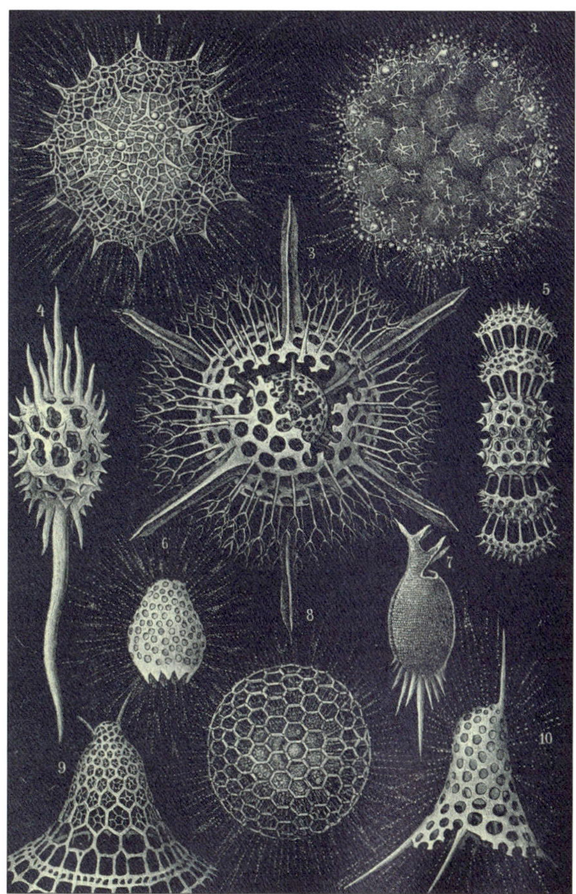

(2)

Radiolaria also have a "pebbly" skeleton that contains organic components in addition to silicon dioxide. Variants from the group of Acantharea are an exception, as they form spikes out of strontium sulphate. Drawings of radiolarian skeletons made by Ernst Haeckel and published in 1862 in the monography "Die Radiolarien" became very well known.

The round or hat-shaped skeletons usually measure between 50 and 500 µm. The axopodia help them float in water and take in food. Radiolaria are heterotrophic and absorb dissolved nutrients from the water or particulate nutrients that get caught in the axopodia. Some types form colonies that are held together by jelly. Within the skeleton capsule you will find mitochondria, the cytoplasm outside of the capsule contains vacuoles (a space filled with fluid and separated by a cytoplasmic membrane). The outer cytoplasm sometimes also absorbs algae as phototrophic symbionts. (...) /

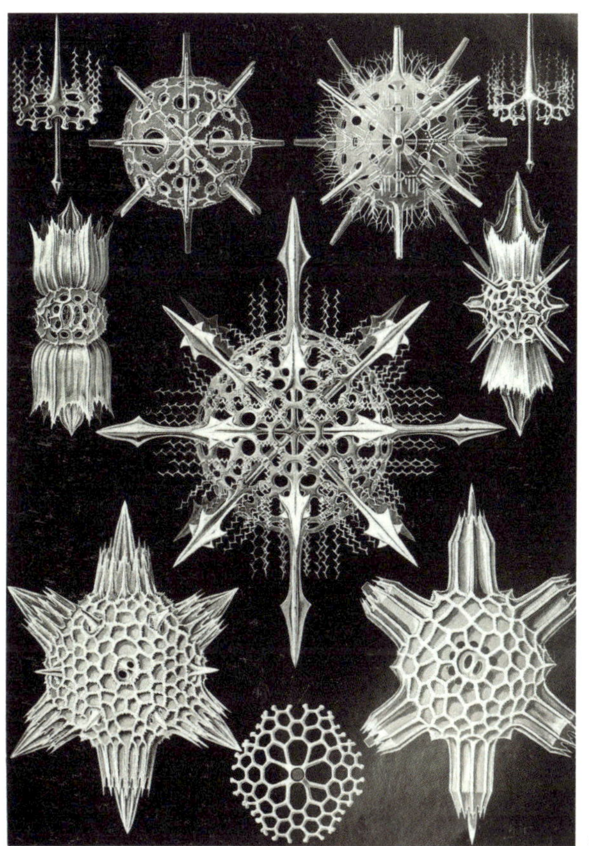

(1)

E 066 ←
→ E 263

176 Tarot

Text source:
https://de.wikipedia.org/wiki/Tarot

Image sources:
(1) Tarot card 9 Wands from the Rider-Waite Tarot deck; https://de.wikipedia.org/wiki/Tarot#/media/Datei: Tarot_Nine_of_Wands.jpg
(2) Tarot card The Lovers from the Rider-Waite Tarot deck; https://de.wikipedia.org/wiki/Tarot#/media/Datei:TheLovers.jpg
(3) Trump II in Tarot de Besançon; https://de.wikipedia.org/wiki/Tarot#/media/Datei:Tarot_de_Besan%C3%A7on_-_Junon.jpg
(all details: see sources)

/ Tarot (...) is a deck of 78 playing cards used for psychological purposes or as fortune-telling cards. It is divided into the Major Arcana, 22 trump cards numbered from 0 to 21, and the Minor Arcana, which includes 56 color cards: ten numbers and four picture cards, each in four colors (e.g., wands, coins, cups, and swords). Arcanum stems from the Latin and means secret, it is derived from arca, meaning box (something that sits in a box is invisible from the outside and therefore secret).

Tarot cards belong to a larger family of tarot playing cards. Up until the late 18th century, they all developed in an identical manner. From this point onward, tarot card decks pictured increasingly symbolic content, as they have been used explicitly as fortune-telling tools ever since. In several languages (including English, French, and Spanish), the word tarot is used synonymously for both fortune-telling and tarot game cards.

"Origin of the word tarot"
One thing is certain: The word tarot stems from the French and is the name of a card game that is also called tarocchi (Italian), Tarock (German), or troccas (Rhaeto-Romanic). In the Italian, German, and Rhaeto-Romanic versions, the trumps have the same name: (...) the word tarocchi is synonymous with the word trump. In the French-speaking region, this is not the case. It cannot be fully clarified whether tarot has the same roots as tarocchi and Tarock. (...) /

(1)

(2)

(3)

E 067 ←
→ E 264

177 A comparison of blackletter fonts

Image source:
Left: https://de.wikipedia.org/wiki/Gebrochene_Schrift#/media/Datei:Gebrochene_Schriften.png (see sources)
Below: https://de.wikipedia.org/wiki/Gebrochene_Schrift#/media/Datei:Gebrochene_Schriften_klein.png (see sources)

Recommended books:
(1) "Fraktur. Form und Geschichte der gebrochenen Schriften," Albert Kapr; with contributions by Hans Peter Willberg and Friedrich Forssman; Verlag Hermann Schmidt, Mainz, 1993; [in German]
ISBN 978-3-8743-9260-0
(2) "Schriften erkennen," Daniel Sauthoff, Gilmar Wendt, Hans Peter Willberg; Verlag Hermann Schmidt, Mainz, 2011; [in German]
ISBN 978-3-8743-9373-7

Blackletter fonts are based on the Latin alphabet and characterized by special features: The arcs of the letters are "broken" through abrupt changes in direction, meaning they display visible bends in their lines. This is one difference to Antiqua fonts, whose letters appear even due to the fluid writing movements. Blackletter fonts held an equal position alongside Antiqua fonts for many centuries in Central and Western Europe. Just like the latter, they changed over time. In the 15th century, the initial texture, which is attributed to the category of "Gothic," was replaced by Rotunda, whose breaks were less pronounced. This is one of the reasons it received the name "Round Gothic." In the same century, the collective name "Schwabacher" emerged, encompassing the traditional fonts that were used at the time. These fonts were characterized by a lighter typeface. "Fraktur," developed in the 16th century (around 1540), eventually became the leading font of the centuries that followed, even though it was subject to various modifications. In the early 20th century, Antiqua fonts and the new creations of the time – "Grotesk" fonts, "Egyptienne" fonts, and monospaced variants – eventually ousted blackletter fonts. (eds.)

A	B	C	D
a	a	a	a
d	d	d	d
g	g	g	g
n	n	n	n
o	o	o	o
A	A	A	A
B	B	B	B
H	H	H	H
S	S	S	S

A = Textura; B = Rotunda; C = Schwabacher; D = Fraktur

Gotisch (Textur)

Rundgotisch (Rotunda)

Schwabacher

Fraktur

E 067 ←
→ E 264

178 Afrikan Alphabets

Image sources:
(a) https://commons.wikimedia.org/wiki/File:Tizi_Ouzou_Tasdawit.jpg
(see sources)
(b) https://de.wikipedia.org/wiki/Tifinagh-Schrift#/media/Datei:
2008_-_Mbrocko_-_berbertext_utanf%C3%B6r_kaf%C3%A9_i_Agadir_3.JPG
(see sources)

Recommended books:
(1) "Afrikan Alphabets, The Story of Writing in Africa," Saki Mafundikwa;
Mark Batty Publisher, New York, 2004;
ISBN 0-9724240-6-7
(2) "The Politics of Design," Ruben Pater; BIS Publishers, Amsterdam, 2016;
ISBN 978-90-6369-422-7

a

b

In present-day Africa, the Latin alphabet is most commonly used – even though this continent is home to around 25% of all of the world's languages (up to 2,100). If we contemplate this circumstance a little longer, it unravels the whole dark history of the continent's colonization. Because the colonial rulers (mostly European/ Christian, but also Islamic) always had the goal of controlling the occupied countries and thereby also influencing their culture. The Hausa language, for example, which is one of the most widely spoken languages of midwestern Africa (particularly Nigeria), was written in an alphabet related to the Arabic one. But then the British arrived and forced the implementation of the Latin alphabet in the 1930s. This pattern of colonial obliteration repeated itself on the entire continent, with very few exceptions. Because Africa contained many languages and many alphabets: for example, the N'Ko script in West Africa, the Vah script in Liberia, or the Tifinagh script of the Tuareg (fig. a,b) in northern Africa. The end of colonialism revitalized the cultures and traditions of the various regions of the continent. As a result, many African regions use the language and script of the respective former colonizers, which remains in place to this day, alongside competing native alphabets that help shape everyday visual communication. Not only have the traditional alphabets been revived, they have also been developed. They have found their way into apps and social media and are taught at schools. (eds.)

E 069 ←
→ E 265

179 Digitale Bildkulturen

Bibliographic information and quotation sources:
(1) "Krypto-Kunst," Kolja Reichert; from the series
"Digitale Bildkulturen;" Verlag Klaus Wagenbach, Berlin, 2021;
[in German] ISBN 978-3-8031-3711-1
Page 19, line 20 – page 20, line 15

(2) "Gesichtserkennung," Roland Meyer; from the series
"Digitale Bildkulturen;" Verlag Klaus Wagenbach, Berlin, 2021;
[in German] ISBN 978-3-8031-3705-0
Page 08, lines 04 – 10; page 09, lines 02 – 07

(3) "Selfies," Wolfgang Ullrich; from the series
"Digitale Bildkulturen;" Verlag Klaus Wagenbach, Berlin, 2019;
[in German] ISBN 978-3-8031-3683-1
Page 35, line 14 – page 36, line 14

accompanying text: eds.

In 2022, the publishing house Verlag Klaus Wagenbach published a book series on the topic of various image phenomena in relation to digitality. It particularly highlights the aesthetic, political, and societal dimensions. The topics included in the series are: "Netzfeminismus" ("Online Feminism"), "Bildproteste" ("Image Protests"), "Screenshots," "Modebilder" ("Fashion Images"), "Hassbilder" ("Images of Hate"), "Meme," "Gifs," "Bodybilder" ("Body Images"), "Emojis," "Copyright," "Videospiele" ("Video Games"), "Krypto-Kunst" ("Crypto-Art"), "Selfies," and "Gesichtserkennung" ("Facial Recognition").

Each booklet of about 80 pages deals with a topic whose current significance, processes, and backgrounds are generally only partly familiar to those who feel more than at home in the digital world. Or could you, dear reader, explain in a few words what NFTs are, how they are created, and how they influence the art market? A quote from "Krypto-Kunst" (1) by Kolja Reichert:

ʼ(…) For a long time, Blockchain wallets exchanged only one thing: coins, Bitcoin, or ether. Each of these coins works in the same way as a chip at a casino: I can purchase a certain amount of them with euros or dollars, use them as payment for all kinds of things within the closed system, and then exchange them into fiat money (this is the term for government-supported currencies) again at the daily rate (the simplest option would be a crypto platform). From an information technology point of view, coins are tokens: standardized counting units. Tokens of the same currency are no different from one another, just like two-euro coins are no different from one another. They are interchangeable. This is not the case with non-fungible tokens: Every NFT has a uniquely identifiable number, refers to other data, and is therefore one-of-a-kind. This means that NFTs are comparable to works of art. It therefore comes as no surprise that NFTs mentioned in discussions over the past years usually referred to art, although in principle, all possible assets can be securitized. But when it comes to unique goods, works of art are simply the paradigm. (…)ʼ

Or let us look at the topic of "Gesichtserkennung" (facial recognition) (2). Roland Meyer writes the following:

ʼ(…) What exactly is facial recognition? Many would say: a technology for "biometric" identification. However, this definition, which applied to the beginnings of the technology, is now rather misleading. Because "biometrics" in the sense of measuring stable physical features no longer plays an important role in today's commonly used processes. (…) Aside from exceptions such as Apple's FaceID, which actually measures the face's three-dimensional geometry to unlock an iPhone, the current facial recognition methods generally do not measure physical features, but rather statistically evaluate an automated image comparison. (…)ʼ

One final example. On the topic of "Selfies" (3), Wolfgang Ullrich writes:

ʼ(…) Due to their popularity, selfies belong to the image categories in which codifications are already easily recognizable. Since many people are focused on their facial expression in selfie mode, but primarily endeavoring to garner reactions from those they are addressing, this encourages expressions that resemble slapstick or caricatures, that are fun to imitate, or that allow for a lot of variation. And if a specific facial expression or the result of certain filters has a particularly positive effect on the responses received, the creator will repeat this successful format, while at the same time responding more strongly to funny or striking facial expressions themselves. Gradually, this allows communication patterns to emerge – similarly to language, where, conventionally, an idiom – firmly established – is answered with another idiom. Selfies have even given rise to facial expressions that didn't exist in our natural body language beforehand – especially not on a global level. For example, a popular option is to wink and simultaneously stick out your tongue. This seems like a challenge, but often also makes fun of the recipient or turns a situation into a funny or silly one (and is therefore comparable to the use of the monkey filter). It took just a few years for these facial expressions to spread and appear in selfies in Asia, Europe, the Arabic world, or in Africa, without any noticeable regional difference in usage or meaning. (…)ʼ

The book series describes the current status quo (of 2022), but also offers a foundation to understand further developments – that will inevitably arrive.

E 070 ←
→ E 266

180 Manifesto of Futurism

Source of the Manifesto of Futurism:
https://www.societyforasianart.org/sites/default/files/manifesto_futurista.pdf
(see sources)

"Futurism" was the name of an avantgarde movement in and through which artists wanted to establish a new culture. Italian Filippo Tommaso Marinetti (1876 – 1944) founded the movement of futurism with his "first manifesto of futurism." It was published in the French newspaper "Le Figaro" on February 20, 1909. (eds.)

/ **MANIFESTO OF FUTURISM**

1. We want to sing the love of danger, the habit of energy and rashness.

2. The essential elements of our poetry will be courage, audacity and revolt.

3. Literature has up to now magnified pensive immobility, ecstasy and slumber. We want to exalt movements of aggression, feverish sleeplessness, the double march, the perilous leap, the slap and the blow with the fist.

4. We declare that the splendor of the world has been enriched by a new beauty: the beauty of speed. A racing automobile with its bonnet adorned with great tubes like serpents with explosive breath ... a roaring motor car which seems to run on machine-gun fire, is more beautiful than the Victory of Samothrace.

5. We want to sing the man at the wheel, the ideal axis of which crosses the earth, itself hurled along its orbit.

6. The poet must spend himself with warmth, glamour and prodigality to increase the enthusiastic fervor of the primordial elements.

7. Beauty exists only in struggle. There is no masterpiece that has not an aggressive character. Poetry must be a violent assault on the forces of the unknown, to force them to bow before man.

8. We are on the extreme promontory of the centuries! What is the use of looking behind at the moment when we must open the mysterious shutters of the impossible? Time and Space died yesterday. We are already living in the absolute, since we have already created eternal, omnipresent speed.

9. We want to glorify war - the only cure for the world - militarism, patriotism, the destructive gesture of the anarchists, the beautiful ideas which kill, and contempt for woman.

10. We want to demolish museums and libraries, fight morality, feminism and all opportunist and utilitarian cowardice.

11. We will sing of the great crowds agitated by work, pleasure and revolt; the multi-colored and polyphonic surf of revolutions in modern capitals: the nocturnal vibration of the arsenals and the workshops beneath their violent electric moons: the gluttonous railway stations devouring smoking serpents; factories suspended from the clouds by the thread of their smoke; bridges with the leap of gymnasts flung across the diabolic cutlery of sunny rivers: adventurous steamers sniffing the horizon; great-breasted locomotives, puffing on the rails like enormous steel horses with long tubes for bridle, and the gliding flight of aeroplanes whose propeller sounds like the flapping of a flag and the applause of enthusiastic crowds. (...) /

E 071 ←
→ E 267

181 Karawane, Hugo Ball. Cigarren, Kurt Schwitters. fmbsbw, Raoul Hausmann.

KARAWANE
jolifanto bambla ô falli bambla
grossiga m'pfa habla horem
égiga goramen
higo bloiko russula huju
hollaka hollala
anlogo bung
blago bung
blago bung
bosso fataka
ü üü ü
schampa wulla wussa ólobo
hej tatta gôrem
eschige zunbada
wulubu ssubudu uluw ssubudu
tumba ba- umf
kusagauma
ba - umf

(1)

Image source:
(1) https://de.wikipedia.org/wiki/Hugo_Ball#/media/Datei:
Hugo_ball_karawane.png (see sources)

(2) "Cigarren" is a reconstruction (by u.v) of the original, pictured in the following book:
"Das Lachen DADAs – Die Berliner Dadaisten und ihre Aktionen," Hanne Bergius; from the series "Werkbund-Archiv," Werkbund-Archiv, Verlag Anabas (eds.), Gießen, 1989; ISBN 3-87038-141-8; [in German]
Page 289, Schwitters: Cigarren, 1921

Recommended websites:
https://en.wikipedia.org/wiki/Hugo_Ball
https://en.wikipedia.org/wiki/Kurt_Schwitters
https://en.wikipedia.org/wiki/Raoul_Hausmann

https://de.wikipedia.org/wiki/Ursonate
https://en.wikipedia.org/wiki/Sound_poetry

CIGARREN
[elementar]

Cigarren
Ci
garr
ren
Ce
i
ge
a
err
err
e
en
Ce
CeI
CeIGe
CeIGeA
CeIGeAErr
CeIGeAErrEr
CeIGeAErrErr
CeIGeAErrErr
ErrEEn
EEn
En
Ce
i
ge
a
err
err
e
en
Ci
garr
ren
Cigarren
[Der letzte Vers wird gesungen.]

(2)

Hugo Ball (1886 – 1927) was a German author. He is the co-founder of the Dada movement. Alongside Kurt Schwitters, Hugo Ball belongs to the pioneers of the sound poem, which served as a central stylistic device of Dada art. Ball composed his poem "Karawane" in 1917. The image (1) shows the original typography of the first publication from 1920.

Kurt Schwitters (1887 – 1948) was an important German Dada artist who worked in many genres: as an author, poet, painter, decorator, and advertising designer. Under the term "Merz," he created a Dadaist "overall world view." In addition to Dadaism, the styles of his work also encompass constructivism and surrealism. He gained fame with some of his sound poems, such as "Ursonate," which he worked on between 1923 and 1932. His sound poem "Cigarren" from 1921 is pictured on the right.

Austrian-German artist Raoul Hausmann (1886 – 1971) was also a Dadaist. His work comprises paintings, collages, sculptures, and text work (including Dadaist manifestos). He was particularly devoted to photo collages and is considered a pioneer of this technique along with Hannah Höch. He also dabbled in sound poems. For a time, he worked together intensively with Schwitters and inspired the creation of "Ursonate" with his sound poem "fmbsbw." (eds.)

Audio sample of "fmbsbw":
https://www.youtube.com/watch?v=2lVqiCURmFQ

E 072 ←
→ E 268

182 Schatzkammer der Revolution. Russische Kinderbücher von 1920 – 1935

Bibliographic information:
"Schatzkammer der Revolution. Russische Kinderbücher von 1920 – 1935: Bücher aus bewegten Zeiten," Julian Rothenstein, Olga Budashevskaya (Ed.), Lars Müller Publishers, Zurich, 2013; [in German] ISBN 978-3-03778-343-6

The book "Schatzkammer der Revolution. Russische Kinderbücher von 1920 – 1935" ("Treasure Chest of the Revolution. Russian Children's Books from 1920 – 1935") highlights children's books published in the early days of the Soviet Union. The following Marxist motto applied: Those who want to influence the spirit of future generations must start with the children. This fundamental attitude is not surprising, as adults still try to teach children values and present role models while at the same time entertaining them – and adults are always the ones who conceptualize and design children's books. In the so-called Golden Age of the young Soviet Union, this was of course also the case. And so countless children's books emerged, devised and designed by outstanding minds and artists. A remark made by Lenin in 1918, which is quoted in the book, demonstrates the ideological value they held: "Give me four years to teach children, and the seed that I sowed will never fade." A "Prawda" article from the same year stated: "Within the big armory with which the bourgeoisie went to battle against socialism, the children's book played a special role. When we chose our cannons and weapons, we overlooked those that spread poison. We needed to snatch this munition out of their hands."

The recommended book shows a cross-section of various children's books, textbooks for children, and poetry collections. This book is a must-read for aspiring illustrators. All other designers who recognize the propagandistic perfidy in the works from the young Soviet Union should remember the prevailing mood of the dawn of a new era after World War II and after a czarist dictatorship in which the impoverished proletariat had no voice. And they should also remember that the west has and still does operate with the same ideological bandage. I would like to mention Scrooge McDuck, the epitome of radical capitalism, who – all things considered – was portrayed as a popular figure despite his greed. As I said at the start, adults are the ones who create visual communication that targets children. And adults always have an agenda. (u.v)

Image source:
https://de.wikipedia.org/wiki/El_Lissitzky#/media/Datei:Design_by_El_Lissitzky_1922.jpg
(see sources)

Cover created by El Lissitzky for the children's book "Four Billy Goats" from 1922.

E 073 ←
→ E 269

183 Jan Tschichold and his relationship with the avantgarde

Bibliographic information:
"Jan Tschichold – Meister der Typographie – Sein Lebenswerk in Bildern," Cees W. de Jong, Alston W. Purvis, Martijn F. Le Coultre, Richard B. Doubleday, Hans Reichardt; Verlag Bernd Detsch, Cologne, 2008;
[in German] ISBN 978-3-940602-01-5

The book "Jan Tschichold – Meister der Typographie – Sein Lebenswerk in Bildern" ("Jan Tschichold – Master of Typography – His Life's Work in Pictures") is dedicated, as the title indicates, to one of the most famous typographers of the 20th century. An astonishing aspect described by the book is the network of celebrities that influenced him and his relationships with them. As an abbreviated cutout, this reads as follows:

In 1923, the young typographer Tschichold (1902 – 1974) visited the first Bauhaus exhibition in Weimar. He got to know the work of architects Walter Gropius (1883 – 1969) and Ludwig Mies van der Rohe (1886 – 1969), painters Oskar Schlemmer (1888 – 1943) and Vasily Kandinsky (1866 – 1944), and the Hungarian constructivist designer, photographer, and former law student Lázló Moholy-Nagy (1895 – 1946). For Tschichold, the exhibition was a revelation. And so it continued. He became acquainted with the work of Dutch graphic designer Piet Zwart (1885 – 1977), Russian suprematist painter Kazimir Malevich (1878 – 1935), and Russian constructivists El Lissitzky (1890 – 1941) and Alexander Rodtschenko (1891 – 1956). These countless influences and impulses left their mark on Tschichold's work. He started to correspond in great detail with the key figures of the avantgarde: with Lissitzky, Kurt Schwitters (1887 – 1948), Josef Albers (1888 – 1976), Willi Baumeister (1889 – 1955), Herbert Bayer (1900 – 1985), Max Bill (1908 – 1994), Walter Dexel (1890 – 1973), and Moholy-Nagy, among others. Other pen pals included Piet Mondrian (1872 – 1976), Ben Nicholson (1894 – 1982), Gustav Klutsis (1895 – 1938), Ladislav Sutnar (1897 – 1976), Friedrich Vordemberge-Gildewart (1899 – 1962), Malevich, and the Dutch constructivists Piet Zwart and Paul Schuitema (1897 – 1973). Tschichold got to know El Lissitzky better. This turned into a productive friendship. The optimism that emerged with the Russian revolution inspired Tschichold to change his name – in 1923, his original name of Johannes Tzschichhold became Iwan Tschichold. And he wasn't the only one to do so at the time. Surrealist photographer Emmanuel Radnitzky (1890 – 1976) turned into Man Ray, and later the American designer Peretz Rosenbaum would become better known as Paul Rand. The book reports meticulously on this network of relationships and illustrates how the exchange of ideas and friendships impacted Tschichold's work. As a designer living in the 21st century, it is absolutely astonishing to see who worked with, corresponded, or was simply friends with whom. Such an intellectual climate would be a dream to have right now and for the present day. (u.v)

E 074 ←
→ E 270

184 Mit voller Kraft. Russische Avantgarde 1910 – 1934

Bibliographic information:
"Mit voller Kraft. Russische Avantgarde 1910 – 1934," Wilhelm Hornbostel, Karlheinz W. Kopanski, Thomas Rudi (Ed.); Edition Braus im Wachterverlag, Heidelberg, 2001; [in German] ISBN 3-926318-92-9

Text source:
From the chapter "Kunst für den Aufbau der neuen Gesellschaft," page 137, 1st column, lines 04 – 26; 2nd column, lines 05 – 24

Image sources:
(1) https://de.wikipedia.org/wiki/Suprematismus#/media/Datei:Supremus_55_(Malevich,_1916).jpg (see sources)
(2) https://de.wikipedia.org/wiki/Konstruktivismus_(Architektur)#/media/Datei:Van_Nelle_Fabriek_-_Van_Nelle_Factory_(5709126091).jpg
(see sources)

The book "Mit voller Kraft. Russische Avantgarde 1910 – 1934" reports on the awakening that took place with the Russian revolution in 1917. The protagonists of this awakening had already started to question the political and cultural circumstances in Russia. The following quote from the book gives a first impression (eds.):
"(…) Every design era has its "heroes." The character of design in the 1920s in Soviet Russia was established by avantgarde artists. They were young, around 30, they called each other "constructivists," "production practicians," or "engineers." They were still unfamiliar with words like "designer." They were followers of a project method in design that did not embellish the object, but instead reconstructed it. The idea of constructing objects emerged in the evolutionary process of abstract art from the picture and object to the project.

→

(1)
Kasimir Malewitsch, Suprematism (Supremus No. 58), 1916

Just a few years earlier, in the late 1910s, these artists had been romantics: They overthrew academic art. From 1921 – 22, they became rationalists. Even their outward appearance resisted the standards of the time: The men were shaven, the women smoked cigarettes and sewed themselves dresses with materials depicting geometric patterns, printed in line with their designs. (…) The secret of the originality of 1920s Russian design lies in the interplay between social conditions and the cultural situation of those years. Art history in the 1910s and early 1920s was so eventful that new "isms" were proclaimed almost on a weekly basis. After they had tapped into French impressionism and cubism, the Russian artistic avantgarde created its own original variations of global trends very quickly, followed by completely independent concepts of abstract art – suprematism, non-objective art, constructivism. The object, the avantgarde's world in images, which did without the conventional sense and representational meaning, disintegrated into individual elements: into simple geometric shapes and surfaces, into lines, dots, colors, factures, and volumes. These abstract fantasies featured two levels of meaning. The first captured the world, the view of the new reality: visually offered abstract categories of space, time, energy, and movement as such. The second was the dream of the future of science and technology that would make all these buildings possible and bridge huge distances by means of telegraph, radio, and aviation. (…) ʼ

(2)
Constructivism in architecture:
Van der Vlugt with Brinkman and Stam: 1926–30, Van-Nelle-Fabrik, Rotterdam.

E 074 ←
→ E 270

184.1 Futurismus

Bibliographic information:
"Metzler Lexikon Ästhetik," Achim Trebeß (Ed.), Verlag J.B. Metzler, Stuttgart, 2006; [in German] ISBN: 3-476-01913-6

Text source:
From the entry "Futurismus" by Achim Trebeß, Page 122, 2nd column, line 47 – page 123, 1st column, line 49

Achim Trebeß describes futurism as follows:
ʼ Futurism is one of the first trends of the avantgarde. It was founded by the writer F.T. Marinetti, who became a leading figure of Italian futurism. After the publication of Marinetti's Manifesto of Futurism (1908), many other manifestos followed. Futurists look for scandal and provocation and lead their internal disputes loudly and in public. Futurism spreads to all traditional arts, as well as photography, film, and architecture. (…) The goal of futurism is radical destruction of everything old and construction of something completely new with the rubble. Sound poems are typical of this, breaking with the conventional lexis and syntax and constructing new words that reach beyond the national languages and aim to lead to the origin of language. With the artistic form, which is given priority, futurists want to revolutionize the content. – Noisy and passionate advocacy of modernism, urbanism, traffic, and speed determine the appearance of futurism and its designs, according to the architectural visions of the Italians.
(…) The technological euphoria of Italian futurism also does not shy away from enthusiasm in light of war technology and war. Marinetti takes a stand during the so-called Second Futurism after World War I (Marinetti: Futurismo e Fascismo, 1924). Russian futurism distances itself from this stance, instead trying to relate the revolution in art to the political revolution of 1917 in Russia. Here, futurism increasingly conflicts with the Marxist aesthetic and later with Stalin's politics. (…)
Within the avantgarde, futurism is very influential, especially for dadaism, surrealism, constructivism, and cubism. ʼ

E 074 ←
→ E 270

184.2 Suprematismus

Bibliographic information:
"mit voller Kraft. Russische Avantgarde 1910 – 1934," Wilhelm Hornbostel, Karlheinz W. Kopanski, Thomas Rudi (Ed.); Edition Braus im Wachterverlag, Heidelberg, 2001; [in German] ISBN 3-926318-92-9

Text source:
From the glossary, compiled by Roland Nachtigäller, page 312, 1st column, line 14 – line 33

ʼ (…) In the fall of 1915, Kazimir Malevich campaigned for a radical change using artistic devices in the circle of Moscow-based futurists: The icon of the black square as a non-objective, pure sensation on a white surface as the nothing outside of this sensation (first shown in 1915 at the exhibition 0,10) marked the radical awakening of suprematism. Malevich put art that was liberated from all references to objects in a cosmic context; his pure, absolute surfaces in few, vibrant colors reflected the world as energy, overcoming gravity, and the rejection of useful functionality in art. Malevich's students, including I. Kljun, L. Malewitsch, L. Popowa, and W. Tatlin, joined forces with him in 1916 for a year to establish the Supremus group (Lat.: highest, top, superlative) in Moscow, and in 1920, he founded the association UNOWIS together with El Lissitzky in Vitebsk. (…) ʼ

E 074 ←
→ E 270

184.3 Konstruktivismus

Bibliographic information:
"Metzler Lexikon Ästhetik," Achim Trebeß (Ed.), Verlag J.B. Metzler, Stuttgart, 2006; [in German] ISBN: 3-476-01913-6

Text source:
From "Konstruktivismus" by Matthias Hennig, Page 202, 2nd column, line 39 – page 203, 1st column, line 30

Metzler's "Lexikon der Ästhetik" ("Lexicon of Aesthetics") explains the term constructivism. Matthias Hennig writes:
ʼ (…) As an avantgarde trend that emphasizes a fine objectivity and exactness, functionality, and logical organization, constructivism is characterized by its affinity with industry and technology as well as its methodical proximity to the formalizable sciences. Constructivism, which started in Russia and continues to have a global effect today, and whose offshoots and branches can be found in all fine arts as well as in photography, design, theater, film, and literature, experienced its golden era in the 1910s and 1920s; its most famous representatives include V. Tatlin, A. Rodtschenko, El Lissitzky, N. Gabo, and A. Pevsner. The ideas of Russian constructivism are in part closely related to the concepts and designs of Bauhaus and the De-Stijl movement. As a style phenomenon, constructivism uses its compositions to try and develop an objective, abstract, and universally understandable design vocabulary that is primarily based on the purposive discipline of a manageable number of geometric structural elements such as circles and lines or rectangles and polygons, clear and precise color schemes, and the use of industrially produced materials. Like futurists and dadaists (see Futurism and Dadaism 181), constructivists also bury the traditional artistic ideal with revolutionary pathos in their manifestos in order to replace it with a new aesthetic order in a bold historical-philosophical way. In addition to the rejection of decorative playfulness and the tendency to synthesize art, this rigorous anti-traditionalism is just as much of a trademark of constructivism as the desire to put art into the center of life's service and to recreate and design the world from scratch in the opening towards practical questions of the here and now, whereby artists should become the intervening "engineers" and operators of this society-shaping process. (…) ʼ

E 075 ←
→ E 271

185 Moholy-Nagy and the New Typography

Bibliographic information:
"Moholy-Nagy and the New Typography," Petra Eisele, Isabel Naegele, Michael Lailach (Ed.); Kettler Verlag, Bönen, 2019;
ISBN 978-3-86206-754-1

Image sources:
(1) The book's front cover;
(2) Page 140/141

Text source:
The text from the publisher's website (see sources)

'In 1929, ten years after the Bauhaus was founded, Berlin's 184.1
Martin-Gropius-Bau launched the exhibition "New Typography."
László Moholy-Nagy, who had left Dessau the previous year and
had earned a reputation as a designer in Berlin, was invited to 184.2
exhibit his work together with other artists. He designed a room—
entitled "Wohin geht die typografische Entwicklung?" ("Where is 184.3
typography headed?")—where he presented 78 wall charts illustrating the development of the "New Typography" since the turn 185
of the century and extrapolating its possible future. To create
these charts, he not only used his own designs, but also included 186
advertising prints by colleagues associated with the Bauhaus.
The functional graphic design, initiated by the "New Typography" movement in the 1920s, broke with tradition and established a new advertising design based on artistic criteria. It aimed to achieve a modern look with standardized typefaces, industrial DIN norms, and adherence to such ideals as legibility, lucidity, and straightforwardness, in line with the key principles of constructivist art.
For the first time, this comprehensive publication showcases Moholy-Nagy's wall charts which have recently been rediscovered in Berlin's Kunstbibliothek. Renowned authors provide insights into this treasure trove by each contributing to this alphabetized compilation starting with "A" for "Asymmetry" and ending with "Z" for "Zukunftsvision" ("vision of the future"). By perusing through the pages and allowing a free flow of association, the typographical world of ideas of the 1920s avant-garde is once again brought back to life.'

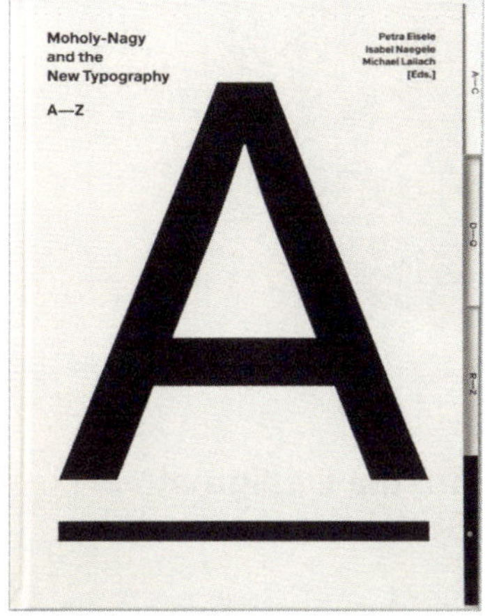

(1)

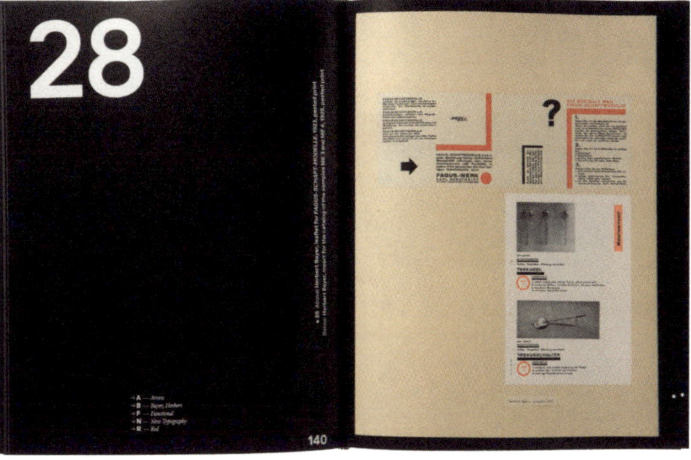

(2)

The quick brown
fox jumps
over the lazy dog
Airport

E 075.1 ←
→ E 272

186 Helvetica, Helvetica Arabic and Hebrew

The fonts are a component of the Apple computer's High Sierra operating system.

Based on the example of the Helvetica font in the Latin alphabet, its Arabic and Hebrew equivalents, we can detect the attempt to equip different scripts with comparable graphic detailed solutions – for example regarding the line width or the avoidance of ink spots. This results in typefaces for different alphabets that are easily combinable – for example, when needed for visual communication at an airport. (eds.)

البني السريع
الثعلب يقفز
فوق الكلب الكسول
مطار

החום המהיר
שועל קופץ
על הכלב העצלן
שדה תעופה

E 076 ←
→ E 273

187 Arts & Crafts.

William Morris

Bibliographic information:
"William Morris," Victoria and Albert Museum, Anna Mason (Eds.);
Thames & Hudson, London, 2021;
ISBN 978-0500480502

Image source:
https://de.wikipedia.org/wiki/William_Morris#/media/Datei:Kelmscott_
chaucer.jpg (see sources)

Websites:
https://en.wikipedia.org/wiki/William_Morris
https://en.wikipedia.org/wiki/Arts_and_Crafts_movement

William Morris (1834–1896) was a pioneer of the Arts & Crafts movement. From the mid-19th century through to the 1920s, the movement focused on the connection between art, culture, and work. In light of the advancing industrialization, members of this movement called for a return to handicrafts and care in dealing with materials and nature. Morris was a man of many talents: He was a writer and poet, he was one of the first socialists in Great Britain, he was committed to protecting nature, and also gained fame as a designer. He designed church decorations, furniture, tiles, and dishes, did calligraphy, and worked in publishing.

The recommended book introduces his work and lets many Morris experts have their say. (eds.)

Page from the "Kelmscott Chaucer." Printed byDruck Kelmscott Press, illustration by Edward Burne-Jones, typography by William Morris, 1896;

Textiles by Gunta Stölzl on the chair with colorful strap covering by Marcel Breuer (1921).

E 076 ←
→ E 273

188 Textile Design at Bauhaus: Gunta Stölzl

Image design:
https://de.wikipedia.org/wiki/Gunta_St%C3%B6lzl#/media/Datei:Marcel_
breuer_con_stoffe_di_gunta_st%C3%B6lzl,_sedia,_1922_01.JPG
(see sources)

Recommended website:
https://en.wikipedia.org/wiki/Gunta_St%C3%B6lzl

Gunta Stölzl (1897–1983) was a textile designer and weaver born in Switzerland. After her studies at Bauhaus, in the weaving workshop, and following brief stays in Krefeld and Switzerland, she returned to Bauhaus and started teaching in the weaving workshop as a master. During this time, she established intensive contacts with the industry. Due to political conflicts and her marriage to architect Arieh Sharon, she left Bauhaus in 1931 and returned to Switzerland, where she created many designs for rugs and upholstery fabric as a self-employed textile designer. Her credo of establishing a connection between functionality and aesthetic demands shaped her work as well as the communication with teaching staff during her Bauhaus period, including Johannes Itten, Paul Klee, Marcel Breuer, and Vasily Kandinsky. Thanks to her, the area of industrial design found its way into the Bauhaus workshop she ran. This made her the most important weaver who managed the leap from artistic single piece to industrially producible design. She therefore deserves the credit for "Bauhaus materials" becoming a trademark. (eds.)

E 076 ←
→ E 273

189

TextielMuseum Tilburg, NL

Address: Goirkestraat 96, 5046GN Tilburg, NL

Website:
https://textielmuseum.nl/

The TextielMuseum in Tilburg (Netherlands) presents the past and present of the Dutch textile industry. Tilburg has always been one of its centers, which is why the museum is housed in a factory. A comprehensive textile collection awaits visitors. At the integrated research facility, the "TextielLab," artists and designers experiment with new fabrics, materials, and designs. The museum's communication follows the latest findings in museological knowledge transfer. For communication designers, a visit is highly recommended, as the museum presents graphic forms on a large scale. In addition, the interplay between the designed surfaces and the respective materials is highly interesting and inspiring for all designers who almost only work with screens as graphic surfaces. (eds.)

E 076 ←
→ E 273

190 Textile Design at Bauhaus: Anni Albers

Bibliographic information:
"Anni Albers," Nicholas Fox Weber, Pandora Tabatabai Asbaghi;
Peggy Guggenheim Collection, USA, 1999

Image sources:
(1) "Intersecting," p. 60; (2) "Pasture," p. 55 (see sources)

Recommended websites:
https://en.wikipedia.org/wiki/Anni_Albers
https://www.wikiart.org/en/anni-albers/

Anni Albers, née Annelise Fleischmann (1899–1994), was a German-American artist, weaver, and graphic designer. She spent time at Bauhaus, both as a student and later as a teacher. She studied textile design with Gunta Stölzl at the Bauhaus weaving workshop, whose position she would take over in 1931. In 1925, she married Bauhaus teacher Josef Albers.

During National Socialism, she emigrated to the USA and taught at Black Mountain College in North Carolina. She also worked as a freelance artist. In the decades that followed, Anni Albers received the highest accolades in the art world, exhibited in the Museum of Modern Art New York, Tate Modern in London, and in Germany. As a student, she struggled with the limiting factor of a lack of real equality, even though it was touted. Male students could choose between working with paper, glass, ceramics, fabrics, clay, or metal. Women were gently – or not so gently – pressured into weaving to develop their artistic skills. This shortcoming also expressed itself in the evaluations of whether

(1)

something was art or handcraft. Textile work was attributed to the latter. Part of the reason for this absence of equality at Bauhaus stemmed from the

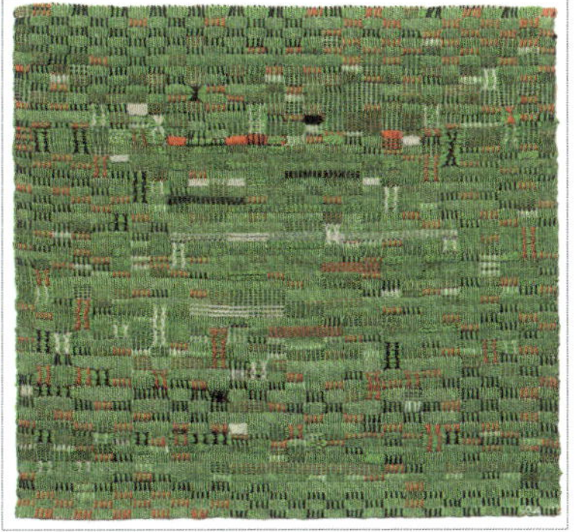

(2)

(justified or unjustified) concern that the industry that supplied Bauhaus with commissions could take offense at the high proportion of women.

Despite the social climate, Anni Albers received plenty of recognition for her textile work over the years. It wasn't until the last third of her life that she turned to paper as a working material and printing techniques. According to Wikipedia (see: recommended website), art critics speculate whether Albers could have made (even) more of herself than one of the most renowned personalities of Bauhaus, namely an important artist of the 20th century – if she had been able to train and express herself in all artistic genres early on. (u.v)

Images: left: (1) Intersecting, 1962, right: (2) Pasture, 1958
This piece of work created on a handloom alternates between traditional handicraft and modern art.

E 077 ←
→ E 274

191 Die Neue Rechte und ihr Design

Bibliographic information:
"Die Neue Rechte und ihr Design. Vom ästhetischen Angriff auf die offene Gesellschaft," Daniel Hornuff; Transcript Verlag, Bielefeld, 2019; [in German] ISBN 978-3-8376-4978-9

Text sources:
(1) Preliminary remark: Ulysses Voelker;
(2) From the publisher's preface, lines 01 – 14;
(3) Page 19, line 37 – page 20, line 32

(1) Right-wing extremists can be recognized by their bald heads, combat boots, Imperial War Flags, and hollow slogans – at least that is the widespread opinion on their visual appearance. The fact that this image is clichéd, no longer corresponds to reality, and that this undifferentiated assessment prevents solution strategies for dealing with right-wing extremists – these are the questions the book from which I will quote in the following discusses:

(2) ' What is new about the New Right is not its ideology, but its public appearance. It primarily uses aesthetic devices to attack the open society. The New Right uses design and images as corrosive tools. It adopts an originally progressive aesthetic and turns it subversive: It transforms racism into diversity management, National Socialism into a feel-good lifestyle, the "hipster Nazi" is not satire, and sexist feminism is not a contradiction. Daniel Hornuff's analysis shows that defending the open society is not only a political, but also an aesthetic task. But this dimension is often overlooked or underestimated. He therefore issues a warning: If aesthetic arrogance or indifference spreads in the political field, this opens the floodgates for the machinations of the New Right. A plea to hone aesthetic powers of judgment anew in order to rebut anti-pluralist subversions on an intellectual level too. (...) '

(3) ' (...) Those who want to establish the suggestion of a binding clarity – a collective identity – must consider the design in which they want this to appear. In any case, it must be a design that stands out from other designs – from the creations of other collective identities. The relationship seems clear: The establishment of a collective, homogenously closed, cultural identity necessitates the development of a design language that divests itself. The appearance should convey information through itself, in order to be physiognomically tangible and thereby readable. But the problem is: Movements of the New Right avoid exactly this meticulously and cautiously. Their political desire for a collective being specifically does not take place through an aesthetic desire for a being. Their ideological essentialism does not express itself in thing-essentialism. Instead, the complexity of modern society – its structural ambiguity – is declared the creative self-image in order to turn the ideologically defined goals into practical actions. Therefore, in the case of the New Right, we are dealing with very convoluted access to collective identity: Identity is politically enforced as a concept by reducing societal complexities to the ostensible essential cores of culture, nation, and people. This in turn occurs under the stipulation of an aesthetic diversification of complexity. Consequently, the ideological one-sidedness of western societies is to be achieved through its design-related reproduction: Antipluralism sails under the flag of pluralism. The New Right are children and residents of modern societies. Accordingly, they are practiced in dealing with the mechanisms of modern societies. Countering them in an effective way can therefore only mean an attempt to interpret these societies more precisely than they do – also and especially on the level of aesthetic practices. (...) '

E 079 ←
→ E 275

192 Anton Stankowski et al.

Bibliographic information:
"Visuelle Kommunikation: ein Design-Handbuch," Anton Stankowski, Karl Duschek (Ed.), preface by Otl Aicher, introduction by Abraham Moles; Dietrich Reimer Verlag, Berlin, 1989; [in German] ISBN 3-496-01061-4

Recommended websites:
http://www.reimer-mann-verlag.de
https://en.wikipedia.org/wiki/Anton_Stankowski
https://de.wikipedia.org/wiki/Karl_Duschek
https://de.wikipedia.org/wiki/Hans_Georg_Hillmann
https://de.wikipedia.org/wiki/Gunter_Rambow
https://de.wikipedia.org/wiki/Christof_Gassner
https://de.wikipedia.org/wiki/Otl_Aicher
https://en.wikipedia.org/wiki/Abraham_Moles

Anton Stankowski (1908 – 1998) was a German graphic designer, painter, and photographer. He started working in Zurich and then moved to Stuttgart, where founded a graphic design studio together with Karl Duschek (1947 – 2011) in 1972. Stankowski was a representative of functional typography. His logo for Deutsche Bank – which still exists in its essence today – is very well known. On top of this, he developed numerous corporate designs for renowned companies, domestically and abroad. In 1989, he and Karl Duschek published the book "Visuelle Kommunikation: Ein Design-Handbuch", which also features contributions from other designers. Otl Aicher (1922 – 1991) wrote the preface, Abraham Moles (1920 – 1992) penned the introduction. The book includes contributions by: Matthias Götz (*1952, *Das grafische Zeichen*), Fritz Seitz (1926 – 2017, *Farbe und Entwurf*), Peter von Kornatzki (*1942, *Text und Bild*), Otto Sudrow (*1941, *Industrial Design*), and Fred Oed (*1944, *Moderne Medien*). Stankowski focused on "Visualization," Duschek on "Grids and Layouts."

I would like to discuss three other authors in more detail:
Hans Hillmann (1925 – 2014) was a German graphic designer and illustrator. He designed over 150 movie posters and shaped generations of graphic designers with his style. He also taught at the University of Fine Arts Kassel. Hillmann worked as an illustrator for renowned magazines. He achieved a design milestone with the book "Fliegenpaper" ("Flypaper"), a short story by Dashiell Hammett for which he provided the illustrations. With this work, he helped establish the genre of the graphic novel in Germany. His contribution in the book deals with the role of "Illustration".
Gunter Rambow (*1938) is a German graphic designer and photographer. His main focus lies on photography and posters or poster series, which he designed for literature, theater, and on other social topics. A few names of the protagonists for whom he created graphic work in the 1970s: Peter Weibel, Günter Brus, Otto Mühl, Valie Export. Rambow taught at the University of Fine Arts Kassel and at Karlsruhe University of Arts and Design. His contribution discusses "Photography".
Christof Gassner (*1941) is a Swiss graphic designer who lives and works in Germany. His work focus is corporate design, editorial design, posters, and postage stamps. He teaches at Darmstadt University of Applied Sciences and the University of Fine Arts Kassel. His best-known magazine design includes the "ÖkoTest-Magazin" in the 1980s. His topic in the book: "Typography". (eds.)

E 085 ←
→ E 276

193 Farbfächer / Color fans

Text source:
https://de.wikipedia.org/wiki/Farbf%C3%A4cher

Image sources:
(1) https://upload.wikimedia.org/wikipedia/commons/4/40/Farbf%C3%A4cher_RAL.jpg
(2) https://upload.wikimedia.org/wikipedia/commons/d/dc/HKS-K-Farbfaecher.jpg
(3) https://upload.wikimedia.org/wikipedia/commons/d/dd/Nuancier_Pantone_2_%28Cut_out%29.jpg
(all details: see sources)

Recommended websites:
https://www.ral-farben.de/
https://www.hks-farben.de/
https://www.pantone.com/eu/en/

ʻ (...) A color fan is a catalog structured in a fan-like fashion that contains all defined colors of a color system in the form of paints or prints on paper or a special substrate. The individual shades in the fan are based on a defined composition with which the shades from individual components can easily be blended in different color (coat) qualities. The use of color fans becomes restricted as soon as the bases or the substrate of the fan differs from the target surface. That is why color fans are available with different surfaces (for example, matte and glossy or painted and printed).

Application
Color fans serve as tools to select and compare colors in the production process (for example, between the client and the printer). They are used primarily by graphic designers and printers for the creation of printed material. But color fans also prove useful in other fields (such as industry or construction) that regularly deal with paints, lacquers, or design.

Common color fans
Essentially, there are three commonly used color fans: HKS color fans, RAL color fans, Pantone color fans. (...) ʻ

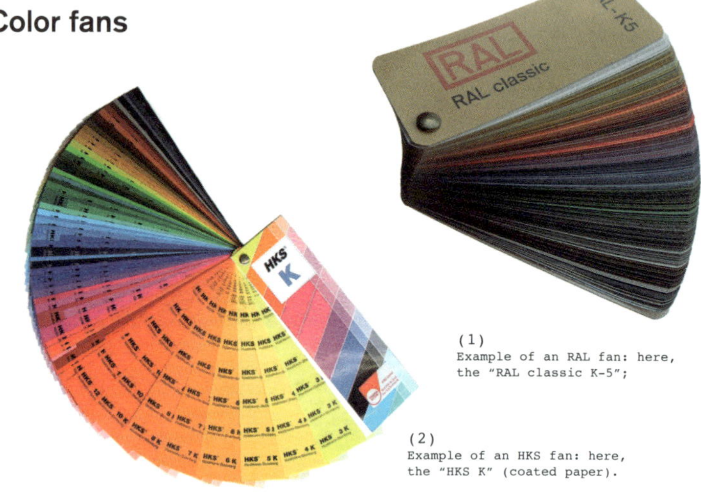

(1)
Example of an RAL fan: here, the "RAL classic K-5";

(2)
Example of an HKS fan: here, the "HKS K" (coated paper).

(3)
Example of a Pantone fan: here, "Pantone Solid Coated."

E 085 ←
→ E 276

194 The Pantone Color of the Year

Text source:
(1) https://de.wikipedia.org/wiki/Pantone_Matching_System
(see sources)

Recommended website: https://www.pantone.com/eu/en/
In 2016 and 2021 two colours were chosen each.

To start with, a preliminary remark: The depicted colors are only recreated to imitate the real Pantone colors, as they are printed in CMYK here. The designation above the color fields (e.g., 17-5104) is included to help you find the colors with Pantone. The line below (c50 m23 y30 k49) indicates the color values in CMYK mode. The goal of this depiction is also to illustrate the approximate trend-setting decision that Pantone makes every year to crown a "color of the year." The Pantone colors can only be properly evaluated in the original color fan. Caution is advised when using CMYK mode in lieu of the

Year	Name	Pantone	CMYK
2023	Viva Magenta	18-1750	c0 m100 y27 k22
2022	Very Peri	17-3938	c69 m62 y7 k0
2021	Ultimate Gray	17-5104	c44 m33 y33 k12
2021	Illuminating	13-0647	c8 m8 y74 k0
2020	Classic Blue	19-4052	c96 m69 y25 k9
2019	Living Coral	16-1546	c0 m68 y52 k0
2018	Ultra Violet	18-3838	c74 m76 y16 k3
2017	Greenery	15-0343	c54 m12 y82 k1
2016	Rose Quartz	13-1520	c1 m28 y15 k0
2016	Serenity	15-3919	c48 m29 y7 k0
2015	Marsala	18-1438	c29 m70 y56 k28
2014	Radiant Orchid	18-3224	c37 m72 y10 k0
2013	Emerald	17-5641	c81 m18 y64 k3
2012	Tangerine Tango	17-1463	c7 m85 y85 k1
2011	Honeysuckle	18-2120	c10 m80 y36 k2
2010	Turquoise	15-5519	c67 m3 y40 k0
2009	Mimosa	14-0848	c7 m27 y69 k0
2008	Blue Iris	18-3943	c75 m66 y9 k0
2007	Chili Pepper	19-1557	c26 m98 y69 k25
2006	Sand Dollar	13-1106	c14 m20 y25 k1
2005	Blue Turquoise	15-5217	c66 m9 y36 k0
2004	Tigerlily	17-1456	c7 m76 y73 k0
2003	Aqua Sky	14-4811	c54 m3 y27 k0
2002	True Red	19-1664	c18 m98 y73 k8

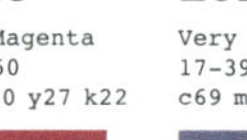

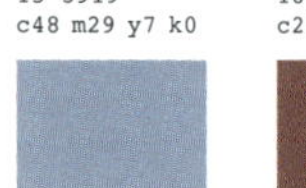
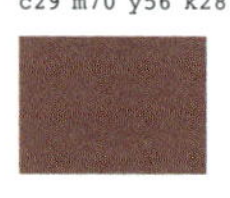
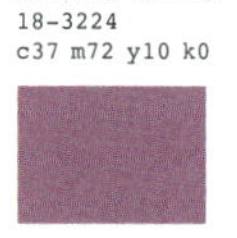

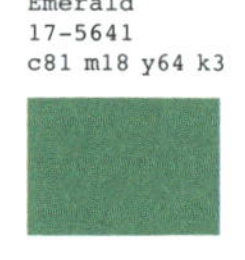
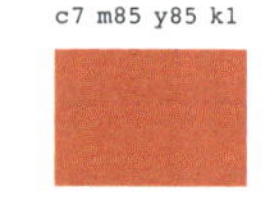

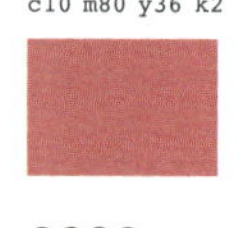
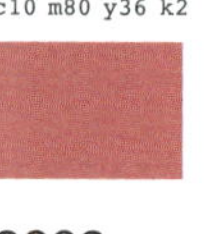
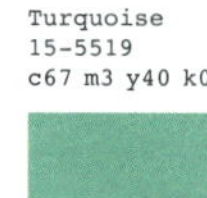

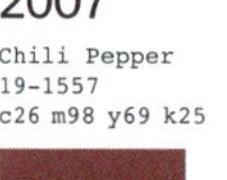

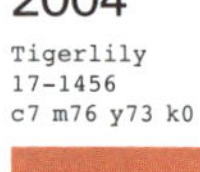
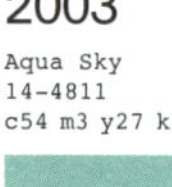

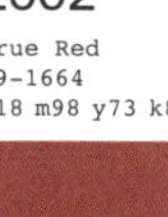

original Pantone colors: The brilliance and depth of the original colors cannot be achieved. The following quoted passage is taken from the Wikipedia entry:

/ (...) Since 2000, the Pantone Color Institute selects a color of the year. The colors are chosen from the pallet of the 14 base colors and their blends, which was introduced in 1963. The selection from the Pantone system takes place after considerations have been made concerning the impression of the time of the respective year. The selection is supposed to serve as inspiration for fashion companies, for example. The "Pantone Color of the Year" has an influence on product development in numerous industries, such as fashion, interior design, and industrial product design as well as product packaging and graphic design. The process evaluates and considers color trends from the entertainment and movie industry, art collections and the work of new artists, fashion, and the socioeconomic environment. (...) /

2024
Peach Fuzz
13-1023
c0 m33 y41 k0

E 085 ←
→ E 276

195 Club colors 1st and 2nd Bundesliga

1st and 2nd Bundesliga, spring 2024. Promotions from and relegations to the 3rd league following the 23/24 season are not taken into account.

The club colors shown here are approximate values. Source: kicker.de

Every soccer club in the world has a logo and club colors. Some colors have established themselves as identifying features (e.g., "the white ballet," Real Madrid), are included in club songs ("Blau und weiß, wie lieb ich dich," Schalke 04 (English: "Blue and white, how I love you"), or form part of the nickname or battle name ("the red devils," Kaiserslautern). This makes it all the more astonishing that clubs' traditional color schemes opt for the same colors so frequently. Here is an overview of the 1st and 2nd Bundesliga in Germany. Abroad, club colors play a fairly important role, as a few examples show: "I Nerazzurri" (Inter Milan), "The Reds" (FC Liverpool), "I Bianconeri" (Juventus Turin). (eds.)

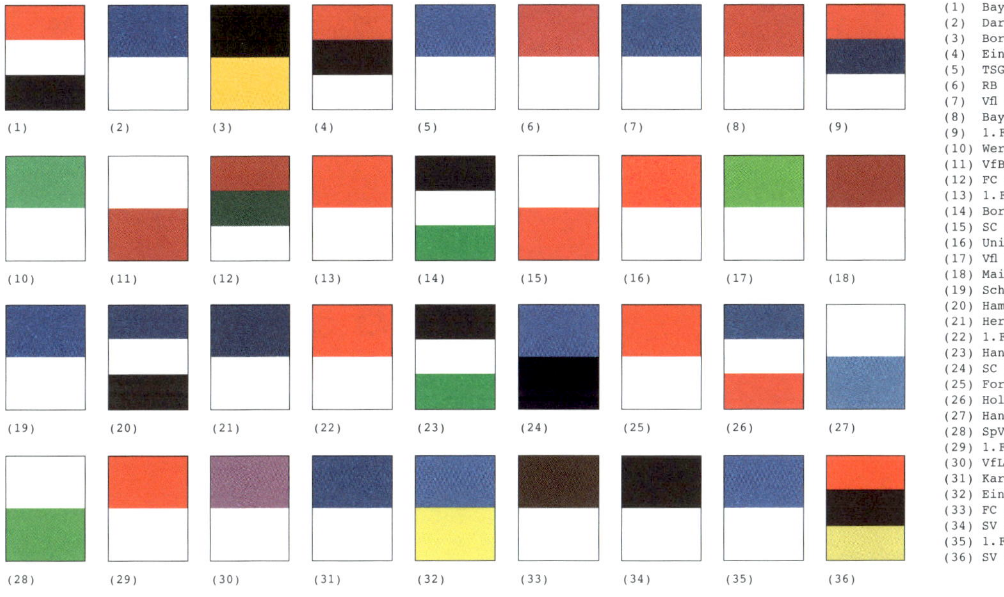

(1) Bayer Leverkusen
(2) Darmstadt 98
(3) Borussia Dortmund
(4) Eintracht Frankfurt
(5) TSG Hoffenheim
(6) RB Leipzig
(7) Vfl Bochum
(8) Bayern München
(9) 1.FC Heidenheim
(10) Werder Bremen
(11) VfB Stuttgart
(12) FC Augsburg
(13) 1.FC Köln
(14) Borussia Mönchengladbach
(15) SC Freiburg
(16) Union Berlin
(17) Vfl Wolfsburg
(18) Mainz 05
(19) Schalke 04
(20) Hamburger SV
(21) Hertha BSC Berlin
(22) 1.FC Kaiserslautern
(23) Hannover 96
(24) SC Paderborn 07
(25) Fortuna Düsseldorf
(26) Holstein Kiel
(27) Hansa Rostock
(28) SpVgg Greuther Fürth
(29) 1.FC Nürnberg
(30) VfL Osnabrück
(31) Karlsruher SC
(32) Eintracht Braunschweig
(33) FC St. Pauli
(34) SV Elversberg
(35) 1.FC Magdeburg
(36) SV Wehen Wiesbaden

E 086 ←
→ E 277

196 Investigative aesthetics

Bibliographic information:
"Investigative aesthetics: Conflicts and Commons in the Politics of Truth,"
Matthew Fuller, Eyal Weizman; Verso, 2021;
ISBN 978-1788739085

The book "Investigative Aesthetics" examines power, corruption, human rights violations, environmental crimes, and other similar offenses. What's special about this: Those who are conducting these analyses are not lawyers or politicians, but increasingly networks that are establishing themselves and include architects, designers, artists, computer scientists, journalists, and interested citizens. The collaborations take place in laboratories, in studios, in galleries, or on the street. The authors of the book, Matthew Fuller and Eyal Weizman, call the procedure and results "investigative aesthetics."

The protagonists rely on scientific findings and research models, resort to artistic processes, use open-source videos, analyze satellite images, and try to uncover shortcomings by means of radical practices. The authors of the book talk about "counter forensic." An example of this is the investigation of the murder of Turkish Internet cafe owner Halit Yozgat in Kassel, committed by the extreme right-wing terror group NSU – while a liaison officer from the Office for the Protection of the Constitution, who had infiltrated the right-wing spectrum, was at the scene and claimed not to have witnessed any part of the murder.
The "Forensic Architecture" collective started investigating, virtually reconstructed the crime scene, analyzed the development of smoke residue that must have resulted from the shots fired, and was able to prove that the liaison officer must have been lying based on the resulting chain of evidence and the computer-animated reconstruction.

Recommended websites:
https://forensic-architecture.org/
https://en.wikipedia.org/wiki/Forensic_Architecture

https://www.bellingcat.com/
https://en.wikipedia.org/wiki/Bellingcat

https://wikileaks.org/
https://en.wikipedia.org/wiki/WikiLeaks

https://www.borderforensics.org/

https://correctiv.org/
https://en.wikipedia.org/wiki/Correctiv

See also: https://www.youtube.com/watch?-v=Z5XXcl2G_yo
"Forensic Architecture" was represented at at documenta 14 with their investigative work. Another event took place at the Frankfurter Kunstverein: https://www.youtube.com/watch?v=byE9fuMF-Z4

In addition to "Forensic Architecture," other collectives with a forensic approach, such as "WikiLeaks," "Bellingcat," "border forensics," and "correctiv" also became known to a wide audience. (eds.)

E 086 ←
→ E 277

197 Exploded-view drawings

Image source:
https://upload.wikimedia.org/wikipedia/commons/d/d7/Internal_hub_3_speed_Shimano.jpg
(see sources)

Recommended links:
There are many online tutorials that can be found with the keyword "exploded-view drawings."

Exploded-view drawings enable the depiction of complex constructions, their details, and their relationship to one another in a communicative way. But the technique can also be used to visualize simple constructions to create a better understanding for future reproductions, for example. This form of depiction has earned its name based on the way the individual components and modules of the drawn objects "fly apart" as if they've exploded. They are mainly used for infographics. They are particularly prevalent in assembly instructions, technical drawings, as well as spare-part catalogs, where they designate the orientation of individual parts and visualize their appearance and quality. In architecture, they create a better understanding of complex buildings, such as functional units, wayfinding systems for visitors, emergency exits, and escape plans at airports. Exploded-view drawings generally do not serve as a technical foundation for manufacturing processes. Special plans are required for this that depict an object from different sides. The principle (that is expanded in line with the complexity) is: frontal view, side view, top view. (eds.)

Exploded-view drawing of a Shimano three-speed hub gear (1977).

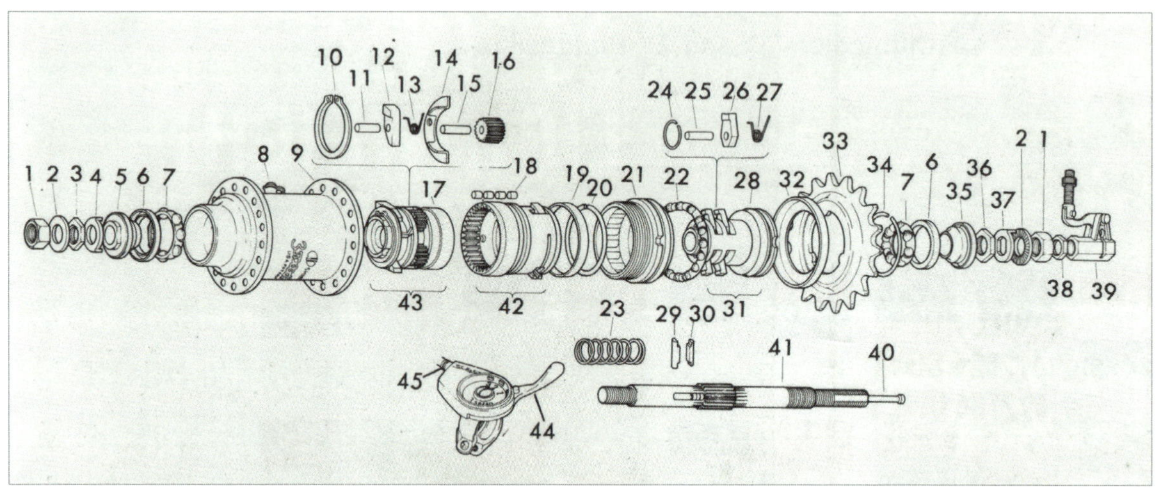

E 086 ←
→ E 277

198 Central projection; Parallel projection

Image sources:
(1), (2) Drawings by Michael Schmitz;
(3) https://de.wikipedia.org/wiki/Perspektive#/media/Datei:Zimmerbild_78.jpg, (see sources)

Recommended websites:
https://en.wikipedia.org/wiki/Parallel_projection
https://en.wikipedia.org/wiki/3D_projection

There are several options for spatially depicting objects. The one that most closely corresponds to human perception is the depiction in a central projection, also called central perspective (1). It is a component of descriptive geometry and aims to create clarity. The main feature is a vanishing point towards which all edges and vanishing lines run. It always sits on an imaginary horizon. This allows a larger depiction of nearby objects and a smaller depiction of objects in the distance. The central projection is thereby linked to the position of the observers. It is used in architecture, technology, various areas of analog and digital graphic design, cartography, and art.

In contrast to central projections, all lines run parallel in parallel projections (2), which results in an unnatural perspective. The advantage of this depiction is that it can provide true-to-scale values. (eds.)

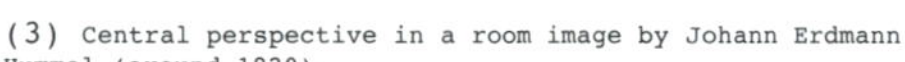
(3) Central perspective in a room image by Johann Erdmann Hummel (around 1820).

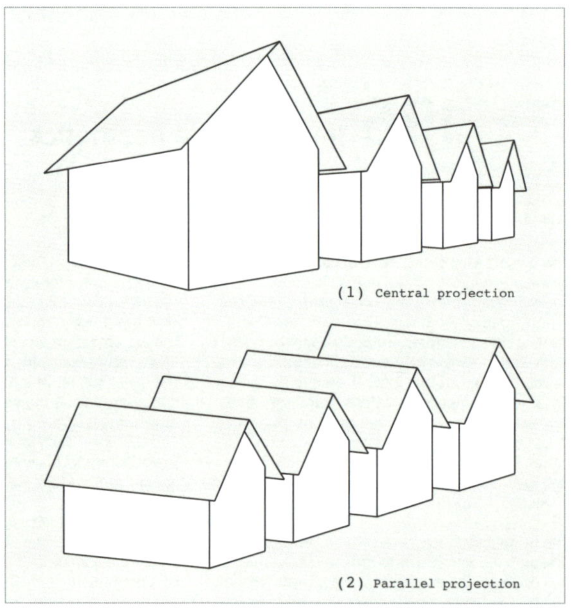
(1) Central projection

(2) Parallel projection

E 087 ←
→ E 278

199 Laws of UX: Using Psychology to Design Better Products & Services.

Bibliographic information:
"Laws of UX: Using Psychology to Design Better Products & Services", Jon Yablonski, O'Reilly Media (ed.), Sebastopol, 2020;
ISBN: 9781492055310

Text sources:
example one: https://lawsofux.com/hicks-law/
example two: https://lawsofux.com/millers-law/
example three: https://lawsofux.com/peak-end-rule/

Recommended website:
https://lawsofux.com/

There are a few key principles of psychology that can make designers' everyday work much more efficient if they acquaint themselves with these. These principles deal with the insight that humans should not be the ones to adapt to design, but that design should adapt to humans. Excessive demands, in whatever form, are conterproductive. But they are easy to prevent in communication.

The guidelines "Laws of UX" by Jon Yablonski include 12 simple rules to take into account.

They are: 1. Jakob's Law, 2. Fitts's Law, 3. Hick's Law, 4. Miller's Law, 5. Postel's Law, 6. Peak-End Rule, 7. Aesthetic-Usability Effect, 8. Von Restorff Effect, 9. Tesler's Law, 10. Doherty Threshold, 11. With power comes responsibility, 12. The application of psychological principles in design.

As an illustration, three of the rules are described here. (eds.)

/ Example one. "Hick's Law" states:
The time it takes to make a decision increases with the number and complexity of choices.

How should we respond to this insight? Answer:
1 Minimize choices when response times are critical to decrease decision time.
2 Break complex tasks into smaller steps in order to decrease cognitive load.
3 Avoid overwhelming users by highlighting recommended options.
4 Use progressive onboarding to minimize cognitive load for new users.
5 Be careful not to simplify to the point of abstraction. (...) /

/ Example two. "Miller's Law" states:
The average person can only keep 7 (plus or minus 2) items in their working memory.

How should respond to this insight? Answer:
1 Don't use the "magical number seven" to justify unnecessary design limitations.
2 Organize contents into smaller chunks to help users process, understand, and memorize easily.
3 Remember that short-term memory capacity will by vary per individual, based on their prior knowledge and situational context. (...) /

/ Example three. The "Peak-End Rule" states:
People judge an experience largely by how they felt at its peak and at its end, rather than the total sum or average of every moment of the experience.

How should we respond to this finding? Answer:
1 Pay close attention to the most intense points and the final moments (the "end") of the user journey.
2 Identify the moments when your product is most helpful, valuable, or entertaining and design to delight the end user.
3 Remember that people recall negative experiences more vividly than positive ones. (...) /

E 091 ←
→ E 279

200 Ticket machines

Image sources:
(1) Private photo of an RMV machine in Königstein/Ts.;
(2) https://upload.wikimedia.org/wikipedia/commons/f/f8/Ticket_machine_at_Tagawaita_Station_198708.jpg (see sources)

Ticket machines serve as important equipment in everyday life. They must meet the goal of being usable by all people – whether locals or foreigners, people with or without disabilities, intelligent or less intelligent people. This means that designers face a considerable challenge. (see 091)
If we take a look at Japanese machines from 1987, I, as someone who is unfamiliar with Japanese, would say: As attractive as it may be, it is just as mysterious. Intuition wouldn't get me very far, at least that is my first impression. Foreigners in Germany will have felt the same way in those years. A leap to the year 2023 shows that new techniques have replaced the confusing attractiveness of the old displays. It isn't clear at first glance whether the machine offered by the Rhein-Main-Verkehrsverbund is accessible to everyone. But the touchscreen makes it easy to follow the steps of purchasing a ticket.
The customer- and service-oriented country of Japan has also stepped up: In 2023, many of the machines are bilingual (jpn/eng) and can hold their own when it comes to "good usability." (u.v)

(1)
A ticket machine from the Rhein-Main-Verkehrsverbund (Germany) from Jahr 2023, with a choice of languages, touchscreen, and four different payment options. The user navigation via the touchscreen gives the rest of the display great clarity.

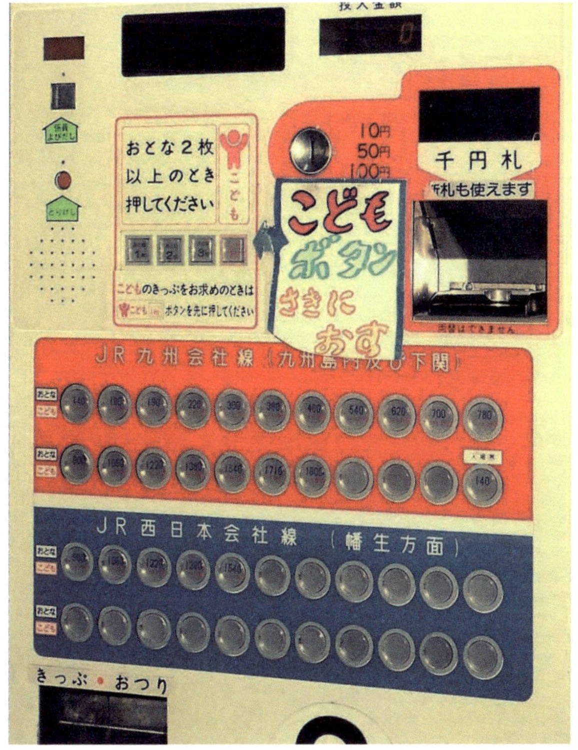

(2)
A ticket machine at JR Kyushu Tagawa-Ita station (Tagawa, Fukuoka) by the "Japanese National Railway," 1987;

E 094 ←
→ E 280

201 Adobe Express Tool

Text source:
https://www.adobe.com/express/ (see sources)

Recommended website:
http://www.adobe.com/de/express/

Sometimes, a few words say a lot. This certainly applies in the case of the Adobe Express tool. A quote from Adobe:

ʹ Save time with templates. Adobe Express makes it easier to get started with thousands of attractive templates and assets for social media content, logos, and more. You can feel as though you have a trustworthy designer by your side with the entire license-free photo collection from Adobe Stock as well as a complete library of Adobe fonts. (...) ʹ

Yes, this is what the future will look like. More and more tools will produce uninspired, average, sometimes even quite nice, but in any case functional graphic design – and thereby make communication designers redundant. However, only those who already cannot come up with more than the tools are capable of. As you will easily have noticed, this is precisely what this book is about: to help you acquire and expand your skills in such a way that the limited tool capacities cannot keep up – whether in conception, visual rhetoric, and/or your mindset. In the future, every dentist and tax accountant may be able to conjure up their own website (and many are already doing so). But when it comes to the complex matters of communication, of knowledge transfer, and questions of visibility among the competition, then they will turn to you – this is the case now and won't change in the future. (eds.)

E 097 ←
→ E 283

202 Chaos Computer Club (CCC)

Image source:
https://de.wikipedia.org/wiki/Chaos_Computer_Club#/media/Datei:Logo_CCC.svg

Text source:
https://de.wikipedia.org/wiki/Chaos_Computer_Club
(see sources)

ʹ Chaos Computer Club (CCC) is a German association in which hackers have joined forces. The association has developed into a crucial non-governmental organization (NGO) in all matters of computer security. According to the CCC, the information society needs "a new human right to global, unimpeded communication," which is why the club "advocates for freedom of information across borders and focuses on the impacts of technology on society as well as individuals." Membership is open to anyone who can identify with these goals. The CCC is a registered association under German law, based in Hamburg, and has over 8,000 members according to its own figures. (...) ʹ

The CCC's media archive is highly recommended for anyone who wants to learn more about topics such as computer security, technological developments, and current debates on topics such as artificial intelligence. Currently (as of April 2024), it contains 9,127 hours of video material that is available for free (74,884 documents from 12,966 recordings of 360 events). (eds.)

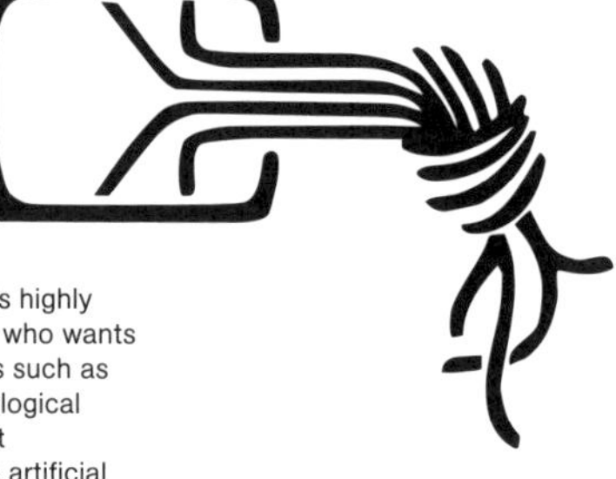

Chaos Computer Club logo

Recommended websites:
https://www.ccc.de/
https://media.ccc.de/

E 100 ←
→ E 281

203 The decolonizing (or puncturing, or de-Westernizing, and SHIFTING), Design Reader, 2021 – 2023

Image source:
Screenshot from https://docs.google.com/document/d/1Hbymt6a3zz044xF_LCqGfTmXJip3cetj5sHlxZEjtJ4/edit# (see sources)

Project source:
https://docs.google.com/document/d/1Hbymt6a3zz044xF_LCqGfTmXJip3cetj5sHlxZEjtJ4/edit#heading=h.92tkp5yoljb9
(see sources)

ʹ The decolonizing, (or puncturing, or de-Westernizing, and SHIFTING), Design Reader, 2021–23 edition[1].

An in-progress, collaborative project[2] since 2018.
Ramon Tejada / Decolonizing Design Reader
Tinyurl address: https://tinyurl.com/y43sukuu

([1]Decolonizing is a term that can mean many things to many people.)

For me, decolonizing is about making space (sometimes taking space…) to allow people that look like me (especially BIPOC people) to be active and essential participants around the table. It is about physical visibility, structural change, representation (not tokenism), acknowledgement (of ideas, land, values that were stolen, repressed, etc), giving up (taking) space, "responsible expansion" (recognizing what design has ignored and not valued) of narratives, points of view, perspectives, stories, theories, ideas, geographical references (not just of Northern European and American lineages, which erases everybody else's identity (colonialism), a diversity of lineages (not just the Bauhaus and all it's grandchildren) etc.
It is about unearthing, shifting the glance, [and] decentering; giving agency, being vulnerable, making mistakes, thinking about our communities (not the design community), thinking about mom/dad/grandparents/your neighbor, our chosen families, acknowledging not knowing and making the periphery the center.*
This will not happen overnight, in one class, in one syllabus. This is a long and slow process. A collaborative process that demands we all work on this.

*Another term that can be used is de-westernized design. —Arturo Escobar

[1] Edits as of Summer 2022.
Thanks to Michiel Teeuw for organizational edits on 10/2021.
[2] *If you would like to contribute or have comments, please email me. I had to turn the comments feature off. (...) ʹ

←
What Does 'Cultural Appropriatio...
https://www.theatlantic.com/polit...
André Alexis: The complex issues...
https://www.theglobeandmail.co...
The Ground on Which We Stand: ...
Arturo Escobar: Designs for the P...
Achille Mbembe. Rethinking Dem...
—Posing Modernity: The Bla...
—The History of the Renaissance...
"Decolonizing Means Many Thi...
Pluralism and Power Dynamics in ...
Interview – Walter Mignolo/Part 1...
Interview – Walter Mignolo/Part 2...
Helvetica, Modernism and the St...
—Building Raíces, Latinx Creative...
Divine collaboration: on Lemi Gh...
In the '90s, Rajeev Prakash Rei...
Sadie Red Wing // F* The Stereot...
Decolonising 'decolonisation' wit...
Long Read | Never Again: Refusin...
Algorithmic Colonisation with Ab...
A New Bauhaus? The Debate for ...
The Cheryl D Miller Portfolio 2020
https://www.youtube.com/watch?...
Once Overlooked, Black Abstract...
https://www.nytimes.com/2021/0...

Beyond the Bauhaus: How a Chicago-Based Art Collective Defined Their Own Aesthetic
https://educators.aiga.org/beyond-the-bauhaus-how-a-chicago-based-art-collective-defined-their-own-aesthetic/

"Decolonizing Means Many Things to Many People"—Four Practitioners Discuss Decolonizing Design
https://eyeondesign.aiga.org/decolonizing-means-many-things-to-many-people-four-practitioners-discuss-decolonizing-design/

Making & Being*
by Susan Jahoda and Caroline Woolard of BFAMFAPHD
Making and Being offers a framework for teaching art that emphasizes contemplation, collaboration, and political economy.
2019, Pioneer Works Press
*This also exists as a very thorough website where you can download the book and the exercises.
*Website, pdf (excerpt) of the book

Pluralism and Power Dynamics in Indian Design: November Studio
https://walkerart.org/magazine/pluralism-indian-design-november-shiva-nallaperumal-juhi-vishnani

This Bridge Called my Back: Writing by Radical Women of Color, edited by Cherrie Moraga and Gloria Anzaldua
https://monoskop.org/images/e/e2/Moraga_Cherrie_Anzaldual_Gloria_eds_This_Bridge_Called_My_Back_Writings_by_Radical_Women_of_Color-Kitchen_Table_Women_of_Color_Press.pdf

Designing an Experimental Technology Curriculum By—and For—Black Creatives, Evan Nicole Brown
https://eyeondesign.aiga.org/afrotectopia/

Who's Bad? Jerome Harris
https://2019.typographics.com/schedule/jerome-harris/

Excerpt from the link list in the Google Doc
(see sources)

E 102 ←
→ E 282

204 Design as an Attitude

Bibliographic information:
"Design as an Attitude," Alice Rawsthorn, JRP editions, Geneva, 2022;
ISBN 978-3037645826

Text source:
Quote from page 8, line 24 – page 9, line 18

The book by Alice Rawsthorn (*1958) is titled "Design as an Attitude." She describes what she means by this at the start, in the form of an homage to Lazlo Moholy-Nagy. Her main goal, as quickly becomes clear, is to shine a light on the designer's mindset, which she considers to be more crucial than ever before. (eds.)

′ (...) As design has adopted so many different meanings at different times and in different contexts, and been prone to muddles and clichés, it seems sensible to begin by defining what I believe it is. In all of its manifold guises, design has always had one elemental role as an agent of change that interprets changes of any type—social, political, economic, scientific, technological, cultural, ecological, or whatever—to ensure that they will affect us positively, rather than negatively. Design as an Attitude explores how designers, professional and otherwise, are fulfilling this role at an extraordinarily turbulent, often perilous time when we face changes of unprecedented speed and scale on many fronts.

Among them are global challenges like the deepening environmental and refugee crises; the rise of poverty, prejudice, intolerance and extremism; the recognition that many of the systems and institutions, which organised our lives in the last century, are no longer effective; and the torrent of ever more complex and powerful technologies that promise to transform society, though not always for the better.
"Design as an Attitude" describes how designers are responding by planning and executing projects to tackle climate change; to reinvent dysfunctional areas of health care and social services; to provide emergency support for the victims of man-made and natural disasters; to help asylum seekers to settle into new communities; and to champion social justice. It charts the evolution of design's relationship to other disciplines, such as art and craft, and its role in the resurgence of interest in making, whether by hand, mechanically or digitally. The book also maps the recent shifts in design culture as it becomes more diverse and inclusive, not only in terms of gender, geography and ethnicity, but by embracing people from very different fields, who did not train to be designers, yet are eager to engage with design. (...) ′

E 103.1 ←
→ E 283

205 UN Sustainable Development Goals

Image source:
https://de.wikipedia.org/wiki/Ziele_für_nachhaltige_Entwicklung#/media/Datei:Sustainable_Development_Goals.svg
(see sources)

Text source:
https://www.un.org/sustainabledevelopment/development-agenda/ (see sources)

′ (...) 17 Goals for People, for Planet

The Sustainable Development Goals are a universal call to action to end poverty, protect the planet and improve the lives and prospects of everyone, everywhere. The 17 Goals were adopted by all UN Member States in 2015, as part of the 2030 Agenda for Sustainable Development which set out a 15-year plan to achieve the Goals.

Today, progress is being made in many places, but, overall, action to meet the Goals is not yet advancing at the speed or scale required. 2020 needs to usher in a decade of ambitious action to deliver the Goals by 2030. (...) ′

Notes on the
Reference information in E3:

The note below explains how the informational headings that precede the references in E3 should be read. If you follow the numbers from E2, they will take you here.
The comments on the entries – unless designated as quotations by the characters '...' – are written by Ulysses Voelker.

Back reference to the origin of the entry and the semi-bold confirmation of receipt here in E3

Title of the origin reference

The marked content is presented.

← E2 106 (Behavioral communication and its cultural influences)

206 **Selection of additional topics:**

- "Struwwelpeter," H. Hoffmann, book → p. 326 (poisonous pedagogy)
- Anti-authoritarian education | bit.ly/406uldV (educational concept and criticism)
- Rules Hell's Angels have to follow | bit.ly/3Qt6irX (closed societies)
- Diocesan code of conduct | bit.ly/3YCWfCR (behavior in religious communities)
- ⊙ Russian prison tattoos **(physical distinguishing features)**
- Skulls | bit.ly/3XBFXIY (symbolism of death in different applications)
- Etiquette at the "NYT" | bit.ly/3kHeg3M (social networks and netiquette)
- Forbidden signs in Germany 2022 | bit.ly/41eypiD (emergency response)

206
⊙ Russian prison tattoos
Image source:
https://www.flickr.com/photos/central-asian/8266172707 (see sources)

Title, references, etc.

Marked content that is presented here

List of possible additional topics.
The limited number is owed to space restrictions. Many more connections are conceivable. With "bit.ly" – also for reasons of space – long links were converted into short ones.

Additional topics: 206 – 283

The associative chain of references that started in chapters A–D and led first to E1 and from there to E2, is completed in this chapter E3.
It presents conceivable continuations of the topics – making it clear that the associations relating to visual communication could essentially be continued infinitely.

E 3

← E2 106 (Behavioral communication and its cultural influences)

206 Selection of additional topics:

- "Struwwelpeter," H. Hoffmann, book → p. 326 (poisonous pedagogy)
- Anti-authoritarian education | bit.ly/406uldV (educational concept and criticism)
- Rules Hell's Angels have to follow | bit.ly/3Qt6irX (closed societies)
- Diocesan code of conduct | bit.ly/3YCWfCR (behavior in religious communities)
- ⊙ Russian prison tattoos **(physical distinguishing features)**
- Skulls | bit.ly/3XBFXIY (symbolism of death in different applications)
- Etiquette at the "NYT" | bit.ly/3kHeg3M (social networks and netiquette)
- Forbidden signs in Germany 2022 | bit.ly/41eypiD (emergency response)

206
⊙ Russian prison tattoos

`Image source: https://www.flickr.com/photos/central-asian/8266172707 (see sources)`

For many years, tattoos were a sign of stigmatization – and that was exactly what the images looked like. People with images on their hands either belonged to specific professional groups (military, seafaring) or operated on the fringes of society. Today, tattoos are essentially par for the course.

Questions: What distinguishing groups of and for fringe groups exist today? Who determines social worth? Why is the image on the right in the public domain?

207
⊙ Das eigensinnige Kind

`Text source: "Die Märchen der Brüder Grimm, Vollständige Ausgabe," Verlag Neues Leben, Berlin (GDR), 1984; page 508`

The book features all of Brothers Grimm's fairy tales – even those that are very brutal and those that don't seem to offer a solution at first glance. It would be interesting to discuss this circumstance with experts: How should children interact with the story? Is it even meant for children? When does it cross the line of what is acceptable? What answers can be found in Bruno Bettelheim's book?

← E2 107 (Kinder brauchen Märchen)

207 Selection of additional topics:

- Little Red Riding Hood (diversity of illustrative depictions)
- ⊙ "Das eigensinnige Kind," book → p. 326 **(fairy tales and poisonous pedagogy)**
- Chemtrails and other conspiracy theories | bit.ly/3RaZkHt (opinion vs. science)
- Unicorns, dinosaurs (significance of mythical creatures for children's imagination)
- "Kindchenschema" – the science of cute | bit.ly/3WLblyJ (protective mechanisms in nature)
- The Teletubbies (children's show and critical appraisal)
- News in simple language (complexity and simplification, inclusion)
- "Papa Tatuato," D. Nesquens, book → p. 326 (example of unusual illustration styles)
- "Emma," Spider, book → p. 326 (example of unusual illustration styles)
- "Fliegenpapier," H. Hillmann, book → p. 326 (illustrations for adults)

Here is the complete fairy tale: Once upon a time, there was a stubborn child who did not do what his mother asked. Therefore, God was not pleased with the child and let him fall ill, and no doctor could help him. Within a short time, he was on his deathbed. Once he had been lowered into his grave and covered with earth, he suddenly raised his arms again and reached up, and every time he was laid down again and had fresh earth placed over him, it did no good, and the poor child emerged over and over again. The mother had to go to the grave herself and hit his arms with a switch, and as soon as she had done so, he retreated, and the child finally found peace beneath the earth.

208
⊙ Schalke 04 badge

`Image source: private`

The seventh-largest club in the world based on membership numbers – Schalke 04 from Gelsenkirchen, Germany, and its club badge for members.

The proportion of merchandising in soccer clubs is steadily growing and constitutes an important source of income. Most clubs have almost everything in their online shops – coffee cups, flags, T-shirts, lucky charms. Jersey sales play an important role.

Question: How much wiggle room do designers have within the strict corporate identity? What clubs around the world are most creative?

← E2 108 (Patches for Space Missions)

208 Selection of additional topics:

- Metal patches | bit.ly/3YUoVa4 (visual language of belonging)
- Badges (visual signals)
- ⊙ Schalke 04 badges **(visual language of belonging)**
- Button (visual signals of belonging)
- Cowls in soccer | bit.ly/3I7AFiL (visual signal s of belonging)

Index librorum prohibitorum

Der **Index librorum prohibitorum** („Verzeichnis der verbotenen Bücher", kurz auch **Index Romanus**, „römischer Index", genannt) war ein Verzeichnis der römischen Inquisition, das für jeden Katholiken die Bücher auflistete, deren Lektüre als schwere Sünde galt; bei manchen dieser Bücher war als kirchliche Strafe die Exkommunikation vorgesehen.

Erstmals erschien das Verzeichnis 1559,[1] seine letzte amtliche Ausgabe datiert von 1948 mit Nachträgen bis 1962 und nannte zuletzt 6000 Bücher. Der *Index* wurde nach dem Zweiten Vatikanischen Konzil 1965 bzw. 1966 nicht mehr weitergeführt.[2]

Inhaltsverzeichnis [Verbergen]

Titelkupfer zum *Index librori prohibitorum*. Der Heilige G entzündet das Feuer, das zu Bücherverbrennung dient, K

← E2 109 (Stop Signs in various cultural circles)

209 Selection of additional topics:

- Design of the police and warning apps in Germany (sovereign aesthetic)
- Critical infrastructure and supply for the population (communication)
- ⊙ Books banned by the Catholic church (1966) **(boundaries for what can be shown and said, censorship)**
- Forbidden signs in Germany 2022 | bit.ly/3GgoSPp (emergency response)
- Nina app, Covid app (design of warning apps)

209
⊙ Books banned by the Catholic church

`Image source: https://en.wikipedia.org/wiki/Index_Librorum_Prohibitorum (see sources)`

Who bans books and why? Are books dangerous? Does religion restrict freedom? What do good and evil look like in religious publications?

← E2 109 (Stop Signs in various cultural circles)

209.1 Selection of additional topics:

- Warning signs in the public sphere (visual warnings)
- Greenwashing | bit.ly/3k0BF0e (image and deception)
- Package inserts (visual consumer information)
- ⊙ Atomic bomb **(the aesthetic of horror)**
- Anti-nuclear movement | bit.ly/3XCRGql (protest movement)
- ⊙ Hier waak ik! **(language and aesthetic of dog warning signs)**
- "Codes of the Underworld," D. Gambetta, book → p. 326 (communication among criminals)

209.1
⊙ Atomic bomb
⊙ Warning sign

Image sources:
(1) https://de.wikipedia.org/wiki/Kernwaffe#/media/Kernwaffentest, VR China, 1964; (see sources)
(2) Photo: private

Questions: What do the visual statements have in common? What design devices issue warnings? How do you trigger fear visually? Is there any research on this?

← E2 110 (Bilder, die lügen; Exchanging the "Flag Iwo Jima" image)

210 Selection of additional topics:

- "Chinese Propaganda Posters," B. Taschen, book → p. 326 (succinctness, kitsch)
- "Iron Fists," S. Heller, book → p. 326 (visuality of totalitarian systems)
- ⊙ "Hoffnung und Widerstand," H. R. Lutz, book → p. 326 **(see title)**
- Deepfake | bit.ly/3YUWoB7 (perception and trust)
- ChatGPT | bit.ly/3kc2rTb (artificial intelligence)
- Fake news platforms (design of "alternative facts")
- Radical advertising | bit.ly/411BL8e (attention economy)
- Body shaming, Instagram, and TikTok (self-image)
- FaceApp | bit.ly/3lKaBTq (perception and trust)

210
⊙ Hoffnung und Widerstand

Hans Rudolf Lutz, Bruno Margadant; Verlag Hans Rudolf Lutz u.a., 1998; ISBN 3-907065-77-8
Image source: pages 70 – 71

Questions:
Do you have any role models in poster design? Do you use your graphic skills for worthwhile purposes? Why do communication designers tend to be apolitical?

← E2 111 (Top Secret. Bilder aus den Archiven der Stasi)

211 Selection of additional topics:

- ⊙ Ministry for State Security loyalty badge **(symbols of power in the GDR)**
- The visual language of the BND | bit.ly/3YWVgNr (symbols of power, Germany)
- The CIA's logo | bit.ly/3XFaWUq (symbols of power, US)
- Masonic cipher | bit.ly/3KezGQo (pigpen ciphers)
- ⊙ Wanted posters **(the aesthetic of calls for wanted people)**
- The Enigma code | bit.ly/3l7toj4 (communication in WWII)
- Visuality of North Korea/South Korea (political systems)
- Space telescopes (aesthetic of observation posts)
- Dragnet investigation | bit.ly/3xuKL8o (mass data processing)
- Targets in the USA, magazine | bit.ly/3tG7krW (concept of the enemy)

211
⊙ Wanted posters

Image source: bit.ly/401x5zm (see sources)

Art already delved into the genre of "wanted posters" 50 years ago. I suggest googling "Thirteen Most Wanted Men" by Andy Warhol (1964).

Questions: Is there a specific aesthetic for wanted posters? Is it acceptable to turn the faces of wanted people into art?

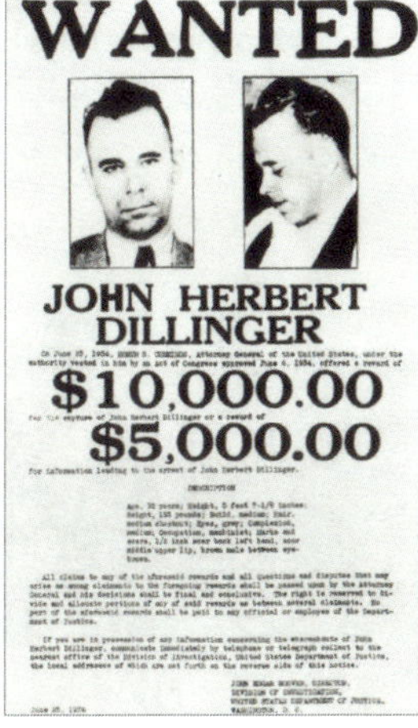

211
⊙ Ministry for State Security loyalty badge (GDR)

Image source: bit.ly/3k3U8ZH (see sources)

Questions: How would you depict trust? Does trust have a color and is there a symbol for it?

← E2 112 – 112.3 (Principles for setting up a supermarket, Focus on children in the advertising industry, Advertising psychology researches purchasing behavior, Compulsive buying promotes antisocial tendencies)

212 Selection of additional topics:

- Candy wrappers for children (spectrum of visual incentives)
- Shopping cart | bit.ly/3FqSRDg (consumption and perception)
- Standard rate for ALG 2 (unemployment benefits) | bit.ly/3I8CYLa (social security systems in consumer societies)
- Impulse buys | bit.ly/3Jgdgwd (purchasing incentives and purchasing behavior)
- Goods in cash register zone | bit.ly/40aGwex (purchasing incentives and purchasing behavior)
- ⊙ Exclusive font for the Plus retail chain **(influencing perception through micro-typography)**
- Developing brand names (marketing and branding)
- Mirroring neurons | bit.ly/42hylPm (empathy as a neurobiological trait)
- "Cock Indian Firework Art," L. Giannuzzi, book → p. 326 (culture-specific advertising languages)

(1)

Da Marco
Cantuccini
Haselnuss

Italienische Gebäckspezialität
je 150g Beutel
100 g 0,57 €

(2)

Da Marco
Cantuccini
Haselnuss

Italienische Gebäckspezialität
je 150g Beutel
100 g 0,57 €

(1) "Compatil Fact,"
(2) "Plus Exklusiv Medium"

212
⊙ Exclusive font for the Plus retail chain

Image source:
"Werkbericht Nr. 12," Johannes Bergerhausen, Lukas Schneider, Ulysses Voelker, © 2006 – 2009 Institut Designlabor Gutenberg, HS Mainz, 2009; ISBN 978-3-936723-20-5

In 2006, Institut Designlabor was commissioned to develop an exclusive font for the Plus retail chain (part of "Netto" today). The aim was to replace the previously used font. Eventually, the font was developed into Greek, Cyrillic, and Bulgarian versions. The most important goal that the font had to fulfil: better readability from a distance while taking up less space, especially when used for price labels. In addition, the font had to possess an unmistakable character that solely represented the Plus retail chain. The font is not for sale.

213
⊙ The Principality of Sealand

Image source: https://de.wikipedia.org/wiki/Sealand#/media/Datei:Flag_of_Sealand.svg (see sources)

In 1967, Patrick Roy Bates from England founded the Principality of Sealand on a former British sea fortress off the coast of Suffolk. Up until his death, he defended his island judicially and demanded recognition as an independent state under international law.

← E2 113 (Maslow's Hierarchy of Needs)

213 Selection of additional topics:

- The prepper movement | bit.ly/3JnLYnw (catastrophes and visual communication)
- Reichsbürger | bit.ly/40aGLWZ (conspiracy theories and associated symbolism)
- ⊙ The Principality of Sealand **(corporate design of a private state)**
- Oligarchies | bit.ly/3JcqSZ6 (presentation of wealth)
- Self-realization | bit.ly/3Io4l3H (individualism and collective thinking)
- Less is more (origin and approach)
- Ascetic design vocabulary | bit.ly/3lcnnKy (minimalism in art)
- Minimalist program | bit.ly/3yFV61T (minimalism in linguistics)
- Simple life | bit.ly/3Fs3beu (minimalism as a lifestyle)
- Decadence | bit.ly/3JEH7jh (description of a social behavior)
- Uncover Designfest Mannheim | bit.ly/3ZQYEu7 (design and decadence)
- ⊙ Pictograms for people with disabilities **(accessibility)**

(1)

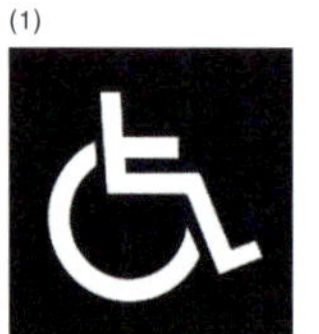

(2)

(1) Design: Susanne Koefoed, 1968
(2) Design: Karl Montan, 1969
(3) Design: Brian Glenney, Sara Hendren, Tim Ferguson Sauder, 2009

The development of pictograms is always linked to social values and points of views. In 1968, even just acknowledging people with disabilities and their needs was considered progress (in 1969, the mind followed the body), while today, emphasizing independence and activity is a given.

(3)

213
⊙ Pictograms for people with disabilities

Image sources: (1) https://99percentinvisible.org/episode/icon-for-access/ (2)/(3) https://accessibleicon.org/ (see sources)

← E2 114 (Dazzle Camouflage, Flecktarn)

214 Selection of additional topics:

- McDonald's and the switch from red to green | bit.ly/3yGjOiJ (greenwashing)
- Color of weapons | bit.ly/3QqFLvE (hierarchy through design)
- Yakuza | bit.ly/3JEQkIn (secret societies and identifications)
- Secret societies | bit.ly/3nansvu (communication and outside world)
- Wagara | bit.ly/42snx1d (Japanese patterns)
- ⊙ Sapeur, Congo **(colonialism, fashion, self-confidence)**
- Prison clothing, prison uniforms | bit.ly/3ZuhMNG (features of hierarchies)

214
⊙ Sapeur, Congo

Text source:
https://de.wikipedia.org/api/rest_v1/page/pdf/Sapeur

Image source:
https://en.wikipedia.org/wiki/La_Sape#/media/File:Men's_Sapeur_inspired_looks_from_SS_15_lookbook.jpg (see sources)

A sapeur, from the colloquial French term **"sape"** meaning "clothes," is a both strikingly and elegantly dressed man in Africa whose appearance stands in stark contrast to his living conditions. Sapeurs emerged as a social movement in the 1960's in Brazzaville, capital of today's Republic of the Congo, and received another boost on the opposite shore of the Congo in Kinshasa, the capital of today's Democratic Republic of the Congo. Protesters who opposed the politics of the former Zairean president Joseph Mobutu used their formal clothing to express that they were not rebels and troublemakers. Papa Wemba particularly shaped the style at the time. In the form of La sape, the sapeur movement is one of the few trends that made its way from the region of the Congo into other parts of the world. The term was later explained through the backronym "Société des Ambianceurs et des Personnes Élégantes" (which translates to "society of entertainers and elegant people"). (…) The most important feature of a sapeur is their lifestyle focused on fashionable elegance and individuality, visually based on the features of a classical dandy and gentleman. However, wearing fancy and elaborately combined clothing does not say anything about their social or financial status, but rather illustrates the contrast between the inner freedom of a sapeur and the external circumstances that surround them. The striking appearance serves primarily as resistance against the dreariness and poverty of a sapeur's home region. (…) ᐟ

215
⊙ Everest Mini Market
Image source: Private, Nightshop in Antwerp (B)

This night shop opts for clever advertising with a name that makes you take a second look. Good typography: trashy, but with a sense for design.

← E2 115 (Typography is culture)

215 Selection of additional topics:

- "Art and Text," A. Selby, book → p. 326 (typography and art)
- The cards "Spain," "UP 12" | bit.ly/3G5TF0H (typography and art)
- "Die Schrift," V. Flusser, book → p. 326 (typography and culture)
- ⊙ Everest Mini Market, Antwerp **(font, culture, advertising)**

← E2 116 – 116.2 (Braille, Braille in the unicode system, Dialog im Dunkeln, Dialog Museum)

216 Selection of additional topics:

- Guidance for blind people | bit.ly/3ZO5sbT (accessibility)
- Visual markings for the visually impaired | bit.ly/3JHVPGc (accessibility and visual communication)
- City maps for disabled people (accessibility and orientation)
- The blind men and the elephant | bit.ly/3ZLHhuK (parable of reality)
- Blind study | bit.ly/3sSommH (medical and psychological research)
- Dummy text | bit.ly/3Jo2G6e (simulation of real text)

(1)

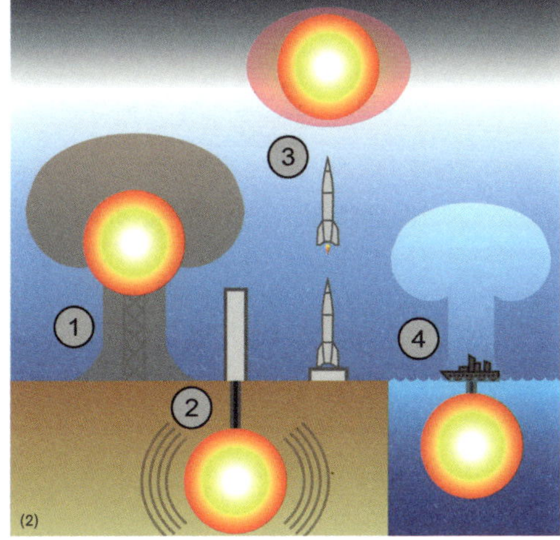

(2)

← E2 117 (Marshall Islands stick charts)

217 Selection of additional topics:

- David Carson | bit.ly/3FqctYm (surf cult and design)
- Pacific | bit.ly/3MY0hlw (depiction of expedition routes)
- ⊙ Marshall Islands **(corporate design)**
- ⊙ Nuclear weapons test scheme **(graphics as relativizing information)**
- Maori Tatau | bit.ly/3yEgwwo (South Sea tattoo)
- ⊙ Tiki style **(design style from Hawaii)**
- Hydrogen bomb scheme | bit.ly/3WicXZV (infographic)
- ⊙ Radiation symbol **(graphic depiction of danger)**

217
⊙ Tiki style, Nuclear weapons test scheme, Radiation symbol, Marshall Islands
Image sources: (1) https://de.wikipedia.org/wiki/Tiki-Kultur#/media/Datei:BaliHaiNO-LA59Postcard.jpg, (2) https://de.wikipedia.org/wiki/Kernwaffentest#/media/Datei:Types_of_nuclear_testing.svg, (3) https://commons.wikimedia.org/wiki/File:Seal_of_the_Marshall_Islands.svg, (4) https://de.wikipedia.org/wiki/Strahlenwarnzeichen#/media/Datei:Radiation_warning_symbol_5.svg (see sources)

Between 1946 and 1958, the USA carried out 20 nuclear weapons tests in the South Sea. The destruction is still visible today. Images:
(1) A South Sea postcard of tiki-style architecture;
(2) the different ignition schemes in the air, on land, and in the water.
(3) The Marshall Islands coat of arms, Pacific;
(4) radiation symbols on the fin of the Convair, 1955;

Questions: Are vivid graphics – ones that are even appealing to the eye – obscene if they depict a form of horror – or are they justified because "nuclear weapons ensure freedom"? Would you accept such a job?

(3)

(4)

← E2 118 – 118.1 (Punkt und Linie zu Fläche, Das grafische Zeichen. Kommunikation und Irritation)

218 Selection of additional topics:

- Arabic SMS in the Lat. Unicode System | bit.ly/3LrTTD8 (language and technology)
- "Pictorial Depth Perception in Sub-Cultural Groups in Africa," W. Hudson, book → p. 326 (spatial perception in cultures)
- Prototype testing in product design | bit.ly/3w5yzhv (functional tests in design)
- The Measure of Man, Henry Dreyfuss | bit.ly/3ZTpu5L (standards through measurements)
- Fashion campaigns and body shaming | bit.ly/40VAfny (role models in advertising)
- ⊙ Seaworthiness certificate **(visuality of certificates)**
- Judo club ID | bit.ly/3TZ0Xtb (visuality of certificates)
- "Bürokratie – Die Utopie der Regeln," D. Graeber, book → p. 326 (governmental communication)

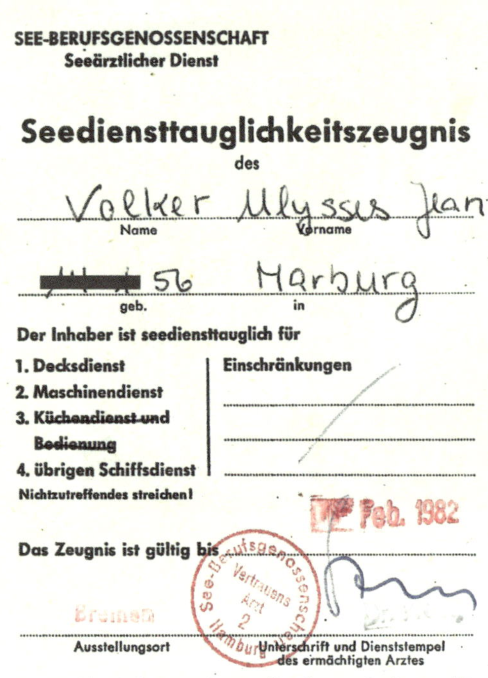

SEE-BERUFSGENOSSENSCHAFT
Seeärztlicher Dienst

Seediensttauglichkeitszeugnis
des

Volker Ulysses Jean
Name Vorname

56 Marburg
geb. in

Der Inhaber ist seediensttauglich für

1. Decksdienst
2. Maschinendienst
3. ~~Küchendienst und Bedienung~~
4. übrigen Schiffsdienst

Nichtzutreffendes streichen!

Einschränkungen

Feb. 1982

Das Zeugnis ist gültig bis

Bremen
Ausstellungsort

See-Berufsgenossenschaft Vertrauens Arzt 2 Hamburg
Unterschrift und Dienststempel des ermächtigten Arztes

Der Umschlag darf nur von einem zur Vornahme von Seediensttauglichkeitsuntersuchungen ermächtigten Arzt geöffnet werden.

Ohne gültiges Seediensttauglichkeitszeugnis darf kein Seemann anmustern. Es ist deshalb sorgfältig zu verwahren.

218
⊙ Seaworthiness certificate
Image source: private

There are forms, lists, tables, certificates, attestations for anything and everything. Designers generally don't give this topic too much thought because it is viewed as unappealing, it doesn't allow them to live out their creative identity. But is that really true? As a rule, agencies communicate with other authorities in this way – and what this communication looks like says a lot about the sender's understanding of hierarchy, proximity to citizens, friendliness. For designers, this design area is therefore highly interesting and relevant.

← E2 119 (Apolitical murals)

219 Selection of additional topics:

- Tag writing | bit.ly/3lW474m (typography in the city)
- Banksy in museums | bit.ly/3KAZVR7 (art – commerce)
- Pictures on house walls | bit.ly/3QNrVnh (advertising)
- Painted menus | bit.ly/3ZCR8SN (authenticity)
- Leipzig-Charta | bit.ly/40BbfCf (guidelines for transformative forces in the city)
- "Building and Dwelling: Ethics for the City," R. Sennett, book → p. 326 (ethics, future)

← E2 120 (Political murals)

220 Selection of additional topics:

- Reclaim Award | bit.ly/3TZ2r6J (public design interventions)
- Ethnic communities in cities | bit.ly/49QUsjk (visual and cultural inheritance)
- Hacking the city | bit.ly/3m2AHBm (interventions in urban space)
- Floating University Berlin | bit.ly/3JVY5Za (open learning forum and participation)
- raumlabor Berlin | bit.ly/3ZACwTO (architecture firm)
- Exhibition: GEO-Design 2020 Eindhoven | bit.ly/3m0MDDS (globalization)
- "Pioneers of the Downtown Scene New York, 1970s," L. Yee, book → p. 326 (see title)
- "Useful Photography 011," Kesselskramer (ed.), book → p. 326 (US target motifs)

← E2 121 – 123 (visual codes 1: Sign Language, visual codes 2: SignWriting, visual codes 3: The Flag Alphabet, visual codes 4: Morphological Tables)

221 Selection of additional topics:

- Free texts (open source) | bit.ly/3PTG54R (licenses and usage)
- ⊙ Blackmail letters **(individual coding)**
- General terms and conditions and the small print | bit.ly/40YjQPb (hard-to-access information)
- Lecture on communication techniques | bit.ly/3JlXUAO (communication forums)
- Stateless Democracy with the Kurdish Women's Movement | bit.ly/3QdS1Qd (Statelessness and outward visual rhethoric)
- "Destination Branding," M. Nigel, A. Pritchard, R. Pride, book → p. 326 (visuality and state identity)
- Ted Talk – Alice Rawsthorn: Pirates, nurses and other rebel designers | bit.ly/3Kr3s4b (rebelliousness in design)

221
⊙ Blackmail letters
Image source: Graphics M. Schmitz

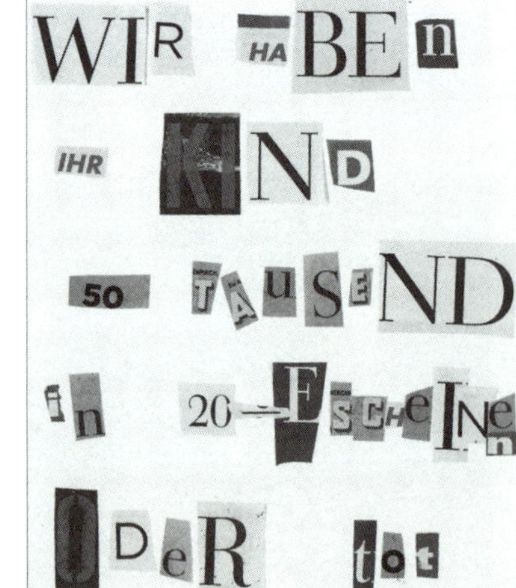

The "Jolly Roger" was the identifying mark of piracy, i.e., predatory undertakings on sea. Pirates were not subject to any governmental control, but were also commissioned by authorities to carry out raids. Condemnation of this practice began in the mid-19th century. Modern pirates, such as those at the Horn of Africa, now use camouflage techniques to sneak up on and raid ships.

222
⊙ Jolly Roger
Image source: https://commons.wikimedia.org/wiki/File:Skull_and_crossbones.png (see sources)

← E2 124 (Visual communication using the example of the "pictogram")

222 Selection of additional topics:

- Drawing stencils for children | bit.ly/40viuLQ (education and pictures)
- Paint by number | bit.ly/3JVwJm8 (creativity and structure)
- Rob Scholte / Back Stage: Die Rückseite | bit.ly/46StBRF (embroidery as art)
- Stencil alphabet | bit.ly/3ZupyHr (transfer techniques)
- City flags, lecture by Roman Mars | bit.ly/3nGXl2C (flag design)
- ⊙ Jolly Roger **(pirates and flags)**
- Standard lettering (EN ISO 3098) | bit.ly/3TZVvGI (standardization)
- ⊙ Traffic signs in NL, GER, CH, and F **(differences between NL, GER, CH and F)**

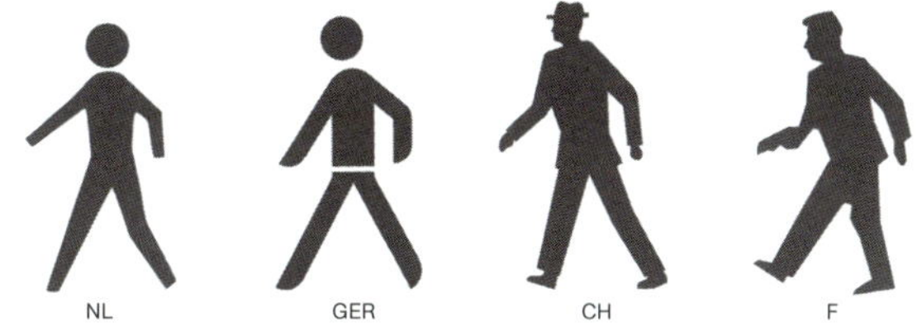

222
⊙ Traffic signs in NL, GER, CH, and F

Image source:
Work report "497 – Die visuellen Sprachen längs des Rheins," Ulysses Voelker, Institut Designlabor Gutenberg, HS Mainz, 2009; ISBN 3-936723-05-2

Globalization is a keyword in the present day. It is accompanied by ongoing efforts to unify standards.
In a seminar in 2006, we addressed the question of the extent to which globalization has progressed. For this purpose, we examined visual language along the Rhine and stopped in Basel, Strasbourg, Mainz, and Rotterdam. Back then, 17 years ago, we were surprised by the many regional particularities, as can be seen in the depictions on the left. The evaluation is conflicting today. On the one hand, in a best-case scenario, a schematic simplification is inclusive. Based on this judgment, there shouldn't be a depiction of a man if, after all, the "pedestrian" symbol refers to all people. Hardly anyone wears a hat anymore either, and suits are not exactly the norm. On the other hand, regional cultures would lose their specific modes of expression. A dilemma that designers, notably, must confront.

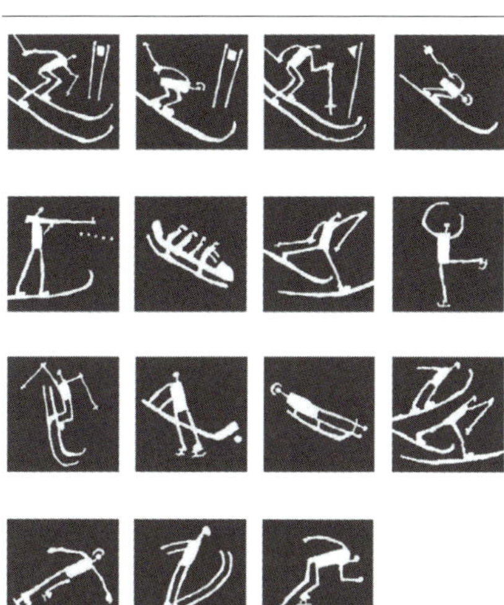

← E2 125 (Die XX. Olympiade München 1972: Richtlinien und Normen für die visuelle Gestaltung)

223 Selection of additional topics:

- ⊙ 1994 Winter Olympics, Norway **(pictograms)**
- Soccer world championship/mascot | bit.ly/3ZTVxTd (identification figures)
- DIN standards | bit.ly/3ZW6hQN (standardization in the graphic design industry)
- Color profiles | bit.ly/3m5Q6kn (standardization in the graphic design industry)
- Master HS Mainz, admissions procedure | bit.ly/3KoOOKG (shortage and talent)
- Reading competitions at schools | bit.ly/3KqJc2u (learning and performance)
- Charlie Hebdo, Mohammed caricatures | bit.ly/3m0OHvC (satire, taboo, terror)
- "Deutsch für junge Profis," W. Schneider, book → p. 326 (language and communication)
- "Die Sprache", J. Trabant, book → p. 326 (language and communication)
- "Was soll an meiner Nase bitte jüdisch sein?", T. Meyer, book → p. 326 (communication and prejudice)

Rødøymannen, 4,000-year-old depiction of a skier

223
⊙ 1994 Winter Olympics, Norway

Image sources:
https://library.olympics.com/Default/doc/SYRACUSE/161826/the-sports-pictograms-of-the-olympic-winter-games-from-grenoble-1968-to-beijing-2022-the-olympic-stu?_lg=en-GB (see sources)
https://de.wikipedia.org/wiki/Olympische_Winterspiele_1994#/media/Datei:Urzeit_rodoy.gif (see sources)
see also: https://de.wikipedia.org/wiki/Olympische_Winterspiele_1994#

The 1994 Winter Olympics took place in February of 1994 in Lillehammer (Norway). The gold, silver, and bronze medals were made of granite. The respective sports were depicted as pictograms on the back. The design template for these was one of the oldest known depictions of a skier that was found in the Norwegian town of Rødøy in 1932. The rock painting is about 25 cm wide and around 4,000 years old. Norway showed courage by choosing this graphic form of expression, because it prioritized regional ties over internationalization. The design received plenty of criticism.

← E2 126 (About diversity and antidiscrimination at FU Berlin)

224 Selection of additional topics:

- Annette Lenz, Paris | bit.ly/3m3oVXB (renowned designers)
- ⊙ Irma Boom, Amsterdam **(renowned designers)**
- Linda van Deursen, Amsterdam | bit.ly/3KtCWr6 (renowned designers)
- The Rodina, Teresa Ruller, Amsterdam | bit.ly/3GaScWW (renowned designers)
- Paula Scher, New York | bit.ly/3G9eBUG (renowned designers)
- Ellen Lupton, Maryland, USA | bit.ly/3Krfr1B (renowned designers)
- April Greiman | bit.ly/40Anuiq (renowned designers)

224
⊙ Irma Boom

Image source:
Scan of the book of a cardboard box, format of the book: 43 x 55 mm; lecturis, ISBN 978-94-6226-035-1

Irma Boom belongs to the most renowned contemporary book designers. She and others on the list of women work in many creative areas. Ellen Lupton, for example, is a globally known design author; Annette Lenz's poster art is on display in museums around the world; Teresa Ruller works as a designer and performer. The mentioned women are a few examples among many more.

← E2 127 (Lexicon der Tatoeages van Aarsgewei tot Zwitserland)

225 Selection of additional topics:

- ⊙ The Anchor as a Symbol **(cultural codes in different applications)**
- Indigenous tattoo styles as western fashion | bit.ly/3ZzuVFd (cultural appropriation)
- Font styles on Asian street-food packaging | bit.ly/3Maw5nC (ethnic typography)
- North American sports logos | bit.ly/40Vj3ye (cultural appropriation)
- Hindu swastika and Nazi swastika | bit.ly/3G8EjJ3 (misuse of symbols)
- Gibberish | bit.ly/3zqn0zi (language and code)
- Twelve-tone technique, Arnold Schönberg | bit.ly/40Mcpus (methods in music)

(1)

(2)

(3)

225
⊙ The anchor as a symbol

Image sources:
(1) https://de.wikipedia.org/wiki/Aldus_Manutius#/media/Datei:Aldus-symbol.jpg; (2) Privat; (3) https://de.wikipedia.org/wiki/Mariupol#/media/Datei:Mariupol_gerb.png
(see sources)

The anchor is the symbol of trust. In Christianity, it stands for hope and is often used in coats of arms. (3: municipal coat of arms of Mariupol, Ukraine).

The anchor is a frequently chosen tattoo motif for seafarers (see 2). The "anchor and dolphin" symbol (1) was the sign of the printer Aldus Pius Manutius (1449 – 1515). He was a Venetian book printer and publisher. Manutius was one of the most important printers of Greek texts of his time.

← E2 127.1 – 128 (Tattoos as cult and identification model, Forever – The New Tattoo; Forever More – The New Tattoo, The artistic font "AK Shavcat")

226 Selection of additional topics:

- Calligraphy in hip-hop subcultures | bit.ly/3M5lHMZ (typography, subcultures)
- "Poesie der Großstadt. Die Affichisten," E. Schlicht, R. Wetzel, M. Hollein, book → p. 326 (visual communication and art)
- ⊙ "Silence," J. Cage, book **(language, typography, and art)**
- "Denken. Reden. Machen," Stiftung Museum Schloss Moyland (ed.), book → p. 326 (art and creative practice)
- "Beuys. Die Revolution sind wir," E. Blume, C. Nichols, book → p. 326 (art)

Dieser Vortrag wurde in Incontri Musicali, *August 1959, gedruckt. Es gibt vier Takte in jeder Zeile und zwölf Zeilen in jeder Einheit der rhythmischen Struktur. Es gibt achtundvierzig solche Einheiten, jede zu achtundvierzig Takten. Das Ganze ist in fünf große Teile im Verhältnis 7, 6, 14, 14, 7 gegliedert. Die achtundvierzig Takte jeder Einheit sind ebenfalls so gegliedert. Der Text ist in vier Kolonnen gedruckt, um ein rhythmisches Lesen zu erleichtern. Jede Zeile ist quer über die Seite von links nach rechts zu lesen, nicht senkrecht den Kolonnen nach. Das sollte nicht in einer gekünstelten Weise geschehen (was aus dem Versuch resultieren könnte, die Stellung der Wörter auf der Seite strikt einzuhalten), sondern mit dem* Rubato, *das man beim alltäglichen Sprechen anwendet.*

VORTRAG ÜBER NICHTS

Ich bin hier , und es gibt nichts zu sagen .
Wenn unter Ihnen
die sind, die irgendwo hingelangen möchten , sollen sie gehen,
jederzeit . Was wir brauchen ist
Stille ; aber was die Stille will
ist, daß ich weiterrede .
Gib einem Gedanken

6

einen Stoß : er fällt leicht um
; aber der Stoßende und der Gestoßene er-zeugen die Unter-
haltung die man Dis-kussion nennt .
Wollen wir nachher eine abhalten ?

Oder wir könnten einfach be-schließen keine Diskussion abzuhalten . Wie sie wollen . Aber
nun gibt es Stille und die
Wörter erzeugen sie, helfen mit diese
Stille zu erzeugen .

Ich hab nichts zu sagen
und ich sage es und das ist
Poesie wie ich sie brauche .

Dieses Stück Zeit ist gegliedert
. Wir brauchen nicht diese Stille zu fürchten. –
wir könnten sie lieben .
Dies ist ein komponierter
Vortrag , denn ich mache ihn

7

226
⊙ Silence, John Cage

Image source: "Silence," John Cage, Bibliothek Suhrkamp, Frankfurt, 1996, Original edition 1954, USA, ISBN 3-518-22193-0, pages 06 – 07;
Text source and recommended website:
https://de.wikipedia.org/wiki/John_Cage (see sources)

' John Milton Cage Jr. (1912 – 1992) was an American composer and artist. With his over 250 compositions, many of which are considered key works of 20th century classical music, he ranks among the most successful composers of the 20th century worldwide. He also wrote fundamentally important music and composition theory work. In addition, Cage is considered a key figure of the "happening" movement that emerged in the late 1950's and an important stimulator for the Fluxus movement and free improvisation. Aside from his composition work, he also dabbled in painting and mycology, the science of mushrooms. '

In the epilog of his book "Silence" from 1961, Cage wrote: ' (...) The way I see it, poetry is simply not prose because poetry is tied to a certain form. It isn't poetry due to its content or ambiguity, but because it allows us to incorporate musical elements into the world of words. (...) '

← E2 128.1 – 129 (Handwritten fonts, Designing Type)

227 Selection of additional topics:

- Stencil technique | bit.ly/46us3xv (typography and production)
- Lettering stencils for technical drawings | bit.ly/45yR1ux (typography and clarity)
- Bar codes and their reading techniques | bit.ly/3m8pork (data and reading)
- "Lesen," S. Dehaene, book → p. 326 (reading backgrounds)
- ⊙ Children's reading primer 1962, FRG **(reading course in the 1960's)**

227
⊙ Children's reading primer 1962, FRG

Image source: Meine Fibel, Ernst Klett Verlag, Stuttgart;
Image source: pages 10 – 11

This is the double page from my school reading primer from the year 1962. I received it at the start of the first grade. In addition to the learning goal of learning to read, the images and division of roles, the landscapes and displayed objects formed a canon that reflected the perspective of adults in the 1950's. On one page, Mother and Lotte are crying because Hans has left. Even the dog and the hedgehog shed a few tears. Hans, in the meantime (who wasn't a vegan yet at the time, as evidenced by the sausage in his pocket) takes the liberty of leaving his home at age six.

Even though the song "Hänschen klein, ging allein…" (English: "Little Hans, left on his own…") serves as the basis for the image, it would be interesting to see how today's designers and educators would depict this subject.

225
226
227
228
229

← E2 130 (Digital Cuneiform)

228 Selection of additional topics:

- Gutenberg-Museum Mainz | bit.ly/3ZAlDal (font and history)
- "The Graphic Art of Tattoo Lettering," B. J. Betts, N. Schonberger, book → p. 326 (font and tattoos)
- Lettering in Comics | bit.ly/3ZVrxq0 (typography and authenticity)
- Bionic reading technique | bit.ly/40PthAV (reading and technology)
- iA Writer | bit.ly/3MamTj9 (software for writing and reading)
- Museum for East-Asian Arts in Cologne | bit.ly/3nJFgRu (Japan and art)
- ⊙ Kimonos **(clothing and communication)**
- Reading direction in newspapers: Japanese, Arabic, Latin script | bit.ly/48X9bsQ (culture and convention)

(1)

(2)

228
⊙ Kimonos

Image sources:
(1) https://de.wikipedia.org/wiki/Kimono#/media/Datei:Kone.jpg (2) https://de.wikipedia.org/wiki/Kimono#/media/Datei:Uchikake.JPG (see sources)
see also: https://en.wikipedia.org/wiki/Kimono

The kimono is a Japanese item of clothing with a long history. It resembles a caftan and is tied together with a wide belt. Between 794 and 1192, the form of the kimono that we see today started to take shape. The clothing item consists of a robe that reaches down to the ankles and features a collar as well as wide sleeves. Men and women both wear kimonos, although men prefer dark muted colors. The preferred material is silk, but kimonos can also be made of wool, linen, or cotton. The name of the kimono differs depending on the occasion.

← E2 131 (Globally valid media "laws")

229 Selection of additional topics:

- The Bengali language as the foundation for the formation of Bangladesh | bit.ly/3Kqsdxj (language, communication, identity, and the foundation of a nation)
- National and international newspaper formats | bit.ly/3M92ElK (editorial design)
- Why the US can't decolonize their design? | bit.ly/3G8Am6Y (decolonization and education)
- ⊙ Soccer in Greenland | bit.ly/40AW4sz **(shared activities around the world)**

Flag of Greenland (DK)

229
⊙ Soccer in Greenland

Image sources:
(1) https://commons.wikimedia.org/wiki/File:Flag_of_Greenland_(2000_World_Factbook).svg,
(2) https://de.wikipedia.org/wiki/Gr%C3%B6nland#/media/Datei:Uummannaq-football-game.jpg
(see sources)

There are few cultural rituals that are practiced around the world while following the same set of rules. Soccer is one of them. While searching for the most remote fields of the world (which really depends on the perspective), I stumbled upon this picture from Greenland – and a beautiful flag.

← E2 132 (The Voynich Manuscript)

230 Selection of additional topics:

- European Voynich Alphabet | bit.ly/3K0iOvb (decoding)
- Rosetta Stone | bit.ly/40WEAGK (translation and writing)
- "Die schreckliche deutsche Sprache – The Awful German Language," M. Twain, book → p. 326 (transculturality)
- Ernst Jandl, poet and writer | bit.ly/3K1fdgl (communication and art)
- ⊙ Secret signs **(encrypted communication)**
- Calligraphy courses/instructions | bit.ly/3uzNxed (tools and writing)
- Character/personality traits and writing style | bit.ly/3sRpGGs (psychology and writing)
- Sütterlin script | bit.ly/40xuMn9 (time-related conventions)

230
⊙ Secret signs

Image source:
https://de.wikipedia.org/wiki/Zinken_(Geheimzeichen)#/media/Datei:Gaunerzinken.svg (see sources)
Recommended websites:
https://en.wikipedia.org/wiki/Hobo#Hobo_signs_and_graffiti
https://en.wikipedia.org/wiki/Hobo

A secret sign or mark is a communication device used by "traveling people". This takes place either through sounds, facial expressions, or gestures – but primarily through graphic signs.
"Secret signs" as a means of communication are largely a thing of the past. There is a classification of secret signs: "Beggars' signs" serve to mark worthwhile locations. "Swindlers' signs" are used as communication within the criminal milieu. "Identifying signs" designate individuals or groups (families). And "directional signs" offer orientation in the public space.

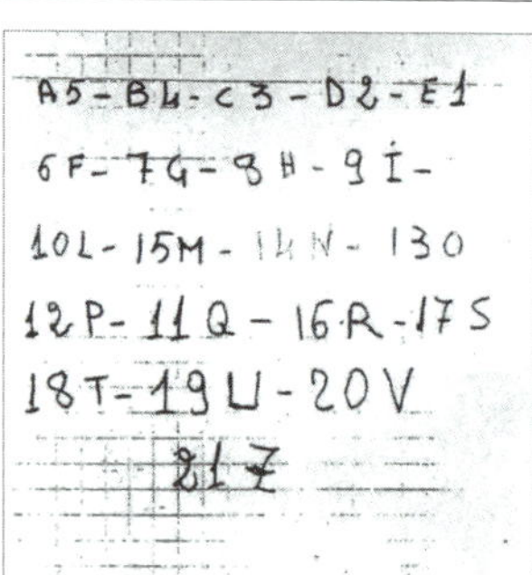

The secret code of Bernardo Provenzano: The letters of the alphabet are shifted by five positions.

← E2 133 (Cryptography)

231 Selection of additional topics:

- Zodiac Killer | bit.ly/40vvz7U (communication and blackmail)
- The Nazi Enigma machine in World War II | bit.ly/3l7toj4 (tools and encryption)
- Alan Turing – code breaker | bit.ly/3KqocJd (mathematics and communication)
- ⊙ Pizzino, the mafia's communication device **(hidden communication)**
- Secret message | bit.ly/3KqocJd (hidden communication)

231
⊙ Pizzino

Image source:
https://de.wikipedia.org/wiki/Pizzino#/media/Datei:Pizzino_Provenzanos.jpg (see sources)
Recommended website: https://de.wikipedia.org/wiki/Pizzino#/media/

Pizzino (plural: pizzini; English: little note) refers to a written note and stems from the Italian. The note is generally intended for communication, for example as work instructions or a shopping list. Since electronic communication isn't tap-proof, this method of communication is preferred by mafia and Cosa Nostra circles. In the past, pizzini were verifiably used to arrange crimes. In the 2000's, the Italian police succeeded in decrypting the secret messages, which led to a slew of arrests. Among others, they tracked down Cosa Nostra godfather Bernardo Provenzano, whom they had spent many years searching for. Provenzano used the "symmetrical Caesar encryption," which shifts the meaning of letters by a set number of positions.

← E2 134 (Communication design and subjectivity)

232 Selection of additional topics:

- Traffic light colors and their signal effect | bit.ly/3m0QSPH (convention and color)
- Information transmission during the Chernobyl reactor catastrophe | bit.ly/3nD8Ubd (power and flow of information)
- ⊙ Clichés in music **(genre-typical codes)**
- Umbrella revolution Hong Kong | bit.ly/42XNPbL (politics and alternative communication media)
- "Die große März-Kassette," Area Verlag (ed.), book series → p. 326 (recognizability and broadcasting)
- Willy Fleckhaus and the publisher Suhrkamp Verlag | bit.ly/3lYwUVJ (recognizability and succinctness)
- Willy Fleckhaus and "Twen" magazine | bit.ly/40Vq4zm (zeitgeist and transitions)

232
⊙ Clichés in music

Image source: Private

Clichéd depictions as identification features form part of the visual repertoire of groups. Interestingly, we only tend to notice clichés when others resort to them. In the 2000's, the newspaper "Süddeutsche Zeitung" presented a photo series in its weekly magazine that pictured attendees of various rock concerts. As expected, their appearance gave away the respective band's music genre. The photos revealed metal fans, hip hop fans, intellectual Bob Dylan fans, or rapt Tom Jones disciples. So before you start gossiping about Franky Bodet (left) and his feeble attempts to pass as Mexican, you might want to take a good look in the mirror.

← E2 135 (How Real is Real?)

233 Selection of additional topics:

- Disinformation campaigns in elections | bit.ly/3M6i8XK (disinformation)
- "Miteinander Reden," F. Schulz von Thun, book → p. 326 (psychology)
- Conspiracy theories | bit.ly/3ZATq4E (disinformation)
- ⊙ Optical illusions **(senses and perception)**
- Provocation as a creative technique | bit.ly/4bodvBG (brainstorming strategies)
- "Finnegan's Wake," J. Joyce, book → p. 326 (experimental literature)
- Retro trendy wallpaper in interior design | bit.ly/3U1gRTC (fashions)
- Wigs | bit.ly/3K2vkdp (taste and zeitgeist)
- "DDR Design," G. Höhne, book → p. 326 (taste formation following the top-down principle)

230
231
232
233
234
235
236
237
238

233
⊙ Optical illusions
Image source: private

If you look at the black center of the top image, it gets larger.
If you glance across the bottom image, it will move.

← E2 136 (Adbuster Media Foundation)

234 Selection of additional topics:

- Culture jamming | bit.ly/40WPpsm (guerilla communication)
- Urbane Liga Jugendforum Stadtentwicklung (Urban League – Youth Forum for Urban Development) | bit.ly/3MaMbxj (participation and urban planning)
- Reverse graffiti | bit.ly/4302ByD (guerilla marketing technique)
- Die with me – chat app only in use with less than 5% power | bit.ly/3Ku0Q5O (communication and addiction)
- iPhone and Fairphone | bit.ly/3MeoB2O (consumption criticism)
- Chicks who love guns | bit.ly/3Gde97C (visually represented violence)
- HBKN - Kalashnikov Girl - Russian Girls and Russian Guns | bit.ly/3Gba7Nq (visually represented violence)
- Graphic announcements in everyday life (aesthetics between chance and intention)

← E2 137 – 140 (Guerrilla marketing, The Yes Men, Guerrilla communication, Dries Depoorter, The Lookout, 2021 – 2024, Werbekodex des Deutschen Werberats)

235 Selection of additional topics:

- ⊙ "I love NY" merchandise **(global advertising success)**
- Addictive UI Design | bit.ly/3zq0KWh (psychological design marketing mechanisms)
- Gambling addiction | bit.ly/3K83qwG (stimuli, addiction, and advertising for it)
- Body shaming | bit.ly/40VAfny (stereotypes, role models)
- Influencer culture | bit.ly/3zoibGM (advertising and social media)

235
⊙ I love NY
Image source: https://de.wikipedia.org/wiki/Milton_Glaser#/media/Datei:I_Love_New_York.svg (see sources)

American graphic designer Milton Glaser (1929 – 2020) created this signet in 1973.

Love sculpture by Robert Indiana in New York City, USA

"Pop Art" is the name of an art genre that grew popular in the fine arts (painting, sculptures) in the 1950's and became a dominating art form in North America and Europe in the 1960's. Pop art integrated everyday culture into its expressive repertoire, particularly elements of consumption and the mass media.

← E2 141 (Der Typografiestreit der Moderne – Max Bill kontra Jan Tschichold)

236 Selection of additional topics:

- "Delirious New York," R. Koolhaas, book → p. 326 (architecture in modernism)
- "Learning from Las Vegas," R. Venturi, D. S. Brown, S. Izenour, book → p. 326 (architecture in modernism)
- The Daily Heller | bit.ly/4e2iGJV (Design blog)
- ⊙ Pop Art **(art genre)**
- "Pop Art," K. Honnef, book → p. 326 (art and revolt)
- "The Complete Cartoons of THE NEW YORKER 1925 – 2004," R. Mankoff, book → p. 326 (cartoons as a mirror of the time)
- "The Medium is the Massage: An Inventory of Effects," M. McLuhan, book → p. 326 (media theory)
- "The Book Cover in the Weimarer Republik," J. Holstein, book → p. 326 (aesthetics in early modernism)

236
⊙ Pop Art
Image source: https://de.wikipedia.org/wiki/Pop_Art#/media/Datei:LOVE_sculpture_NY_cropped.jpg (see sources)
Recommended website: https://de.wikipedia.org/wiki/Pop_Art

← E2 142 (Richard Paul Lohse – Konstruktive Gebrauchsgrafik)

237 Selection of additional topics:

- "Rückblick auf sieben Kapitel konstruktive Bilder. Etc," K. Gerstner, book → p. 326 (graphic design, art, and algorithm)
- Constructivism in psychology | bit.ly/3Gat96s (psychology and communication)
- Drip painting | bit.ly/433dyzp (chance in art)
- "World Transformers," M. Weinhart, M. Hollein, book → p. 326 (crossover artists)

← E2 143 – 143.1 (Ausbildung in typografischer Gestaltung, Typoundso)

238 Selection of additional topics:

- "Altitude. Contemporary Swiss Graphic Design," N. Bourquin, R. Klanten, C. Mareis, buch → p. 326 (Swiss design in the 2000's)
- Corporate design of banks | bit.ly/3R9F6iP (capital and look)
- Blingee GIF | bit.ly/3ZPQcuB (design and kitsch)
- Goods as a sensory physical commodity | bit.ly/3Rb5B7v (commodity fetishism)

← E2 144 – 144.1 (False Flat: Why Dutch Design is so Good, Sandberg Instituut, Werkplaats Typografie, KABK Den Haag)

239 Selection of additional topics:

- Black Mountain College | bit.ly/3nlFl2M (Bauhaus in the USA)
- Wim Crouwel | bit.ly/3zrl0a8 (Dutch designers)
- Jan van Toorn | bit.ly/3U58Mxx (Dutch designers)
- Fred Smeijers | bit.ly/3U05FXy (Dutch designers)
- Karel Martens | bit.ly/3m34utG (Dutch designers)
- Erik Kessels | bit.ly/3zncA3A (Dutch designers)
- Kesselskramer | bit.ly/3KoZNE3 (Dutch design studio)
- Experimental Jetset | bit.ly/3Gyrqs7 (Dutch design studio)
- Thonik | bit.ly/42YBeVG (Dutch design studio)
- Metahaven | bit.ly/431wQVO (Dutch design studio)

240
⦿ Ads in crime books, 1980s

Image source: private

Take a look at the ad for remote teaching – "Fernunterricht." It lists "graphic designer" as a learning opportunity. As you can see, when it comes to the professional self-image, it entirely depends on the environment in which one operates. Of course, the job of a "graphic designer" can be understood in a completely different way from our conception. This also explains the questioning glances of relatives and acquaintances when you tell them what you're studying. Another aspect: The ads were designed, who knows by whom. The question: Does this constitute good design because the offer corresponds to the target group?

← E2 145 (DDC Wettbewerb 2023: "Was ist gut" – Kriterien)

240 Selection of additional topics:

- Dutch Design Week Eindhoven | bit.ly/3GmJk1B (design and publicity)
- Red Dot Award | bit.ly/3Mclqsu (design and publicity)
- German Design Award | bit.ly/40YOyHX (design and publicity)
- Windmills in Holland | bit.ly/4442BOW (cliché and reality)
- Anfachen Award | bit.ly/3Q8Kj9v (competition design)
- ⦿ Ads in crime books, 1980's **(advertising, standard, target groups)**

Trophy "Keizer St-Godelievevink, Ruddervoorde 1992," Belgium.

← E2 145.1 (German Sustainability Award 2024 – Design Criteria)

241 Selection of additional topics:

- German Ecodesign Award | bit.ly/3Maflww (competitions)
- Germany's most beautiful books | bit.ly/47mCnlz (competitions)
- Design Award of the Federal Republic of Germany | bit.ly/3UioFAR (competitions)
- ⦿ Trophy, Belgium, 1992 **(trophy design)**

241
⦿ Trophy, Belgium, 1992

Image source: private

Questions: What should a good trophy look like? Who designs trophies? Who needs to find the trophies appealing? How much tradition does a trophy need to exude? Does a trophy need to visualize the respective sport?

(1)

(2)

← E2 146 (Symbolism and use of the White and Red Cross)

242 Selection of additional topics:

- Corporate design of the Swiss government (Flag use regulation) | bit.ly/40R9vEy (order and design)
- Branding of the Dutch police | bit.ly/3nGSI92 (authority and visual identity)
- "Models," E. Kessels, book → p. 326 (design and collecting)
- Religious symbols | bit.ly/3UaKli3 (significant visual language)
- ⦿ Highway permit stickers **(sovereign communication)**

242
⦿ Highway permit stickers

Image sources:
(1) https://de.wikipedia.org/wiki/Autobahnvignette#/media/Datei:Vigcz2007.jpg
2) https://de.wikipedia.org/wiki/Autobahnvignette#/media/Datei:Vignetten_1997-2011.jpg (see sources)

Questions:
What criteria could apply to the design of highway permit stickers? Protection against forgery, potentially created through graphic complexity? Or a good long-distance effect thanks to minimalism? What role do sovereign insignia play? What role does color play? Who even designs these stickers?

(1) (2)

243

⊙ The Seal of the USA

Image sources: (1) https://de.wikipedia.org/wiki/Liste_der_Flaggen_der_Vereinigten_Staaten#/media/Datei:Great_Seal_of_the_United_States_(obverse).svg (2) https://de.wikipedia.org/wiki/Liste_der_Flaggen_der_Vereinigten_Staaten#/media/Datei:Great_Seal_of_the_United_States_(reverse).svg/ (see sources)

The Great Seal of the USA is the official seal and national emblem. The front features the head of a bald eagle. The back shows an incomplete pyramid above which floats the Eye of Providence.

(3)

Since 1987, the flag of the Bikini Atoll acts as a reminder of the USA's great guilt in first evacuating the atoll's residents and then partly destroying and completely contaminating it during the nuclear weapons tests of 1954.

239
240
241
242
243
244
245
246
247

243

⊙ The flag of the Bikini Atoll

Image source: (3) https://de.wikipedia.org/wiki/Liste_der_Flaggen_der_Vereinigten_Staaten#/media/Datei:Flag_of_Bikini_Atoll.svg (see sources)

← E2 147 (The German Federal States' Coats of Arms)

243 Selection of additional topics:

⊙ The Seal of the USA **(sovereign communication)**
- The flags of the US Space Force | bit.ly/40OR4kU (sovereign communication)

⊙ The flag of the Bikini Atoll **(sovereign communication and criticism)**
- Flags of the federal subjects of Russia | bit.ly/3Gdagjw (sovereign communication)
- Flags of the federal states/union territories, India | bit.ly/3U4NEay (sovereign communication)

← E2 148 (Josef Müller-Brockmann. Ein Pionier der Schweizer Grafik)

244 Selection of additional topics:

- Halftone screening | bit.ly/3zoAprw (preliminary stage of printing)
- Design grids | bit.ly/42XiSo3 (layout and order)
- Public transport line networks | bit.ly/3nDX00K (abstraction of reality)
- Tabular figures / old style figures | bit.ly/3lZq3eG (typography)
- Widow line and club line | bit.ly/3zoVfaj (typography)
- Paper formats | bit.ly/3Krj9lt (different standards vs. globalization)

245

⊙ Woodcut

Image source: https://de.wikipedia.org/wiki/Die_gro%C3%9Fe_Welle_vor_Kanagawa (see sources)

The Great Wave off Kanagawa (around 1830), Woodcut by Katsushika Hokusai.

← E2 149 – 150 (The "Opendyslexic" font, "Ryman Eco" font)

245 Selection of additional topics:

- Silkscreen technique | bit.ly/40PTtLL (graphic printing processes)
- "A – Z of Letterpress," A. Kitching, book → p. 326 (typographic art)

⊙ Woodcut **(graphic printing processes)**
- Linocut | bit.ly/42TqfwR (graphic printing processes)
- Etching | bit.ly/3Gaz4bV (graphic printing processes)
- Lithography | bit.ly/3ZzoC4u (graphic printing processes)
- Potato print | bit.ly/3GcD6Ax (graphic printing processes)

These fighter bomber groups existed into the 1990's in Germany. Question: How can weapons convey that one has peaceful intentions, but is capable of the opposite? Are weapons directed at the enemy or do they serve as internal motivation?

246

⊙ Fighter bomber groups 41, 49

Image sources: (1) https://de.wikipedia.org/wiki/Jagdbombergeschwader_49#/media/Datei:COA_JaBoG_49.svg / (2) https://de.wikipedia.org/wiki/Jagdbombergeschwader_41#/media/Datei:COA_JaboG_41.svg (see sources)

← E2 151 (Font development for documenta 15)

246 Selection of additional topics:

- Font designer Peter Bil'ak | bit.ly/3GaOzka (font distribution)
- Font manufacturer Monotype | bit.ly/3U6PyHQ (font distribution)
- Illiteracy | bit.ly/3lY9vnv (living without writing)
- Bundesverband Alphabetisierung und Grundbildung e.V. (Federal Association for Literacy and Basic Education) | bit.ly/3zvOyTO (living without writing)

⊙ Fighter bomber groups 41, 49 **(war aesthetics)**
- The Brevity Code | bit.ly/3MaHAev (military communication)
- Non-violent communication | bit.ly/42Y9f8E (non-violent conflict resolution)
- Pacifism | bit.ly/3m1bTK5 (ethical attitude)

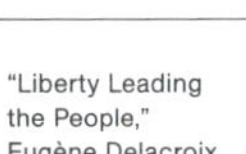
"Liberty Leading the People," Eugène Delacroix (1830)

247

⊙ Symbol of the French Revolution from 1830

Image source: https://de.wikipedia.org/wiki/Marianne#/media/Datei:Eug%C3%A8ne_Delacroix_-_La_libert%C3%A9_guidant_le_peuple.jpg (see sources)

Task: Draw a picture that symbolizes the battle of the "Last Generation."

← E2 152 (Liberation movements)

247 Selection of additional topics:

⊙ Symbol of the French Revolution from 1830 **(visual identification features)**
- ISIS branding and its appearance | bit.ly/3lSXBLK (violence and design)
- Look of weapons exhibitions in the USA | bit.ly/49REHZy (weapons and normality)
- Che Guevara T-shirts in commerce | bit.ly/42YaFQw (pop and revolution)
- "Gegen den Hass," C. Emcke, book → p. 326 (doubt and dogma)
- "Branding Terror," A. Beifuss, book → p. 326 (the visual language of terrorist organizations)
- "The Complete Crumb Comics Vol. 4," R. Crumb, book → p. 326 (underground comics)
- "Complete Freak Brothers, Vol. 1," G. Shelton, book → p. 326 (underground comics)

248

⊙ British Guiana 1c Magenta (1856)

Image source: https://upload.wikimedia.org/wikipedia/commons/4/4d/%28Enhanced%29_British_Guiana_1856_1c_magenta_stamp.jpg (see sources)

As of 2014, this stamp is the most expensive collector's item in the world. Estimated value: between 10 and 20 million US dollars.

← E2 153 (Manual typesetting for children)

248 Selection of additional topics:

- ⊙ British Guiana 1c Magenta (1856) **(most expensive postage stamp in the world)**
- "Lechts und Rinks," E. Jandl, book → p. 326 (communication according to one's own laws)
- The Stedelijk Museum (Amsterdam) for children | bit.ly/3K2lebq (museum education)
- The Städelmuseum (Frankfurt) for children | bit.ly/430gi0n (museum education)
- The Museum Boijmans van Beuningen (Rotterdam) for children | bit.ly/3KrnmMk (education)
- Robert Indiana, US artist | bit.ly/3m1qcOU (pop art and signal art)
- Jenny Holzer, US artist | bit.ly/3MsO8Wn (art, text, and public space)
- Barbara Kruger, US artist | bit.ly/3MgnSyl (art and text)

← E2 154 (Computers and their designs 1979 – 1986)

249 Selection of additional topics:

- Apple marketing events and the hype surrounding them | bit.ly/40Ynp99 (successful brands)
- Cell phones | bit.ly/40AYgAu (technological development and their design)
- Rotary phones | bit.ly/40PYSm1 ((technological development and its design)
- Life without a cell phone | bit.ly/40zXBPL (technology and dependence)
- The whistle-blowing platform Wikileaks | bit.ly/3G6zWhF (David vs. Goliath)
- War game "Call of Duty" | bit.ly/3U2zjLG (psychology, ethics, and design)

← E2 155 (Anarchy of Signs)

250 Selection of additional topics:

- Random.org – True random number service | bit.ly/3MdcHGE (random numbers, based on atmospheric noise)
- Lottery aesthetics | bit.ly/3U0emRG (order within arbitrariness)
- "design – design," A. Petruschat, J. Petruschat, specialist German/English dictionary, book → p. 326 (transcultural communication)

← E2 156 (The Risograph)

251 Selection of additional topics:

- Fanzine culture | bit.ly/40xUXtV (DIY and visual communication)
- Bitmap aesthetics | bit.ly/40Y4GL2 (technological development and aesthetics)
- ⊙ Fluxus **(idea vs. work of art)**
- Hipster | bit.ly/40RYpiK – (2) | bit.ly/40AVY4k (subculture)
- Hipster hairstyles | bit.ly/3JW6vzW (fashion and subculture)
- Minimalist tattoos | bit.ly/42WX4ce (fashion and subculture)

251

⊙ Fluxus

Image source: https://de.wikipedia.org/wiki/Fluxus#/media/Datei:Fluxus_manifesto.jpg (see sources)

The "Fluxus" art movement acquired its name from the Latin word meaning "to flow" and emerged in the 1960's. After Dadaism, Fluxus was another attack on the traditional concept of works of art. Fluxus propagated that the creative idea should be the main focal point, not the work of art, as this in itself was viewed as a bourgeois fetish. Fluxus was founded by the American George Maciunas (1931 – 1978). Many renowned avantgarde artists shaped the movement: Bazon Brock, John Cage, George Brecht, Mary Bauermeister, Wolf Vostell, Arthur Køpcke, Benjamin Patterson, Emmett Williams, Dick Higgins, Ludwig Gosewitz, Alison Knowles, Yoko Ono, Robin Page, Tomas Schmit, Ben Vautier, Robert Filliou, Joseph Beuys, Nam June Paik, and Charlotte Moorman.

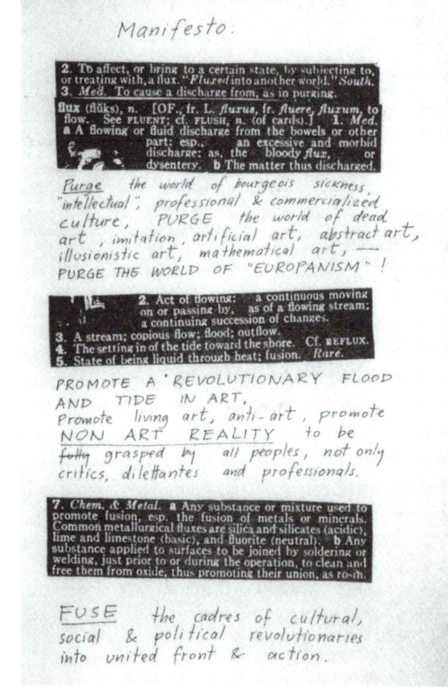

Manifesto.

2. To affect, or bring to a certain state, by subjecting to, or treating with, a flux. "Fluxed into another world." South. 3. Med. To cause a discharge from, as in purging.

flux (flŭks), n. [OF., fr. L. fluxus, fr. fluere, fluxum, to flow. See FLUENT; cf. FLUSH, n. (of cards).] 1. Med. a A flowing or fluid discharge from the bowels or other part; esp., an excessive and morbid discharge: as, the bloody flux, or dysentery. b The matter thus discharged.

Purge the world of bourgeois sickness, "intellectual", professional & commercialized culture, PURGE the world of dead art, imitation, artificial art, abstract art, illusionistic art, mathematical art, — PURGE THE WORLD OF "EUROPANISM"!

2. Act of flowing: a continuous moving on or passing by, as of a flowing stream; a continuing succession of changes.
3. A stream; copious flow; flood; outflow.
4. The setting in of the tide toward the shore. Cf. REFLUX.
5. State of being liquid through heat; fusion. Rare.

PROMOTE A REVOLUTIONARY FLOOD AND TIDE IN ART, Promote living art, anti-art, promote NON ART REALITY to be ~~fully~~ grasped by all peoples, not only critics, dilettantes and professionals.

7. Chem. & Metal. a Any substance or mixture used to promote fusion, esp. the fusion of metals or minerals. Common metallurgical fluxes are silica and silicates (acidic), lime and limestone (basic), and fluorite (neutral). b Any substance applied to surfaces to be joined by soldering or welding, just prior to or during the operation, to clean and free them from oxide, thus promoting their union, as rosin.

FUSE the cadres of cultural, social & political revolutionaries into united front & action.

253

⊙ Stereotypical couple, 1962

Image source: private

"Art can also be attractive, you just need to want it," Jürgen von Manger (1923 – 1994).

← E2 157 (Art Directors Club Germany)

252 Selection of additional topics:

- Type Directors Club New York | bit.ly/40BHhOg (design organizations)
- Payment for design internships in NYC | bit.ly/40UY0Ms (money and work)
- Association Typographique Internationale ATypI | bit.ly/40ydCW9 (design organizations)
- Professional Association of Freelance Photographers and Film Creators BFF | bit.ly/3ZC48rZ (design organizations)
- Organization for illustrators | bit.ly/3KtDeya (design organizations)
- Gesellschaft für Designgeschichte | bit.ly/3KtmtTN (design organizations)

← E2 158 (Sinus Milieus)

253 Selection of additional topics:

- Target-group analysis | bit.ly/3U1MPz4 (marketing management)
- Natural environment | bit.ly/40P2kfW (economic knowledge)
- ⊙ Couples as a stereotype **(target group, simplification)**
- Functional competition | bit.ly/3znQhdY (economic knowledge)
- Cartel, definition | bit.ly/3GcFC9X (economic knowledge)

254
⦿ Orange wrappers
Image source: private

There is a graphic world that is fairly neglected – that of orange wrappers. It offers an incredible variety of motifs and patterns and leaves many designers wondering how they might snag such a commission. The book "Verhüllt um zu verführen" ("Covered to seduce") provides an insight into this world.

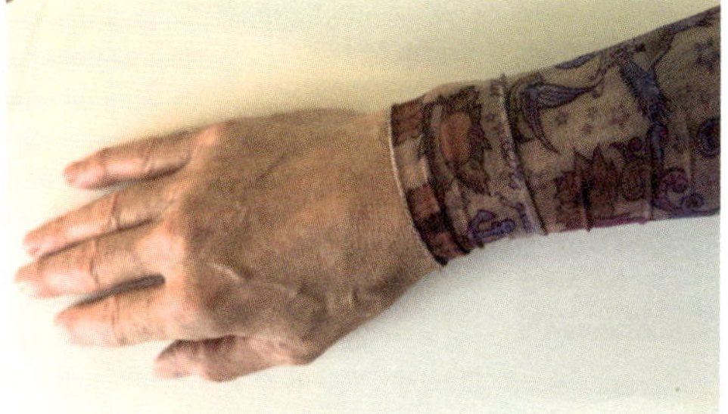

254
⦿ Tattoo sleeves
Image source: private

Fifteen years ago, tattoo sleeves were almost trendy. In the meantime, we could use sleeves that feign tattoolessness – because one in five Germans now has ink on their skin. Although it could also be stylish to pull one over one's own tattoo...

← E2 159 (All-American Ads, 1950s)

254 Selection of additional topics:

- Intercultural communication | bit.ly/3MslUdd (global communication)
- Brands in the supermarket | bit.ly/49ZwOjQ (product comparability)
- Primal Artesian Water/FIJI water | bit.ly/3KtjD15 (water branding and pricing)
- Calvé labels 1949, 1999 | bit.ly/3MQY3UM (graphic zeitgeist)
- "Freaks, Geeks & Strange Girls," L. Stone, book → p. 326 (advertising)
- ⦿ Tattoo sleeves **(self-optimization, fashion)**
- ⦿ Orange wrappers **(advertising)**
- "Verhüllt um zu verführen," D. Oettingen, book → p. 326 (advertising, orange wrappers)
- Cannes Lions International Festival of Creativity | bit.ly/3Mexrxw (competition in advertising, advertising as cult)
- Zirkus Roncalli, circus | bit.ly/3SPmR3f (graphic staging of sensations)
- Riverside stomp open air 2014 | bit.ly/46qjUcQ (gender stereotypes on the eve of gender debates)
- ⦿ Zirkus Charles Knie, circus **(graphic staging of sensations)**

254
⦿ Zirkus Charles Knie
Image source: flyer, Mainz, 2010's

What do we expect of a circus? Sensations, surprises, suspense – in short: stimulation of all senses in a pleasurable sense. If this analysis is correct and included in a briefing, this would mean that the flyer has done quite a few things right here: the choice of color, the layout, and the pictures promise just that. Those of you who find the layout too trashy should attempt to create a design yourselves, just for fun (or google the more poetic Zirkus Roncalli).

← E2 160 (Motivation + Aktion)

255 Selection of additional topics:

- Resistance Design | bit.ly/49lgZO3 (Design as a resistant tool)
- The Austrian resistance movement 05 | bit.ly/3Gauvy1 (code and public)
- What design can do – Festival Amsterdam | bit.ly/3K1SK2B (design and change)
- Creative forms of protest | bit.ly/3wghAZJ (attention, resistance)
- Lo-TEK Design by Radical Indigenism | bit.ly/3zoi9yP (indigenous design)
- Brave New Alps (design collective) | bit.ly/40zRw5T (design and activism)
- "Time for outrage!," S. Hessel, book → p. 326 (social engagement)
- "Génération offensée," C. Fourest, book → p. 326 (zeitgeist criticism and society)
- The Last Generation | bit.ly/47x9bya (society and resistance)

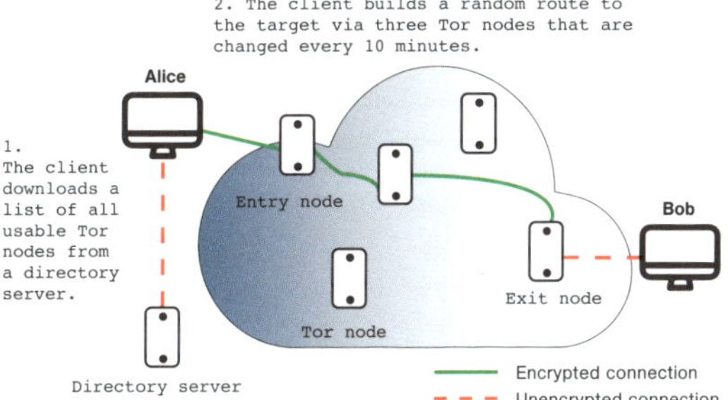

257
⦿ Tor project
Image source: https://de.wikipedia.org/wiki/Tor_(Netzwerk)#/media/Datei:TOR_Arbeitsweise.svg (see sources)
Recommended website: https://de.wikipedia.org/wiki/Tor_(Netzwerk)

← E2 161 – 162 (The Oslo Manifesto, The Last Whole Earth Catalog, 1972)

256 Selection of additional topics:

- "A Dictionary of Color Combinations," Collectif, book → p. 326 (color combinations)
- Word-of-mouth recommendation | bit.ly/3lYm2XW (spread of information)
- Silkscreen technique and reproduction | bit.ly/40PTtLL (independent spread of information)
- Measuring the visual field | bit.ly/49l8B2s (anatomy, field of vision)
- "The Nightmare of Participation," M. Miessen, book → p. 326 (downsides of taking part)

← E2 163 (Anonymous: Rules of the Internet)

257 Selection of additional topics:

- The Internet situation in Russia, China, and the Arabic region | bit.ly/3SRlS2C (deglobalization)
- Hatespeech slam | bit.ly/3sl1Z3q (online phenomena)
- X (formerly Twitter) rules | bit.ly/3QKsxcs (freedom/rules/censorship)
- ⦿ Tor project **(encrypted Internet)**

"Tor" is a network for anonymizing connection data. It is used for TCP connections. Tor shields its users from analyses of their data traffic. It is based on the idea of onion routing. At the end of 2022, up to 2.5 million users took advantage of Tor every day. Tor is a topic of discussion because its secure encryption has led to the establishment of illegal trading platforms, for example for drugs and weapons.

Image source: private

258

⊙ Pikachu

Text source: https://en.wikipedia.org/wiki/Pikachu

' Pikachu (...) is a fictional species of the Pokémon media franchise. Designed by Atsuko Nishida and Ken Sugimori, Pikachu first appeared in the 1996 Japanese video games Pokémon Red and Pokémon Green created by Game Freak and Nintendo, which were released outside of Japan in 1998 as Pokémon Red and Pokémon Blue. Pikachu is a yellow, mouse-like creature with electrical abilities. It is a major character in the Pokémon franchise, serving as its mascot.
Pikachu is widely considered to be the most popular and well-known Pokémon species, largely due to its appearance in the Pokémon anime television series as the companion of protagonist Ash Ketchum. In most vocalized appearances Pikachu is voiced by Ikue Ōtani, though it has been portrayed by other actors, notably Ryan Reynolds in the live-action animated film Pokémon Detective Pikachu. Pikachu has been well-received by critics, with particular praise given for to its cute design, and it has been regarded as an icon of both the Pokémon franchise and Japanese pop culture as a whole. '

← E2 164 (3D printing projects)

258 Selection of additional topics:

- Coworking-Map | bit.ly/3K1QSH7 (see title)
- Arduino software | bit.ly/3m3SJ6r (DIY software & projects)
- 3D-printed drones | bit.ly/4dm45Zc (surveillance)
- Cyberwarfare | bit.ly/3UQS6fb (digitally controlled aggression)
- ⊙ Pikachu, Japan (comic, merchandise, and 3D appearance)
- 3D-printed houses | bit.ly/44yz2VW (architecture and the future)
- Badgir (windcatchers) | bit.ly/4bjgOKE (architecture and the past)

← E2 165 – 167 (Sharing economy, Local sharing platforms, Internet Archive, Texte zur Theorie des Internets)

259 Selection of additional topics:

- Food sharing communities | bit.ly/3U4BWMV (common good)
- "Alles und nichts sagen," E. Menasse, book → p. 326 (digital modernism)
- Criticism of wdcd by ruben pater | bit.ly/3zJkVil (help and criticism)
- coapp.io | bit.ly/3U4BzSx (app for coworking spaces)
- Presentation of the anonymous collective | bit.ly/42YBmEE (hacker culture)
- Invention of the Internet at MIT | bit.ly/3ZB5bbi (history)
- ⊙ Pirate stations **(precursors of uncontrolled information)**

259

⊙ Pirate stations

Image source: https://de.wikipedia.org/wiki/Piratensender#/media/Datei:Plaid_Cymru_broadcasting_%22Radio_Wales (see sources)
Recommended website: https://en.wikipedia.org/wiki/Pirate_radio

Pirate stations were radio stations in the 1960's that broadcast from ships outside of the European nations' territorial waters. They thereby broadcast rock'n'roll, blues, soul, and beat music illegally and without a license. The most famous stations included Radio Noordzee International (off the Dutch coast), Radio Veronica, and Radio Caroline. Due to European legislation, all stations were forced to discontinue their broadcasting operations in the late 1960's.

On August 6, 1959, "Radio Wales" broadcast illegally for the first time in northern Wales. The participants covered their faces.

← E2 168 – 170 (Ästhetisches Denken, Pierre & Gilles, Kitsch! oder: Warum der schlechte Geschmack der eigentlich gute ist)

260 Selection of additional topics:

- The smallest picture in the world: clownfish picture from ETH Zurich (= 0.0092mm) | bit.ly/3KqlQcd (design)
- "Künstler in der Lehre," E. Bippus, M. Glasmeier, book → p. 326 (mindset and aesthetic expression)
- "The Cover Art of Blue Note Records," G. Callingham, Glyn, F. Cromey, Felix, G. Marsh, book → p. 326 (informative prose)
- High Glitz: portrait series on child beauty pageants | bit.ly/40RjrOP (ideal and reality)
- The art of Jeff Koons | bit.ly/3KpbYAC (art and kitsch)
- ⊙ A Sailor's Grave, picture in gold frame **(body art and kitsch)**
- Hacker culture | bit.ly/3znE1ds (digitality and illegality)
- Agitprop | bit.ly/3TZroPr (propaganda)
- Missile tests on TV: the example of North Korea | bit.ly/40vFIBw (propaganda)
- Beauty pageants | bit.ly/40xFXw7 (beauty ideals today)
- Cosmetic surgery | bit.ly/40VZypA (fictitious beauty)
- Edgar Rubin's vase "Vase or Face" | bit.ly/40xUp6Z (faces and illusion)
- Ambiguous images and ambigrams | bit.ly/3nEUI76 (images and psychology)
- Giuseppe Arcimboldo – portraits of fruit | bit.ly/3GafX1n (art)
- ⊙ Behavior in the event of fire **(pictogram language)**

260

⊙ A Sailor's Grave

Image source: Thomas Klefisch 2013

Designers need to understand that kitsch and trash form an indelible component of society. In certain areas, kitsch is a permanent phenomenon, e.g., in the tattoo sector, which is unscrupulously romanticized as it is. And that is the reason for the question, also directed at the "dogmatic" representatives of modernism: What would Sailor's Grave look like if it were "well-designed"? Or should kitsch and tattoos be prohibited? I'd like to hear your suggestions.

260

⊙ Behavior in the event of fire

Image source: private

Another case that causes uncertainty. There is a silent agreement that the left image is clearly better because it sums up the procedure without individualistic details. But is that always true? The image on the right hangs in the Luca School of Arts, Ghent (B).

And somehow the depiction (from the 1950's) suits the surroundings. Conclusion: There are no simple recipes in design. You will always need to think from scratch. Which isn't a bad thing.

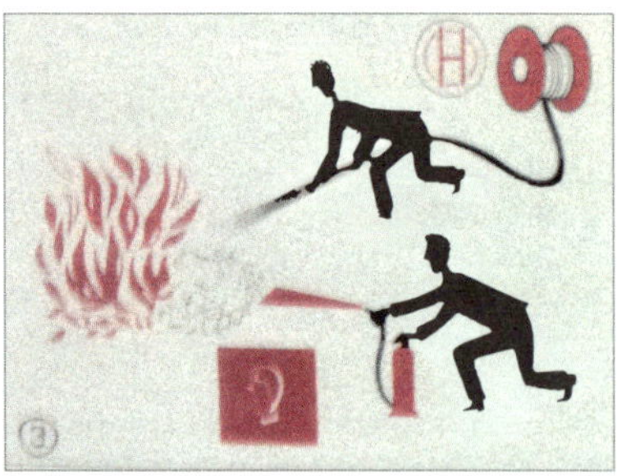

← E2 171 – 173 (The Barbie doll as a beauty ideal, BIG JIM as a beauty ideal, Schöne Hunde)

261 Selection of additional topics:

- Barbie ban in Saudi Arabia & Iran | bit.ly/4319BeQ (dominance of religion)
- Iranian Barbie version: Fulla | bit.ly/3QIHo6o (style and religion)
- 12/16/18 age ratings | bit.ly/3neS4fe (self-restriction)
- Advertising brochure | bit.ly/46mlj2T (everyday design)
- Pavlov's dog | bit.ly/3NiRYxT (conditioning)
- The Bible Belt in the USA | bit.ly/3QPSg30 (style and religion)
- ⊙ Shaker furniture **(style and religion)**

Interior of a room in Mount Lebanon

261

⊙ Shaker furniture

Image source: https://de.wikipedia.org/wiki/Shaker-M%C3%B6bel#/media/Datei:Shaker_furniture8.jpg (see sources)
Recommended website: https://de.wikipedia.org/wiki/Shaker-M%C3%B6bel

The disciples of a Protestant free church, the Shakers, live in the USA. Their ancestors had emigrated from Europe in the 18th century. Their ethos includes an ascetic lifestyle. This attitude is also reflected in the furniture they produce, which is free of ornamentation. The focus lies on the function, the natural material, and precise craftsmanship. This resulted in a style that is considered an important contribution to art history. The design of Shaker furniture influenced functionalist modernism.

262

⊙ Interior of a launderette

Image source: private. Laundrette in Knokke (B)

← E2 174 – 175 (The Grid in Novels, Radiolaria)

262 Selection of additional topics:

- Golden ratio in blossoms and flowers | bit.ly/47Dwiai (nature and aesthetics)
- European garden art in the 18th century | bit.ly/3nBsYe6 (planning and aesthetics)
- Name tags for plants with binary nomenclature (genus/species) | bit.ly/40OJzJE (set informational hierarchies)
- Letter proportions | bit.ly/3ZyzlvZ (font design)
- Paintings in the golden ratio | bit.ly/3tUoO1m (harmony)
- Fractals in nature | bit.ly/3K40m4H (Fibonacci in the environment)
- ⊙ Interior of a launderette **(visual signals for cleanliness and order)**
- Pictures from the scanning electron microscope | bit.ly/42Wzvjl (structures in nature)
- Bionics | bit.ly/39URyzY (learning from nature)
- Fragrances in animals | bit.ly/3zqTtW9 (alternative forms of communication in the animal kingdom)
- Stomping elephants | bit.ly/49GXln1 (alternative forms of communication in the animal kingdom)

One can certainly break open clichés and ask target groups to accept something other than what they are used to. This launderette combines the insignia of cleanliness with stylizing wallpaper, equally sized picture frames, and surprisingly high-quality flooring. But we are, after all, in the affluent town of Knokke (B).

← E2 176 (Tarot)

263 Selection of additional topics:

- Church of Satan | bit.ly/39MDyZf (secret societies and symbolism)
- Freemasons, Illuminati | bit.ly/3KoY55C (secret societies and symbolism)
- Das Alphabet in Mystik und Magie (1925) | bit.ly/3nHCsV2 (mysticism)
- Emergency currency banknotes Germany | bit.ly/3HMArge (banknote aesthetics)
- Sigillum Dei (God's seal) | bit.ly/3tWC7OC (occult diagram)
- Money Museum Frankfurt | bit.ly/3NdBabv (money and design)
- ⊙ The US dollar **(banknote design)**
- ⊙ The guilder (NL) **(banknote design)**

263

⊙ US dollar, the Guilder (NL)

Image sources: https://de.wikipedia.org/wiki/US-Dollar#/media/Datei:United_States_one_dollar_bill,_obverse.jpg; https://de.wikipedia.org/wiki/Niederl%C3%A4ndischer_Gulden#/media/Datei:100_Gulden_(1992)_-_Vorderseite.jpg (see sources)

Both the everlasting (dollar) and the changeable (the NL guilder that preceded the euro) have their justification. However, the Dutch managed to achieve an iconic style with their beautiful banknote design that was regularly renewed. What a shame that the guilder no longer exists.

← E2 177 – 178 (A comparison of blackletter fonts, Afrikan Alphabets)

264 Selection of additional topics:

- Calligraphy | bit.ly/3Zl8i1y (craftsmanship)
- Logos of black and death metal bands | bit.ly/40TyF6w (font and ornamentation)
- MIT Press | bit.ly/3zqZKRW (development of self-publishing)
- Independent publishing fairs (self-publishing)
- "No-ISBN: On self-publishing," B. Cella, L. Findeisen, A. Blaha, book → p. 326 (self-publishing)
- Tagbanuwa font | bit.ly/3KrjDOT (writing direction from top to bottom)
- safo military flags from Ghana | bit.ly/3zrhRHk (art and military)

← E2 179 (Digitale Bildkulturen)

265 Selection of additional topics:

- "Reading Images," G. Kress, T. van Leeuwen, book → p. 326 (visual grammar)
- Pinhole camera | bit.ly/3S8qeBY (DIY)
- "Towards a Philosophy of Photography," V. Flusser, book → p. 326 (philosophy)
- Analog photo creation | bit.ly/46wUN8O (digital and analog)
- Shanzai (term for copying Western ideas on the Chinese market) | bit.ly/3U14QgY (plagiarism, tradition)

Super Hudson, 1937

266

⊙ Streamlined Shape

Image source: https://de.wikipedia.org/wiki/Stromlinienform#/media/Datei:Hudson_locomotive_for_the_New_York_Central.jpg (see sources)
Recommended website: http://de.wikipedia. org/wiki/Stromlinienform

← E2 180 (The Manifesto of Futurism)

266 Selection of additional topics:

- Max Wertheimer (cofounder of gestalt psychology): experiments on movement | bit.ly/3Fkcxbz (movement and gestalt psychology)
- The Whole is More Than the Sum of Its Parts | bit.ly/4buMaxa (gestalt psychology)
- "Ernst May: Das neue Frankfurt," DW Dreysse, book → p. 326 (urban planning 1925 – 1930)
- ⊙ Aerodynamics and Streamlined Shape **(progress and design vocabulary)**
- "Stromlinienform," F. Engler, C. Lichtenstein, book → p. 326 (progress and design vocabulary)
- Future perfect | bit.ly/3MaqMo1 (progress and concept)

Streamlined shape refers to the ideal figure of a body in relation to its flow resistance in water or in the air. The value of resistance is measured by means of the flow resistance coefficient.

The term emerged in the early 20th century when vehicles became increasingly faster thanks to technical progress. To meet this demand, vehicles had to be aerodynamic. The "streamlined shape" is a synonym and symbol of this time.

← E2 181 (Karawane, Hugo Ball. Cigarren, Kurt Schwitters. fmbsbw, Raoul Hausmann)

267 Selection of additional topics:

- "Eile ist des Witzes Weile," K. Schwitters, book → p. 326 (DADA)
- DADA digital project from Kunsthaus Zurich | bit.ly/3ZtF1aA (archive and design)
- ⊙ Poem by Kurt Schwitters **(DADA)**
- "Das Ringelnatz Lesebuch," J. Ringelnatz, book → p. 326 (literature and subversiveness)
- "Will happiness find me?," P. Fischli, D. Weiss, book → p. 326 (artist book)
- "Texte zur Typografie," P. Eisele, I. Naegele, book → p. 326 (textbook)

Die Gazelle zittert

Die Gazelle zittert,
Weil der Löwe brüllt.
Die Hyäne wittert,
Doch die KUNST ERFÜLLT.

267

⊙ Poem by Kurt Schwitters

1947; text source:
"Eile ist des Witzes Weile," Kurt Schwitters
Reclam, ISBN 978-3-15-008392-5

The national coat of arms of the USSR, what it looked like from 1923 – 1931. Right: hammer and sickle.

268

⊙ Appearance of the USSR

Image sources: Coat of arms of the Soviet Union (1923–1936).svg; Hammer and sickle red on transparent.svg from: https://de.wikipedia.org/wiki/Hammer_und_Sichel (see sources)

← E2 182 (Schatzkammer der Revolution. Russische Kinderbücher von 1920 – 1935)

268 Selection of additional topics:

- Alexander Rodtschenko | bit.ly/3KnjwUx (constructivism)
- "El Lissitzky Proun 23 N," K. Simons, book → p. 326 (constructivism)
- Rise of fascism | bit.ly/3M4d05L (aestheticization of politics)
- ⊙ Appearance of the USSR **(aesthetics of Soviet communism)**
- "Liberating Society from the State," E. Mühsam, book → p. 326 (anarchism)
- "War and Peace," L. Tolstoi, book → p. 326 (pre-revolutionary Russia)
- "The Aesthetics of Resistance," P. Weiss, book → p. 326 (literature and politics)

The motto of the USSR was: "Workers of the world, unite!" Question: What would a coat of arms for this slogan look like today?

← E2 183 (Jan Tschichold and his relationship with the avantgarde)

269 Selection of additional topics:

- "How one can make swiss typography?," W. Weingart | bit.ly/411DGtB (Swiss design)
- Communism | bit.ly/3m3sAoo (ideology)
- "Capital in the Twenty-First Century," T. Piketty, book → p. 326 (analysis)
- Oeconomia, documentary, 2020 | bit.ly/3KrfRoH (the abstract rules of capitalism)

← E2 185 (Moholy-Nagy and the New Typography)

271 Selection of additional topics:

- Photograms (Moholy-Nagy) | bit.ly/3M1y8tf (avantgarde communication)
- New Bauhaus / School of Design foundation in Chicago | bit.ly/46LWBeB (design and exile)
- Telephone pictures, Moholy-Nagy | bit.ly/3rWNsAv (first media art images)

← E2 184 – 184.3 (Mit voller Kraft. Russische Avantgarde 1910 – 1934, Futurism, Suprematism, Constructivism)

270 Selection of additional topics:

- Arts & crafts | bit.ly/3trwOcA (avantgarde art movement)
- Brutalism in architecture | bit.ly/3M5j5zz (architecture trend)
- Brutalist websites | bit.ly/3Kr9BNO (web developments)
- Hostile architecture | bit.ly/3Ktr4Fv (architecture)
- ⊙ Spider webs and raindrops **(constructions in nature)**
- Martin Kippenberger | bit.ly/40RYGIx (art and full power)

270

⊙ Spider webs and raindrops

Spider Webs After Rain; image source: private;
Recommended website: https://de.wikipedia.org/wiki/Spinnennetz

266
267
268
269
270
271
272
273
274
275

← E2 186 (Helvetica, Helvetica Arabic and Hebrew)

272 Selection of additional topics:

- Super-font families for various languages | bit.ly/3QdQzNL (internationalization and communication)
- Reading: typeface design | bit.ly/3KqKlax (studying font design)
- OCRB | bit.ly/3QjrTTW (machine-readable font)
- Readsearch Institute | bit.ly/3Qfw9Eb (font and international communication)
- ⊙ I am a deaf person **(sign language, communication)**

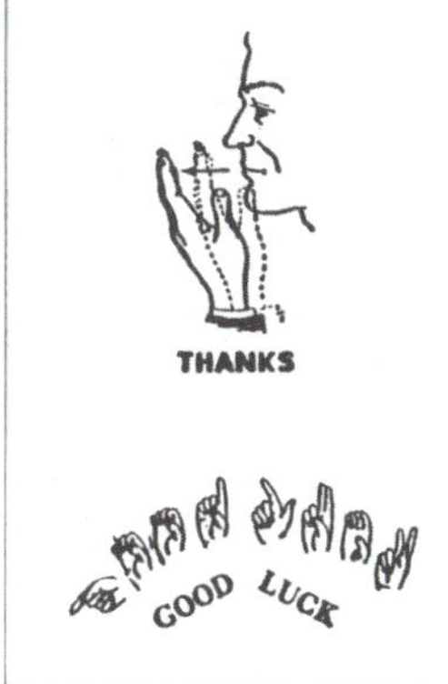

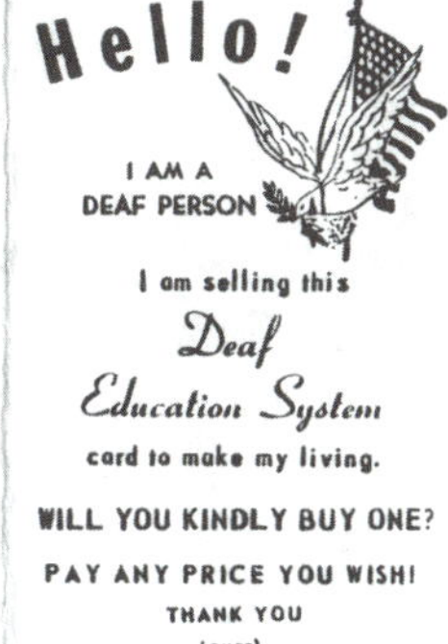

272
⊙ I AM A DEAF PERSON

Image source: private, USA 1998

The communication of the opened A7 carton from New York is asking for donations. What year do you think this is from? What symbols would we use in Europe?

Obi knots in martial arts

273
⊙ Knots with instructions

Image source: https://de.wikipedia.org/wiki/Knoten_(Kn%C3%BCpfen)#/media/Datei:Obi-knoten.png (see sources)

The example shows how to tie a knot. A designer has made an effort to produce a clear depiction. This aspect of our work often goes unacknowledged: We need to graphically depict increasingly complex devices, processes, and connections. Greater attention should be given to this topic at universities.

← E2 187 – 190 (Arts & Crafts. William Morris, Textile Design at Bauhaus: Gunta Stölzl, TextielMuseum Tilburg, NL, Textile Design at Bauhaus: Anni Albers)

273 Selection of additional topics:

- Tapestries of protest, Hannah Rygen | bit.ly/3nD46Tp (protest and ornamentation)
- Atlas, Gerhard Richter | bit.ly/3TZWpCJ (collection in art)
- Palestinian Weaving as Heritage | bit.ly/40xiZVV (ornamentation and identity)
- ⊙ Knots with instructions **(function and depiction)**
- Knot density in silkscreens and their print image | bit.ly/3U2fiVw (grid effects and their origins)
- Marguerita Mergentime: food quiz tablecloths | bit.ly/3m7TNWN (playful communication)
- Aby Warburg, Mnemosyne atlas of pictures | bit.ly/3ZxWM8Q (ornaments and collection)
- The Antwerp six | bit.ly/42XzMTz (Mode Avantgarde)
- ⊙ Space suits **(functional clothing and design)**
- Balenciaga | bit.ly/3GaSqNM (Mode Avantgarde)
- Primark | bit.ly/3Gc5hzz (fashion, textiles, and exploitation)

273
⊙ Space suits

Image source: https://de.wikipedia.org/wiki/Raumanzug#/media/Datei:Bruce_McCandless_II_during_EVA_in_1984.jpg (see sources)
Website: https://de.wikipedia.org/wiki/Raumanzug

Astronaut B. McCandless during STS-41-B.

A space suit is gas-tight and allows the wearer to move through the vacuum of space. It works through overpressure. The suit consists of several layers of textiles, plastics, and metals. A suit like this is meant to be functional. Do design decisions need to be made as well? And who is responsible for them? Does NASA have a designer on staff?

← E2 192 (Anton Stankowski et al.)

275 Selection of additional topics:

- ⊙ Deutsche Bank logo **(icons of logo design)**
- Paul Rand: bees and IBM poster | bit.ly/40Bafht (icons of poster/logo design)
- Bees' waggle dance | bit.ly/3U2baou (communication in the animal world)
- Karl Bühler: organon model (1934) | bit.ly/3nG94P9 (predecessor of the information theory communication model)
- Kurt Weidemann | bit.ly/3U0wBXc (renowned German designers)

The logo as of 1974

The logo from 1957 – 1974

275
⊙ Deutsche Bank logo

Image sources: (1) https://de.wikipedia.org/wiki/Deutsche_Bank#/media/Datei:Deutsche_Bank_logo.svg
(2) https://logos-world.net/wp-content/uploads/2021/02/Deutsche-Bank-Logo-1957-1973.png (see sources)

Anton Stankowski designed the Deutsche Bank logo that was introduced in 1974. The minimalist design corresponded with the zeitgeist and the belief that minimalism increased succinctness. Stankowski once said that a logo is only good if you can draw it in the sand with your toenail. The tabloid Bild-Zeitung deemed this to be too little design for too much money, opting for the following title on April 17, 1974: "A painter earns 100,000 marks with five lines."

But it is simply a basic design fact that the recognition value rises the simpler the sign is. And that it tends to be difficult to find simple forms.

← E2 191 (Die Neue Rechte und ihr Design)

274 Selection of additional topics:

- Compact Magazin | bit.ly/3TZSlgr (longing for the mainstream)
- Appearance of the AfD | bit.ly/40PPs9y (right-wing aesthetics)
- Appearance of "Die Heimat" | bit.ly/4005jD2 (right-wing aesthetics)
- NSU | bit.ly/3m3m0y7 (right-wing underground and visual devices)
- "Keine falsche Toleranz," Wolfgang Kraushaar, book → p. 326 (right-wing terrorism)
- Hammerskins | bit.ly/3rHQNDC (right-wing aesthetics)
- Blood and honour | bit.ly/3rJ53fm (right-wing aesthetics)
- Geert Wilders, Partij voor de Vrijheid | bit.ly/3S1rF5f (right-wing aesthetics)
- Fremdenlegion | bit.ly/3ZUlWjP (outsourcing)
- Proud Boys | bit.ly/48V2Y0f (right-wing aesthetics)
- Banned symbols 2022 | bit.ly/49HpyZB (right-wing aesthetics)
- Redneck woman | bit.ly/3PZHUwZ (right-wing mindset)
- Linguistic codes | bit.ly/3rTTody (clandestine communication)
- "The Circle," Dave Eggers, book → p. 326 (Technology and dystopia)

(1)

(2)

276
⊙ Protective clothing in the military and police

Image sources: (1) https://de.wikipedia.org/wiki/Schutzkleidung#/media/Datei:Sonderschutzbekleidung_ZODIAK.jpg; (2) https://commons.wikimedia.org/wiki/File:Protest_0068.JPG (see sources)
website: https://de.wikipedia.org/wiki/Schutzkleidung

← E2 193 – 195 (Farbfächer / Color Fans, The Pantone Color of the Year, Club colors 1st and 2nd Bundesliga)

276 Selection of additional topics:

- "Male" and "female" colors | bit.ly/3FhIfr0 (gender design)
- Cultural color attributions | bit.ly/3k1RSCm (convention and color)
- The Lüscher test: colors and personality | bit.ly/3k9zXtp (color psychology claims)
- "Die Tafeln zur Farbenlehre und deren Erklärungen," W. Goethe, book → p. 326 (theory of colors)
- Color concepts for interior prison rooms | bit.ly/4a4kS0d (color and psychology)
- ⊙ Protective clothing in the military and police **(function and form)**
- Color concepts for prison clothing | bit.ly/3S6eNZw (color and classification)
- "Englands Fussballwappen," H. Grüne, book → p. 326 (tradition)
- Color analyses along a European line of longitude, Markus Pretnar | bit.ly/3KgqIrn (cultural differences)
- Work clothing and colors | bit.ly/3YGc0cf (safety at work)

Protective clothing and uniforms in the military and police: They also need to be designed. Even if we can assume that the form and design follow strictly defined functions and standards, this still leaves open the question of who makes the design decisions. Are there ministries of design for protective clothing? Would you be interested in such a role?

← E2 196 – 198 (Investigative aesthetics, Exploded-view drawings, Central projection; Parallel projection)

277 Selection of additional topics:

- Descriptive geometry | bit.ly/3Igec3g (perspective and drawing)
- Lens raster pictures (lenticular pictures) | bit.ly/3EjTb6n (perspective and depiction)
- Counter-surveillance | bit.ly/3Ix99fZ (transparency & control in the digital sphere)
- Panopticon by Jeremy Bentham | bit.ly/3I8P6mD (psychology and surveillance)
- Adam Harvey: CV Dazzle project | bit.ly/3YC1jqY (surveillance)
- ⊙ Unknown signs **(coding for specialist groups in the public space)**
- "Das ist Ästhetik" Congress Offenbach (GER) | bit.ly/3KeLimq (aesthetics research)
- Deutsche Gesellschaft für Ästhetik (German Society for Aesthetics) | bit.ly/3XFfF8H (aesthetics and research)
- Iconographic depictions | bit.ly/3YClZzl (ideal and everyday life)
- "Draw it with your eyes closed: the art of the art assignment," D. Petrovich, R. White, book → p. 326 (visual communication and experimentation)
- "Die blinden Flecken der RAF," W. Kraushaar, book → p. 326 (left-wing terrorism)

277
⊙ Unknown signs

Image source: private

Gathering all the signs that are not directed at passers-by, as those shown here from Frankfurt's central station, could be quite a nice project. But humans have the ability to perceive only what they understand to some extent. This finding is crucial for designers because ultimately, communication is always about being understood.

(1) Space Pilot X Ray Gun from the Japanese company Taiyo in the early 1970's.

(2) Buck Rogers U-238 Atomic Pistol in the 25th century (the pistol's packaging).

278
⊙ Ray Gun

Image sources:
(1) Space_Pilot_X_Ray_Gun_made_by_Taiyo.jpg,
(2) Buck_Rogers_in_the_25th_Century_U-238_Atomic_Pistol-NMAH-AHB2015q029270.jpg (see sources)
Website: https://en.wikipedia.org/wiki/Raygun

← E2 199 (Laws of UX: Using Psychology to Design Better Products & Services.)

278 Selection of additional topics:

- Mesoamerican calendar | bit.ly/3xMmGKF (antiquity and good design)
- Olivetti's typewriter | bit.ly/3Sd0QsX (function and good design)
- Ergonomic office furniture | bit.ly/3lHLlHW (product design, occupational health)
- Useless Machines, B. Munari | bit.ly/3lFpZQP (design)
- Traditional costumes from rural areas | bit.ly/3lseHZg (folk art and inheritance)
- "Cornflakes in Cellophane," H. F. Seller, book → p. 326 (American illustrations from the 1950's)
- ⊙ "Ray gun," E. W. Metcalf, F. Maresca, book → p. 326 **(toy from the 1950's and 1960's)**
- "Jack Cole and Plastic Man," A. Spiegelmann, C. Kidd, book → p. 326 (American comics from the 1950's)

A ray gun like the "Space Pilot X-Ray Gun" depicted here can kill and destroy objects with its energy ray – at least that's what those who carry it believe. The toy was a component of a flourishing science-fiction wave from the 1950's to the 1970's. The comics are famous for and popular because of their enchanting aura (from today's perspective), even if the stories were relatively simple. But that was and is true for many comics. And many of today's graphic designers might wish they could draw like this.

← E2 200 (Ticket machines)

279 Selection of additional topics:

- Timetable design | bit.ly/3l89ELY (economy and design)
- "The Stuff of Thought," S. Pinker, book → p. 326 (cognitive science)
- How to tie a tie, instructions | bit.ly/3S8VuyP (planning & convention)
- ⊙ Intersection in Eindhoven (NL) **(order in the city)**
- Identifying marks of the queer community | bit.ly/41cTTwe (identification features)
- Boxing posters | bit.ly/49VZz0E (visual aesthetic of the sport of boxing in the public space)
- Contemporary images of religion | bit.ly/3A4YHst (visuality in religion)
- Cut-off/color | bit.ly/3KdfJte (rocker codes)
- Popular first names in 2023 | bit.ly/3Fja4OQ (individuality and taste of the masses)
- Encrypted information | bit.ly/3Eek77t (formal appeal without content)

279

⊙ Intersection in Eindhoven (NL)

Image source: private

The view from the 6th floor of the Holiday Inn, Eindhoven. Even in Holland, where bicycles have top priority in cities, urban-planning transgressions of the past are still visible (these are evident almost everywhere in Germany): a city built for cars, then for shops, and only then for pedestrians and cyclists. Design is creation, says L. Burckhardt, so a problem like this is also a job for you.

← E2 201 (Adobe Express Tool)

280 Selection of additional topics:

- Fashion eco labels | bit.ly/3IrJCou (greenwashing and fashion)
- Certified paper | bit.ly/412aClzT (ecology & print design)
- ⊙ Lava lamps as a source of encryption **(randomized encryption)**
- Hype cycles | bit.ly/41eoRnN (trend principles)

280

⊙ Lava lamps

Image source: https://de.wikipedia.org/wiki/Lavalampe#/media/Datei:Lavalampe.jpg (see sources)

Once a source of joy for potheads, lava lamps are used for encryption today: Bubbles rise, divide, sink, and rise again – in incalculable variations. A company whose field of business includes encrypting data arranged 100 lava lamps on a shelf and placed a camera in front of them. The unpredictable shapes of the bubbles form the foundation of algorithms that don't depict a transparent scheme due to their random nature.

Further information:
https://www.cloudflare.com/de-de/learning/ssl/lava-lamp-encryption/

← E2 203 (The decolonizing..., Design Reader, 2021 – 2023)

281 Selection of additional topics:

- European Accessibility Act | bit.ly/3lrcf47 (inclusion as a political tool)
- Morphological table | bit.ly/3l9VIGM (intercultural reading directions)
- Consistent Doodles | bit.ly/3lw7nvM (aesthetics and cave drawings)
- Cancel culture | bit.ly/3YYgPgS (political correctness, pattern breakers)
- DB logo, Kurt Weidemann, criticism | bit.ly/3xtoh7K (design)
- A Swedish perspective on critical practice, R. Poynor | bit.ly/3EgazZU (criticism)

← E2 204 (Design as an attitude)

282 Selection of additional topics:

- Consciousness industry, Enzensberger | bit.ly/40YHvzM (psychology)
- Building block for a media theory | bit.ly/3YA0KxL (media psychology)
- Open calls for art | bit.ly/3Kd8G3Z (mindset and participation)
- Co-working concepts | bit.ly/3xqaQFE (work and participation)
- "Wir müssen die Welt verändern," O. Niemeyer, book → p. 326 (motivation)
- Disarming Design from Palestine | bit.ly/3YAWVsn (world and design)
- SLOC (Small-Local-Open-Connected), E. Manzini | bit.ly/3lvpbhh (future)
- "No Logo," N. Klein, book → p. 326 (criticism of capitalism)
- "The Language of the 3rd Reich," V. Klemperer, book → p. 326 (language and power)

← E2 202, 205 (Chaos Computer Club, UN Sustainable Development Goals)

283 Selection of additional topics:

- Circular houses (zero energy emissions) | bit.ly/3lL04ra (sustainability in construction)
- Idea of the circular ECONOMY | bit.ly/3YUhXSn (sustainable economy)
- ⊙ Facade lettering **(using the public sphere for communication)**
- Ten tactics to turn information into action | bit.ly/3EF73lY (instructions to take action)
- 150 strategies of YALE University to increase social capital | bit.ly/3Oj4RKn (improving the world)
- Political theories: anarchy | bit.ly/3ScJFaX (political theories)
- Knowmads Business School Amsterdam | bit.ly/3OhrUVO (anarchy and teaching)
- Urban Interventions Manifesto | bit.ly/3tK2WVD (artistic resistance)
- Guerilla Open Access Manifesto | bit.ly/3YAVdHt (open access)
- Designing digital and political realities | bit.ly/3EHkN5S (design and sociology)

283

⊙ Facade lettering

Image source: private; building wall in Belfast, 2021

Name register

Key terms in chapters A – D for a quick search:

Bibliography

A

Aarsman, Hans u.a., "Useful Photography 011," Kesselskramer (ed.), 2013 E: 220

Aicher, Otl, "die hochschule für gestaltung, neun stufen ihrer entwicklung,"1975 in Archithese, nr.15, 1975 E: 050

Aicher, Otl, "die welt als entwurf," Verlag Ernst & Sohn, 1991 E: 103.1

Aicher, Otl, "Richtlinien und Normen für die visuelle Gestaltung," Niggli Verlag, 2019 E: 125

Aicher, Otl, "typography," 1988, Verlag Ernst & Sohn, reprint, Verlag Hermann Schmidt Mainz, 2005 E: 003, 078

Ambrose, Gavin, Harris, Paul, "Design Th!nking," Stiebner Verlag, 2013 E: 052

Arbeitskreis Bremen (ed.), "5. Bundestreffen Forum Typografie 1988," 1989 E: 040.1

Area Verlag (ed.), "Die große März-Kassette," 2004, E: 232

B

Baldev, Danzig, "Russian Criminal Tattoo Encyclopaedia Volume I," Fuel Publishing, 2009 E: 206

Bandel, Jan-Frederik, Gilbert, Annette, Prill,Tania (eds.), "Under the Radar: Underground Zines and Self-Publications 1965 – 1975," Spector Books, 2019 E: 036.1

Bauer, Thomas, "Die Vereindeutigung der Welt. Über den Verlust an Mehrdeutigkeit und Vielfalt," Reclam Verlag, 2018 E: 006.2, 100

Baumgärtel, Tilman (ed.), "Texte zur Theorie des Internets," Reclam Verlag, Ditzingen, 2017 E: 167

Baumgärtel, Tilman (ed.), "Texte zur Theorie der Werbung," Reclam Verlag, Ditzingen, 2018 E: 049.1

Baur, Ruedi, Felsing, Ulrike, "Visual Coexistence. Informationdesign and Typography in the Intercultural Field," Civic City and HEAD Genève (eds.), Lars Müller Publishers, 2020 E: 020.1

Beifuss, Artur, "Branding Terror – The Logotypes and Iconography of Insurgent Groups and Terrorist Organizations," Merell Publishers, 2013 E: 247

Berger, John, "Sehen. Das Bild der Welt in der Bilderwelt," Fischer Verlag, 2016 E: 069.1

Bergerhausen, Johannes, Poarangan, Siri, "Decodeunicode – die Schriftzeichen der Welt," Verlag Hermann Schmidt Mainz, 2011 E: 017

Bergerhausen, Johannes, "Digitale Keilschrift – 1.063 Glyphen der ältesten Schriftsysteme der Welt," Verlag Hermann Schmidt Mainz, 2014 E: 130

Bergerhausen, Johannes, Schneider, Lukas, Voelker, Ulysses, "Werkbericht Nr. 12," Institut Designlabor Gutenberg, 2009 E: 212

Bergius, Hanne, "Das Lachen DADAs – Die Berliner Dadaisten und ihre Aktionen," out of the series "Werkbund-Archiv," Werkbund-Archiv, Verlag Anabas (eds.), 1989 E: 071, 181

Betsky, Aaron, Eeuwens, Adam, "False Flat: Why Dutch Design is so Good," Phaidon Press, New York, 2004 E: 144

Bettelheim, Bruno, "The Uses of Enchantement", Random House Inc., 2010 E: 107

Bieber, Alain, Feireiss, Lukas (eds.), "Planet B – Ideen für eine Neue Welt," Verlag der Buchhandlung Walther König, 2016 E: 058.1

Bippus, Elke, Glasmeier, Michael (eds.), "Künstler in der Lehre," Philo & Philo Fine Arts / EVA Europäische Verlagsanstalt, 2007 E: 260

Betts, B. J., Schonberger, Nick, "The Graphic Art of Tattoo Lettering," Thames and Hudson Ltd, 2019 E: 228

Beyer, Andreas, Bredekamp, Horst, Fleckner, Uwe, Wolf, Gerhard (authors and eds.), "Bilderfahrzeuge – Abi Warburgs Vermächtnis und die Zukunft der Ikonologie," Wagenbach Verlag, 2018 E: 273

Bill, Max, "Max Bill: Typography, Advertising, Book Design," Niggli Verlag, 1999 E: 028

Bizot, Jean-François, "Free Press – Underground & Alternative Publications 1965 – 1975," Universe Publishing, 2006 E: 036

Blackwell, Lewis, "David Carson. The End of Print," Bangert, 1995 E: 043

Blauvelt, Andrew, Lupton, Ellen, Walker Art Center (eds.), "Graphic Design: Now in Production," Minneapolis, 2014 E: 059

Blume, Eugen, Nichols, Catherine, "Beuys. Die Revolution sind wir.," Steidl Verlag, 2008 E: 226

Boom, Irma, "Irma Boom: The architecture of the book," University of Amsterdam (ed.), lecturis, 2013 E: 224

Bosshard, Hans Rudolf, "Der Typografiestreit der Moderne – Max Bill kontra Jan Tschichold," Niggli Verlag, Salenstein, 2012 E: 141

Bourdieu, Pierre, "Die feinen Unterschiede. Die Kritik der gesellschaftlichen Urteilskraft," Suhrkamp Verlag, Frankfurt, 1979 E: 089

Bourquin, Nicolas, Klanten, Robert, Mareis, Claudia, "Altitude. Contemporary Swiss Graphic Design," Die Gestalten Verlag, 2006 E: 238

Brand, Stewart, "The Last Whole Earth Catalog: Access to Tools," Portola Institute Inc. (ed.), 1971 E: 162

Breuer, Gerda (ed.), "Dialogue, continuity, self-empowerment. Women graphic designers from 1880 until today," Jovis Verlag, 2023 E: 015.3

Brody, Neville, "The Graphic Language of Neville Brody," Verlag C.J. Bucher, 1988 E: 042

Brody, Neville, "Die Grafik-Sprache des Neville Brody 2," Bangert Verlag, 1994 E: 042

C

Cage, John, "Silence," Bibliothek Suhrkamp, Frankfurt, 1996 E: 226

Callingham, Glyn, Cromey, Felix, Marsh, Graham, "The Cover Art of Blue Note Records," Edition Olms Zürich, 1993 E: 260

Cella, Bernhard, Findeisen, Leo, Blaha, Agnes, "No-ISBN: On self-publishing," Salon für Kunstbuch, Verlag der Buchhandlung Walter König, 2015 E: 264

Cheng, Karen, "Anatomie der Buchstaben," Verlag Hermann Schmidt Mainz, 2013 E: 129

Collectif, "A Dictionary of Color Combinations," Seigensha Art Publishing, 2011 E: 256

Crawford, Kate, "Atlas of AI - Power, Politics, and the Planetary Costs of Artificial Intelligence", Yale University Press, 2022 E: 097.2

Crumb, Robert, "The Complete Crumb Comics Vol. 4: Mr. Sixties!" Fantagraphics, 2009 E: 247

D

de Jong, Cees W., Purvis, Alston W., Le Coultre, Martijn F., Doubleday, Richard.B., Reichardt, Hans, "Jan Tschichold – Meister der Typographie – Sein Lebenswerk in Bildern," Verlag Bernd Detsch, 2008 E: 183

Dehaene, Stanislas, "Lesen. Die größte Erfindung der Menschheit und was dabei in unseren Köpfen passiert," btb Verlag, 2012 E: 227

Dettmar, Ute, Küpper, Thomas (eds.), "Kitsch. Texte und Theorien," Reclam Verlag, Ditzingen, 2007 E: 088, 090, 170

Didero, Maria Cristina, "SuperDesign: Italian Radical Design 1965 - 75," Monacelli Press, 2017 E: 056

Dorschel, Andreas, "Gestaltung – Zur Ästhetik des Brauchbaren," Universitätsverlag C. Winter, 2002 E: 082

Dreysse, DW, "Ernst May: Das neue Frankfurt," Verlag Henrich Editionen, 2011 E: 266

Dunne, Anthony, Raby, Fiona, "Speculative Everything," MIT Press, 2013 E: 053

E

Eco, Umberto, "Einführung in die Semiotik," Verlag W. Fink UTB, 2002 E: 014

Eco, Umberto, "Die Geschichte der Schönheit," Verlag dtv, 2012 E: 061

Eco, Umberto, "Die Geschichte der Häßlichkeit," Carl Hanser Verlag, 2007 E: 061.1

Eco, Umberto, "Zeichen. Einführung in einen Begriff und seine Geschichte," edition suhrkamp, 1977 E: 013

Eggers, Dave, "The Circle," Vintage, 2014 E: 274

Eisele, Petra, Ludwig, Annette, Naegele, Isabel (eds.), "Futura. Die Schrift," Verlag Hermann Schmidt, Gutenberg Museum Mainz, Institut Designlabor Gutenberg/ Hochschule Mainz, 2016 E: 075

Eisele, Petra, Naegele, Isabel, Lailach, Michael (eds.), "Moholy-Nagy and the New Typography," Kettler Verlag, 2019 E: 185

Eisele, Petra, Naegele, Isabel (eds.), "Texte zur Typografie," Niggli Verlag, 2012, E: 267

Emcke, Carolin, "Gegen den Hass," Fischer Verlag, 2018, E: 247

Emigre Inc. (ed.), "The Emigre Catalog 02.0," Sacramento, 2001 E: 044

Engel, Peter, Schreiber, Theo (eds.), "Meine Fibel," Ernst Klett Verlag, 1961 E: 227

Engler, Franz, Lichtenstein, Claude, "Stromlinienform," Verlag Lars Müller, 1992, E: 266

Erler, Johannes, "Hallo, ich bin Erik," Gestalten Verlag, 2014 E: 042.1

Erlhoff, Michael, Marshall, Tim (eds.), "Wörterbuch Design," Birkhäuser Verlag, Basel, 2008 E: 001.1, 008, 049

F

Fechner, Gustav Theodor, "Vorschule der Ästhetik," tredition E: 086

Fiell, Charlotte, Fiell, Clementine, "Design von Frauen," Dumont, 2019 E: 015.2

Fischli, Peter, Weiss, David, "Will Happiness find me?" Alberta Press, 2003 E: 267

Fisher, Mark, "Capitalist Realism," Zer0 Books, 2022 E: 058.2

Flusser, Vilem, "Die Schrift," Immatrix Publications, 1989 E: 215

Flusser, Vilem, "Towards a Philosophy of Photography," Reaktion Books, 2000 E: 265

Foresman, Scott and Co. (eds.), "All Around us – Teachers Edition," 1949 E: 001

Forssman, Friedrich, de Jong, Ralf, "Detailtypografie" Verlag Hermann Schmidt Mainz, 2004 E: 018

Fourest, Caroline, "Génération offensée," Grasset; 2020 E: 255

Friedl, Friedrich, Frutiger, Adrian, Alb, Erich (eds.), "Adrian Frutiger Schriften. Das Gesamtwerk," Birkhäuser Verlag, 2009 E: 032.1

Friedl, Friedrich, "Die Univers von Adrian Frutiger," Verlag Form, 1998 E: 032.1

Frutiger, Adrian, "Der Mensch und seine Zeichen," Fourier Verlag, 2013 E: 016, 123

Fuller, Matthew, Weizman, Eyal, "Investigative aesthetics: Conflicts and Commons in the Politics of Truth," Verso, 2021 E: 196

G

Gambetta, Diego, "Codes of the Underworld – How Criminals Communicate," Princeton University Press, 2011 E: 209.1

Gendolla, Peter, Kamphusmann, Thomas (eds.), "Die Künste des Zufalls," Suhrkamp Verlag, Frankfurt, 1999 E: 094

Gerstner, Karl, "Programme entwerfen," Lars Müller Publishers, 2007 E: 033

Gerstner, Karl, "Rückblick auf sieben Kapitel konstruktive Bilder. Etc.," Hatje Cantz, 2003 E: 237

Giannuzzi, Luigi (ed.), "Cock Indian Firework Art," Westzone Publishing Ltd (ed.), 2000 E: 212

Goethe, Johann Wolfgang, "Die Tafeln zur Farbenlehre und deren Erklärungen," Insel Verlag, 1994 E: 276

Graeber, David, "Bürokratie – Die Utopie der Regeln," Goldmann Verlag, 2017, E: 218

Graves, Hannah, "Forever More – The New Tattoo," Gestalten Verlag, Berlin, 2017 E: 127.2

Greif, Mark, Ross, Kathleen, Tortorici, Dayna, Geiselberger, Heinrich (eds.), "Hipster – eine transatlantische Diskussion," Suhrkamp Verlag, Berlin, 2012 E: 047.1

Grimm, Jacob und Wilhelm, "Die Märchen der Brüder Grimm," Vollständige Ausgabe; Verlag Neues Leben Berlin, 1990 E: 207

Groys, Boris, "Über das Neue. Versuch einer Kulturökonomie," Fischer Verlag, Frankfurt, 2002 E: 093

Grüne, Hardy, "Englands Fussballwappen," Verlag Zeitspiel, Hannover, 2023 E: 276

Grunenberg, Christoph (ed.), "Summer of Love. Psychedelische Kunst der 60er Jahre," Hatje Cantz Verlag, 2005 E: 034

Gropius, Walter, "Das Bauhaus-Manifest (1919)," from Wingler, Hans M.: Das Bauhaus 1919 – 1933. Weimar, Dessau, Berlin und die Nachfolge in Chicago seit 1937, Bramsche, 1968 E: 072

H

Haarmann, Harald, "Geschichte der Schrift," Verlag C. H. Beck, 2011 E: 068.2

Haus der Geschichte der Bundesrepublik Deutschland (ed.), "Bilder, die lügen," Bouvier Verlag, Bonn, 2000 E: 110

Heartney, Eleanor, "Postmoderne," Hatje Cantz, 2002 E: 041

Heimann, Jim (ed.), "All-American Ads," Taschen Verlag, 2001 E: 159

Heller, Steven, "Iron fists: Branding the 20th-Century Totalitarian State," Phaidon Press, 2008 E: 210

Helmes, Günter, Köster, Werner, "Texte zur Medientheorie," Reclam Verlag, 2002 E: 282

Hessel, Stephane, "Time for Outrage!," Twelve, 2011 E: 255

Hillmann, Hans, "Fliegenpapier," dtv Verlagsgesellschaft, 2005 E: 207

Hochuli, Jost, "Bücher machen," Agfa Compugraphic, 1989 E: 084.1

Hochuli, Jost, "Detail in typography," Editions B42, 2015, Montreuil E: 084

Hoffmann, Heinrich, "Der Struwwelpeter," Schwager & Steinlein Verlag, 2017 E: 206

Höhne, Günter, "DDR Design," Komet Verlag, 2006 E: 233

Hollis, Richard, "Schweizer Grafik" Die Entwicklung eines internationalen Stils 1920 – 1965, Birkhäuser Verlag, 2006 E: 030

Holstein, Jürgen, "The Book Cover in the Weimarer Republik," Taschen Verlag, 2015 E: 236

Honnef, Klaus, "Pop Art," Taschen Verlag, 2022 E: 236

Hornbostel, Wilhelm, Kopanski, Karlheinz W., Rudi, Thomas (eds.), "mit voller Kraft. Russische Avantgarde 1910 – 1934," Edition Braus im Wachterverlag, 2001 E: 184, 184.2

Hornuff, Daniel, "Die Neue Rechte und ihr Design. Vom ästhetischen Angriff auf die offene Gesellschaft," Transscript Verlag, 2019 E: 191

Hudson W., "Pictorial Depth Perception in Sub-Cultural Groups in Africa," The Journal of Social Psychology, Nr.52, Philadelphia, 1960 E: 218

I

IDZ Berlin (ed.), "Design? Umwelt wird in Frage gestellt.," 1970 E: 091

Itten, Johannes, "Kunst der Farbe," Christopherus Verlag, Wiesbaden, 2021 E: 085

J

Jandl, Ernst, "lechts und rinks. gedichte statements peppermints," dtv, 1997 E: 248

Joost, Gesche, Scheuermann, Arne (eds.), "Design als Rhetorik," Birkhäuser Verlag, 2008 E: 009.1, 010

Joyce, James, "Finnegan's Wake," Double 9 Booksllp, 2022 E: 233

K

Kandinsky, Vasily, "Punkt zu Linie zu Fläche," Benteli Verlag, 1955, 1959, 1963 E: 118

Kapr, Albert, "Fraktur. Form und Geschichte der gebrochenen Schriften," Verlag Hermann Schmidt Mainz, 1993 E: 177

Keedy, Jefferey, "The Global Style," Slanted Art Type, Nr.22, Slanted Publishers, 2013 E: 048

Kessels, Erik, "Models. A collection of 132 German police uniforms and how they should be worn," A Kesselskramer book, 2005 E: 242

Kitching, Alan, "A – Z of Letterpress. Founts from The Typography Workshop," Laurence King Publishing, 2015 E: 245

Klanten, Robert, Bourquin, Mareis, Claudia, "Altitude Contemporary Swiss Graphic Design," Die Gestalten Verlag, 2006 E: 238

Kleine, Susanne, "Martin Kippenberger: BITTESCHÖNDANKESCHÖN," Snoeck verlagsgesellschaft, 2019 E: 270

Klein, Naomi, "No Logo: Taking Aim at the Brand Bullies," Vintage Canada, 2009 E 282

Klemperer, Viktor, "The Language of the 3rd Reich," Continuum International Publishing Group, 2000 E: 282

Knaur, Käte, Ruperti, Marga, "Schöne Hunde," Albert Müller Verlag, 1953 E: 173

Koetzle, Hans-Michael, Wolff, Carsten, "Fleckhaus: Design/Revolte/Regenbogen," Hartmann Projects Verlag, 2017 E: 232

Koetzle, Hans-Michael, Koenig, Thilo et al., "twen – Revision einer Legende," Klinkhardt & Biermann, 1995 E: 232

Koolhaas, Rem, "delirious new york," 010 Publishers, 1994 E: 236

Koop, Andreas, "NSCI-Das visuelle Erscheinungsbild der Nationalsozialisten 1920 – 1945," Verlag Hermann Schmidt Mainz, 2008 E: 077

Kraushaar, Wolfgang, "Die blinden Flecken der RAF," Klett-Cotta, 2017 E: 277

Kraushaar, Wolfgang, "Keine falsche Toleranz," CEP Europäische Verlagsanstalt, 2022 E: 274

Kress, Gunther, van Leeuwen, Theo, "Reading Images," Routledge, 2020 E: 265

L

Lars Müller Publishers (ed.), "Josef Müller-Brockmann. Ein Pionier der Schweizer Grafik," Baden, 2001 E: 148

Le-Mentzel, Van Bo (ed.), "hartzIV-moebel.com, Build more, Buy Less," Hatje Cantz, 2018 E: 057.1

Loos, Adolf, Opel, Adolf (eds.), "Trotzdem. Gesammelte Schriften 1900-1930," Braumüller Verlag, 1982 E: 076

Lupton, Ellen, Miller, J. Abbott (eds.), "Dreieck, Quadrat und Kreis. Bauhaus und Design-Theorie heute," Birkhäuser Verlag,1994 E: 075.1

Lupton, Ellen, Kafei, Farah, Tobias, Jennifer, Halstead, Josh A., Sales, Kaleena, Xia, Leslie, Vergara, Valentina (eds.), "Extra Bold – a feminist inclusive anti-racist nonbinary field guide for graphic designers," Princeton Architectural Press, 2021 E: 105

Lutz, Hans-Rudolf, "Ausbildung in typografischer Gestaltung," Verlag Hans-Rudolf Lutz, 1987 E: 143

Lutz, Hans-Rudolf, Margadant, Bruno, "Hoffnung und Widerstand," Verlag Hans-Rudolf Lutz und Museum für Gestaltung, Zürich, 1998 E: 210

Lutz, Hans-Rudolf, "Typoundso" Verlag Hans-Rudolf Lutz, 1997 E: 143.1

M

Mafundikwa, Saki, "Afrikan Alphabets, The Story of writing in Africa," Mark Batty Publisher, 2004 E: 178

Mankoff, Robert, "The complete Cartoons of the New Yorker," Black Dog & Leventhal Publishers, 2004 E: 236

Mareis, Claudia, Paim, Nina (eds.), "Design Struggles: Intersecting Histories, Pedagogies, and Perspectives," Valiz, 2021 E: 102

Mareis, Claudia, "Experimente zu einer Theorie der Praxis. Historische Etappen der Designforschung in der Nachfolge des Bauhauses," in kunsttexte.de, special issue 1: Kunst und Design, G. Jain (eds.), 2010. E: 051.1

Mareis, Claudia, "Theorien des Designs," Junius Verlag, 2014 E: S. 336

Mason, Anna, Victoria and Albert Museum (eds.), "William Morris," Thames & Hudson, 2021 E: 187

McLuhan, Marshall, "The Medium is the Message: An Inventory of Effects," Penguin Classics, 2008 E: 236

McCarthy, Steven, "The Designer as: Author, Producer, Artist, Entrepreneur, Curator & Collaborator," BIS Publishers, 2013 E: 096

Menasse, Eva, "Alles und nichts sagen – Vom Zustand der Debatte in der Digitalmoderne," Büchergilde Gutenberg, 2024 E: 259

Menichinelli, Massimo (ed.), "Fab Lab – Revolution Field Manual," Niggli Verlag, 2017 E: 057.2

Menner, Simon, "Top secret. Bilder aus den Archiven der Staatssicherheit," Verlag Hatje Cantz, Berlin, 2014 E: 111

Metcalf, Eugene W., Maresca, Frank, "ray gun," Fotofolio Inc., 1999 E: 278

Meyer, Roland, "Gesichtserkennung," out of the series "Digitale Bildkulturen," Verlag Klaus Wagenbach, 2021 E: 179

Meyer, Thomas, "Was soll an meiner Nase bitte jüdisch sein?," Edition Zeitkritik 5, Büchergilde Gutenberg, 2021 E: 223

Miessen, Markus, "The Nightmare of Participation," Sternberg Press, 2011 E: 256

Miller, Alice, "For Your Own Good: Hidden Cruelty in Child-Rearing and the Roots of Violence," Farrar, Straus and Giroux, New York City, 1990 E: 001.2

Morgan, Nigel, Pritchard, Annette, Pride, Roger, "Destination Branding," Butterworth-Heinemann Ltd, 2004 E: 221

Mühsam, Erich, "Die Befreiung der Gesellschaft vom Staat," Rixdorfer Verlagsanstalt, 1984 E: 268

Müller-Brockmann, Josef, "Grid systems in graphic design, a visual communication manual for graphic designers, typographers and three dimensional designers," Niggli Verlag, 2012 E: 031

Müller, Lars, "Helvetica. Hommage to a typeface," Lars Müller Publishers, 2002 E: 032

Museum für Gestaltung (ed.), "Social Design. Partizipation und Empowerment," Lars Müller Publishers, 2018 E: 057.3

N

Nänni, Jürg, "Visuelle Wahrnehmung. Eine interaktive Entdeckungsreise durch unser Sehsystem," Niggli Verlag, 2009 E: 005.1

Naegele, Isabel, Baur, Ruedi, "Scents of the city," Lars Müller Publishers, 2004 E: 013.1

Naegele, Isabel, Eisele, Petra, Ludwig, Annette (eds.), "Neue Schriften. New Typefaces," Niggli Verlag, 2013 E: 032.3

Nemitz, Paul, Pfeffer, Matthias, "Prinzip Mensch. Macht, Freiheit und Demokratie im Zeitalter der Künstlichen Intelligenz," Verlag J. H. W. Dietz, 2020 E: 097

Nesquens, Daniel (text), Mora, Sergio (illustration), "Papa Tatuato," Ediciones A buen Paso, 2009 E: 207

Neurath, Marie, Kinross, Robin, Switzer, Brian (eds.), "Die Transformierer – Entstehung und Prinzipien von Isotype," Niggli Verlag, 2017 E: 015.1

Niemeyer, Oscar, "Wir müssen die Welt verändern," Antje Kunstmann Verlag, 2013 E: 282

O

Oettingen, Dirik von, "Verhüllt um zu verführen – Die Welt auf der Orange," vacat verlag, 2007 E: 254

P

Papanek Victor, Kries, Mateo, Klein, Amelie, Clarke Alson J. (eds.), "The Politics of Design," Vitra Design Museum und Victor Papanek Foundation, 2018 E: 054

Papanek, Victor, "Design for the Real World," Thames & Hudson Ltd, 2020 E: 054.1

Pariser, Eli, "The Filter Bubble. What the internet is hiding from you," Penguin Books, 2011 E: 098

Pater, Ruben, "Caps Lock: How Capitalism Took Hold of Graphic Design, and How to Escape from It," Valiz Publishers, 2021 E: 058.3

Pater, Ruben, "The Politics of Design," BIS Publishers, 2016 E: 002.1, 178

Petersen, Thomas, Schwender, Clemens (eds.), "Die Entschlüsselung der Bilder – Methoden zur Erforschung visueller Kommunikation," Herbert von Halem Verlag, 2011 E: 003.2

Petrovich, Dushko, White, Roger, "Draw it with your eyes closed: the art of the art assignment," Paper Monument, 2012 E: 277

Petruschat, Angelika, Petruschat, Jörg, "design – design, Fachwörterbuch für Gestaltung," German – English – German, form+zweck Verlag, 2009 E: 250

Piketty, Thomas, "Capital in the Twenty-First Century," Harvard University Press, 2014 E: 269

Pinker, Steven, "The Stuff of Thought," Penguin Books, 2008 E: 279

Poynor, Rick, "Anarchie der Zeichen," Birkhäuser Verlag, Basel, 2003 E: 155

Q

Quiring, Claudia, and others, "Ernst May 1886 – 1970," Prestel Verlag, 2011 E: 266

R

Rautenberg, Ursula, Schneider, Ute (eds.), "Lesen – Ein interdisziplinäres Handbuch," De Gruyter Verlag, 2015 E: 012.1

Rao, Sirish, Geetha, V., Wolf, Gita, "An Ideal Boy – Charts from India," dewi lewis publishing, Stockport, United Kingdom, 2001, E: 106

Rawsthorn, Alice, "Design as an Attitude," JRP editions, 2018 E: 204

Reichert, Kolja, "Krypto-Kunst," out of the series "Digitale Bildkulturen," Verlag Klaus Wagenbach, 2021 E: 179

Richard Paul Lohse-Stiftung (ed.), "Richard Paul Lohse – Konstruktive Gebrauchsgrafik," Verlag Hatje Cantz, Stuttgart, 1999 E: 142

Ringelnatz, Joachim, "Das Ringelnatz Lesebuch," Keel, Daniel (ed.), Diogenes Verlag, 1984 E: 267

Rodatz, Christoph, Smolarski, Pierre (eds.), "Wie können wir den Schaden maximieren? Gestaltung trotz Komplexität," transcript Verlag, 2021 E: 100.1

Rogger, Basil, Voegeli, Jonas, Widmer, Ruedi, Museum für Gestaltung Zürich (eds.), "Protest. Eine Zukunftspraxis," Lars Müller Publishers, 2018 E: 035

Rothenstein, Julian, Budashevskaya, Olga (eds.), "Schatzkammer der Revolution. Russische Kinderbücher von 1920 – 1935: Bücher aus bewegten Zeiten," Lars Müller Publishers, 2013 E: 182

Ruder, Emil, "typography," Niggli Verlag, 1996 E: 029

S

Sahihi, Arman, "Altpersische Numerologie," Ariston Verlag, 1992 E: 066.1

Sauthoff, Daniel, Wendt, Gilmar, Willberg, Hans Peter, "Schriften erkennen," Verlag Hermann Schmidt Mainz, 2011 E: 177

Schiffmacher, Henk, "Lexicon der Tatoeages van Aarsgewei tot Zwitserland," Uitgeverij Carrera, 2008 E: 127

Schepers, Wolfgang, Schmitt, Peter (eds.), "Das Jahrhundert des Design, Geschichte und Zukunft der Dinge," Verlag Anabas, 2000 E: 080

Schlicht, Esther, Wetzel, Roland, Hollein, Max (eds.), "Poesie der Großstadt. Die Affichisten," Snoeck Verlagsgesellschaft, 2014 E: 226

Schmitz, Michael, "Motivation + Aktion," Self-Published, 2016 E: 160

Schneider, Wolf, "Deutsch für junge Profis. Wie man gut und lebendig schreibt," Rowohlt Taschenbuch Verlag, 2020 E: 223

Schulz von Thun, Friedemann, "Miteinander Reden: 1 – Störungen und Klärungen. Allgemeine Psychologie der Kommunikation," Rowohlt Verlag, 1981 E: 233

Schranz, Christine (ed.), "Shifts in Mapping. Maps as a Tool of Knowledge," Transcript Verlag, 2021 E: 006.1

Schröder, Jörg, Hof, Bruno, "Die große März-Kassette. Wer die 60er und 70er verstehen will, muss März kennen!," AREA Verlag, 2004 E: 230

Schulze, Floyd, "Forever – The New Tattoo," Gestalten Verlag, Berlin, 2012 E: 127.2

Schwitters, Kurt, "Eile ist des Witzes Weile," Reclam, 2009 E: 267

Selby, Aimee, "Art and Text," Black Dog Publishers, 2009, E: 215

Sennett, Richard, "Building and Dwelling: Ethics for the City," Farrar, Straus & Giroux, 2018 E: 219

Seller, Hank F., "Cornflakes in Cellophane," Greno Verlagsgesellschaft, 1987 E: 278

Shell Deutschland Holding (ed.), "18. Shell Jugendstudie Jugend 2019. Eine Generation meldet sich zu Wort.," Beltz Verlag, 2019 E: 099

Shelton, Gilbert, "Complete Freak Brothers, Vol.1," Knockabout Comics, 2001 E: 247

Simons, Katrin, "El Lissitzky, Proun 23 N," Insel Verlag, 1998 E: 268

Spider, "Emma," Éditions Sarbacane, 2009 E: 207

Spiegelman, Art, Kidd, Chip, "Jack Cole and Plastic Man," DC Comics, 2001 E: 278

Stadt Mainz, Krawietz, Peter, Hanebutt-Benz, Dr. Eva-Maria (eds.), "Gutenberg – Aventur und Kunst. Vom Geheimunternehmen zur ersten Medienrevolution," 2000 E: 067

Stankowski, Anton, Duschek, Karl (eds.), "Visuelle Kommunikation: ein Design-Handbuch," Dietrich Reimer Verlag, 1989 E: 079, 192

Stiegler, Bernd (ed.), "Texte zur Theorie der Fotografie," Reclam Verlag, 2018 E: 069

Stiftung Museum Schloss Moyland (ed.), "Denken. Reden. Machen. Joseph Beuys für Kinder und Jugendliche," Kerber Verlag, 2003 E: 226

Stone, Lisa, "Freaks, Geeks & Strange Girls – Sideshow Banners of the Great American Midway," Hardy Marks Publications, 1996 E: 254

T

Taschen, Benedikt, "Chinese Propaganda Posters," Taschen Verlag, 2003 E: 210

Taschen Verlag (ed.), "Pierre et Gilles," Taschen Verlag, 1993 E: 169

Teipel, Jürgen, "Verschwende deine Jugend," Suhrkamp Verlag, 2021 E: 038

Tilley, Alvin, R., Henry Dreyfuss Associates, "The Measure of Man and Woman: Human Factors in Design," Wiley, 2001 E: 218

Tolstoi, Leo, "War and Peace," Penguin Classics, 2007 E: 268

Trabant, Jürgen, "Die Sprache," Verlag C. H. Beck, 2009 E: 223

Trebeß, Achim (ed.), "Metzler Lexikon Ästhetik," Verlag J.B. Metzler, 2006 E: 023, 184.1, 184.3

Turcotte, Bryan Ray, Miller, Christopher T., "Fucked up + Photocopied: The Instant Art of the Punk Rock Movement," Gingko Press, 2002 E: 039

Twain, Mark, "Die schreckliche deutsche Sprache – The Awful German Language," Nikol-Verlag, 2009 E: 230

TwoPoints.Net (ed.), "Pretty Ugly Design – Visual Rebellion in Design," Gestalten Verlag, 2012 E: 047

U

Uebele, Andreas, "Orientierungssysteme und Signaletik. Führen – Finden – Fliehen," Verlag Hermann Schmidt Mainz, 2006 E: 020

Ueki-Polet, Keiko, Klemp, Klaus, "Less and more. The Design Ethos of Dieter Rams," Die Gestalten Verlag, 2010 E: 087.1

Ullrich, Wolfgang, "Selfies," out of the series "Digitale Bildkulturen," Verlag Klaus Wagenbach, 2019 E: 179

V

van Toorn, Jan, "design's delight," nai010 publishers, 2006 E: 101

Venturi, Robert, Brown, Denise S., Izenour, Steven, "Lernen von Las Vegas: Zur Ikonographie und Architektursymbolik der Geschäftsstadt," Birkhäuser Verlag, 2001 E: 236

Verlag Hermann Schmidt Mainz (ed.), special issue of the "typographical communications" from October 1925, a "journal of the educational association of German book printers in Leipzig," reprint: 1986 E: 073, 074, 074,1

Voelker, Ulysses, "Km 497 – Über die visuellen Sprachen längs des Rheins," Hochschule Mainz, 2007 E: 222

Voelker, Ulysses, "Read + Play," Verlag Hermann Schmidt Mainz, 2015 E: 011, 032.2, 068, 068.1, 070

Voelker, Ulysses, "Structuring Design," Niggli Verlag, 2018 E: 005.2, 019, 021, 022, 084.2, 174

Voelker, Ulysses, »Zimmermann meets Spiekermann«, HfK Bremen, 1992 E: 042.1

von Borries, Friedrich, "RLF, Das richtige Leben im falschen," Suhrkamp Verlag, 2013 E: 104

von Borries, Friedrich, "Weltentwerfen – Eine politische Designtheorie," edition suhrkamp, 2017 E: 103

Vossoughian, Nader, "Otto Neurath – the Language of the Global Polis," NAi Publishers, Rotterdam, 2008 E: 015

W

Watzlawick, Paul, Beavin, Janet H., Jackson, Don D., "Menschliche Kommunikation," Verlag Hans Huber, 2011 E: 011

Watzlawick, Paul, "Wie wirklich ist die Wirklichkeit," Piper Verlag, München, 2006 E: 135

Weingart, Wolfgang, "Weingart: Typographie. Wege zur Typographie," Lars Müller Publishers, 2000 E: 026.1

Weinhart, Martina, Hollein, Max, "World Transformers. The Art of the Outsiders," Hatje Cantz, 2010 E: 237

Weiss, Peter, "The Aesthetics of Resistance," Duke University Press, 2005 E: 268

Welsch, Wolfgang, "Ästhetisches Denken," Reclam Verlag, 2010 E: 168

Willberg, Hans Peter, Forssman, Friedrich, "Lesetypografie," Verlag Hermann Schmidt, Mainz, 2010 E: 012

Wolf, Maryanne, "Das lesende Gehirn," Spektrum Verlag, 2009 E: 016.1

Y

Yablonski, Jon, "Laws of UX: Using Psychology to Design Better Products & Services," O'Reilly Media, 2020 E: 199

Yee, Lydia, "Laurie Anderson, Trisha Brown, Gordon Matta-Clark. Pioneers of the Downtown Scene New York, 1970s," Prestel Verlag, 2011 E: 220

Image sources A–D

1
"All Around us – Teachers Edition"; Scott Foresman and co. (Eds.), US, 1st edition, 1949; front cover

2
"All Around us – Teachers Edition"; Scott Foresman and co. (Eds.), US, 1st edition, 1949; front cover

3
"All Around us – Teachers Edition"; Scott Foresman and co. (Eds.), US, 1st edition, 1949; p. 30–31

4
"All Around us – Teachers Edition"; Scott Foresman and co. (Eds.), US, 1st edition, 1949; p. 1

5
"All Around us – Teachers Edition"; Scott Foresman and co. (Eds.), US, 1st edition, 1949; p. 45

6
"All Around us – Teachers Edition"; Scott Foresman and co. (Eds.), US, 1st edition, 1949; p. 52

7
"All Around us – Teachers Edition"; Scott Foresman and co. (Eds.), US, 1st edition, 1949; p. 51

8
"All Around us – Teachers Edition"; Scott Foresman and co. (Eds.), US, 1st edition, 1949; p. 51

9
"All Around us – Teachers Edition"; Scott Foresman and co. (Eds.), US, 1st edition, 1949; p. 37

10
"All Around us – Teachers Edition"; Scott Foresman and co. (Eds.), US, 1st edition, 1949; p. 51

11
Graphic: Michael Schmitz

12
Image: Ulysses Voelker

13
Graphic: Michael Schmitz

19
Graphic: Michael Schmitz

21
"Fucked Up+Photocopied: Instant Art of the punk rock movement," Bryan Ray Turcotte, Christopher T. Miller, Gingko Press, 1999;
Design: Ken Inouye; p. 194

22
https://de.wikipedia.org/wiki/Datei:Bleiletter.svg, 10.01.23, 16:55;

23
"Gutenberg. Aventur und Kunst," Stadt Mainz (ed.), Verlag Hermann Schmidt Mainz, 2000, p. 191

24
Polen, no.8, 1963, p. 12-13

25
Twen, no.9, 1970, p. 124

26
"Weingart: Typography – Wege zur Typografie," Lars Müller (ed.), Baden, 2000, p. 385

27
"Kulturkampf," Hochschule für Künste (ed.), Bremen, 1990, p. 24-25

28
"032c," no.34, Berlin, 2018, unknown page

29
Bravo, no.1, Germany, 1962, front cover

30
Bravo, no.1, Germany, 2002, front cover

31
Easyriders Tattoo, US, 1990, front cover

32
Tätowier-Magazin, Mannheim, 2017, front cover

33
Deutsche Metall-Arbeiter-Zeitung, no.9, Nuremberg, 1891, front cover

34
"Socialist Worker," No. 924, UK, 1985, front cover

35
"Josef Müller-Brockmann – Pionier der Schweizer Grafik," Lars Müller, Lars Müller Publishers, Zurich, p. 150-151

36
Parapluie, No.04, Paris, 1970, front cover

37
Berkeley Barb, No.508, US, May 1975, front cover

38
Pretty vacant, UK, 1978, front cover

39
Kingdom come, Nr.15, UK, 1977, front cover

40
Touch and Go, US, 1982, unknown page

41
"The graphic language of Neville Brody," Jon Wozencroft (ed.), Bangert Verlag, 1988, p. 121

42
Raygun, No. 28, US, 1995, unknown page

43
Emigre, No. 15, US, 1990, p. 10-11

44
032c, No.13, Berlin, 2007, unknown page

45
Pretty Ugly, Gestalten Verlag, Berlin, 2012, p. 192-193

46
Pretty Ugly, Gestalten Verlag, Berlin, 2012, unknown page

47
https://eyeondesign.aiga.org/knotty-objects-dunne-raby-ab-hi-res/, 11.01.23, 10:17;

48
Image: Ulysses Voelker

49
Graphic: Michael Schmitz

50
Graphic: Michael Schmitz

51
Graphic: Michael Schmitz

52
File:Pentagram (Levi).jpg. (2023, January 6). Wikimedia Commons. Retrieved 10:13, January 11, 2023 from https://commons.wikimedia.org/w/index.php?title=File:Pentagram_(Levi).jpg&oldid=723165164.

53
"read + play. Einführung in die Typografie," Verlag Hermann Schmidt Mainz, 2015, p. 137

58
File:Futura Bold Condensed.jpg. (2023, January 21). Wikimedia Commons. Retrieved 10:24, Jnuary 11, 2023 from https://commons.wikimedia.org/w/index.php?title=File:Futura_Bold_Condensed.jpg&oldid=726711499.

60
Nachbau der Originalgrafik: Michael Schmitz, abgerufen unter: bit.ly/3v-RTvoi, 11.01.23, 10:25;

62
File:1955 Foto-HansGConrad HfGUlm Architekt-MaxBill.jpg. (2023, April 5). Wikimedia Commons. Retrieved 10:15, October 14, 2023 from https://commons.wikimedia.org/w/index.php?title=File:1955_Foto-HansGConrad_HfGUlm_Architekt-MaxBill.jpg&oldid=747483548.

63
Reproduction of the original graphic: Michael Schmitz, retrieved from: https://commons.wikimedia.org/wiki/File:Schematic_teaching_of_HFG_Ulm.jpg, 11.01.23, 10:25;

64
https://www.fontshop.com/families/ff-dirty-three, 26.01.23, 14:00;

65
"1 Typographics," Baird, Anne, 1996, Harper Collins Publishers, New York, p. 70

66
"1 Typographics," Baird, Anne, 1996, Harper Collins Publishers, New York, p. 71

67
Familie mit Herz, edition 113, Bastei Lübbe, Cologne, 2021, front page

68
Graphic: Michael Schmitz

69
Graphic: Michael Schmitz

70
Graphic: Michael Schmitz

71
Graphic: Michael Schmitz

73
"Vorschule der Ästhetik," Gustav Theodor Fechner, Volume 1, 3rd edition, Verlag Von Breitel & Härtkopf, Leipzig, 1925, accessed via: https://archive.org/details/in.ernet.dli.2015.187651/page/n192/mode/thumb, 11.01.23, 10:34;

77
Graphic: Ulysses Voelker, Michael Schmitz

78
Graphic: Ulysses Voelker, Michael Schmitz

79
Graphic: Ulysses Voelker, Michael Schmitz

80
Graphic: Ulysses Voelker, Michael Schmitz

81
Graphic: Ulysses Voelker, Michael Schmitz

82
File:Ilya Repin - Barge Haulers on the Volga - Google Art Project.jpg. (2022, November 21). Wikimedia Commons. Retrieved 10:16, October 14, 2023 from https://commons.wikimedia.org/w/index.php?title=-File:Ilya_Repin_-_Barge_Haulers_on_the_Volga_-_Google_Art_Project.jpg&oldid=708471105.

83
File:L'Aubade Picasso mai 1942.jpg. (2020, October 11). Wikimedia Commons. Retrieved 10:17, October 14, 2023 from https://commons.wikimedia.org/w/index.php?title=File:L%27Aubade_Picasso_mai_1942.jpg&oldid=486678681.

84
Image: Ulysses Voelker

85
Das Magazin, Hamburg, Spring 2024, p. 8-9

86
flow, Hamburg, No..81, 2024, p. 76-77

87
Cicero, Berlin, No.01, 2024, p. 66-67

88
Psychologie heute, Weinheim, February 2024, p. 46-47

89
InStyle, Offenburg, May 2024, p. 40-41

90
Informationen zur politischen Bildung, Bonn, No.354, 2023, p. 58-59

91
Futurzwei, Berlin, No.28, 2024, p. 52-53

92
Cato, Berlin, No.3, 2024, p. 56-57

93
Image: Ulysses Voelker

Image sources / text sources E1

001
"All Around us – Teachers Edition"; Scott Foresman and co. (Eds.), US, 1st edition, 1949; p. 38–39

002
(1) File:The Sounds of Earth Record Cover - GPN-2000-001978.jpg. (2023, May 15). Wikimedia Commons. Retrieved 11:20, October 13, 2023 from https://commons.wikimedia.org/w/index.php?-title=File:The_Sounds_of_Earth_Record_Cover_-_GPN-2000-001978.jpg&oldid=763432484.
(2) File:The Sounds of Earth - GPN-2000-001976.jpg. (2023, October 11). Wikimedia Commons. Retrieved 11:18, October 13, 2023 from https://commons.wikimedia.org/w/index.php?-title=File:The_Sounds_of_Earth_-_GPN-2000-001976.jpg&oldid=810957174.
(3) https://voyager.jpl.nasa.gov/golden-record/whats-on-the-record/images/, 04.07.2024, 21:20.
(4) File:Mounting-the-golden-record 30269499363 o.jpg. (2023, August 20). Wikimedia Commons. Retrieved 11:21, October 13, 2023 from https://commons.wikimedia.org/w/index.php?title=File:Mounting-the-golden-record_30269499363_o.jpg&oldid=794621169.
(5)(6) File:Voyager Golden Record Cover Explanation.svg. (2020, September 7). Wikimedia Commons. Retrieved 11:22, October 13, 2023 from https://commons.wikimedia.org/w/index.php?title=File:Voyager_Golden_Record_Cover_Explanation.svg&oldid=450863111.

002.2
(1) File:Pictogram for nuclear sites, US Department of Energy, 2004.png. (2022, December 22). Wikimedia Commons. Retrieved 11:24, October 13, 2023 from https://commons.wikimedia.org/w/index.php?title=File:Pictogram_for_nuclear_sites,_US_Department_of_Energy,_2004.png&oldid=718689673.

003.1
(1) File:Heatmaps und AOIs.png. (2020, September 24). Wikimedia Commons. Retrieved 11:24, October 13, 2023 from https://commons.wikimedia.org/w/index.php?title=File:Heatmaps_und_AOIs.png&oldid=470094009.

006
(1) File:World map geographical.jpg. (2022, June 12). Wikimedia Commons. Retrieved 11:26, October 13, 2023 from https://commons.wikimedia.org/w/index.php?title=File:World_map_geographical.jpg&oldid=664135541.
(2) File:BlankMap-World-90W.svg. (2022, February 15). Wikimedia Commons. Retrieved 11:29, October 13, 2023 from https://commons.wikimedia.org/w/index.php?title=File:BlankMap-World-90W.svg&oldid=629899168.

015
(1) "Otto Neurath – the Language of the Global Polis," Nader Vossoughian; NAi Publishers, Rotterdam, 2008, p.87.
(2) "Otto Neurath – the Language of the Global Polis," Nader Vossoughian; NAi Publishers, Rotterdam, 2008, p.68.

017
(2) Screenshot: https://decodeunicode.org/en/u+03105, 17.01.23, 23:35.

023
Page „Geschmack (Kultur)". In: Wikipedia - The free encyclopedia. Editing status: September 27, 2023, 07:19 UTC. URL: https://de.wikipedia.org/w/index.php?title=Geschmack_(Kultur)&oldid=237671766 (Accessed: October 13, 2023, 11:35 UTC)

024
Wikipedia contributors. Marketing. Wikipedia, The Free Encyclopedia. April 4, 2024, 14:51 UTC. Available at: https://en.wikipedia.org/w/index.php?title=Marketing&oldid=1217220090. Accessed June 3, 2024.
Wikipedia contributors. Market research. Wikipedia, The Free Encyclopedia. April 5, 2024, 16:43 UTC. Available at: https://en.wikipedia.org/w/index.php?title=Market_research&oldid=1217404092. Accessed June 3, 2024.

025
Wikipedia contributors. (2024, June 15). Typesetting. In Wikipedia, The Free Encyclopedia. Retrieved 08:01, July 5, 2024, from https://en.wikipedia.org/w/index.php?title=Typesetting&oldid=1229139988

026
Wikipedia contributors. (2024, March 18). Phototypesetting. In Wikipedia, The Free Encyclopedia. Retrieved 08:25, July 5, 2024, from https://en.wikipedia.org/w/index.php?title=Phototypesetting&oldid=1214330159

027
(1) https://vimeo.com/301953910, 7.12.2022, 20:30.
(2) https://vimeo.com/301953910, 7.12.2022, 20:30.
(3) Screenshot of https://www.type-together.com/2021-adelle-sans-multiscript, 30.08.2021, 11:46.
(4)(5) Screenshot of https://v-fonts.com/, 04.07. 2024, 21:24.
(6) Screenshot of https://abcdinamo.com/custom/ica-london, 08.10.2023, 12:30.
(7) Screenshot of https://abcdinamo.com/custom/ica-london, 08.10.2023, 12:30.
(8) Screenshot of https://aifont.process.studio/, 28.08.2023, 11:51.
(9) Screenshot of https://aifont.process.studio/, 28.08.2023, 11:51.
(10) Screenshot of http://benjaminschupp.de/html/work.html, 08.10.2023, 11:00.
(11) Graphic: Michael Schmitz

034
(1) Page „Hippie". In: Wikipedia – The Free Encyclopedia. Last edited: July 28, 2023, 10:51 UTC. URL: https://de.wikipedia.org/w/index.php?title=Hippie&oldid=235889983 (Accessed: October 13, 2023, 11:39 UTC)
(1) https://commons.wikimedia.org/wiki/File:White_rabbit.JPG?uselang=de, 04.07.2024, 19:27.
(2) https://bit.ly/3LcNDxw, 04.07.2024, 19:28.

037.1
(1) Page „Rotaprint". In: Wikipedia – The Free Encyclopedia. Last edited: July 27, 2022, 12:03 UTC. URL: https://de.wikipedia.org/w/index.php?title=Rotaprint&oldid=224859499 (Accessed: October 13, 2023, 11:40 UTC)
(2) Page „Kleinoffset". In: Wikipedia – The free encyclopedia. Editing status: February 26, 2023, 12:23 UTC. URL: https://de.wikipedia.org/w/index.php?title=Kleinoffset&oldid=231266979 (Accessed: October 13, 2023, 11:40 UTC)

038
Page „Verschwende deine Jugend". In: Wikipedia – The free encyclopedia. Editing status: February 5, 2023, 11:53 UTC. URL: https://de.wikipedia.org/w/index.php?title=Verschwende_Deine_Jugend&oldid=230567110 (Accessed: October 13, 2023, 11:41 UTC)

040
(1)
Page „Macintosh". In: Wikipedia – The free encyclopedia. Last edited: September 28, 2023, 18:34 UTC. URL: https://de.wikipedia.org/w/index.php?title=Macintosh&oldid=237712494 (Accessed: October 13, 2023, 11:41 UTC)
(2)
File:Macintosh 128k transparency.png. (2023, January 31). Wikimedia Commons. Retrieved 11:42, October 13, 2023 from https://commons.wikimedia.org/w/index.php?title=File:Macintosh_128k_transparency.png&oldid=729232325.

044
(1) Wikipedia contributors. (2023, January 18). Emigre (magazine). In Wikipedia, The Free Encyclopedia. Retrieved 11:44, October 13, 2023, from https://en.wikipedia.org/w/index.php?title=Emigre_(magazine)&oldid=1134321592

045
https://designobserver.com/feature/how-to-be-ugly/5867, 21.12.22, 12:07;

049
Page „Werbung". In: Wikipedia – The free encyclopedia. Editing status: September 20, 2023, 06:04 UTC. URL: https://de.wikipedia.org/w/index.php?title=Werbung&oldid=237480868 (Accessed: October 13, 2023, 11:46 UTC)

051
Wikipedia contributors. (2023, June 26). Design methods. In Wikipedia, The Free Encyclopedia. Retrieved 11:47, October 13, 2023, from https://en.wikipedia.org/w/index.php?title=Design_methods&oldid=1162019855

051.1
"Experimente zu einer Theorie der Praxis. Historische Etappen der Designforschung in der Nachfolge des Bauhauses," Claudia Mareis, in kunsttexte.de, Themenheft 1: Kunst und Design, G. Jain (Ed.), 2010. retrieved 13:44, August 06, 2021 from https://edoc.hu-berlin.de/bitstream/handle/18452/8019/mareis.pdf?sequence=1&isAllowed=y.

055
(1) Wikipedia contributors. (2020, December 5). First Things First 1964 manifesto. In Wikipedia, The Free Encyclopedia. Retrieved 11:50, October 13, 2023, from https://en.wikipedia.org/w/index.php?title=First_Things_First_1964_manifesto&oldid=992561246
(2) http://www.designishistory.com/1960/first-things-first/, 21.12.2022, 12:27.

055.1
(1) https://en.wikipedia.org/wiki/First_Things_First_2000_manifesto, 21.12.2022, 12:28.
(2) https://www.eyemagazine.com/feature/article/first-things-first-manifesto-2000, 21.12.2022, 12:31.

055.2
https://www.firstthingsfirst2020.org/, 21.12.22, 12:29;

056
Wikipedia contributors. (2023, August 21). Studio 65. In Wikipedia, The Free Encyclopedia. Retrieved 11:53, October 13, 2023, from https://en.wikipedia.org/w/index.php?title=Studio_65&oldid=1171472810

056.1
(1) Page „Alessandro Mendini". In: Wikipedia – The free encyclopedia. Editing status: December 25, 2022, 15:02 UTC. URL: https://de.wikipedia.org/w/index.php?title=Alessandro_Mendini&oldid=229176839 (Accessed: October 13, 2023, 11:54 UTC)
(2) File:Alessandro Mendini Poltrona di Proust Studio Alchimia 1979 Musée des arts décoratifs Paris.jpg. (2023, July 31). Wikimedia Commons. Retrieved 11:55, October 13, 2023 from https://commons.wikimedia.org/w/index.php?title=File:Alessandro_Mendini_Poltrona_di_Proust_Studio_Alchimia_1979_Mus%C3%A9e_des_arts_d%C3%A9coratifs_Paris.jpg&oldid=788482260.

058
https://oxfordre.com/environmentalscience/view/10.1093/acrefore/9780199389414.001.0001/acrefore-9780199389414-e-144, 21.12.2022, 12:36.

058.3
https://valiz.nl/en/publications/caps-lock.html, 30.08.2021, 11:30.

060
Wikipedia contributors. (2024, July 5). Aesthetics. In Wikipedia, The Free Encyclopedia. Retrieved 08:40, July 5, 2024, from https://en.wikipedia.org/w/index.php?title=Aesthetics&oldid=1232715872

062
https://www.youtube.com/watch?v=7Zxc22Vd9VQ, 21.12.2022, 12:54.

063
https://mymodernmet.com/eray-eren-asymmetry/, 21.12.2022, 12:54.

068
File:Gutenberg Bible B42 Genesis cropped.jpg. (2023, February 15). Wikimedia Commons. Retrieved 16:27, October 13, 2023 from https://commons.wikimedia.org/w/index.php?title=File:Gutenberg_Bible_B42_Genesis_cropped.jpg&oldid=732620524.

068.2
(1)"Geschichte der Schrift," Harald Haarmann; Verlag C. H. Beck, Munich, 2011, p. 12;
(2)"Geschichte der Schrift," Harald Haarmann; Verlag C. H. Beck, Munich, 2011, . 13;

081
https://ocw.mit.edu/courses/architecture/4-205-analysis-of-contemporary-architecture-fall-2009/readings/MIT4_205F09_Sullivan.pdf, 28.01.2022, 20:52.

092
(1) Page „Allianz deutscher Designer". In: Wikipedia – The Free Encyclopedia. Editing status: November 16, 2022, 11:16 UTC. URL: https://de.wikipedia.org/w/index.php?title=Allianz_deutscher_Designer&oldid=228021137 (Accessed: December 18, 2022, 16:28 UTC)
(2) Page „Professional Association of Communication Design". In: Wikipedia – The Free Encyclopedia. Last edited: September 19, 2023, 12:20 UTC. URL: https://de.wikipedia.org/w/index.php?title=Berufsverband_Kommunikationsdesign&oldid=237462695 (Accessed: December 18, 2022, 12:02 UTC)
(3) Page „German Designer Club". In: Wikipedia – The Free Encyclopedia. Editing status: October 3, 2023, 09:18 UTC. URL: https://de.wikipedia.org/w/index.php?title=Deutscher_Designer_Club&oldid=237833215 (Accessed: October 13, 2023, 16:29 UTC)

095
https://www.youtube.com/watch?v=s-Qy-Q_psTJ0; 13.10.2023, 18:12.

097.1
https://en.wikipedia.org/wiki/Artificial_intelligence, 06.06.2024, 12:14.

097.2
(1) "Atlas of AI – Power, Politics, and the Planetary Costs of Artificial Intelligence" Kate Crawford, Yale University Press, 2022, front cover

097.7
(1) ChatGPT 4.0, https://chat.openai.com/, 12.04.2024, 16:10
(2) ChatGPT 4.0, https://chat.openai.com/, 12.04.2024, 16:12
(3) ChatGPT 4.0, https://chat.openai.com/, 12.04.2024, 16:17

104
https://www.friedrichvonborries.de/de/projekte/rlf-manifest, 03.03.2022, 09:52.

Image sources / text sources E2

108
(1) File:STS-102 Patch.svg. (2021, May 24). Wikimedia Commons. Retrieved 16:36, October 13, 2023 from https://commons.wikimedia.org/w/index.php?title=File:STS-102_Patch.svg&oldid=564029472.
(2) File:Space Shuttle Approach and Landing Test (ALT) Patch.svg. (2023, April 18). Wikimedia Commons. Retrieved 16:37, October 13, 2023 from https://commons.wikimedia.org/w/index.php?title=File:Space_Shuttle_Approach_and_Landing_Test_(ALT)_Patch.svg&oldid=751802788.
(3) File:ISS Yearlong mission patch.png. (2021, May 24). Wikimedia Commons. Retrieved 16:37, October 13, 2023 from https://commons.wikimedia.org/w/index.php?title=File:ISS_Yearlong_mission_patch.png&oldid=564061485.
(4) File:Soyuz TMA 01M-Mission Patch.svg. (2021, May 24). Wikimedia Commons. Retrieved 17:10, October 13, 2021 from https://commons.wikimedia.org/wiki/File:Soyuz-TMA-01M-Mission-Patch.svg.
(5) File:Apollo 14-insignia.png. (2023, September 9). Wikimedia Commons. Retrieved 16:42, October 13, 2023 from https://commons.wikimedia.org/w/index.php?title=File:Apollo_14-insignia.png&oldid=799877469.
(6) File:Soyuz-36-svg.svg. (2022, February 8). Wikimedia Commons. Retrieved 16:42, October 13, 2023 from https://commons.wikimedia.org/w/index.php?title=File:Soyuz-36-svg.svg&oldid=628541227.
(7) File:Skylab1-Patch.png. (2022, September 4). Wikimedia Commons. Retrieved 16:43, October 13, 2023 from https://commons.wikimedia.org/w/index.php?title=File:Skylab1-Patch.png&oldid=686556273.
(8) File:Skylab3-Patch.png. (2021, May 24). Wikimedia Commons. Retrieved 16:43, October 13, 2023 from https://commons.wikimedia.org/w/index.php?title=File:Skylab3-Patch.png&oldid=563926556.

109
Page „Stoppschild". In: Wikipedia – The free encyclopedia. Editing status: August 23, 2022, 11:56 UTC. URL: https://de.wikipedia.org/w/index.php?title=Stoppschild&oldid=225569109 (Accessed: October 13, 2023, 16:43 UTC)

110
(1) Page „X für U – Bilder, die lügen". In: Wikipedia – The free encyclopedia. Editing status: February 17, 2023, 10:16 p.m. UTC. URL: https://de.wikipedia.org/w/index.php?title=X_f%C3%BCr_U_%E2%80%93_Bilder,_die_l%C3%BCgen&oldid=230997782 (Accessed: October 13, 2023, 4:44 p.m. UTC)
(a) File:Raising the Flag on Iwo Jima, larger - edit1.jpg. (2023, September 17). Wikimedia Commons. Retrieved 16:45, October 13, 2023 from https://commons.wikimedia.org/w/index.php?title=File:Raising_the_Flag_on_Iwo_Jima,_larger_-_edit1.jpg&oldid=802302532.
(b) File:First Iwo Jima Flag Raising.jpg. (2023, January 22). Wikimedia Commons. Retrieved 16:45, October 13, 2023 from https://commons.wikimedia.org/w/index.php?title=File:First_Iwo_Jima_Flag_Raising.jpg&oldid=726853574.

111
(1) File:GDR Stasi Fotosnaiper12.jpg. (2020, September 30). Wikimedia Commons. Retrieved 16:46, October 13, 2023 from https://commons.wikimedia.org/w/index.php?title=File:GDR_Stasi_Fotosnaiper12.jpg&oldid=476030369.
(2) File:GDR Stasi Mikrofone Sennheiser.jpg. (2020, October 7). Wikimedia Commons. Retrieved 16:46, October 13, 2023 from https://commons.wikimedia.org/w/index.php?title=File:GDR_Stasi_Mikrofone_Sennheiser.jpg&oldid=483373308.

112.3
Page „Kaufzwang". In: Wikipedia – The free encyclopedia. Editing status: October 6, 2023, 08:39 UTC. URL: https://de.wikipedia.org/w/index.php?title=Kaufzwang&oldid=237918127 (Accessed: October 13, 2023, 16:26 UTC)

113
Page „Maslowsche Bedürfnishierarchie". In: Wikipedia – The free encyclopedia. Editing status: September 25, 2023, 11:53 UTC. URL: https://de.wikipedia.org/w/index.php?title=Maslowsche_Bed%C3%BCrfnishierarchie&oldid=237627230 (Accessed: October 13, 2023, 16:47 UTC)

114
(A) Page „Dazzle camouflage". In: Wikipedia – The free encyclopedia. Editing status: July 28, 2023, 09:27 UTC. URL: https://de.wikipedia.org/w/index.php?title=Dazzle_camouflage&oldid=235886711 (Accessed: October 13, 2023, 16:48 UTC)
(B) Page „Flecktarn". In: Wikipedia – The free encyclopedia. Last edited: June 28, 2023, 17:58 UTC. URL: https://de.wikipedia.org/w/index.php?title=Flecktarn&oldid=235017002 (Accessed: October 13, 2023, 16:48 UTC)
(1) File:Mauretania with dazzle camouflage bringing troops home from Europe.jpg. (2022, December 7). Wikimedia Commons. Retrieved 16:49, October 13, 2023 from https://commons.wikimedia.org/w/index.php?title=File:Mauretania_with_dazzle_camouflage_bringing_troops_home_from_Europe.jpg&oldid=713066794.
(2) File:Flecktarn.jpg. (2020, October 1). Wikimedia Commons. Retrieved 16:49, October 13, 2023 from https://commons.wikimedia.org/w/index.php?title=File:Flecktarn.jpg&oldid=476956120.
(3) File:People's Army of Vietnam – K07 (Type 07) camouflage – Ground Force.jpg. (2022, October 15). Wikimedia Commons. Retrieved 16:50, October 13, 2023 from https://commons.wikimedia.org/w/index.php?title=File:People%27s_Army_of_Vietnam_-_K07_(Type_07)_camouflage_-_Ground_Force.jpg&oldid=696447180.
(4) File:OCP SW2.jpg. (2020, October 13). Wikimedia Commons. Retrieved 16:51, October 13, 2023 from https://commons.wikimedia.org/w/index.php?title=File:OCP_SW2.jpg&oldid=488930800.
(5) File:CADPAT digital camouflage pattern (Temperate Woodland variant).jpg. (2023, May 16). Wikimedia Commons. Retrieved 16:51, October 13, 2023 from https://commons.wikimedia.org/w/index.php?title=File:CAD-

PAT_digital_camouflage_pattern_(Tem-
perate_Woodland_variant).jpg&ol-
did=763718012.

116
https://www.dbsv.org/wie-die-brail-
leschrift-funktioniert.html,
04.07.2024, 21:29.
–
Screenshot of the "Brailleschrift"
page. In: Wikipedia — The Free Encyclopedia. Last edited: October 13,
2023, 12:02 UTC. URL: https://de.wi-
kipedia.org/w/index.php?title=Brail-
leschrift&oldid=238112707 (Accessed:
October 13, 2023, 16:52 UTC)

116.1
Screenshot of https://decodeunicode.
org/en/u+02874, 30.12.20, 00:22;

116.2
Page „Dialog im Dunkeln". In: Wikipedia - The Free Encyclopedia. Last
edited: June 7, 2023, 23:59 UTC.
URL: https://de.wikipedia.org/w/
index.php?title=Dialog_im_Dunkeln&ol-
did=234411730 (Accessed: October 13,
2023, 16:53 UTC)

117
Wikipedia contributors. (2023, May
26). Marshall Islands stick chart. In
Wikipedia, The Free Encyclopedia. Retrieved 16:54, October 13, 2023, from
https://en.wikipedia.org/w/index.
php?title=Marshall_Islands_stick_
chart&oldid=1157128652
(1) File:Micronesian navigational
chart.jpg. (2023, May 13). Wikimedia
Commons. Retrieved 16:54, October 13,
2023 from https://commons.wikimedia.
org/w/index.php?title=File:Microne-
sian_navigational_chart.jpg&ol-
did=762793917.
(2) File:Überseemuseum Bremen 2009
063a.jpg. (2020, September 15).
Wikimedia Commons. Retrieved 16:55,
October 13, 2023 from https://
commons.wikimedia.org/w/index.php?-
title=File:%C3%9Cberseemuseum_Bre-
men_2009_063a.jpg&oldid=459618280.

121
File:Deutsche Fingeralphabet.jpg.
(2023, June 26). Wikimedia Commons.
Retrieved 16:56, October 13, 2023
from https://commons.wikimedia.org/w/
index.php?title=File:Deutsche_Finge-
ralphabet.jpg&oldid=777513458.

121.1
https://www.delegs.de/gebaerden-
schrift, 17.05.24, 20:01.
https://de.wikipedia.org/wiki/
Geb%C3%A4rdenschrift#SignWriting,
27.06.22, 21:18.

122
Wikipedia contributors. (2024, June
12). International maritime signal
flags. In Wikipedia, The Free Encyclopedia. Retrieved 11:12, July 5,
2024, from https://en.wikipedia.or-
g/w/index.php?title=International_ma-
ritime_signal_flags&oldid=1228579116

126
https://www.fu-berlin.de/en/sites/
diversity/antidiskriminierung/in-
dex.html, 03.06.2024, 16:27

132
Page „Voynich-Manuskript". In:
Wikipedia - The Free Encyclopedia.
Editing status: September 15, 2023,
18:43 UTC. URL: https://de.wikipedia.
org/w/index.php?title=Voynich-Ma-
nuskript&oldid=237366825 (Accessed:
October 13, 2023, 17:18 UTC)

133
https://books.google.at/books?id=i-
W85AAAAcAAJ&printsec=frontcover&dq=-
Schreibekunst&hl=de&sa=X&ei=69MyUuS-
NIaq40QWY1YCQDA#v=onepage&q&f=false,
23.12.20, 00:05

137
File:SixtlDSC 1153.jpg. (2023, January 18). Wikimedia Commons. Retrieved
17:18, October 13, 2023 from https://
commons.wikimedia.org/w/index.php?-
title=File:SixtlDSC_1153.jpg&ol-
did=725886466.

140
https://www.werberat.de/content/
leitfaden-zum-werbekodex-des-deut-
schen-werberats, 07.07.22, 21:30;

141
https://www.niggli.ch/Produkt/der-ty-
pografiestreit-der-moderne/, 08.07.22;
17:00;

145
https://www.ddc.de/de/wettbewerb/was-
ist-gut/infos.php, 07.07.22, 22:05;

145.1
www.bit.ly/45OcUI5,01.06.24, 22:05;

146
(1) Page „Fahne und Wappen der
Schweiz". In: Wikipedia - The free
encyclopedia. Editing status: August
23, 2023, 11:35 UTC. URL: https://
de.wikipedia.org/w/index.php?tit-
le=Fahne_und_Wappen_der_Schweiz&ol-
did=236672565 (Accessed: October 13,
2023, 17:21 UTC)
(2) Page „Griechisches Kreuz". In:
Wikipedia - The Free Encyclopedia.
Editing status: March 13, 2023,
20:03 UTC. URL: https://de.wikipedia.
org/w/index.php?title=Griechisches_
Kreuz&oldid=231788948 (Accessed:
October 13, 2023, 17:21 UTC)
(3) Page „Fahne und Wappen der
Schweiz". In: Wikipedia - The free
encyclopedia. Editing status: August
23, 2023, 11:35 UTC. URL: https://
de.wikipedia.org/w/index.php?tit-
le=Fahne_und_Wappen_der_Schweiz&ol-
did=236672565 (Accessed: October 13,
2023, 17:21 UTC)

147
Page „Flaggen und Wappen der Länder
der Bundesrepublik Deutschland". In:
Wikipedia - The free encyclopedia.
Last edited: August 4, 2023, 16:06
UTC. URL: https://de.wikipedia.org/w/
index.php?title=Flaggen_und_Wap-
pen_der_L%C3%A4nder_der_Bundesrepu-
blik_Deutschland&oldid=236112087 (Accessed: October 13, 2023, 17:22 UTC)

149
File:OpenDyslexic3Regular-sample.
svg. (2023, September 5). Wikimedia
Commons. Retrieved 17:22, October 13,
2023 from https://commons.wikimedia.
org/w/index.php?title=File:Open-
Dyslexic3Regular-sample.svg&ol-
did=798777365.

152
File:Logo Tupamaros.svg. (2020,
December 11). Wikimedia Commons.
Retrieved 17:23, October 13, 2023
from https://commons.wikimedia.org/w/
index.php?title=File:Logo_Tupamaros.
svg&oldid=518170585.
File:Emblem of Viet Cong.svg. (2023,
September 28). Wikimedia Commons.
Retrieved 17:24, October 13, 2023
from https://commons.wikimedia.org/w/
index.php?title=File:Emblem_of_Viet_
Cong.svg&oldid=805707068.

154
(1) File:American 286.jpg. (2023,
August 6). Wikimedia Commons. Retrieved 17:26, October 13, 2023 from
https://commons.wikimedia.org/w/
index.php?title=File:American_286.
jpg&oldid=790406736.
(2) File:Intellec-MDS-80--Museum-En-
ter-6094735.jpg. (2022, April 6).
Wikimedia Commons. Retrieved 17:28,
October 13, 2023 from https://
commons.wikimedia.org/w/index.php?ti-
tle=File:Intellec-MDS-80--Museum-En-
ter-6094735.jpg&oldid=647104973.

157
File:ADC Logo 2018.png. (2023, June
13). Wikimedia Commons. Retrieved
17:29, October 13, 2023 from https://
commons.wikimedia.org/w/index.php?-
title=File:ADC_Logo_2018.png&ol-
did=773979863.

158
(1) Page „Sinus-Milieus". In: Wikipedia - The Free Encyclopedia. Editing
status: July 12, 2023, 19:45 UTC.
URL: https://de.wikipedia.org/w/
index.php?title=Sinus-Milieus&ol-
did=235430022 (Accessed: October 13,
2023, 17:29 UTC)
(2) https://www.sinus-institut.de/si-
nus-milieus/sinus-milieus-deutschland
18.05.22, 09:21;

162
(A) https://de.wikipedia.org/wiki/
Whole_Earth_Catalog, 04.07.24,
21:32.

163
(2) https://rulesoftheinternet.com/,
10.01.23, 21:40;

164
File:DDLiberator2.3.jpg. (2020, October 6). Wikimedia Commons. Retrieved
17:31, October 13, 2023 from https://
commons.wikimedia.org/w/index.
php?title=File:DDLiberator2.3.jpg&ol-
did=482714478.

165
https://wirtschaftslexikon.gabler.de/
definition/sharing-economy-53876/
version-384536, 22.09.22, 20:57;

166
http://archive.org/about, 13.10.23,
19:33;

171
(6) File:Barbie Logo.svg. (2023,
September 1). Wikimedia Commons.
Retrieved 17:34, October 13, 2023
from https://commons.wikimedia.org/w/
index.php?title=File:Barbie_Logo.
svg&oldid=797433989.

175
Page „Strahlentierchen". In: Wikipedia - The Free Encyclopedia. Editing
status: August 29, 2023, 05:14 UTC.
URL: https://de.wikipedia.org/w/
index.php?title=Strahlentierchen&ol-
did=236844093 (Accessed: October 13,
2023, 17:36 UTC)
(1) File:Haeckel Acanthophracta.
jpg. (2023, October 23). Wikimedia
Commons. Retrieved 11:48, May 2, 2024
from https://commons.wikimedia.org/w/
index.php?title=File:Haeckel_Acantho-
phracta.jpg&oldid=814438222.
(2) File:The royal natural history
(1893) (14778597471).jpg. (2021,
November 6). Wikimedia Commons.
Retrieved 11:49, May 2, 2024 from
https://commons.wikimedia.org/w/
index.php?title=File:The_royal_na-
tural_history_(1893)_(14778597471).
jpg&oldid=605827908.

176
Page „Tarot". In: Wikipedia - The
Free Encyclopedia. Last edited:
August 15, 2023, 21:16 UTC. URL: https://de.wikipedia.org/w/index.php?ti-
tle=Tarot&oldid=236453488 (Accessed:
October 13, 2023, 17:42 UTC)
(1) File:Tarot Nine of Wands.jpg.
(2022, March 15). Wikimedia Commons.
Retrieved 17:42, October 13, 2023
from https://commons.wikimedia.org/w/
index.php?title=File:Tarot_Nine_of_
Wands.jpg&oldid=638716523.
(2) File:TheLovers.jpg. (2022, March
15). Wikimedia Commons. Retrieved
17:43, October 13, 2023 from https://commons.wikimedia.org/w/index.
php?title=File:TheLovers.jpg&ol-
did=638716683.
(3) File:Tarot de Besançon - Junon.
jpg. (2020, November 18). Wikimedia
Commons. Retrieved 17:43, October 13, 2023 from https://commons.
wikimedia.org/w/index.php?title=Fi-
le:Tarot_de_Besan%C3%A7on_-_Junon.
jpg&oldid=513224141.

177
(1) File:Gebrochene Schriften.png.
(2022, August 18). Wikimedia Commons.
Retrieved 17:44, October 13, 2023
from https://commons.wikimedia.org/w/
index.php?title=File:Gebrochene_
Schriften.png&oldid=683367988.
(2) File:Gebrochene Schriften klein.
png. (2023, January 6). Wikimedia
Commons. Retrieved 17:44, October 13, 2023 from https://commons.
wikimedia.org/w/index.php?title=Fi-
le:Gebrochene_Schriften_klein.png&ol-
did=723367797.

178
(a) File:Tizi Ouzou Tasdawit.jpg.
(2023, May 28). Wikimedia Commons.
Retrieved 17:44, October 13, 2023
from https://commons.wikimedia.org/w/
index.php?title=File:Tizi_Ouzou_Tas-
dawit.jpg&oldid=768110007.
(b) File:2008 - Marocko - berbertext
utanför kafé i Agadir 3.JPG. (2023,
April 13). Wikimedia Commons. Retrieved 17:45, October 13, 2023 from https://commons.wikimedia.org/w/index.
php?title=File:2008_-_Marocko_-_ber-
bertext_utanf%C3%B6r_kaf%C3%A9_i_Aga-
dir_3.JPG&oldid=749918846.

180
Page „Futurismus". In: Wikipedia -
The Free Encyclopedia. Last edited:
August 25, 2023, 2:35 p.m. UTC. URL:
https://de.wikipedia.org/w/index.
php?title=Futurismus&oldid=236737481
(Accessed: October 13, 2023, 5:46
p.m. UTC)

181
(1) File:Hugo ball karawane.png.
(2022, January 5). Wikimedia Commons.
Retrieved 17:47, October 13, 2023
from https://commons.wikimedia.org/w/
index.php?title=File:Hugo_ball_kara-
wane.png&oldid=619475497.

182
File:Design by El Lissitzky 1922.jpg.
(2022, May 21). Wikimedia Commons.
Retrieved 17:48, October 13, 2023
from https://commons.wikimedia.org/w/
index.php?title=File:Design_by_El_
Lissitzky_1922.jpg&oldid=657681104.

184
(1) File:Supremus 55 (Malevich,
1916).jpg. (2022, June 30). Wikimedia
Commons. Retrieved 18:07, October 13,
2023 from https://commons.wikimedia.
org/w/index.php?title=File:Supre-
mus_55_(Malevich,_1916).jpg&ol-
did=669920559.
(2) File:Van Nelle Fabriek - Van Nelle Factory (5709126091).jpg. (2022,
February 26). Wikimedia Commons.
Retrieved 18:07, October 13, 2023
from https://commons.wikimedia.
org/w/index.php?title=File:Van_Nel-
le_Fabriek_-_Van_Nelle_Factory_
(5709126091).jpg&oldid=632990247.

185
https://www.verlag-kettler.de/en/
books/moholy-nagy-und-die-neue-typog-
rafie-ein-a-z/, 05.06.2024, 19:11.

187
File:Kelmscott chaucer.jpg (2007,
December 31). Wikimedia Commons. Retrieved 18:12, January 09, 2021 from
https://upload.wikimedia.org/wikipe-
dia/de/1/18/Kelmscott_chaucer.jpg.

188
File:Marcel breuer con stoffe di
gunta stölzl, sedia, 1922 01.JPG.
(2023, March 31). Wikimedia Commons.
Retrieved 18:13, October 13, 2023
from https://commons.wikimedia.org/w/
index.php?title=File:Marcel_breuer_
con_stoffe_di_gunta_st%C3%B6lzl,_se-
dia,_1922_01.JPG&oldid=745496569.

190
(1) "Anni Albers," Nicholas Fox Weber, Pandora Tabatabai Asbaghi;
Peggy Guggenheim Collection, US,
1999, p. 60;
(2) "Anni Albers," Nicholas Fox Weber, Pandora Tabatabai Asbaghi;
Peggy Guggenheim Collection, US,
1999, p. 55.

193
Page „Color fan". In: Wikipedia -
The free encyclopedia. Last edited:
August 31, 2015, 20:37 UTC. URL: https://de.wikipedia.org/w/index.php?ti-
tle=Farbf%C3%A4cher&oldid=145604749
(Accessed: October 13, 2023, 18:16
UTC)
(1) File:Farbfächer RAL.jpg. (2022,
February 20). Wikimedia Commons.
Retrieved 18:16, October 13, 2023
from https://commons.wikimedia.org/w/
index.php?title=File:Farbf%C3%A4cher_
RAL.jpg&oldid=631054581.
(2) File:HKS-K-Farbfaecher.jpg.
(2020, October 15). Wikimedia Commons. Retrieved 18:17, October 13,
2023 from https://commons.wikimedia.
org/w/index.php?title=File:H-
KS-K-Farbfaecher.jpg&oldid=490674661.
(3) File:Nuancier Pantone 2 (Cut
out).jpg. (2021, April 25). Wikimedia
Commons. Retrieved 18:18, October 13,
2023 from https://commons.wikimedia.
org/w/index.php?title=File:Nuan-
cier_Pantone_2_(Cut_out).jpg&ol-
did=555344807.

194
Page „Pantone Matching System". In:
Wikipedia - The Free Encyclopedia.
Editing status: October 7, 2023,
17:01 UTC. URL: https://de.wikipe-
dia.org/w/index.php?title=Panto-
ne_Matching_System&oldid=237962168
(Accessed: October 13, 2023, 18:18
UTC)

197
File:Internal hub 3 speed Shimano.
jpg. (2021, November 7). Wikimedia
Commons. Retrieved 18:20, October 13,
2023 from https://commons.wikimedia.
org/w/index.php?title=File:Inter-
nal_hub_3_speed_Shimano.jpg&ol-
did=605927918.

198
(3) File:Zimmerbild 78.jpg. (2023,
January 5). Wikimedia Commons. Retrieved 18:21, October 13, 2023 from
https://commons.wikimedia.org/w/
index.php?title=File:Zimmerbild_78.
jpg&oldid=723029156.200

200
(2) https://bit.ly/3zyaTUo,
13.10.2023, 14:12.

201
https://www.adobe.com/express/,
06.06.24, 21:37.

202
https://de.wikipedia.org/wiki/Chaos_
Computer_Club#/media/Datei:Logo_CCC.
svg, 27.05.2024, 12:34.
https://de.wikipedia.org/wiki/Chaos_
Computer_Club, 27.05.2024, 12:29.

203
https://bit.ly/4eREhVO, 24.04.24,
13:09.

205
https://de.wikipedia.org/wiki/Zie-
le_für_nachhaltige_
Entwicklung#/media/Datei:Sustainab-
le_Development_Goals.svg, 04.02.24,
09:08.
https://www.un.org/sustainablede-
velopment/development-
agenda/, 04.02.24, 08:56.

Image sources / text sources E3

206
File:Sergei Vasiliev - Russian Criminal Tattoo Encyclopaedia Print No.7
(2010) (2021, December 12). Sergei
Vasiliev. Retrieved 13:38, October
15, 2023 from https://www.flickr.
com/photos/centralasian/8266172707,
author: Sergei Vasiliev, Attribution
2.0 Generic, no changes were made,
link to licence: https://creativecom-
mons.org/licenses/by/2.0/.

209
Screenshot of the page „Index librorum prohibitorum“. Wikipedia
contributors. (2024, May 6). Index
Librorum Prohibitorum. In Wikipedia,
The Free Encyclopedia. Retrieved
18:22, June 3, 2024, from https://
en.wikipedia.org/w/index.php?tit-
le=Index_Librorum_Prohibitorum&ol-
did=1222576909

209.1
File:1965-01 1964年首次原子弹爆炸3.jpg.
(2023, May 8). Wikimedia Commons.
Retrieved 18:30, October 13, 2023
from https://commons.wikimedia.org/w/
index.php?title=File:1965-01_1964%E5
%B9%B4_%E9%A6%96%E6%AC%A1%E5%8E%9F%E
5%AD%90%E5%BC%B9%E7%88%86%E7%82%B83.
jpg&oldid=760912304.

211
File:Dillingerwantedposter.jpg.
(2021, April 19). Wikimedia Commons.
Retrieved 18:34, October 13, 2023
from https://commons.wikimedia.org/w/
index.php?title=File:Dillingerwanted-
poster.jpg&oldid=553998414.
File:Treueorden des MfS 20, 25,
30.jpg. (2020, December 6). Wikimedia
Commons. Retrieved 18:34, October 13,
2023 from https://commons.wikimedia.
org/w/index.php?title=File:Treue-
orden_des_MfS_20,_25,_30.jpg&ol-
did=517019520.

213
File:Flag of Sealand.svg. (2023,
October 9). Wikimedia Commons. Retrieved 18:35, October 13, 2023 from
https://commons.wikimedia.org/w/
index.php?title=File:Flag_of_Sealand.
svg&oldid=810258185.
(1) https://99percentinvisible.org/
app/uploads/2014/02/wheelchair-sym-
bol-susanne-koefoed.jpg, 13.10.23,
20:39;
(2) https://accessibleicon.org/img/
icon-original.png, 13.10.23, 20:39;
(3) https://accessibleicon.org/img/
accessible-icon.jpg, 13.10.23, 20:40;

214
Wikipedia contributors. (2023, June
6). La Sape. In Wikipedia, The Free
Encyclopedia. Retrieved 18:41, October 13, 2023, from https://en.wikipe-
dia.org/w/index.php?title=La_Sape&ol-
did=1158859665
File:Men's Sapeur inspired looks from
SS 15 lookbook.jpg. (2020, September
16). Wikimedia Commons. Retrieved
18:41, October 13, 2023 from https://commons.wikimedia.org/w/index.
php?title=File:Men%27s_Sapeur_inspi-
red_looks_from_SS_15_lookbook.jpg&ol-
did=461799892.

217
(1) File:BaliHaiNOLA59Postcard.jpg.
(2022, April 25). Wikimedia Commons.
Retrieved 18:42, October 13, 2023
from https://commons.wikimedia.org/w/
index.php?title=File:BaliHaiNOLA59Po-
stcard.jpg&oldid=651660951.
(2) File:Types of nuclear testing.
svg. (2022, November 27). Wikimedia
Commons. Retrieved 18:43, October 13,
2023 from https://commons.wikimedia.
org/w/index.php?title=File:Types_of_
nuclear_testing.svg&oldid=710140159.
(3) File:Seal of the Marshall
Islands.svg. (2023, January 1). Wikimedia Commons. Retrieved 18:44, October 13, 2023 from https://commons.
wikimedia.org/w/index.php?title=-
File:Seal_of_the_Marshall_Islands.
svg&oldid=721977661.
(4) File:Radiation warning symbol
5.svg. (2023, February 10). Wikimedia
Commons. Retrieved 18:45, October 13,
2023 from https://commons.wikimedia.
org/w/index.php?title=File:Radiation_
warning_symbol_5.svg&oldid=731498358.

222
File:Skull and crossbones.png. (2020,
October 28). Wikimedia Commons. Retrieved 18:45, October 13, 2023 from
https://bit.ly/3VJCE3q.

223
(1) Screenshot from https://li-
brary.olympics.com/Default/doc/
SYRACUSE/161826/the-sports-picto-
grams-of-the-olympic-winter-games-
from-grenoble-1968-to-beijing-2022-
the-olympic-stu?_lg=en-GB, 02.05.24,
13:56;
(2) https://de.wikipedia.org/wiki/
Olympische_Winterspiele_1994#/media/
Datei:Urzeit_rodoy.gif, 13.10.23,
21:02;

225
(1) File:Aldus-symbol.jpg. (2023,
July 30). Wikimedia Commons. Retrieved 19:03, October 13, 2023 from
https://commons.wikimedia.org/w/
index.php?title=File:Aldus-symbol.
jpg&oldid=788310993.
(3) File:Mariupol gerb.png. (2023,
March 31). Wikimedia Commons. Retrieved 19:03, October 13, 2023 from
https://commons.wikimedia.org/w/
index.php?title=File:Mariupol_gerb.
png&oldid=745637927.

226
Page „John Cage“. In: Wikipedia -
The Free Encyclopedia. Last edited:
August 16, 2023, 09:28 UTC. URL: https://de.wikipedia.org/w/index.php?ti-
tle=John_Cage&oldid=236462915 (Accessed: October 13, 2023, 19:06 UTC)

228
(1) File:Kone.jpg. (2020, September
11). Wikimedia Commons. Retrieved
19:09, October 13, 2023 from https://
commons.wikimedia.org/w/index.php?ti-
tle=File:Kone.jpg&oldid=455354320.
(2) https://de.wikipedia.org/wiki/
Kimono#/media/Datei:
Uchikake.JPG, 13.10.23, 21:07;

229
(1) File:Flag of Greenland (2000
World Factbook).svg. (2022, May 15).
Wikimedia Commons. Retrieved 19:12,
October 13, 2023 from https://com-
mons.wikimedia.org/w/index.php?tit-
le=File:Flag_of_Greenland_(2000_Wor-
ld_Factbook).svg&oldid=656289173.
(2) File:Uummannaq-football-game.
jpg. (2020, September 27). Wikimedia
Commons. Retrieved 19:10, October 13, 2023 from https://commons.
wikimedia.org/w/index.php?title=Fi-
le:Uummannaq-football-game.jpg&ol-
did=473126636.

230
File:Gaunerzinken.svg. (2020, September 26). Wikimedia Commons. Retrieved
19:12, October 13, 2023 from https://
commons.wikimedia.org/w/index.
php?title=File:Gaunerzinken.svg&ol-
did=471550695.

231
File:Pizzino Provenzanos.jpg. (2023,
April 8). Wikimedia Commons. Retrieved 19:13, October 13, 2023 from https://commons.wikimedia.org/w/index.
php?title=File:Pizzino_Provenzanos.
jpg&oldid=748265928.

235
File:I Love New York.svg. (2023,
September 17). Wikimedia Commons.
Retrieved 19:14, October 13, 2023
from https://commons.wikimedia.org/w/
index.php?title=File:I_Love_New_York.
svg&oldid=802547094.

236
File:LOVE sculpture NY cropped.jpg.
(2021, June 2). Wikimedia Commons.
Retrieved 19:14, October 13, 2023
from https://commons.wikimedia.org/w/
index.php?title=File:LOVE_sculpture_
NY_cropped.jpg&oldid=566723999.

242
(1) File:Vigcz2007.jpg. (2022, November 16). Wikimedia Commons. Retrieved
19:15, October 13, 2023 from https://
commons.wikimedia.org/w/index.
php?title=File:Vigcz2007.jpg&ol-
did=706650792.
(2) https://de.wikipedia.org/wiki/
Autobahnvignette#/media/Datei:Vignet-
ten_1997-2011.jpg, 13.10.23, 21:16;

243
(1) File:Great Seal of the United
States (obverse).svg. (2023, February
7). Wikimedia Commons. Retrieved
19:18, October 13, 2023 from https://
commons.wikimedia.org/w/index.php?-
title=File:Great_Seal_of_the_United_
States_(obverse).svg&oldid=730671778.
(2) File:Great Seal of the United
States (reverse).svg. (2023, September 1). Wikimedia Commons. Retrieved
19:19, October 13, 2023 from https://
commons.wikimedia.org/w/index.php?-
title=File:Great_Seal_of_the_United_
States_(reverse).svg&oldid=797612864.
(3) File:Flag of Bikini Atoll.svg.
(2023, June 25). Wikimedia Commons.
Retrieved 19:19, October 13, 2023
from https://commons.wikimedia.org/w/
index.php?title=File:Flag_of_Biki-
ni_Atoll.svg&oldid=777349132.

245
File:Katsushika Hokusai - Thirty-Six
Views of Mount Fuji- The Great Wave
Off the Coast of Kanagawa - Google
Art Project.jpg. (2023, September
8). Wikimedia Commons. Retrieved 19:22, October 13, 2023 from
https://commons.wikimedia.org/w/
index.php?title=File:Katsushika_Ho-
kusai_-_Thirty-Six_Views_of_Mount_
Fuji-_The_Great_Wave_Off_the_Coast_
of_Kanagawa_-_Google_Art_Project.
jpg&oldid=799618380.

246
(1) File:COA JaBoG 49.svg. (2020,
April 20). Wikimedia Commons. Retrieved 19:24, October 13, 2023 from
https://commons.wikimedia.org/w/
index.php?title=File:COA_JaBoG_49.
svg&oldid=413305792.
(2) File:COA JaboG 41.svg. (2020,
April 20). Wikimedia Commons. Retrieved 19:25, October 13, 2023 from
https://commons.wikimedia.org/w/
index.php?title=File:COA_JaboG_41.
svg&oldid=413305755.

247
File:Eugène Delacroix - La liberté
guidant le peuple.jpg. (2023, August
12). Wikimedia Commons. Retrieved
19:26, October 13, 2023 from https://
commons.wikimedia.org/w/index.php?-
title=File:Eug%C3%A8ne_Delacroix_-_
La_libert%C3%A9_guidant_le_peuple.
jpg&oldid=792532350.

248
File:(Enhanced) British Guiana 1856
1c magenta stamp.jpg. (2023, June
22). Wikimedia Commons. Retrieved
19:32, October 13, 2023 from https://
bit.ly/3zt2ocZ.

251
File:Fluxus manifesto.jpg. (2022,
July 31). Wikimedia Commons. Retrieved 19:33, October 13, 2023 from
https://commons.wikimedia.org/w/in-
dex.php?title=File:Fluxus_manifesto.
jpg&oldid=679240666.

257
File:TOR Arbeitsweise.svg. (2023,
March 13). Wikimedia Commons. Retrieved 19:33, October 13, 2023 from
https://commons.wikimedia.org/w/in-
dex.php?title=File:TOR_Arbeitsweise.
svg&oldid=740303345.

258
(1) Wikipedia contributors. (2024,
May 26). Pikachu. In Wikipedia, The
Free Encyclopedia. Retrieved 13:27,
June 4, 2024, from https://bit.
ly/4bqxoYw

259
File:Plaid Cymru broadcasting „Radio
Wales“ illegally for the first time in
North Wales (4478261757).jpg. (2023,
January 31). Wikimedia Commons.
Retrieved 19:35, October 13, 2023
from https://commons.wikimedia.org/w/
index.php?title=File:Plaid_Cymru_bro-
adcasting_%22Radio_Wales%22_illegal-
ly_for_the_first_time_in_North_Wales_
(4478261757).jpg&oldid=729043911.

261
File:Shaker furniture8.jpg. (2020,
November 3). Wikimedia Commons. Retrieved 19:37, October 13, 2023 from
https://commons.wikimedia.org/w/in-
dex.php?title=File:Shaker_furniture8.
jpg&oldid=509592378.

263
File:United States one dollar bill,
obverse.jpg. (2023, September 28).
Wikimedia Commons. Retrieved 19:38,
October 13, 2023 from https://
commons.wikimedia.org/w/index.php?-
title=File:United_States_one_dollar_
bill,_obverse.jpg&oldid=805704250.
File:100 Gulden (1992) - Vordersei-
te.jpg. (2023, May 20). Wikimedia
Commons. Retrieved 19:39, October 13,
2023 from https://commons.wikimedia.
org/w/index.php?title=File:100_Gul-
den_(1992)_-_Vorderseite.jpg&ol-
did=765228370.

266
File:Hudson locomotive for the New
York Central.jpg. (2021, December
31). Wikimedia Commons. Retrieved
19:40, October 13, 2023 from https://
commons.wikimedia.org/w/index.php?ti-
tle=File:Hudson_locomotive_for_the_
New_York_Central.jpg&oldid=617898638.

268
File:Coat of arms of the Soviet Union
(1923–1936).svg. (2023, September
29). Wikimedia Commons. Retrieved
19:41, October 13, 2023 from https://
commons.wikimedia.org/w/index.php?-
title=File:Coat_of_arms_of_the_So-
viet_Union_(1923%E2%80%931936).
svg&oldid=806162640.
File:Hammer and sickle red on trans-
parent.svg. (2023, August 26). Wikimedia Commons. Retrieved 19:42, October 13, 2023 from https://commons.
wikimedia.org/w/index.php?title=Fi-
le:Hammer_and_sickle_red_on_transpa-
rent.svg&oldid=796005589.

273
File:Obi-knoten.png. (2023, May 8).
Wikimedia Commons. Retrieved 19:43,
October 13, 2023 from https://
commons.wikimedia.org/w/index.
php?title=File:Obi-knoten.png&ol-
did=760823166.
File:Bruce McCandless II during EVA
in 1984.jpg. (2023, June 5). Wikimedia Commons. Retrieved 19:43, October
13, 2023 from https://commons.wikime-
dia.org/w/index.php?title=File:Bruce_
McCandless_II_during_EVA_in_1984.
jpg&oldid=771211258.

275
(1) File:Deutsche Bank logo.svg.
(2023, February 17). Wikimedia Commons. Retrieved 19:45, October 13,
2023 from https://commons.wikimedia.
org/w/index.php?title=File:Deutsche_
Bank_logo.svg&oldid=733256942.
(2) https://logos-world.net/wp-cont-
ent/uploads/2021/02/Deutsche-Bank-Lo-
go-1957-1973.png, 04.07.2024, 21:35.

276
(1) File:Sonderschutzbekleidung
ZODIAK.jpg. (2020, September 13). Wikimedia Commons. Retrieved 10:18, October 14, 2023 from https://commons.
wikimedia.org/w/index.php?title=Fi-
le:Sonderschutzbekleidung_ZODIAK.
jpg&oldid=457507757.
(2) File:Protest 0068.JPG. (2020,
September 14). Wikimedia Commons.
Retrieved 10:18, October 14, 2023
from https://commons.wikimedia.org/w/
index.php?title=File:Protest_0068.
JPG&oldid=458994174.

278
(1) File:Space Pilot X Ray Gun made
by Taiyo.jpg. (2023, February 25).
Wikimedia Commons. Retrieved 10:19,
October 14, 2023 from https://com-
mons.wikimedia.org/w/index.php?tit-
le=File:Space_Pilot_X_Ray_Gun_made_
by_Taiyo.jpg&oldid=735569175.
(2) File:Buck Rogers in the 25th
Century U-238 Atomic Pistol-NMAH-AH-
B2015q029270.jpg. (2022, December
5). Wikimedia Commons. Retrieved
10:20, October 14, 2023 from https://
commons.wikimedia.org/w/index.php?ti-
tle=File:Buck_Rogers_in_the_25th_Cen-
tury_U-238_Atomic_Pistol-NMAH-AH-
B2015q029270.jpg&oldid=712711624.

280
File:Lavalampe.jpg. (2020, October
18). Wikimedia Commons. Retrieved
10:20, October 14, 2023 from https://commons.wikimedia.org/w/index.
php?title=File:Lavalampe.jpg&ol-
did=493673375.

Author
Ulysses Voelker

Concept, research, editing, design
Ulysses Voelker, Michael Schmitz

Editor and proofreader
Renate Noack

Scientific editor and proofreader
Dr. Katrin Simons

Translation
Anja Wiest (London, UK)

Paper
Munken pure rough, 100g/m^2

Fonts
Arnhem, Akzidenz Grotesk,
Courier

© 2024 Niggli,
imprint of Braun Publishing AG, Salenstein
www.niggli.ch

This work is protected by copyright. Any use outside the narrow confines of copyright law that has not been granted permission by the publisher is unauthorized and liable for prosecution. This especially applies to duplications, translations, microfiming, and any saving or processing in electronic systems.

1st edition, 2024
ISBN 978-3-7212-1040-8

Title of the German edition:
»was Komunikationsdesign kann«, Niggli,
Salenstein, 2024;
ISBN 978-3-7212-1042-2

We would like to thank our colleagues

Henning Eichinger (Reutlingen), Professor of Artistic Design,
Florian Jenett (Frankfurt), Professor of Media Informatics and Digital Design,
Robert Paulmann (Bielefeld), Professor of Communication Design,
Anna-Lisa Schönecker (Mainz), Professor of Information Design,
Dr. Katrin Simons (Wiesbaden), Professor of Art History,
Dr. Wolfgang Storz (Frankfurt), Publicist, Communications Consultant,

for their feedback over the course of creating this book.

The following institutions at Hochschule Mainz supported this book project: the *Department of Design* and the research institute *Designlabor Gutenberg*. We thank them for their support.

We would like to extend special thanks to the *VG Bild-Kunst*, Bonn, for the support provided as part of the publication funding.

Jean Ulysses Voelker (*1956) is a professor of typography and editorial design and taught these subjects at Hochschule Mainz from 2000 to 2019. He is a member of the Designlabor Gutenberg research institute (Hochschule Mainz), which he co-founded and directed for many years. He lives in Frankfurt/Main and in the Netherlands.

ulyssesvoelker.com
designlabor-gutenberg.de

Ulysses Voelker is the author of other books and book contributions:

"read + play. An Introduction to Typography,"
Designlabor Gutenberg, Mainz, 2010; (ENG/GER)
ISBN 978-3-936723-26-7

"read + play. Einführung in die Typografie,"
Verlag Hermann Schmidt Mainz, 2015; (revised and expanded edition, only in German)
ISBN 978-3-87439-868-8

"Structuring Design," Niggli Verlag, Salenstein, 2019;
ISBN 978-3-7212-0994-5; this book has also been published in German, title: "Ordnung in der Gestaltung," 2018; ISBN 978-3-7212-0995-2;
the book is also available in a Polish (2020) and Japanese version (2021).

In addition, Ulysses Voelker composed the chapter "Design" in "Handbuch Zeitschriftenforschung," which was published in December 2022 in "Edition Medienwissenschaft" by Transcript-Verlag.
Editors: Dr. Sabina Fazli, Prof. Dr. Oliver Scheiding; (in German)
ISBN 978-3-8376-5113-3

Michael Schmitz (*1992) studied at Hochschule Mainz and works as a communication designer. The clients of his design studio in Cologne include cultural institutions and political foundations as well as companies and publishing companies. He designed the book "Structuring Design" together with Ulysses Voelker. He also contributed to the design of the German edition.

www.studiomichaelschmitz.eu

"As human beings, we continuously create things that help form the basis of the world as we know it. When we create these new things—tools, organizations, processes, symbols and systems—we engage in design. To come up with an idea, and to give form, structure and function to that idea, is at the core of design as a human activity."

Harold Nelson, Erik Stolterman (from: The Design Way. International Change in an Unpredictable World. Englewood Cliffs, NJ: Educational Rechnology Publications 2003)

see also: "Theorien des Designs," Claudia Mareis, Junius Verlag, Hamburg, 2014; ISBN 978-3-88506-086-4